N

W · E

S

*Atlantic
Ocean*

Cape Cod

Cape Cod
Bay

Yarmouth

Detail of
Massachusetts Bay

1692

THE
WITCHES

ALSO BY STACY SCHIFF

Cleopatra: A Life

A Great Improvisation: Franklin, France, and the Birth of America

Véra (Mrs. Vladimir Nabokov)

Saint-Exupéry: A Biography

THE
WITCHES

Salem, 1692

STACY SCHIFF

LITTLE, BROWN AND COMPANY

New York   Boston   London

Little, Brown and Company
Hachette Book Group
1290 Avenue of the Americas, New York, NY 10104
littlebrown.com

First Edition: October 2015

Little, Brown and Company is a division of Hachette Book Group, Inc. The Little, Brown name and logo are trademarks of Hachette Book Group, Inc.

The publisher is not responsible for websites (or their content) that are not owned by the publisher.

Front endpaper: Map illustration by Debra Lill.
Back endpaper: Samuel Parris's notes for his March 27, 1692, sermon, "occasioned," he noted, "by dreadful witchcraft broke out a few weeks past." With the announcement of his text—"Have not I chosen you, and one of you is a devil"—Sarah Cloyce stormed out of the meetinghouse. A week later she was accused of witchcraft. (MS 101740 Samuel Parris sermon notebook, 1689–1695. Connecticut Historical Society.)

ISBN 978-0-316-20060-8 (hardcover)/978-0-316-38774-3 (large print)/
978-0-316-35370-0 (signed edition)/978-0-316-39100-9 (signed Barnes & Noble edition)
LCCN 2015939026

10 9 8 7 6 5 4 3 2

RRD-C

Printed in the United States of America

For Wendy Belzberg

Contents

———◇———

Cast of Characters

———⌾———

INGERSOLL, HANNAH, about sixty, the tavern owner's wife and a parsonage neighbor.

INGERSOLL, NATHANIEL, sixty, militia lieutenant, early village deacon, owner of the tavern in which accusations, hearings, judicial conferences, spectral stabbings, and much speculation takes place. A Putnam and Parris confidant.

NURSE, FRANCIS, seventy-four. Worldly-wise, steadfast husband of accused witch Rebecca Nurse. Displeased with his minister well before the crisis.

POPE, BATHSHUA, forty, a bewitched, sermon-interrupting matron. Lobs a shoe at a defendant; levitates in court.

PUTNAM, THOMAS, forty-year-old militia sergeant and veteran of King Philip's War. Court recorder, parish clerk, stout Parris supporter. Lives with four witchcraft victims; presses first charges and initiates nearly half the rest.

PUTNAM, EDWARD, thirty-eight, Thomas's younger brother, a church deacon. Cosigns first witchcraft accusations.

SIBLEY, MARY, a pregnant, concerned thirty-two-year-old parsonage neighbor. Suggests and supervises witch-cake baking in the Parris household.

WALCOTT, JONATHAN, fifty-three. A village militia captain and Putnam brother-in-law; Mary's father.

THE CORE ACCUSERS

BIBBER, SARAH, a quarrelsome, meddlesome thirty-six-year-old village matron. Stabbed by pins in the courtroom.

CHURCHILL, SARAH, about twenty, a refugee and servant in the Jacobs household. Tries unsuccessfully to recant. Distantly related to Mary Walcott.

HOBBS, ABIGAIL, a headstrong, unruly Topsfield fourteen-year-old, earlier a servant in Maine. Second to confess to witchcraft; an accuser thereafter. Sends both parents to prison.

HUBBARD, ELIZABETH, sixteen, an orphan and a servant in the household of her uncle, Dr. Griggs. Among the five most frequent accusers.

LEWIS, MERCY, nineteen; a two-time refugee and orphan. Previously a Burroughs servant in Maine; in 1692 a Putnam servant in Salem. Reliably identifies invisible attackers and offers most detailed testimony; known as a "visionary girl."

PUTNAM, ANN, JR., twelve, the eldest of six siblings. Can predict events and recall others that predate her birth. Sole accuser living at home with two parents.

PUTNAM, ANN, SR., Ann Jr.'s pregnant, pious mother, about thirty. Incapacitated by ghosts and witches. Entranced; at one juncture carried bodily from the courtroom.

SHELDEN, SUSANNAH, an eighteen-year-old, two-time Maine refugee. Witnessed Indian atrocities; recently buried her father. Tends to reveal murders.

WALCOTT, MARY, sixteen, daughter of a village militia captain, living with her Putnam cousins. Also an Ingersoll niece. Charges at least seventy with witchcraft, far more than any other accuser.

Cast of Characters

WARREN, MARY, twenty, an orphaned refugee and a servant in the Procter household. Afflicted, accused, then afflicted. Strikingly pretty; endures bloody, extreme courtroom tortures.

SOME OF THE ACCUSED

ALDEN, JOHN, midsixties. Shrewd Boston-based fur trader, militia officer, sea captain. Longtime associate of Salem merchant Bartholomew Gedney; Willard parishioner; Samuel Sewall friend and neighbor.

BARKER, WILLIAM, forty-six, a silver-tongued farmer in debt.

BISHOP, BRIDGET, a Salem town widow in her early fifties; belligerent, provocative, brash. Confused at trial with Salem village's Sarah Bishop.

CARRIER, MARTHA, an abrasive mother of five in her late thirties; well before 1692 seemed a likely candidate for "queen of hell." Scoffs that the afflicted are "out of their wits." First arrested Andover witch.

CARRIER, RICHARD, eighteen, and ANDREW, sixteen. Martha's strapping sons, both tortured, after which Richard names more diabolical confederates than any other confessor.

CARY, ELIZABETH, early forties. Wife of a feisty Charlestown shipbuilder. Sails to Salem to clear her name; leaves in chains.

CLOYCE, SARAH, forty-four. Rebecca Nurse's much younger, ill-starred sister. A village church member; a Dane relative by her first marriage.

COLSON, ELIZABETH, gutsy Reading sixteen-year-old; only teenager to elude arrest, if temporarily.

COREY, GILES, a fearless, pugnacious farmer in his seventies. Initially accuses his wife; ultimately defies the court.

COREY, MARTHA, sixties, Giles's third wife. Straight-spined, stubborn, dogmatic. Makes the tour of Massachusetts prisons.

ENGLISH, PHILIP, forty-two, born Philippe l'Anglois, outspoken, sharp-elbowed Jersey native. Immensely successful immigrant entrepreneur; Salem town's richest merchant and a newly elected selectman.

ENGLISH, MARY, about forty, his wife. Daughter of a prominent Salem merchant and of a woman earlier accused of witchcraft. Escapes with her husband.

ESTY, MARY, fifty-eight, kindhearted Topsfield mother of seven, youngest of the three Towne sisters. Charms even her jailers.

FOSTER, ANN, a quiet widow in her seventies. Mother of a murdered twenty-two-year-old; mother-in-law of an executed murderer. Picks up on early hints of flight and connects them to diabolical Sabbaths.

GOOD, SARAH, thirty-eight, local beggar woman, sullen, combative, unkempt. The first to be interrogated on suspicion of witchcraft; mother of an accused five-year-old.

HOAR, DORCAS, a mischief-making, fortune-telling fifty-eight-year-old widow with a gift for petty larceny. Singular-looking; easily frightens children.

HOW, ELIZABETH, early fifties, dutiful wife to a blind Topsfield farmer; a Dane, Carrier, and Nurse relative. Long suspected of witchcraft.

JACOBS, GEORGE, a jaunty, convivial, illiterate, elderly farmer.

JACOBS, MARGARET, seventeen, his articulate, soulful granddaughter. Confesses, recants, sobs mightily in Salem's dungeon.

LACEY, MARY, JR., eighteen, a self-described disobedient daughter. Highly voluble, with a theatrical bent.

LACEY, MARY, SR., forty, Mary Lacey Jr.'s mother and Ann Foster's daughter.

MARTIN, SUSANNAH, seventy-one, diminutive Amesbury widow, steely, self-possessed. Accused and cleared of witchcraft charges in 1669.

NURSE, REBECCA, seventy-one, a nearly deaf, sickly, sensitive great-grandmother. Presents the court with its greatest challenge.

OSBORNE, SARAH, about fifty, frail, among the first three suspects. Embroiled in a long-standing dispute with her Putnam in-laws.

PROCTER, ELIZABETH, forty-one, pregnant mother of five and stepmother to six. Temperamental, fond of reading. Granddaughter of a 1669 witch suspect.

PROCTER, JOHN, her older, outspoken husband, a bluff sixty-year-old farmer and tavern keeper. Swears the afflicted should hang. First 1692 man accused of witchcraft.

TOOTHAKER, MARY, forty-four, Billerica widow of an accused wizard. Ruminative, candid, petrified. Martha Carrier's sister; a niece of Reverend Dane.

WARDWELL, SAMUEL, forty-nine. A feckless fortune-teller and carpenter, at the bottom of the Andover tax lists. Colorfully confesses; later recants. Father of seven.

WILDS, SARAH, a hay-enchanting Topsfield carpenter's wife in her midsixties. Also accused sixteen years earlier; mother of the town constable.

WILLARD, JOHN, about thirty, village deputy constable, former Putnam farmhand. An abusive husband, reviled by his in-laws.

THE AUTHORITIES

BRADSTREET, DUDLEY, the forty-four-year-old son of the colony's previous governor. Leading Andover citizen; justice of the peace; selectman, 1692 council member. Orders a slew of witchcraft arrests; flees when accused.

CORWIN, GEORGE, twenty-six, opportunistic high sheriff of Essex County. Nephew of two witchcraft justices and son-in-law of a third.

CORWIN, JONATHAN, fifty-two, town merchant and liquor retailer. Longtime Hathorne confederate and experienced justice of the peace; a fixture at the hearings. Related by marriage to Winthrop, Hathorne, and Sergeant.

DANFORTH, THOMAS, sixty-nine-year-old Charlestown landowner. Reversed a guilty verdict in an earlier witchcraft case; conducts first 1692 examination of wizards. Elicits initial report of witches' meeting; ultimately opposes trials.

Cast of Characters

GEDNEY, BARTHOLOMEW, fifty-two. Risk-taking sawmill owner and entrepreneur; a respected town physician, magistrate, militia major. A Corwin relative.

HATHORNE, JOHN, fifty-one, a high-handed, intimidating, prosperous local magistrate. Hails from one of Salem town's first families; a Putnam relative.

HERRICK, GEORGE, well-born, handsome Salem deputy sheriff in his thirties, an upholsterer by trade. Spends 1692 rounding up and transporting witches.

HIGGINSON, JOHN, JR., forty-six, Reverend Higginson's eldest son, a militia officer, engaged in the fishing business. Newly appointed justice of the peace; a witch examiner.

PHIPS, SIR WILLIAM, forty-one, unschooled, enterprising, blustery sea captain and adventurer; newly appointed Massachusetts governor.

RICHARDS, JOHN, at sixty-seven, eldest member of the court. Related to three colleagues; applies for judicial direction. Boston merchant, Harvard College treasurer, leading Mather patron.

SALTONSTALL, NATHANIEL, fifty-three, a short-lived member of the court. Thought "the most popular and well principled" of Massachusetts military officers.

SERGEANT, PETER, a fabulously wealthy forty-five-year-old Boston merchant and witchcraft justice. Loaned Massachusetts funds; owner of a palatial home. A Samuel Sewall business partner.

SEWALL, SAMUEL, a round Bostonian of forty, genial, sensitive, sophisticated, devout. Youngest member of the court and its clerk's brother.

SEWALL, STEPHEN, thirty-five-year-old court clerk and keeper of its papers. Salem town merchant and military officer; takes in bewitched Betty Parris.

STOUGHTON, WILLIAM, chief justice of the Court of Oyer and Terminer. A large, starched, small-eyed sixty-year-old. Highly discerning; expertly versed in theology; New England's most trusted judicial authority. A land speculator and lifelong bachelor.

WINTHROP, WAIT STILL, fifty-one, grandson of John Winthrop, Bay Colony founder. A major general and an influential landholder; apolitical, fashion-conscious, a reluctant public servant. Close to Samuel Sewall; a Mather intimate.

AMONG THE MINISTERS

BARNARD, THOMAS, thirty-four, Andover's excitable orthodox associate minister. Arranges touch test.

DANE, FRANCIS, seventy-six, senior Andover minister, in that pulpit since 1648. Cautious regarding witchcraft; autocratic, uncompromising. No formal education.

HALE, JOHN, Charlestown-born Beverly minister, congenial, compassionate, fifty-six. Fascinated by the proceedings and with the mechanics of witchcraft. As a child, watched Massachusetts hang its first witch; a Noyes relative by marriage.

HIGGINSON, JOHN, seventy-six, in his thirty-third year in the Salem town pulpit. Sober, well spoken, highly respected.

MATHER, COTTON, twenty-nine, son of Increase Mather and assistant minister at Boston's Second Church. A Harvard student at eleven; a master of theology at eighteen. The rising star of the New England ministry, adroit, brilliant, prolific, a champion conversationalist.

Cast of Characters

MATHER, INCREASE, Second Church minister since 1664. At fifty-three, most prominent New England cleric and its leading intellectual; Harvard College president, 1685 to 1701. Procurer of the colony's new charter.

MOODY, JOSHUA, fifty-nine, First Church of Boston minister, a Willard schoolmate. Firmly believes in witchcraft; less convinced by Stoughton's court. Assists in escapes.

NOYES, NICHOLAS, forty-five, a Harvard schoolmate of Burroughs's, assistant minister to Higginson. A portly, ebullient bachelor, author of deadly doggerel. Samuel Sewall's closest friend in Salem town.

WILLARD, SAMUEL, fifty-two-year-old Third Church minister. With the Mathers, most eminent of Boston clerics. Erudite, diplomatic, clear-minded, discreet.

A FEW SKEPTICS

BRATTLE, THOMAS, accomplished scientist and logician, Anglican-leaning. Fresh from a trip to England spent largely in Samuel Sewall's company; attends various Salem hearings. A thirty-four-year-old bachelor.

CALEF, ROBERT, forty-four, a Boston textile merchant of some wit. Attended trials and at least one hanging; the Mathers' chief antagonist afterward.

MAULE, THOMAS, a contentious, quick-witted, forty-seven-year-old Salem town shopkeeper. Accused Bishop; later a Quaker and a cogent critic of the trials.

MILBORNE, WILLIAM, fifties, former Bermuda resident; a troublemaking Baptist minister with a background in law. Arrested for sedition.

PIKE, ROBERT, council member and militia captain, Salisbury's leading resident. Outspoken; midseventies; probably the first public official to voice concern about the trials.

WISE, JOHN, Ipswich's forty-year-old minister, a Parris contemporary and Harvard schoolmate. Bold, magnetic, articulate. A local hero; had served jail time for protesting government abuses.

THE
WITCHES

I

---◇---

THE DISEASES OF ASTONISHMENT

We will declare frankly that nothing is clear in this world. Only fools and
charlatans know and understand everything.
—ANTON CHEKHOV

IN 1692 THE Massachusetts Bay Colony executed fourteen women, five men, and two dogs for witchcraft. The sorcery materialized in January. The first hanging took place in June, the last in September; a stark, stunned silence followed. What discomfited those who survived the ordeal was not the cunning practice of witchcraft but the clumsy administration of justice. Innocents indeed appeared to have hanged. But guilty parties had escaped. There was no vow never to forget; consigning nine months to oblivion seemed a more appropriate response. It worked, for a generation. We have been conjuring with Salem—our national nightmare, the undercooked, overripe tabloid episode, the dystopian chapter in our past—ever since. It crackles, flickers, and jolts its way through American history and literature.

No one burned at the stake. No midwives died. The voodoo arrived later, with a nineteenth-century historian; the half-black slave with Longfellow; the casting of spells in the forest with Arthur Miller. (A movie delivered the chicken blood and the boiling cauldron.) Erudition plays a greater role in the story than ignorance. It is however true that fifty-five people confessed to witchcraft. A minister was hanged. And while we will never know the exact number of those formally charged with having "wickedly, maliciously, and feloniously" engaged in sorcery, somewhere between 144 and 185 witches and wizards were named in twenty-five villages and towns before the crisis passed. Reports had it that more than seven hundred witches flew about Massachusetts. So many stood accused that witnesses confused their witches. Even a careful chronicler afterward sent the wrong woman flying through the air on a singularly inauspicious flight.

The youngest of the witches was five, the eldest nearly eighty. A daughter accused her mother, who in turn accused her mother, who accused a neighbor and a minister. A wife and daughter denounced their husband and father. Husbands implicated wives; nephews their aunts; sons-in-law their mothers-in-law; siblings each other. Only fathers and sons weathered the crisis unscathed. A woman who traveled to Salem to clear her name wound up shackled before the afternoon was out. In Andover—the community most severely affected—one of every fifteen people was accused. The town's senior minister discovered he was related to no fewer than twenty witches. Ghosts escaped their graves to flit in and out of the courtroom, unnerving more than did the witches themselves. Through the episode surge several questions that touch the third rail of our fears: Who was conspiring against you? Might you be a witch and not know it? Can an innocent person be guilty? Could anyone, wondered a group of men late in the summer, think himself safe?

How did the idealistic Bay Colony arrive—three generations after its founding—in such a dark place? Nearly as many theories have been advanced to explain the Salem witch trials as the Kennedy assassination. Our first true-crime story has been attributed to generational, sexual, economic, ecclesiastical, and class tensions; regional hostilities imported from England; food poisoning; a hothouse religion in a cold climate; teenage hysteria; fraud, taxes, conspiracy; political instability; trauma

induced by Indian attacks; and to witchcraft itself, among the more reasonable theories.* You can blame atmospheric conditions, or simply the
weather: Historically, witchcraft accusations tended to spike in late winter. Over the years various parties have played the villain, some more
convincingly than others. The Salem villagers searched too to explain
what sent a constable with an arrest warrant to which door. The pattern
was only slightly more obvious to them than it is to us, involving as it did
subterranean fairy circles of credits and debits, whispered resentments,
long-incubated grudges, and half-forgotten aversions. Even at the time, it
was clear to some that Salem was a story of one thing behind which was
a story about something else altogether. Much of its subtext is lost to us,
like the jokes in Shakespeare.

America's tiny reign of terror, Salem represents one of the rare
moments in our enlightened past when the candles are knocked out
and everyone seems to be groping about in the dark, the place where all
good stories begin. Easy to caricature — it is the only tragedy that has
acquired its own annual, unrelated holiday — it is more difficult to com-
prehend. The irresistible locked-room mystery of the matter is what
keeps us coming back to it. In three hundred years, we have not adequately penetrated nine months of Massachusetts history. If we knew
more about Salem, we might attend to it less, a conundrum that touches
on something of what propelled the witch panic in the first place. Things
disturb us in the night. Sometimes they are our consciences. Sometimes
they are our secrets. Sometimes they are our fears, translated from one
idiom to another. Often what pinches and pricks, gnaws, claws, stabs,
and suffocates, like a seventeenth-century witch, is the irritatingly
unsolved puzzle in the next room.

The population of New England in 1692 would fit into Yankee Stadium

* Most accomplish only part of the job. As a proponent of the witchcraft theory conceded:
"There are departments in twentieth-century American universities with as long and as
vicious a history of factional hatreds as any to be found in Salem, and the parties to these
hatreds accuse each other of all sorts of absurdities, but witchcraft is not one of them."

today. Nearly to a person, they were Puritans. Having suffered for their faith, those families had sailed to North America to worship "with more purity and less peril than they could do in the country where they were," as a minister at the heart of the crisis put it. They believed the Reformation incomplete, the Church of England insufficiently pure. They intended in North America to complete the task. On a providential mission, they hoped to begin history anew; they had the advantage of building a civilization—a "New English Israel," as one clergyman termed it in 1689—from scratch. Nonconforming Protestants, they were double dissenters, twice in revolt. That did not make them popular people. They tended toward fissions and factions, strong opinions, righteous indignation. Like any oppressed people, they defined themselves by what offended them, which would give New England its gritty flavor and, it has been argued, America its independence. Rigorous Calvinists, they had come a great distance to worship as they pleased; they were intolerant of those who did so differently. They were ardent, anxious, unbashful, incurably logical, not quite Americans, of as homogeneous a culture as has ever existed on this continent.

A visitor exaggerated when he reported that New Englanders could "neither drive a bargain, nor make a jest, without a text of Scripture at the end on it," but he was not far off. If there was a book in the house—as almost inevitably there was—it was the Bible. The early modern American thought, breathed, dreamed, disciplined, bartered, and hallucinated in biblical texts and imagery. Witchcraft judge Samuel Sewall would court an attractive widow with published sermons; she held him off with the Apostle Paul.* Railing that the people would rather starve him to death than pay his salary, the New Hampshire lieutenant governor cited Corinthians. His constituents countered with Luke. Saint John the Baptist might well turn up in a heated Cambridge land dispute. A prisoner cited Deuteronomy 19:19 in his own defense. And when a killer cat came

---

* To prepare his seventeen-year-old for a suitor, Sewall read her the story of Adam and Eve. It proved less soothing than expected; she hid from her caller in the stable.

flying in your window—to take hold of your throat and crush your chest as you lay defenseless in bed at night—you scared it away by invoking the Father, the Son, and the Holy Ghost. The creature thereupon leaped to the floor and flung itself out the window while you concluded that your irascible neighbor had paid a call, in feline form. A village away, a wheelwright came to the same conclusion when, just after sunset on a wet, windy evening, a black dog lunged at his throat. The ax in his hand proved useless; the name of the Lord alone spared him as he ran for his life.

The New World constituted a plagiarism of the old with a few crucial differences. Stretching from Martha's Vineyard to Nova Scotia and incorporating parts of present-day Rhode Island, Connecticut, New Hampshire, and Maine, the Bible commonwealth perched on the edge of a wilderness. From the start it tangled with another American staple: the devilish savage, the swarthy terrorist in the backyard. Even the colony's less isolated outposts felt their fragility. A tempest blew the roof off one of the finest houses in Salem as its ten occupants slept. A church went flying with its congregation inside. The early American lived not only on a frontier but in many ways out of time. A foreign monarch could be dead one minute and alive the next, so unreliable was the news. The residents of Massachusetts Bay did not always know who sat on the throne to which they owed allegiance. In 1692 they did not know the terms of their government. They had endured without one for three years; finalized at the end of 1691, a new charter was only just sailing their way. For three months of the year they could not be certain what year they were living in. Because the pope approved the Gregorian calendar, New England rejected it, stubbornly continuing to date the start of the new year to March 25. (When witches assaulted their first victims in Salem village, it was 1691 in North America, 1692 in Europe.)

In isolated settlements, in dim, smoky, firelit homes, New Englanders lived very much in the dark, where one listens more acutely, feels most passionately, imagines most vividly, where the sacred and the occult thrive. Their fears and fancies differed little from ours, even if the early

7

American witch had as much in common with our pointy-hatted crone as Somali pirates do with Captain Hook. Their dark, however, was a very different dark. The sky over New England was crow black, pitch-black, Bible black, so black it could be difficult at night to keep to the path, so black that a line of trees might freely migrate to another location or that you might find yourself pursued after nightfall by a rabid black hog, leaving you to crawl home, bloody and disoriented, on all fours. Indeed eyeglasses were rare in seventeenth-century Massachusetts. Hard cider was the drink of choice. Still, the thoughtful, devout, literate New Englander could, in the Salem courtroom, at times sound as if he were on a low-grade acid trip.

In all of New England, it would have been difficult to find more than a few souls to whom the supernatural was not eminently real, part and parcel of the culture, as was the devil himself. Most had a story to tell you, as many of us do today. We have all observed the occult in action, even if we do not quite subscribe to it. A year after the witchcraft crisis had passed, Cotton Mather, among the best-read men in America, visited Salem. He lost his sermon notes, which turned up a month later, scattered through the streets of a neighboring town. He concluded that diabolical agents had stolen them. One no more doubted the reality of sorcery than the literal truth of the Bible; to do so was to question the sun shining at noon. Faith aside, witchcraft served an eminently useful purpose. The aggravating, the confounding, the humiliating all dissolved in its cauldron. It made sense of the unfortunate and the eerie, the sick child and the rancid butter along with the killer cat. What else, shrugged one husband, could have caused the black and blue marks on his wife's arm?

For some of the things that plagued the seventeenth-century New Englander we have modern-day explanations. For others we do not. We have believed in any number of things—the tooth fairy, cold fusion, the benefits of smoking, the free lunch—that turn out not to exist. We all subscribe to preposterous beliefs; we just don't know yet which ones they are. We too have been known to prefer plot to truth; to deny the evidence before us in favor of the ideas behind us; to do insane things in the name of reason; to take that satisfying step from the righteous to the self-righteous; to drown our private guilts in a public well; to indulge in a little delusion. We have all believed that someone had nothing better to do than spend his day plotting against us. The seventeenth-century world appeared full of inexplicables, not unlike the automated, mind-reading, algorithmically enhanced modern one.

Though we tend not to conclude that specters have stolen our notes, we live with—and continue to relish—perplexity every day. We love to hear that when the flash of lightning struck the man at prayer, it carried away the book of Revelation but left the rest of the Bible intact. Even those of us who do not occupy the Puritans' high spiritual plane are susceptible to what Mather termed the "diseases of astonishment." Our appetite for the miraculous endures; we continue to want there to be something just beyond our ken. We hope to locate the secret powers we didn't know we had, like the ruby slippers Dorothy finds on her feet and that Glinda has to tell her how to work. Where women are concerned, it is preferable that those powers manifest only when crisis strikes; the best heroine is the accidental one. Before and after the trials, New England feasted on sensational tales of female daring, the prowess its women displayed under Indian assault. Those captivity narratives provided something of a template for witchcraft. Everyone has a captivity narrative; today we call it memoir. Sometimes too we turn out to be captives of our ideas. Salem is in part the story of what happens when a set of unanswerable questions meets a set of unquestioned answers.

Rich in shape-shifting humans, fantastical flights, rash wishes, beleaguered servants, evil stepmothers, bewitched hay, and enchanted apples, the crisis in Salem resembles another seventeenth-century genre as well: the fairy tale. It took place in the wilderness, the address to which the hunter transports you when instructed to cut out your lungs and liver, where wolves follow you home. Salem touches on what is unreal but by no means untrue; at its heart are unfulfilled wishes and unexpressed anxieties, rippling sexual undercurrents and raw terror. It unspools in that fertile, dreamlike expanse between the uncanny and the absurd. There had been New England witch trials before, but none precipitated by a cohort of bewitched adolescent and preadolescent girls. Also like a fairy tale, Salem is a story in which women — strong-minded women and trembling, subservient women, upright matrons and wayward teenagers — play decisive roles. It includes a tacit salute to unsettling female power in the sheer number of women accused. A group of young, disenfranchised girls unleashed the crisis, displaying forces no one could contain and that disturb still today. Which may or may not have something to do with why we have turned a story of women in peril into one about perilous women.

Women play the villains in fairy tales — what are you saying when you place the very emblem of lowly domestic duty between your legs and ride off, defying the bounds of community and laws of gravity? — but those tales are as well the province of youth. Salem is bound up on every level with adolescence, that immoderate age when, vulnerable and invincible, we skip blithely along the border between the rational and the irrational, when interest surges both in the spiritual and the supernatural. The crisis began with two prepubescent girls and came quickly to involve a group of teenagers, understood to be enchanted by individuals most of them had never met. The girls hailed from a village clamoring for its autonomy and from a colony itself in the throes of a painful adolescence. For years the Crown had attempted to impose royal authorities on New England, the most recent of which the leading citizens of Massachusetts — including nearly all the future witchcraft judges — had overthrown. They had every reason to demand English protection against marauding Indians and designing Frenchmen. But while bemoaning their vulnerability — they were an "orphan plantation" — the settlers simultaneously resented oversight. They braced from the start for interference, vowing to reject it when it came and finding themselves humiliated when it did. The relationship with the mother country had devolved into a running quarrel; for some time the people who were meant to protect the colonists seemed rather as if they persecuted them. (By contrast, London found New Englanders to be of "peevish and touchy humor.") The Massachusetts authorities suffered too from another anxiety that would play a role in 1692. Every time they looked back in admiration at the men who had founded their godly common-wealth, every time they lauded that greatest of generations, they grew just a little bit smaller themselves.

HISTORICAL TRUTHS EMERGE only with time. With Salem they have crept out haltingly at best and with some deformation. Avid record keep-ers, Puritans did not like for things to go forgotten. Yet mid-1692 is a period when, if you take the extant archives at face value, no one in Mas-sachusetts kept a regular diary, including even the most fanatical of dia-rists. Reverend Samuel Willard's *Compleat Body of Divinity*—a compendium so voluminous that no New England press could print it—makes a spec-tacular lunge from April 19 to August 8. Willard elided no months in 1691 or 1693. A venerable Salem minister wrote his eldest son that summer that the son's sister had been deserted by her miserable husband. He did not mention that she also happened to be detained on witchcraft charges. On his way to eminence, twenty-nine-year-old Cotton Mather remained largely in Boston but so much dwelled on Salem afterward that he essen-tially wrote himself into the story. He composed much of his 1692 diary after the fact. Salem comes down to us pockmarked by seventeenth-century deletions and studded with nineteenth-century inventions. We tend to revisit our national crack-up after miscarriages of justice, some parts of the country with more enthusiasm than others. (The Massachu-setts misstep was a Southern favorite around 1860, except in South Caro-lina, which later jailed a witch for over a year.) The Holocaust sent Marion Starkey toward Salem witchcraft in 1949. She produced the vol-ume that would inspire Arthur Miller to write *The Crucible* at the outset of the McCarthy crisis. Along with Nathaniel Hawthorne, Miller has largely made off with the story.

No trace of a single session of the witchcraft court survives. We have accounts of the trials but no records; we are left with preparatory papers—depositions, indictments, confessions, petitions—and two death warrants. The Salem village record book has been expunged. No newspaper yet circulated in a North American colony. While the bewitched commanded a rapt audience for much of a year, their voices are lost to us. Their words come to us exclusively from men who were far from thorough, seldom impartial, and not always transcribing in the room in which they heard those statements. They mangle and strangle the voices of the accused; they are equally inattentive to the accusers, not all of whose statements they committed to paper. We have few full transcripts of preliminary hearings. The testimony came too fast; the pandemonium in the courtroom made it impossible to hear. It is difficult to say with any certainty whose lines are whose. The recorders quickly gave up on faithful transcribing, summarizing instead, adding flavor as they went. One simply noted that a defendant adopted "a very wicked, spiteful manner." Another interrupted his work to call the suspect a liar. After a certain date, the keepers of the accounts did not dwell on denials, understood to crumble soon enough into confessions. Which poses another problem: The testimony is sworn, on oath. It is also full of tall tales, unless you happen to believe—as one woman confessed, having vowed to tell the truth, the whole truth, and nothing but the truth—that she flew on a stick with her church deacon and two others to a satanic baptism, and that she had, the previous Monday, carried her minister's specter through the air along with her, having earlier conferred in her orchard with a satanic cat. Over one hundred reporters took down testimony. Few were trained to do so. They were maddeningly inconsistent. Even when they recorded an answer, they did not always bother to note the question, although it is fairly easy to extrapolate what that was when a nineteen-year-old standing before three of the most imposing men she would meet in her lifetime cried, "I will tell! I will tell!"—and proceeded to confess to witchcraft.

Accusers confused suspects; later chroniclers conflated them further. Several had the same name. In many cases all we can glimpse of an individual is what emerged under withering interrogation as transcribed by court reporters antipathetic to her and who in some cases testified against her. We know little about most of them except that they were accused of witchcraft or confessed to it. They are like fairy-tale figures too in that we recognize them by a sole detail—a quirk of dress, a turn of phrase, an inner tremor. This leaves us to make much of a single characteristic: Mary Warren was fair-faced. Abigail Hobbs was shameless. George Jacobs had a rollicking sense of humor; Samuel Parris had none. What do we want those implicated in the trials to tell us? What were they thinking when they confessed to flying through the air or smothering the neighbor; deposing a perfectly lucid woman who insisted she knew nothing of witchcraft; sharing a cell with a convicted wizard; standing at the gallows as the man they accused of sorcery insisted, with his last breath, on his innocence? Where was the devil in Salem and what was he really up to? How did those who withstood the vicious accusations find the strength to do so? All went to their graves believing still in witches. At what point did it occur to them that though the sorcery might be real, the trials were a sham? Theirs is a little story that becomes a big one, much more than our national campfire story, the gothic, genie-releasing crack-up on the way to the Constitution. The witch hunt stands as a cobwebbed, crowd-sourced cautionary tale, a reminder that—as a minister at odds with the crisis noted—extreme right can blunder into extreme wrong.

There is a very great deal we cannot know: How did two people who had accused each other of witchcraft fare together for months on end in a tiny cell? What if they were mother and daughter? How did a ghost differ from an apparition? Which terror was worse, that the next knock would be at your door, that the witchcraft would skid next into your home, or that the man you were sentencing to hang might not be a wizard after all? We go back to their words again and again to wring answers from parched Puritan prose and pursed Puritan lips, to unlock the meaning of an episode that originated in allegory and that burst — an electrifying pop-up book — into incandescent history, only to settle back into allegory. A prayer, a spell, a book; the hope is the same: if we can just fix the words in the right order, the horizon will brighten, our vision improve, and — uncertainty relaxing its hold — all will fall wondrously into place.

II

⎯⎯⎯⎯◦◦⎯⎯⎯⎯

THAT OLD DELUDER

But who can tell what miraculous things I may see before this year be out!
—COTTON MATHER, 1692

SKIMMING GROVES OF oak, mossy bogs, and a tangle of streams, Ann Foster sailed above the treetops, over fields and fences, on a pole. In her pocket she carried bread and cheese. It was mid-May 1692; after a wet spring, a chill hung in the air. Before Foster on the pole sat Martha Carrier, half Foster's age and the dauntless mother of four. Carrier had arranged the flight. She had persuaded Foster to accompany her; she knew the way. A plush carpet of meadows and hillocks unfurled beneath the women as they flew southeast across the Ipswich River, over red maples and blossoming orchards, the wind in their faces, a bright moon pasted in the sky. For years Foster and Carrier—near neighbors, their families of Scottish descent—had attended the same church, in Andover, Massachusetts.

They traveled at high speed, covering in a flash ground that would have required three and a half hours by a good horse and that until recently had been stony and uneven, impassable in the dark. Their flight was all the same not without incident. Aloft one minute, the women found themselves in freefall the next when—nearing a thick woods—their pole snapped suddenly beneath them and they plunged to the ground. Elderly Foster felt her leg crumple under her. Instinctively, she flung her arms around Carrier's neck, to which she held fast. In such a way, Foster later explained—and her account never varied in the slightest—the two women soared off again, to land safely in a Salem village meadow. The meeting had not yet begun; they had time to picnic in the grass, under a tree. On her knees, Foster drank from a nearby brook. Theirs was not the first such aerial malfunction. Two decades earlier a little girl in Sweden, also en route to a momentous, late-night meeting in a meadow, had precipitously fallen from a great altitude. She wound up with an "exceeding great pain in her side."

Foster and Carrier overflew twelve miles between sparsely settled communities. That no one saw them streak through the sky made sense. That no one heard the crash was more surprising. Sound echoed and ricocheted through the New England air, which had an amplifying effect on the ear and the imagination. The slap of a beaver's tail against the water could be heard a half a mile off. The "hideous noise with roaring" of fat black bears carried far and wide, as did the screech of the crowd when a scaffold fell. Each disturbance begged for an explanation. That crash of the ocean in the landlocked distance? A flock of pigeons, alighting in a tree. The freakish bellow? In Boston, Samuel Sewall discovered it to be the lament of his cow, bitten by a dog. Dogs howled nightly at marauding wolves. But sometimes the wild barking, the predawn crack of timber, indicated something more sinister. Sometimes it meant that— board by board—the neighbors were disassembling the house next door, the deft resolution of a bitter property dispute. Who would have guessed that what sounded like a washerwoman beating her linen deep in the forest would turn out to be giant tortoises propagating?

Nor did it necessarily make sense to believe your eyes. Sometimes the scuffling and stomping in the dark revealed brilliantly uniformed foreigners. They left visible tracks before evaporating into cornfields, orchards, and swamps. They fired real bullets but—over two nerve-racking weeks—proved impervious to those returned by sixty Ipswich militiamen. They were understood to be phantom Frenchmen and Indians. That was a better explanation than some. You might wake to commotion in the night to discover a family of frisky cats. The bright moonlight could as easily reveal the scrabbling at the window to have been Susannah Martin, who had crashed into your bed and was settled on your stomach, reaching for your throat. In broad daylight, Ann Putnam's uncle saw Mrs. Bradbury vanish into her yard, to reappear seconds later as a blue boar. When a live calf came hurtling down the chimney and into the kitchen, a mischievous teenager prowled about. But what of the glow-in-the-dark jellyfish in the late-night fireplace? There were at least a dozen of them, marveled Elizer Keyser. The maid saw them too! The mare was there one minute, gone the next. Who had moved the landmarks, leaving an Amesbury man to stumble about the brush — and into a nonexistent pit — three miles from home, on a moonlit Saturday night? Eighteen-year-old Susannah Shelden rubbed her eyes: a saucer had transported itself out of doors. What was the broom doing lodged in the apple tree again?

Shapes emerged from the darkness to resolve into different entities altogether. The troop of men and horses on the beach in the mid-distance turned out to be a lame Indian with a fishing net over his shoulder. When an apprentice in the Sewall household clubbed a dog outside the door, he in fact leveled a nine-year-old boy. And when Reverend Samuel Parris's slave Tituba came upon a hairy, three-foot-tall creature with wings and a long nose warming itself in a dark room before the parsonage fire, she naturally took it to be peevish Sarah Osborne. She swore it was, in fact. Beverly minister John Hale was perhaps more correct in surmising that when something came tearing down the chimney, ripping an eight-foot hole in the roof, rattling the pewter, and paralyzing his arm, it was lightning. In an equally sure-handed attempt to reconcile perception with understanding, several eminent ministers standing in a refurbished kitchen on a hot April afternoon discussing why "heaven's artillery" seemed disproportionately fond of clergymen's homes had every reason to conclude — as buckets of hailstones suddenly crashed through the brand-new windows and skittered across the floor — that someone, somewhere, was making a point. Neighbors gaped at the heap of broken tile and shattered glass. It remained only to discern the message. A Puritan did not waste a catastrophe.

Ann Foster had soared into Salem on her stick three years before that hailstorm. She needed no witness to corroborate her aerial misadventure; she had reason to remember the flight with vivid clarity, down to the hoofprints in the sandy path along the meadow. Moreover, her leg continued to trouble her for months.

TWO THINGS FLEW even more swiftly than two Andover women through the New England air. Indians darted out of forests to glide soundlessly into villages. "Horrid sorcerers and hellish conjurers," they seemed the true princes of darkness. Without a knock or a greeting, four armed Indians might appear in your parlor to warm themselves by the fire, propositioning you while you cowered in the corner with your knitting. You could return from a trip to Boston to find your house in ashes and your family taken captive, all courtesy of an invisible enemy. "It is harder to find them than to foil them," noted Cotton Mather, the brilliant, fair-haired young minister.* They skulked, they lurked, they flitted, they committed atrocities—and they vanished. Even their wigwams dematerialized from one minute to the next. "Our men could see no enemy to shoot at," lamented a Cambridge major general. A fifteen-month contest between the settlers and the Native Americans, King Philip's War ended in 1676. It obliterated a third of New England's one hundred towns, pulverized its economy, and claimed 10 percent of the adult male population. Every Bay Colony resident—and especially every resident of Essex County, to which Salem belonged—lost a friend or relative. In 1692 colonists referred to those grisly months as "the last Indian war" for a reason: another had begun to take shape. A series of devastating raids portended a new conflict with Wabanaki Indians and the

---

* He was citing Caesar on the Scythians, from whom Mather understood the Native Americans descended. Others believed them in some vague way descended from a tribe of Israel.

French who made them their allies in an extension of a European war. The frontier had recently moved to within fifty miles of Salem.

Rumor was the other nimble traveler, melting through floorboards and floating through windows, insensible to mud, snow, fatigue, a light-footed fugitive from lumbering truth. As a seventeenth-century bookseller observed, "The whole race of mankind is generally infected with an itching desire of hearing news." The condition was more acute for the lack of newspapers. A New Englander made do with what he had; when word failed to filter through knotholes or curtainless windows, it was coaxed. A Salem couple took a servant to court for spying on them and retailing what he saw. Given the shared beds and cramped, cluttered quarters—the average Salem village household consisted of six people in four rooms, the beef in the parlor and the loom in the kitchen—privacy proved a New England rarity. More than a few Massachusetts residents woke to giggling, sometimes in the very bed in which they slept.*

Small towns subvert the natural ratio of mystery to secrecy. With a population of no more than five hundred and fifty people, Salem village knew plenty of the former, little of the latter. Hearsay enjoyed a long life, sustained by accretion as well as repetition. Everyone in 1692 Andover knew that Ann Foster had three years earlier suffered a horrific loss. Her son-in-law and her daughter had quarreled one evening over a land sale; Foster's son-in-law had ended the argument by slashing his wife's throat. She had been hugely pregnant with what would have been the couple's eighth child. The murderer repented on the gallows, publicly testifying to the virtues of family harmony. (That account too is hearsay, but at least ministerial hearsay.) Also in 1689, Foster's grandson miraculously survived an Indian ambush. Partially scalped, he had been left for dead. It was no secret either that Martha Carrier, Foster's flying companion, had had a son before she married the child's father, a penniless Welsh servant. In 1690 the Carriers contracted smallpox. Andover had ordered

---

* And some of those who tittered wound up thereafter in meeting with signs reading "I Stand Here for My Lascivious and Wanton Carriages" around their necks.

them to leave town. They refused. The Andover selectmen quarantined the family, concerned that—if they had not already done so—the Carriers might "spread the distemper with wicked carelessness." Decades earlier, Martha had been rumored to be a witch.

So it was that in late January 1692—about the time that a vicious Indian attack razed York, Maine, leaving its mutilated minister dead on his doorstep; as a thaw released New England from an uncommonly brutal winter; as word arrived that an ocean away a new Massachusetts governor had kissed the ring of William III and would be sailing home with a new charter, one that promised at last to deliver the colony from months of anarchy—reports flew about that something was grievously wrong in the household of Samuel Parris, the Salem village minister.

It began, over a week of inky black nights, with prickling sensations. Abigail Williams, the reverend's blond, eleven-year-old niece, appears to have been afflicted first. Soon enough nine-year-old Betty Parris exhibited the same symptoms. The cousins complained of bites and pinches by "invisible agents." They barked and yelped. They fell dumb. Their bodies shuddered and spun. They went limp or spasmodically rigid. Neither girl ran a fever; neither suffered from epilepsy. The paralyzed postures alternated with frantic, indecipherable gestures. The girls launched into "foolish, ridiculous speeches, which neither they themselves nor any others could make sense of." They crept into holes or under chairs and stools from which they were extracted with difficulty. One disappeared halfway down a well. Abigail attempted to launch herself into the air, flinging her arms and making flying noises. Neither appeared to have time for prayer, though until January, both had been perfectly well behaved and well mannered. At night they slept like babies.

It had all happened before. Most memorably, four equally sensible Boston children—the sons and daughters of a devout Boston stone layer, children of "exemplary temper and carriage"—had suffered from a baffling disorder. "They would bark at one another like dogs, and again purr like so many cats," noted Cotton Mather, who observed John Goodwin's children in 1689. They flew like geese, on one occasion for twenty feet. They recoiled from blows of invisible sticks, shrieked that they were sliced by knives or wrapped in chains. Pains ricocheted around their bodies faster than an observer could record them. The children could neither dress nor undress for their contortions. They attempted to strangle themselves. Jaws, wrists, necks flew out of joint. "Sometimes they would be deaf, sometimes dumb, and sometimes blind, and often, all this at once," recorded Mather, under normal circumstances a perfect working definition of adolescence. Parental reproof sent them into agonies; chores defied them. They could scrub a clean table while a dirty one left them paralyzed. Household mishaps produced gales of laughter. "But nothing in the world," reported Mather, "would so discompose them as a religious exercise." Any mention of God or Christ sent them into "intolerable anguish." Martha Goodwin could read the *Oxford Book of Jests* but seized up when handed either a more edifying volume or one with the name Mather on it.

He that summer took in thirteen-year-old Martha to see to her cure. She cantered, trotted, and galloped about the Mather household on her "aerial steed," whistling through family prayer and pummeling anyone who attempted it in her presence, the worst houseguest in history. Samuel Parris and his wife, Elizabeth, had moved to Salem over the same season; they acquainted themselves with the village as, in Boston, Martha threw books at Cotton Mather's head. Parris could only have thought instantly of the Goodwins in 1692; he would have known every detail of that family's trials from Mather's much reprinted *Memorable Providences, Relating to Witchcraft and Possessions,* which included their story. His own minister had endorsed the volume, having observed the contorting children. The "agitations, writhings, tumblings, tossings, wallowings, foamings" in the Salem household were identical, only more acute. Abigail and Betty cried that they were being stabbed by fine needles. Their skin burned. In a two-story parsonage that measured forty-two by twenty feet, Parris could nowhere have escaped their shrieks, audible from a distance; they could only have been grateful the steep-roofed, clapboard home sat back from the road. The household also included ten-year-old Thomas Parris and four-year-old Susannah, neither of them afflicted, both presumably petrified.

Although they kept two Indian slaves, Tituba and John, the family had reason to feel practically as well as spiritually besieged. When she was not tending livestock, the garden, or a fire, when she was not baking or candle-making, a Puritan girl was meant to be knitting, spooling, or weaving. A five-year-old could be relied upon to sew a counterpane or spin flax. The flailing girls utterly disrupted the family routine. They could not be left alone. Nor could Parris have easily prepared a sermon upstairs given the mayhem downstairs. The most gifted of his colleagues devoted seven hours of fevered concentration to that exercise; others allotted a week of solitary study to each discourse, reading and meditating on his subject. If the Puritan minister spent a good deal of time parsing silences, Parris's ordeal was now reversed. He worked to ear-piercing screams. He was accustomed to being the one visitors came to hear, a role his daughter and niece usurped.

At all times, the parsonage welcomed callers; as of February, it was overrun. Illness was a public event in the seventeenth century, unexplained illness a province-wide one. The curious and the well-wishers crowded in, gooseflesh rising on their arms. The howls and grotesque writhings disturbed. They were riveting. They were the kind of thing that made you flee in horror, gape in hair-raising, heart-racing disbelief, or faint dead away. In similar cases as many as forty or fifty pressed into the sickroom. Some were repeat visitors and helpful neighbors enlisted to watch and restrain the frenzied children. The neighbor who did not call was the exception, as one would be reminded soon enough. Others traveled from miles away to sit in the smoky, opaque light of the Parrises' low-ceilinged parlor. Between prayers they sang psalms together, as had a great crowd at the Goodwin household for days on end. Sometimes they got more than they bargained for; those children were abusive with ministers and insolent with visitors.*

A natural list-maker and scorekeeper, Samuel Parris was impatient and exacting, but he did not act precipitously. From his disordered household some hints of the affliction crept into his sermons, which he delivered regularly, once on Thursday, twice on Sunday. Those were uninspired affairs; Parris was an unoriginal thinker to whom markedly original things would happen. He did not deviate substantially from his previous themes, dilating on Christ's ascension, on his mediation between God and man. Through February Parris looked largely to fasts and prayer. He consulted with fellow clergymen. His cousin and contemporary the Milton minister may have been particularly helpful; his daughter had earlier suffered convulsions. With cider and cakes, Samuel and Elizabeth Parris entertained the well-wishers who crowded their home. They prayed ardently. But when he had had enough of the "odd postures and antic gestures," the deranged speeches, when it became clear that Scripture alone would not relieve the girls' preternatural symptoms, Parris called in the doctors.

Years later the practice of medicine in Boston would be deemed "perniciously bad" by a university-educated physician; in 1692 no university-trained physician had yet arrived in either Salem town or its neighbor, tiny Salem village, where the girls twitched and snapped. A basic medical kit of the time looked little different from an ancient Greek one, consisting as it did of beetle's blood, fox lung, and dried dolphin heart. In powders or plasters, snails figured in many remedies. They were at least easier to harvest than unicorn's horn. The fat of a roasted hedgehog dripped into the ear constituted "an excellent remedy for deafness." The most informed medical man in the colonies at the time swore by saltpeter for measles, headache, and sciatica. Cotton Mather believed sixty

---

* In a Connecticut case later in 1692, the father of a convulsing girl encouraged callers; it was important they observe the unnatural happenings for themselves. He wanted to make it clear that no one was playacting.

drops of lavender and a mouthful of gingerbread cured memory loss. For epilepsy a wolf-skin girdle purportedly worked wonders, as did burnt black-cow dung or frog-liver powder administered five times daily. Hysteria had been cataloged well before 1692. A Salem physician treated it with a brew of breast milk and the blood from an amputated tomcat ear.

Salem village consisted of some ninety families; it had one practicing physician that January. William Griggs was new to the community, having recently bought a farm about a mile and a half from the parsonage. An active, pious citizen, he had complained of taverns near meeting-houses; he had testified against those who absented themselves from worship. Griggs owned nine medical texts. He could read but not write. He is the likely candidate — or among the likely candidates, as Parris evidently reached out to several — to have examined the girls. Years earlier Griggs had been a member of Parris's Boston congregation; the two were close to the same Salem families. There is at least one concrete reason to assume Parris called for the seventy-one-year-old: the contagion followed Griggs home. Better traveled, more sophisticated physicians had examined the Goodwin children, who had turned blue in the face and complained of being roasted alive on invisible spits. Prolonged, violent fits were assumed to be sent by the devil; the first question a victim asked under the circumstances was "Am I bewitched?" The doctor who had examined a seizing, strangled Groton girl a generation earlier initially diagnosed a stomach disorder. On a second visit he refused to administer to her further. The distemper was diabolical; he prescribed a town-wide fast. Whoever examined Abigail and Betty came to the same conclusion. Clearly the supernatural explanation was already the one on the street. The "evil hand" was a diagnosis "the neighbors quickly took up," noted Reverend Hale, the only chronicler to observe the girls' initial pinches and pricks. It likely terrified the cousins, whose symptoms worsened.

Hale had some experience in that realm, having as a child joined a delegation that visited a jailed witch on her execution day in the hope of eliciting a confession. The suspect was a neighbor, the first woman to be hanged for witchcraft in Massachusetts. She denied her guilt all the way to the gallows. Hale had spoken with another accused witch after her 1680 reprieve. Officiating in nearby Beverly, the amiable fifty-six-year-old counted himself as among Parris's closest colleagues. As did most everyone in New England at the time, he believed in witches, if not also in angels, unicorns, and mermen. How did he receive the diagnosis? He could not have been surprised; he may well have been relieved. "Hellish operations," as he termed them, dissolved any doubts about the girls' souls and absolved him of responsibility. He had every reason to prefer satanic mischief to a divine frown; possession would have been more problematic.* As alarming as was the diagnosis, it was also pulse-quickening. Witchcraft was portentous, a Puritan favorite. Never before had it broken out in a parsonage. On the scale of ministerial humiliations, a diabolical invasion was at least more exciting than the birth of an illegitimate grandson, a stain with which Cotton Mather would later contend. A decade younger than Parris, Mather was only twenty-nine in 1692. He was also already ubiquitous, on his way to becoming the best-known man in New England, which is what happens when you are handsome, tall, gifted, and tireless, enter Harvard at eleven, preach your first sermon at sixteen, and combine in your very name two legends of the early Massachusetts ministry.

Parris made no attempt to shrink from the celestial drama in which he found himself; divine love could be glimpsed behind every misfortune. From his upstairs study in a bewitched house he continued his meditations on the 110th Psalm. God was "angry and sending forth

---

* If a serious discussion of witchcraft versus possession took place, it is lost to us. Not everyone distinguished between them or so much as attempted to; the symptoms were largely the same. Mather noted their "near affinity," conjoining the two even in the title of *Memorable Providences*. One could invite the other: "It is an ordinary thing," the minister at the center of the Groton case observed, "for a possession to be introduced by a bewitching." (In that he followed Mather's father, Increase, who believed one could simultaneously suffer from both.) Fumbling toward an explanation, Parris early on hinted at demonic possession. It was understood that the possessed experienced no bodily harm, however; visible marks bloomed on the girls' bodies. Soon enough apparitions corroborated the witchcraft, a diagnosis Parris had cause to prefer. Complicity made all the difference: a willing host to impurity, the possessed person was guilty. The bewitched was innocent.

destroyers," he alerted his parishioners. It was essential to persevere, "to beware of fainting when we are chastened," to battle bravely against "all our spiritual enemies." The explanation was to some degree satisfying. It was perversely flattering to be singled out to combat evil; there was a reason for those selective lightning strikes, the bolts from the blue, through the window, down the chimney. "I am a man greatly assaulted by Satan," Mather would observe privately, sounding nearly boastful. "Is it because I have done much against that enemy?" Or as the father of the Goodwin children had phrased it, playing the adversity-shouldering game with grace, a dangerous condition was—spiritually speaking—a profitable one. "If we want afflictions we shall have them, and sanctified afflictions are choice mercies," concluded the godly mason. Simultaneously he wrung his hands over a question that must have haunted Parris as well: What had he done to incite this heavenly rebuke? A minister's home was meant to be a "school of piety," not "a den for devils."

How the village received the diagnosis was clear from what came next. On February 25, Parris and his wife left Salem under teeming rain. In their absence a close neighbor paid a call. The Parrises presumably asked Mary Sibley to look in on Abigail and Betty, roaring now for over a month. The mother of five, Mary Sibley was six months pregnant. Among the wealthier couples in the community, she and her cooper husband were pillars of the church; Samuel Sibley stepped in when an estate needed to be settled or a bond guaranteed. His wife felt comfortable in the Parris household. Less comfortable with the pace at which her minister resolved the mystery there, she arranged a furtive experiment. The question was no longer what afflicted the children but who; Sibley determined to catch a witch. At her instruction, John, the Parrises' Indian slave, mixed the girls' urine into a rye-flour cake, baked amid the embers on the hearth. Sibley then fed the concoction to the family dog. There was some fogginess about how the countermagic worked—by drawing the witch to the animal, by transferring the spell to it, or by scalding the witch—but the old English recipe could be trusted to reveal the guilty party.

Parris was livid to learn of the experiment. Countermagic had no place in a parsonage. He remained intent on the scourge not escaping his home; in his place, Boston ministers had taken great pains to suppress the names of alleged witches. Sibley courted greater perils as well. She had favored superstition over religion, a practice Parris decried as "going to the devil for help against the devil." Her meddling unleashed occult, little-understood forces; she had set up a kind of satanic lightning rod. A month later—the intervening weeks proved tumultuous—the belea-guered minister would summon her to an interview in his study. He reproached her severely. Sobbing, she offered abject apologies. She had acted only unthinkingly, Sibley explained, "from what she had heard of this nature from other ignorant, or worse, persons." She would be cir-cumspect in the future. Parris read her the stiff reprimand he intended to share with the congregation after Sunday's sermon. Her cake had occa-sioned much mischief. "By this means (it seems) the Devil has been raised amongst us," Parris announced before administering communion on March 27, "and his rage is vehement and terrible, and when he shall be silenced, the Lord only knows." He warned his congregants to be on the alert against "Satan's wiles and devices." From the pulpit, in a dark gown and a flat white linen collar, Parris asked them to bear collective witness to Mary Sibley's misdeed, to call "our sister to deep humiliation for what she has done." Might he have a show of hands? All agreed. Turning to the heavily pregnant Sibley, Parris asked if—assuming she admitted to her sin and repented for it—they might hear as much from her own mouth. Public expiation was essential. Sibley offered an emotional apology. Parris continued: "Brethren, if herein you have received satisfaction, testify by lifting up your hands." Every (male) hand in the room went up, the last time a consensus would prove possible in the 1692 village meetinghouse.

At the parsonage Parris reproached the servants as well. Already charged, the atmosphere there must have crackled with resentment. By that time the minister had larger matters with which to contend, how-ever. While his niece and daughter made a great deal of noise, it had been impossible to decipher what precisely they meant to say. The cake worked its diabolical magic; within days, Betty and Abigail named names. Not one but three witches were loose in Salem. The girls could see them perfectly. And by the sodden end of February—sheets of rain fell all week, flooding fields and turning the village into a coursing river of mud—those witches were on a pole flying through the air.

SALEM VILLAGE OWED its existence in part to its fear of ambush. The oldest settlement in Massachusetts Bay and very nearly New England's capital, the town of Salem had been named in 1629. A fine, flourishing community about a mile long, scented by salty sea air and the rich, crisp hint of pine, it counted among the most agreeable addresses in the colony. Salem's gem of a harbor was second only to Boston's; the town enjoyed a brisk trade with Europe and the West Indies. Built on a peninsula, surrounded by velvety green hills and idyllic coves, it was home to thriving fisheries and shipyards. When a new king ascended to the English throne in 1685, he did so with acclamations and celebrations in Boston but with proclamations as well in Salem, the only other Massachusetts town of more than two thousand people. Quieter and less cosmopolitan, Salem was every bit as refined as Boston, with an array of painted, gabled, multiple-storied homes and a number of newly minted fortunes.

As early as 1640, farmers had begun to venture north and west, away from the prosperous port, beyond the town's rolling hills, in search of more arable land. Their loose-limbed settlement became Salem village (and modern-day Danvers). Soon enough, those enterprising villagers— known locally as the Salem farmers—began to lobby for institutions of their own. While their families disliked making the five- to ten-mile trek through driving snow to attend meeting, there were additional considerations as well. In 1667 the villagers petitioned the general court in Boston. Did it really make sense for them to trudge to Salem town to take their turns at military watch? It was awfully far for them, particularly onerous after dark, "in a wilderness that is so little cleared and [by] ways

so unpassable." Many of them lived a full mile from their nearest neighbors. The farmers' departures struck terror in the hearts of their wives,
"especially considering what dreadful examples former times have
afforded in that respect, in this country, from Indians (and from others
also), in the night season, when their husbands have been absent."

Moreover, they continued with unassailable logic, was it not profan-
ing the Lord to travel so far armed to watch a town in peacetime? The
older community insisted on the unceasing danger. (Its leaders preferred
to reduce neither its tax base nor its territory.) But were the farmers—in
a rustic settlement of fifty isolated farmsteads, then without even a meetinghouse at their center—not more vulnerable than those in the compact, commercial lanes of Salem, with its larger population and its many
fine homes? Surely the town could keep watch without the villagers. Its
leaders balked, countering that only recently a French ship had somehow
managed to sail undetected into port after nightfall. How was that possible? scoffed the farmers, who knew well that the innocuous ship had
been sighted well before dark. They occupied the front lines. Would it
not make more sense for the townspeople to come watch them rather
than the other way around? The farmers prevailed, though not without
Nathaniel Putnam, one of the wealthiest villagers, being fined for "bitterly affronting and abusing" the town officials.

Tempers flared anew several years later when the town of Salem proposed to build a larger meetinghouse. We won't pay for it, announced the
defiant villagers, unless you help pay for one of our own. Repeatedly
they lobbied for an independent parish, succeeding in the last days of
1672. Salem town supplied a hand-me-down pulpit along with a deacon's
seat, probably of riven oak, like the pews. The two Salems continued to
annoy each other, the village because it was obliged to appeal to the
town for legislation, extracted only with difficulty; the town because the
villagers remained perpetually at odds, unable to resolve their disputes.
Meanwhile the town could not seem to liberate itself from the farmers'
pesky questions about their church affairs. Could they not keep their
antipathies to themselves? They seemed intent on devouring one

another. Shortly after the Parris family settled into the parsonage, the town leaders essentially advised the villagers to leave them alone.

The village officially hired its first minister in 1672. Sixteen years later, with Samuel Parris, it hired its fourth. Each would prove indelibly involved in the events of 1692, when their paths crossed with varying degrees of awkwardness. One man literally haunted those proceedings, while another recorded them. The third would return as a powerful wizard. A recent Harvard graduate, James Bayley preached his first Salem sermon in October 1671. He had turned twenty-two and married weeks earlier. The community did not unanimously take to him. Bayley was unqualified; he was offensive; he was negligent; he imagined his post to be more permanent than it was. A guest who spent three weeks at his home swore in court that she had never heard Bayley read or expound on any part of the Scripture with his family. His home life was doubtless tense. His congregants had agreed to build him a parsonage, an offer on which they failed to make good. The minister constructed a house himself; he and his new wife evidently lost two daughters in it before 1677. Meanwhile the community divided along party lines. Matters proved so incendiary that the parishioners could not agree on so much as who might arbitrate. Thirty-nine church members supported Bayley. Sixteen did not, including several of the most influential men in the community.

Bayley's tenure caught something of the flavor of Salem village. With him came his wife's twelve-year-old sister, who at seventeen would marry into the redoubtable Putnam clan. Her husband was Thomas Putnam Jr., a son of the richest man in the village and a nephew of the elderly Nathaniel. Salem was composed in large part of Putnams, to whom both Mary Sibley, the impulsive baker, and William Griggs, the physician, were related by marriage. The two young couples—the Bayleys and the Thomas Putnams—grew close. That did not prevent other Putnams from attacking Bayley. It might even have encouraged them in their campaign. Samuel Parris knew of what he spoke when, on a Sunday afternoon in 1692, just before his home erupted in chaos, he observed from the pulpit that "not seldom great hatred ariseth even from nearest relations." He took as his text Mark 13:12: "Brother will betray brother to death, as father his child. Children will rebel against their parents and have them put to death."

The Salem farmers carried their bitter allegations and implacable grudges to the mother church in Salem, ultimately to court. Bayley meanwhile filed a slander suit. The court ruled in his favor and ordered that he continue in his position. It could not enforce its decision; while the majority of his congregants continued to support him, by late 1679 Bayley understood that he had no future in Salem. He moved across the village. Within a year the committee formed to name his successor settled on George Burroughs, a handsome, diminutive, dark-haired man who, though older, had been just behind Bayley at Harvard, where he had earned a master's degree. The grandson of an eminent minister, Burroughs had since served at a number of frontier parishes, at the last of which he had heroically endured an Indian attack. He was twenty-eight.

Again the Putnams played a crucial role. Burroughs and his family lived with a Putnam family for much of 1681, moving into the parsonage — the Parrises' future address — only in the fall. Keenly aware of the collisions and disappointments that vexed New England ministries, Burroughs attached an arbitration clause to his contract. He would serve on the condition "that in case any difference should arise in time to come, that we engage on both sides to submit to council for a peaceable issue." He landed in court all the same; it seemed an obligation of one church faction to make the life of the other faction's choice miserable. From the start, Burroughs's salary was not collected. When his young wife died shortly after the move to the newly built parsonage, he could not afford the funeral. On April 10, 1683, the villagers complained in county court that Burroughs had not preached for a month. He was hastily packing to leave — he expected to be gone that very week — but refused to explain himself. (His reluctance may have had something to do with the fact that John Putnam had loaned Burroughs funds, then threatened to have the minister arrested for debt when Burroughs could not reimburse him. The village was to blame on both counts, having neglected to pay its minister in the first place.) Burroughs continued unresponsive, prefer-ring to wash his hands of the fractious community. What I had wanted to ask when I called on you, explained one parishioner, an obsessive, out-spoken potter, was how a village might prosper "when brother is against brother and neighbors against neighbors, all quarreling and smiting one another?" Their minister, the potter reminded Burroughs, was meant to be their spokesman and guardian, an intellectual light. Burroughs had been unwilling to organize private meetings or cool village tempers. He preached what he felt like. For his lucid if indelicate analysis, the potter was admonished by the court. Burroughs departed that spring.

In February 1684 the Salem church committee brought Reverend Deodat Lawson to Salem. Unlike his predecessors, Lawson was British-born. He had arrived in the colony some five years earlier from Norfolk, where his father was a Cambridge-educated minister. Intended from birth for the clergy—Deodat, he explained, meant "given to God"—Lawson had somewhere acquired a formal education, although he took no degree. He wrote easily in Latin and Greek, in an exquisite hand. He benefited from some socially prestigious family connections in London, where he had worked briefly as an apprentice to a prosperous ironmon-ger and even more briefly as a royal physician before emigrating, early in the 1670s. Having served fewer than two of the expected seven years of a pastorate on Martha's Vineyard, Lawson returned in 1682 to secular pur-suits, in Boston. With his wife and two young children he settled in Salem. He was then in his early thirties. A third child, a daughter, was born and died in the village, where Lawson suddenly lost his wife as well. Given to drama and formal turns of phrase, he had a keen ear for nuance. He could be pragmatic; he praised family prayer so long as it was not overtedious. "God is not moved by a multitude of words," he would note, though one wishes Lawson had felt differently. He supplied the only contemporaneous account of the events of 1692.

The villagers voted to deliver firewood to their new minister but in the end paid him and advised him to forage for his own. If the decision rankled, Lawson left no record of ill will. He preferred to please. Two years into his tenure, his future divided the community. Were he ordained, Salem would constitute a covenanted church at last. It would also relinquish the land on which the parsonage sat, a New England sticking point. The Putnams supported the ordination, which several other families opposed on theological ground, because Lawson disappointed in some way, or simply because he was the Putnams' man. Again the farmers submitted the matter to cooler minds in Salem town, where the authorities professed themselves heartsick to witness such a vast supply of "uncharitable expressions," "settled prejudice and resolved animosity." Why did they persist in making one another miserable? It was at this juncture that the town fathers asked again not to be disturbed by the villagers' recriminations. "If you will unreasonably trouble yourselves, we pray you not any further to trouble us," they scolded. Lawson opted to leave before relations deteriorated completely. The villagers were not unembarrassed by their behavior. They voted to purge the record book, which in 1687 Thomas Putnam rewrote, the squabbling of the Burroughs and Bayley decade omitted. It was thought those toxic entries might prove damaging in the future.

Without an independent church and with no civic authorities of its own, the village was hamstrung when it came to settling communal differences. It was far from alone in its troubled church politics. The relationship between pastor and flock, it was said, should be like that between husband and wife. Indeed it proved as contentious as cordial. A Puritan devoted himself to examination and interrogation; he held his minister in a similar embrace. Plenty of clergymen inserted escape clauses into their contracts. Increase Mather, the most conspicuous cleric in New England and Cotton's illustrious father, allowed that he was free to leave his Boston parish if the Lord called him elsewhere, if his pay proved insufficient, or if he suffered "persecution" by his congregation. Jobs were difficult to come by, as was job security; ministers were dismissed and ordinations delayed. One patient cleric waited twenty-seven years. At a 1720 ordination, malcontents launched water and missiles from the gallery. Arguments erupted even when a congregation liked its minister. Two years before he kept vigil with the Parrises at a larger and more lavishly furnished home than his own, Beverly's John Hale was ordered to serve as chaplain on a Quebec expedition against the French and Indians. His congregation objected. The case went to court. Hale sailed with the militia.

Ministerial salaries ranged from sixty to a hundred pounds a year, more than sufficient—it put the minister among the topmost ranks of his parishioners—if collected. Voluntary contributions had given way to compulsory ones, resented by many in the community, a minority of them church members, all of them taxed. Regularly maligned and occasionally mauled, the fee-collecting constable fled from axes and vats of boiling water. The Salem constable suffered a painful run-in with a warming pan.* The people's reluctance to support the clergy demoralized them; the ministers, Mather would thunder in 1693, felt cheated and starved. In the course of a protracted campaign to secure his salary, Topsfield's minister announced to a town meeting that he hoped the parsonage would burn to the ground—with certain members of his congregation inside. Clergymen were keenly aware of what they earned, which they could not help but translate into self-worth. Cotton Mather at one point calculated his daily wage. Expectations were precariously high on both sides. In the mutual recriminations it was difficult to say which came first, the difficulties in collecting the ministerial salary or the griping about getting what one paid for from the pulpit. What felt like ingratitude to one party felt like extortion to the other.

The spirited Salem potter who had queried Burroughs deplored the fact that the minister delivered what he liked, for which the community paid. The reverse was also true. Parishioners contributed whatever was on hand, which could mean a barrel of oysters, a bushel of peas, a pound

* Many sympathized with a farmer whose home—just north of Salem village—straddled the Topsfield-Ipswich line. When a constable approached from one direction, the farmer removed to the far side of his house. (Constable Wilds finally settled the matter by force. Enlisting some sturdy friends, he seized a choice pig and declared the account settled. The collecting of witches, he was about to discover, was less straightforward.)

of linen, a beehive.* Congregants paid in labor as well, planting a minister's beans or slaughtering his cow. This rather blurred the lines of command, terrifically distinct though they appeared to some. "Are you, sir, the parson who serves here?" asked a visitor to nearby Rowley. "I am, sir, the parson who rules here" came the reply. While the community rose when the minister entered the meetinghouse, where his family occupied a special pew, while farmers felt intimidated by their learned minister, it was unclear who precisely worked for whom. As a modern scholar put it, there was some confusion as to whether the pastor was the congregation's employee, spiritual companion, or representative from "some nebulous and distant ecclesiastical galaxy."

While railing against the barbarous starving of clergymen, Cotton Mather had to admit that—in his plea for their maintenance—he artfully included passages "that might render the ministers themselves more deserving persons than, it may be, some of them are." Even with a surfeit of pastors, a great deal of mediocre preaching went on. So did a lot of sleeping in the pews. The Puritan was intensely alert, preternaturally attentive, neurotically vigilant about the state of his soul. He was not invariably so at meeting. Some would "sit and sleep under the best preaching in the world," clucked Increase Mather. Doubtless someone slumbered through that 1682 sermon too. (In fairness there may have been no better place to rest for a New England farmer, who had few opportunities to do so.) Mary Rowlandson, whose account of her 1675 Indian captivity electrified New England, occasionally nodded off during her husband's preaching.

Two months into his tenure Samuel Parris complained of the inertia of his parishioners, senseless before him. He chided them for "useless whispering, much less nodding and napping." While he noted the

---

* Harvard tuition—which ran about fifty-five pounds for the four-year course of study—was paid the same way, most commonly in wheat and malt. The occasional New England father sent his son to Cambridge with parsnips, butter, and, regrettably for all, goat mutton. A 141-pound side of beef covered a year's tuition. Translating in another direction, four years' tuition amounted to the cost of a small home.

"unnecessary gazing to and fro," he made no mention of the walnuts that flew from the galleries; the antics on the stairs; the spitting, laughing, flirting, and whittling; the elbows in the ribs and the knees in backs and the occasional punch in the nose; the woman who installed herself in her neighbor's lap when the neighbor refused to make room for her in the pew. The New England meetinghouse was a decorous but lively place; that spring, Martha Carrier roughly jostled a twelve-year-old girl there mid-psalm. It was at meeting that you learned why your sister's eyes were puffy from crying, that a pirate had been captured, a lion killed in Andover. The sermon, the centerpiece of the week, represented its social and spiritual touchstone. The sole regular means of shared communication, it served educational and journalistic purposes as well. Over the course of a lifetime, the average New England churchgoer absorbed some fifteen thousand hours of sermons. Seldom if ever had so many people literally been on the same page. Many took notes. Others discussed those homilies for days afterward. Bits and pieces of Parris's addresses from the pulpit would surface in the weeks to come; the audience was listening. Attention was not always so rapt, however, that when your neighbor yawned in the next pew, you failed to notice the devil's mark under his tongue.

SAMUEL PARRIS PREACHED his first Salem sermon in November 1689. He came to the village with little pastoral experience. Born in 1653 in England, he spent his youth largely in Barbados, where his family flourished as merchant-planters. While the ministry may once have been Parris's profession of choice—he attended Harvard for several years but left in 1673, on the death of his father—his background was in business. At twenty, having inherited a plantation and seventy slaves, he returned to Barbados. Parris fared only adequately, struggling to maintain both the 170-acre estate and a generous inheritance from an uncle. Within a few years he sold the property at a loss. By 1680 he had reappeared in Boston, where he set himself up as a West Indies merchant. He married. He thrived initially, but while Massachusetts offered a more favorable economic climate than Barbados, his career remained one of misfires and false starts. Parris spent a year in and out of court over a disputed loan. He grew as accustomed to financial scrambling as to deal-making. Opportunities regularly came his way. Each got the better of him.

When the Salem delegation found him in 1688, Parris was a member of Boston's First Church and the father of three. It is unclear how or why he made the decision to enter the ministry; clergymen more often left the pulpit for mercantile pursuits than the other way around. He had previously thought of himself as a merchant and a gentleman, enough so to have his portrait painted in miniature. Just this side of handsome, with crisp, angular features, wide-set eyes, dark hair to his shoulders, and a voluptuous mouth, he bore a distinguished air. He is the only villager to whom we can put a face. His older brother was a minister in England; an uncle had preached at Boston's First Church. Parris had served briefly in a remote Massachusetts hamlet. He spoke at informal prayer groups. He was on intimate terms with several local clergymen, including his Milton cousin. The Salem overture made, Parris stalled. "The work was weighty," he explained. The farmers would have his decision in due course. He had any number of reasons to hesitate even if he knew nothing of Salem history, which was unlikely. His immediate predecessor, Deodat Lawson, was a member of the same Boston congregation. The two had mutual friends. The long courtship of Parris, a reluctant candidate without a bachelor's degree at a time when Harvard MAs could not find pulpits, says as much about Salem village as about its future minister. Neither qualified as anyone's first choice.

When finally it began, the negotiation was long and arduous. While he demonstrated little aptitude for business, Parris relished negotiation. At thirty, he was more seasoned than the ministers Salem had worn out before him. He had seen more of the world; he had limited experience of life in a backwater, of what he would term "this poor little village." A bustling town of about eight thousand, Puritan Boston—with its ruffles and ribbons, silver lace coats and scarlet petticoats—dazzled by comparison with rustic Salem, of a very different palette altogether, all muted greens, muddy purples, and deep reddish browns. Both contrasted vividly with Barbados. The village presented its best offer, entirely in line with the going rate. A hard-bitten bargainer, Parris was unimpressed. Deeming the terms "rather discouraging than encouraging," he countered with eight conditions. The most onerous concerned firewood. If a minister's battle for respect translated into a salary discussion, the battle for wood served as the combustive flash point. Its delivery burdened the community; a message was conveyed when it failed to arrive or proved substandard. "Isn't that pretty soft wood?" observed a later parson as a congregant unloaded his cart. "And don't we sometimes have pretty soft preaching?" came the response.

Parris wanted his firewood delivered. Again the villagers preferred to contribute to a fund from which he might arrange for his own. They had no village commons; wood was difficult to come by. Already scarce by 1692, timber represented a persistent, pervasive New England concern. Its use and misuse, its felling and export, were tightly regulated. Village proposal and counterproposal followed, relations fraying. An obstinate man with a rickety ego, Parris objected to the preferred fund. The price of firewood might well rise. Discussion persisted through much of 1689, a year that saw the overthrow of the colony's Crown-imposed Anglican governor followed by profound political unrest, the intensifying Indian skirmishes, and the publication of *Memorable Providences,* the Mather volume that included the account of the bewitched Goodwins. "After much urging," Parris remembered later, "I replied I would try them for one year. And so debate upon this point was ended."

Even as negotiations continued, Parris, Elizabeth, their three children, and slaves moved into the parsonage at the village crossroads. A comfortable two-story home on two acres of land, it was configured around a cavernous chimney with four fireplaces. Parris constructed a large lean-to behind the parsonage's four whitewashed rooms; the children presumably lodged upstairs with the help. Eighteen months after their arrival, the family lost the young black slave who had moved with them. In a momentous step for both the village and its new minister, on a windy mid-November Tuesday, Parris was ordained in the presence of several neighboring clergymen, John Hale and Salem town's two reverends among them. Parris discoursed on Joshua and a new era. With his ordination, the village could now offer the all-important sacrament. Acknowledging the villagers' travails, he reassured them. The years in the wilderness were over. God that day rolled away his reproach; the farmers could move forward compatibly and constructively. In that undertaking the new minister included himself. His work was great but he would be zealous in its exercise. In conventional terms, he acknowledged that he would administer cordials to some but corrosives to others. "You are to bear me a great deal of love," Parris instructed his congregants. In a less orthodox vein, he leaned on the homage part. "You are indeed highly to love every minister of Christ Jesus but (if you can, notwithstanding the vast disproportion between myself and others) you are to love me best."

Some did, and some did not. He did not make it easy. Plenty of towns made life miserable for plenty of ministers, but few of them dealt as severely with their congregants as did Parris. He could be tedious, mulish, sulky. In possession of standards, he liked for things to be done properly. He applied great energy to small matters; he had the proclivity for tidiness that creates a shambles. When the wife of tailor Ezekiel Cheever went into labor early in 1690, Cheever impulsively borrowed a horse from his neighbor's stable without permission, presumably to summon a midwife. The neighbor protested. Resolving the matter fell to Parris, who required three meetings to do so. He demanded a public apology. Cheever readily submitted one. Parris deemed the effort "mincing"; he ordered the new father to repent again in the meetinghouse the following week. He was the type of person who believed he alone could do the job adequately and afterward complained that no one had helped. He could be petty, unlike the elderly Salem town minister who had ordained him, from whom it was said "consolations dropped like dew."

Parris tried to cram a great deal into a sermon; he could belabor, and exhaust, a point. He knew he often fell short but did not like to concede.

The pewter tankards on the communion table were an eyesore. Could they not be replaced? (Wealthier congregations used silver communion pieces.) To the parsonage he brought a number of items rare in Salem village: his own silver tankard, a writing desk, and a mirror. He boasted a coat of arms, a rarity among Massachusetts ministers. Parris had come of age in Barbados, the richest colony in English America, at the height of its power. He knew splendid homes and sumptuous hospitality. Salem looked shabby and—given the size of the Barbados household staff—doubtless also lonely to him. He quickly began lobbying for ownership of the parsonage and its land. The request was not inappropriate but it was premature; towns made such grants to their ministers after longtime service. The Salem villagers demurred.

Less than a year after his ordination, Parris compiled a numbered list of complaints, which he attempted to read to his congregants. Tempers twice prevented him from finishing. He managed finally to air his grievances at a special meeting in his parlor. Neither the house nor the fence and pasture nor the salary nor the firewood supply met with his approval. Already the eight-year-old parsonage was in dire need of repairs. His fence was rotten and on the verge of collapse. Brush overran two-thirds of his pasture. He could not subsist on an unpaid salary. Firewood he left until last. After much trouble on his part, he had received two small loads in three weeks. It was now the end of October. Without wood, he warned his congregants, they would hear no further Scripture. "I cannot preach without study. I cannot study without fire. I cannot live quietly without study," Parris explained. He demanded a speedy consideration of each matter and "a loving and Christian answer, in writing." The air was icy with grievances, taut with apprehension and frustration, discomforts his family inevitably shared. They greeted the disgruntled parsonage visitors and heard the raised voices, the outraged stomp of boots. The minister found his congregants insulting in the extreme. To his petition Parris affixed a line in his signature brand of high-handed self-pity: "Let me add if you continue contentious, your contentions will remove me either to the grave, or some other place." He understood that his parishioners had been kinder to his predecessors. None had fared as poorly. Nor presumably were his predecessors as sensitive to the cold as was he, after nearly a decade in the tropics.

The villagers met repeatedly to discuss their minister's predicament. Within months of his ordination, his salary was in arrears; as early as the fall of 1690, a movement was afoot to dismiss him. The committee to collect his salary voted late in 1691 not to do so. He was also out of wood. A bitterness seeped into the sermons. The parsonage meanwhile grew colder and colder, as he emphasized from the pulpit. Were it not for a visiting Salem town deacon who made a last-minute delivery, Parris informed his congregants on October 8, he would have frozen. He made no appeal for the relief of his family, acutely aware of the challenges to his authority and presumably shivering as well in the rabid weather; November brought heavy snows and howling winds. Parris informed the committee that came to see him early that month that they should be more mindful of him than of other people. Having dug out from banks of snow, he complained on November 18 that he "had scarce wood enough to burn 'til tomorrow." It did not help that the winter of 1691–1692 was especially arctic. Bread froze in communion plates, ink in pens, sap in the fireplace. The chimney delivered icy blasts. Parris preached to a chorus of rattling coughs and sniffles, to the shuffling of cruelly frostbitten feet. For everyone's comfort he curtailed his afternoon sermon of January 3, 1692. It was simply too cold to go on.

Village quarrels aside, Parris had ample reason to complain. His was grueling work for which he was little prepared. He had taken on several occupations at once. The minister in a "little village" read divinity one minute and trimmed his mare the next, left off repairing the garden fence to preside over a prayer meeting. Parris might well hang a map of the world in his parsonage, he might appear to be the village intellectual, having at Harvard translated the Old Testament into Hebrew and Greek, but he devoted himself equally to turnip-sowing, cider-making, and squirrel-killing. "So perplexing it is to have the affairs of the ministry and of a farm to manage together," lamented one Massachusetts minister.

Parris—who speculated in real estate and came late in life to tending his own fields—could only have felt similarly. The pastoral work alone was arduous and endless. "Now of all the churches under heaven there are none that expect so much variety of service from their pastors as those of New England," wailed Cotton Mather, who did not thrill to the pastoral visit. Parris called on parishioners to inquire after religious instruction at home. He served as scribe, judge, counselor, confidant. He kept fasts and performed baptisms, arranged lectures and conferred with neighboring congregations. He comforted the sick and the bereaved, which over the summer of 1689 included four families who had lost sons to Indian attacks. Marblehead's minister calculated that he went eight years at one stretch without so much as a half a day off. There was cause to be bone-tired under the best of circumstances, which Parris's were not. Already primed for affront, he came increasingly to harp on Christ's wounds and bruises. Well before the pitiless winter of 1692, he sounded better suited to a calamity than a ministry.

In addition to all else came the family devotions that had landed Bayley in such trouble. Morning and evening, Parris prayed and read Scripture with his household, including his slaves, their souls his charge as well. He gathered the family before the hearth for the singing of psalms and in weekly catechism. Many ministers' children heard a preview on Saturday evening of the next day's sermon; the Sabbath ended with a digest of the day's service. Parris reinforced basic principles, stressing covenant obligations. Man was born in sin and embarked on a pilgrimage toward grace. A spiritual war was afoot, separating the godly from the damned. Church sacraments were paramount. Puritan parenting constituted a full-time activity; Mather was forever devising exercises for his sons and daughters. While Parris was less creative, he paid close attention to his children's education, indistinguishable from their spiritual welfare. Well before the girls began to tense and twitch, their souls were closely monitored, daily palpated; the state of New England's young qualified as something of a preoccupation. Parris devoutly hoped that all of his parishioners were so vigilant. He feared they were not. He took up the popular refrain that family order was disintegrating; what was the matter with kids today? At a Cambridge ministers' meeting he led a charge to see what could be done.

Five years older than her husband, a member of Boston's First Church before her marriage, surrounded by five Putnam wives in her Salem pew, Elizabeth Parris would have shared in those tasks. She was expected to be constant in her devotions and compassionate toward the neighbors. Her obligations increased after the distractions of 1692; under any circumstances, she would have read and discussed the Bible with the parsonage children, whose education fell to her and whom she taught to read. Basic literacy was a New England requirement, thanks to the 1647 statute establishing schools, to which Massachusetts owes its educational eminence. That law too amounted to a defensive measure. It was understood that the "one chief project of that old deluder, Satan, [was] to keep men from knowledge of the Scriptures." The point was to outwit him, to stave off demonic ambush; even in the midst of an arctic New England winter, his hot breath could be felt on the cheek. The Salem town father who had not taught his children to read found a notice posted on the meetinghouse door offering them as servants to someone who would. And while basic literacy was a requirement, it was hardly a sufficiency. One future minister made his way three times through the Bible before he turned six. It was not unusual to have done so a dozen times before adolescence or be able to recite long passages by heart.

The ideal Puritan wife was self-effacing, and Elizabeth Parris obliged; little trace of her survives beyond her initial on a fragment of dark pewter plate. Of Parris as a father we have a few glimmers. As he warned his congregants: "Wise parents won't suffer children to play with their food." The sage mother engaged "rod and reproof." He may have sounded more ferocious in the pulpit than he did at the dinner table but it is difficult to believe that his children ever won an argument with their standard-upholding, apology-rejecting father when his parishioners so rarely did. Parris could not ignore missteps; he pried open closed issues; he never made one point when he might make three. He delivered another hint of his paternal style with the abbreviated January sermon. As the Salem villagers curled and uncurled aching fingers and toes, as the shutters rattled in the wind, Parris illuminated a dim meetinghouse with the lessons of affliction. They made one more vigilant. They humbled and instructed. The Lord delivered afflictions, preached Parris, in the same spirit that parents, "seeing their young children over-bold with fire or water," will bring them "near to the fire, or hold them over the water, as if they would burn them or drown them." Naturally no parent intended to do anything of the sort. He endeavored merely, Parris explained, "to awe and fright them, that they may hereafter keep farther off."*

The chilly parsonage was soon enough steeped both in awe and fear. In that it was not alone. Just before or just as the February witch cake introduced Abigail and Betty to their tormentors, twelve-year-old Ann Putnam, the daughter of Parris's stalwart supporter Thomas Putnam, began to shudder and choke. Three miles down the road in the other direction, Elizabeth Hubbard, Dr. Griggs's sixteen-year-old niece, convulsed as well. A creature had followed her home from an errand, through the February snow. She now realized it had not been a wolf at all. All four girls could say with certainty who pinched and pummeled them. For the remainder of 1692 Samuel Parris left no further mention of firewood.

* In the same vein, Cotton Mather felt it necessary to prepare his eight-year-old daughter for his imminent death. He went on to outlive her by twelve years.

III

◄►

THE WORKING OF WONDERS

I have seen too much not to know that the impression of a woman may be more valuable than the conclusion of an analytical reasoner.
—ARTHUR CONAN DOYLE

OVER THE DAYS that followed Mary Sibley's witch-cake experiment, rainstorms gusted through Essex County, swelling rivers with snow-melt. They overspilled their banks, inundating homes, sweeping away livestock, mills, and bridges, flooding freshly tilled fields. On every count the village was a seething, muddy morass. Having consulted with his minister, Thomas Putnam braved the tempests to ride to Salem town on February 29 with three friends. The girls now understood who tormented them; that Monday, the middle-aged farmers in mud-splattered cloaks appeared before two Salem justices to press formal witchcraft charges. Hours later, his black, brass-tipped staff in hand, the village constable knocked at a door just over a mile southwest of the parsonage. He carried a warrant for Sarah Good's arrest. She was to appear before the authorities the following morning to account for having, over the previous two months, tortured two girls in the Parris household as well as Thomas Putnam's daughter and Dr. Griggs's maid. Sin and crime were close cousins in seventeenth-century Massachusetts, which drew its list of capital offenses from the Bible.

A semi-itinerant beggar, Sarah Good constituted something of a local menace. She would seem to have wandered into the village directly from the Brothers Grimm, were it not for the fact that they had not been born yet. And she came trailing a backstory of pitiless downward mobility. When she was eighteen, her French-born father, a wealthy innkeeper, committed suicide. His considerable estate passed in its entirety to her stepfather. When Sarah was in her twenties, her husband died suddenly; she inherited his debts. A series of suits followed, leaving her disaffected and destitute. To the dismay of their orderly, industrious neighbors, she and her family lived for long stretches on charity, in barns and fields. She and her second husband, William, did not appear always to share an address. Recently she had turned up at the parsonage, her five-year-old daughter in tow. Parris offered something to the youngster. Good had stalked off, muttering under her breath. The encounter with their disheveled, snarling neighbor seriously unsettled the members of the household. Relief of the poor was a chronic problem in Massachusetts, where resources were scant and where idleness posed a riddle to most minds. All preferred to drive the destitute from town. The two Salems were over these weeks contending with this very issue, especially urgent as King Philip's War had produced an unwieldy number of widows and orphans. If they were to provide for their own poor, wondered the Salem farmers, bargaining yet again for their independence, might the town exempt them from highway maintenance?

As it happened, Sarah Good had been unsettling Salem households for some time. Three years earlier she and her family had found themselves homeless; a well-intentioned couple lodged them. Good proved so "turbulent a spirit, spiteful, and so maliciously bent" that after six months, her hosts turned her out. They could not bear another moment of her presence. Retaliating for their kindness, Good insulted their children and threatened the family. That winter their livestock began unaccountably to fall ill and die. Told of the misfortune, Good swore she did not care if they lost every head of cattle. When another villager refused to admit her to his house for fear she carried smallpox—Good clearly carried a whiff of something foul about her—she scolded and cursed. If the family did not mean to extend their hospitality, she fumed, she would confer something on them! Sure enough, the next morning the family cow died "in a sudden, terrible and strange unusual manner." Constable Herrick's brother himself turned the muttering Good away when she came in search of lodging. As she continued to wander about the property, he enlisted his son to keep her from the barn. Fond as she was of her pipe—she was far from the only Massachusetts woman who had discovered tobacco—she was likely to set the place on fire. Good had promised that the Herricks too would pay for their lack of hospitality. She may have cast only dark hints; we have her words as they were heard, not as they were delivered. In no way did she make anyone feel comfortable. Several of the Herricks' prize cows moreover subsequently vanished. All three families would have cause to review those inauspicious encounters soon enough.

The constable delivered Sarah Good at ten in the morning on March 1 to Ingersoll's ordinary, or tavern, where her interrogation was to take place. Insofar as the village had a nucleus, Ingersoll's was it. Steps from the meetinghouse, just south of the parsonage, on a rise along the Salem-Andover road, the ordinary was the address at which Parris's congregants refreshed themselves between Sunday sermons. Only the absences were notable that morning. Sarah Good's upright neighbor Martha Corey elected not to attend. She attempted to detain her husband as well, going so far as to unsaddle his horse. She lost the battle; Giles Corey missed not a minute of the week's examinations. By the time the town justices arrived, it was clear that Ingersoll's could not accommodate the crowd. They moved the hearing to the village's austere, raftered meetinghouse, a dim chamber at the best of times, dimmer now after years of neglect. The Salem farmers had long deferred repairs, boarding up broken windows and leaving others open to the air. The place was so dark as to be nearly unusable. All the same, a heady, holiday atmosphere prevailed. The colony was without theater, considered a "shameful vanity." While all of Shakespeare's plays existed, no copy had turned up in North America, where the first organ would not arrive for another nineteen years. In the feverish air that Tuesday the usual rules and all hierarchy evaporated, as, in the weeks to come, inhibitions, obligations, and curfews would fantastically lift. The farmers knew very well their places in the dark, planked pews—among contentious issues, seating was nearly toxic, determined by an ego-bruising, oft-contested algorithm of age, rank, and estate—and that morning they were not sitting in them.

From a table before the pulpit, justices of the peace Jonathan Corwin and John Hathorne presided. Widely respected, they counted among the first men of Salem town. A successful land speculator and quick-thinking militia captain, dark-haired Hathorne lived in a fine mansion. A skilled and harsh interrogator as his father had been before him, Hathorne had been hearing cases since 1684. He was the father of six, though as yet had no experience with teenage girls. Corwin owned sawmills, several in conjunction with Hathorne. The son of one of Salem's wealthiest merchants, he had inherited one fortune and married another. The justices were close confederates, in their early fifties, and related by marriage. They lived a block from each other. Together they had seated the Salem town meetinghouse, where Hathorne played a leading role. They had recently traveled together to the Maine frontier to evaluate Indian defenses. And while neither had a background in the law—men with formal legal training did not immigrate to the colonies, which had no law school—both knew the business of the community, the offenders and the offenses, inside out. Hathorne had sat on the committee that five years earlier had urged the villagers to spare the town their animosities. He had devoted hours to adjudicating Putnam family disputes. No doubt with relief, both men had attended Parris's ordination. Corwin had rescued the Parris family from the cold with the emergency October firewood delivery.

After an opening prayer, Hathorne took charge of the hearing from the long table at which Parris and his deacons normally conducted the communion service. "Sarah Good," Hathorne asked, "what evil spirit have you familiarity with?" She replied, "None." Working from prepared notes, Hathorne continued as if she had said just the opposite. Had she contracted with the devil? Why did she hurt these children? What creature did she employ to do so? He proceeded less like a judge than a police interrogator; it fell to him to establish not the truth of the charges but the guilt of the suspect. When an alleged thief had appeared before Hathorne eight years earlier, he had begun: "What day of the week did you steal the money from Elizabeth Russell?" The second question was, When did you take it?; the next, Where is the money you took?

The contest was asymmetric. For all her misdemeanors, despite the suit against her stepfather, Good had never testified before a magistrate when she stood that sodden morning—several feet and a waist-high rail separating them—before Hathorne and Corwin. It was the kind of confrontation that reduced responsible men to gibberish. All the same Hathorne got nowhere. Good continued in her sullen denials, as unforthcoming in the courtroom as she was intemperate on doorsteps. Hathorne tried a different tack. What was all that muttering about at the parsonage? She had merely thanked the Reverend Parris for his charity, she explained. She was falsely accused. She knew nothing of the devil. Hathorne directed the four girls, assembled together, to rise. Was this the woman who hurt them? Not only did all testify that she had—three had suffered at her hands that very morning—but as they came face to face with Good before the canopied pulpit, each began to thrash. Hathorne had no choice but to move them away. "Sarah Good, do you not see now what you have done? Why do you not tell us the truth? Why do you thus torment these poor children?" he chided. The wrenching and writhing continued; Good could not help but agree that something afflicted the girls. But what did she have to do with it? she asked bitingly. Like everyone else, she knew that Hathorne had arrested two other women. One of them was his culprit.

The fourth or fifth time Hathorne asked who bewitched the children Good supplied an answer. She named Sarah Osborne, apprehended the same afternoon, her house turned upside down for evidence. Recovered, the girls clarified that Osborne and Good together tortured them. Hathorne returned to the muttering. What was it Good said when she stalked away from people's houses? He implied that she was either tossing off an incantation or conferring with her devilish accomplices. Muttering qualified as something else too, New England code for all that was suspect and subversive. The word smacked of iniquities and insurrections. It led directly to anarchy; where murmuring broke out, mutiny could not be far behind. To the minds of their captives, Indians muttered. Cotton Mather had recently written off murmuring as "the devil's music."

Good was caustic at best, insolent at worst. "Her answers were in a very wicked, spiteful manner," noted one of the court reporters, detouring into the third person, his editorial comment supplanting Good's voice. Appearances were on his side. Weather-beaten and bedraggled, Good looked as miserable as her reputation. A child would have taken her to be aged. She was in fact thirty-eight; she had had a baby three months earlier. She continued to resist her well-dressed examiner, who had to drag answers out of her. As for the muttering, she finally relented: "If I must tell you, I will." She had recited the Commandments. Pressed for details, she changed her story. It had been a psalm. She paused, silent, before floundering ("muttering," in the opinion of a clerk) through a portion of it. "Who do you serve?" persisted Hathorne, swerving slightly. "The God that made heaven and earth," Good replied, though perversely she hesitated to pronounce the Lord's name. She could explain her Sunday absences: she had not come to meeting as she had no proper clothes.

If she did not seal her fate with her acrid answers, her husband did so for her. Someone in the room volunteered that William Good had voiced suspicions of his wife, submitting that she "either was a witch or would be one very quickly." Hathorne pressed the hapless weaver for specifics. Had he witnessed any diabolical acts? He had not. But his wife had comported herself rancorously with him. Tears welling in his eyes, he felt compelled to admit "that she is an enemy to all good." If there were gasps in the room, they went unrecorded; Ezekiel Cheever—enlisted that day as one of several clerks—had no reason to preserve them. The years of poverty had not been kind to the marriage; the report of Sarah Good's lack of sympathy for their hosts' livestock had also originated with her husband. The night before his wife's arrest, William Good would reveal, he had noticed a witch mark—a sign the devil was known to stamp on his recruits—just below her right shoulder. It had never been there before. He wondered if anyone else had seen it. Hathorne remanded Good to prison.

He grilled middle-aged Sarah Osborne, his second suspect, with the same rigor. Like Good, Osborne had tenaciously pursued a substantial inheritance, in her case after the 1674 death of her husband. That claim proceeded slowly. In the meantime, she had taken up with and married her Irish farmhand. Rumors had circulated about her for years, the most recent of which she had spent bedridden. Hathorne met again with denials, if from a better-humored, less shabby defendant. Osborne refused to implicate Good, whom she had not seen in some time and knew only in passing. But Sarah Good implicated you, Hathorne needled her. Osborne neglected to rise to the bait. Again Hathorne asked the girls to stand. Would they approach the witness? Each identified her positively. When she had pinched and strangled them, they said, she had worn precisely the clothes she did that afternoon. In an acknowledgment of her looking-glass predicament, Osborne had been heard since her arrest to sigh that she was more likely bewitched than a witch. This too came to Hathorne's attention. What, he asked, had she meant by the remark? Osborne related a familiar nightmare. In her sleep, she either saw or dreamed she saw— the distinction passed without comment—an Indian-like figure. He pinched her neck and dragged her by her hair to her front door. What to do under the circumstances was something most Massachusetts women had already contemplated. In her bestselling narrative, Mary Rowland-son noted that before her Indian abduction, she had regularly concluded that she would prefer death to being taken alive by savages.* All had heard of infant heads dashed against trees, of pregnant women disemboweled. Impatient though the villagers were with the destitute, they willingly contributed to a fund for the relief of former Indian captives. In February, the village collected thirty-two pounds, or half of Parris's annual (unpaid) salary.

Again someone in the packed meetinghouse volunteered a bit of stale history. Between the girls' contortions and the salvos of unsolicited evidence, Hathorne's courtroom, bathed in anemic, late-winter light, was far from orderly. Even on paper the hearings sound chaotic; there is a reason, notes a scholar of the seventeenth century, that we shout "Order in the court!" today. It seemed Osborne had once mentioned having heard a suspicious voice. Was that the devil speaking to you? Hathorne asked. "I do not know the devil," Osborne replied evenly. She had thought she heard a voice proposing she skip meeting. She ignored it. Hathorne persevered. "Why did you yield thus far to the devil as never to go to meeting since?" he demanded. She had been ill, as anyone named Putnam knew full well; Osborne had been absent from worship for some time, embroiled in a lawsuit with the village's first family for far longer. Her first husband's will named as its executors Thomas and John Putnam, Osborne's adversaries in her decades-long litigation. Her current husband helpfully specified that she had not attended meeting for fourteen months. That day or the next, the innkeeper's wife inspected both Good and Osborne for witch marks.

While arresting Osborne, Constable Herrick had performed a diligent search for any images, ointments, or apparatus associated with witchcraft. He appears to have added the fillip himself; his warrant included no such instructions. At one address, the rifling must have been especially awkward. The third name twelve-year-old Ann Putnam sup-

---

* In the minds of most Indian captives, there was only one thing worse. An English settler would prefer to have his brains dashed out by a hatchet than to kiss a crucifix. Fearing for his soul, one starving youngster refused even a Jesuit-proffered biscuit. He buried it under a log.

plied was that of Tituba, her minister's Indian slave. She had lived with the family for some time, since at least the Boston years. She may have worked for Parris earlier, in Barbados. It is notable that the parsonage girls—at whose side Tituba lived, prayed, took her meals, and likely slept at night—did not name her. Nor did Parris. He also twice stated that John, whom the villagers understood to be Tituba's husband, had baked the witch cake, following Mary Sibley's instructions. Deeply attached to Betty, well versed in Scripture, Tituba was by no means the usual suspect. All kinds of slaves and servants got into all kinds of trouble. She had not. She had never before landed in court. For years Tituba had sung psalms and recited her catechism before the Parris hearth; she was as integrated into every aspect of family life as the Goods had been shut out. She knew no pinch of hard luck that might discomfit the community. Both Good and Osborne lived on the outskirts of town and attended meeting irregularly. Traditionally witches were marginals: outliers and deviants, cantankerous scolds and choleric foot-stampers. They were not people of color. On all counts Tituba failed to fit the profile. She proved spellbinding, however.

Again Hathorne began with a presumption of guilt. "Why do you hurt these children?" he demanded. In what was clearly not her first language ("I no hurt them at all"), Tituba denied having done so. Who was it then who tortured the girls? continued Hathorne. "The devil, for all I know," she rejoined before—moments later, to a hushed room—she was describing him. She was as expansive as Sarah Good had been curt, less the scapegoat of myth than a sort of satanic Scheherazade. Lifting liberally from the Puritan playbook, in supersaturated 3-D, she introduced a full, malevolent cast, their animal accomplices, their various superpowers. She was masterful and gloriously persuasive.

Only the day before, while she cleaned the parsonage lean-to, a tall, white-haired man in a dark serge coat had appeared. He ordered her to hurt the children. With him were four accomplices, including Good and Osborne. The others were Bostonians. The man threatened to kill Tituba if she did not torture the girls. Had the man appeared to her in any other guise? asked Hathorne. Here Tituba made clear that she must have been the life of the corn-pounding, pea-shelling Parris kitchen; her tale grew more intricate as she warmed to it.* What she reported was vivid and sensational, lurid and harebrained. While earlier the girls had violently twisted and screeched, none now flexed a muscle or emitted a sound, their relief attributed to Tituba's confession.

A yellow bird accompanied her visitor. He appeared as two red cats, an oversize black one, a black dog, a hog. If she served him, she could have the yellow bird. The cats had appeared at the Parris home as recently as the night before, just after prayer when they had scratched her, nearly driven her into the fireplace, and commanded her to torture the girls. Sarah Good had also appeared that evening while the family prayed. She had a yellow bird on her hand and a cat at her side. She had attempted to bargain with Tituba, stopping her ears so that she could not hear the Scripture. Tituba remained deaf for some time afterward. If she lived in fear of Parris — servants and slaves could expect to be beaten, by ministers as often as anyone else — she was more terrified still of her serge-coated caller. He visited four times, threatening to slice off her head if she mentioned him. In their spectral disguises, Good and Osborne had kept her extremely busy, sending her to the doctor's to pinch sixteen-year-old Elizabeth Hubbard; to the Putnams' to afflict twelve-year-old Ann. They commanded Tituba to kill Ann Putnam with a knife, testimony that was instantly corroborated; from the pews came reports that Ann had complained that her supernatural tormentors had tried to lop off her head! Tituba had traveled a great deal in and out of houses during a week of drenching rains, flying as far south as Boston. She was a brilliant raconteur, the more compelling for her simple, declarative sentences. The accent may have helped. She was as utterly clear-minded and cogent as one can be in describing translucent cats. And she was obliging; her examination is five times as long as Sarah Good's. No one

---

* The phenomenon was not new. Under repeated interrogation, hardy details tend to blossom and grow more lush. The same had happened with an earlier "infernal nuisance," Joan of Arc.

objected that the previous day, when Tituba held the conversation in the lean-to, or that morning, when she claimed to have pinched Elizabeth Hubbard, she had been in custody. Nor did anyone ask why the visitor directed Tituba's attention to only two of the parsonage's four children or point out that Tituba dated her newfound acquaintances to after the girls had experienced their first pains. But then no one seemed inclined to interrupt her either. Finally, they were getting somewhere.

How had Tituba managed her travels? Hathorne wanted to know. "I ride upon a stick or pole, and Good and Osborne behind me," she confessed, elaborating a little; the three traveled with their arms around each other. She could not say if they sailed through the trees or over them as they flew so swiftly. Time and distance held no meaning for them. Tituba may have been smallish; she several times asked her examiners to believe that Good and Osborne strong-armed her into those excursions. She cleared up a few other mysteries as well. That wolf that had stalked Elizabeth Hubbard? It was Sarah Good, transformed. The hairy creature with the wings and the long nose that warmed itself before the Parris fire? Sarah Osborne. She claimed not to know the words to describe the creature but fared admirably. She could not name the tall man's accomplice but knew the woman from Boston; she recognized her white-lined hood. Tituba neither stinted on the visual details nor failed to deliver on any of Hathorne's leading questions. If he mentioned a book, she could describe it. If he inquired after the devil's disguises, she could provide them. She had had time that morning to talk to Good and Osborne. She had had weeks to wonder at, worry about, and care for Betty and Abigail. She adored the girls and deferred to her master, of whom she lived in some fear; a clergyman was meant to show more love than terror to his children and more terror than love to his servants. Tituba was as desperate for a resolution as anyone. Her life was upended. Here was a performance through which no one slept. Only at the end of her testimony did the girls again begin to convulse. "Do you see who it is that torments these children now?" demanded Hathorne. It was Sarah Good, Tituba assured him. The girls agreed. They continued to howl, but Tituba ran out of words. She could not manage another syllable. "I am blind now, I cannot see," she protested before the March 1 hearing concluded with a prayer.

BY THE END of the afternoon Tituba and Osborne were locked in the Salem jail. It had been a stimulating, destabilizing day for all involved. More prosaic business followed the justices' departure. A town meeting had been called for one o'clock; it began late. The Salem villagers wrangled still with their obligations to Salem town. The differences, it was decided, remained irreconcilable. The farmers resolved to petition the court for full autonomy, appointing a constable to spearhead that effort. They voted as well to reject the town's offer to trade highway maintenance for their support of the village poor. Charity was an unaffordable luxury.

That evening after dark a persistent, unearthly noise startled a village cooper and a laborer. Drawing near, William Allen and John Hughes discovered a "strange and unusual" beast on the ground. As they approached it dissolved in the silvery moonlight; two or three women materialized in its place and flew swiftly away. More or less concurrently, Elizabeth Hubbard heaved at the Griggs homestead. "There stands Sarah Good upon the table by you!" she cried to Samuel Sibley, Mary's husband, who was tending to her in her sickness. Shockingly, Good was barefoot, bare-legged, and bare-chested. "If I had something I would kill her!" roared Sibley, reaching for his walking stick. With it he struck the spectral beggar woman across the arm. Hubbard's account was easily corroborated. Constable Joseph Herrick held Sarah Good that evening at his farm so as to deliver her the following day to the Ipswich jail. Somehow the irascible prisoner managed to elude her guards and slip out into the night, taking her infant but leaving her shoes and stockings behind. In the morning, Herrick's wife noticed lacerations along Good's arm, from elbow to wrist. There had been no sign of blood the evening before. Sibley's blows had evidently struck home.

Herrick's deputy could only have been relieved to deliver the suspected witch to Ipswich, a trip of several hours that she made as difficult for him as possible. She rode pillion, on a cushion behind the saddle. It made for slow going; three times that afternoon she also leaped from the horse in attempts to escape. She was not a witch, she railed. Nor would she confess she was one. They had only Tituba's word. It would be absurd to believe a smooth-talking slave, Good protested, simultaneously fretting that someone actually might. She cursed the magistrates. Addled, she tried to kill herself; it was difficult to say who was more terrified in the wake of Tituba's hypnotic performance. On Wednesday, March 2, the authorities clapped Good into the Ipswich jail, an insalubrious address even by her standards. It was squalid and stinking. That evening found John Hughes at the Sibley home, where some account of Sarah Good's antics and his encounter with the flying beast were doubtless discussed. Hughes left around eight o'clock, followed for some time by an unfamiliar white dog. When he was in bed at home, behind locked doors, a great gleam suddenly illuminated his room. He sat up to discover a fat gray cat at the foot of his bed. The twenty-two-year-old cooper, William Allen, also suffered a restless night. A fluorescent Sarah Good landed on his bed. She sat on his foot, though when he kicked, she vanished, taking her light with her. It was as if Tituba had handed out hallucinogens. The terrifying, psychedelic confession, rather than the voodoo of legend, was to be her contribution to the events of 1692.

Who should Ann Putnam Jr. discover in her room the following day but Dorothy Good, the itinerant Sarah's five-year-old daughter. The pint-size witch bit, pinched, and choked Ann, all the while urging her to sign a diabolical pact. Meanwhile Hathorne continued to interrogate the suspects in jail, where Tituba continued, over the course of four days, to deliver revelations. She had entered into an agreement with the devil. "He tell me he God and I must believe him and serve him six years and he would give me many fine things," she related. What else had he said, asked Hathorne, nearly supplying the answers; the first mention of a satanic compact is his. He had suggested pacts with the devil to Good and Osborne as well, neither of whom picked up on them. "Did he say you must write anything? Did he offer you any paper?" he asked Tituba. He had. She had told him she could not accept him as God and tried to run upstairs to confer with Reverend Parris, but the visitor had prevented her. He traveled with his confederates. He forced her to torture the girls. He arranged things so that Parris could see neither himself nor Tituba, a well-known maneuver. Tituba knew her Bible and traded in all the right imagery; if she was not obedient, she understood how obedience sounded. On a subsequent visit—generally the devil called around prayer time—he produced a book from his pocket in which she was to inscribe her name. She was spared from doing so as Mrs. Parris called for her at that very moment from the next room. Tituba was meant to sign in blood, though she muddled her account of how this was arranged. How many marks were in the book? inquired Hathorne. Tituba could say exactly: there were nine, in red and yellow, Sarah Good's and Sarah Osborne's distinct among them. In custody Good confirmed the mark was hers. Osborne scoffed at the notion.

Before Tituba's initial testimony the tall man had reappeared, she revealed, to warn her not to breathe a word. Were she to do so, he would decapitate her. Pressed for other names she was hopeless. She began to veer into incoherence, or at least the account of her testimony does. Could Tituba at least say where the nine lived? "Yes, some in Boston and some here in town, but he would not tell me who they were," she replied. This was unsettling news, as were the blood signatures and the hint of conspiracy. Tituba had seen something of which every villager had heard and in which all believed: an actual pact with the devil.

John Hale, the thoughtful Beverly minister, lived two miles from the village. Having attended hangings as well as prison examinations, he knew his witches. He had observed the parsonage girls in their first fits; he was among those on hand when Hathorne deposed Tituba in jail. The magistrates interrogated her four times, more extensively than they would any other suspect. Three men took copious notes; they dared not miss a febrile word. Tituba insisted she was not a witch, though she had previously worked for one. Her mistress had taught her how to identify witches and how to avoid being bewitched, a lesson she had evidently forgotten. In prison she was reexamined for suspicious marks, which she turned out to have after all. Were further evidence necessary, as Hale and the justices looked on, she began to writhe and shriek. Her diabolical confederates tortured her for having betrayed them.

A week after their arrest, Sarah Good, Sarah Osborne, and Tituba were carted off to await trial in Boston's prison, Good's infant along with them. Even assuming no one jumped from her horse, that journey constituted a full-day affair. It could only have been tense, given the mutual accusations. As for their destination, with its fetid air, dirt floor, and armies of lice, the Boston jail constituted "a grave of the living." John Arnold, the Boston jail keep, was notoriously cruel, said to be as obdurate as the shackles with which he fixed the suspects in place. The chains had no locks; a blacksmith alone could remove them. At the same time, Arnold opened accounts for the women's charges, for which they would be billed. He was soon buying blankets for the prisoner-infant, settled in the dungeon. The chains were as much a testimony to the women's preternatural force as the defects of the Massachusetts jails. It was understood that witches could control their victims with their every gesture; if they could not move, they could not enchant. Prison breaks however occurred with stunning regularity. An Ipswich prisoner blithely decamped by lifting the boards over his head. Salem inmates at one point dismantled not only the door but an entire wall of the facility. A year earlier, two had called for a pot of beer. They were in a canoe paddling to freedom by the time the jail keep's wife delivered it.

Assuming Tituba was convinced by her own testimony, she must have been petrified. Not even a sturdy prison could prevent the tall man from decapitating her. The justices found her entirely credible. She suffered for her confession. She repented. Her details were precise; they tallied unerringly with the reports of the bewitched. Tituba had moreover been consistent from beginning to end. "And it was thought that if she had feigned her confession, she could not have remembered her answers so exactly," Hale later explained. A liar, it was understood, needed a better memory. Tituba had absorbed all of Parris's teachings, even if her incandescent account was notably short on professions of piety; she mentioned God only once. Assured throughout, she held up remarkably well for someone caught between a merciless inquisitor and a ghastly decapitator. The irony was that all might have turned out very differently had she been less accommodating. Confessions to witchcraft were rare. Convincing, satisfying, and the most kaleidoscopically colorful of the century, Tituba's changed everything. It assured the authorities they were on the right track. Doubling the number of suspects, hers stressed the urgency of the investigation. It introduced a dangerous recruiter into the proceedings. "And thus," wrote Hale evenly of an affair that had seemed modest, local, and—Salem town's senior minister implied—so ordinary as to be uninteresting, "was this matter driven on."

WHAT EXACTLY WAS a witch? Any seventeenth-century New Englander could have told you. Adversarial though the relationships were, Hathorne and Corwin, the court officials, the accused, and the accusers all envisioned the same figure, as real to them as had been the February floods, if infinitely more pernicious. Directly or indirectly they drew their definition from Joseph Glanvill, a distinguished English academician and naturalist. With unimpeachable authority, the Oxford-educated Glanvill had proved that witchcraft existed as plainly as heat or light. As he defined the term: "A witch is one who can do or seems to do strange things, beyond the known power of art and ordinary nature, by virtue of a confederacy with evil spirits." From those pacts, witches assumed their power to transform themselves into cats, wolves, hare. They had a particular fondness for yellow birds. A witch could be male or female but was most often female. An English witch in particular maintained a kind of menagerie of imps or "familiars," demonic mascots that did her bidding. Those companions could be hogs, turtles, weasels. Cats and dogs were prevalent, though toads were a universal favorite. The witchcraft literature is thick with toads: burned toads, exploding toads, dancing toads, groaning toads, pet toads, pots of toads, human-born toads, cats disguised as toads. The sixteen-year-old servant who slipped a plump toad into the family milk pitcher delivered an explicit message, as she fully intended.

The witch bore a mark on her body indicating her unnatural compact with the spirits that engaged her. Those marks could be blue or red, raised or inverted. They might resemble a nipple or a fleabite. They came and went. Essentially any dark blemish qualified, though a mark in the genital area was particularly incriminating. As had Tituba, a witch signed an agreement in blood, binding her to her master, to whom she pledged her services. He recruited by means of customized bribes. Witchcraft tended to run in families, along matrilineal lines. While a witch's power was supernatural, her crime was religious. She could be relied on to stumble over the Lord's Prayer, anathema to the devil. She worked her magic with charms or ointments—incriminating news for Salem's Elizabeth Procter, whose maid was about to reveal that her mistress kept a greenish, foul-smelling oil on hand. To work her magic at a distance, a witch resorted on occasion to poppets, the doll-like figures for which Constable Herrick had ransacked the Osborne and Parris cupboards. And the witch's connection to the wildly convulsing Salem children? An Englishman had long known precisely what enchantment looked like. According to an early legal guide on several Salem desks in 1692, it manifested as senseless trances, paralyzed limbs, fits, jaws clapped shut or grotesquely deformed, frothing, gnashing, violent shaking. The author of that volume tendered as well some vital advice: in the presence of such symptoms, consult your physician before blaming your neighbor.

Witches had troubled New England since its founding. They drowned oxen, caused cattle to leap four feet from the ground, tossed skillets into the fire, tipped hay from wagons, enchanted beer, sent pails crashing and kettles dancing. They launched apples, chairs, embers, candlesticks, dung through the air. They sent forth disembodied creatures, in one case a man's head connected to a white cat tail by several feet of nothingness— a Cheshire cat centuries before Lewis Carroll. (It should be said that there were a fair number of taverns in the colony. Salem town was particularly well served, with fifteen taverns, or one establishment for every eighty men, women, and children.)* Witches alternately charmed and disabled. Out of the blue, Hathorne asked Tituba if she knew anything about Justice Corwin's son. Most likely Hathorne wondered if she had crippled Corwin's lame nine-year-old, although there were other candidates; in quick succession, Corwin had buried three boys. Witches managed to be two places at once or emerge dry from a wet road. They walked soundlessly over loose boards. They arrived too quickly, divined the contents of unopened letters, spun suspiciously fine linen, cultured uncommonly good cheese, knew secrets for bleaching cloth, smelled figs in someone else's pocket, survived falls down stairs. Witches could be muttering, contentious malcontents or they could be inexplicably strong and unaccountably smart. Indeed they often committed the capital offense of having more wit than their neighbors, as her former minister had said of the third Massachusetts woman hanged for witchcraft, in 1656.

Compared to their European counterparts, New England witches were a tame bunch, their powers more ordinary than occult. They specialized in disordering the barn and kitchen. When the New England witch suspended natural laws, those laws tended to be agricultural ones. She had no talent for storms or weather of any kind; she neither called down plague nor burned Boston.† Continental witches had more fun. They walked on their hands. They made pregnancies last three years. They turned their enemies' faces upside down and backward. They flew

---

* Following a prickly conversation with the governor in which he asserted that more drunkenness could be observed in six months in North America than in the course of an English lifetime, Increase Mather noted in his diary: "No wonder that New England is visited when the head is so spirited." At around the same time, his son complained that every other house in Boston was an alehouse. The Salem town minister shared their concern. The New England visitor eager to write the Puritans off as sanctimonious hypocrites found them "the worst of drunkards," muddy-brained at the end of each day but never so incapacitated as to desist from spouting Scripture. All exaggerated, to different ends. Strong cider was nonetheless as constant a feature of seventeenth-century New England as the belief in witchcraft. As one modern historian noted, "The 'Puritan' who shuddered at the very sight (or thought) of a glass of beer or wine, not to mention hard liquor, did not live in colonial Massachusetts."
† One New England witch did nearly sink a Barbados-bound ship. That witch was a man.

internationally. They rode hyenas to bacchanals deep in the forest; they stole babies and penises. They employed hedgehog familiars. The Massachusetts witch's familiars—which she suckled, in a maternal relationship—were unexotic by comparison. She did not venture very far afield. Even in her transgressions she was puritanical. She rarely enjoyed sexual congress with the devil.* When she visited men in the night she seemed interested mostly in wringing their necks. Prior to 1692, the New England witch seldom flew to illicit meetings, more common in Scandinavia and Scotland. While there was plenty of roistering in New England, little of it occurred at witches' Sabbaths, which seldom featured depravity, dancing, or voluptuous cakes and took place in broad daylight. Revelers listened to sermons there! (The Salem menu consisted primarily of bread, wine, and boiled meat.) The witch's ultimate target, the point of all those pricks and pinches, was the soul rather than the body. And despite her prodigious powers, she did not break out of jail, something many less advantaged New Englanders managed with ease.

Among the abundant proofs of her existence—where proofs were needed—was the biblical injunction against her. "Thou shalt not suffer a witch to live," commands Exodus, although there was some debate about that term; in Hebrew it more accurately denotes "poisoner." As workers of magic, as diviners, witches and wizards extend as far back as recorded history. They tend to flourish when their literature does. The first known prosecution took place in Egypt around 1300 BC, for a crime that would today constitute practicing medicine without a license. (That supernatural medic was male.) Descended from Celtic horned gods and Teutonic folklore, Pan's distant ancestor the devil was not yet on the scene. He arrived with the New Testament, a volume notably free of witches. Nothing in the Bible connects the two, a job that fell, much later, to the church. It took religion as well for anyone to propose satanic pacts, more

---

* The New England minister could barely entertain the possibility of an erotic encounter even when a witch confessed to it. When several such cases came to his attention, Increase Mather insisted that the devil had planted false memories. Those poor women hallucinated!

popular in Scotland than in England. You could not really bargain away your soul before it was established that you had one.

The witch as Salem conceived her materialized in the thirteenth century as sorcery and heresy moved closer together; she came wholly into her own as a popular myth yielded to a popular madness. In 1326 Pope John XXII charged his inquisitors with the task of clearing the land of devil worshippers; the next two centuries proved transformative. When she was not being burned alive, the witch adopted two practices under the Inquisition. In her Continental incarnation she attended lurid orgies, the elements of which coalesced early in the fifteenth century, in the western Alps. At the same time, probably in Germany, she began to fly, sometimes on a broom. Also as the magician molted into the witch, the witch—previously a unisex term—became a woman, understood to be more susceptible to satanic overtures, inherently more wicked. The most reckless volume on the subject, the *Malleus Maleficarum*, or *Witch Hammer*, summoned a shelf of classical authorities to prove its point: "When a woman thinks alone, she thinks evil." As is often the case with questions of women and power, elucidations here verged on the paranormal. Weak as she was to devilish temptations, a woman could emerge dangerously, insatiably commanding. According to the indispensable *Malleus*, even in the absence of occult power, women constituted "a foe to friendship, an inescapable punishment, a necessary evil, a natural temptation, a desirable calamity, a domestic danger, a delectable detriment."

The fifteenth century—the century of Joan of Arc—introduced the great contest between Christ and the devil. The all-powerful Reformation God required an all-powerful enemy; the witch came along for the ride. For reasons that appeared self-evident, the devil could not accomplish what Lawson would term his "venomous operations" without her. Frenzied prosecutions began at the end of that century with the publication of the *Malleus*, the volume that turned women into "necessary evils"; witchcraft literature and prosecutions had a habit of going hand in hand. And while Satan worship was a useful charge to level at a rival religious sect—Catholics hurled it at Protestants as vigorously as Protestants hurled it back—all agreed on the prosecution of witches.* For their part, witches were perfectly ecumenical. They frequented Catholic and Protestant, Lutheran and Calvinist parishes. Exorcism alone remained a Roman Catholic monopoly. Nor had witches any preferred address. They were neither particularly English nor exclusively European.

As to what country engaged in the greatest hunts, the competition is fierce. Germany was slow to prosecute, afterward fanatical. A Lorrain inquisitor boasted that he had cleared the land of nine hundred witches in fifteen years. An Italian bested him with a thousand deaths in a year. One German town managed four hundred in a single day. Between 1580 and 1680, Great Britain dispensed with no fewer than four thousand witches. Several years after Salem, at least five accused witches perished in Scotland on the testimony of an eleven-year-old girl. Essex County, England, from which many Massachusetts Bay settlers hailed, proved especially prosecution-happy, though it convicted at a steady rate rather than in the flash-flood manner of Salem. A diabolical rooster figured among the many hunt victims, as did the mayor of a German city and several British clergymen. For the most part, English witches were hanged while French ones were burned. This posed a riddle for the Channel island of Guernsey when three witches turned up there in 1617. Ultimately, they were hanged according to British law, then burned, according to French.

The witch made the trip from England to North America largely intact. With her came her Anglo-Saxon imps. Similarly, the contractual aspects—the devil's mark, the book, the pact—represented Protestant preoccupations. The Sabbaths, like the flights, derived from the Continent; English witches evinced no interest in broomsticks. The little

---

* The devil boasts a similarly catholic heritage, as he reminds Daniel Webster in Stephen Vincent Benét's 1937 story: "'Tis true the North claims me for a Southerner, and the South for a Northerner, but I am neither. I am merely an honest American like yourself—and of the best descent—for, to tell the truth, Mr. Webster, though I don't like to boast of it, my name is older in this country than yours."

Swedish girl who had plummeted from her stick had also been on her way to a riotous, open-air meeting to enter her name in a satanic book. The devil swooped in after her crash to minister to the injury that caused the "exceeding great pain in her side."* (He proved less obliging in New England; Ann Foster would benefit from no such rescue in 1692.) When he was not proffering pacts or practicing medicine, the devil was very busy. He baited deviously and worked stealthily, specializing in the perverse. He assured the skeptic that witchcraft did not exist. He knew his Bible, from which he quoted strategically, to odious ends. He interfered with the ministerial message by lulling men to sleep during sermons. He impeded scientific progress. A gifted medic, he understood more of healing than any man. He was the best scholar around. He too had a serious work ethic; agile and labile, he was always present, always recruiting. He knew everyone's secrets. And he came to the job with six thousand years' experience! As William Perkins, the early Puritan theologian, noted, he could cause you to believe things of yourself that were untrue. (A number of distressed Massachusetts residents asked themselves a related question in 1692, one that assumed greater urgency as spring turned to summer: Could I be a witch and not know it?) These ideas the New England settlers imported wholesale, derived primarily from the work of Glanvill, with whom Increase Mather corresponded, and Perkins, from whom Cotton Mather cribbed. When the colonists established a legal code, the first capital crime was idolatry. The second was witchcraft. "If any man or woman be a witch, that is, has or consults with a familiar spirit, they shall be put to death," read the 1641 body of laws, citing Exodus, Leviticus, and Deuteronomy. Blasphemy came next, followed by murder, poisoning, and bestiality.

While he was not cited in that statute by name, the devil was soon up to his usual tricks in New England. The first person to confess to enter-

---

* A Swedish volume that turned up in seventeenth-century Delaware included the warning that a cross be cut in brooms to prevent witch hijackings.

ing into a pact with Satan had prayed for his help with chores. An assistant materialized to clear the ashes from the hearth and the hogs from the fields. That case turned on heresy rather than harm; the Connecticut servant was indicted in 1648 for "familiarity with the devil." Cotton Mather—who could not resist a calamity, preternatural or otherwise—disseminated an instructive account of her compact. Early New England witchcraft cases included no broomsticks, satanic gatherings, or convulsing girls. Rather they featured bewitched pigs and roving livestock, proprieties trampled, properties trespassed. They centered on the overly attentive acquaintance or the supplicant who, like Sarah Good, was turned away. Most involved some stubborn, calcified knot of vexed, small-town relations. Many charges had a fairy-tale aspect to them: spinning more wool than was possible without supernatural assistance, completing housework in record time, enchanting animals, inquiring too solicitously about a neighbor's illness, proffering poisoned treats.

In the years since its laws had been codified, New England indicted over a hundred witches, about a quarter of them men. The flying, roaring, religion-resisting Goodwin children accounted for the most recent Massachusetts trial. The culprit in their case turned out to be the mother of a neighborhood laundress, whom the eldest Goodwin girl accused of theft. The older woman erupted in fury, upbraiding Martha Goodwin; the teenager's fits began immediately. Within the week, three of her siblings heaved and screamed. On the stand, the accused was unable to recite the Lord's Prayer in English, having learned it in Gaelic, the only language she spoke. A search of her house turned up poppets; through an interpreter, she offered a full confession, if one foggy on the devil.* (Years earlier the woman's husband had accused her of witchcraft, establishing a role that would be reprised at Salem.) The Irish Catholic witch

---

* This too Cotton Mather attributed to witchcraft. She had communicated with her employer perfectly well in English. Clearly a confederate had cast a spell on her "to prevent her telling tales, by confining her to a language which 'twas hoped nobody would understand." He certainly did not and spoke to her through interpreters.

was hanged on November 16, 1688, warning as she rode to the gallows that the children's fits would not abate with her death. She proved right; they grew more severe. Martha continued to kick ministers and ride her aerial steed for some time.

Of late-seventeenth-century Boston, a Dutch visitor remarked that he had "never been in a place where more was said about witchcraft and witches." Indeed the word "witch" got batted around a good deal there. So did witchcraft diagnoses. The first settlers had emigrated from England when that country's witch craze was at its height; they came in large part from the most enchanted counties. Newly arrived in town, a stranger might take one look at a convulsing child and—all goodwill and sympathy—inform his family that a witch lived nearby. They might beg to differ, reassuring him that their neighbors were models of piety, but he knew better: "You have a neighbor that is a witch and she has had a falling out with your wife and said in her heart your wife is a proud woman, and she would bring down her pride in this child." When Sarah Good, Sarah Osborne, and Tituba were fitted with chains in March, they joined another accused witch, languishing in prison since the previous October. Sorcery adapted well to New England—a howling wilderness haunted by devilish Frenchmen and satanic Indians—as it did to Puritanism, an immersive, insecure-making creed that anticipated conflict if not downright cataclysm, having nearly been persecuted into existence. New England trials were nonetheless on the wane in 1692, as they were in the mother country. Connecticut had been more troubled by witches than Massachusetts. That colony had executed a series of them in the early 1660s then relented, never to hang another. Other cases erupted sporadically rather than in frenzied outbursts.

Nor did New England demonstrate any particular eagerness to convict. "We inclined to the more charitable side," noted John Hale following a controversial 1680 reprieve, when the court had refused to convict a woman for injuries caused by a demon in her guise. Justices proceeded cautiously; magistrates dismissed cases and overturned jury convictions.

One accused witch was fined for lying, another whipped for chatting with the devil. The Plymouth woman who swore that a neighbor had appeared to her in the shape of a spectral bear was interrogated closely. What kind of tail did the bear have? asked a shrewd magistrate. The woman could not tell; the animal had faced her straight on. Bears, she was reminded, did not have tails. For her fiction she was offered the choice between a whipping and a public apology. Of the 103 pre-Salem cases in New England, the conviction rate hovered around 25 percent. In all, Massachusetts hanged only six witches before 1692. On the initial day of hearings, when a deacon from Parris's Boston congregation placed a copy of William Perkins's famed book into the village minister's hands, no one, with the exception of the Goodwins' tormentor—the three women jailed in Ipswich would be reassured to remember—had been executed for witchcraft in well over a quarter century.

In the decades prior to 1692, a great debate over the reality of witchcraft had raged in Britain, where prosecutions essentially halted. That discussion fell to the elite; the witch was a subject for the academician and the educated clergyman. Skeptics argued their case a full century before Salem, though to Joseph Glanvill—writing late in the 1670s—it was still just possible to believe that all intelligent men were on your side. The existence of witches, it was understood, was something on which men of all ages, wise and unwise, Jewish, Muslim, Christian, and heathen, could agree. It remained as obvious that a spirit could convey men and women through the air as it was that the wind could flatten a house. The first steps away from the belief were tentative ones. The rationalist came up always against Perkins, than whom no one defended witchcraft more cogently. Of course there were all manner of frauds, cheats, and counterfeits, he conceded, sounding a variation on the paranoiac's anthem. Just because there were impostures did not mean the genuine article did not exist! The cheats rather proved the case; there would be no counterfeits were there not things to be counterfeited. Cotton Mather echoed that argument, as he would a great deal of Perkins.

Sorcery did not account for all dubious accidents. But some things could be explained no other way.* To doubt its efficacy was, as Perkins had noted, Mather reiterated, and Massachusetts believed, to doubt the sun shining at noon.

Glanvill elaborated on Perkins's contention that we should not deny the existence of something because one fails to understand it. We did not know how the soul operated either, observed Glanvill. Why did the Bible warn against witches if they did not exist? Every nation had a word for the phenomenon. How had they all managed to name a nonentity? There were moreover plenty of confessions. Here as elsewhere, consistency proved the point. "We have the attestation of thousands of eye and ear witnesses, and those not of the easily deceivable vulgar only, but of wise and grave discerners, and that, when no interest could oblige them to agree together in a common lie," asserted Glanvill. It was inconceivable that "imagination, which is the most various thing in all the world, should infinitely repeat the same conceit in all times and places." Proof was elusive but by no means impossible. By the same logic, argued the royal academician, among the keenest minds of his century, touching up against the nature of knowledge, how can we prove that Julius Caesar founded the Roman Empire? (In Mather's version, this was tantamount to ranking the entire history of Great Britain among the tales of Don Quixote.) To disbelieve was to reduce history to fiction.†

Indeed the imagery was startlingly similar, as were the convulsions, trances, shrieks, and stranglings. A New Englander knew what a witch looked like as today we recognize a leprechaun or a vampire, although we have (presumably) never met one. Which was no proof of anything. Just because you did not see the robbers on the road, argued Mather, did not mean they failed to exist. The skeptic insisted witchcraft was absurd

* Logic worked some wonders of its own in the realm of witchcraft. Argued one German authority: "Many things are done in this world by the force of demons which we in our ignorance attribute to natural causes."
† At the apogee of this coiled logic sits Thomas Hobbes, himself a vicar's son. The great political philosopher was a skeptic. He felt witches should however be prosecuted for perpetuating a blatantly false belief.

and impossible, a fantasy, as one doubter would contend, propagated by "little imposters." But that was precisely the point, countered Glanvill. Witchcraft was so far-fetched, so preposterous, so improbable, it had to be true. You couldn't make this stuff up! To the impossibility of a shared delusion was added the most compelling reason to believe in witchcraft, one pinched from the title page of the *Malleus:* "Not to believe in witchcraft is the greatest of heresies." The seventeenth-century skeptic was made to appear an appeaser. "Flashy people may burlesque these things," sniped Mather in 1702, taking aim at the "learned witlings of the coffee-house," the latte-sipping liberals of the day. But sober minds did not make sport of the invisible world, especially in light of the evidence. Mather was very close to a larger theme from his father's 1684 *Illustrious Providences,* stuffed with mind-boggling portents and prodigies, an occult *Ripley's Believe It or Not.* Without mystery there was no faith. To deny witchcraft was to deny religion, a small step from a more provocative assertion: to deny witchcraft was to advocate it.

As for the wily figure who came to the job with six thousand years' experience, the master of disguise who could cause things to appear and disappear, who knew your secrets and could make you believe things of yourself that were not true? Here matters grew murkier. Perkins assigned the devil a concrete form but did not describe him. No New Englander seemed particularly clear as to who he was or what he looked like. There were no bat wings or forked tails in sight, though in one Salem account, he stuck out a cloven foot, and in another he turned up as a hybrid monkey, man, and rooster. It was uncertain whether he was male or female. One accused witch wondered if he might be a mouse or a fast-moving turtle. If he had a physical existence, the devil the New Englander knew was a "little black man" or a "great black rogue" or a "black hog." In the more or less official 1692 version, he was barely taller than a walking stick, tawny, with straight, dark hair and a high-crowned hat. While he was allergic to Scripture—the Swedish girl had fallen from the air because she uttered the Lord's name in flight—it was unclear what language the devil spoke. Even Cotton Mather did not know. He was however a pervasive presence. The air pulsed with his minions. There were more devils than men in the world, warned the Mathers. We inhaled them with every breath.

Not only were his infernal armies everywhere, but the devil was invoked regularly. Having beaten her and turned her out in the January snow, a Haverhill husband bellowed that his wife "was nothing to him but a devil in woman's apparel." The young woman discovered in the wrong bed when giggling erupted late one night was convicted as a "lying little devil." An Ipswich man testified that his abusive neighbor "had so much of the devil in him that he was a great affliction to those who lived near him." The fiend emerged often in the heat of argument—"the devil take you" served precisely as do two short, spiked syllables today—though that was not a necessary precondition. He took well to the uncongenial New England climate; naturally, the Indians worshipped Satan, as did the Quakers. (Which justified appropriating the Friends' Salem land. On it stood the 1692 prison.) With their "spirit of contention," the Salem villagers had, according to the 1675 court ruling, offered the devil a leg up. In the opinion of at least one Massachusetts cleric, religious tolerance qualified as a satanic idea. The starving of ministers, Cotton Mather warned, was a way for Satan to take over the land.* The foreigner in an unusual hat was a devil. He figured as the codefendant in most criminal indictments and graced a fair number of sermons, the ravening wolf to the minister's shepherd. Parris's were no exception, reliably though not disproportionately Satan-heavy. On January 3, 1692, Parris noted that the village church seemed on stable footing. He also cautioned that "it is the main drift of the Devil to pull it all down."

In a New England twist, a group of ministers observed that sometimes God sent devils expressly to silence the naysayers. That was the lesson Mather extracted from the Goodwin episode. He vowed to make ample use of that assault and, with *Memorable Providences,* to settle the

---

* He met his match in the Barnstable man who credited the devil with the law exacting ministers' maintenance.

matter once and for all. With a gentle pat on its spine, he sent forth his little volume—a lackey to the great British works, as he saw it—to assure mankind that there were devils at large. Massachusetts knew of the little Swedish girl, her flying accident, the un-English, clandestine meeting in the meadow, the blood pact, and the man in the high-crowned hat, thanks to Mather, who plucked them from Glanvill. No wonder Massachusetts was troubled by witches, noted Mather, quoting a Glanvill disciple who, in a bit of transatlantic log-rolling, was quoting him. "Where will the Devil show most malice but where he is hated, and hated most?" Mather demanded. The devil's appearance was nearly a badge of honor, further proof that New Englanders were the chosen people. He touched down like spiritual lightning on the ministerial roof. He was not altogether unwelcome; if the devil was about, God could not be far behind. The book of Revelation predicted that he would descend accompanied by his "infernal fiends"; Mather had long been on the lookout for the Apocalypse, imminent in New England since the 1650s. And the devil earned a promotion in 1692. He became a megalomaniacal conspirator laboring to subvert God's kingdom, a feat he had never before attempted in Massachusetts.

By the time the Massachusetts witches took flight, the European witch craze had exhausted itself. Holland had abolished prosecutions in 1610, Geneva in 1632. France's Louis XIV dismissed all witchcraft cases fifty years later, although several shepherds burned in 1691. In the age of Boyle, Newton, and Locke (all of whom believed in witchcraft), prosecutions stuttered to a stop all over Europe. Any number of texts discrediting witchcraft existed, although you could not read a skeptical page on the subject printed in Boston before 1692. Faith and a tightly controlled press insulated the Massachusetts settler; by 1692 the New England witch differed from her English counterpart primarily in that she was more real. What you could read in Massachusetts were the tirades against witchcraft with which Cotton Mather throttled its doubters, few of them in evidence. It was like studying ecstatic creationist literature without knowing that Darwin had ever lived. To that end, Mather laid out the

Goodwin case in explicit detail. He included only those particulars he had personally observed or for which he could unequivocally vouch. They were conclusive; he defied anyone again to deny witchcraft. He would never trust another man who did.

PRAYER, EVERY MASSACHUSETTS minister agreed, was the sole powerful and effective remedy against the devil. And it was prayer that Parris embraced in 1692. Massachusetts had held colony-wide fasts to counteract witchcraft as early as 1651. Parris convened a series of them at his home, in the village, and in nearby congregations. On Friday, March 11, a group of ministers assembled at the parsonage for a day of devotions. The girls remained largely quiet, though at the conclusion of each prayer, noted Hale, himself the father of three children under the age of seven, "they would act and speak strangely and ridiculously." More severely affected, blond Abigail Williams wound up in a fit, her limbs pretzeled. At some point thereafter Parris decided to separate the children, opting to send off his daughter. The choice may have been practical; the family could not spare Abigail, the servant. They lodged nine-year-old Betty with Stephen Sewall, the town court clerk, soon to grapple with contorting young women both day and night. A distant cousin, he was a magnanimous man. The Sewalls were themselves parents of three children under the age of four. And Betty's fits persisted, leaving her hosts disheartened. Late in the month, the "great black man" of whom Tituba spoke visited, offering Betty anything her heart desired. He would carry her to the city of her dreams, evidently neither Salem village nor Salem town.* That was the devil, explained Mrs. Sewall, herself a minister's daughter. If he returned, the child was to inform him he was a liar from beginning to end.

All talk was of witchcraft; increasingly, the day began with an account of what had transpired in the night and how the afflicted had fared. It

---

* It says something about the relative expectations of a New England slave and a minister's daughter that the devil promised Tituba "pretty things" and a pet canary. He enticed Betty with a visit to the "Golden City."

was the wrong moment to sound a dubious note, as it was the wrong season to be the one whose premonitions turned out to be true. Between
the time the Boston jailer clapped irons on the three Salem suspects and
March 12, a new specter began to pinch Ann Putnam Jr. Her distraught
father turned to his brother, Edward Putnam, and Ezekiel Cheever, the
horse-borrower, serving as court recorder. A church deacon, Edward
Putnam had joined in pressing the initial witchcraft charges. On Saturday morning, March 12, the two resolved to call on Ann's latest tormentor. She was a church member in good standing. Before riding the few
miles south they stopped at the Putnam farm to speak with Ann. Was
the twelve-year-old possibly mistaken about the identity of her afflicter?
Could she describe her clothes? Unfortunately, that afternoon Ann could
converse with the witch but not see her. The spirit had blinded her until
evening, when she vowed to reckon with her. In doing so she had however also introduced herself by name.

Martha Corey was alone at her home in southwestern Salem when
her visitors arrived. All smiles, she invited them in. She also anticipated
their question—a misstep. Putnam and Cheever had barely settled when
she announced: "I know what you are come for. You are come to talk
with me about being a witch." She was not one. "I cannot help people
talking of me." Corey shrugged. Edward Putnam revealed that his
bewitched niece had indeed named her. Corey was prepared, or thought
she was: "But does she tell you what clothes I have on?" she asked. So
flabbergasted were her callers by the prescient question that they asked
her to repeat it. The twelve-year-old had been unable to do so, they
reported, as Corey had "blinded her and told her that she should see you
no more before it was night, that she might not tell us what clothes you
had on." Corey could only smile at this subterfuge. She had no cause for
concern, she assured her callers. She was a devout woman who "had
made a profession of Christ and rejoiced to go and hear the word of
God," as both men knew she unfailingly did. Her deacon reminded
her that professions of faith alone would not clear her name. Witches
had infiltrated churches for centuries. Neither party appears to have

mentioned the only obvious stain on Corey's record: before her first marriage, in Salem town, she had borne a mulatto son, now a teenager.

Cheever and Putnam had no need to resurrect that fifteen-year-old history, as Corey incurred a new stain that afternoon. She took her doctrine seriously; she relished the opportunity to discourse on it. She considered herself "a gospel woman." She found herself explaining why she had unsaddled her husband's horse in her failed attempt to keep him from the hearing. It struck her as distasteful; how could any good come of such a thing? In that she was correct. Her husband had reported that the girls identified specters by their clothing, a dangerous shard of information. Cheever and Putnam emphasized the seriousness of the charge. Corey remained unmoved, intent on squelching idle gossip. She did not necessarily believe there were witches about, an inflammatory assertion at the best of times but impossible now. Tituba had confessed, Putnam and Cheever reminded her. The evidence was conclusive.

Corey backtracked a little, though not without acknowledging another form of blindness. She promised to "open the eyes of the magistrates and ministers," a particularly imprudent remark. The three spoke for some time; Corey was articulate and steadfast, a little given to lecturing. She proved an attentive listener too, paraphrasing their minister's apocalyptic assertion that the devil had come down in a great rage among them. As for Tituba, Good, and Osborne, she would not be altogether surprised if the three turned out to be witches. "They were idle, slothful persons and minded nothing that was good," Corey huffed. Her case was altogether different. Secure in her piety, she believed herself invulnerable. Her callers rode home by way of the Putnam household, where they discovered Ann to be at peace. Only that evening did the fits resume. They continued through the following day, when another unidentified specter shimmered into the room. Ann did not know her by name, though she could say that the pale, serious woman sat in the meetinghouse pew Ann's grandmother had previously occupied.

·Two days later Martha Corey rode north to the Putnam household, to which she had been summoned, presumably by Thomas Putnam. He may have wanted to charge Corey to her face. She had no sooner dismounted and entered the house than Ann began to choke. In a strangled voice she accused her visitor; her tongue then darted from her mouth, to be clamped sharply between her teeth. Her hands and feet twisted. When she regained her ability to speak, she pointed to a canary sucking between Corey's second and third finger. "I will come and see it," she announced. "So you may," challenged Corey, rubbing the spot. The bird vanished, after which Ann lost her sight. Drawing near Corey, she crumpled to the planked floor. Ann accused Corey of blinding another woman in meeting that week, demonstrating with her hands, which could thereafter not be unfastened from her face. She described a spectral spit on which a man was impaled, roasting, under Corey's supervision. No one else saw the spit but all knew of it from the Goodwin children. At this, the Putnams' nineteen-year-old maid, Mercy Lewis, stepped in, waving a stick at the apparition. It disappeared, only to return. She offered to strike again. "Do not if you love yourself!" warned Ann, but too late. Mercy recoiled from a terrific blow to her arm. "You have struck Mercy Lewis with an iron rod," Ann informed the nonspectral Corey, who must have been as stunned as everyone else. She had not budged. She saw no spit. So severe were the girls' pains that the Putnams demanded that Corey leave. Mercy's condition deteriorated. As she sat before the glowing fire that evening, her chair crept toward the hearth, propelled by invisible hands. Only with difficulty did three adults manage to save her from being delivered feetfirst to the flames. As he stepped in to help, one man observed bites along Mercy's skin. Her fits lasted until eleven that night.

With both her daughter and her maid afflicted—the two in no way conformed to Cotton Mather's 1692 description of women as "the people who make no noise at all in the world"—Ann Putnam Sr. weighed in four days later. She had been the child who arrived in Salem with Reverend Bayley, the first village minister, when he had married her older sister. Now thirty, she had in the intervening years lost that sister and a brother. The previous spring, she had lost her mother as well. She had also recently lost a crucial court case. After a decade of litigation, she was deprived of any claim to her father's large estate, one that had included several islands, meadows, and a ferry. In thirteen years she had borne seven children, of which Ann Jr. was the eldest. Having lost an eight-week-old baby in December, she was again pregnant. To those strains was added a new one. As she reported, she found herself exhausted on March 18, consumed by "helping to tend my poor afflicted child and maid. About the middle of the afternoon I laid me down on the bed to take a little rest, and immediately I was almost pressed and choked to death." Soon Martha Corey's specter materialized, inflicting indescribable tortures; had it not been for the men of the household, she would have been torn to shreds. Between assaults, Corey offered "a little red book in her hand and a black pen." Corey commanded Ann to inscribe her name in it.

The warrant for Martha Corey's arrest went out the following morning, a Saturday. Corey could not be apprehended until after the Sabbath, which left her time to attend meeting along with her accusers. It was no doubt a sensational occasion; congregants did not often pray with a flesh-and-blood witch in their midst. Already she had claimed several additional victims, including Parris's niece and Dr. Griggs's maid. That Saturday evening, Giles Corey, now in his seventies—no model citizen himself—sat by the fire alongside pious Martha. She was his third wife; the two had married seven years earlier. She encouraged him to go to bed. He attempted first to pray but found himself speechless; he could not so much as open his mouth. Martha noticed as much and ministered to him, after which the spell lifted. Her arrest seemed generally to jog her husband's memory. Five days later he confided in a Salem town minister that there had been—as William Perkins termed it in the book in Samuel Parris's study—some "working of wonders" on the Corey farm that week. His ox had suffered a strange episode. A cat had behaved oddly. Needlessly, Martha had suggested he put the animal out of its misery. Now that he thought about it, his wife had lately been given to sitting up after he went to bed. "I have perceived her to kneel down on the hearth as if she were at prayer, but heard nothing," he mused. The unheard words proved nearly as incriminating as mangled, muttered ones. Why would a woman drop silently to her knees by herself, late at night, before the fire? Corey intimated she was casting spells. It was equally possible that his wife had come to wonder, heart sinking, if she had perhaps spoken too plainly when her deacon had called two weeks earlier.

IV

———— ⟨•⟩ ————

ONE OF YOU IS A DEVIL

Two errors: 1. To take everything literally. 2. To take everything spiritually.
—BLAISE PASCAL

DEODAT LAWSON, THE previous village minister, was the first to try to make sense of things. He arrived late on the afternoon of March 19, hours after the order had gone out for Martha Corey's arrest. He stayed just over a week. Resettled in Boston, Lawson assisted at Parris's former congregation. He frequented the homes of prominent ministers, including Cotton Mather. He had been away from Salem for four years but knew the villagers, their affections and antipathies, as well as anyone; were it not for their bristling and snarling, he would still be among them. What he saw astonished him. By the time he set his wide-eyed account to paper, three weeks later, the Salem infestation could legitimately be termed "as rare an history as perhaps an age has had."

Lawson could not have returned to the village without an express invitation from Parris, overwhelmed and overworked in the pulpit as elsewhere. He managed to keep only sporadic notes on his sermons that spring, transcribing none at all between the end of March and mid-September, when he lost whole days to hearings. He also remained unpaid. Consumed by the needs of his distraught family and the long hours in court, he must have felt like a man struggling to contain a fire with a rolled-up newspaper. Reports of the Salem afflictions reached Lawson swiftly, the more so as they had broken out in his former home. Already the diabolical descent was the talk of Boston. Lawson equably noted that the distemper erupted among the villagers "after I was removed from them"; he pointed no fingers. He remained a welcome figure in the fractious community, to which he claimed he had returned out of concern for friends. He had had some rudimentary medical training in England, where twenty years earlier he had served, at least decoratively, as a royal physician. He took expert notes. He was in many ways the perfect man for the job. He had a personal incentive as well. An early victim claimed that witchcraft had dispatched Lawson's wife and infant daughter in 1689; their ghosts fluttered about, demanding vengeance. If indeed his family had been sacrificed to "malicious operations of the infernal powers," Lawson ached to know more. So did the concerned members of the Boston court. They encouraged him to investigate.

Lawson made his way that Saturday to Nathaniel Ingersoll's, an inn as well as a tavern. He had no sooner dropped his bags than he received a visit from Mary Walcott, the daughter of a village militia captain. A close neighbor of both the Parrises and the Putnams, Jonathan Walcott had served as a Lawson deacon. No less pertinently, Mary Sibley, the witch-cake enthusiast, was Mary's aunt, as was Ann Putnam Sr., in whose household Mary Walcott lived. The sixteen-year-old spoke for several minutes with the minister. As she turned to leave she stopped dead in the doorway. She had been bitten! It was already late afternoon; the room was dim. Candle in hand, Lawson examined Mary, whom he would have remembered as a child rather than as a young woman. He found two distinct sets of wounds. Something had clamped its jaws around her wrist, imprinting teeth marks on both sides.

Early that evening Lawson strolled across the road to the parsonage, just north of the inn, in the company of Ingersoll's wife. Sabbath prayer may already have begun in the first-floor parlor. Parris had little need to describe the commotion of the prior months as Abigail treated Lawson to a vivid display. The pale girl raced back and forth through the room, "making as if she would fly, stretching up her arms as high as she could and crying 'Whish, whish, whish!' several times." Without success Hannah Ingersoll tried to restrain her. Transfixed, Abigail pointed to a figure invisible to the others: "Do you not see her?" she asked. "Why there she stands!" Could they really not make out old Rebecca Nurse in the parlor, clear as day? Even in the presence of two ministers, Nurse dared offer Abigail a book, from which the eleven-year-old emphatically and repeatedly shrank. "It is the devil's book for ought I know," she chided the specter. She did not need to sign; it would suffice merely to touch the volume, Nurse assured the petrified youngster. This was the first Lawson had heard of the dark acts of Rebecca Nurse, a devout mother, grandmother, and great-grandmother who turned up elsewhere as well that day. She was the hazy second specter Ann had glimpsed in the old Putnam pew. Racing to the fire—it was the same hearth before which Tituba had met the winged creature—Abigail began to remove chunks of burning wood. These she tossed blithely around the house. Lawson thought that she intended to run straight up the chimney as, he learned, she had attempted many times. It was that evening, several miles away, before the fire in another village parlor, that some malignant force stopped Giles Corey when he opened his mouth to pray.

Parris had arranged for Lawson to deliver the following day's sermons. They are lost to us, though the texts could not have been remotely as memorable as their reception. Amid the pews sat five contorting girls and women, along with Martha Corey, the fear mounting inside her; all knew she was to be arrested for witchcraft. Justices Hathorne and Corwin as well as at least one of the town's two ministers joined the congregation. Lawson began the service, to be interrupted by writhing girls. Pastors were accustomed to preaching past disturbances, through the stamping of feet on the wood floor, the chirps of birds in the rafters, the wails of infants, the dog that vomited or congregant who fainted dead away. The convulsions stopped Lawson cold, however. He had never seen such a thing. Normality returned with the singing of the psalm, after which he prepared to rise from his pulpit seat for the sermon. A voice rang out in the stillness. "Now stand up and name your text!" commanded Abigail Williams. Some minutes into Lawson's discourse a second voice rang out. "Now there is enough of that," announced Bathshua Pope, a forty-year-old matron, newly afflicted. The propriety-minded Parris could only have burned with shame. Women did not speak in meeting, demurely or impudently. The fine for interrupting a minister was five pounds or two hours on the block. Those who had done so previously were Quaker women, who ventured eerily similar-sounding commentaries. "Parson! Thy sermon is too long!" one had offered. "Parson! Sit down! Thee has already said more than thee knows how to say well," instructed another. From the front of the rough-hewn meetinghouse, Parris's niece sounded the same note after Lawson obliged her by naming his text. "It is a long text," carped Abigail.

She behaved no better that afternoon. From the pulpit Lawson announced his doctrine for the day. "I know no doctrine you had," she countered. "If you did name it, I have forgot it." She went on to disrupt that sermon too, pointing to an astounding sight. All eyes must already have scuttled and darted in Martha Corey's direction. Abigail redirected the congregation's attention skyward. "Look where Goodwife Corey sits on the beam," cried the eleven-year-old, gesturing to the rafters, "suckling her yellow bird between her fingers!" Young Ann Putnam indicated something more dangerous yet: the canary perched on Lawson's hat, hanging from a peg in the high pulpit. Adults reached out to silence both girls. It was neither the first nor the last such interruption. A fair number of Parris's 1692 sermons would be sacrificed, a parishioner later complained, to the "distracting and disturbing tumults and noises" of the bewitched.

The next day Martha Corey stood before the meetinghouse as she had done precisely two years earlier when she became a full church member. This time the room was packed, the gallery and pulpit stairs overflowing. Portly Salem town minister Nicholas Noyes opened the noon hearing with what Lawson described as "a very pertinent and pathetic prayer." The magistrates took seats behind the refectory table. Gently at first—the Coreys were not only church members but substantial landowners—Hathorne posed his questions. Why did she afflict these people? If she had not, who did? By way of response Martha Corey asked permission to pray, a request the justices denied. She persisted. "We did not send for you to go to prayer," Hathorne crisply informed her; they were there to discuss witchcraft. Corey insisted that she had had nothing to do with sorcery in her life, again contending that she was "a gospel woman." She appealed to the Lord to "open the eyes of the magistrates and ministers" so that they might apprehend the guilty party. Hathorne chafed at the sanctimony as at the implication that he was anything less than clear-sighted already. Growing more caustic, he broached the matter gnawing at all minds: If she was not a witch, how had she known that Ann Putnam would ask about her clothing? Corey had barely opened her mouth to reply when clerk Ezekiel Cheever interrupted. She had better not begin with a lie, he cautioned. Putnam weighed in as well. "You speak falsely," Corey's deacon contended as she tried to explain. Her husband had reported on the earlier examinations. Hathorne turned to Giles Corey. Had he indeed told his wife as much? He had not. "Did you not say your husband told you so?" Hathorne needled the accused. Either she fell speechless or Parris could not make out her answer amid the commotion. He left a blank in the record.

Even had Corey attended Tituba's hearing, she would not have been prepared for Hathorne's tone. Stringent then, he turned vicious now. He reminded her that she stood before the authorities. "I expect the truth," he intoned. "You promised it." The idea that she had anticipated the deacons' question was highly problematic. Hathorne harped on it for some time, pummeling Corey for an explanation. The girls several times interrupted his inquiry to indicate a man whispering in her ear. "What did he say to you?" demanded Hathorne. Corey had neither seen nor heard a thing. She ventured a bit of counsel, however. "We must not believe all that these distracted children say," she asserted, eliciting fresh agonies. Hathorne quibbled with his spirited suspect about the definition of "distracted," a word she used three times in a matter of minutes. By its nature, Hathorne noted, distraction was fleeting and changeable. The girls were utterly consistent. She alone believed them mad. "It was the judgment of all that were present," both Hathorne and a Salem town minister reminded Corey, that "they were bewitched."

She could not help with reports of the spit, the book, the canary, or a suspicious ointment unearthed at her home. As it would continue to do, ignorance registered in the courtroom as defiance; Hathorne urged her to confess. "So I would if I were guilty," she rejoined. Corey was formidable but not imperturbable; she bit her lip and wrung her hands throughout the interrogation, the most punishing of the preliminary hearings. She was on her feet for a very long time, interrupted by witnesses bearing clarifications and suffering afflictions; Parris transcribed in fits and starts between outbursts. "Now tell me the truth, will you," demanded Hathorne, "why did you say that the magistrates' and ministers' eyes were blinded and you would open them?" Framed as such, the question struck Corey as absurd. She laughed as she answered. Mercilessly Hathorne pressed on, leading his defendant to pose a preposterous query of her own. "Can an innocent person be guilty?" she asked.

The court seemed to expect special powers of her; she had none to display. You say we are blind, challenged Hathorne. "If you say I am a witch," huffed Corey. He begged her to elucidate, as she seemed in her doctrinaire way to have promised. If not, he had a different question. "What did you strike the maid at Mr. Thomas Putnam's with?" Hathorne asked. "I never struck her in my life!" Corey cried. Two witnesses disagreed. Had she no iron rod, no familiar, no covenant with the devil? She had not. Did she truly believe she would go unpunished? "I have nothing to do with witchcraft," she vowed, as the room stirred and as Hathorne introduced the subject of the March 1 hearings. Why had she attempted to prevent her husband from attending? "I did not know that it would be to any benefit," she answered. From the long, narrow pews came a different answer: Martha Corey had no desire to root out witches. She smiled to see her meaning so willfully misconstrued. Hathorne reprimanded her; were the girls' troubles a laughing matter? "You are all against me and I cannot help it," Corey conceded. Did she not believe there were witches about? She could not be certain. But Tituba had confessed as much, Hathorne reminded her. "I did not hear her speak," she replied coolly.

The crowd was incensed. Corey grew more and more flippant ("If you will all go hang me, how can I help it?"), the girls bolder and bolder. Yelping and snapping, they mocked her replies. She was no gospel woman, they sniggered. She was a gospel witch! Observers informed Hathorne that when his suspect bit her lip, teeth marks bloomed on the arms and wrists of her accusers. Thenceforth court officers observed Corey more closely. Indeed each time she clasped her hands together the girls shuddered. When she shifted her weight, they involuntarily, raucously stamped their feet. If she leaned against the bar—she stood for well over an hour, probably closer to two—they crumpled in agony. While she had registered no complaint before Lawson's return, forty-year-old Bathshua Pope now felt the witch reach deep into her bowels as if to tear them from her body. Howling in pain, she threw her muff at Corey. The room was thirty-four by twenty-eight feet; afflicters and afflicted stood in awkward proximity, a foot or two from one another. Witnessed at close range, in the cramped pews, amid the smudged light and fretful whispers, the writhings and screechings were as terrifying as any sorcery. The muff failed to reach its mark. Pope leaned down to remove a shoe. Launched more effectively, it hit Martha Corey squarely in the head. She could not have found it easy to defend herself, as her hands appear by this time to have been bound, for the protection of her victims.

Hathorne allowed Corey's accusers to interrogate her. There were now ten, almost as many women as girls; they fired questions from all sides. Why had Corey not joined the other witches mustering before the meetinghouse? For how long was the covenant she had signed with the devil? (They answered for her: ten years, of which she had served six.) Hathorne tossed out a catechism question. Corey answered correctly, though in Lawson's view she did so oddly. At the girls' instruction, the authorities examined her hands. Had the canary left a mark between her fingers? A pin she had stuck in one of her victims turned up in the child's hair. Before the hearing wound down, Reverend Noyes announced himself satisfied that Corey practiced witchcraft before their very eyes.

Hathorne was beside himself with frustration. He was intent on a confession, nowhere in sight. He got only senseless shrieking and stamping; his suspect remained alternately bemused and self-righteous. The case, he reminded her, appeared open-and-shut. Did she not see that the afflicted were every bit as rational and sober as their neighbors? Here Corey appeared blind. They could not prove she was a witch, she informed the Salem justice, who—like Noyes, a hard-liner from the start—believed they had irrefutably done so. That afternoon a constable led the self-declared gospel woman to the town jail. She would spend the next six months in chains, awaiting trial.

WHILE THE AFFLICTED saw nothing further that day of Martha Corey, they enjoyed little peace. Ann Putnam Sr. woke the next morning to a visitor. At dawn Rebecca Nurse pounced upon her, dressed only in a linen undergarment. She carried a little red book. For two hours the women wrestled, Nurse denying the power of God and Christ and threatening to wrench Ann's soul from her body. Meanwhile the beggar Sarah Good's five-year-old daughter flew about the village, sinking her teeth into Mary Walcott and Ann Putnam Jr. Both displayed raw imprints of her miniature mouth. With a glance, tiny Dorothy Good sent the girls into crippling spasms. She choked and pinched them, goading them to write in the devil's book, of which suddenly there were a profusion in Salem village.

Probably the same day a delegation assembled to pay a call on the Nurse homestead. Though not among the original settlers, Rebecca and Francis Nurse had firmly established themselves in the village, where they acquired a three-hundred-acre farm from a Boston minister who had inherited it. Over the course of nearly fifty years of marriage, they had raised eight children, along with an orphaned Quaker boy. Theirs was a thriving, close-knit clan, the marriage a solid one. All of the children had survived; they demonstrated no inclination to sue one another. A woodworker by trade, Francis Nurse had emerged as one of Salem's most active citizens, serving as juror and constable, appraising properties, surveying borders, and arbitrating land disputes. He had sat on the committee that made the initial overture to Parris, though the two men's relationship had since soured; more recently, Nurse had served on the committee that withheld Parris's wages. Prosperous and widely respected, the Nurses had strong ties to the Sibleys and much of the community, as was clear from the late-March delegation. It included three members of another prominent village family as well as Peter Cloyce, a Nurse brother-in-law. None were related to a bewitched girl or the men who had filed the original complaints. (Also among the delegation was Justice Hathorne's sister, Elizabeth.) Someone—most likely Parris or Hathorne—had dispatched the group to tease out any knowledge Rebecca Nurse might have of recent events and to gauge her reaction to their disquieting news.

They arrived at the spacious Nurse home to find seventy-one-year-old Rebecca sick in bed. She had not ventured out for over a week but assured her visitors that she only felt closer to God in her infirmity. She asked immediately after the convulsing girls, in particular about the Parrises, among her closest neighbors. She had not called at the parsonage. She felt remiss but had her reasons: she had suffered fits when younger. She feared their return, she explained, offering a little, lost nod to contagion. She did grieve and pray for her neighbors, the more so as she knew of the severity of the symptoms; she had heard they were shattering to observe. She worried too as she understood that villagers as innocent as herself had been accused of witchcraft. As gently as they could at high volume— Nurse had lost much of her hearing—her visitors broke the news that she had in fact been named. The old woman sat dumbfounded for some time. Finally she allowed that she was "as innocent as the child unborn."

Her callers left satisfied that she had had no inkling of their mission until they revealed it.

If the delegation intended to clear Nurse's name, they ran into trouble soon enough. Probably the next day Reverend Lawson called on Ann Putnam Sr. He found her lying in bed, surrounded by visitors. Wednesday was baking day in New England; the yeasty smell of fresh bread replaced the spiked, acidic scent of wet ash. Ann was particularly pleased to see her former minister, of whom she was fond. Husband and wife requested that Lawson pray with them while Ann could manage to do so. She followed Lawson for a short while before she began to seize. At prayer's end her husband attempted to lift her from her bed to his lap; her limbs were so stiff she could not be coaxed into a sitting position. She went on to twitch violently, arms and legs flailing, while she disputed, eyes closed tight, with a Rebecca Nurse whom she alone could see. "Be gone! Be gone!" she instructed Nurse. "What hurt did I ever do you in my life?" she pleaded. She knew what Nurse wanted. She would not have it, Ann informed the wraith, with whom, in a trance, she debated a description of Judgment Day. Nurse insisted that the biblical passage did not exist. Ann struggled to name it, her mouth twisting grotesquely, her breath jagged, her limbs contorted. Finally, she succeeded. She had in mind the popular third chapter of Revelation, the reading of which she defied Nurse to endure, appealing to the minister at her side. Lawson hesitated. He felt out of his depth, alarmed by the forces at play in the room and apprehensive of unleashing more; he stood at the edge of bibliomancy. Having now watched an anguished, intelligent friend struggle for a full half hour however, he decided to risk one small experiment. Before he reached the end of the first verse, Ann Putnam's eyes fluttered open. She was perfectly well. It had been the case before, those around the bed informed him, that the texts she named in her fits — there seemed no rhyme or reason to her choices — brought immediate relief. From Salem town, warrants went out for Rebecca Nurse and five-year-old Dorothy Good.

At ten the following morning, elderly Rebecca Nurse stood before Hathorne and Corwin. Hathorne turned first to Parris's niece and Ann Putnam Jr. Would the eleven- and twelve-year-old repeat their charges? Abigail contended that Nurse had beaten her that very morning. Ann howled. Hathorne invited others to register their complaints. Two girls stepped forward, as did a former constable. "Are you an innocent person relating to this witchcraft?" Hathorne asked Nurse, posing the question for the first time in an open-ended manner. Before she could reply, Ann Putnam Sr. cried out: Nurse had brought the black man to her and tempted her to defy God! "O Lord, help me!" cried Nurse, spreading her arms heavenward. As she did so the girls hurled themselves about, choking, ribs heaving. Did she not see how much agony she caused when her hands were loose? Hathorne asked.

For the most part Hathorne inclined that Thursday toward generosity. Before him stood the unlikeliest of suspects. His sister may have vouched for Nurse. It remained possible that she did not yet know she was a witch and had been led astray; he allowed that he was himself uncertain as to what to make of the wispy apparitions. The evidence before him was, however, irrefutable. Tituba—who continued to run the show from the Boston prison—had professed her love for Betty Parris while simultaneously torturing her, Hathorne reasoned. Had Nurse no familiarity with spirits? Like Corey, she could see neither the black man whispering at her side nor the birds in the rafters to which the girls pointed. Hathorne invoked shame: What a sad thing it was that upstanding church members should be charged with witchcraft! "A sad thing sure enough," echoed the shoe-hurling Bathshua Pope, launching into convulsions. They set off an unbridled chain reaction. Hathorne attempted to extract an answer as to whether Nurse thought the afflictions voluntary or involuntary. She hesitated to opine. Hathorne turned the puzzle around. If Rebecca Nurse thought the girls counterfeited, then she "must look upon them as murderers." It was a weighty remark; already he had thought his way past the judicial leniency of the previous years. They were dealing in death sentences.

In fatigue or despair, Nurse at one point dropped her head to her chest. Elizabeth Hubbard's neck seemed automatically to snap. Abigail Williams warned that if Nurse's neck were not righted, Elizabeth's would break; several villagers stepped forward to correct the older woman's posture. The sixteen-year-old instantly recovered. Shrieking, Mary Walcott, the Putnam cousin, displayed a fresh set of teeth marks. Biting and pinching disrupted the room. Ann Putnam Sr. went stiff as a plank in the course of the hearing, from which her husband carried her. She left chaos in her wake. Lawson did not see her go as he had excused himself after two hours, to prepare his sermon. Screeches and roars reached him some distance from the meetinghouse. Even at close quarters Hathorne and his half-deaf suspect could barely hear each other, for which others offered an alternate explanation: Nurse missed Hathorne's questions because the black man whispered in her ear.

While many in the room wept with fear, Nurse remained dry-eyed. Hathorne found this curious and incriminating, especially as it was understood that a witch could not cry. (More exactly, she could shed only three tears, only from the left eye.) The villagers too professed themselves appalled by her indifference. Hathorne continued to poke around, less than constructively. Why had she not visited the Parrises? And what ailed her exactly? "Do you believe these afflicted persons are bewitched?" he asked at last. "I do think they are," she agreed, surveying the bedlam. Lawson was himself stupefied by the disjointed limbs and distracted minds, as awed as the villagers, who whispered "they were afraid that those that sat next to them were under the influence of witchcraft." He could nearly make out the hammering hearts, the raised hairs on the backs of necks, the tickle of fear in the throats. Whatever they were in the presence of appeared contagious, as he allowed in his Thursday-afternoon sermon. Rebecca Nurse was not among those who reconvened for it. Several saw her riding by the meetinghouse with the unidentified black man. She perceived things differently, en route as she was to the Salem town jail.

The crisis thus far had been met with more action than analysis.

Lawson attempted to redress the balance. The villagers hungered for solace and elucidation; over the course of several hours, in the overflowing, unpainted meetinghouse, he delivered on both counts. He had prepared carefully, well aware that he was sitting in a tinderbox, addressing the justices and Salem ministers, families of the afflicted and of the accused. Picking up on Parris's tropes and texts, Lawson permitted that the devil ranged and raged among them. He delivered a short biography of Satan, one that allowed him to display his knowledge of Hebrew and Greek. The flourish of erudition aside, the hybrid creature he summoned—it boasted "the subtlety of the serpent, the malice of the dragon, and strength of the lion"—sounded like a cousin of the furry, fiery beast Tituba had met in the Parris parlor. That that beast was especially eager to "distress, delude, devour" should come as no surprise: the more pious a people, the more vigorously did Satan persecute them. Lawson registered a special plea for his beleaguered colleague. Reverend Parris deserved their spiritual sympathy at all times but especially now, when he and his family labored under such dreadful circumstances.

Lawson ventured a few additional reasons for Satan's particular grudge against Salem. The villagers might consider whether the Lord had singled out their address for this diabolical rendezvous as a sign of "holy displeasure, to put out some fires of contention that have been amongst you." Three signatories of the 1687 Salem town letter advising the villagers to take their animosities elsewhere sat in the pews that afternoon in the felted gray light. They could not have disagreed. Lawson inveighed too against charms and superstitions; he knew all about the witch cake. He understood that the villagers needed answers, but such experiments merely gratified the devil. He added a pestilential note: Satan "spread the contagious atoms of epidemical diseases" in order to destroy more effectively. Lawson warned against false accusations and premature conclusions. There was but one antidote to the old serpent's venomous operation: prayer!

Everyone was guilty in this provocation, lectured Lawson. And everyone should apply himself to solemn self-examination. All the villagers—not only those jolted awake in the electrifying presence of the bewitched—were to search their hearts and embrace their faith. A legion of devils should be met with a multitude of prayers. Lawson's lyrics were soothing but his melody martial: Satan had descended, armed, among them. As he mustered his troops, the villagers were to prepare for spiritual warfare. They should assume every piece of godly armor; this was a trial greater than any they had faced. They must and should be afraid. At the same time, Lawson begged the justices to do all in their power to "check and rebuke Satan." They should prove "the terror to and punishment of evil-doers." Glancing off the question of whether Satan might borrow the shape of an innocent, he called for a vigorous investigation and a firm prosecution.

Solemn self-examining may have transpired over the next days but so did plenty of biting and devouring. That Thursday Martha Corey's husband admitted to a town minister that he suspected his wife of witchcraft. Corey was the third husband to suggest the woman to whom he was married was a witch. Rebecca Nurse—whose husband alone did not step forward—continued to torture Ann Putnam Jr., flaying her for thirty minutes with an invisible chain. Tender, ringed welts rose across the twelve-year-old's skin. Little was discussed in and around the village that week besides the Nurse testimony, the Lawson sermon, and the arrest of Dorothy, Sarah Good's daughter. Both Lawson and the senior town minister, John Higginson, accompanied Hathorne and Corwin to prison to examine the child. She had demonstrated a remarkable ability to cripple with a glance, a feat she managed even while several men held her head in place. Dorothy confessed that she too had a familiar, a little snake that nursed at the lowest joint of her index finger. Holding out her hand, she displayed a red spot about the size of a fleabite. Had the black man given her the snake? the justices asked. Not at all, replied the five-year-old, who was to spend the next nine months dragging herself about in heavy irons. Her mother had.

Amid the "terror, amazement, and astonishment," Lawson entreated all to sympathy and compassion on March 24. While the two ministers conferred closely, while they invoked similar imagery, Parris delivered a different message in the meetinghouse three days later. That Sunday he tangled with a definition of who precisely the devil was. He could be a wicked angel or spirit, the prince of evil spirits, or simply "vile and wicked persons, the worst of such, who for their villainy and impiety do most resemble devils and wicked spirits." Where Lawson invoked Job, Parris favored Judas. He took as his text John 6:70; as there had been a devil among the disciples, so, too, were there devils "here in Christ's little church." He was vehement to the point of accusatory. "One of you is a devil," Parris lectured his tense congregants, making a singular leap and arriving at an exclusionary, door-closing extreme. It provoked an immediate echo. "We are either saints or devils; the Scripture gives us no medium," Parris preached. He dispelled any doubts that had begun to crystallize around another question too. Hathorne remained perplexed as to whether the devil could assume an innocent's form, but the minister was certain: he could not. Parris drew no distinction between those who covenanted with Satan and those whose bodies he appropriated.

The remarks were pointed, transparently so to some. No sooner had Parris announced his text—"Jesus answered them, 'Have not I chosen you twelve, and one of you is a devil?'"—than forty-four-year-old Sarah Cloyce rose and stormed out of the meetinghouse. To the amazement of the congregation, she either slammed the outer door behind her or left the wind to do so. The heavy door banged shut, its metal latch grating. She would miss Mary Sibley's tearful confession that afternoon but had already heard enough; Cloyce was Rebecca Nurse's much younger sister. Her husband had joined the Nurse delegation. All eyes followed her, although it would be three weeks before anyone connected the conspiratorial hints in Parris's sermon with her exit. And while many villagers understood her to have stomped off in rage, only one sharp-eyed eleven-year-old saw Cloyce curtsy to the devil just outside the meetinghouse entry.

A few misgivings surfaced before Lawson left the village. Probably on the morning of March 25, John Procter, a sixty-year-old tavern owner and farmer, fell into conversation with Mary Sibley's husband. Procter stopped for a drink on his way into town to pick up his maid, Mary Warren, who would become one of the more unusual witnesses for the prosecution. A straight shooter, earnest and forthright, Procter had no patience for either the inquest or the afflictions. He would rather have paid Mary, he roared, than allow her to attend a hearing. Why did he rail so? Sibley asked. Mary had suffered fits too, Procter explained, but he had handily dispensed with them. He had kept her at her spinning wheel and threatened to beat her if she misbehaved again. Only in his absence had she started all over with her nonsense. He intended now to "thresh the devil out of her." (He partly succeeded. Mary soon suggested that the girls were acting.) Were the malingerers to continue, Procter informed his startled friend, they would all wind up charged with witchcraft. The girls should hang! Dutifully Sibley reported every word of that rant to their minister.

The morning after Sarah Cloyce's resounding exit, Rebecca Nurse's son-in-law Jonathan Tarbell headed to the Thomas Putnams. He had a number of questions for the women of the house. By this point, interrogations and accounts of interrogations were so frequent in Salem village it is difficult to believe dinner appeared regularly on the table. In a household crowded with well-wishers and small children, Tarbell asked the Putnams: Had Ann Jr. been the first to name his mother-in-law? The girl had after all initially noted only that her tormentor was the pallid woman in her grandmother's pew. She could not identify her. Mercy Lewis, the maid who had struck the specter on Ann Jr.'s behalf, confirmed that Ann Sr. had first named Rebecca Nurse. Ann Sr. claimed Mercy had done so. No one seemed willing to assume responsibility, thirty-eight-year-old Tarbell reported. The same day a group of young men discussed new allegations over drinks at Ingersoll's. Several afflicted girls were on hand. Suddenly one cried out that Procter's wife, Elizabeth, was in the room. She was a witch. She deserved to hang! Objecting that he could see nothing, a man accused the youngster of lying. Ingersoll's wife reprimanded her as well; this was no laughing matter. The teenager conceded she had misspoken, with a heavy admission: she did it for "sport, they must have some sport." The same day two young men helping to care for the bewitched Putnams claimed they overheard the family putting words in nineteen-year-old Mercy Lewis's mouth.

Lawson returned to Boston soon thereafter to write up his notes on the diabolical descent. He missed the fast of March 31, a Thursday the farmers spent in prayer for the afflicted. Over the next month accusations flew throughout and beyond the village, their tempo accelerating wildly. Five witches were accused in March. Twenty-five would be accused in April. The next hearing would be conducted by a Boston magistrate before a larger crowd in Salem town's more comfortable meetinghouse. Among the first of the new arrests were Sarah Cloyce and Elizabeth Procter.

LAWSON'S ACCOUNT OF the Salem witches was published nearly as soon as he finished it, on April 5. The rush to narrative was not solely the work of an enterprising bookseller, although Benjamin Harris was very much that. (He billed the ten-page pamphlet as an account of "the mysterious assaults from hell.") The rush to narrative was a Puritan proclivity, the reflex of a logic-loving, literal-minded people, questing and causation-obsessed. Scripture provided the bedrock of New England law and served as its fundamental text; all answers could be found there. You fortified yourself, restored and refreshed yourself with those passages, familiar to all; at a moral or practical crossroads, you might turn to a page at random. At the same time, God was silent and maddeningly inscrutable. To discern his will, to decode his purpose, was the lifework of a Puritan, who grappled with the terrible, impenetrable riddle at the heart of his faith: One was selected before birth for salvation or damnation; to which camp did one belong? That puzzle left the Puritan on edge, inwardly focused, worrying his way through the world. Long before Lawson's March instructions, he was an ardent, unsparing observer, a compulsive self-examiner.

Watching stood at the heart of the enterprise, whether that meant scanning the heavens, scouring the self, or scrutinizing the neighbors. The word figured in all church covenants. The minister was himself a seer and watchman. Together parishioners joined in "holy watchfulness" over one another. Very little went unnoticed, as the couple who had a child five months after their marriage inevitably discovered. There was every reason the villagers should have scoffed at the assertion that a ship could dock undetected in Salem town. All was supervised; in addition to fence viewers and wheat surveyors, every community supported a surveillance team in its tithing men. The tithing man monitored families and taverns, where he intervened if liquor ran too freely. (He risked attack by chair and andiron.) He served as tax collector and moral guardian, enforcer and informer. He was to examine anyone out after ten p.m. He encouraged catechism at home and confiscated flying walnuts at meetings. He watched for Indians and, on Sundays, for delinquent parishioners. The town watch was itself watched, twice a week. One could never be too sure, as an insecure people perched on the uncomfortable edge of an unpredictable wilderness—squinting into the murk of their parlors, through the woods, into their uncooperative souls—well knew.

Salvation depended on communal virtue, the reason that Mary Sibley and Ezekiel Cheever offered apologies to the village as a whole and the reason that hesitating to identify a witch might seem tantamount to abetting the devil. "If the neighbor of an elected saint sins, then the saint sins also," Mather reminded his congregants. As a result you wound up intimately acquainted with your neighbor's wardrobe, feuds, temper, inheritance, and idiosyncrasies, as well as the state of his cider supply and the brand on his cow's ear. No one was monitored as closely as the children, whose moral well-being was not yet assured and seemed at times distinctly improbable. The surveillance was not always malignant. Had a passerby not peered into the Mathers' Boston windows one autumn evening, he might not have noticed the daughter whose bonnet had caught fire and who, alone at home, would seconds later have been consumed by flames.*

The Massachusetts Puritan also knew—or devoutly hoped—that he was being watched. If you inhabited a city on a hill, by definition you stood onstage. That gaze did not discomfort the settlers. It made them—in the words of former deputy president William Stoughton, who helped the colony define itself and would soon define Salem witchcraft—a civilization of which great things were expected. "If any people in the world have been lifted up to heaven as to advantages and privileges," Stoughton proclaimed, "we are the people." That was one way to put it. A modern historian suggested a less exalted one. Having traveled three thousand miles, New Englanders "had willingly risked life and property to come to the wilderness so they could sit on benches in drafty, gloomy barns for three to six hours on Sundays hearing the Word as it should be preached." The combination was in other words ideal. The Puritan was wary and watchful. His faith kept him off balance and on guard. And if you intended to live in a state of nerve-racking insecurity, in expectation of ambush and meteorological rebuke—on the watch for every brand of intruder, from the "ravening wolves of heresy" to the "wild boars of tyranny," as a 1694 narrative had it—seventeenth-century Massachusetts, that rude and howling wilderness, was the place for you.

So far as what Mather in March termed "fiery rebukes from heaven" went, the Lord had amply delivered. Since the Puritans' 1630 arrival, the Almighty had sent them immoderate rains and blasting mildew, caterpillars and grasshoppers, drought, smallpox, and fire. For several decades he had spoken only with displeasure. Over the first two generations, the colonists had assumed a de facto independence from England, which in

* And had a neighbor not peered through the window, the mystery of William Morse's haunted house—through which cats, hogs, spoons, stones, and chairs periodically flew—might never have been solved. There was Morse, deep in prayer. And there was the teenage grandson, flinging shoes at his grandfather's head. Having grown up nearby, Ann Putnam Sr. would have known every wrinkle of that long-running mystery, one that had produced an earlier witchcraft accusation.

1684 had led King Charles II to revoke their charter, a document of near-sacred status; decades of prosperity came to a shuddering halt. The settlers had been refractory and disruptive, coining their own money, ignoring the Navigation Acts, oppressing Quakers. They seemed to believe the laws of England did not extend across an ocean; they had taken it upon themselves to found a self-governing republic while no one was looking. Several years later, the Crown imposed a royal governor on Massachusetts to address the settlers' irregularities, resolve "the petty differences and animosities" among the colonial administrations, and coordinate defenses. When Edmund Andros arrived to head up a Dominion government in 1686, he exercised absolute authority over all territory from Maine to New Jersey. He curtailed town meetings and abolished the Massachusetts legislature. He threw Puritan hegemony and land claims into question — and left a Boston congregation to wait outdoors for several hours, in March, while he appropriated their meetinghouse for an Anglican service. To many New Englanders, he qualified as both a wolf of heresy and a boar of tyranny.

In March 1689 the uniformed Andros passed through Salem with a large retinue. Throwing down the gauntlet, he asked John Higginson, the town's vigorous senior minister, if all the land in New England did not rightfully belong to the king. His conversation described as "a glimpse of heaven," Higginson was too tactful a man to gratify his visitor with an answer. He replied that he could speak only as a curate; Andros had broached a matter of state. That was all the more reason he should like an answer, persisted the iron-fisted governor. Higginson allowed as how he felt the lands belonged to those who occupied them and who had bartered with the Indians for them. At great expense to themselves, over two generations, the settlers had subdued a wasteland. They had tamed what an early visitor termed a "remote, rocky, barren, bushy, wild-woody wilderness." The Salem minister and the royal governor went back and forth for some time, weighing the laws of God and Englishmen. The king, Higginson argued, had had no stake in North

American lands before the settlers arrived. At which Andros exploded, positing another binary choice, if eighty-seven years prematurely: "Either you are subjects or you are rebels."

Andros lasted until April of 1689, when the colonists removed him in a military coup. Instigated by the Boston ministers, it was led by many of the men who would exterminate witches three years later. Even before that revolt Increase Mather had secretly sailed to London — he narrowly avoided arrest — to clarify the colony's grievances and plead for a new charter. The negotiation took the better part of three years, during which time Massachusetts knew no political authority. Only in April 1692 was it emerging from what Topsfield's minister called its "fears and troubles." A disgruntled official was not wrong when he noted that Massachusetts was as close to establishing a viable government as it was to building the Tower of Babel; civil affairs remained in a shambles. There was much fear that a royal punishment was forthcoming, that Anglicanism would be imposed. Massachusetts felt acutely vulnerable, the more so as Bay Colony calamities registered as verdicts. Each time God frowned — whether in the form of a hailstorm, plague, overbearing English officials, or witchcraft — he was assumed to do so for a reason.

The settlers watched then for many things in 1692 besides marauding Indians and nonphantom Frenchmen. They watched for a charter that would restore their rights and for the return of the indispensable, accomplished Mather. They watched for an explanation of and a deliverance from their misery. For some time, Cotton Mather and others had been on the lookout as well for the Second Coming. Given the calamities that had visited New England, it felt imminent. Witchcraft in Salem further proved that time was short; Mather calculated the golden age to be five years in the future. His exactitude points up another feature of the seventeenth-century mind. Described as "that strange agglomeration of incongruities," it consisted of a crazy quilt of erudition and superstition.*

---

* The great Enlightenment thinkers were not altogether different. Robert Boyle proposed interviews with miners who in their excavations had met with "subterraneous demons." Newton divided his time between the occult and physics, practicing alchemy and devot-

The natural bordered on the supernatural—one eminent minister received the news that his wife had given birth not from the midwife but from the Lord—as medicine blurred into astrology, science into nonsense.

Plenty of clergymen dabbled in alchemy while inveighing against the occult; popular magic was one thing, elite magic another. A great deal of bet-hedging and base-covering went on; just because you were eminently pious did not mean you hesitated to serve up a witch cake. Like any people under a sentence of predestination, the Puritans developed an obsession with fortune-telling. Almanacs sold briskly, offering astrological wisdoms.* Harvard's 1683 commencement was postponed due to an eclipse. By any account the Puritans were very far from kitchen-sink realism; God spoke to them in rolls of thunder, in what sounds like dragon smoke, in glittering comets. It said something about Samuel Sewall that where others looked for heaven's artillery, Sewall, whose brother had taken in little Betty Parris, kept particularly close track of rainbows—comforting rainbows, noble rainbows, perfect rainbows, a rainbow directly out of the book of Revelation. Sewall installed angel-head carvings on the gate before his home as protective cover. In the anxious murk, religion sometimes seemed a kind of halfway house between reason and superstition.

The Bay Colony may have constituted the best-educated community in the history of the world before 1692. Rarely have so many been able to parse a sentence in the presence of so few books. The majority of adolescent girls in Salem village could read, even if they could not sign their names. (Ann Putnam Jr. numbered among the few who could.) Theirs was also a society in which the most literate happened to be the most literal. The New England clergy collected proofs of the supernatural in part to fend off the surging forces of rationalism. Increase Mather had

---

ing 300,000 words to the book of Revelation; Keynes termed him "the last of the magicians." Isaac Newton identified the Antichrist. John Locke applied astrology to the harvest of medicinal herbs.
* The 1692 almanac warned that the March alignment of the stars portended feuds and skirmishes: "In short mankind in general are about this time inclined to violence."

harvested prodigies and portents in his 1684 *Illustrious Providences,* the precursor to his son's *Memorable Providences,* the pulpy volume through which news of the Swedish flight and satanic rescue reached New England. A grab bag of apparitions, possessions, earthquakes, shipwrecks, and flying candlesticks, *Illustrious Providences* was a stunning hybrid of folklore and erudition, produced to satisfy the ministers who in 1681 requested a collection of "prodigious witchcrafts, diabolical possessions, remarkable judgments." Those "native wonder tales" served a political purpose, reaffirming God's commitment to the New England mission in the face of royal incursions.

The Puritan overlooked nothing by way of sign or symbol. When he headed into the marsh with a gun to hunt waterfowl for dinner and his best pig followed him, it meant something. The fury of hailstones that would shatter Sewall's new kitchen windows delivered a providential message. (Mather assured his disconsolate friend that the damage was Apocalypse practice.) The thirst for meaning introduced an obsession with causality; explanations were a regular feature of Puritan life. A comet was never simply a comet. A burn in the linen was ripe with meaning. As the Goodwin children twisted and writhed, their father naturally assumed he was being punished for his sins. If Parris read a rebuke in his convulsing children he did not say so publicly. It was the obvious conclusion, however. Cotton Mather would infer as much when another daughter—the Mather home was a dangerous place—fell into the fire.

Human frailty was thought to account for inclement weather; teeth chattering, toes numb, the Massachusetts Puritan had every reason to believe he sinned flamboyantly. Immoderate behavior claimed a fair number of casualties; Increase Mather suggested that King Philip's War followed from excessive silk- and wig-wearing. A Connecticut cleric wrote down his widowhood to the fact that he had too much enjoyed sex with his wife. Others attributed the deaths of children to their outsize affections for them. Negligence constituted the workhorse of explanations, especially for a generation convinced of its inferiority. They were not the pious men their fathers had been; the idyllic age was behind them. The Cambridge minister who went hoarse was being chastised for his poor preaching. Was his left knee lame, Increase Mather wondered, in the thirty-fourth year of his sixty-four-year ministry, as witches began to fly through the air, because he had been insufficiently diligent in his service to God? (He spent no fewer than sixteen of every twenty-four hours in his study.) One could not be too careful; Cotton Mather accidentally omitted a daughter's name from his morning prayer. He finished to discover that an hour earlier the child's nurse had accidentally suffocated her. When in 1690 Samuel Parris attributed New England's suffering to lapses in family devotions, he took the problem to a Cambridge ministers' meeting. The solution was simple: the Massachusetts clergymen were to do their utmost to call on each of their parishioners to "inquire, instruct, advise, warn, and charge, according to the circumstances of the families."

The full-scale embrace of causality sent the Puritan in two seemingly opposite directions. On the one hand it made of him an enthusiastic litigant. Prior to the 1690s, there were no lawyers in the Bay Colony. There were no accidents either. Every conceivable offense found its way to court, as, it seemed, did most Massachusetts residents, seduced by the irresistible idea—when things fall apart, disappoint, go awry or astray—that someone, somewhere, must be to blame.* (Much of what we know about the upright Salem villagers comes from the court records, a catalog of their misdeeds. It is at once a dazzling compendium of major and minor infractions and a tribute to a hypertrophied faith in reason.) The residents of seventeenth-century Massachusetts were not more given to transgression than others, only more in love with justice. Even when they rewrote the official record, they remained ledger-keepers and score-settlers. A testifying people whose salvation depended on a public confession, they made for natural witnesses. There seemed never to be a shortage of volunteers to report on what had been said, or what they had

---

* Rare was the New Englander who agreed with Samuel Sewall's suit-adverse father-in-law who remarked, "I observe the law to be very much like a lottery—great charge, little benefit."

heard had been said a generation earlier. Mutual surveillance could sound like something else altogether in the courtroom. What Cotton Mather had in mind when he exhorted his congregation in 1692 to remain one another's eagle-eyed guardians was probably not what William Cantlebery's wife had in mind when—standing in a tree—she invited a friend to join her in spying on the neighbor who shoved Cantlebery off her property, pelting him with a rain of objects.

Vigilant though the settlers were, many things went missing, from mares to fences to virtue. Debt and drunkenness were the popular legal favorites, but trespass in all its forms came close behind. That was unsurprising when land grants were defined as "beginning at a stump and running east four rods, to a stake" or bounded "easterly to a tree 'pretty big' either black oak or yellow oak, upon a ridge by the highway." Even where borders were exact, livestock chose not to respect them. Freewheeling New England pigs sowed havoc for generations; the neighbor's swine seemed perpetually to be rooting in the peas. Serene Rebecca Nurse had erupted in fury one Saturday morning when the next-door neighbor's pigs turned up in her garden. She had called to her son to bring his gun. (It would not help her case that the pig owner died soon thereafter.) When Parris petitioned the village to repair his rotten, decomposing fence, he described it as a "make-bait" between himself and his neighbors. Every spring his livestock ventured to their side, their hogs, cows, and sheep to his. Year in and year out, Salem discussed the minister's pasture fence, which—joining fears of impiety, famine, and invasion—crammed the New England conundrum into a three-word nutshell.

Locks do not appear to have functioned in seventeenth-century Massachusetts, where all kinds of boundaries were trampled and thresholds penetrated. The Salem villagers had every reason to advertise their wives' fears when left alone; a woman risked assault from a visiting neighbor when her husband descended to the cellar for more cider. Consciously and not, men slipped into beds not their own. (It is interesting that spectral women so frequently disturbed men in their beds throughout 1692 when in the visible world the opposite occurred with some frequency.) Dark barns proved especially perilous places. The candle knocked from her hand, a Newbury girl informed the assailant who lured her into the stable that "she would as soon be gored by the cows as to be defiled by such a rogue as he." There was a conflagrative nature to those complaints; angry words between two parties regularly begat angrier exchanges among their relatives, who handed them down, intact and still smoldering, from one generation to the next. In such a way the Putnams' feud with several Topsfield families had gathered legendary force over the decades; Rebecca Nurse's family and the Putnams had sued and countersued each other in an epic land dispute. The courts functioned efficiently, with English procedures and remarkable speed. Prison sentences were rare. The workforce beckoned, as did redemption— or a renewed court case.

While the punishments were highly original, the catalog of offenses was less so. Servants suffered regular verbal and physical abuse. They sought revenge by raiding the cellar, stealing the kettle, or planting stones in beds. Before running away with his master's shoes and horse, one servant informed his mistress she was "an ordinary whore, burnt-tail bitch and hopping toad." Few were as creative as the girl who slipped the toad into the milk pitcher. Hauled into court over and over—he had an irritating Quaker habit of working, and requiring his help to work, on the Sabbath (he was spotted through a shop window)—Salem merchant Thomas Maule landed there in 1681 for abuse of his maid. He had taken to delivering thirty or forty lashes with a horsewhip to her naked back. She spat blood for two weeks. Why did he so cruelly beat the girl, he was asked, when he could just as easily have sold her? "Because she was a good servant," explained Maule, who largely sat out the events of 1692 but did not mince words afterward.

What a court could not always do was make sense of things. Sometimes, in the headlong pursuit of reason, the best explanation turned out to be the otherworldly one. Sometimes, the most eminent of New England ministers collectively pointed out, it was the only explanation. Certainly it was the most versatile. One husband blamed his impotence on witches in the woods outside. If Sarah Good had not enchanted them, how to construe the death of those village cattle? Witchcraft tied up loose ends, accounting for the arbitrary, the eerie, and the unneighborly. As Samuel Parris was discovering, it deflected divine judgment and dissolved personal responsibility. The devil not only provided a holiday from reason but expressed himself clearly; for all their perversity, his motives made sense. You did not need to ask what you had done to deserve his disfavor, preferable to celestial rebuke—or indifference. And when diabolical machinations were what you were watching for, they quickly became what you saw. Amid glaring accountability, witchcraft broke up logical logjams. It ratified grudges, neutralized slights, relieved anxiety. It offered an airtight explanation when, literally, all hell broke loose.

NO ONE IN Salem village lived alone. But suddenly—after Deodat Lawson's alarm and Parris's inflammatory sermon—they seemed less alone than ever. A riot of shadowy sightings followed. On the evening of April 6, Parris reported, John Procter visited the parsonage to attack his niece. He inflicted similar punishments at the Putnam household. The same Wednesday, several miles off, a twenty-five-year-old farmer named Ben Gould woke to find Giles and Martha Corey standing by his bed. They delivered two sharp pinches to his side and returned the following night, Procter in tow. For several days Gould could not fit a shoe to his foot for the pain. He was the first in what would be a series of young male accusers. Men now practiced witchcraft on other men, although they tended not to assault one another in the presence of justices. Nor did they fend off invisible specters in public assemblies, with one notable exception. Parris's April 10 sermon was interrupted by John Indian, the parsonage slave. John was as aware as anyone that Tituba had now been in prison for five weeks. The spectral Sarah Cloyce descended on him as he sat in his pew; she sank her teeth into him with such force that she drew blood. She assaulted eleven-year-old Abigail as well. Following the sermon, the Putnams' maid convulsed again at Ingersoll's. When she returned to her

senses, she could not identify her afflicter. A roll call of suspects was submitted; the same names were on all minds. Had the witch been ancient
Rebecca Nurse? Or straight-spined Martha Corey? Sarah Cloyce seemed
a safe choice, the warrant having already gone out for her arrest. Twenty-
five miles away, in Boston, Cotton Mather that day exhorted his congregants to shake off their sinful sleep, to watch against the devil, for the
coming of the Lord, as the "stupendious revolution" was near.

Word of the preternatural events in Salem reached Boston through a
variety of channels. Either because Hathorne and Corwin felt they
needed reinforcements, because those reinforcements felt compelled to
investigate the curious matter for themselves, or because for the first
time a male suspect was to take the stand, acting deputy governor
Thomas Danforth traveled to Salem to conduct the April 11 preliminary
hearing. With him rode a host of officials, including Boston judge and
merchant Samuel Sewall. Among the colony's most eminent public servants, sixty-nine-year-old Danforth had for decades tended to Harvard's
survival as the university's treasurer and steward. He served simultaneously in the Massachusetts legislature. He had fought to defend the colony's lost charter and participated in the Andros coup. He cut an
impressive figure. For some of the same reasons that brought him to
Salem, the April hearing was moved to the less rustic, better-lit town
meetinghouse, nearly twice the size of the village one, with an extensive,
newly built gallery and stylish boxed pews.

Danforth appointed Parris court clerk that Monday, leaving the minister to record his slave's account of events that had taken place in his
own home. Parris struggled to keep up. The words regularly came too
quickly for the Salem recorders. With quill and ink wholly unsuited to
the fast-paced, stereophonic scene, they leaped from direct quotes to
paraphrase, from unidentified voices in the courtroom to specters,
half noting the changes of speakers as they did so. The blots on the page
testify to their labor; it was not easy to keep the ink flowing. They corrected themselves as they went. They summarized and editorialized.
(For Parris, the fits before them could be "dreadful," "extreme," "horrible,"

"miserable," or "grievous.") Thomas Putnam beefed up accounts after the fact. It was sometimes easier to rest their pens, to state that the defendant said nothing worth repeating, that the witchcraft was altogether obvious, that the testimony amounted to a mass of lies and contradictions. The clerks noted what they deemed most significant (impertinence, laughter, dry eyes), omitting what they deemed insignificant (denials). The logic of accusations tended to win out over the illogic of alibis. What wound up on the page was not always what the reporter heard but what he remembered or believed; few would prove as fastidious as he had been with Tituba. On April 11, amid the restive crowd, Parris could not always hear or see. Errors crept into his transcripts.

Thomas Danforth orchestrated a sort of chorus, with each of the afflicted—three adult women joined the girls—chiming in. Certain truths emerged quickly. First Elizabeth Procter and later Sarah Cloyce had visited John at the parsonage, pinching and biting him in broad daylight, choking the slave to within an inch of his life, insisting he sign their book. A far more imposing figure, Danforth proceeded less harshly than Hathorne. He had dismissed a 1659 witchcraft case, twice overturning the verdict of the jury. He wanted now to be certain: Did John Indian recognize his two tormentors? Indeed he did, replied the slave, indicating one of them, Sarah Cloyce, standing as if spotlit at the front of the room. Cloyce had known her share of misery; she had fled an Indian raid and spent years in poverty as the widowed mother of five. Her life had been far more difficult than that of her older sister, Rebecca Nurse. "When did I hurt thee?" she protested. "A great many times," John rejoined. "Oh, you are a grievous liar!" cried Cloyce.

Cloyce's hearing proceeded more tautly than her sister's, which she had almost certainly attended. The girls did the bulk of the talking. "Abigail Williams!" Danforth called, having been briefed in advance. "Did you see a company at Mr. Parris's house eat and drink?" The first to use the word, she replied: "Yes, Sir, that was their sacrament." A devil's Sabbath had taken place the day of the public fast. Cloyce and Good served as deacons at that service, held just behind the parsonage. For the second time, details of the diabolical meeting issued from the minister's household; over and over, Parris was to hear of witches congregating just outside his home, an idea that may have buttressed his position in the community—it pointed up his righteousness—or shamed him. In either event, he had cause to flinch at this sudden interest in his overrun, under-fenced pasture. A white man before whom all the witches trembled presided. Abigail supplied a detail more disturbing than even the blood-drinking: there had been some forty witches in attendance! At this juncture Cloyce asked for water, collapsing into her seat "as one seized with a dying fainting fit," noted Parris. It was ten years to the day since the disgruntled Salem potter had warned that the village would never amount to a town if its inhabitants did not desist from their quarreling.

Danforth turned next to forty-one-year-old Elizabeth Procter, newly pregnant with her sixth child, a fact of which she may not yet have been aware. Here the magistrate ran into difficulties. One of the girls protested that she had never seen Elizabeth before. Two were struck dumb. Asked if Elizabeth afflicted her, Parris's niece plunged her fist into her mouth. The doctor's niece fell into a long trance. The girls had either lost their thread or succumbed to a greater power. Danforth may have intimidated them; the father of twelve, he knew how to speak to a child. John Indian alone obliged him. Scantily clad, Elizabeth Procter had, John revealed, choked him. Twice Danforth asked if he was certain of her identity. John was. Gradually most of the girls rallied, supplying additional details of Elizabeth's demonic book.

It was probably at that point—the words flew from every side—that Parris's niece and Ann Putnam Jr. reached out to strike the accused. Abigail's fist magically unclenched in midair. As the tips of her fingers brushed the older woman's hood, she howled in pain. They were scorched! When not in fits the two took over for John, directing the room's attention. The girls would announce: "Look to her! She will have a fit presently"—as the bewitched would. At other times they warned, "We shall all fall!" and seven or eight girls would collapse, raving, to the floor. For their predictive power the eleven- and twelve-year-old were soon dubbed the "visionary girls." They pointed to the meetinghouse beam: Elizabeth Procter, the wizard's wife, balanced there. And soon enough, they cautioned, Procter—who had pronounced their claims pure nonsense—would make the muff-throwing Bathshua Pope levitate. At precisely that moment Pope's feet rose from the floor. What did he say to this, Danforth demanded of John Procter, suddenly on trial. He barely had time to reply when Abigail pointed to two older women. Procter was on the verge of attacking them, she cried as both began to twist in pain. "You see the devil will deceive you," Danforth warned the accidental suspect. "The children could see what you were going to do before the woman was hurt." He strongly advised repentance; Satan toyed with him. "Woe, woe, woe," Boston magistrate Samuel Sewall noted in his diary that evening, in Latin, the language to which he reverted for delicate matters, like the lustful dream about his wife or his father-in-law's criticisms. Only later did he add the loaded word "witchcraft" to the line.

Procter singlehandedly attempted to restore some sanity. Brusque if genial, he was of Danforth's generation. The mother of five of his eleven children, Elizabeth, his much younger wife, assisted with the couple's tavern. They owned as well a seven-hundred-acre farm. Procter lost no time in informing all who would listen—including the husband of the woman whom he had caused to levitate—that if Parris would allow him a few minutes with John Indian, "he would soon beat the devil out of him." It was the same blustery note he had sounded earlier. The threat could not have been welcome to Parris, well beyond the point where he believed devils could be thrashed away. At least a few others shared Procter's opinion. A Salem farmer named Edward Bishop returned John Indian to the village late that afternoon on horseback. The slave fell into a violent fit. Lurching forward, he bit the rider before him, holding on with his teeth alone. Bishop struck him with a stick, lifting the spell. John promised it would not happen again. Bishop heartily assured him it would not, vowing in such a way to cure all the bewitched.

The following morning found Parris in the town meetinghouse

attempting, in his tight, precise hand, to draft a faithful record of the previous day's astonishments. He met with nothing but interruptions. John and Abigail roared and twisted around him. Mary Walcott, the Putnam maid, sat calmly knitting nearby, though went glassy-eyed for stretches at a time. Emerging from a trance, the sixteen-year-old confirmed what Abigail abruptly asserted: John Procter sat in the marshal's lap! John Indian corrected her: Procter sat astride the minister's dog under the very table at which Parris expanded on his courtroom shorthand. John coaxed the animal—presumably the witch-cake eater—out from under the refectory table. He then cried to an invisible Sarah Cloyce "Oh you old witch!" before convulsing so wildly that four men could not calm him. Still at her knitting, Mary Walcott casually looked up to note that the Procters and Cloyce together tortured the Indian. John and Abigail were carried off. Mary remained behind as Parris read his account to the marshal. As he finished, she pointed across the room, knitting in hand: the entire coven—Good, the Procters, Nurse, Corey, Cloyce, Good's daughter—had assembled. Everyone she named sailed to the Boston prison that day, including Procter, who may have wound up incarcerated without first having been arrested. Giles Corey rode with Martha as far as the Salem ferry but could continue no farther. He did not have the money to cross. He vowed to join his wife the following week, a promise on which he could not make good. He too would be in custody Monday.

Various ground rules had begun to emerge, some of them unprecedented. Witches could be male or female, itinerant beggars or prosperous farmers, young or old, full church members or outsiders. As Giles Corey would discover, expressing sympathy for a convicted spouse—even one whom you had previously maligned—was imprudent. Implicating one was more acceptable; William Good never found himself on trial. The skeptic was a marked man. Having observed both the accused witches and the accusers at closer range than anyone other than the Parrises, John Indian may have reasoned that it was wise to name names before anyone mentioned his. Certainly it was safer to be afflicted than accused. Suspicions ran wild over an otherwise eerily quiet week. All hung in a state of suspended stillness. Danforth's interrogation, with the girls' reports of the witches' Sabbath, had been the lightning. Now came the thunder, from which even a dog under a meetinghouse table warming his master's feet was not safe.

MORE AND MORE often, when one of the girls pointed to a specter, someone else saw it too. Vision grew sharper in Salem village. Memories improved. As early-morning swallows announced the spring, Constable Herrick rounded up four more witches; he ran himself ragged over the next days, corralling witnesses and arresting suspects. Danforth had lent a legitimacy to the proceedings but in no way altered them. The only tangible result was that, picking up where his superior had left off, Hathorne revised his opening gambit, more neutral in April than it had been in March. He may have felt he was now playing on a larger stage.

The first of four very different suspects, Giles Corey walked into the meetinghouse at eight o'clock that April morning, trailing behind him a colorful, seven-decade-long past. While the ferry-side date he had made with his wife sounded to some like demonic collusion, Corey was an obvious target for other reasons. When he had joined the Salem town congregation a year earlier, reference was made to his scandalous reputation. A half century earlier, Corey had stolen wheat, flax, tobacco, and a host of other items from a warehouse. (It belonged to the father of Justice Corwin.) Corey had fetched a canoe load of wood while he was meant to be serving watch, then lied about it in court. He had exchanged blows with the local schoolmaster whom he doused with filthy water; he had been prosecuted for brawling and disturbing the peace. In 1676 he savagely beat a thief with a stick, delivering nearly a hundred blows, pretending afterward that the disoriented young man had taken a fall. He died of his injuries within days.

Uprooting fences and threatening horses, Corey trafficked in Sarah Good's brand of spite. He warned a neighbor that if his orchard fence did not burn this year, it would the next. Either way, his trees would yield no fruit. (That neighbor happened to be the father of Corey's son-in-law. The account of the curse came from his daughter's twenty-five-year-old husband, testifying against Corey.) Another in-law reported that Corey had stolen wood, hay, carpentry tools, and twelve bushels of apples. Corey tossed a malediction at him too: the neighbor's sawmill would work no more. Over these years Corey amassed a hundred acres of farmland, a feat that even the most affable of men could not manage without sharp words and bruised egos. By all accounts—including one taken in the courtroom of Hathorne's father, who heard the assault case—he was "a very quarrelsome and contentious bad neighbor." His name surfaced regularly in connection with missing mares and dead pigs. There had long been some animus against the Coreys and something ominous about their house.

When flames had shot out of the roof of a Procter home fifteen years earlier, Corey seemed the obvious culprit. He narrowly skirted a different accusation when it was noted that the house could have burned "but by some evil hand." Corey did not address the witchcraft imputation but did prove he was in bed that evening; he was acquitted. Inevitably he sued John Procter for defamation. Procter's bluff good nature was such that when the two later met on the road, Corey hauling a load of wood, Procter teased: "How now, Giles, will thou never leave thy old trade? Thou hast got some of my wood here upon thy cart." Corey admitted as much. The two proceeded to make peace over a glass of wine, bantering and manifesting an "abundance of love," as one observer recalled. It would come in handy; the men were about to share close quarters.

Plenty of old scores surfaced at the April 19 hearing. Corey did his best to beat them away. "Which of you have seen this man hurt you?" Hathorne asked. Four girls stepped forward. Corey denied the charges. He had entered into no contract with the devil. "What temptations have you had?" Hathorne demanded. "I never had temptations in my life," scowled Corey, who took the same tack when, from the pews, came three reports that Corey had that very morning suffered a scare in his barn. "What was it frighted you?" inquired Hathorne. "I do not know that ever I spoke the word in my life," Corey rejoined, sending his accusers into paroxysms. For their protection Hathorne requested the marshal fasten Corey's hands. Was it not enough to indulge in witchcraft at other times, Hathorne reprimanded Corey, "must you do it now in the face of authority?" He seemed personally affronted. "I am a poor creature, and cannot help it" came the reply of the ornery old man, sounding—in one of the unlikeliest transmutations that spring— suddenly sympathetic.

Hands bound, Corey did his best to explain. He had no recollection of having been frightened in the cowshed. Nor could he shed light on the green ointment with which Martha had been arrested. It came from a neighbor, whose husband, it turned out, Corey had called a "damned, devilish rogue." Others introduced some enduring, equally unsavory language. It seemed that Corey had at one time contemplated suicide, for which he considered framing a relative, no great surprise for someone whose in-laws testified against him in court. But you said you suffered no temptations, Hathorne needled. "I meant temptations to witchcraft," clarified Corey. "If you can give way to self-murder, that will make way to temptation to witchcraft," Hathorne scolded, rather anticipating Corey's grisly end, if getting the terms backward.

Another suspect that Tuesday—the only one of the four to have formally faced an earlier witchcraft accusation—proved more defiant. A middle-aged resident of Salem town, probably in her early fifties, Bridget Bishop had a history of petty theft. She and a former husband had fought bitterly; she had turned up once with blood on her face, on another occasion with bruises all over her body. In 1677 she had landed in court for having called her husband an old rogue and old devil on the Sabbath; the couple had been whipped eight years earlier for the same offense. The second time both stood for an hour, gagged, back to back, on lecture day in the public market, a paper advertising their offense fastened to their foreheads. Soon thereafter Bishop's husband died under suspicious circumstances. Within eight months, at odds with her neighbors and with her stepchildren, saddled by debts, she stood trial for witchcraft. A slave had been leading his horses through the November woods when they had panicked and plunged into a freezing swamp. Astonished onlookers declared the animals enchanted. A week later, the slave walked into the barn to discover a transparent Bridget Bishop balancing on a beam. She vanished when he reached for a pitchfork.

Those visions—and the Bishops' quarrels—were well enough remembered that her accusers referred to her still as Bridget Oliver, her previous husband's name. "They say you bewitched your first husband to death," Hathorne observed, reaching back into the swirl of rumor. "If it please your worship, I know nothing of it," she answered, shaking her head. Parris implied that she did so respectfully. Cheever felt she did so angrily. Given that she had fielded the same questions before, she sounds uncommonly patient. In both men's accounts, the girls jerked with each turn of her head. When she looked to the heavens for help, their eyes floated up in their sockets. Bishop contended that she knew neither the devil nor her accusers. In fact, she knew no man, woman, or child in the room, having never lived in the village. Her accusers disagreed. Putnam cousin Mary Walcott had more compelling evidence yet. When Bishop's specter descended on her, she had cried out; her brother had thrust his sword at Bishop's coat. Mary heard the fabric tear. Was there a hole in her coat? Hathorne inquired of the suspect. There was not, Bishop assured him. Hathorne ordered a search. Two corresponding rents turned up. Constable Herrick, an upholsterer when he was not apprehending witch suspects, interposed a question of his own: How had Bishop managed to slip into his bedroom one morning? (Massachusetts witchcraft again proved itself unlike any other: she appeared there, Herrick claimed, to ask if he had any curtains to sell.)

Bishop could be arch if not provocative; unwisely, she sounded a few skeptical notes. She could not say what ailed the girls, nor had she given consent for any evil spirit to parade about in her likeness. She was not a witch. She could not even say what one was. She had the bad luck to be appearing before a fine logician. "How do you know, then," countered Hathorne, "that you are not a witch?" She failed to grasp his meaning.

"How can you know that you are no witch, and yet not know what a witch is?" persisted Hathorne. Bishop bristled. Were she a witch Hathorne would know of her powers, she replied. Hathorne heard the remark as a threat. He would not forget it. Did she not know that others had confessed that very day? She did not. Two men stepped forward, sputtering. They had specifically told Bishop as much! "Why look, you are taken now in a flat lie!" Hathorne berated her.

By the time Hathorne examined Bishop that Tuesday, he had struck gold with his previous two suspects. One was pretty Mary Warren, whose initial fits Procter had thrashed out of her. Hathorne attempted to do the same with the truth. Since Procter had beaten her, the two had been engaged in a steely battle. For relief from her distemper she had posted a note of gratitude on the meetinghouse door, a common practice. That door functioned as a community bulletin board; it was where you learned who the new fence viewer was or who had not properly educated his children, now offered in service. The Procters were furious at the advertisement of the disorder in their home. An impulsive twenty-year-old given to outbursts of emotion, Mary also defected from her peers. She passed in her recovery from victim to suspect, possibly accusing her friends of fraud on the way. Soon enough she would confess to witchcraft, then submit to afflictions all over again. She seemed to want all the roles to herself.

As Mary approached the bar the bewitched choked; they could not speak when Hathorne asked if Warren hurt them. Dr. Griggs's maid managed to compose herself only long enough to confirm that the older girl did so. She was joined by John Indian and Bathshua Pope, the muff thrower. "You were a little while ago an afflicted person, now you are an afflicter: How comes this to pass?" demanded Hathorne. Mary choked and spun. She seemed uncertain herself as to which side she was on. For some time she stood entranced, then launched into a tearful, hand-wringing apology. She promised to tell all, though it remained unclear to which party she was apologizing and what she meant to tell. Each time she attempted to speak she contorted. Hathorne several times dismissed her from the room to recover; the ministers and justices finally deposed her in private.

The twenty-year-old was more forthcoming after a night in prison. The evening after she had posted her note, Elizabeth Procter had forced her from bed. She informed Mary that she was a witch—Salem witches tended to supply formal introductions and helpful exposition, presenting their credentials up front*—something that, on reflection, Mary might have surmised, given that her mistress read so much. Elizabeth owned a number of books, traveling always with one in her pocket. Mary implicated Giles Corey, whose attire she astonished her examiners by describing in detail. Corey abused her for a very earthly reason: Mary had advised her master to raise the price of a meadow Corey had hoped to buy. She described an equally vexed spiritual transaction on April 21. While resisting various prompts, she admitted that she had signed some sort of portentous tome urged on her by her employers while she drank cider at their table. Her finger had left a strange black blot on the volume. It took three days to extract those details from her; Mary cried she would be "torn in pieces" if she divulged them. Procter had indeed bullied her privately, although if he had threatened to burn her out of her fit, drown her, or run her through the hedges, as she claimed, he may have done so for non-sorcerous reasons. He had clearly banked on her discretion. He had confided in Mary that his wife exasperated him. His confidences, or that intimacy, proved a burden. Mary carried about another fear too. She had yielded to Procter's demand that she sign the book because he warned that if she did not, he would not save her in her next fit, when she tumbled into fire or water. She used precisely the terms Parris had used in describing parents dangling children before dangers only to rescue them, educating by way of false alarms.

Hathorne's second suspect that Tuesday delivered the richest rewards. The bad girl of neighboring Topsfield, fourteen-year-old Abigail Hobbs lived just over the village line. For some time she had bragged of a most

---

* The saints who appeared to Joan of Arc also thoughtfully identified themselves

un-Puritan childhood. She cavorted in the woods at night. She mocked her stepmother, who despaired of her. Several weeks earlier a friend had chided the visiting Abigail for her rudeness. Had she no shame? Hobbs directed her to hold her tongue or she would raise a ruckus. She boasted of her invincibility; she feared nothing, having sold her soul to Satan. In a Tituba-inflected testimony, she edged as close to a unified theory of Salem as was to emerge. She also set off an avalanche. You knew you were making progress when the afflicted girls sat stock-still; none flinched while lusty Abigail testified. "I will speak the truth," she began. "I have been very wicked." She had spoken with the devil. In exchange for finery, she had agreed to pinch the girls. Dogs, cats, and semi-human creatures had urged her on. She had signed several pacts, the first of them in the woods, in broad daylight—but not in Topsfield. Abigail led Hathorne to an essential address: she entered into that compact in Casco Bay, eighty miles north, in the province of Maine, where she had survived an Indian raid three years earlier. She added a few names, including the mother of the Topsfield constable who had wrung the pig from the tax-withholding farmer. She lacked Tituba's flair for detail but with her cat-proffered book she would do. The girls evidently thought so; only when Abigail had exhausted herself and seemed no longer able to hear did they cry out for the first time. Her eyes wide open, Abigail went blind, although she did eke out a final explanation: the beggar woman Sarah Good had silenced her.

Hathorne could only have been relieved. His hearings moved ploddingly, in a claustrophobic space, amid trying interruptions and tedious repetitions. Accounts emerged in bits and pieces. He had a family and a business of his own; witchcraft threatened to consume his life. Abigail illuminated a number of matters, as she would continue to do from prison. The next day she described how she managed the spectral pricks: the devil provided her with thorns that she drove into wooden images. Had she by chance stuck a thorn in a victim's midsection? Why, yes, she had! Though at her hearing she had known nothing of meetings, by the following day, in prison, she did. She had attended a great witches' assembly, where she had eaten red bread and drunk red wine. There had been nine celebrants in all, she announced, confirming Tituba's tally by introducing a celebration Tituba had not mentioned. They met in Parris's ill-tended pasture.

The next evening, a new and especially bold apparition taunted Ann Putnam Jr. He materialized again the following day. On the morning of April 21, before her uncle's lecture, Abigail Williams accosted Benjamin Hutchinson, Ingersoll's adopted son, about a decade her senior, outside the inn. He carried a pitchfork. Abigail pointed out a sinister little man by the side of the path. She marveled over his uncommon strength and his various feats: he had killed three women and recruited nine Salem witches! He could fire the heaviest musket with one hand! Where was he? Hutchinson valiantly inquired. Abigail motioned; Hutchinson launched his pitchfork. She convulsed but recovered in time to assure the young man that he had hit his mark. She had heard the intruder's coat tear. At the inn about an hour later the eleven-year-old sought Hutchinson out again, in the main room; she was neither shy about enlisting older men to defend her nor slow to secure their attention. "There he stands," she informed Hutchinson, who, peering all about him, brandished his rapier, in an odd variation on blindman's bluff. By this time, the apparition had dissolved into a gray cat; Hutchinson struck all the same. Abigail assured him that he had prevailed. She watched spectral Sarah Good, the beggar woman, carry away the animal.

It was now noon; the two headed off for Parris's lecture. Shortly before four o'clock, Abigail again sought out Hutchinson at the tavern, this time arriving with his cousin, Mary Walcott. They were just able to report that a Topsfield woman had bitten Mary before both girls began to shudder. As they calmed, they pointed to a table: the witch's husband stood upon it! Hutchinson plunged his rapier into what he understood to be their tormentor's side. He withdrew it to learn that the room swarmed with spirits, an Indian and a "great black woman" among them. Wildly Hutchinson and a friend struck left and right, directed by the bewitched, who described the carnage for their defenders; they now lived in a world where when a girl pointed to a notional figure, you assumed she was right and you were blind. The sanded floor was slick with blood. On the hill outside, the girls spotted a coven of witches, three of them dead.

Warrants went out on April 21 for nine witch suspects, the majority of them in Topsfield; accusations spread across town lines as a local affair bloomed into a provincial crisis. Among those to be apprehended before the weekend were the wife of Salem town's richest merchant, Rebecca Nurse's second sister, Abigail Hobbs's parents, and a black slave. The Topsfield constable dutifully arrested his own mother. So quickly did the allegations pile up that it proved difficult to keep suspects straight. Even to meticulous Reverend Hale, Salem town's Bridget Bishop and Topsfield's Sarah Wilds became one person. Over the next seven weeks, fifty-four witches would be named.

Thomas Putnam's name figured first on the mid-April complaints. On the twenty-first, he felt the need to weigh in personally with the Salem justices as well. Expressing his gratitude for their "great care and pains," he begged the magistrates to continue "a terror to evil-doers." The villagers would assist them in any way possible. He offered support and benediction but something else too. Events were evolving quickly; he knew of alarming, late-breaking news that had yet to make its way to the magistrates' attention. There was, Putnam warned, a plot afoot, "a wheel within a wheel, at which our ears do tingle." He had biblical prophets Ezekiel and Jeremiah to thank for his phrasing, as he did Reverend Lawson, who had incorporated the tingling ears and the terror to evil-doers into his late-March sermon.*

Putnam's was a pay-attention-to-the-man-behind-the-curtain letter, a timely bit of stage management. He had a flair for the sensational; in his hands, witchcraft victims were never less than "grievously afflicted" or "dreadfully tormented." He would make over a hundred and twenty accusations in all, nearly a third of the total number. He would testify

---

* Consciously or not, Putnam deferred to two prophets who experienced trances and visions.

against seventeen suspects. For whatever reason, he felt it necessary that Thursday to add a drumroll to the proceedings. The technique was one he might have learned from the Mathers; when you predicted an apocalypse, you needed sooner or later to produce one. Putnam made no mention of his ailing wife or daughter or his own run of bad luck: His sheep had escaped. A cow had died, as had his favorite horse. He had recently lost a contested inheritance to a much younger half brother. He spoke instead for the community, or at least insinuated that others soon would. Confining himself to dark hints—Jeremiah heralded imminent disaster—he stopped short of the sensational details. He left it to the visionary girls to deliver the "high and dreadful" news: there was an ingenious mastermind at work.

V

―❖―

THE WIZARD

In the terror of seeing the figure, and in the terror of being certain that it had not been there a moment before, I at first ran from it, and then ran towards it. And my terror was greatest of all when I found no figure there.
—CHARLES DICKENS

IF PUTNAM'S HINTS struck the justices as cryptic, the suspense lasted all of two days. Already Hathorne was receptive to their tenor, having ordered the additional arrests. Any number of discrepancies had presented themselves over the previous six weeks; he barreled past each and every one. When an unlikely charge surfaced—at one point someone accused Dr. Griggs's wife—it evaporated. Tituba's tall man from Boston too disappeared in the shuffle. He would return as a short man from Maine.

Hathorne never asked saucy Abigail Hobbs to produce the finery the devil had promised. Nor did he quarantine the girls or interview them separately, as every legal manual advised. He made no attempt to match teeth marks to dentistry, which would have yielded some surprising results, one of the accused having, noted a contemporary, "not a tooth in his head wherewith to bite." Hathorne does not appear to have questioned how—despite all the grievous pinching, choking, biting, punching—

the bewitched remained in the pink of health. He trusted their spectral sight even when he himself could not make out a middle-aged parishioner perched, in her skirts, on the rafters. He viewed the descent of witchcraft as did Cotton Mather: the business was "managed in imagination yet may not be called imaginary."* When the girls contradicted themselves, when they fumbled with an inconsistency, he turned a blind eye, discarding the facts that failed to fit his extraordinary case. Neither the fists in the mouth nor the timely trances nor Mary Warren's charge that the girls dissembled gave him pause. All signs indicate a prosecutor single-mindedly pursuing a preordained end.

At Hathorne's elbow, throughout hearings and in prison interrogations, sat Reverend Nicholas Noyes, a plump, uncompromising poet.† A Salem fixture for a decade, Noyes was good company, vivacious and witty, the owner of the best local library, a Massachusetts mark of distinction. The son of an Essex County justice, the forty-five-year-old minister was comfortable in a courtroom. Noyes was friendly with the Putnams; the Sewall brothers considered him an intimate. He assumed a vocal role, challenging suspects before their testimonies, validating bits of evidence, offering his expert opinion, and making it impossible for suspects to get a word in edgewise. At one point he performed a courtroom experiment with burning poppets. He tackled any suspect who attempted to invoke Scripture in his or her defense. Neither Noyes nor Hathorne seems to have wondered why, when Bishop pressed herself upon her victim in bed, nearly stopping his breath, the wife at his side did not see her, or why children carted away by the devil never went missing from their households. Some things were illogical. Others made less sense. Why, for example, had Tituba flown on a stick to a meeting that took place in her own backyard?

---

* Or as Dumbledore assures Harry Potter: "Of course it is happening inside your head, Harry, but why on earth should that mean that it is not real?"
† His verses, it was said, "certainly ought to establish the fame of Nicholas Noyes as the most gifted and brilliant master ever produced in America, of the most execrable form of poetry to which the English language was ever degraded." No surviving evidence contradicts that claim.

Hathorne interrogated ruthlessly and incarcerated reflexively. If there was a crime in your past, he would unearth it, with the "cross and swift questions" recommended under the circumstances. Through April 22 every suspect who appeared before him wound up in prison to await trial, whether he pleaded innocent or confessed to witchcraft. On the one hand, Hathorne was taking no chances. Salem homes echoed "with the doleful shrieks of their children and servants," as Mather would put it. Their symptoms were nerve-rackingly, bloodcurdlingly authentic; the raving disrupted all affairs. The ground had thawed. The busiest season of the year was upon the villagers. It was time to plow and plant, to sink peg holes into the earth for seeds of Indian corn, to shear sheep and wash wool. On the other hand, Hathorne had reason to proceed with caution. Witchcraft constituted the gravest of crimes. Its facts were simple; its forensics difficult. Three possibilities presented themselves: the girls were bewitched; the girls dissembled; some kind of conspiracy was afoot. The situation was baffling. And like all baffling matters, this one seemed at once inexplicable and obvious. Hathorne opted for witchcraft and fixed on rooting it out. Not everyone shared his conviction. Under blistering interrogation, several of the first suspects agreed that something ailed the girls but would not concede it to be sorcery. Hathorne proceeded as if he knew better. What else, after all, was a witch likely to say on the stand? Moreover he had in hand—had had in hand for seven weeks—incontestable evidence, the sole certain proof of witchcraft. "It is no rare thing for witches to confess," observed the British legal expert most regularly consulted at Salem. Tituba had made Hathorne's case. Tiny Dorothy Good and wild Abigail Hobbs buttressed it.

Hathorne all the same entertained some small, discomfiting kernel of doubt. In receipt of Putnam's enigmatic letter, he designed an experiment for April 22. That Friday two extraordinary gatherings took place in Salem. Hathorne's hearing was the less sensational, which was saying a great deal. The largest crowd yet piled into the dark pews and galleries of the village meetinghouse; they obscured the windows and Parris's view. Amid the crush of bodies, accusers squinted and craned their necks to make out faces. With a full docket of suspects, Hathorne arranged for the marshal to lead in the first defendant without introduction. "Mercy Lewis," Hathorne challenged the nineteen-year-old at the front of the room, "do you know her that stands at the bar?" The mounting number of witches may have alarmed Hathorne. Or the irregularities among testimonies had begun to tug at him; he may have singled out the Putnams' maid because of her earlier foot-dragging. Among the eldest of the girls, Mercy seemed the likely ringleader. She could not name the suspect.* Hathorne appealed to the next accuser, almost certainly young Abigail, Parris's niece. She was struck dumb.

Ann Putnam Jr. saved the day, correctly identifying Abigail Hobbs's stepmother, Deliverance Hobbs. Ann claimed the Topsfield woman had tortured her. Turning to the accused, Hathorne posed the usual round of questions: Why did Hobbs hurt these people, how had she come to practice witchcraft, whom did she suppose afflicted them if she did not? He had tried to trip up the girls. Having succeeded, he moved on. Meanwhile, in the half-light, the suspect engaged in some table-turning of her own. She too was afflicted! In that very room a week earlier she had seen birds, cats, dogs, and a human apparition—who happened to be none other than Mercy Lewis, the Putnam maid. Deliverance Hobbs proceeded to reject each of Hathorne's prompts. No apparition had introduced a book or demanded she sign one. A tug-of-narrative-war ensued, Hathorne growing irritable as the story slipped from him. He prodded Hobbs, dubious that in a matter of days she had gone from tormentor to tormented. She was spared having to explain by the girls' assertion—the two youngest pointed excitedly to the rafters—that Hobbs was at that moment not before the bar, where they could not see her at all, but above their heads, on the meetinghouse beam. This made more sense to Hathorne, who returned to his familiar line of inquiry. He left the

---

* The reluctance was particularly odd as Lewis did know Hobbs. Evidently she had more to lose by admitting as much than she did by feigning ignorance. We too are left squinting in the pewter light; there were many more agendas in Hathorne's courtroom than are visible to the twenty-first-century eye.

incriminating Mercy Lewis comment to fall by the wayside, where it remained.

What did Hobbs have to say about the apparition above their heads? Who threatened her if she confessed her pact? Hathorne pounded the Topsfield woman with questions. "I have done nothing" were her last words before she swerved again. If something happened in the room to change her course, Parris did not record it. Hobbs may have deemed it futile to attempt to outmaneuver Hathorne; plenty of defendants admitted to having been overawed by magistrates. She had lost contests to her stepdaughter before. She now blurted that Sarah Wilds, the Topsfield constable's mother, had two nights earlier brought her a book, with pen and ink; that with pins and images, Deliverance Hobbs had afflicted the girls; that she had made the acquaintance of "a tall black man, with a high-crowned hat." Hathorne had his confession. He was very soon to have a good deal more. Over the next twenty-four hours, Hobbs lent the conspiracy its binding logic, connecting the village afflictions, Putnam's prophecies, Tituba's black man, and Abigail's insidious reference to the Maine woods.

Hobbs managed as well to make sense of the bloody battle waged the previous afternoon at Ingersoll's. Following her testimony, Hathorne asked her privately if she had suffered any pains that Thursday. She reported a sharp stab to her right side, still sore. The justices ordered several women to examine her. Hobbs undressed behind closed doors, revealing evidence of a rapier wound. She now learned how she had acquired it: it seemed she was the woman into whom—at Abigail's direction—Hutchinson had sunk his dagger at the inn. William Hobbs resurrected himself from that battle to appear before Hathorne on the twenty-second. He professed himself as innocent as a newborn babe. How, asked Hathorne, did he explain his ability to strike people down with his eyes? At this, Abigail called out that Hobbs intended to assault Mercy Lewis, who began to writhe. Could William Hobbs truly deny his complicity? demanded Hathorne. "I can deny it to my dying day," vowed the middle-aged farmer, one of Topsfield's earliest settlers, a man whose wife had now confessed to witchcraft and whose wayward daughter had testified against him, asserting that he read no Scripture at home. Had he not known for some time that his daughter was a witch? Hathorne asked. Hobbs had not. He agreed that something preternatural ailed the girls. "Do you think they are bewitched?" asked Hathorne. That Hobbs could not say. Constable Herrick carted Abigail's parents, along with six additional suspects, to jail that afternoon.*

The following day the justices interrogated Deliverance in prison. They could not have done so out of earshot of the others, closely confined in the cramped space. Expanding on her confession, the Topsfield woman described the other Salem assembly that Friday. Summoned by a diabolical trumpet, a group of witches had descended on the village, to hold a parody of a communion service. Deliverance eventually produced eleven names. The numbers rarely agreed but steadily increased, from Tituba's nine to the twenty-three or twenty-four of whom Deodat Lawson heard to Abigail's forty. Later reports would put attendance at one hundred, a tally that rose to three hundred and seven, ultimately to an eye-popping five hundred, nearly the population of the village itself. The witches assembled in Parris's pasture, not too derelict for their diabolical purposes, which Hobbs revealed: they were to bewitch each of the villagers, although they were instructed to do so gradually. Parris's niece had emerged from the parsonage in time to see the witches assembled at a long table, tankards in hand. For their sacrament, they took "red bread, and red wine like blood." Deliverance Hobbs affirmed that those previously accused were in attendance, omitting only the names of the confessed witches.

Most crucially, Hobbs explicated her stepdaughter's reference to the Maine frontier and the visit Ann Putnam Jr. had received just before her

---

* One long-haired, severely pockmarked Topsfield man was released when the girls could not agree he was the witch in question. The authorities led him outside the meetinghouse, where the light was better. Still the girls hesitated. "How did you know his name?" Hathorne challenged, puzzled by their indecision. "He did not tell me himself, but other witches told me," one of them explained. Sixty-year-old Nehemiah Abbott would be the only accused witch to walk free from a Hathorne hearing.

father composed his loaded letter. A terrifying, dark-coated apparition had alighted in the village. "What, are ministers witches, too?" Ann demanded of the specter. He racked and choked her and nearly tore her to pieces, only then introducing himself. He had murdered several women and—evidently a secret agent, in the employ of the French and Indians—dispatched a number of frontier soldiers. He had murdered Lawson's child and wife. He had bewitched Parris's niece. He confided that his mission was a frightful one: he who should have been teaching children to fear God had now "come to persuade poor creatures to give their souls to the devil." Witches not only identified themselves to their victims but preened a little, like the James Bond villain who inventories the tortures to which he is about to subject his prey.

The figure impaled by the pitchfork outside Ingersoll's, Ann Putnam's self-pitying minister, the officiant at the witches' Sabbath, and the mastermind behind Thomas Putnam's conspiracy turned out to be the same person. He was no mere wizard, warned Ann Putnam. A New England child had every reason to be acutely sensitive to hierarchy; it permeated all. Ann's April visitor bragged that he outranked a witch. More powerful yet, he was a conjurer. (Days later, he introduced himself to Abigail with the same credentials.) He happened also to be a little black man who lived in the woods. He was strong, devious, and omniscient. And he was familiar. While Ann Putnam Jr. knew him as a bloodthirsty conjurer, she had also met him as a child of four. Mercy Lewis knew him as her ex-employer, having served in his household in the 1680s. Abigail Hobbs knew him as a leading citizen of Casco, Maine, before the Indian raid of 1688. Hathorne knew him as his former brother-in-law. Everyone in Salem village—where he had never administered any kind of sacrament to his congregants, who had never ordained him—knew him as their former minister. On April 30, a warrant went out for the arrest of Lawson's predecessor. By the time a constable delivered George Burroughs to Salem from the far reaches of Maine a week later he could not be incarcerated. The jail would not accommodate another prisoner.

Under close supervision, Burroughs lodged in an upstairs room at a Salem town tavern. Despite his preternatural powers, he was allowed visitors; the handsome, headstrong minister still had friends in Essex County. Urged to visit by a local militia captain, Elizer Keyser begged off. A forty-five-year-old tanner, Keyser was terrified, convinced Burroughs was "the chief of all the persons accused for witchcraft or the ringleader of them all." Under duress, he ventured a peek at the superhuman mastermind. Burroughs stared steadily back at him. Later that evening in a pitch-black room, twelve quivering, glow-in-the-dark jellyfish swam up Keyser's fireplace. He called excitedly to his servant. Tilting her head, she marveled at the creatures gliding up the immense chimney. They remained invisible to Keyser's wife, proof they were "some diabolical apparition."

As Keyser collected himself before his village hearth, Burroughs paid a second spectral visit to the Putnam household, an address where—in corporeal form—he had never been entirely welcome; he had after all supplanted Ann Putnam Sr.'s brother-in-law, Reverend Bayley. On May 8 Burroughs warned twelve-year-old Ann that his first two wives would soon appear to tell a great many lies. She was to pay them no heed. Sure enough, two chalk-white women disturbed the air, dressed in linen burial shrouds; ghosts now fluttered freely about amid wizards and witches. Red with fury, "as if the blood would fly out of their faces," the spirits demanded justice. Burroughs should be "cast into hell." At these words the minister vanished. His wives explained that he had murdered them. One unwound her shroud to display the fatal wound under her left arm; the next morning Ann saw Deodat Lawson's dead wife and young daughter, with whom she had been friends. Burroughs had killed them as well. These were the crimes to which Abigail had alluded in recruiting Hutchinson and his pitchfork two weeks earlier.

Why Burroughs allowed Ann to converse with his articulate, avenging dead wives was not discussed; he worked in strange and mysterious ways. Nor would the record include another word from the faithful militia captain who had insisted the village tanner look in on Burroughs, assuring Keyser that he had nothing to fear as their ex-minister was "a child of God, a choice child of God, and that God would clear up his innocence."

FROM THOSE THINGS the devil promised we can glimpse what the seventeenth-century girl dreamed of: splendid finery, travel abroad, fashion books, leisure, gold, a husband, help with the housework. Her longings differed little from those of any other orphaned semi-adolescent farm girl stalled in a bleak, storm-prone landscape where animals strayed into the gardens of peevish neighbors who turned up on the doorstep to fulminate, disabling the adults of the house. Insofar as they dared to dream, these girls dreamed—at the ashen end of a New England winter—of journeys to exotic realms and in supersaturated color. From Tituba's on down, the Salem testimony explodes with invigorating, over-the-rainbow intensity. It is all bluebirds and canaries, yellow dogs, red rats, red meat, red bread, red books. Deprivation, however, had its limits. Even with the regular fasts, there was no hungering after (or enticing with) food. No daughter, niece, cousin, servant, or slave longed for a roast beef with pumpkin sauce or a luscious apple pudding or a dish of sugared almonds. Rather the girls appeared starved for color, expressionist splashes of which light up their testimonies, nearly conjuring ruby slippers.

At twelve and eleven, Ann Putnam Jr. and Abigail Williams, Parris's niece, were the youngest of those under Satan's supernatural spell. Nineteen-year-old Mercy Lewis, the Putnam maid, and twenty-year-old Mary Warren, the wavering Procter maid, were among the eldest. None of the four left a diary. Nor did any other Puritan girl. Even assuming she had paper and could write, she would have had little opportunity to do so in the course of a day spent milking and spooling, churning, weeding, washing, and candle-making. Only in the devil's presence did the girls enunciate their desires, which come to us by way of the court clerks; we get the girls' hankerings under duress and at a remove.* In the rare cases where their words come to us directly, the bewitched speak in what sounds like borrowed syntax and vocabulary. It is doubtful that Griggs's niece actually said that an Andover matron "did most grievously torment" her with such tortures "as no tongue can express" — especially as Mary Walcott used identical words in denouncing the same woman, whom both girls pronounced "a most dreadful witch." (Thomas Putnam, the adverbial master, drafted both complaints.) Ventriloquism aside, the bewitched girls exercised uncommon power, the small and the meek displacing the great and the powerful. History is not rich in unruly young women; with the exception of Joan of Arc and a few underage sovereigns, it would be difficult to name another historical moment so dominated by teenage virgins, traditionally a vulnerable, mute, and disenfranchised cohort. From the start, the Salem girls made themselves heard. Theirs quickly proved the decisive voices. By April a core group of eight girls assumed oracular import. Twitching and thrusting, they played the role of bloodhounds, soothsayers, folk healers, moral authorities, martyrs to a cause.

From any number of clergymen we know what the ideal Puritan girl looked like. She was a sterling amalgam of modesty, piety, and tireless industry. She spoke neither too soon nor too much. She read her Scripture twice daily. Her father was her prince and judge; his authority was understood to be absolute. She deferred to him as she would to the man she would marry, in her early twenties. The father was the master of the family, its soul, the governor of all the governed. He was often an active

---

* Excepting the work of Parris, Cheever, and a few others, the written record is a sampler of phonetic idiosyncrasies. Proper names appear in every conceivable variation, as if conjugated. Indeed "Tituba" could be spelled eight different ways (three of them on the same day), but "Hollingworth" appeared in nearly as many mutations as well. The governor, his wife, and his son each spelled "Winthrop" differently. Individuals submitted affidavits that suggested their authors were, as was said of one Burroughs (or, as he sometimes wrote, "Burrough") accuser, "sublimely unaware of punctuation and a pioneer in spelling reform." Orthography proved as fluid as the Salem-Topsfield border.

and engaged parent. He sat vigil in the sickroom; he fretted over his children's bodies and souls. It is not difficult to imagine how deeply his absence would be felt. A majority of the bewitched girls had lost fathers, most of them to Indian attacks. It left them unsteady on their feet in terms of marriage and inheritance, if not starved for male attention; an afflicted girl in 1693 begged the young man at her bedside who tried to bid her good night to stay. She would die if he left. Another challenged the devil directly, when he mentioned the matter one too many times: "Well; and what if I am fatherless?" Mothers were less visible but equally sovereign. Youths who disregarded them could expect to "come to the gallows, and be hanged up in gibbets for the ravens and eagles to feed upon them," warned Increase Mather. For all of the emphasis on discipline, for all the indictments of juvenile willfulness, there was plenty of seventeenth-century tenderness. "Charm the children of New England unto the fear of God," urged Cotton Mather, a champion of sweet authority. Lawson too discouraged harshness and formality in child-rearing. Stiffer than his predecessor, even Parris advocated not "penal and wrathful blows, but strokes issuing from parental love." There was indeed a New England statute against disobedience to one's parents; the child over sixteen who struck or cursed a father was to be executed. The law was never invoked.

A mother dispatching her daughter in 1680 reminded her that she was to carry herself respectfully, dutifully, soberly. She was to pray regularly and—above all—work diligently. The idea was smilingly to outlabor the industrious; already the idle brain qualified as the devil's tool.* If Mather can be used as a measure, the attention to a youngster's spiritual state, unflagging from the start, intensified at Ann Putnam Jr. and Abigail Williams's age, when children became simultaneously more capable of reason and less reasonable. Fourteen stood as the dividing line in law, for slander among other matters. After it, one was meant to embrace

---

* "When the devil finds an idle person," Cotton Mather warned in 1689, "he as it were, calls to more of his crew, 'Come here! Come here! A brave prize for us all!'"

sobriety and "put away childish things," as a father reminded his Harvard-bound son. A boy's seven-year apprenticeship commonly began at that age. As fourteen-year-old Abigail Hobbs demonstrated, the regular hand-wringing over disobedience—like the reminders to dispense with frivolities and the frequent inveighing against the occult—indicated a certain degree of noncompliance with the Puritan ideal. As occupied as she was with her spinning and weaving, the seventeenth-century Massachusetts daughter wound up on occasion in taverns, an address at which the bonds of propriety relaxed, even for clergymen; where a rate-collecting constable might be informed that a man would prefer to hang than contribute to the Salem senior minister's salary; where plenty of flirting went on, with and without rapiers.

The dream of a perfect woman—the pious, industrious, and blushingly submissive female—was as venerable as the seventeenth-century medical chest. What set the early New England girl apart was her nightmares. Samuel Sewall would return to his beautifully furnished home early one winter evening in 1696 to find his wife anxiously awaiting him in the entry. Fifteen-year-old Betty Sewall had burst out sobbing just after dinner, upsetting her siblings. A line from the Gospel according to John ran over and over in her precocious mind; some Mather pages haunted her. She concluded she would go to hell, her prayers unheard, her sins unpardoned. (Again, the account is her father's.) It was not Betty's first yelp of terror. When she was seven, the tumultuous Judgment Day scenes in Isaiah had undone her. Her brother was similarly fretful when advised, at eleven, to prepare for death.

In Betty's collision with John 8:21, Sewall sent for the eminent Samuel Willard, minister of Boston's Third Church. Willard prayed for Betty, confused in her thinking and long in recovering. Six weeks later she sought out her father at dawn to report that she was destined for hell. For what should they pray? Sewall asked the distraught teenager at his bedside. In a rare case of a desire articulated out of the devil's hearing, Betty wished for God to "give her a new heart." In tears, on their knees, father and daughter together beseeched the heavens. Betty remained inconsolable. In August she was packed off to Salem to recover at the home of her uncle Stephen, who several years earlier had taken in a girl suffering other agonies, nine-year-old Betty Parris. (Sewall made no connection between the muffled cries of one child and the piercing screams of another.) Betty Sewall wept through November. She was a reprobate. She did not love God's people as she should. There was, she warned her father, no shred of hope for her salvation.

The distress was not altogether unwelcome. "I had rather find my children praying and weeping in a corner that they cannot love God more, than to have all the wealth in the world," declared one minister in a popular text. Nor was Betty Sewall alone in her distress, part and parcel of a Puritan upbringing.* The idea that life constituted a pilgrimage from sin to grace did not bode well for the formative years. It was never too soon to address one's depravity, to meditate on death and damnation. The few early New England children's books were accounts of the holy lives and exemplary deaths of the preteen set: the little girl who at four wept for her everlasting soul, the boy who repented at nine for his life of sin. The spasms of despair were frequent; a seventeenth-century New Englander knew as well as anyone ever has that we are all guilty of something. Lost in the 1688 witchcraft shuffle was John Goodwin's remark on his daughter's initial anguish; weeks before the phantom horseback riding, the teenager had groaned "that she was in the dark concerning her soul's estate, and that she had misspent her precious time." In respites between fits, a violently convulsing Groton sixteen-year-old admonished those gathered around to use their time to better purpose than she had done.

Piety correlated to literacy; especially in religious homes, mothers taught the children, servants, and slaves of the house to read. Writing

---

* Betty's would not be the last meltdown in the pious Sewall household. In 1713 a servant knocked on her master's bedroom door after midnight; the day's sermon had left her too petrified to sleep. The Sewalls comforted her before the fire. She illustrated a familiar Salem phenomenon: visions—whether in the form of suffocating women, apple-scattering goblins, or avenging ghosts—tended to appear on the Sabbath, when people had been (or should have been) in church.

came later, if it came at all. Elizabeth Parris could write, a skill she likely passed on to the parsonage dependents. The village girls freely deciphered the diabolical books proffered them. Mary Warren could write well enough to post the news of her (short-lived) recovery on the meetinghouse door. Young minds were suffused with the language and imagery of the book they knew best. And the disquieting sermons and baleful visions endured, as they were meant to; one did not easily tame the apocalyptic horses and blood-vomiting dragons of one's youth. The great error came not in fixating on one's miserable condition but in feeling secure. As ever, the thorny paradox of Puritanism loomed: to be confident of one's salvation was to prove unworthy of it. As a modern scholar has noted, "To fail to be frightened was a sure sign that one was either spiritually lost, or stupid, or both."*

The orthodox childhood may have been particularly steeped in fear; it is difficult to say if pious homes bore higher-strung children, as the ministers are the ones who left the diaries. Certainly the girls of the Salem village parsonage would have felt especially constrained, held to a higher standard by Parris's expectations and the village's attention. They made for a little city on a hill unto themselves, even if Parris did not devise the kind of incessant exercises Mather did. He never left the house without a parable or crossed a youngster's path without a monitory word. He saw his children's birthdays as occasions to offer up "lively and pungent admonitions": What were their earthly errands, and how had they addressed them? When he warned five-year-old Katy that she should prepare for his imminent death he cautioned too that, as an orphan, she should brace herself for far greater trials.† Like any besieged minority,

---

* The Indians did childhood differently. Indian mothers bore fewer children, doled out liberties rather than punishments, and wept freely over the children they lost. The kids had leisure time! That pampering was not lost on the Puritans. "Let not English parents be as indulgent and negligent as they report the Indians are," warned Mather, defensive on the subject. A fair number of Indian captives elected to remain. One boy returned only when bound, arms and legs; he escaped soon afterward to rejoin his Indian family.
† Mather however hesitated to share tales of evil angels with his children, a son remembered, lest they "entertain any frightful fancies about the apparitions of devils."

the Puritans paid emphatic, extravagant attention to their progeny, on whom their survival rested. They wrote compulsively on the subject.

Along with the apocalyptic imagery and the vivid descriptions of hell (if one night's toothache was painful, imagine what it would feel like to roast for millions upon millions of years over everlasting fire!) were grisly tales like Mary Rowlandson's, a kind of martyrdom porn to the impressionable youngster. Everyone knew a story about a dismembering or an abduction. That was especially true of the convulsing Salem girls, of whom at least half were refugees from or had been orphaned by attacks in "the last Indian war." Mercy Lewis, the Putnam maid, had twice known tragedy, at three, when the Wabanaki torched her Maine town and abducted the women and children, again at sixteen, when she was orphaned in a second raid. (She dated her compact with Satan to just before that crisis.) A two-year-old might well recite stories from Scripture. But a three-year-old was sufficiently schooled in adult anxieties that he was said to warn from his cradle that the French—at war with England after 1689—were coming.

Terror rumbled close to the surface, erupting regularly. A neighbor who came to the doorstep with a carpet over his head could send the panicked children screaming through the house to their mother. And a full catalog of dangers beckoned close to home. As obsessively attentive as was a New England parent, she was also short-armed. Children swallowed pins, fell down wells, through ice, beneath barrels, under horses, upon knives, into fires, ponds, washtubs. For good reason, parents had nightmares about their children. (Samuel Sewall dreamed in 1695 that all but one were dead. He would bury eight.) Though healthier than their English counterparts, they regularly succumbed to disease; a Salem mother could count on losing two or three of her sons and daughters. Rebecca Nurse was a remarkable, possibly unforgivable, exception to that rule.

Thrifty with names, the Puritans bestowed few and recycled often; several children in a family might bear the name of a parent. It was not uncommon to share one with a dead sibling.* If that did not make you feel replaceable, the brother or sister who came along just behind you might. At twelve, Ann Putnam had lost her mother's attention to younger siblings six times. She had viewed and sat vigil over miniature corpses and attended funerals, most recently one late in 1691 for her six-week-old sister. They were no less emotional for their regularity; the Sewall children wept freely on the return from burying a baby brother. A village girl could ably describe the dead as they lay in their coffins.

In her day, in her earth-toned wardrobe, the New England girl resembled her mother in painstaking miniature. Surrounded by siblings, she had before her as well advertisements for the endless round of childbearing, nursing, and burying to which she could look forward. Childbirth produced plenty of orphans, along with great gushers of guilt for the child who dispatched his mother in the act of being born. This introduced what could prove an especially earthly terror to the mix: the malignant stepmother. She reliably reordered affections and complicated successions. Reverend Bayley and the Putnam household charged that Ann Putnam's stepmother cheated her daughters out of the inheritance their father had intended for them; the trouble began the night of the funeral and continued for a decade. (Ann received twenty pounds of an estate valued at fourteen hundred.) Widowers remarried quickly, given the families to be raised and the work to be done. At times stepmothers were not much older than the eldest of their new children. Deliverance Hobbs wondered aloud what she had done to deserve Abigail, who, after pelting her with water, announced that she had now baptized her heathen of a stepmother. Cotton Mather sent a daughter away to escape his tempestuous new wife. At the time of George Burroughs's arrest, his Maine household included seven children under the age of sixteen. Their stepmother left all but her own daughter to fend for themselves.

---

* By 1692 Justice Jonathan Corwin had lost seven children, among them three boys named John.

Mather's daughter was far from alone in having been farmed out. Neither Mercy Lewis, the orphaned Putnam maid, nor Mary Warren, the orphaned Procter maid with the dramatic bent, lived at home. Of the initial accusers, only Ann Putnam and Betty Parris did. For reasons that made sense at the time but have not been adequately explained since, a third of New England children left home to lodge elsewhere, usually as servants or apprentices, often as early as age six. (The servant had no contract; the apprentice typically served seven years.) As a result, most households included several unrelated adolescents. Boys learned a trade while girls mastered what was advertised to a later nine-year-old as the "art, craft, and mystery of housewifery." All were sent off to be disciplined by adults other than their parents; it was understood that they might learn better manners elsewhere. "Binding out," as it was called, occurred across the social spectrum. Rebecca Nurse's enterprising husband began as a servant, as did any number of future ministers and at least one witchcraft judge. Often the children landed in families no more privileged than their own. Some left in tears. (One Sewall son fainted at the very prospect.) A surrogate family introduced new rules and expectations; the separation felt like—was perhaps intended to feel like—practice for the more traumatic one to come. If nothing else, binding out reinforced discipline at a hot-blooded, high-spirited, self-intoxicated, notoriously subversive, devilishly difficult time of life. "Puberty," it has been said, "is everyone's first experience of a sentient madness."

Binding out introduced a fresh set of perils. Servant girls fended off groping hands and unwanted embraces from lascivious swineherds, from the men of the house, and from visitors to the house, often at appallingly early ages. Isolated, semi-orphaned, they seldom knew someone to whom they could appeal to wield pitchforks or pray at dawn on their behalf; the daughters of one Salem magistrate, the elder of whom was six, were for two years routinely sexually abused by their master. Removed to the home of an upstanding church member, they were molested all over again before the elder girl had turned ten. The court record reveals a full inventory of harassments, from stolen kisses to lunging assaults. They occurred while women were bringing in linen or lending canoes or riding to help an assailant's wife give birth. A nineteen-year-old servant boy attempted to rape a ten-year-old maid in the same house. Women retired for the evening to stumble over piles of clothes on the floor and to find strange men in their beds. They bit attackers' noses. One Massachusetts man sat in a cage with a paper around his neck reading "A married man for committing fornication in his own house with his servant maid."

Abuse came in other forms as well. Masters and mistresses beat servant girls for being disrespectful, disorderly, abusive, sullen, saucy; for not caring properly for their mistresses; for crimes no greater than laziness, which — given the amount to be done — was surely a relative term. An exasperated husband defended his wife's brutal treatment of their maid. The girl slipped out after dark, slept in, never learned to milk the cow or goat, was slatternly, could not be trusted to so much as feed the pigs: "She is so fat and soggy she can hardly do any work." The Newburyport preacher whipped his servant at the slightest provocation, tying her tongue to her big toe. When his hired girl let the baby fall on her head, Reverend Thacher, a Parris intimate, beat her with a sturdy walnut stick. Servants ran away, to be swiftly returned. Flight was difficult.* With greater success they petitioned the courts. More often than not, rulings came down in their favor.

In the 1690s, with insubordination on the rise all around, the problem the New England adolescent faced was that of the colony writ indecipherably small. For decades Massachusetts had distinguished itself for its misdemeanors. London accused the settlers of lurching toward independence and disciplined them accordingly. They had no choice, moaned a prominent Bay Colony merchant, railing at onerous trade regulations; were they to comply with all English demands — with the kind

---

*The hired help was in no danger of disappearing. The moment anyone went missing, a Huguenot settler observed, you had only to notify the Indians, who for a modest fee would locate him for you. Flight was in any event rare, "for they would know not where to go, there being few trodden roads."

of restrictions that had hobbled Parris's Boston business — "this orphan plantation will be crushed." Having ousted Andros, the colonists lived in a state of sullen suspension, expecting life to return to normal. Stubbornly it would not. The far-off government to which they were incomprehensible was to them unintelligible. Was it, wondered the author of a 1691 tract, because they had been "disobedient, disobliging, and disingenuous children" that God rained calamities down upon them, leaving them to be "tormented and butchered by bloody barbarians?" Unmoored from the mother country, regularly scolded for insubordination, the vulnerable, intractable New Englanders bargained for their self-respect, struggling to reconcile autonomy with the demands of a clueless authority, one that struck them less as a beneficent guardian than a protection racket.

IN DIFFERING WAYS, servants and the children of the house absorbed family confidences. They disseminated slanders and perpetuated neighborly grudges, a form of filial loyalty. As ever, the servants imbibed the secrets; to the psychological perils was added the fact that these children knew too much. Though he thrashed Mary Warren, John Procter also consulted with her about a land deal and complained of his temperamental wife. The woman nearly drove him to suicide! The servant — and seven of what would ultimately be thirteen bewitched girls were domestics — knew where the money was kept, the bedcovers unrumpled, the fires of contention smoldered. She could in turn pose a terror to the children of the house. In the spring of 1678 Reverend John Hale discovered that one of his servants had been stealing from him. She disappeared at night to deliver her haul, which included flour, butter, jewelry, money, oatmeal, candles, silk, and colored ribbon. His wife confronted the girl, Margaret Lord, so defiant that Mrs. Hale thought it best to hide the kitchen knives. Upon investigation, it turned out that twelve-year-old Rebecca Hale had known all along of Margaret's thieving. Every one of the Hale children did. Margaret had threatened to throw Rebecca into the fire or hang her from the barn rafters if she breathed a word; she held her over the well, dropping her to the bottom in the bucket. She assured Rebecca she had a book with which she could summon the devil, who would kill her little sister. Flourishing an ax, she wondered aloud if she should murder Mrs. Hale; the children begged her to reconsider. She threatened to burn another Hale child with a red-hot iron. Rebecca was no pushover. "I told her if she killed me it would be discovered," she reported. In her response Margaret hinted that not everyone was impressed by colonial law enforcement: "She said that was in England but it could not so easily be discovered here." Further details of the reign of terror came to light in May, when one of Margaret's accomplices appeared before the Salem magistrates for witchcraft.

Ministers devoted sermons to masters, who were to issue orders humanely, and servants, who were to follow them cheerfully. Seven years was hardly an eternity, a Boston cleric reminded the apprentices in his audience. As for the maids, if they comported themselves well, they might find that their mistresses counted them among their children, clearly a thing to be desired. All the same, when summoned to a dark room, not every servant girl saw the shimmering creatures in the chimney to which her master frantically pointed. Nor was every girl summoned for that purpose. Saucy maids and disrespectful daughters choked on authority, proving anything but the voiceless, noiseless creatures of a Mather sermon. At home or in the households of others, they catapulted past guilt, shame, and self-loathing to land in trouble, if rarely with Abigail Hobbs's strapping insouciance. Teenage daughters spoke impertinently to fathers, as did the eighteen-year-old who—having spent a day complaining—exploded: "Pray sooth, Father, are you deaf?" Hale described the pilfering Margaret to be "exceedingly addicted to lying and very obstinate to stand in her lies." She turned up in the barn when she was meant to be at meeting. She stayed out until two in the morning. Her accomplices lurked in the pigsty, spooking the children. A Mather maid got pregnant. And, clearly, despite the parental attention, the continual employment, the inhospitable climate, girls arranged to congregate at the local inn, where their masters might collect them for a ride home or where they might divert the attentions of a few eligible men in the long hours between witchcraft hearings. Two days after the Boston jailer had affixed chains to Good, Osborne, and Tituba, Plymouth voted unanimously to apply itself to the reformation of its children, "who were much given to sensuality, intemperance, long tarrying, drinking, and gaming at ordinaries."

Women too had troubled New England since its founding; they claimed starring roles as heretics and rebels. Beginning with Anne Hutchinson, the charismatic religious leader who encouraged women to walk out of sermons and who disputed church doctrine, they had been speaking their minds, otherwise known as disturbing the peace. At her 1640 trial, Ann Hibbins cited the Old Testament, a text she claimed exhorted husbands to heed their wives. She also took the opposite tack; sixteen years earlier, she refused in court to answer her accusers on the grounds that God demanded silence of women. Defying repeated orders to leave Massachusetts, Mary Dyer, an outspoken Quaker, would hang as well. A Salem church member claimed she hoped to live long enough to tear the flesh off Justice Hathorne's father. The New England woman had no political rights. She neither voted nor served on juries. Officially voiceless, she nonetheless found plenty of ways to make herself heard and demonstrated a vaulting need to speak her mind. In legal records she hectors, shrieks, quarrels, scolds, rants, rails, tattles, and spits.*

Massachusetts women turned their backs on the ministers who excommunicated them. They informed magistrates who sentenced them to hang that they preferred to be beheaded. They drank until they "could not tell ink from liquor"; one woman returned from Salem so inebriated it was unclear if she had traveled "upon her head or her feet." They dragged men from taverns or punched the Salem market inspector in the chest until he could barely breathe. They beat and clawed husbands, in one case breaking a skull open with a pot of cider. They threw

---

* Mather acknowledged their formidable force when, late in life, he griped that women had heaped more opprobrium on him than on any man alive. Were there more than twenty women in Boston who had not "at some time or other, spoken basely of me?" he asked.

themselves at widowed ministers twice their age, as a flustered Cotton Mather would discover three months after his wife's death. They shredded warrants before the officers who delivered them. Two women fell to fighting after one called the other a "lousy slut," mocked her for owning only one dress, and, her daughter in tow, assaulted her with a stick. They threw stones at mothers-in-law and scratched sons-in-law. They landed in court with regularity, a trend that increased through the 1690s when — the events in Salem aside — women participated in more crimes than they had in any other decade. Even when they did not scrabble at the late-night windowsill or materialize as balls of light, they managed to suffocate and paralyze the men in their lives.

While women were understood to be more susceptible to witchcraft because of their weaker wills, the evidence remains inconclusive. For every Giles Corey who defied his wife and resaddled his horse, there was a beguiling Mary Warren who won an argument with her master over whether she could attend a witchcraft hearing. The original wonder-workers, women transformed milk into cheese and thread into lace. They could coax pudding from dry moss. They ran taverns, assisted cobbler husbands, and haggled with craftsmen. They conferred with husbands on land deals and represented them in court. Boston justice Samuel Sewall entrusted the household management to his wife, who he thought "has a better faculty than I at managing affairs." Women sued fathers, brothers, stepsons over estates. In a land where labor was infinite and the workforce small, they could be assured of their value; absent women, sick women, jailed women, cost a household dearly. Mothers led prayer when fathers were busy; Mather pointed to a biblical precedent for the practice. While a group of Ipswich men petitioned for the right to build a meetinghouse, their wives raised it by themselves.

As ever, society proved most elastic in a period of unrest. Women constructed bulwarks across the river to protect Boston from invasion in the course of King Philip's War, when Indian raids decimated entire towns. Boston in 1690 allowed thirty women to saw lumber and manufacture potash. That year nearly half the town's innkeepers were female.

During one 1692 assault, the women in the Wells, Maine, garrison fired on the enemy. Others overpowered guards to beat, behead, and dismember two bound Wabanaki captives. A quick-thinking Dorchester maid hid the children under brass kettles when an Indian appeared at the door one July Sunday; she then pitched shovelfuls of live coals at his face. Hannah Dustin tomahawked her Indian captors after they murdered her newborn baby before her eyes. She scalped her victims before escaping— or at least Cotton Mather said she did. The captivity narrative glorified those formidable women and their daring displays. At a time of shuddering devastation, they stepped in as the dragon-slayers.

While ministers paid infrequent attention to maternal roles, they tended closely to female piety. They had compelling reason to do so: the majority of every congregation was female. Twenty percent of Mather's were widows. And although no Puritan lacked for cause to berate herself, there is evidence that women found their faith more disabling than did men, even if they did not always show it with the blazing display of a Betty Sewall. Generally it is a woman who is so convinced of her iniquity that she chooses to drown herself in a puddle, who worries she has sinned against the Holy Ghost, who fears she is "in a worse condition than any toad." She took a very personal religion very personally. "It amazes me to think one so young as I, scarce 20 years old, should have heaped up so much sin and guilt," one woman rebuked herself in 1727. Men blamed their sins for corrupting their souls. Women blamed their souls, which is to say themselves. With dismay Reverend Thacher noted that his wife was "ready to draw up deadly conclusions against herself" for having tripped over a chair while pregnant.* A seven-year-old girl could not eat for fear of damnation.

Well before screams disrupted the Salem parsonage, women had a lock on the captivity narrative, accounts of Indian abductions that inflamed the popular imagination. Rich in lurid detail and crackling

---

* As Hilary Mantel writes retrospectively of her six-year-old self: "What I am experiencing is the beginning of compunction, but is it the awakening of a sense of sin, or is it the beginning of femininity?"

with sexual undercurrents, those tales matched satanic savages with the unlikeliest of adversaries: plucky women who met with—and mastered—every manner of hardship. Recast as religious allegory, the melodramas would not have worked as well with male heroes. Their protagonists were pricked with stones and pinched with ice, as Hannah Swarton would note in describing the harrowing ordeal that swept her from Casco Bay in 1690, an attack George Burroughs survived as well. Swarton's account of being carried over mountains and swamps by demonic Indians was broadcast by Mather, initially from the pulpit, in 1697 in print. (Here the accounts parted company with traditional fairy tales. Captivity narratives inverted the tale of the rescued princess to celebrate resourceful, resilient women rather than damsels in distress.) The wrinkle with Salem's infernal onslaught of 1692 was that both the spirited victims and their oppressors were predominantly female. And in a New England first, women's voices proved so commanding that the spectral testimony of two dead wives could prevail in court against an articulate, Harvard-educated minister.

THE BOSTON AUTHORITIES issued a warrant for the arrest of George Burroughs on April 30. Burroughs then lived seventy miles north of Salem, in Wells, on the Maine frontier. Though he did so "with all speed," the Maine and New Hampshire constable was several days in conveying the minister to the village. He arrived on May 4. Hathorne and Corwin had issued fifteen warrants as they awaited his delivery, doubling the number of witch suspects; it was a season when you had more than the usual cause to worry about the stains on your conscience or the wart on your chest. One of Ann Putnam Jr.'s uncles was said to have kept a horse saddled at all times. Again allegations jumped town lines; the early-May arrests included several Beverly suspects. The Salem justices worked overtime to process the complaints, testimonies, and prisoners. They must have felt as beleaguered as the minister dislodged from his home and transported—against his will and as fast as rocky horse paths would allow—to his former parish.

As Burroughs rode south, as Deliverance Hobbs settled into the prison on what is today Salem's Washington Street, Hathorne and Corwin interrogated several new suspects, all accused by the village girls. Fifty-eight-year-old Dorcas Hoar was well known to the court. A practiced palm reader, she had predicted deaths and infirmities. She had a tendency to appear just before people fell ill. Decades earlier she had consulted a borrowed book of fortunes; she apologized to John Hale when he discovered as much. That was before she became an accomplice of her minister's thieving servant, so devoted to Hoar that she called her "Mother." The maid further terrorized Hale's daughter with reports that old Dorcas Hoar would kill or bewitch her should Rebecca reveal their larceny. Rebecca Hale supplied a convincing digest of Hoar's witchcraft; she had worked all kinds of sorcery in the Hale household. A singular-looking character, Hoar fit the part, a middle-aged woman who trimmed her gray hair short save for a dark, matted, four-and-a-half-foot-long ponytail. Even to a minister, it appeared "like an elf-lock." Hoar's fisherman husband had died suddenly the previous winter. When the coroner's jury called to examine the body, she had insulted the men, stamping her feet for effect. They were wicked wretches if they took her for a murderer! Like Sarah Good, Hoar was downwardly mobile, having lost out on an ample estate.

As she entered the meetinghouse on May 2 the girls greeted her with convulsions. They explained that she had admitted to the murder of her husband; she boasted that she had killed a Boston woman as well. A new accuser had joined in the chorus. Like Mercy Lewis and Abigail Hobbs, eighteen-year-old Susannah Shelden had grown up largely on the Maine frontier, from which Indians twice drove her family. In the process, she had lost a father, a brother, and an uncle. The brother's body was recovered, scalped and mutilated. In 1688 the remaining Sheldens had settled in Salem; the village contributed to their support. It seemed that Dorcas Hoar had visited Susannah as well, with her book and two black cats. As Hoar denied the litany of charges, two girls cried that a bluebird melted

Frontispiece to Joseph Glanvill's much consulted 1681 volume. With unassailable logic, the Royal Society fellow proved the existence of witchcraft; nothing so preposterous could be a sham. And how was it possible, asked Glanvill, "that imagination, which is the most various thing in the world, should infinitely repeat the same conceit in all times and places?" The "wonderful story of certain Swedish witches" traveled to New England with Glanvill as well. *(© The British Library Board 084228)*

From a pamphlet on a sixteenth-century English witchcraft case. Four women stood accused of various misdeeds; three hanged within weeks of their arrest. English witches in particular maintained menageries of "familiars," demonic mascots that did their bidding. This one feeds her blood to her diabolical toads.

A sixteenth-century French woodcut, probably from a text that argued that witches could not perform magical feats but deserved to be prosecuted anyway as heretics. The prying neighbor observes a sort of time-lapse sequence as the witch spirits herself up the chimney. *(The Bridgeman Art Library)*

The cover of a pamphlet on a Northamptonshire trial, at which several women were accused of murder and pig-bewitching. One of their victims suffered "such a gripping and gnawing in her body that she cried out and could scarce be held by such as came unto her."

A late-arriving, probably eighteenth-century set of English broomsticks. The devil rides along with two confederates; the woman on the ground is either an accomplice or a potential recruit. (© *The British Library Board C13724-46, T. 1855 [19]*).

Sam: Parris

Reverend Samuel Parris, in whose contested meadow the witches congregated. The miniature probably dates from just before the move to Salem. Parris had the proclivity for tidiness that creates a shambles. He could be sharp. "I cannot preach without study, I cannot study without fire, I cannot live quietly without study," he warned his disobliging parishioners, slow to provide firewood over the wretched winter of 1691–1692. *(The Bridgeman Art Library/Massachusetts Historical Society)*

Fragment of a monogrammed pewter plate—a rarity in seventeenth-century Salem village excavated at the parsonage site. It is the only physical trace of Elizabeth Parris's existence. *(Photograph by Richard B. Trask)*

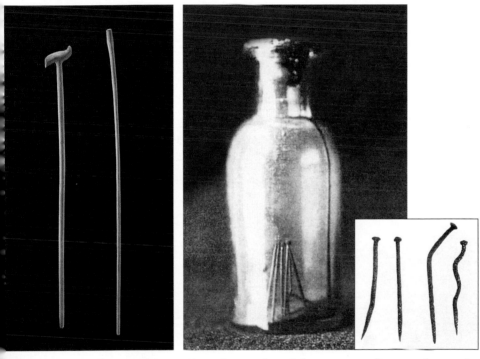

The homemade walking sticks on which George Jacobs hobbled into court, to inform the justices he was as likely a buzzard as a wizard. *(Peabody Essex Museum)*

Pins from the Salem proceedings, where they punctured throats and protruded from arms. They were removed, noted an eyewitness, "by the judges' own hands." One was found sticking upright in a victim's hair; another pierced an enchanted girl's upper and lower lips, binding them together, leaving her unable to testify. *(Courtesy Danvers Archival Center)*

The restored Nurse homestead, where four villagers called on seventy-one-year-old Rebecca in March to break the news that she had been accused of witchcraft. "What sin has God found in me unrepented of that he should lay such an affliction upon me in my old age?" she asked once she had recovered from the shock. She hanged four months later. *(Photograph by Richard B. Trask)*

The Salem village meetinghouse, reconstructed in 1985 and in better shape today than it was in 1692. Adolescent girls interrupted both hearings and sermons in the dimly lit 34-by-28-foot structure. *(Photograph by Richard B. Trask)*

Witchcraft y^e practice of deluded minds,
Where grace is wanting soon admission finds.
With golden promisses of life, & wealth,
The Tempter takes unwary souls by stealth.
In this his seeming clemency appears,
That he will give them back a lease for years.
But y^t expir'd, how dismall is their end!
And casse, when he a Feind shall for them send.
Tis death to think of mending when too late,
And glories given for so vile a rate.
As power to hurt another, & to sin
With greater freedom, from controll within.
That Laws Divine, & humane, should not be
The least restraint, to their impiety,
That reason should be set aside, & death
Become their choice, when they resigne their breath
That piety should be of no esteem,
Now Faith in him, that only can redeem.
All their conceited pleasures come to this,
When yelling they descend ye grand Abyss.

From the account of a 1621 English case, in which three young women—falling into fits and trances—conversed with dead siblings and specters. Among the accused was an old widow, known to have consorted for over forty years with a spirit in the shape of a great black cat; she appears here with her demon familiar as well. She was acquitted. (© *The British Library Board B20051-69, Add. 32496 f.2*)

Increase Mather, Cotton's father, Harvard's president and New England's most eminent minister. The portrait dates from 1688, four years after the publication of *Illustrious Providences*, a treasure trove of shipwrecks, portents, tempests, and possessions collected to political end. Those oddities proved New Englanders to be a chosen people on an exceptional mission. *(American Antiquarian Society)*

Increase Mather

Cotton Mather, later in life. Although largely absent from Salem, the twenty-nine-year-old minister wrote himself into the story; no one in Massachusetts poked as insistently into and around the subject of witchcraft. Nor did anyone offer such contradictory opinions. In June, Mather advised the court to exercise "very critical and exquisite caution," five paragraphs later endorsing a "speedy and vigorous prosecution." *(American Antiquarian Society)*

Cotton Mather.

into her body. A marshal struck furiously at the air; several saw a pale gray moth fly through the meetinghouse.

Hathorne met his two most combative suspects that spring Monday. As the girls described Dorcas Hoar's cats, the book, the black man whispering in her ear, she exploded: "Oh! You are liars, and God will stop the mouth of liars." Hathorne reprimanded her: "You are not to speak after this manner in the court." Hoar was unmoved. "I will speak the truth as long as I live," she spat back. Hathorne denounced her "unusual impudence"; it paled next to that of Susannah Martin, a blacksmith's widow. The tiny, seventy-one-year-old Amesbury woman could hardly take Hathorne's proceedings seriously. She had already once been accused of witchcraft decades earlier. Her husband had sued for slander; he won, although the accusations continued. Martin was said to have bewitched a woman to insanity, murdered her own infant, borne an imp. On a more pedestrian plane, she had accused a man of theft and quarreled freely with her children. She challenged her seat in the meetinghouse. Disinherited once by a stepmother and again by a nephew-in-law, she had sued, unsuccessfully. Eight accusers contorted as Martin took her place before them on May 2; Ann Putnam managed nonetheless to throw a glove at the older woman. Martin chuckled. "What?" gasped Hathorne, startled. "Do you laugh at it?" "Well I may at such folly," scoffed Martin. Hathorne upbraided her: "Is this folly? The hurt of these persons?" She had hurt no one, Martin contended, Mercy Lewis tumbling to the ground at her feet.

Precise and self-assured, Martin could only laugh anew at the girls' antics. "Do you not think they are bewitched?" asked Hathorne. "No, I do not think they are," Martin replied. Hathorne challenged her to provide a better explanation. Perhaps they dealt in black magic, she suggested. Did Hathorne not remember the Witch of Endor? She too had disguised herself as a saint; the devil could wrap himself in any shape. Martin's truculence elicited more agitation and some jeering. "You have been a long time coming to the court today, you can come fast enough in the night," taunted the Putnams' maid. "No, sweetheart," replied the elderly woman, injecting a rare note of sarcasm into the proceedings. If they were going to toss gloves at her, she would hurl words back. "Have you no compassion for these afflicted?" asked Hathorne. "No, I have none," she snapped. It was believed that if a witch touched a victim, her spell would flow back into her, reabsorbed, like electricity. The authorities ordered the afflicted to approach Martin. Four did so, John Indian vowing as he stepped forward to kill the sorceress. Repelled by her power, he collapsed to the floor.

The entire community believed her guilty, Hathorne informed Martin. "Let them think what they will," she sniffed as a litany of incomprehensible events were dredged up and laid at her feet. Witchcraft worked a tidying effect: Not only had Martin bewitched cows and drowned oxen, she had transformed herself into a black hog. Eighteen years previously she had walked several miles by foot in the muddiest of seasons without getting so much as her shoes wet. (How had she managed the feat? her accuser asked. She should have been muddy to the knees after such a journey! Martin had been matter-of-fact. She did not enjoy being wet. Swift, nimble traveling — especially travel that sounded to be airborne — was suspect. It was what Indians did. Martin's crime was worse: heavy, sodden skirts kept women confined; she had slipped her moorings.) On a clear moonlit night, Martin had appeared as a ball of fire. She had turned a dog into a keg. It was she who — disguised as a cat — had leaped through a window to strangle a man in his bed. More than anyone else, the seventy-one-year-old seemed to allow men to reveal that they were scared out of their wits, in fields, in forests, at night in their beds. Did she truly believe the girls dissembled? Hathorne prodded. She could not say. But did she? "I dare not tell a lie if it would save my life," Martin replied, again acknowledging what, by May, was rumored to be at stake. Others had arrived at the same conclusion; for the first time that week constables failed to locate a suspect. On Monday Salem merchant Philip English actually did vanish into thin air. A wealthy man, he would manage over a month in hiding.

Hathorne had scheduled Burroughs's examination for May 9; the minister's specter flew about madly in anticipation. When not enchanting Keyser's fireplace, Burroughs tempted Mercy Lewis with a fashion book—she swore it had not been in his study when she worked in his household—and carried her up an exceedingly high mountain. Below her stretched "all the kingdoms of the earth." They were hers, promised the specter, if she would but sign over her soul. (Burroughs had taught Lewis well: she drew the description nearly verbatim from the book of Matthew, in which the devil tempts Christ, a text Lawson had cited in his March 24 sermon.) Burroughs assaulted the doctor's niece, one of the few accusers who had not met him before. He was unknown as well to thirty-six-year-old Sarah Bibber when, in somber minister's garb, he pinched her and proposed she accompany him as she made her way to the village for that morning's hearing. He introduced himself neither as a conjurer nor as a wizard; only in the meetinghouse would she realize who her dark-suited escort had been.

The day before Burroughs's hearing, Parris administered the village sacrament, warning that those who partook of the devil's fare were not to drink of the Lord's cup. Through the summer, he reminded his congregants that there were but two parties in the world: "Everyone is on one side or the other," he would warn, unnecessarily. As those in his household well knew, each member of the community was already either with him or against him. The village was in the thick of a cosmic battle, one the devil and his troops would wage as long as they could. By the fall Parris compared their siege to biblical trials, cataloging enemies from Herod to Louis XIV, who seven years earlier had revoked the Edict of Nantes, depriving Protestants of their liberties; the Puritan devil reliably enjoyed a French connection, whether to kings, dragoons, priests, or fashion. Parris reproved anyone who doubted the conspiracy. "If ever there were witches, men and women in covenant with the devil, here are multitudes in New England," he proclaimed. Those infernal fiends occupied the most civilized and the most remote precincts. They had evolved from their traditional form. Where previously "some silly ignorant old woman" might have pestered, now highly knowledgeable, ostensibly devout sorcerers of both sexes preyed upon the settlers, a most pernicious state of affairs.

Less than twenty-four hours later, George Burroughs walked into the same raftered room, wearing a sober black suit and waistcoat if not the distinctive flat, white collar of his profession. Having preached in the meetinghouse three times weekly for over two years, he knew its every plank intimately; he could not have retained fond memories of the building. In a contentious discussion there nine years earlier, he and John Putnam had attempted to settle their accounts, a resolution that eluded both men. In the course of that meeting Putnam encouraged a skittish marshal to extract payment from his former houseguest. Burroughs shrugged him off. He had nothing with which to settle his debt apart from his body. He then issued a challenge: "Well, what will you do with me?" The marshal appealed to Putnam. "What shall I do?" he asked, quailing a little before a clergyman. Thomas Putnam signaled to his brother; the two conferred outside. On their return, they were firm. "Marshal," John commanded, "take your prisoner." He secured Burroughs overnight at Ingersoll's. Ultimately the level-headed innkeeper saved the day; Ingersoll managed to persuade the Putnams that the debt had been paid. Burroughs could not have expected ever again to set foot in the village meetinghouse as either a minister or a wizard.

Hathorne and Corwin approached Burroughs's 1692 hearing differently from that of any previous suspect. By the time they deposed him on May 9 they had collected formal testimony and sat flanked by two additional justices. The first was forty-year-old Samuel Sewall, round-faced, with small, glinting eyes, thin lips, and a tumble of gray-brown curls. His brother, Stephen, housed Parris's daughter down the street from the town meetinghouse. The second was William Stoughton, former Massachusetts deputy president. The presence of the two men spoke to the gravity of the situation. It also made it more ticklish. Burroughs and Sewall had known each other at Harvard. They had socialized over the intervening years; Sewall had loaned Burroughs money. Both Hathorne and Corwin knew Burroughs from their 1690 trip to Maine.

The grandson of a Cambridge-educated, Suffolk County rector, Burroughs grew up in Maryland, to which his parents had immigrated. The family was small and itinerant. An only child, Burroughs moved with his mother to Massachusetts, where she joined the Roxbury church in 1657. His father, a merchant mariner, traveled the coast. Burroughs graduated from Harvard in 1670, a year behind Sewall and Bayley, the village's first minister. (He narrowly missed Parris, who arrived in Cambridge as he left.) Both parents returned to England, leaving Burroughs on his own. At least initially, he fell in with the Massachusetts establishment. Sewall would journey to hear Burroughs lecture as late as 1691, eighteen months before he sat in judgment of him. In 1674, having married and served as a schoolmaster, Burroughs joined the Roxbury church and became a father. Shortly thereafter he accepted a pulpit in Casco, a prosperous settlement slightly smaller than Salem village, today a part of Portland, Maine. It was not a plum posting. Generally relations were frosty between eastern Maine and the Puritan establishment. Irregularities tended to creep into the preaching there, as Maine clergymen made concessions to their heterogeneous flocks. On a large bay, amid miles of farm- and marshland, Burroughs ministered to a collection of Anglicans, Baptists, and Puritans, to frontiersmen, seagoing traders, and recent immigrants. The frontier towns submitted to Massachusetts's jurisdiction at about the time that Burroughs moved to Roxbury; in the process, they traded religious freedom for military protection. That did not relieve them of the need to appeal to provincial authorities for their scant share of resources. Massachusetts delivered grudgingly and desultorily, despite the fact that much of the colonial elite — the Salem justices included — had large financial interests in Maine fishing and lumber industries. Over and over officials washed their hands of the vulnerable frontier.* In 1690, Corwin and Hathorne had recommended that Massachusetts withdraw its soldiers, with disastrous results.

---

* It was a lousy bargain. Eager to discuss the area's defense, the newly installed New Hampshire lieutenant governor complained to Crown authorities in the fall of 1692 that he "could after tedious waiting get no other answer but neglect, slights, and reproaches"

Casco could not offer Burroughs an organized church; he was never to be ordained. Nor could it offer him a house, Indians having destroyed that of their previous minister. The town did grant Burroughs two hundred acres of prime land, bounded on three sides by rocky coastline and affording misty, majestic ocean views. On that promontory he built a home. The attacks continued—the Wabanaki in Maine outnumbered the English six to one—but Burroughs did not budge. He was in his midtwenties when Indians again fell upon Casco in August 1676, obliterating the town. Burroughs managed to lead a group of ten men, six women, and sixteen children to a lush island, where they subsisted for some time on fish and berries before being evacuated to safety. In the wake of that attack the family of three-year-old Mercy Lewis temporarily fled to Salem. Burroughs wound up twenty-five miles north, in Salisbury. He eked out a living as an occasional minister until the Salem villagers found him, to install him with the Putnams.

Burroughs's steeliness can be read in the Putnam contretemps, for which he returned to Salem, proposing to settle his debt with his body. With equal determination he resettled in Casco in 1683. His former parish heartily welcomed him back.* Six years later, Casco—by now larger than Salem village—again found itself besieged when what would be known as King William's War erupted. Tensions between the French and English settlers ran high well before England declared war on France in May 1689. That September, more than four hundred French and Indians descended on the town with a roar. Burroughs joined in the seven-hour battle, waged in a field and orchard; a veteran Boston militia captain lauded him for his unexpected role. The assault cost the poorly equipped

---

out of Massachusetts governor William Phips, despite the enemy skulking in the woods. In April 1693, he warned that "by the next ships you will hear the province of Massachusetts and the province of Hampshire are in civil war."

* To encourage others to settle among the ruins, town officials asked Burroughs if he might relinquish three-quarters of his waterfront tract. They could offer a hundred acres farther inland in exchange. Graciously Burroughs ceded an even greater part of the original property. And in an unprecedented move for a New England minister, especially one with a large family, he declined the offer of additional land, settling for thirty coastal acres of salt marsh.

settlers dearly; two hundred and fifty of them were killed or taken captive. It was in that attack that fifteen-year-old Mercy Lewis was orphaned. She moved in with the Burroughs family, who must have seen her in even greater distress than she demonstrated before Hathorne. These were the raids that flooded Salem with refugees. Again widowed, still not ordained, Burroughs retreated down the coast to Wells, seventy-five miles north of Boston but now the frontier. Everything to the east had been destroyed.

Studded with two-story, thick-walled garrison houses, extending over both sides of a river thick with sturgeon and salmon, handsome Wells was the best-defended town in Maine. That was fortunate, as the summer of 1691 amounted to a protracted siege. Burroughs spent it behind rows of pickets while nearby settlements went up in flames. As a visitor noted of the Wabanaki, "It is taken for granted, without some speedy help coming, that they will not leave a beast alive in the whole province." In a sustained mid-June siege, they destroyed the Wells livestock and trampled the fields. (They were well armed thanks to the business-minded colonists. It was a poor Indian, noted a visitor, who did not own two guns.) Burroughs joined in signing an abject, late-July appeal for provisions to the Massachusetts council. He pleaded anew for clothing in September. They were in rags, and without salt; the corn supply would last six months. They expected the enemy daily. Indians captured a seventeen-year-old who ventured out that week for wood. The winter was an agony and got worse; in a predawn raid on February 5, 1692, a hundred and fifty Indians plundered and burned the prosperous town of York, Wells's closest neighbor. Burroughs submitted an apocalyptic account to the provincial authorities late that afternoon. As the first witchcraft accusations emerged fifty miles south, Indians killed or carried off half of York, marching fifty captives through the snow to Canada. They slaughtered sheep, cattle, and horses. Having spoken with an escaped youth, Burroughs painted a hellish picture of "pillars of smoke, the raging of merciless flames, the insults of the heathen enemy, shouting, shooting, hacking (not having regard to the earnest supplications of men, women, or children, with sharp cries and bitter tears in a most humble manner), and dragging away others (and none to help)."

The ravages reminded him of the passage in Samuel in which David and his people discover their families taken hostage at Ziklag. Viewing the blackened, leveled city, they "lifted up their voices and wept, until they had no more power to weep." Evoking the destruction of Jerusalem, Burroughs switched to Lamentations: "And saith Jeremiah, mine eye affecteth mine heart, because of all the daughters of my city." He read the devastation as divine rebuke. "God is still manifesting his displeasure against his land," he wrote three months before his arrest. "He who formerly hath set to his hand to help us, doth even write bitter things against us." He closed with a variation on God's promise of deliverance in Jeremiah, which he hoped the Massachusetts council might share: "If you will remain in this land, then I will build you up and not pull you down; I will plant you and not pluck you up." Burroughs stressed the "low condition and eminent danger" in which the settlers found themselves. Wells was next, and would soon have no choice but to surrender. The York raid had moreover claimed an eminent casualty. Shubael Dummer, the only ordained minister in Maine and a Sewall cousin, stepped out that Friday morning to be butchered on his doorstep, "barbarously murdered, stripped naked, cut, and mangled," as an eyewitness reported. Dummer's wife was carried off. She would not survive.

Cotton Mather too reported on York, in an address on the corruption of New England manners. The details and the atrocities were the same. Families were butchered, hostages in danger of being roasted alive. Hearts, Mather preached, should bleed over the carnage. But congregations should also wake, with a start, to York's warning. Where Mather wrote allegory, Burroughs submitted an SOS, if one ripe with biblical allusions. Like Sarah Good, he was both ferocious and needy, a musket-wielding man of the cloth and a public-spirited supplicant. He might well have observed that the hated Andros had better protected Maine than the inept, homegrown government that had ousted him; the insurrection — and the subsequent chaos — had only encouraged the enemy. Boston had withdrawn its forces, leaving men like Burroughs to beg for protection. Some went so far as to petition the king after the Boston coup, there being, under the interim government, "no peace, order or safety in New England."

HATHORNE AND CORWIN built a careful case against Burroughs, soliciting evidence from sixteen people. They also took the exceptional step of deposing their suspect privately. That interview took place at Ingersoll's, although on this occasion the sixty-year-old innkeeper—familiar with the Maine skirmishes, which had sent his own family scurrying south as well—made no move to defend his former minister. To some extent we are left to extrapolate the charges from Burroughs's denials. The first was the gravest and surely weighed as heavily against him as the slaughtered wives. When, inquired the justices on the morning of May 9, had Burroughs last taken communion? The Maine frontier was thinly populated; fewer than four thousand English settlers made their homes there. They were not always eager to expose themselves to the dangers of travel for the sake of the Sabbath, a day on which much ceased but Indian ambushes did not. If only out of necessity, Burroughs was less orthodox than his inquisitors. He was also either blunt to the point of self-destruction or Parris—who recorded his testimony—made him seem so. When had he last taken communion? It had been so long he could not say exactly, Burroughs replied, though on a recent Sabbath, he had attended a morning meeting in Boston and an afternoon one in Charlestown. He remained a full member of the Roxbury church. He had baptized only the eldest of his children, among the original residents of the Salem parsonage. Parris did not note that the minister lived far from any address at which he might conceivably have baptized the others.*

The interrogation veered swiftly from the orthodox to the occult. Burroughs's second wife had complained of visitations in the night. What of the terrifying creature that had bolted from the roof, raced along the chimney, and flown down the stairs? A slave swore it had been

---

* If indeed Burroughs said as much, he misspoke. He had baptized a second child in 1691.

a white calf. On another occasion something rustled by the bed, breathing on Sarah Burroughs while she lay at her husband's side. It dematerialized when he woke. Burroughs denied that his house was haunted although—he had a perverse habit of raising questions, if not hackles—he could not help but add that there were toads. He sounds nearly to have been amusing himself. He had no particular reason to think himself vulnerable; witches were women of sour disposition and humble circumstances. They were more often acquitted than convicted. Massachusetts did not try ministers for witchcraft; he still had his champions. As recently as three months earlier he had been holed up, half starved, in a lice-infested garrison surrounded by several feet of snow, a vicious enemy bearing down. He had twice barely escaped with his life. He had witnessed appalling sights; he knew of ears and noses hacked off and stuffed into mouths. He had little time for diabolical toads.

The dead wives came next. There was some reason why various Burroughs women might be flying about Salem posthumously denouncing the minister. The Putnams were far from alone in testifying that over the weeks their minister had lodged with them, "he was a very sharp man to his wife." In Maine, Sarah Burroughs had lived in a fear that had nothing to do with enchanted white calves. Her husband scolded mercilessly and controlled obsessively. He convinced her that he heard every word she uttered in his absence. It was reported that, returning from a strawberry-picking expedition with Sarah and his brother-in-law, Burroughs had vanished into the brush. His companions hollered for him. He was nowhere to be found. They rode home; somehow he had preceded them, on foot and with a basket of berries. He afterward admonished his wife for the vile things she had said about him in his absence. The devil could not know as much, protested the brother-in-law, to which Burroughs cryptically replied: "My God makes known your thoughts unto me."*

* The 1656 offense of Ann Hibbins—said after her witchcraft execution to "have had more wit than her neighbors"—had been that she knew when others were speaking about her. Burroughs boasted of and demonstrated a cleverness that seemed clairvoyant.

y

w

b

A week after his wife had given birth, Burroughs kept her on her feet to berate her at length. When his daughter blamed him for the resulting illness he chided her as well. (The night before Burroughs's hearing, Shelden testified, the spectral wizard told her that he had killed two of his own children. The charge may have seemed plausible to those who knew the family, in which daughters sided with a stepmother.) While Burroughs had neither choked nor smothered his wives—or stabbed them, as others maintained; again the discrepancies tended to flit about unnoticed—the choice of verbs was interesting. Burroughs believed in secrets, something that sat poorly with a community dedicated to mutual surveillance. It would emerge that he had attempted even to silence the woman to whom his daughter complained. Should his wife fail to survive, the neighbor was not to mention the tongue-lashing. Burroughs may have mistreated Mercy Lewis as well; a special violence crept into her accounts of her former employer. She would not write in his book, she insisted, "if he threw me down on 100 pitchforks." Avenging females hovered everywhere in 1692 Salem.

A fairly consistent portrait emerges, if not of a sinister black man who abducted girls on whom he pressed diabolical books, then of a tyrannical husband. During their stay with the Putnams, he and his first wife had quarreled so violently that they appealed to their hosts to arbitrate. (The request may have amounted to mere politeness. It would have been impossible to argue privately, even in the comfortable Putnam home.) Again roguish Burroughs either kept or hoped to keep secrets. He had insisted his wife sign an agreement that she would reveal none of his private affairs, a request that in itself sounded incriminating, the more so at a time when document signing assumed a diabolical taint. He discovered as much that morning. The justices had done their homework: Had he made his wife swear that she would write her father only those letters of which he approved? Burroughs denied the charge, of special interest to Hathorne. Sarah Ruck, the second Mrs. Burroughs, currently flitting about in her funeral shroud, was his brother's

widow.* Her father lived in Salem, where he was about to serve as foreman of a grand jury.

The Salem marshal led the compact, dark-haired Burroughs into the
meetinghouse, where he was instructed to look only at the justices.
Susannah Shelden, the Maine refugee who had buried more relatives
than any of the other girls and whose father had died months earlier,
offered up her conversation with the two dead wives. The justices asked
Burroughs to face his accuser, standing several feet from him. As he
turned, all or nearly all of the bewitched fell screaming to the ground;
Parris could not properly say how many contorted amid the mayhem.
What, the justices asked, did Burroughs make of all this? He agreed they
had before them "an amazing and humbling providence." He understood
nothing of it. He doubtless cited Scripture; he was as fluent in biblical
wonders as anyone in the room, something Parris had no reason to indicate in his notes and that Reverend Noyes did his best to suppress. Burroughs did point up one irregularity—"Some of you may observe that
when they begin [to] name my name, they cannot name it," he observed
of his accusers—but was drowned out.

A very different set of incriminating reports followed. Several men
testified to Burroughs's strength. It was legendary, especially as he was a
small man, even "a very puny" one, in the estimation of statuesque Cotton Mather. Burroughs had hoisted a barrel of molasses with two fingers.
He had fired a seven-foot shotgun with one hand. While a companion
had gone off to the fort for help, he had unloaded an entire canoe of provisions. In September 1689, a time when a prodigiously strong, stout-
hearted leader came in handy, many had admired his fortitude; it was
that month that the minister won praise for his role in the Casco battle.
"None of us could do what he could do," recalled a forty-two-year-old
Salem weaver, who had attempted to lift the shotgun but—even with
two hands—could not steady the weapon. What had inspired awe at the

---

* Sarah Ruck was unlucky in love. Her first husband entered simultaneously into two
marriages. Having legally untangled herself from him in 1664, she married William
Hathorne, Justice Hathorne's older brother. Burroughs was her third husband.

time appeared as wizardry now. Many had heard secondhand of Burroughs's exploits; others had heard directly from him. He displayed as prodigious a talent for boasting as did his specter. Where once he might have solicited those tributes, Burroughs now disowned his feats. (He had, he explained, merely rested the shotgun on his chest.) Lurking behind the accounts was what may have been the most pertinent charge against him. He had survived every devastating Indian attack unscathed. Abigail Hobbs, Mercy Lewis, and Susannah Shelden had not been so lucky; others who might have testified about Burroughs's wielding an impossibly heavy musket could not do so because they were dead. By no account an agreeable man — plenty of supercilious baiting and blustering accompanied the domestic cruelty — Burroughs managed to join abusive behavior at home with miraculous feats abroad. All evidence pointed to the same conclusion: he was a bad man but a very good wizard.

Though he rode to jail in Boston directly from the hearing, Burroughs continued to haunt the week's proceedings. He may still have been in transit when toothless, gray-haired George Jacobs hobbled into his hearing the next day, his long figure bent over two canes. Jacobs was at least seventy and possibly closer to eighty, in the eyes of his neighbors an exceptionally old man. A prosperous, longtime Salem farmer, Jacobs sounds like nothing so much as an aging rascal. Before his interrogators, he chortled and quipped. As the justices introduced his accusers, Jacobs invited the girls to speak up. He eagerly awaited their story. Parris's niece offered her testimony. Jacobs could only laugh. Asked to explain himself, he interrogated his interrogators: "Your worships, all of you, do you think this is true?" Their credulousness struck him as incredible. He did not shy from a challenge; he would admit to witchcraft if they could prove it!

Like George Burroughs and the take-no-prisoners John Procter, Jacobs had been firm with his servant, whom he very likely beat. A sixteen-year-old boy would later testify that Jacobs had threatened to drown him. The charge resonated. A generation earlier, Jacobs had been prosecuted for having drowned several horses, trapping them in a river with a barrage of sticks and stones. (He claimed he had simply attempted to run the trespassing animals off his property.) Over two days of hearings, it emerged that the spectral Jacobs had beaten the girls with his canes. Several produced pins that the old man had stuck into their hands. Sarah Churchill, his former servant, urged Jacobs to confess. "Have you heard that I have any witchcraft?" he asked, looking not at her but at the magistrates, as directed. "I know you have lived a wicked life," Sarah chided, which seemed sufficient.

Did Jacobs tend to family prayer? inquired Hathorne and Corwin. He did not. A prayerless house was understood to be a haunted one; the magistrates pressed the old farmer to account for his negligence. He did not worship with his family, Jacobs explained, because he could not read. That was no impediment; "Can you say the Lord's Prayer?" prompted the justices. "Let us hear you." All understood those lines to be a sort of talisman before which evil fled. Jacobs made multiple attempts, stumbling every time. Nearly every witness who appeared before Hathorne and Corwin would do the same; as another wizard nervously quipped a week later, himself mangling a clause, the accused appeared to be every bit as bewitched as their accusers.* Otherwise words came easily to Jacobs. He bantered with the justices. He could not help them with their inquiry, he feared. They could burn him or hang him; he knew nothing of witchcraft. He was no more guilty than his examiners. "You tax me for a wizard. You may as well tax me for a buzzard," he protested. "I have done no harm." Having been beaten black and blue by the elderly farmer, having been urged to write in his book, having been offered gold and many fine things—all before she had yet learned his name or set eyes on his nonspectral self—Mercy Lewis offered a more convincing explanation: Women were if anything more dangerous in 1692 than the men who claimed that they flew into bedchambers to lie heavily on their chests for

---

* "Deliver us from all evil" raised suspicions. "Hollowed be thy name" sounded like a sly curse, as Elizabeth Procter discovered.

hours, were aware. "I verily believe in my heart that George Jacobs is a most dreadful wizard," swore Lewis. Along with nine additional witches, Jacobs that week followed Burroughs to jail in Boston, where the old man who beat girls with his canes and the minister who abused wives had occasion to get to know each other intimately, enough so that Burroughs may even have caught sight of the triangular witch's teat that officials discovered below Jacobs's right shoulder.

Accusations exploded in the wake of a minister's imprisonment; hearings and prison depositions could barely keep pace. Mercy Lewis took the lead in testifying, to become the most active accuser. Ultimately she would be afflicted by fifty-one people. A retentive girl, she wove psalms and sermons into her visitations, offering the most imaginative testimony. (Maine refugee Susannah Shelden tended to divulge murders. She emphasized witches who suckled birds, hairless kittens, pigs, turtles at their breasts. Ann Putnam Sr. made a sideline of dead infants. Her daughter introduced new suspects.) At some point, Lewis moved to the household of Constable Jonathan Putnam, who had just lost a baby to what the family assumed to be witchcraft. Mary Warren, the Procter maid, waffled as recently as the day of Burroughs's Salem return, when she was heard to say that the magistrates might just as well listen to Keyser's crazy daughter as to any of the afflicted girls. Within the week she reversed course again; she would prove the most sensational witness for the prosecution. She plucked pins from her body. She spat blood in the meetinghouse. Her tongue protruded from her mouth for so long it turned black. Her legs locked together and could not be separated by the strongest of men. The court reporter did not elaborate on this unconventional intercession: here were grown men attempting to pry apart a twenty-year-old girl's knees.

Phantoms and specters meanwhile commingled. Ann Putnam Sr. reported on several milky-white figures at her bedside. Two were ghosts, but the third was John Willard, her dark-haired neighbor. Willard had evidently helped to round up several initial suspects until he tired of the girls and swore they should all hang. In spectral form he confided in Ann that he had murdered at least thirteen villagers, whom she named. The litany of unfortunate explanations left everyone scrambling to reexamine domestic misfortunes and mysteries, of which there is never a shortage. All over Essex County, stomach cramps, bladder problems, numbness, deafness, and every brand of deviance—including unexpected kindness—suddenly made sense.

Not every terror was airborne. Sarah Churchill, George Jacobs's principal accuser, left the May 10 hearing in tears, wringing her hands. She took her distress to Ingersoll's niece. Though she had sworn as much, she sobbed, she had never set her hand to the devil's book. What she had testified was "altogether false and untrue." Her confidante would not accept her recanting. In tears, Churchill insisted. Why on earth then had she lied? asked the older woman. The justices had threatened to lock her in the Salem dungeon with Burroughs, Sarah explained. She preferred to perjure herself than be chained in a dark hole with a wizard. The problem, she moaned, was one of disbelief rather than credulity. If she told Reverend Noyes a single time that she had signed the devil's book, he would believe her, "but if she told the truth and said she had not set her hand to the book a hundred times, he would not believe her."

Late in May, as eighty-one-year-old Salem farmer Bray Wilkins prepared to ride to Boston, his granddaughter's husband paid a call. Would Wilkins pray for him? The young man—it was John Willard, the Putnam neighbor—was frantic. He had been accused. Wilkins put him off as politely as he could. The two had long been at odds; the Wilkins clan had not taken to Willard. Who should turn up just as Bray Wilkins sat down to table days later in Boston but the young man. He cast an evil eye on the family patriarch; for days afterward the old man suffered an excruciating urinary blockage. On the painful return to Salem—Wilkins felt "like a man on the rack"—he appealed to Mercy Lewis. By May the girls served as traditional witch-finders; parents of ailing children made pilgrimages to consult with them. They might only be eleven or twelve, but under Parris's supervision, they could explain how several head of cattle a community away had come to freeze to death six years in the past. Mercy saw Wilkins's grandson-in-law pressing on the old man's stomach, clear as day.

The witchcraft claimed its first fatality that month. Early in May, Bray Wilkins's seventeen-year-old grandson Daniel also ranted about John Willard. Daniel may have been among those who knew that Willard beat his wife. He may already have heard rumors of witchcraft. He swore that Willard should hang. Several days later, the teenager fell ill. He was soon unable to eat or speak. A doctor attributed the sickness to preternatural causes, a diagnosis with which the visiting Mercy Lewis agreed. At Daniel's bedside at dusk she watched a gauzy Willard torture the limp, dazed boy. He gasped for breath. Over the next day Lewis, Mary Walcott, and Ann Putnam Jr. all reported Willard at his throat and chest, choking him. The specter spoke with the three girls. On Saturday the fourteenth, he announced he would shortly murder Daniel "if he could." He had not, he explained, strength enough; he would apply to Burroughs for renewed powers. On Tuesday, the specter vowed he would kill Wilkins that moonless evening. Three hours later, he breathed his last. "Bewitched to death," Parris wrote after the seventeen-year-old's name in the village church record.

The culprit turned up forty miles away, having eluded arrest for nearly a week. His flight seemed to confirm his guilt; he caused such a stir in the watch house that the marshal had no choice but to shackle him. Alarmed, the marshal urged the justices to press ahead in their investigations, to prevent further casualties. Hathorne and Corwin examined the suspect promptly. "What do you say to this murdering and bewitching your relations?" they challenged the young man. Willard insisted he wished no harm to any human being. The girls' testimony was read aloud. It was familiar, down to the charges of wife-beating. Several relatives—and nearly all who testified against Willard were family—recalled the sticks he had broken while thrashing his wife. He had left her cowering under the stairs; she had not expected to recover from the blows. Through the hearing, ghosts flew about the room, clustering around Willard. Did he believe the girls were bewitched? Hathorne inquired. "Yes, I really believe it," replied Willard, the next to trip, perilously and five times, over the Lord's Prayer.

Quietly, having been wrenched from her sickbed in February and mentioned only occasionally since, Sarah Osborne—the frail villager who had worried Indians might drag her off by her hair—died that week in prison. It took a sturdier soul to survive nine weeks and two days in a raw, rank cell through the coldest months of the year on scant rations and in heavy irons. On May 10 Boston's jailer removed Osborne's body from among the villagers who had watched her slip away, none of whom would have quibbled with the 1686 description of the Court Street lockup as a "suburb of hell." At the time no one ascribed her death to witchcraft. She, rather than Wilkins, would be Salem's first casualty.

VI

⎯⎯⎯◁▷⎯⎯⎯

A SUBURB OF HELL

Hell seems a great deal more feasible to my weak mind than heaven. No doubt because hell is a more earthly-seeming thing.
—FLANNERY O'CONNOR

AT AN IDEOLOGICALLY fraught moment, a group of children suffer from an incapacitating disorder. Their bewildered families cast frantically about for a diagnosis; meanwhile the symptoms intensify under observation and the disorder spreads. A group of experts—ministers, in this case—weigh in, an unverifiable explanation gains favor, allegations bloom left and right, and seventy people find themselves clapped in airless cells, accused of offenses they can only half imagine. These things happen, and not only in the seventeenth century. What could not yet happen in 1692 was any resolution. Hathorne could investigate the charges and incarcerate the suspects. Neither he nor any Massachusetts magistrate could advance to the next steps—grand jury hearings and formal indictments—until the acting governor allowed the Salem cases to proceed to trial. An eighty-nine-year-old political moderate, very much a placeholder, he seems to have elected to stall. Sixteen years earlier he had reprieved an accused Newbury witch, the woman with whom John Hale spoke after her pardon. The colony teetered between governments or, more exactly, "between government and no government." It awaited the charter it knew to be en route. It awaited its new governor. All was in a holding pattern. "Salem is one of the few dramas in history with a beginning, a middle, and an end," Arthur Miller observed in 1953. The middle act opened now, as the panic gathered force and the jails of Essex County bulged with shackled witches.

Deliverance—or at least judicial relief—arrived at dusk on May 14 in the rotund and improbable form of an erstwhile Maine shepherd.* Sir William Phips, the new Massachusetts governor, sailed past the spray of islands and into Boston's majestic harbor late that Saturday. The snap of New England spruce met him even before he set foot on shore. Built on the slope of three rolling hills, the town—of handsome churches, extensive wharfs, a two-story town house, and a marketplace packed with well-furnished shops and tradesmen of all kinds—was surrounded by water on nearly every side. Boston was small enough still that you could walk easily from one end to the other in search of your lost cow. Brick, pitched-roofed mansions had begun to rise among its tight huddle of wooden homes. Still, you were more likely to meet a hog than a coach in its narrow streets. The interim administration had assembled at the wharf to welcome Phips; shouting acclamations, well-wishers thronged the pebble-stone streets, which echoed with celebratory cannon shots. Along with the new governor sailed Increase Mather and the colony's revised charter. The three were to rescue Massachusetts, that "shaken and shattered country," from its post-Andros anarchy, from the "thousand perplexities and entanglements" that beset its people.

The rugged forty-one-year-old who made his way to the town house, accompanied by several hundred flag-bearing militiamen, some wielding muskets and pikes, others in breastplates or heavy leather doublets, was an odd man for the job. A burly, pleasant-faced gunsmith's son, Phips had spent his early years in the remote reaches of Maine; at twenty-two,

---

* Whether or not Phips actually tended a flock is open to debate. Mather asserted he did in a work conflating New England's history with that of the Promised Land; he had every reason to make the colony's savior a shepherd if he had not been one already.

he moved to Boston as a shipwright. Rough-hewn and wildly ambitious, he could not settle for being merely one of the first self-made men in American history. As Samuel Parris was setting up shop next door, Phips determined to seek his fortune, sailing to the West Indies in search of sunken treasure. An initial expedition yielded only two mutinies, the first of which he essentially suppressed with his bare hands. A third journey yielded a cache of gold, silver, and precious stones off the coast of Haiti. English patrons had underwritten the voyage; to London Phips sailed with thirty tons of silver. Writing centuries later, Keynes deemed his feat "one of the most extraordinary records of improbable success." The haul altered England's financial future, triggering an early stock-market boom and leading directly to the foundation of the Bank of England. At a time when five hundred pounds constituted a small fortune, Phips's share alone came to eleven thousand pounds.*

While the exploit won him medals and a knighthood, it did nothing to burnish his manners. Phips might be compared to Jason fetching the Golden Fleece, as a minister asserted before Harvard's 1688 graduates, but he remained a rude and rascally frontiersman who proceeded by brawn and bluster, colorful overreaching and vigorous head-bashing, earning reprimands from many, as he had done even from the aged provisional governor he now replaced. A decade earlier constables attempted to break up Phips's men, brawling late in a Boston bar. He stepped in on their behalf. When the constables threatened to notify the authorities, Phips roared that he "did not care a turd for the governor, for he had more power than he had," a sentiment he expressed less decorously on other occasions. Brought to trial, he flung his papers at the justices. (Stoughton, about to become Phips's deputy governor, sat on the court that fined him.) His swearing and cursing impressed even veteran sailors. The fortune did nothing to suppress an appetite for bribery and extortion.

---

* The sunken treasure was Spanish, from a forty-five-year-old wreck. Indian divers salvaged it, allegedly managing forty-five minutes underwater at a time, using tubs lowered over their heads.

It took a great deal to transform a rabble-rousing adventurer into an angel, but New England's preeminent mythmaker managed to do so, later describing Phips arriving in Boston at this critical juncture as if "dropped from the machine of heaven." While his contemporaries would have choked on the celestial equation, the timing was more problematic yet. "We are in daily expectation of Sir William Phips," Samuel Sewall had noted—nearly four months earlier, as the Parris girls shuddered with their first convulsions and weeks before the new governor had so much as embarked.* The charter Phips carried was already six months old, months that had worn down Massachusetts, that "distressed, enfeebled, ruined country."

For all his recklessness, Phips could be said to have been a habitual late-arriver. Having learned to read and write at twenty-two, his grasp of both skills remained shaky.† He apparently could not distinguish Dutch from English on the page and may or may not have been able to decipher his own December 1691 commission. It established him as governor by royal prerogative; under the old charter, his had been an elected position. In March of 1689 Phips had raced from London to Boston to deliver the news of England's Glorious Revolution, in which William III overthrew James II, a Protestant king supplanting a Catholic one. Aboard ship, Phips crowed that he would personally unseat Andros, the reviled royal governor; he arrived to discover the job had been done six weeks earlier. A year later Phips found his way to the North Church, where Cotton Mather baptized him, clinching his political future. In his case, the delayed rite raised no eyebrows. There had been, Mather explained, no settled minister on hand in Maine to perform the task.

In 1690 Phips led a combined naval and land expedition against Quebec, the capital of French Canada. Rumors of a Wabanaki-French alli-

* In fairness, these were years when you could die of smallpox in four days but word that you had done so could take fifteen months to cross an ocean, as would be the case with Queen Mary. When she had ordered Massachusetts to establish a proper postal system, the letter took ten months to reach Phips. He ignored it.
† He was fortunate in that a gentleman was not expected to write well. Penmanship remained a clerk's art.

ance haunted New England, as they would continue to do; word flew that the enemy intended to destroy every town in the colony. Phips had enjoyed an earlier success against a French outpost in Nova Scotia, a success only slightly soiled by his men's pillaging. The 1690 expedition was rashly planned and repeatedly delayed; the French greeted him with heavy fire. He sacrificed hundreds of men to a ruinously expensive campaign, one London deemed "a shameful and cowardly defeat." Phips would play a role in altering North American financial history too; without funds to pay the returning soldiers and sailors or recruit new ones, the colony issued paper currency. Crippling inflation ensued. The economy in tatters, a French retaliation expected, trade at a standstill, a state of near-anarchy prevailed. The "poor people," noted a Boston visitor, "are ready to eat up one another." None of which stopped Phips from sailing to London to ask William III to bankroll an attempt to dislodge the French from North America once and for all. Maine's fur trade and fisheries stood in peril. (England would have cause for regret too, argued the settlers, should the French get their hands on the Massachusetts shipyards.) It was on that trip that Phips and Increase Mather joined forces in the charter negotiation.

As Phips walked that late-spring Saturday afternoon from the Boston wharf the light drained completely from the sky. A hush fell on the city. From the town-house balcony he delivered half a speech—God had sent him to preserve his country, where all prior laws and liberties would obtain—then paused. The light was gone. He would not infringe upon the Lord's Day. The acclamations, the salutes, would have to wait until Monday. By candlelight the militia accompanied him to his red-brick mansion at the corner of today's Salem and Charter Streets, a beautifully appointed home with a brilliant harbor view. The crowd continued around the corner to the home of Increase Mather, to whom Phips owed his appointment. On Monday morning the authorities reconvened in the pillared town house, where they engaged in a six-hour debate as to whether the reading of Phips's commission should be resumed where it had been left off or whether it should be read anew, politics and religion stumbling over each other. At the same ceremony sixty-year-old William Stoughton, a veteran of two decades of civil service and of four regimes, took the oath as deputy governor.

Published two days later, the charter failed to accomplish all the colony—henceforth a province—had hoped. The colonists were to pay the price for having arrogated powers not their own; the Crown expanded Massachusetts boundaries but curtailed its privileges. The charter demolished the political basis of the first decades, granting religious tolerance to all (except Catholics). Any man with substantial income could vote, irrespective of church membership. The colonists lost the right to choose their own governor; the installation of Phips was a compromise worked out in London by Increase Mather. Surely the province could overlook a royal appointment if its governor was a New England Puritan, reasoned Mather, who knew that the king preferred a military man at the Massachusetts helm. Meanwhile, various Crown advisers lobbied for someone who shared their economic interests. Phips proved acceptable to all parties, in part because he belonged to none. Nor had he any political experience. He replaced what the Mathers referred to as "a knot of people that had no design but to enrich themselves on the ruins of this flourishing plantation." The province could now count on better protection, the vacuum of authority having proved more traumatic than the royal invasion, the "alien incubus" that was Andros. Most important, the charter put an end to three years of gnawing uncertainty.

Increase Mather set about selling the document aggressively; he knew he proffered an imperfect bill of goods.* His countrymen might wonder how he had not obtained more. The real wonder, he proclaimed, was that he had secured so much. Indeed autonomy was a thing of the past. But their governor and lieutenant governor hailed from their ranks. Spared a Crown-imposed Anglican aristocrat, Massachusetts got a

---

* He had himself been against the new charter before he was for it. After having huffed that he would rather die than consent to a document that so cramped Massachusetts liberties—the colony preferred to elect its own officers, as it had done earlier—he was reminded that he did not hail from a sovereign state.

Mather-baptized native son. The new document had its defects. But was not half a loaf better than none? Mather challenged in a spring sermon. Property rights were confirmed, religious rights guaranteed, political liberties and regular town meetings restored. Their governor could not pass laws or levy taxes unilaterally, as had Andros, whose courts were a mockery, who extorted monies, and who had exercised more power over New Englanders than did the king over Englishmen. Pleading and shaming, Increase Mather beseeched his compatriots to be happy with their lot and — appreciative, obedient children — to support their sovereigns. The last thing Massachusetts needed was "an unthankful murmuring generation of men." Cotton Mather jumped on the bandwagon, selling the charter to the Second Church congregation, Boston's largest. He had already reminded his fifteen hundred parishioners that the Lord had spared them three years earlier. He had rescued them from those who declared them "a people fit only to be rooted off the face of the earth." Mather meant Englishmen rather than Indians.

A roar of dissatisfaction could be heard in the propagandizing. A people disobliged God, Cotton Mather submitted, in a sermon delivered on a day of thanksgiving for his father's safe return, when they comported themselves like "vultures and harpies." Men who had shown "unfainting industry" for their countrymen should not be thanked with infamy. In that sunny address Mather extolled ministers, magistrates, and civic leaders of all kinds, hardworking, underappreciated public servants, each of whom "must carry two handkerchiefs about him, one to wipe off sweat of travail, another to wipe off the spit of reproach." He reminded his audience of their good fortune and ample privileges. They should avoid divisions and contentions. Those invited malignant "breaches in God's hedge about us," allowing devils to break in, of which there was currently a "stupendous instance" nearby.

Two disgruntled camps weighed in: those who would settle only for the restoration of the original charter (the orthodox, for the most part), and those who preferred a return of Dominion rule to an ineffectual New England regime (the merchants). Many felt the colony had been

shortchanged, that something had been irretrievably lost, always a summons to conservatism. The interregnum had taken its toll; not everyone
was eager to fling himself into the arms of the new administration.*
Prominent men who endorsed the charter bristled at Phips, who had so
often run afoul of the law in his pre-angelic incarnation. Grumbling
could be heard throughout the city of eight thousand, to the delight of
the remaining Andros supporters. Increase Mather conveyed none of
that disappointment to London, reporting instead on June 23 "that the
people are very well pleased with their new charter." For his part, Phips
had his hands full not only with the discontent but with Indians who ravaged the frontier—the devastating raid Burroughs described had taken
place fourteen weeks earlier—and French privateers who ravaged the
coast. The restoration of order, the dire need for sailors, a strategy by
which to foil French and Indian designs, constituted his immediate concerns, as did the empty Massachusetts treasury. For a loan the government turned to the ever-obliging Samuel Sewall, who had bailed out
Burroughs several years earlier.

Phips could not have expected the supernatural assault, having left
London the day Boston's jailers clapped irons on the first three suspects.
It is impossible to say what he made of the ambush, more an annoyance
than an urgent matter of state. Witch-hunting offered none of the glory
of sunken treasure or Indian scalps. The conquest of Canada—rich in
furs, fish, and precious metals—remained his priority. He was neither a
reflective man nor a letter writer; the realities of his career have been
largely subsumed by Mather's fantasies. Phips directed his attention to
reconstituting a government. From sheriffs to justices, he had positions
to fill all around; many awaited audiences with him. He would mention
Salem's "perplexed affair" to his British superiors only in mid-October,
by which time both he and the Mathers had reason to reframe the
onslaught of the invisible world. On his arrival, Phips would note five

* Some refused to associate with those who did. One prominent New Englander in London
in 1692 so violently disapproved of the new charter—the instructions had been to safeguard
the old—that he refused to sail to North America on any vessel that carried Increase Mather.

months later, "I found this province miserably harassed by a most horri-ble witchcraft or possession of devils, which had broke in upon several towns. Some scores of poor people were taken with preternatural tor-ments; some were scalded with brimstone; some had pins stuck into their flesh; others were hurried into fire and water, and some dragged out of their houses and carried over the tops of trees and hills for many miles together."* He was operating wholly on hearsay. Neither he nor Mather had witnessed any of those phenomena.

Although Phips mentioned satanic possession in October, the pros-pect surfaced rarely in the interim.† Cotton Mather instead urged upon Phips the parallel with Sweden's earlier scourge. In that assault a "hellish crew" of no fewer than seventy witches had preyed upon three hundred children, ages four to sixteen, carrying them over central Sweden by var-ious conveyances, assisted by cats and birds. They assembled in a lush meadow, where they met Satan himself and—with blood—inscribed their names in his book. The Swedish witches threatened to kill commis-sioners and tormented ministers, one of whom had earlier been unable to make sense of a searing headache. Mather noted that those who had rooted out the Swedish malefactors had so well acquitted themselves of their task that they were instantly rewarded "with a remarkable smile of God," a fact that appears nowhere in accounts of that witchcraft. (He did not yet mention that seventy were put to death, of which only twenty-three had confessed, or that hundreds of Swedish children afterward admitted that they had lied. He must have noticed that what began with quotidian curses bloomed rapidly into a satanic cult. In Sweden too a knot of young children targeted a group of families, very often their own.)

---

* The brimstone appears to have been added between Salem and Boston. There is no trace of it in the court papers.

† Phips would later hold that he had established a court to discern whether witchcraft or possession was at work. The word "possession" falls in and out of favor; whole months went by without its mention, although on the day of his Boston return Increase Mather used it too. He found the country in a dire state "by reason of witchcrafts and possessed persons."

Sweden's was the witchcraft crisis from which derived the dizzying aerial malfunction that resembled Ann Foster's. And it was the week of Phips's return that Martha Carrier and Ann Foster crash landed as they soared over the treetops to Parris's much-discussed meadow, Foster's leg folding beneath her. Around the same time, Carrier jostled a twelve-year-old neighborhood girl at meeting. The child afterward heard the older woman's disembodied voice in the bushes; Carrier threatened to poison her. The first to be served in Andover, a warrant went out for Martha Carrier's arrest on May 28. Three days later, in an ill humor, she appeared before Hathorne to defend herself against charges that she had bewitched Abigail Williams and Ann Putnam Jr., on whom she had never before set eyes.

HATHORNE AND CORWIN had postponed their mid-May hearings on account of Phips's arrival. With it came a rash of new allegations. Orders went out to round up the extended family of George Jacobs, the jocular old man who had invited the justices to burn or hang him if they could prove him guilty but who bore that telltale sign below his right shoulder. When the Salem constable arrested Jacobs's daughter-in-law, a half-sane woman then nursing a baby, her three older children ran after her in tears until she disappeared from sight. Charitable neighbors took in the orphans. Their uncle, a close neighbor, could not do so; also accused, he had fled, along with Jacobs's son. That brand of flight was less available to women. George Jacobs's bright, soulful seventeen-year-old granddaughter landed in jail.

The caseload for Hathorne and Corwin was tremendous; on May 18, nine people testified to nineteen different afflictions. That Wednesday Rebecca Nurse's younger sister Mary Esty was released from jail, where she had spent the previous three weeks. She had figured in no recent testimony. (There was no bail in capital cases.) Her husband, a Topsfield cooper, had served in every civic office, from selectman to tithing man to highway surveyor to grand jury man. He knew how the system worked; he fought to convince the court that the earlier testimony was in error, not entirely difficult to believe of his mild-mannered wife. One witness violently disagreed. Within two days of Esty's release, Mercy Lewis hovered near death. Her mistress summoned Ann Putnam Jr., who arrived with Parris's niece; the girls appear to have been joined at the hip all spring. At Mercy's bedside they described the same sight: Esty and her accomplices savagely choked their friend. She did so, they explained, because Mercy, her breath now ragged, refused to clear Esty's name. Toward early evening on May 20 a diaphanous Mary Esty warned the teenager that she would not live past midnight. Under a sliver of new moon, a marshal raced to Topsfield to rearrest the fifty-eight-year-old mother of seven. By the time she sat shackled in Boston's prison, Mercy Lewis had fully recovered.

Over the same days Susannah Shelden, the two-time Maine refugee, revealed that when Philip English, the town merchant who had for weeks eluded arrest, visited her with his book and a knife, he threatened to murder their new governor, "the greatest enemy he had." Shelden was not alone in plaiting together the two conspiracies. Cotton Mather would do the same. The devil, Mather warned, angled "to sink that happy settlement of government wherewith Almighty God has graciously inclined Their Majesties to favor us." The complots easily aligned: Five of the men who were to become witchcraft judges had together ousted Andros, an insurrection partly planned at Mather's address. Hathorne took affidavits in that affair; Sewall responded to its critics. The justifications sounded familiar: having invaded New England, a crimson-coated, Crown-worshipping gang had subjected its people to barbarous usages. Their leader penetrated the colony's meetinghouses. He collaborated with the French. He suborned Indians, one of whom swore that Andros had given him a book with the picture of the Virgin Mary; anyone who did not own that volume was to be killed. Andros intended to sacrifice the settlers to their "heathen adversaries." He had summoned additional redcoats. He plotted to topple every town in New England, beginning with Boston.

At dawn on May 23, Nathaniel Cary, a wealthy, middle-aged Charlestown ship captain, sailed with his wife to Salem village. Over the previous days, disturbing reports had reached the couple that Elizabeth Cary, then in her early forties, had been accused of witchcraft. At the advice of friends, they made the half-day trip to Salem. They could resolve the matter easily enough; the afflicted would not so much as recognize Elizabeth, none having met her before. The justices had crammed a great number of hearings into that Monday's schedule; after conferring with them, Cary maneuvered himself into a prime meetinghouse seat. He watched with fascination as officials led in the prisoners, positioning them seven or eight feet before the bench and ordering them to face Hathorne and Corwin. Marshals remained at the defendants' sides, holding arms aloft to disable their powers. It hardly mattered. Along with three older girls, Parris's little niece Abigail stood between the suspects and the justices. If the eyes of the accused so much as drifted toward the bewitched, they shrieked. When they fell quiet, the justices pronounced them struck dumb. Cary labored to understand the difference between silent and entranced; he did not immediately grasp that, as Parris described it, the girls' mouths had been supernaturally stopped. "Which of you will go and touch the prisoner at the bar?" Hathorne inquired. The most courageous fell to the floor before she had taken three steps. Hathorne ordered her carried forward, to pronounce her cured once the touch test had been administered. "I observed that the justices understood the manner of it," Cary noted drily, unable to detect any change in the girls' behavior himself. They roamed freely about, several times approaching his wife to ask her name. The improvised courtroom was a disorderly place; in the midst of it, Cary discussed his predicament with John Hale, whom he had known for years. The Beverly minister suggested a private interview with Elizabeth's accuser, one he would arrange. Cary commanded ships; he knew something about making himself understood. He entrusted the matter to Hale.

Elizabeth's accuser turned out to be Abigail Williams. Parris would not consent to the parsonage interview Hale had promised, however; his niece would meet the couple only at Ingersoll's. The Carys crossed the road to the bustling inn, where they found John Indian waiting tables. Court days were exuberant alehouse days; justice — for which neighborhoods turned out and for which court officers enjoyed generous liquor allowances — came as a gift to Ingersoll. John introduced himself as one of the bewitched; in exchange for a bowl of cider, he treated the Carys to his story, displaying his wounds. At an earlier hearing, court officials had bound a suspect's hands with a cord. John's hands had magically fused together as well, tied by a rope that cut into his flesh. He in no way connected his affliction to Tituba, a confessed witch who had now been in prison, he told the couple, for nearly three months. In the midst of his account the band of girls filed in, "to tumble down like swine," Cary noted. A sort of demented acrobatics troupe, they had been together since the court's adjournment. Someone called for a few women to calm them; time stood still as all waited tremulously for the girls to pronounce. Revived, they cried out in unison: Elizabeth Cary tormented them! Instantly an official stepped from an adjoining room, where the justices had congregated. He bore an arrest warrant. With or without the connivance of Reverend Hale, the Carys had walked into a trap.

Having traveled to Salem to clear her name, Elizabeth Cary found herself under interrogation. Hathorne and Corwin do not appear to have decamped from the ordinary when they instructed the Charlestown matron to stand, arms stretched wide, her neck twisted away, so as not to torment the girls. Two of them accused her. She explained that she had never so much as heard of either one in her life. Her husband asked if he might at least support one of his wife's hands; Hathorne denied the request. Elizabeth began to cry. Might her husband, at her side, wipe the tears from her eyes and the sweat from her face? This Hathorne permitted. The room was stifling; Elizabeth felt faint. Could she lean on her husband? Hathorne barked that "she had strength enough to torment those persons, and she should have strength enough to stand." The ship captain railed at the cruelty; Hathorne instructed him to remain silent or leave the room. Who should appear next but John Indian, tumbling about on the floor although he had sat drinking cider only hours earlier with Elizabeth Cary, impervious to her supernatural powers.

Hathorne appealed to the bewitched. Who afflicted John? They could see Elizabeth Cary upon him. Again Hathorne enlisted the touch test, now in regular use; on those occasions when it failed to produce results, he urged the suspect to grasp harder, then harder still, until it did. Often the suspect did so blindfolded. Her touch, it was understood, enabled the poisonous particles emitted from the witch's eye to return to her body; the blindfold allowed it to be reabsorbed without the victim's being leveled by the witch's gaze. Noyes in particular subscribed to the practice, to the distress of some suspects. Hathorne ordered Elizabeth to touch John but under no circumstances to look upon him; court officers carefully guided her hand. Grasping it, John pulled the Charlestown matron to the ground. The sight of his wife sprawled roughly on the floor alongside an Indian slave shocked Captain Cary into a hasty speech. He had just enough time to sputter that he hoped that God would take vengeance on the heartless justices when a jail warrant appeared for his wife. With much difficulty Cary secured her a room for the night, which would have proved sleepless even if there had been a bed in it, which there was not.

Along with Mary Esty and six others, Elizabeth Cary traveled the following day to Boston's prison. It was the second delivery of witches since Phips's return. He would remember that he ordered all suspects to be chained that Monday, but according to the jailer's record — meticulous, as the accused bore every expense of her incarceration, from straw to blankets to chains — the prisoners' arms and legs were already shackled. Puritan punishment was meant to be public, reforming, and swift; it required an audience. A malefactor was sentenced "to sit in the stocks one hour next lecture day, if the weather be moderate," not for his comfort, but that of the requisite spectators. The entire community stood to suffer for a delinquent's misdeed, his redemption crucial to their peace of mind.

Boston's jail was that May also a crowded one; the majority of the accused bedded down there. The stone facility announced itself from a distance with a stench of refuse and rotting wounds. Neighbors suffered along with the inmates. Visitors did not tarry long. In close quarters, at least some of the Salem suspects terrified one another. Others terrified passersby. Iron bars covered the open windows; one could reach out for provisions or in to touch a loved one's hand. One could also spit and jeer; some came to the prison expressly for those purposes. When a seventeen-year-old servant girl visited on a May errand, Sarah Good, the Salem beggar woman, recognized her and pleaded for tobacco. What remained of her clothing barely covered her body. The girl replied by tossing a handful of wood shavings in her face, adding: "That's tobacco good enough for you!" Good cursed her, working the same effect she had five months earlier on the Parris children. The teenager raved and fainted for weeks afterward.

It was impossibly cold in the prisons, so arctic in midwinter that the authorities had not always been able to justify holding an inmate there. They had sent a shivering 1678 constable attacker home. In December 1685, Hathorne's father had dispatched a horse thief to Barbados as a servant, convinced that if the man remained in prison, he would freeze to death before he could be tried. The wind whipped through the ramshackle structures; ocean humidity penetrated all. While the winter of 1692 was colder still, witches did not sail for Barbados. Mercy was not generally in great supply. (The irascible Boston jailer was said to resemble a man but to manifest "the fierceness and currishness of a tiger." He twice reinforced his facility with extra lumber and with additional locks.) By law a prisoner was to be supplied with flax or hemp for bedding and with bread and water. No one had counted on a Tituba or a Sarah Good spending months behind bars under conditions that made the noxious, lice-infested pen—by no means designed for extended stays—"a grave of the living." In the most sophisticated of New England facilities, the deposed Andros and his attorney general could count, in 1689, on at least six inches of water in their cell when it rained. In the dark much of the time, famished at all times, the witch suspects set a miserable colonial record. At considerable expense, some family members—including the Topsfield constable—made regular daylong trips to deliver food, drink, and fresh linen to incarcerated relatives. The daughters of an accused Ipswich woman led their blind father to visit twice weekly.

Salem's jail was little better. The four-hundred-square-foot facility included an unlit dungeon, in which George Burroughs spent his spring and summer; he could only have felt "buried alive," as had an Andros official in a larger space. In an earlier incarnation, the jail had been described as "a noisome place not fit for a Christian man to breathe in." A minister's son who found himself rotting there thought he would die of cold, already "almost poisoned with the stink of my own dung and the stink of this prison." No human being, he contended, could bear "so pestiferous a stink." In ten freezing weeks he had not enjoyed a breath of fresh air. William Dounton, a town carpenter, presided over the Salem facility. Dounton seemed to wind up with all the unpleasant civic chores: he stood watch over the boys who attempted to escape meeting early, served on coroner's juries, and collected taxes. He and his family resided in the Washington Street building, where his wife sold refreshments to the prisoners. Security had been stepped up since the day a year earlier when, fetching the pot of beer, she had inadvertently assisted in an escape. (The days of jailbreaks were not over, though they proved impossible for those with eight-pound shackles on their legs.) To sixty-four-year-old Dounton fell the unsavory task of searching the bodies of wizards for telltale marks and jabbing at blemishes with a pin. Unflappable George Jacobs felt nothing, additional proof of guilt.

Nathaniel Cary managed to spare his wife a Boston incarceration. Special privileges were extended to the wealthy, not only because jail keeps tended to be eminently bribable; Boston's jailer did nothing to disprove the notion that such men could exact more from their operations than from the best acre of English corn land. When finally he was apprehended, Philip English would pay four thousand pounds to lodge in the jailer's house rather than in the prison itself. Elizabeth Cary wound up transferred on the morning of May 24 across the river to the Cambridge prison, closer to home. The weights on her legs brought on convulsions. Her husband did not think she would survive to the following day, when the province joined in a fast to rebuke Satan. Repeatedly Cary petitioned for the eight-pound irons to be removed. Repeatedly he learned that his wife must remain shackled, even at the risk of her life. She posed a dreadful public danger.

By the end of May at least sixty suspects had been jailed, more than the Massachusetts prisons had ever accommodated. Those who had frozen through the winter began to roast in the sweltering spring. The situation cried out for resolution, as did the accused. Earlier in the month, a petition had circulated for pious Rebecca Nurse; thirty-nine villagers had affixed their names. She would have heard news of it from her family, who visited regularly, as from the fresh arrivals that week, which included her rearrested sister. The torrent of complaints meanwhile continued. Two weeks after his arrival, in an order that made reference to the stifling prisons but not to the multitude of witches, Phips established a special court to try the cases in Salem. He appointed nine justices; a quorum of five was required at any session. Most had served on the bench at one time or another; all sat on the governor's council. Merchants and landowners, they constituted the leading men of Massachusetts Bay. Their fortunes and influence entitled them to the prize meetinghouse pews. No rabble-rousing treasure hunters figured among them. The usual suspects, they would manage to wreak as much havoc as a cabal of church-toppling witches.

ONE OF THE reassuring things about witchcraft was that it answered to certain neat and immutable laws. It ran in families, primarily along matrilineal lines. Tainted reputations remained stubbornly so; the infamy endured long after the offenses had been forgotten. One Scotswoman preferred to burn rather than live as even an acquitted witch. Her family had disowned her and her friends deserted her. Unable to draw water from neighborhood wells, an acquitted Charlestown woman found herself reduced to drinking from puddles. Bridget Bishop, the occasional thief, could not escape the name she had already made for herself. To most of her accusers she remained Goody Oliver. Totaling her expenses at two shillings, five pence a week, the Boston jailer referred to her as "Bridget Bishop alias Oliver." The new Massachusetts governor notwithstanding, status too descended to a large extent genetically. Civic leaders produced civic leaders. At least a few selectmen in every town were raised by selectmen, as were nearly three-quarters of Salem's. Almost without exception, the witchcraft judges were the sons of merchants or ministers. Cotton Mather, John Hathorne, Jonathan Corwin, and William Stoughton all reprised roles their fathers had played. The prominent, accomplished parent proved nearly as difficult to sidestep as the one who, three decades earlier, had warned that a pig would keel over before dawn, and who had the misfortune to prove correct.

In establishing a Court of Oyer and Terminer—literally, "to hear and determine"—Phips assembled the "people of the best prudence and figure that could be pitched upon," as he put it. No member of that panel had any formal training in the law. Two had trained as ministers. Three were Harvard graduates. At least five were merchants, one an amateur physician. Most bore long lists of civic titles. The enterprising Bartholomew Gedney, who early on visited the parsonage girls and had attended a number of preliminary hearings, owned a Salem wharf and shipyard as well as several Maine sawmills. As Salem town residents, Hathorne and Gedney assured the court of a connection to—and a tenor consonant with—the hearings of the previous four months. They sat feet from each other among the front pews in Salem's First Church before the deacons, where together they absorbed Higginson's and Noyes's homilies. They had attended Parris's ordination; they fielded the villagers' unremitting complaints. Possessed of a flowing and elegant round hand, Stephen Sewall continued, with his pot of ink and his goose-feather quill, as court clerk. He organized the paperwork, which went home with him in a document box at night to the address he presumably still shared with Parris's daughter. Parris returned to preaching. At the court's head, Phips installed lieutenant governor William Stoughton, who weeks earlier had traveled to Salem for the Burroughs hearing.

For their pains, the justices earned about what an eminent schoolmaster did, or twice what the survivor of a 1694 Indian raid received for the ten scalps she redeemed in Boston. That was of little import to the magistrates, all men of wealth. No one would have quibbled with Phips's choices. He had assembled an irreproachable cast. At a time when much was in flux—when even the New England vocabulary was evolving, the colony now a province, its marshals sheriffs, its twenty-eight assistants councillors—this was reassuring. These were Massachusetts's well-traveled, civic, economic, and militia leaders, the sons (and in several cases also the sons-in-law) of its first families, men of established rank with distinguished names, each of which figured in New England's new charter. Among them they owned hundreds of thousands of New England acres. Nearly all had prior experience adjudicating witchcraft cases, if none with an outbreak of 1692 proportions.

Newly sworn in, the justices applied for guidance. It did not help that their orders were to determine what crimes had been perpetrated according to the laws of both England and Massachusetts, two bodies of law that differed. They turned naturally to the available expert. Four of the nine members of the court—including sixty-seven-year-old John Richards, the Boston merchant who solicited the advice—were close friends of Cotton Mather. He more than anyone grasped the slender dimensions of the administration. As he exulted that month in his diary, not only was the governor one of his dearest friends and someone he had personally baptized, but "all the councilors of the province are of my own father's nomination; and my father-in-law, with several related unto me, and several brethren of my church, are among them."

Eleven new warrants went out even before jurors could be assembled. The plaintiffs appeared only half acquainted with most of the accused, identified by surnames alone. Among the May 28 suspects, however, one name boldly jumped out, familiar to all: that of sixty-six-year-old John

Alden, a hard-edged Boston sea captain and merchant, the firstborn son of Plymouth's founding family. Among the sturdiest soldiers in Massachusetts, Alden was newly returned from Maine, where he had negotiated for the release of the captives carried off from York. Alden belonged to the same church as did three members of the witchcraft court. He was especially close to Samuel Sewall, having long done business with his father-in-law. On May 31, accused by several villagers, the enterprising Alden appeared before his friends and peers in the makeshift Salem courtroom.

The newly appointed king's attorney, Thomas Newton, traveled to that hearing as well, to glean a sense of what the Court of Oyer and Terminer might contend with at its first session, scheduled for June 2. It fell to Newton to decide the order of the trials. Stephen Sewall may have advised him; he knew the Salem cast and cases better than anyone. Already Chief Justice Stoughton had summoned eighteen "honest and lawful men" to serve as grand jurors and forty-eight men to serve as regular jurors. All hailed from the neighboring communities. They were to appear at the town house that Thursday morning at eight. The word "witchcraft" appeared nowhere in their summons but the men knew the nature of their charge. They were courtroom veterans drawn from a familiar cohort of local leaders. Their experience rather than their impartiality recommended them; they brought an invaluable knowledge of the community to the job. They would hear no other cases.

An Anglican and a trained barrister, Thomas Newton was fairly new to the colony. Like Deodat Lawson, the former village minister, Newton was a worldly man. Also like Lawson, he was dumbfounded by the scene before him. Possibly for his benefit, Hathorne again tested the accusers, arranging for Alden to attend his hearing without a guard. The sea captain strode into the village meetinghouse, his sword at his side, and took his place discreetly in the crowd. Hathorne then challenged the girls to identify their afflicter. They hesitated before pointing to another military man in the room. A little adult prompting, Alden noted later, helped. (He left an account of his hearing, not something many would have the opportunity to do.) As it had earlier, the dark meetinghouse further obscured matters. Alden was ordered outside, where the girls formed a circle around him, snapping and sneering. One—most likely Ann Putnam Jr.—taunted him for his lack of deference. He was awfully bold not to remove his hat before the justices!

The girls had absorbed plenty of reports on Alden in Massachusetts and in Maine, where he spent a great deal of time; it has been estimated that he had made at least sixteen round trips to the frontier since late 1688. He knew the territory well. His father-in-law had owned Maine sawmills; Alden had served valiantly in King Philip's War. He traded with the Wabanaki and had negotiated the truce that had indirectly pre-cipitated the York raid. He supplied the Maine garrisons. He had long been suspected of preferring arms sales to captive redemptions, putting his own business before that of the public; he had been ordered to travel with only restricted quantities of ammunition. Certainly Alden did not see the Wabanaki purely as "bears and wolves," as his February instruc-tions on the York exchange described them. Sure enough, the bewitched accused Alden of selling munitions to the enemy. He slept, they jeered, with Indian women! And he afflicted the girls with his sword, of which, to his chagrin, Alden was relieved. A marshal led him out to await his interrogation, probably at Ingersoll's. Whatever the truth to the charges of profiteering, he had thrived in Maine, amid dense fogs and blood-thirsty Indians where others had lost families.

Alden spent several hours in suspense while Hathorne summoned Martha Carrier, accused by Parris's niece and eighteen-year-old Susan-nah Shelden. Carrier hailed from a hot-headed family whose reputation she upheld. When Hathorne inquired about the spectral black man with whom the girls accused her of consorting, Carrier snorted. She saw no black man aside from the dark-haired, dark-gowned magistrate himself. As instructed, she locked eyes with him upon entering the room. Hathorne challenged her to turn to the girls without incapacitating them. "They will dissemble," she objected—it was the first use of the word—"if I look upon them." From a trance, Susannah Shelden, the fatalities expert, asked how Carrier had managed to murder thirteen people. The girls trembled as they described the spirits in the room; they complained of pins in their flesh, which they produced. Did Carrier not see the ghosts? Hathorne inquired. "If I speak you will not believe me," she scoffed, accurately enough. The girls shrieked that she lied.

No word had yet emerged regarding Carrier's flights or recruits. Nor was it yet clear that, as her own children would testify, the devil had promised their imperious mother that "she should be Queen of Hell." Still, the attorney general blinked in disbelief at the girls' visions, their pins, their agonies. "Staring in people's faces," they roamed about. "It is a shameful thing that you should mind these folks that are out of their wits," Carrier observed before the disorder reached crisis proportions, the flailing so severe that some thought the girls' lives in peril. Hathorne ordered Carrier to be tied, hand and foot, and carted away. Newton may or may not have managed in the pandemonium to hear Mary Walcott, who months earlier had displayed the bites on her wrist for Deodat Lawson, tell the justices that Carrier had boasted she had been a witch for forty years. Carrier was thirty-eight.

John Alden returned to the meetinghouse later that afternoon. To facilitate viewing, Hathorne instructed him to stand on a chair, another humiliation in itself; the girls appeared to be disciplining their elder. A marshal then restrained his hands. Alden was not as easily silenced. Why in the world, he protested from his awkward perch, would he come all the way to Salem village to hurt people he neither knew of nor had ever met? Bartholomew Gedney, the fifty-two-year-old Salem merchant, pressed him to confess. Alden answered that he had no intention of gratifying the devil with a lie. He challenged the assembly to supply a shred of evidence that he practiced witchcraft. Hathorne arranged for a touch test; a bewitched girl calmed the minute Alden set a finger on her. Among the remarkable things Newton observed that day the most remarkable may have been what came next. From his seat at the front of the room, Gedney allowed that he had known Alden for years. The two had sailed together. They were business associates. Gedney had defended his opportunistic colleague from earlier charges of collusion with a different enemy. He informed Alden that he "had always looked upon him to be an honest man, but now he did see cause to alter his judgment." He could not disregard that touch test. It was the height of a crisis when decades-long loyalties crumbled or proved inconvenient. A member of the same exclusive Boston prayer group, Samuel Sewall elected not to rise to Alden's defense either. His family had entrusted Alden to sail their ships across the ocean. Some sort of seismic shift had occurred.

Alden could say nothing more to his former colleague than that he was sorry. He trusted God would clear his name. For his part, he would, "with Job, maintain his integrity till he died." He was a man who— permitted a few minutes with Indian hostages—reinforced their faith, assuring them, when their captors barred them from prayer, that they suffered for Christ. Ordered to look upon his accusers, he watched them tumble to the ground. What could explain the fact, he challenged, that his gaze had no deleterious effect on Gedney? His old friend did not deign to answer. Alden launched into a spirited discourse on the plight of innocents, only to be silenced by Reverend Noyes, who offered a long speech of his own. What did the sea captain know of divine providence? Alden managed a final appeal to Gedney. "I can assure you," he insisted, "that there is not a word of truth in all these say of me." Sword confiscated, hands bound, he traveled that evening to Boston's prison.

It had been a long and exhausting day, not one, Thomas Newton marveled, anyone would believe had he not observed it with his own eyes. "I have beheld most strange things scarce credible but to the spectator," he reported to the secretary of the province. They made a convert of him. He left convinced that Alden was as deeply implicated as anyone else; the conspiracy, he feared, extended even to persons of quality. The long day of hearings also caused Newton to rethink his trial strategy. The very names of the accused elicited strangling, trances, yowls. The girls lay for prolonged periods as if dead. It made for slow going. He had sent for nine suspects; he now saw he could not possibly prosecute so many. He submitted two requests to the secretary. He asked that the confessors—Tituba and a servant who worked in the household of Justice Corwin's extended family—travel separately from the accused. And he asked for the records of Bridget Bishop's 1680 witchcraft trial.

The same day, in one headlong burst and with a minimum of corrections, Cotton Mather composed a thoughtful, seven-part letter. So eager was he to commit his thoughts to paper that he did not bother even to consult his vaunted library. The Court of Oyer and Terminer would convene in forty-eight hours; he labored to shed some light on its assignment. It was not unusual for a court to solicit advice from the clergy, even less for John Richards, the eldest member of the court, to have appealed to his pastor. Others clearly had questions as well. The previous Sunday, Samuel Willard—the only Boston minister to rival Increase Mather in his influence—went out of his way to expound on the devil and how to recognize him. Willard affirmed that the Old Deluder tempted, afflicted, and worked his infernal art through witchcraft. He missed no opportunities to recruit. He did so handily, given that he promised—Willard cited Matthew 4:8, as had Mercy Lewis—"all the kingdoms of the world."

Like most of his colleagues, sixty-seven-year-old Richards held many titles: He was a selectman and militia captain. He did not shrink from unpopular assignments. He had accepted a 1681 charter-negotiating mission to London that William Stoughton had managed to dodge, engaging while abroad in the requisite colonial groveling: the Massachusetts Bay irregularities had arisen only inadvertently! Long among the most influential members of the North Church, Richards contributed more than any other parishioner to his ministers' salaries. In turn Cotton Mather consulted him regarding church matters, on which Richards was a staunch conservative. He was as well a close and accommodating North End neighbor, having lodged the Mathers in his stately brick mansion when their home burned. Cotton Mather was a teenager at the time; a decade later, Richards officiated at his wedding. Understandably, then,

Mather was at his service; Richards's desires were always, Mather assured him, his commands. He offered up his thoughts concerning the mysterious matter. The entire province fasted and prayed on the justices' behalf; it placed itself in their righteous hands. Mather invoked his favorite analogies, trotting out the "stupendous witchcraft, much like ours," in Sweden. Personally he had begun to fear that devils worked more mischief than was generally understood. The "murmuring frenzies of late" provided ample opportunities for the great deluder to present himself and inquire: "Are you willing that I should go do this or that for you?" By accepting a simple favor, an innocent all too easily found himself ensnared. "And yet I must humbly beg you," cautioned Mather, loud and clear, sending up a crimson flag, "that in the management of the affair in your most worthy hands, you do not lay more stress upon pure specter testimony than it will bear."

He touched there on the heart of the matter, addressing the question with which the Salem justices wrestled from the start: Could the devil pass himself off as an innocent — and could a defendant be prosecuted on evidence only some could see? Mather rejected the idea, which had discomfited the justices in the 1676 Newbury case. They had not been able to bring themselves to convict a suspect for mischief caused in her likeness. The devil had disguised himself as an innocent before. Those who indulged in "malignant, envious, malicious" behavior might all too easily be taken for his confederates without ever having caught sight of him, much less having signed any kind of pact. To presume guilt, warned Mather, was to play into devious, diabolical hands.

He offered a few tips. A credible confession was worth its weight in gold, although, warned Mather, there was credible and credible. A "delirious brain, or a discontented heart" could produce false results. As for eliciting confessions, he could not condone torture. He recommended clever storms of cross, swift questions. Otherwise he subscribed to the traditional tactics. Could the accused recite the Lord's Prayer? Interestingly for an anguished ex-stutterer, he placed a great deal of faith in "confounding the lisping witches." He trusted in hard evidence, such as poppets. A witch could as well use her own body as a poppet, inducing suffering in her victim's eye, for example, by touching her own. While he had never seen one himself, a good physician could recognize a witch's mark.* He endorsed the water test; devils infused their recruits with a venom that rendered them buoyant.† He addressed neither the touch test nor the evil eye.

At every turn he opted for leniency. Rather than shackle every wretched witch, why not consider lesser punishments? Surely those might exact "some solemn, open, public, and explicit renunciation of the devil" sufficient to chase the Old Deluder from the neighborhood. Here Mather caught himself; he was writing his elder and a family benefactor. With a bow and a scrape, he apologized for getting ahead of matters. He would pray that Richards and his venerable colleagues sagely resolve the "thorny affair" before them. He rambled a little, although he was on one point perfectly explicit. He distrusted spectral evidence, visible only to the bewitched. An innocent could be used unwittingly to diabolical ends. No one should be convicted for a crime he committed in someone else's imagination.

Unsurprisingly for a man who had already met with a shimmering, winged, white-robed angel in his study—and who over the next years would note that the heavens advised, assured, and irradiated him— Mather also cast a vote for the invisible world. "Our dear neighbors are most really tormented, really murdered, and really acquainted with hidden things. Which are afterwards proved plainly to have been realities," he asserted. It was perfectly just to execute an individual "who in the sight of men shall with a sword in his hand stab his neighbor into the heart." In other words, Mather assured the justices, they could very well believe their eyes. Visible wounds—John Indian's scars, Mercy Lewis's

---

* As a sixteenth-century French physician had assured Henry IV, those who said that it was difficult to distinguish a devil's mark from a natural blemish were not good doctors.
† Massachusetts never attempted that experiment, although the day after Mather wrote Richards, an accused Connecticut witch requested it. The method had a quirk: the innocent could exonerate herself only by near-drowning.

bite marks—could not be ignored. Richards had every reason to share Mather's wisdoms with his colleagues, who in the weeks that followed consulted precedent in witchcraft cases, reading in Richard Bernard's *Guide to Grand-Jury Men* and Joseph Keble's treatise on common law, studying Glanvill, Baxter, and Perkins, as well as Mather's *Memorable Providences*. Their orders were to uphold the laws of England; they had paid a price for having deviated from them in the past. Richards reached out for an ecclesiastical opinion not from any shortage of legal manuals but because the senior justice knew he had an authority at hand. His minister would never sound more assured on the subject. As for Richards and his colleagues, they represented the best minds in America. The events in Salem utterly confounded them.

PREVIOUS CAPITAL CASES had been heard in Boston. Given the number of suspects and the multitude of witnesses, it made more sense to hear the witchcraft cases in Salem's town house, a spacious, two-story brick structure on an open square. Richards traveled there the day after Mather composed his letter so as to be on hand for the early-morning opening of the court. As the sheriff impaneled grand jurors, Newton's nine suspects—seven women and two men—returned to Salem. We do not know how they were transported or where room was found for them in an already congested prison, but they quickly made their presence felt. As the jail transfer took place that Wednesday a transparent Rebecca Nurse tackled Ann Putnam Sr. She boasted of various murders, claims buttressed by the huddle of ghosts around her. Ann Jr. reported on a set of matching apparitions.

Speculation must have run rampant throughout the village: With which witch would Newton begin? If the Putnams supposed it to be Nurse, they were mistaken. Newton did not select the criminal mastermind who posed the greatest danger, whom he left to molder in Boston. Nor did he choose the first accused witch, against whom he inventoried the evidence. His initial suspect was neither a confessed witch nor even a Salem villager. Newton was a level-headed civil servant, discerning and decisive. He acted as would any seasoned prosecutor, choosing what appeared from every angle an open-and-shut case, one that would ease the way for future prosecutions and deliver a clear signal to all. Cooperation was prudent, he could remind perpetrators. Guilt was easily determined, he could reassure the nervous jurors. Conviction was handily obtained, he could demonstrate to the judges. The star attraction could wait.

Since Newton's arrival in Salem, one name had recurred repeatedly. He heard it even from girls who had not mentioned it previously. Though in chains, his first defendant continued to afflict. She had attended the meeting in Parris's pasture. She had murdered six people, including a husband. A confessed witch had implicated her. Her case could be argued without recourse to spectral evidence. She had threatened a justice, assuring Hathorne that if she were a witch, he would know it. She had little family and none of the combative Nurse variety. Newton could call up a body of evidence against her from an earlier witchcraft trial. While judges and an assembly of minor officials journeyed to Salem, Newton prepared formal indictments against Bridget Bishop, charging her with having practiced her black art on five girls. What would be said of a Charlestown woman in 1693 applied equally to the ornery, peace-disturbing petty thief who had been walking around with a gash in her coat that corresponded perfectly to a lunge made at her specter; "If there were a witch in the world, she was one."

With the break of dawn on Thursday, ghosts alighted all over Salem. Soon thereafter a crowd began to assemble in the second, galleried floor of Salem's town house. A school occupied the ground floor; the large chamber above was fitted with benches. The justices presided from raised seats above a long table. Shortly after eight that morning, Newton stood before Chief Justice William Stoughton. Did the attorney general swear, asked Stoughton, "that according to your best skill, you will act truly and faithfully on Their Majesties' behalf, as to law and justice doth appertain, without any favor or affection, so help you God?" Newton did. Stephen Sewall took the oath to serve as clerk. A court officer, most likely the sheriff, swore in eighteen grand jurors, men of local influence who were to determine if sufficient evidence existed for the case to proceed. Newton laid out his evidence against Bishop, charging her with having "hurt, tortured, afflicted, pined, consumed, wasted, and tormented" the village girls. With little fuss, the girls testified to their statements. Newton may have presented evidence from Bishop's prior case as well; she was on trial as much for her character as her crime. The grand jury—its foreman was Burroughs's onetime brother-in-law—handed down five formal indictments against Bishop.

She submitted meanwhile to an intimate and invasive examination. Either under the supervision of a male surgeon or at his direction, a group of women scoured the bodies of the six female suspects for witch's teats. Several of the examiners were experienced midwives, although that was not saying a good deal. Where available, seventeenth-century treatises on childbirth tended to omit the finer details; its practitioners—usually older women from prominent families—knew relatively little about bodily functions. Nor was there much guidance as to what the women were looking for. A fleabite, a wart, a mole, anything raised or discolored could qualify as a teat. A panel of Connecticut women engaged in the same task scanned a woman three times but could not agree on their findings; they were unconvinced the suspect's anatomy differed from theirs. A bystander felt similarly at a Connecticut hanging. After close inspection of the body cut down from the gallows, she announced that if the victim's marks were preternatural, she too was a witch. Knowledge of anatomy was still primitive enough in New England that at a 1676 autopsy, a heart removed from a corpse was affirmed to be the stomach.

The midwives probed and pressed in tender areas, gauging sensitivity with pins or needles; you had to hope you would bleed when the three-inch pin went in. A Quaker woman subjected to the indelicate procedure swore that she had suffered greater abuse at the hands of church members than she had in bearing five children. While the Salem examiners did not entirely agree among themselves, they did locate several incriminating signs; three of Newton's suspects turned out to have "a preternatural excrescence of flesh between the pudendum and anus."* These were abnormal protrusions, unnaturally positioned. They appeared in precisely the same place on all three women, which by some logic indicated sorcery. At least some of her examiners were surely known to Bishop, among the three suspects with unusual growths.

The justices seated, officers escorted her into the courtroom for her arraignment. A court clerk called out her name; she stepped forward and held up her hand to acknowledge her identity. The indictments against her were read. How did she plead? Bishop had no choice but to speak for herself, there being no counsel for the defense. Early New England did not like lawyers. (More to the point, lawyers did not like early New England. Their value had been recognized only seven years earlier, when a call went to London to send over a few honest attorneys, if such a thing existed.†) Newton was the only trained lawyer in the room. It was felt that the innocent could make her case better than anyone else; left to her own devices, the guilty would prove unable to conceal the truth. Then in her late fifties, Bishop had spent six weeks on meager rations in a foul, dank jail. She had been threadbare from the start. She stood before the court filthy and haggard, under intense scrutiny, a sour woman in a cloud of sour air. She pleaded not guilty. "Culprit, how will you be tried?" the clerk then asked, to which Bishop replied with the formulaic, mandatory phrase: "By God and my country."

---

* There was some confusion as to what purpose the marks served. As the great seventeenth-century English witch-finder general explained, the devil was a spirit. He had no need for human blood. The teats served not for nourishment but to aggravate the witch, remind her of her covenant, and allow the devil to enter her body, the better to control it. The teat could look like any number of things, from the footprint of a hare to that of a mouse. Whole pamphlets were devoted to the subject, although it is unlikely that anyone in Salem had read them. Those who examined Tituba found scratches, understood to have been left by the devil in the course of their bodily tussle.

† The only member of the Massachusetts bench with a legal education—instrumental in formulating Massachusetts's first body of law—had left a will so convoluted that, after several years' dispute, the court chose to ignore it. Massachusetts would not allow lawyers to practice for fees until 1704.

By law, court cases were to be scrupulously documented; Stephen Sewall sat before the judges stabbing his quill in his ink bottle, transcribing as furiously as had Parris during the preliminary hearings. Nothing Sewall set down that day — or during any other 1692 witchcraft trial, for which Bishop's set the precedent — has come down to us. Three decades of evidence against Bishop has. She had been tried and reprieved before; while the stakes appeared greater this time — she had never before witnessed such a formidable gathering — she did not believe herself to be a witch. Once she had entered her plea, witnesses were sworn in, taking the oath to speak "the truth, the whole truth and nothing but the truth." One told of having been carried from her spinning wheel to the river, in which Bishop threatened to drown her. Another reported on murders of which Bishop boasted; a third described a ghost of one of her victims. Many — little Betty Parris and Ann Putnam Jr. among them — recounted tortures they had endured at the April hearing. Bishop's touch had revived the girls, others testified, fulfilling the crucial Deuteronomy-determined requirement of two witnesses to a crime. Deliverance Hobbs swore that Bishop had whipped her with iron rods to force her to retract her confession. Together they had attended the "general meeting of the witches" in Parris's field. The jurors heard testimony from the villager who had stabbed at Bishop's shape to produce the gash displayed in her coat. She and her specter were manifestly one and the same.

Any number of suspects could have been said to have enchanted neighbors and afflicted the village girls. Bishop alone could be convicted of having lied in court, several times, during her preliminary hearing. Her history represented such a prosecutorial gold mine that some testimony never made its way to court. Susannah Shelden reported that Bishop had been a witch for more than twenty years; that she knelt and prayed before a black man in a high-crowned hat; that a snake familiar had crept "into her bosom." Newton did not use that deposition. The court may have heard of a more earthly incident: not only had Bishop stood before Hathorne four years earlier when accused of theft, but she had spent several weeks in jail that year. A town miller accused her of having stolen a piece of brass. She returned it and twice begged his forgiveness, on her knees. Asked at her 1688 trial to confirm as much, she had denied all. She had stumbled upon the brass in a corner of her garden while weeding. She had never apologized. A most irritating woman, she on that occasion drove Hathorne to frustration.

The court heard other charges that had nothing to do with demonic conspiracies, red books, or petty theft. Newton summoned a sailor who recounted having been awoken one Sabbath at sunrise to find Bishop standing by his bed. With a smile, she struck him on the head and melted out the window. At about noon the same day she caused an apple to fly from his hand and travel more than six feet across the room. Twelve years earlier, "muttering and menacing," she had thrown hatter Samuel Shattuck's son around the house, bludgeoning him and separating him completely from all reason. (This was the unsuspecting family warned by a visitor—after one look at the child—that a witch lived in their vicinity.) She had paid the son of the miller with whom she tangled in 1688 in disappearing currency. She had caused his cart to sink into a hole that appeared out of nowhere and afterward vanished. She had bewitched a bag of corn. She slipped through locked doors and closed windows. None of those charges was remotely recent; many clustered around her earlier trial. One involved three generations. These were the ancient, dredged-up, multiply resurrected accusations that the New England air seemed to stimulate and sustain, that defied the laws of nature by growing hardier with age.

Bishop knew she occasioned whispering and that townspeople believed her a witch. She could not have been unaware that she unsettled for other reasons as well. In April the Salem marshal had cited a nocturnal visit; the June jury heard of at least five more. Bishop seemed to have a habit of hopping around young men's bedrooms, incapacitating them and striking them dumb, symptoms commonly associated with a different form of enchantment. Wanton or flirtatious, she burned bright in men's minds; they tended to recall her wardrobe precisely. When she visited the miller's son years earlier, she had professed a great affection for him, more, he testified, than was proper. He described her flashy red coat with the multicolored edging; Bishop had clapped it around her legs as she jumped into his bed. Samuel Shattuck reported that she called on him frequently for trumped-up reasons and in a "smooth, flattering manner." She pressed her lips to those of defenseless young men. Although she could not have looked it on June 2—Sewall saw her only as "an old woman"— she may once have been very beautiful.*

Salem tailor John Louder testified to a protracted, moonlit tangle with Bishop. Confronted afterward, she claimed no knowledge of that bedroom tryst; she did not intend to be held responsible for men's dreams. Shortly thereafter, home sick on a Sabbath afternoon, Louder received a terrifying visitor: a black monster leaped through his window, to stand inches away from him. A cousin of Tituba's hearthside goblin, it had the face of a man, the body of a monkey, and the feet of a cock. It had come, it announced, to rule Louder. In exchange, it promised to satisfy his every desire. "You devil, I will kill you," the tailor swore, attempting to clasp the creature but grasping only thin air. The flying monkey and Louder went a few rounds, Louder injuring his arm in the process. Lunging through a window, the creature reappeared through a locked porch door. It lured the tailor outside. As he struggled to chase it away—"The whole armor of God be between me and you!" he cried—he spied Bishop in her orchard. Ultimately the goblin launched itself over the trees, churning up a storm of dirt and fruit; Bishop would several times find herself mixed up with snakes and apples.

In her April 19 hearing Bishop had shaken her head in disbelief, grown hot under interrogation, and appealed to those in the room to clear her name. (No one volunteered.) In the case of the stolen brass, she had quarreled with testimony before a justice. Once Louder delivered up his account of the apple-scattering goblin—it left him dumb for three

* The Bishop testimony reinforces Somerset Maugham's quip: "A woman may be as wicked as she likes, but if she isn't pretty it won't do her much good." Mather stamps out any smoldering innuendo in his account, where the kisses are nowhere to be found.

days!—she weighed in. Though without counsel, she had the right to question her accusers. She did not even know Louder! She was reminded that their orchards adjoined. They had quarreled over the years. Here she stumbled upon a Catch-22 of the seventeenth-century system. Self-incrimination was not yet an issue. Questioning evidence was risky. As a justice had chided an earlier suspect, his "answer was thought overbold and uncomely for a man under such apparent guilt."

Among the reheated charges against Bishop was one piece of testimony that trumped all. It happened also to be the most ancient. Seventeen years earlier, she had hired two workmen to demolish a wall of her house. Buried within it were several rag-and-bristle poppets, headless and stuck through with pins. Pressed to explain, Bishop could offer up no reasonable explanation. She made as little progress in attempting to defend herself on June 2. Urged to confess, she insisted on her innocence. The gross lying in court, the muttering and menacing, the various enchantments, the murders, the bedroom visits, were one thing. With the poppets, with the rent in her coat, with the news that Bishop bore a supernatural mark on her body, Newton had material evidence. He received a supplementary gift as well. Probably the day before the trial, as she rode under guard past the empty town house, Bishop glanced up at the stately, heavy-timbered building. A plank crashed down from an upper story, later turning up some distance away.*

The trial proceeded smoothly and swiftly. While she could challenge the choice of jurors, Bishop could not probe them for their views. In the absence of lawyers, there were no points of procedure to be discussed. There was no voir dire, no cross-examination. The justices represented both parties, interrogating the suspect as well as her accusers. Testimony went according to plan, not only because much of it had been delivered before; Bishop appeared unable to dispute or derail it. Though distressed,

---

* We have the account solely from Mather, who has Bishop accomplish the deed with the help of an invisible demon.

the bewitched girls seem to have been relatively quiet. In his account—written later, from court papers—Mather suggested there was more evil on hand than the court knew what to do with. He did not bother to describe the charges that had landed Bishop in the courtroom in the first place for a similar reason: "There was little occasion to prove the witchcraft, it being evident and notorious to all beholders."

A seventeenth-century magistrate did not hesitate to tell jurors what they thought or how to evaluate evidence. He might direct them to find a defendant guilty. In the absence of sufficient evidence, strong suspicion would do. Reputation carried great weight, which explained how so many ostensibly nongermane testimonies against Bishop wound up in court. If guilt seemed likely but not certain—"reasonable doubt" was still nearly two centuries in the future—a sentence might be adjusted accordingly. You could be convicted of a lesser crime than that for which you had been indicted. In a closing statement, Stoughton summarized the case and reminded the jury that they were to prove the evidence. He offered some instruction that June afternoon. The jurors were to disregard the girls' robust good health. Bishop's intention alone mattered. The court did not need to prove that witchcraft had been inflicted, only that it had been deployed. That, explained the sober, much-respected chief justice, was the meaning of the law. His instructions surprised at least one observer. They flew in the face of Mather's May 31 advice; in the face of Perkins, the authoritative English expert; and in the face of New England judicial history.

Stoughton likely had his verdict by midafternoon. While the jurors had no confession, they had much else. The evidence was overwhelming. Their foreman stood to announce the decision: for having practiced witchcraft on the five village girls on April 19 and "on diverse other days and times before and after," they found Bishop guilty. The goblin in the apple tree, the bedroom visits, the poppets may have done the trick. The jury convicted however for the afflictions. The ancient histories could not be corroborated. The courtroom tortures had been witnessed by all.

In one of Salem's more unusual twists, the court found Bishop guilty for enchanting village girls she did not know, as opposed to the men in town she did.*

Doomed, she returned to prison, where just before four o'clock, the women submitted to a second strip search. Bishop's unnatural growth was nowhere to be found, proof that she had communicated with an evil spirit in the course of the day. All three suspects' marks had in fact mysteriously vanished. The protuberance discovered on the body of Rebecca Nurse had by afternoon deflated to a spot of dry skin. Its variation proved its diabolical origin; she had evidently suckled a demonic imp. (During her preliminary hearing, Hathorne had asked about any wounds. "I have naught but old age," the village great-grandmother had replied.) As for Susannah Martin, the tiny, contemptuous Amesbury widow, where her breasts had appeared full in the morning, they were lank and flattened by afternoon. She too had suckled a familiar in the course of the day. Nurse was outraged; the most practiced midwife disagreed with her colleagues. And Nurse could account for her deformities, the result of difficult labors. They had caused her trouble for years. She had not visited men's bedrooms, transformed herself into a goblin, or pried boards from public buildings with a glance. For having practiced "certain detestable arts called witchcrafts and sorceries" on four village girls, the court however indicted her on June 3.

In the village Hathorne and Corwin meanwhile continued to issue warrants and hear complaints. The Salem constable that week found a new suspect at her spinning wheel and delivered her posthaste to the authorities. Forty-year-old Ann Dolliver would have been especially easy to locate as she lodged, with her children, at the home of her father, Salem town's seventy-six-year-old senior minister, round-faced, beak-nosed John Higginson. (A Gloucester sea captain, Dolliver's husband had abandoned the family.) Dolliver was not only the daughter but also the

---

* As if her fate were not grim enough, Bishop appears to have been confused with another uncooperative suspect. John Hale testified against that Bishop; the testimony was mistakenly attached to Bridget.

granddaughter and great-granddaughter of ministers. The three men who signed the warrant for her arrest were her father's parishioners, as were her examiners. Her brother was a newly appointed magistrate. Like Abigail Hobbs, Dolliver was a wanderer, at odds with her stepmother. Long crippled by melancholy, she seemed, as one Salem resident put it, "crazed in her understanding."

Presumably out of deference to her family — a minister's daughter, she was Mrs. Dolliver in the eyes of the court — Hathorne interrogated her gently, in private. Had she ever practiced witchcraft? "Not with intent to hurt anybody" came the troubling reply. She may have been simple; she was certainly naive. She had slept in the woods late at night. She had run away from home to avoid her stepmother. After some coaxing from the girls, she revealed some additional oddities. Had she any poppets? Hathorne asked. She had two, of wax. She had made them about fourteen years earlier, when she had believed herself bewitched. She had felt the telltale pinches. (Everyone seemed to know what a witch's tweak felt like.) She read in a book that she could reverse the spell.

On the page as in person, her father was flinty and direct, a man of "soft words but hard arguments." He had forcefully expressed himself in the past, in his attacks on Quakers, on points of doctrine, an epidemic of drinking, the abuses of a royal governor, the obstreperous Salem villagers. He had had no particular use for the diabolical in his sermons, which included none of the sense of siege, the alarmist, assaultive sparks that lit up a Parris or Mather performance. Six years earlier, reconciled to the fact that he would never see the five hundred pounds of back salary the town owed him, Higginson had arranged for Salem to keep the funds but provide for his adult children, an arrangement to which the town had agreed, perhaps less cheerfully than it seemed at the time. He was not the last minister in 1692 to find his daughter accused of witchcraft. Nor does he appear to have objected to the proceedings, even when they reached his doorstep. He had not a thing to say about witchcraft, despite an unassailable position in his community, which he had energetically served for thirty-two years. Having jousted with Andros, having tangled with angry, obstinate Baptists, he went silent in 1692. He labored, he explained later, "under the infirmities of a decrepit old age." He made no mention of his daughter, imprisoned on June 6.

Three days later, Chief Justice Stoughton ordered the Salem sheriff to conduct Bridget Bishop on Friday, between eight o'clock and noon, to the appointed place of execution, "and there cause her to be hanged by the neck until she be dead." He was afterward to attest he had done so. The sheriff, Stoughton added—in an uncommon turn of phrase; there seemed some fear of escape — was to fail only at his peril.

AT SOME POINT on the morning of June 10 George Corwin—Justice Corwin's nephew, who was also one witchcraft judge's son-in-law and another's nephew—removed Bishop from prison. He arranged for her to travel by open, two-wheeled cart from the prison on what is today St. Peter Street, west along Essex Street, through central Salem, turning sharply north on the Boston road, a route of about fifteen minutes on foot. The idea was to dispense with the convicted witch as publicly as possible; Bishop rode to her death as an enchantress and an example. A full panoply of marshals and constables accompanied the procession as it rattled across a tidal inlet, up the steep path, and to a rocky ledge along a pasture overlooking the town. There a rope hung from a freshly installed gallows. Beyond lay a panoramic view of fields and marshes, inlets, head-lands, and sparkling ocean.

No eyewitness account of the hanging survives, though plenty might have. So many had streamed to a 1659 execution of a Quaker woman that the bridge over which they returned to Boston collapsed under their weight.* The stampede to a lecture before a murderer's execution in 1686 nearly brought down the First Church gallery. Five thousand turned out for that execution, some traveling from more than fifty miles away; they began to assemble a week in advance. Female malefactors were especially

---

* On the ladder, her skirts tied and face covered, the woman was reprieved. Sixty specta-tors suffered injuries on the bridge.

compelling, only more so in Bishop's case: Who doesn't care to know what a witch looks like? There had been no such execution since Mary Glover, hanged four years earlier on Boston Common for having bewitched the Goodwin children. Not only was the event so horrible as to be irresistible, but it was intended as moral instruction. It was the kind of thing to which you took the children, the well-schooled of whom learned, among other five-syllable words, "abomination," "edification," "humiliation," "mortification," "purification." A carnival atmosphere prevailed.

Ministers attended eagerly to the condemned, who on the scaffold reliably attested to the beauties of family discipline or the wisdom of the court and admonished the crowd against following in their wicked footsteps. It was not easy to rival those last-ditch expressions of remorse; a condemned pirate's regret that he had scorned his parents, embraced vice, and entangled himself with foul company made an impression. A witch merited no such treatment, however. She offered no stirring lessons in deterrence, no soul-purifying shame. Meanwhile the onlookers ached with suspense. In her final minutes would she at least confess?

Under the gallows, an officer of the court read Bishop's death warrant. Had she anything to say? She insisted on her innocence even as she climbed the ladder. There was to be no tidy satisfaction like that offered by a Connecticut witch who—repenting for her sins—"died in a frame extremely to the satisfaction of them that were spectators of it." (She was the first New Englander to confess to a devil's pact.) As Bishop's minister and at her request, John Hale seems to have offered a few last words at the foot of the gallows. A Salem shopkeeper scoffed that were he asked to pray at her execution, he would not do so; Hale heard the comment as a reproach. No doubt speaking for many, the shopkeeper excoriated Bishop. She had covenanted with the devil. He would happily have testified against her. (His wife had.) We do not know if Parris was present, although it is difficult to believe that any local minister could have absented himself, much less one who had signed four indictments against Bishop. Many of her accusers stood in the crowd, along with at least some of the bewitched girls and much of the village. A few unexpected parties turned up as well. A Salem matron watched the devil help George Jacobs up to a perch on the gallows. Mary Walcott saw Jacobs too; he beat her with his spectral walking sticks. The members of the court were themselves in Boston, at a meeting of the governor's council.

We know nothing of Bishop's last words, of who tied her skirts around her ankles or her hands behind her back, who urged her up the ladder, placed the cloth over her head, or fitted the noose around her neck. Hangmen were not easy to come by. Sheriff Corwin may himself have delivered the push that left her suspended by the neck, thrashing desperately, twitching spasmodically, finally dangling, still and silent, in mid-air. She died by slow strangulation; the end could have taken as long as an hour. It was not necessarily quiet. It could be preceded by bloodcurdling groans and—in one case—a shocking request: Having hung for some time, a 1646 malefactor asked what her executioners proposed to do next. Someone stepped forward "and turned the knot of the rope backward, and then she soon died." In New York a year earlier, the condemned was still alive when he was cut down from the gallows. The blow of an ax finished the job. Agonized cries went up from the spectators; at a later hanging, the screeches as the body dropped could be heard a mile away. Afterward it swayed in the air for some time, the crowd dispersing slowly. Bishop's could be seen across the fields for miles around and from the far side of Salem town. She died before noon; Corwin arranged for the corpse to be buried nearby, a detail he added to his report and later crossed out, presumably as he had exceeded his instructions. It is difficult to imagine who might have claimed the body. Bishop's husband appears to have absented himself from the scene. From an earlier marriage, she had a twenty-five-year-old daughter, who could only have kept her distance that season.

Across both Salems, villagers and townsfolk breathed a collective sigh of relief. They had dispatched a nuisance and a notorious sinner. Together they had engaged in a cathartic, calming ritual. They had discharged their fear; there would be no more confounding bedroom intrusions. As would be observed much later, such things were "painful, grotesque, but a scandal was after all a sort of service to the community." The wise magistrates whose praises Mather sang in his charter-selling sermon—the authorities who were to clear the woods of Indians and the sea of pirates—were on their way to clearing the air of evil; the charter enjoined those men to "kill, slay, destroy, and conquer" anyone who attempted to invade or annoy Massachusetts. Wrongs were righted and reason returned—in one case, quite literally. A decade earlier Bishop had pried a woman from her bed and nearly drowned her. The woman was thereafter insane, "a vexation to herself and all about her." With Bishop's arrest, her condition improved. And as Bishop swung from the gallows, the woman miraculously emerged from her decade of madness. The execution worked a spell of its own over Essex County, where—Mather would note—many "marvelously recovered their senses." Accusations ceased over the next weeks, as did arrests. The girls appeared symptom-free, the jailed witches incapacitated. Both Salems had reason to believe themselves safe.

One other person might have as well. The day after Bishop's execution, five hundred Wabanaki and French descended upon Wells, Maine, with shouts, shots, and flaming arrows, "a formidable crew of dragons, coming with open mouth upon them, to swallow them up at a mouthful," as Mather later described it. Over two days a band of fifteen men managed to hold off the attackers. The Wabanaki all the same made off with a captive. In full view of the settlers, just beyond musket range, they stripped, scalped, and castrated him, slicing open his fingers and toes and inserting burning coals under the skin before leaving him to die. George Burroughs was spared that sight and the horrific, two-day siege of his parishioners, safe as he was in the eternal dark of Boston's dungeon.

The remainder of the summer was, Mather noted in his diary at some indeterminate point later in the year, "a very doleful time, unto the whole country."

VII

---◇---

NOW THEY SAY THERE IS ABOVE
SEVEN HUNDRED IN ALL

*Nature has given women so much power that the law has very
wisely given them little.*
—SAMUEL JOHNSON

GOVERNOR PHIPS SPOKE accurately when he hailed the Salem justices
as the best and brightest. Well-read, widely traveled, they were men of
integrity, familiar with the workings of the court, an inevitable stop on
the way to a New England fortune.* Many had handed down unpopular
decisions. Several had witnessed trials in London. They lived in the finest
brick mansions and gabled homes in their respective towns. The burden
of proof rested on the prosecution, but the prosecution enjoyed a few
seventeenth-century advantages. An English trial of the time was inquis-
itorial, an informal, free-form, hectic, rapid-fire contest best described as
"a relatively spontaneous bicker between accusers and accused." Across
the board, standards of proof were imprecise. A suspect had no idea of
the evidence against her until she stepped into the courtroom, where she
could be convicted of a different crime than the one for which she stood

---

* As one scholar put it, the accepted wisdom appeared to be that if you sued, you were better off socioeconomically. "If you sued a lot, you were better off still."

206

indicted. She had the right to defend herself but no guarantee she would be heard. Protests of innocence carried little weight. "I am no thief," a defendant in a larceny case insisted two generations later. "You must prove that," replied the judge. A valued legal treatise recommended deposing the defendant's adversaries, for such people "will pry very narrowly into everything." As only witnesses for the prosecution testified under oath, their word carried greater weight. Hearsay was perfectly acceptable, which explained how — at Bishop's trial — Samuel Shattuck could testify about a stranger who divined that Bishop had bewitched a child. That was the guest who insisted a quarrelsome witch lived nearby. Only then did Shattuck recall a tense encounter between his wife and Bishop, who had stalked off, muttering. Soon afterward, Shattuck's son fell ill. The stranger had acted no differently from the fortune-teller who intuits that you have recently suffered a setback; she is unfailingly correct. Witchcraft merely supplied the culprit, sometimes in advance of her crime, often many years later. There was in 1692 a certain amount of relitigating ancient offenses. It was not a summer when you wanted to appear in your neighbor's dreams.

No fewer than five men sat in judgment over Bridget Bishop. We can be certain of the identities of only three. They did not hear the case the same way. All had graduated from Harvard, approximately a decade apart. Each had opted for a more secular career than the one for which he had been educated.* Amiable, heavyset Samuel Sewall was the only one of the three courteous enough to leave a diary. Salem witchcraft was something one talked of endlessly but wrote about very little; Sewall made no entries over the month of June, remaining silent until mid-July. He would write more expansively on Salem later. The kind of father who devoted his morning to a teenager's spiritual crisis, Sewall worried always that he did "much harm and little good," an equation he struggled to invert. He shrank from the censure of friends; he was appalled in 1701

---

* An Oxford MA in divinity presided over the 1692 trials while a minister with no degree preached in Salem village. Both were anomalies for the time.

when, at the top of his lungs, Cotton Mather excoriated him—Mather could be heard from the street—in a bookstore. (Sewall the next day attempted to placate his irate friend with a fine haunch of venison. He failed.) He wrote even a cordial dunning letter. He compared himself unfavorably to his mother-in-law. Sewall moved at a deliberate pace; with reason, colleagues accused him of temporizing. He did not naturally oppose authority, something that on occasion also discomfited him. He had been displeased with himself for having bowed to pressure when—his dear friend and fellow witchcraft justice Wait Still Winthrop forcing his hand—agreed at the last minute to reprieve a pirate. Never before had he adjudicated a witchcraft case.

Two days after Bishop's hanging, Sewall took his place in the pews of Boston's Old South Church for Samuel Willard's afternoon sermon. Several other justices joined him there. The son of one of Massachusetts's founding families, Wait Still Winthrop, sat nearby, as did Peter Sergeant. What Willard had to say that afternoon both reassured and disturbed. Taking 1 Peter 5:8 as his text, he reminded his congregants that they were to be sober-minded and watchful. The devil ranged among them, eager to pounce. He reserved his greatest malice for the pious. Willard confirmed Mather's millennial note; the fiend was at his most violent when his time was short. The devil, noted Willard, could represent anyone he pleased; he required no pact. Willard appealed for charity and compassion. Some matters, he held, should be left to divine adjudication.

That possibility—that one might well work witchcraft without having consented, much less contracted, to do so—struck Chief Justice Stoughton as unlikely. The eldest of the three Harvard-educated judges, sixty-year-old Stoughton demonstrated a gift for extracting himself from controversies that tended to sink lesser men. Far steelier than Sewall, he knew a great deal about law enforcement. Massachusetts legal code carefully and clearly enumerated crimes but could be opaque regarding court procedures. On the one hand, leniency was preferred. On the other hand, offenses that undermined society as a whole demanded swift prosecution. And the province faced a crisis of unprecedented proportions.

Never before had it suffered a witchcraft epidemic. Even those unsympathetic to the Puritan establishment were astonished. To a half-amused New York Anglican, it seemed as if Cotton Mather had been prescient two years earlier when he had warned that Satan schemed to wrench the colony from Puritan hands. The devil indeed now seemed on the verge of depopulating Massachusetts. There were over one hundred suspects in jail, most of them church members, elders, and deacons, reported the New Yorker. A minister rotted in prison, as did another's daughter. The wife of a third had been named. The wretches betrayed one another so quickly that "now they say there is above seven hundred in all." (That was untrue, although it was true that more witches were jailed than had been convicted in all the years of New England history combined.) To someone like Stoughton, it seemed as if everything in which he believed stood in jeopardy. That fear galloped across New England. On June 22, Connecticut established a witchcraft court to address an epidemic of its own.

Enforcing the laws of New England qualified as a sacred duty. The justices approached it scrupulously, consulting authoritative legal texts and following the letter of the law. Some dissension nonetheless arose among the ranks. Within days of Bishop's hanging, fifty-three-year-old Nathaniel Saltonstall, the third Harvard-educated justice, resigned from the Court of Oyer and Terminer. An Ipswich native, the grandson of an early Bay Colony leader, Saltonstall sat regularly on the Massachusetts bench. He had lobbied in London on New England's behalf alongside Increase Mather. A highly popular militia captain, he had served on the Maine frontier. Principles had tripped him up before and may have done so again; in 1687 he had refused to cooperate with Andros, an offense for which he spent fifteen days in prison. It is unclear if Saltonstall caviled with the Bishop verdict or the execution. An observer later allowed simply that "he has left the court, and is very much dissatisfied with the proceedings of it." He was not replaced.

Although he excused himself from the court, Saltonstall does not seem to have offered a public statement. When you questioned the proceedings, specters had a habit of assuming your shape; it was a short step from urging caution to fending off accusation. Already Mather peered nervously over his shoulder, wondering when the devil would begin to masquerade in his guise. (It would not be long.) An Andover constable would balk at further arrests, dubious about the charges; he landed in prison. Indeed, within the year, a report of Saltonstall's specter began to circulate. More than ever it was true that—as Baxter had it, paraphrasing Luke, in a line Parris would adapt—"If you are not for Christ and his works, you are against him."

Skepticism tended to burst forth, execute a few mincing steps, then burrow underground, spooked by its shadow. No one pointed out that thirty-six-year-old Sarah Bibber—whom the spectral Burroughs had accompanied to his hearing and who now writhed alongside the girls— was a known scandalmonger, double-tongued and mischief-making. On no front were lips more suddenly pursed than when it came to counter-suits. Prior to 1692, defamation had represented a lively New England business. In one of the earliest Massachusetts witchcraft proceedings, a woman received twenty lashes for calling another a witch. The Salem woman of whom it had been said that "she was a witch and if she were not a witch already she would be one and therefore it was as good to hang her at first as last" sued successfully for defamation. Often the cases pitted men against each other, one having lobbed an accusation at the other's wife. Susannah Martin's husband had filed and won a defamation suit after her 1669 witchcraft trial.

Francis Nurse had sued successfully both for defamation and slander. He brought no such action in 1692, when it might too easily have mis-fired. What prevailed instead was Mather's admonition that "if the neigh-bor of an elected saint sins, then the saint sins also." There was no odium attached to delivering up your fellow villager; in 1692 it was better to accuse than be suspected of complicity. To fail to report an offense con-stituted an offense of its own. Moreover, by informing, you did your part for the community. Hostile words that had earlier produced slander suits seemed in 1692 diverted to witchcraft accusations.

A rustle of doubt all the same made itself felt. Three days after Bishop's execution, Phips met with his council, which included Chief Justice Stoughton. They requested some guidance. Over the next days, twelve ministers conferred. Cotton Mather drafted their joint reply, delivered on June 15. While pages seemed to issue from Mather in his sleep, "The Return of Several Ministers Consulted" was a circumspect, eight-paragraph document over which he labored.* In two paragraphs Mather acknowledged the enormity of the crisis and issued a paean to good government. In two more he urged "exquisite caution." He addressed procedural issues: The courtroom should be as quiet and neutral as possible. Susceptible as they were to abuse by the "devil's legerdemains," practices like the touch test should be deployed carefully. The same went for the evil eye, by no means infallible. Yet again Mather held up English authorities Perkins and Bernard as the gold standard. He sounded a more tentative note than he had two weeks earlier in his discursive letter to John Richards.

In the lines that surely received the greatest scrutiny, Mather reminded the justices that convictions should not rest purely on spectral evidence, to which only the enchanted were privy. He had said as much already; he would insist on the point through the summer. Other considerations must weigh against the suspected witch, "inasmuch as 'tis an undoubted and a notorious thing" that a devil might impersonate an innocent, even a virtuous, man. In a contorted penultimate paragraph, Mather wondered if the entire calamity might be resolved were the court to discount those very testimonies. With a sweeping "nevertheless"—a word that figured in every 1692 Mather witchcraft statement—he then executed an about-face. His "very critical and exquisite caution" became, five

---

* Mather could have an anxiety dream about an unprepared sermon and go on to compose it in his sleep. Between 1689 and 1691, he published twenty-two volumes. He knew people disliked him for publishing so much. He was unrepentant. On a 1699 list of "favors of heaven" came, in third place, "that I should be a more silly and shallow person than most in this country; and yet write and print more books, and have greater opportunities to do good by my published composures, than any man that ever was in this country, or indeed in all America."

paragraphs later, a vote for a "speedy and vigorous prosecution." The ministers endorsed the prosecution of those who had "rendered themselves obnoxious, according to the direction given in the laws of God, and the wholesome statutes of the English nation, for the detection of witchcrafts." Equivocal though he remained, Mather came down emphatically on two points: Their case was extraordinary. The New England magistrate was no less so. Mather would apologize several times for his incoherence on a devilish subject.

Other clergymen were more cogent. In June a Baptist preacher named William Milborne submitted two petitions to the Massachusetts General Assembly. Milborne had preached for some time in Saco, Maine; Burroughs's plight may have occasioned his protest. (In all ways, one had to be wary of one's friends. Milborne's defense may have encouraged the idea that Burroughs was a Baptist, considered heretics and nearly as dangerous as Quakers.) "Several persons of good fame and of unspotted reputation," Milborne pointed out, were jailed on witchcraft charges. They had committed imaginary crimes. He urged the justices to discount specious evidence; they stood in grave danger of convicting innocents. Milborne had come to the ministry with a legal degree and a background in whaling. He was also a known troublemaker who hailed from a family of troublemakers. He tussled with both congregants and political authorities.*

Phips ordered Milborne's arrest, yet another acknowledgment of the churning tide in 1692; the two had previously been allies, having made common cause with common friends. Milborne had helped foment the rebellion against Andros. On June 25, the minister found himself summoned to explain his "seditious and scandalous papers." For his potent "reflections upon the administrations of public justice," the court offered him his choice between jail and a crushing two-hundred-pound bond. Cotton Mather had bought his home and a tract of land for the same

---

* Milborne's younger brother had been beheaded for treason in New York a year earlier; he was the criminal not yet dead when cut down from the gallows. Thomas Newton had prosecuted the case.

sum. Milborne was not heard from again. Two days after his arrest—by which time it was clear the New England ministers might differ from the magistrates but would entrust witchcraft to their better judgment—the Court of Oyer and Terminer called its next eight suspects.

THE PURITAN MINISTER in an apocalyptic frame of mind, the Crown prosecutor preparing his case, and the Massachusetts farmer pondering the sudden death of his cow all engaged in the same exercise. Mind quickening, pulse hammering, each went into analytic overdrive. How to make sense of the ominous and inexplicable without clobbering the dog that was really a child? Rummaging about for the pattern that had to be there somewhere, he ventured into the coincidence-free sector between faith and paranoia, both invested in global, half-visible designs. And he did so as only a fundamentalist, a prosecutor, or an adolescent will: with the heady conviction that he was incontestably, blindingly right.

No other witchcraft suspect could rival Bridget Bishop for supernatural activity or bedroom disturbances. One other could account for yellow birds, cats, stalking wolves. Five confessed witches—including her own daughter—had named her. Her husband noted the strange mark on her shoulder. She had suckled a familiar on her finger. Her name turned up in the devil's book. She had ridden on a pole to the parsonage meadow for Burroughs's "hellish meeting." On a fresh sheet of paper, Thomas Newton outlined his case against Sarah Good, the Salem beggar, noting with satisfaction that the testimony of the bewitched and the confessors regarding the witches' Sabbath conformed. Newton relied on a detailed abstract he had made of Tituba's account, tidy in its cause and effect: Good visited the parsonage. She mumbled under her breath. The children fell ill. Moreover, only their victims and their confederates could see the witches. Good had seen Osborne, whose powers did not level her. Good, reasoned the attorney general, "must consequently be a witch." The pieces fit together seamlessly.

The call for jurors had hardly gone out when Sarah Good began afflicting again. On June 28 Susannah Shelden contorted before the grand jury to whom she submitted testimony that, as recently as two days earlier, Good had pricked, pinched, and nearly choked her to death. Good had lashed her hands together so tightly that two men had had to rescue her; they understood it was the fourth time in two weeks the eighteen-year-old had found her wrists bound. It was on one such occasion that the broom had wound up in the apple tree; between fits, Shelden told of invisible hands that had stolen a saucer from the table. She had watched Good carry it outside. The Procters' maid also writhed before the grand jurors; Shelden explained that Good assaulted her. Under oath Sarah Bibber swore that Good had bewitched her four-year-old. Parris swore to the sufferings of the girls during the March preliminary hearing. The grand jury handed down at least three indictments against Good, whose trial began immediately. Although she was about Bibber's age, she looked decrepit. For weeks already her clothes had been in shreds. If earlier she had mumbled like a witch, she had come to resemble one. She had been in jail since February with a nursing child, and, for some length of time, with the dying Osborne.

Good tended to seize opportunities to speak her mind, a reason she stood before a panel of black-gowned justices in the first place. It is more likely that she entered a screed into the record than a hopeless, half-hearted denial. A guilty plea at this juncture would in any event have accomplished little. Between the girls' flailing and the mountain of evidence, her arraignment and trial extended over two days. At its end, the jury delivered a guilty verdict. It little surprised one Boston observer, who commented on the formulaic, one-size-fits-all approach in Salem. As he saw it, "The same evidence that served for one would serve for all the rest."

Neither John Hale nor Deodat Lawson, both present, wrote about Sarah Good. Nor did Cotton Mather. A burden to her community, a menace and a malcontent, she was not noteworthy. The case against her was largely spectral. The two accused witches who followed—over the course of the week the grand jury heard eight cases and the trial jury five — interested Mather more. No confederate had implicated Susannah Martin, the tart-tongued, seventy-one-year-old Amesbury woman who had scoffed at the idea that the girls were bewitched, suggesting that they practiced black magic themselves. Martin had stood accused once already for witchcraft, however. Evidence suggested that in the course of Bishop's trial, she had nursed an imp. As in that case, Newton could appeal not only to the bewitched girls but to a procession of afflicted men as well. Constables located a dozen in all. They had no need to resort to fits to express themselves, testifying straightforwardly, persuasively, and without interruption.

Martin too pestered men in their beds. She bit fingers and transformed herself into a black hog. She specialized in animals; the justices heard of drowned oxen, crazed cows, blighted cattle, flying puppies, dogs transformed into kegs, killer cats. Martin made sense of other oddities as well, having had several decades to do so. Over two years, a Salisbury man had been carried about by demons. For six months of that time, they rendered him mute. He now swore that at their hellish meetings, meetings at which he was offered a book to sign in exchange for "all the delectable things, persons, and places that he could imagine," he had seen Martin. A fifty-three-year-old who many years earlier could not find his way home one Saturday night — although he was but three miles away and walking in bright moonlight — attributed his disorientation to Martin. Just beyond her field he stumbled into a ditch that he knew full well was not there.

Susannah Martin had quibbled over church seating. She drove a hard bargain. She exchanged cross words with her brother-in-law. She scorned those who had testified against her in 1669, as many colorfully recalled. When a Salisbury carpenter allowed in the course of that trial that he believed her to be a witch, Martin had promised "that some she-devil would shortly fetch him away." The killer cat had pounced the next night, lunging at his throat as he lay in bed. After a Salisbury woman had appeared before the earlier grand jury, Martin startled her while she was out milking the cow. "For thy defaming me at court," she swore, "I'll make thee the miserablest creature in the world." Two months later, out of the blue, the woman began to spew nonsense. Physicians declared her bewitched, as she remained for two decades.*

It is difficult to say which came first: Was Martin, like Bridget Bishop, strident because she had stood trial previously, or had she stood trial previously because she was strident? Witchcraft inscribed a vicious circle, its allegation generating witchlike behavior. There appeared no other response to an accusation than a malediction, which explained at least some of Martin's unminced words. Singled out earlier, she attracted charges; 1692 was a good time to revive old ones. Once questions arise we sift for answers. And when it comes to blame, none of us draws a blank; only after Bridget Bishop told the miller's son of the rumors swirling around her did odd things begin to happen to him. We have no record of what Martin said—to her accusers or the magistrates—on June 29, though she remained defiant throughout the proceedings. "Her chief plea," Cotton Mather noted, based on pages lost to us, "was that she had led a most virtuous and holy life." That struck him as blasphemous. The jurors agreed, returning a guilty verdict. Months later, the court documents in hand, Mather offered the last word on Susannah Martin, whom he had not met and no longer could: "This woman was one of the most impudent, scurrilous, wicked creatures in the world."

Two other cases that week turned on natural grudges and preternatural pranks. The evidence against Topsfield's Elizabeth How featured a full collection of fairy-tale marvels: leaping pigs, poisoned turnips, self-emptying vessels, dissolving fence posts, amnesia-inducing apples. Her case differed from Martin's in two crucial respects. The ox sacrificed to the turnip belonged to one brother-in-law, the leaping sow to another. When named in May, Elizabeth How had applied to the first brother-in-law for assistance. Might he accompany her to Salem? Her blind husband could not make the trip; she had no desire to go alone. She

---

* The doctor concluded that "some evil person" had bewitched her. In his account, Mather preferred "some devil had certainly bewitched her."

too discovered how difficult it was to outrun the cloud of suspicion that, once raised, wafted about the neighborhood. For any other reason he would readily accompany her, the in-law replied. Here he drew the line. He bargained with her: "If you are a witch, tell me how long you have been a witch and what mischief you have done and then I will go with you." The next day his sow leaped three to four feet in the early-evening air, "turning about, squeaking, falling, and dying."

In his account of her trial Cotton Mather did not note a significant advantage fifty-five-year-old Elizabeth How had over the previous suspects: No fewer than twelve people testified in her defense, two ministers among them. She had never been anything other than a good Christian, faithful in her promises, just in her dealings, pious in her beliefs. Her husband's family did not abandon her entirely; her ninety-four-year-old father-in-law described her devotion to his blind son, whom she gently led about by the hand. She tended their farm. She cared for their six children. An Ipswich shoemaker testified that How spoke no ill of her accusers, who she thought harmed themselves more than they did her. All kinds of alarm bells sounded in the How testimony. The Rowley assistant minister took it upon himself to join How on a visit to a ten-year-old girl whom she had allegedly bewitched. The child said nothing of her, in her convulsions or afterward. She managed even to take How's hand in the minister's presence. Had she hurt her? "No, never," replied the child. The minister later sat outdoors with the girl. From an upstairs window her brother called down: "Say Goodwife How is a witch, say she is a witch!"

The Salem jurors heard of enchanted hay and bewitched rope when Sarah Wilds came before them the same day. Her case prominently featured malicious relatives. She had been an easy target, arriving too promptly in a family that still mourned Wilds's previous wife. Though confined to the home, women were the geographically mobile ones in New England; they were the strangers who came to town. The Topsfield constable had weeks earlier rounded up and delivered the Hobbses to Salem; he was Wilds's son. "I have had serious thoughts many times since," twenty-eight-year-old Ephraim Wilds told the court, "whether my seizing of them might not be some cause of her thus accusing my mother." Retaliation seemed likely; in arresting Hobbs, he "almost saw revenge in her face, she looked so maliciously on me." At a time when it still seemed possible to walk out of court with a reprieve, How and Wilds no doubt insisted on their innocence. Generally the courtroom rejoinders seem to have fallen somewhere between Joan of Arc's straight-spined "People have been hung for telling the truth before now," and Dorothy's wide-eyed, back-in-Kansas "Doesn't anybody believe me?" No demonic Sabbaths or diabolical pacts figured among the charges against either woman. Both had defenders. Wilds was a full church member. Flying pigs, bewitched hay, and misbehaving scythes made indelible impressions, however. The jury found both women guilty of witchcraft.

Mather elected not to write of another case tried that Wednesday or of a suspect to whom the adjectives "impudent, scurrilous, and wicked" had never been applied. No one had accused Rebecca Nurse of witchcraft before 1692. She had never so much as appeared in court. Nor since the arrival of the marshal on her doorstep, weeks earlier, had anyone launched as concerted a defense as the large and influential Nurse clan. Theirs was a family in which brothers-in-law rode to the rescue rather than prodding the accused to confess to witchcraft. Francis Nurse had energetically canvassed the village, riding door to door with a petition asserting that his wife was, as she had claimed in March—five girls and two grown women flailing about her—as innocent "as the child unborn." Thirty-nine villagers signed Nurse's petition, although it did nothing to free his wife from jail or exempt her from two brutal physical examinations. Samuel Sibley, husband of the witch-cake baker, signed, as did seven Putnams (including one of Nurse's original accusers), the father of an afflicted eleven-year-old, and three of the four church members who had called on Nurse to tell her of her plight, a group that included Justice Hathorne's sister. (Parris remained staunchly on the other side, his niece among the four signatories to the indictments.) No case so sharply divided the community.*

Francis Nurse launched a more targeted offensive as well. On June 29 the jury heard evidence not only against his wife but also her accusers. A villager swore that Dr. Griggs's maid had lied about having attended meeting the previous month. Having sat at Rebecca's bedside over the previous weeks, a neighbor pointed out several inconsistencies in Susannah Shelden's story. The witches had hauled Susannah through the grass and over stone walls on her belly, like a snake. No; she had surmounted the wall herself. She had flown on a pole to Boston. No; the devil had carried her through the air. A Beverly couple who had employed the Putnams' maid several years earlier observed that the nineteen-year-old enjoyed an arm's-length relationship with the truth. Francis Nurse had no trouble discrediting spiteful Sarah Bibber; for all the love of her neighbors, she sounds like someone who, had she not joined the girls, would have been accused of witchcraft herself. She had a testy relationship with her husband. She wished her child ill. She spoke obscenely; she had long taken to falling into fits when crossed. Three different villagers denounced her as an "unruly, turbulent spirit." The resolute Nurses corroborated what witchcraft allegations tended to prove: No one was misdemeanor-free.

The case against Rebecca Nurse was thin on the occult; her husband did his best to tug the supernatural rug wholly out from under it. The parents of an alleged victim testified that their child's death was due purely to "a malignant fever." They entertained no witchcraft suspicions. Nathaniel Putnam, who had waged an interminable battle against the Nurses over their neighboring lands, testified in Rebecca's defense, although his nephew had pressed the initial charges. Putnam had known the pious great-grandmother for years. She had raised and educated a

---

* It divided individuals too. Imperative as it was to take sides in 1692, some villagers took several. John Putnam Sr. seems to have been both for and against Nurse.

good and godly family. While she had differed with neighbors, he had never heard a whisper regarding sorcery. The defendant did what she could to return common sense to the scene. Before the court reconvened, she submitted a request. She had endured two invasive physical examinations. The experienced woman on that panel—"the most ancient, skillful prudent person of them all"—had disagreed with the rest. Might the authorities dispatch a professional? Nurse suggested a few names. Two of her daughters confirmed that their mother had been troubled for years by complications from childbirth, though "the jury of women seem to be afraid it should be something else."

In the jittery courtroom the girls impressed their infirmities on the jury. Already pins punctured their lips, in one case binding them together; Ann Putnam plucked another from her hand at the How hearing. During Rebecca Nurse's trial, Sarah Bibber clasped her hands to her knees and howled in pain: the witch had pricked her! Unfortunately Nurse's daughter had kept an eye on Bibber; she saw her pull pins from her clothing and jab herself. At one point court officers escorted Abigail and Deliverance Hobbs into the room. Nurse knew the Topsfield mother and daughter from prison. What were they doing there? she asked, startled. The question would return to haunt her. And it did nothing to derail the account of the occult Sabbath at which Nurse had officiated, seated, asserted Parris's niece, in the place of honor, at the devil's side.

Some discreet backpedaling took place. Ann Putnam Sr. figured among Nurse's original accusers. She had disputed Scripture with the spectral Nurse in Deodat Lawson's presence. Ann's husband had carried her out of Nurse's March hearing, at which Ann had gone stiff as a plank. She was nowhere near the Salem courtroom that Wednesday. Nurse's case involved no flying apples and, at best, one malediction: she had railed against a wandering pig. The family had stature in the community; there was a solid sliver of hope. After a short deliberation—the suspect presumably remained in the courtroom, dimly aware of the clamor and clatter around her—the jury returned to their seats. Stoughton called for their verdict. It sent a ripple of astonishment through the room. Standing, the foreman declared the defendant not guilty. Any cries of relief on the part of the Nurse clan were drowned out by the accusers, who erupted in hideous roars. An echo rose to meet them from outside. Not everyone had expected the Nurses to prevail, least of all the judges, who made their irritation known. One openly declared himself disappointed. Another swore to re-indict Nurse, as he well could.

Stoughton turned to the jurors. He had no intention of imposing his opinions on them. But had they duly considered Nurse's reaction to Deliverance Hobbs? At the sight of her, the prisoner had let slip something along the lines of "She is one of us," always loaded words. Hobbs was by her own admission a witch. With that remark, had Nurse not acknowledged, Stoughton wondered, that she was one too? Perhaps that was a confession they had heard? (Judges did not hesitate to question jury decisions, although they more often challenged, and commuted, convictions. It was exceedingly rare for one to question an acquittal.) Distressed by the pandemonium they had created, the jurors asked to re-deliberate. It is impossible to know how the strain felt to the Nurse family, much less to the stunned, half-deaf defendant, an invalid well before her nine weeks in prison.

Behind closed doors the jury did its best to parse Rebecca Nurse's outburst. Had she meant that she and Hobbs were fellow prisoners or fellow witches? The twelve men could not agree; the court awaited not only a decision but a unanimous one. The foreman remained mystified. "I could not tell how to take her words," he afterward explained. By themselves, they did not appear to incriminate. The jurors reassumed their seats for some clarification. Nurse stood at the bar. The foreman repeated the baffling line to her. As recorded, she had asked: "What? Do these persons give in evidence against me now? They used to come among us." What exactly, he asked, had Nurse meant? She stood silently, in an unresponsive daze. The jury waited for but received no elucidation, "whereupon," the sixty-year-old foreman revealed days later, "these words were to me a principal evidence against her." For a third time the jury deliberated. They handed Stoughton a guilty verdict.

Francis Nurse pressed them: What could account for their reversal after twelve men had agreed they had insufficient evidence to convict? And Rebecca Nurse explained herself soon enough, having conferred with someone familiar with the law. She submitted a paper to the court; she had intended nothing by her remark other than that the Hobbs women were her fellow prisoners. She had been taken aback. How could accused criminals provide legal evidence against another? (They could, as accomplices.) She may have meant only that the two women—with whom she had shared every minute of a shameful, terrifying incarceration—were her friends. It had not occurred to her that her remark could be interpreted differently. As for her silence, she was, she reminded the magistrates, "hard of hearing, and full of grief." Not having grasped that they had misconstrued her words, she had had no opportunity to set the matter straight. Even at her March examination she had had difficulty understanding precisely what was asked, hardly the first defendant to report as much. (Of course she had not heard the magistrates, sneered her accusers. The devil whispered at her ear!) She remained deaf not only to the proceedings but to any nuance in her statement. From the jury's point of view, she had baldly incriminated herself.

Francis Nurse lost no time in requesting the court transcripts. Sewall provided what he could. Some testimony was oral, as Hobbs's must have been; Sewall had nothing on paper. His wife's statement and the villagers' signatures in hand, Nurse prepared a fresh appeal, petitioning Governor Phips for a reprieve. Meanwhile Reverend Noyes arranged for Rebecca to make another public appearance. The following Sunday, he brought her to the meetinghouse in which she had prayed for decades. It was a communion day; the portly, stiff-necked minister had a full house. Should a convicted witch remain a member of the congregation? Phrased as such, the answer was entirely obvious. It was the church's godly duty to purify their ranks; Nurse defiled them all with her crimes. After the sacrament, with a unanimous show of hands, the Salem congregation voted to issue a formal sentence of excommunication, something of a rarity by 1692. It carried no legal ramifications; a parishioner was excommunicated for trampling the laws of God, not man. Under normal circumstances the penalty was temporary. A sinner could repent, be absolved of his sin, and rejoin the parish. A witch could not.

On the afternoon of July 3 the Salem elders assumed their seats before the congregation, the deacons in the first rows. Nurse stood in the center aisle, chained. Her minister pronounced her an unclean person, an admonition that could be lengthy and that detailed her offenses all over again. He then delivered some version of the vituperative sentence handed to Ann Hibbins and Anne Hutchinson a half century earlier: "I do here and in the name of Christ Jesus and His Church deliver you up to Satan and to his power and working." The sentence was a dreadful one; the shame for a woman whose life had revolved around her faith, whose neighbors now reviled her as a witch, whose two sisters lay in chains in Boston, would have been excruciating, the more so as Noyes did vituperation well. He barred Nurse from the congregation, a formality given her current prison address though an insult to her crusading husband, who had demonstrated that many in no way shunned his wife. The fragile seventy-one-year-old who had assured her March callers that she felt closer to the Almighty in her sickness than she did in good health was henceforth to withdraw herself, like a leper, from the parish. She would never again be allowed to take communion. Noyes consigned her soul to everlasting hell.

THE COURT OF Oyer and Terminer proceeded with all five late-June suspects as they had with Bridget Bishop three weeks earlier. In the intervening weeks, the justices had hanged a witch and solicited counsel; the ministers submitted their recommendations. Where they warned against "noise, company, and openness," the Salem town house reverberated with cries. The clergy denounced the touch test and the evil eye. They expressed doubt about spectral evidence, a matter that continued to preoccupy them; late in June, as the court reconvened, the Massachusetts ministers settled on that question for their late-summer meeting. Might the devil disguise himself as an innocent in order to work his diabolical art? If he could, those who afflicted did so involuntarily. The judges meanwhile had moved on. Ultimately the clergymen's counsel carried as much weight as the remark of a young citizen who preferred the evidence before his eyes to the wisdom of the crowd. The emperor, cried the little boy, wore no clothes! Indeed he did not. But he stiffened his spine as his procession continued, a page holding high the imaginary, multicolored mantle.

A Puritan minister appeared black in dress from head to toe; plenty of somber suits graced the Salem courtroom. Deodat Lawson returned for some portion of the June trials. A Watertown minister—he happened to be Jonathan Corwin's stepson—made the trip to Salem to observe the extraordinary events. He left utterly flummoxed. The only lessons he could extract were to tread gently and demonstrate great care for those around him. Parris was in the courtroom daily. He and John Hale testified against both Topsfield witches, Sarah Wilds and Elizabeth How. Noyes was unlikely to have missed a session; for weeks he had interrogated witnesses, gathered evidence, and challenged testimony. Along with pin-wielding Sarah Bibber, the girls held the room rapt; they continued to be "struck dumb, deaf, blind, and sometimes lay as if they were dead for a while," noted an observer. The eyeballs rolling back in the heads, the flailing limbs made all acts of malfeasance seem plausible. By June the bewitched were themselves instruments in more expert hands, however; the narrative had swallowed them up. They could be sidelined or corrected. The bench openly reprimanded one girl for lying. Another accused Samuel Willard, minister to three of the justices, a signatory to Mather's June 15 letter, and among the most respected men in Boston. Over the searingly hot, uncommonly dry summer, Willard preached a cycle of sermons on the devil. He expertly elicited false confessions and conjured false reports; his quarry might be oblivious to—and therefore innocent of—the abuse. Willard's point was unmistakable. His reward was to be accused of witchcraft. The bench dismissed his accuser from court, letting it be known that the girl "was mistaken in the person."

As was clear from Rebecca Nurse's short-lived acquittal, jurors arrived freely at their decision. The afflicted indeed shrieked in response. But it was the bench that officially frowned on the verdict. And it was the chief justice who stepped in to ask if those twelve upstanding men might have overlooked a clue. He drew their attention to crucial bits of evidence. He may well have interpreted Nurse's silence for them; it was in his power to elicit a response from the bewildered defendant, whom he did not pursue. His disapproval weighed heavily on the jurors, much in the thrall of "the honored court" to which they submitted their decision. There was no question to whom the Salem courtroom belonged.

Sixty-year old William Stoughton assumed the ego-trampling, alibi-crushing role of John Hathorne, a decade his junior. To the job Stoughton brought more judicial experience than anyone in the province. As deputy governor, he was second only to Phips in the new administration. Pale and long-faced, with a high forehead, deep-set eyes, and a collection of chins, he was among the court's eldest members. A fine orator, persuasive and widely admired, he summed up evidence for the jurors at trial's end and issued their instructions. We have no sense of Stoughton's voice, though we know it impressed his peers. Presumably he spoke with the harsh, high-pitched scrape of New England. Whether one desired a speedy and vigorous prosecution, to resolve a dispute over the location of a meetinghouse, to effect a prisoner exchange with the Wabanaki, or to discipline an obstreperous political official, Stoughton was the man to call. With a crisp command of both old and New England code, he had for years been the go-to person for legal advice.* He was specifically requested when tempers flared. English officials repeatedly bemoaned the dearth of qualified civil servants in Massachusetts; they cited Stoughton as a rare exception. He knew how to proceed with exquisite caution, dampening explosions, tacking gracefully among egos and administrations. He would smooth the waters when, in council, William Phips

---

* By the laws of England, Stoughton assured Plymouth's governor in 1681, a jury's verdict of not guilty could mean nothing other than not guilty. In colonial practice, the prisoner could be dealt a grievous punishment regardless, commensurate with the magnitude of his crime.

informed the New Hampshire lieutenant governor he was "an impudent, saucy, pitiful jakanapes."

A lifelong bachelor, Stoughton was the second son of an early Massachusetts magistrate, a leading colonial light and early Harvard benefactor, a founder of Dorchester, a pleasant town of about two hundred homes, scenically spread along two lazy rivers, lush with orchards and gardens. Socially, Stoughton ranked highest in his Harvard class. He completed a master's degree at Oxford. He afterward preached part-time in Dorchester but resisted regular calls to accept its pulpit. Well-connected, beautifully educated, he was a choice candidate. Six attractive ministerial offers came his way; he declined each, opting instead for a political career. He enjoyed a meteoric rise. He settled into a Dorchester mansion surrounded by extensive pastures, meadows, orchards, cornfields, and a salt marsh.

At thirty-six, the first of his generation to do so, Stoughton preached the influential 1668 election sermon in Boston, essentially a state of the union address, distributed afterward to town leaders. In a cool-headed discourse, Stoughton ably burnished New England's founding myth. It reverberated; his words were still being cited twenty-four years later. American exceptionalism was not born with him, but—forty-eight years after the landing of the *Mayflower*—Stoughton articulated it as well as anyone. They were God's firstborns, his favorites, his most privileged; "What could have been done more for us than hath been done?" Stoughton dilated on divine expectation and paternal example, a cramped combination for a generation that preferred to luxuriate in their unworthiness. The colonists represented, Stoughton reminded his compatriots, the choice grain. A torrent of celestial blessings and expectations, mercies, advantages, privileges, liberties rained down upon them. Did they intend to flower or to molder in the wilderness? In light of the occasion, Stoughton cast a lordly vote for hierarchy. His compatriots submitted wisely to their "civic and spiritual guides." Also by necessity—it was the second-generation theme song—he despaired of a people who had grown less vigilant, "sermon-proof and ordinance proof." He injected the obligatory millennial note; the Lord would soon "finish his great works in the world." He nodded vaguely to adversaries in the murky middle distance. The Antichrist and his brood were on the march, for what promised to be a close battle. A generation before Parris had, Stoughton stressed "that this is the time wherein he that is not with Christ is against him." There were to be no neutral parties.

From the age of forty, Stoughton devoted himself to public office and land speculation, a traditionally lucrative combination, more so at a time when a thousand square miles of Connecticut could be purchased for fifty pounds and a coat. With English partners, usually in association with his closest political ally, Joseph Dudley, briefly president of the colony, Stoughton went on a land-accumulating spree through the 1680s. (As a royal agent groused, it was impossible to contest the Crown's claim to land titles when Massachusetts justices inevitably turned out to be the owners of those lands.)* While settling Indian land claims in 1681, Stoughton and Dudley carved out two thousand acres—dense with stands of massive white pine—for themselves. Five years later they presided over a (failed) venture to secure one hundred thousand acres along the Merrimack River.

In the two decades between the time he was appointed to the bench and the time he addressed Rebecca Nurse's jurors, Stoughton proved that while there might well be no neutrals, there are men who will flourish in any regime. At the outset of King Philip's War, he sailed to London, among the earliest in a century-long series of colonial agents who were to defend the independent-minded colony against charges of noncompliance and overreaching. He heard firsthand of their impertinence; in English eyes they were, as an official put it, all adolescents—and intemperate, bigoted adolescents at that.† Stoughton made little headway. He listened

---

* Stoughton had humbly protested the installation of that royal official in 1678. Given his lack of fortune, he was unlikely to be honest. It was a particularly rich remark under the circumstances. As the too-poor-to-be-principled official observed nine years later, Stoughton and his associates had "amassed great quantities of this country."
† As a British official informed Boston's wealthiest merchant in 1684, "I find all are mad in your country."

with humiliation to accounts of colonial misdemeanors and to the earliest discussions of the voiding of the charter. He returned to Boston—by which time Burroughs had been driven from Casco and Salem's first minister from his pulpit—to a chilly reception. A moderate in English eyes, Stoughton appeared an appeaser at home.

Over the next years he executed a feat of acrobatic agility. He practically seemed a traitor when in 1684 the Crown revoked the Massachusetts charter. Even Increase Mather declared him an enemy of the people. Stoughton served as deputy president under the temporary Dominion government, against the counsel of Willard and Increase Mather, who opposed that regime. (He would not, however, land in prison for ten months afterward, as did the less pliable Dudley.) He cooperated with Andros when the scarlet-coated governor arrived in December of 1686 to rein in wayward New England.

Displaying the gift for which he truly deserves his place in history and that must have kept the Nurse family monitoring his every move through July, Stoughton managed three years later to help unseat the royal governor on whose council he sat and whose courts he headed. He was the first to address Andros in the aftermath of the coup, informing his prison-bound superior that "he might thank himself for the present disaster that had befallen him." A year before the Parris girls began to twitch, Stoughton helped to outline the people's grievances against the regime they had toppled. The excesses, the intrusions, the humiliations, the abuses of power were such that a level-headed man would skid off topic for a long digression when reminded of Andros even a decade later.

In "The Revolution in New-England Justified," the only self-exculpating document in which Stoughton would have a hand, he celebrated colonial liberation from its years of oppression. It now turned out that that "rascally petty tyrant" under whom he had served had paid his council no heed. Andros had allowed Harvard to fall into decay, framed legislation in private (and then ignored it), curtailed town meetings, levied arbitrary taxes, subjected the people to venal fees. Justice had come to a standstill under a corrupt administration that stacked juries, toyed with due process, and solicited bribes. Rumors flew that Andros had bribed the Wabanaki to attack the colonists; that he provided them with gunpowder and bullets; that he had converted them to Catholicism. It was sabotage.* The Indians themselves assured the settlers that Andros conspired with the French and Irish to destroy Boston. And of course in invalidating land titles, Andros disrupted speculative ventures, seizing property from Stoughton's closest friends, leaving them without legal recourse, and redistributing their lands to cronies.†

From London's point of view, the colonists recognized no authority, mismanaged their affairs, and suffered a thousand divisions. The Anglican Church had felt the Puritans' fury "by having the windows broke to pieces, and the doors and walls daubed and defiled with dung." New Englanders were hopeless at self-defense; they eagerly sold powder and ammunition to the French and Indians. Had they refrained from doing so, the Wabanaki would long before have sued for peace. It was sabotage. Whoever incited it, the new conflict—to be known as King William's War—took an immediate toll. Captain Higginson, the Salem town minister's son, had been a comfortable man in 1689. Since that time, trade having decayed, he knew only losses. Of Salem's sixty ketches, six remained. No Massachusetts town, he believed, had suffered so acutely.

Out of favor after the Andros coup, Stoughton had the Mathers to thank for his resurrection. It required a certain amount of artistry. In the course of six convulsive years, Stoughton had served in four different regimes. He resigned, recused himself, sidestepped, and turned coat more than anyone else of his time; in seventeenth-century New England terms, it was as if, through the years of captivity, he had played both Moses and Pharaoh's adviser. The Nurses could not have had an easy time second-guessing him. The shortage of Massachusetts manpower

---

* The suspicion reached back a generation. In the 1660s, Sewall's father-in-law had fumed that the English had no right to come to North America to "seek the subversion of our civil and ecclesiastical politics."

† There was no question that all was in disarray under Andros, especially for speculators. Land sales were impossible at the time, as no one knew if payment should be made to the proprietors or to the king.

worked in Stoughton's favor. By 1692 he had held nearly every exalted position Massachusetts could offer and may already have had his eye on the governorship, for which he was inarguably better qualified than Phips. Even when he ascended to that office he continued as chief justice, a position he would hold to the end of his life. Political offices had a habit of attaching themselves to him in clumps.

Second generations distinguish themselves for being more orthodox than their fathers, as new regimes tend to be more oppressive; both have something to prove. High-minded and doctrinaire, Stoughton nonetheless understood the value of dexterous accommodation. It may have been impressed upon him early. When he was very young, his father, Israel, published a pamphlet pressing for a more representative Massachusetts government. The result was a bitter attack from Governor Winthrop, Wait Still's father, who termed Stoughton "a worm" and "an underminer of state." Israel Stoughton issued a craven apology, in which he pressed the authorities to burn his offensive, wrongheaded book. He found himself barred from political office for three years. Stoughton had no intention of landing in that wilderness. As an English official had noted of him approvingly, Stoughton sided with the Puritan ministers but—a nimble man—could be counted on to attend to the king's interests. He was also a pious, eminently able public servant; a Mather did not hesitate to indulge in a certain amount of contortionism on his account. As Cotton reminded his father late in 1691: "Mr. Stoughton is a real friend of New-England, and willing to make any amendment for the miscarriages of the late government." He should be restored to favor.

If there was a spot on Stoughton's record, it was not the hastily reconstituted loyalties or the hoard of titles. In 1688, the year that Parris preached his first Salem sermon, Stoughton traveled to Maine to negotiate a prisoner exchange with the Wabanaki. He bungled the assignment, leaving the Wabanaki incensed. Sixteen English settlers died afterward in retaliatory attacks. Here was cause for some legitimate concern about measuring up to earlier generations; as militia captain, Stoughton's father had massacred an Indian tribe in 1637, returning to Dorchester in triumph. It was from the Maine fiasco that the Mathers and the revised charter saved Stoughton in 1692.

Known as someone who "never yields a point without a protest," Stoughton was short-tempered. He could be contemptuous. He had been setting high moral standards since 1668, when he first reminded his compatriots that—as the elect—they could count on Satan nipping at their heels. He did not believe God would allow the righteous to work evil against their will; he recognized no grounds on which the spectrally represented could fail to be guilty. If the girls saw Rebecca Nurse choke Ann Putnam Jr., then Rebecca Nurse must be a witch. He had judged such cases before; he sat on the court that sent Glover to her death for having enchanted the Goodwin children. He had warned earlier of invisible enemies; by July 1692 they seemed to be everywhere. Sixty miles from Salem, a Lancaster man returned home to find his wife and three children lying in a pool of blood, tomahawked to death. Nocturnal invasions began to plague nearby Gloucester in midsummer, when, over a series of moonless nights, scuffling could be heard near the town garrison. A dozen men soon materialized, alternately dressed as Frenchmen and as Indians. At times they spoke English, at others a foreign tongue. Impervious to gunshot, they jammed firearms and dissolved into bushes. They left no tracks. After two terrifying weeks, Gloucester called for reinforcements; a unit of sixty militiamen fared no better. Bullets turned up in trees, just as, in court, crochet needles materialized in aprons. Salem shuddered at that assault, which did nothing to divert the Nurse clan from its tireless campaign. They looked anxiously to Boston for their reprieve.

Impressive even to his enemies, Stoughton was—with his fiery temper, starched presence, and fluid command of ideas—intimidating to his peers. To someone like Francis Nurse, his was a towering presence. Unfailingly conscientious, Samuel Sewall was often at Stoughton's side; Sewall may have had the best attendance record of all the justices. If only because they lived a short walk from the Salem town house, Hathorne and Corwin seem to have been consistently in the room. Fifty-two-year-old Bartholomew Gedney, the wealthy Salem landowner with Maine interests, had also urged accommodation with England. He too had served under Andros before joining to oust him. A physician, Gedney had a taste for the finer things. He may have been the best dressed of the justices; he owned one of the few velvet saddles in Salem town. All three Salem men made their leanings clear in the preliminary hearings. Much-respected John Richards had applied to Cotton Mather and received his answer. Wait Still Winthrop too remained an Andros councillor until the day of the revolt. Public office did not overly tax his attention, which tended more toward real estate, litigation, and fashion.* He was neither an energetic nor an original thinker; he tended to wilt before imposing men. Justice Peter Sergeant, a fabulously rich Boston merchant, remains something of a cipher, possibly because he kept his distance from Stoughton's courtroom.

As were several of his colleagues, Stoughton was in Cambridge on July 6, 1692, for the festivities surrounding Harvard's commencement, a raucous civic holiday complete with peddlers despite the Latin, Greek, and Hebrew orations. The celebration could include salmon and capers, oranges and pineapples; so much did it incline to excess that graduates had been restricted to three gallons of wine. As university president, Increase Mather that morning bestowed bachelor's degrees on six young men. At least one celebrated in his father's absence: among the graduates was a son of John Alden, the indefatigable trader, then jailed on witchcraft charges. (The new graduate's brother too missed the revelry. He remained in Indian captivity, from which his father had not managed to rescue him.) In Salem village, the Nurse family engaged in its own celebration, without dignitaries or delicacies: days after her

---

* Three summers earlier he had noted the crimp of public service on his wallet. Tempted though he was to "eat up the poor as bread and squeeze them to death by virtue of an office," he looked about for other means of supporting himself.

excommunication, Governor Phips overruled Stoughton, to reprieve Rebecca Nurse.

Phips did so as he prepared a new Maine expedition, ordering provisions and returning several hundred militiamen to active duty. He arranged to leave Stoughton in charge in his absence. The deputy governor had no doubt expected from the start to take over for the blustering, semiliterate governor under whom he served. There was no particular affection between the two men, who had nearly come to blows in the past and would again. (Stoughton reported in 1692 to a man he had been discreetly asked to lock up in case of treachery years earlier. There had been some concern that Phips might defraud the Crown, something Stoughton agreed seemed likely.) In pardoning Nurse, Phips expressed doubt if not about witchcraft then about the courts' ability to identify it. He was not entirely alone. In mid-July a prominent Dutch merchant wrote Increase Mather directly with his qualms. Surely God was again punishing New England. But satanic pacts struck the merchant as implausible, as did the idea that witches could torment victims at a distance or topple a church. Meanwhile the bewitched acted "as if they were deprived of their sanity and unable to come to their senses." If not downright lunatic, were they perhaps possessed? Might Mather supply some text to refute their "superstitions and mistakes"?

The Nurse reprieve eased the breathing in a fair number of village households. In others it provoked a clamor. So great were the "dismal outcries" on the part of her accusers that a Salem justice—Hathorne or Gedney—persuaded Phips to reconsider his pardon. Nurse women did not remain easily behind bars. To some that proved that they lobbied most effectively; to others it confirmed their iniquity. No other family caused such distress, a point Mercy Lewis had nearly died making on Mary Esty's brief release in May. The Nurse family was to know another reversal: shortly after its issue, Rebecca's pardon was revoked. The timing is unclear. The Salem justice may have presented Phips with a convincing case. As acting governor, Stoughton may have seized the opportunity to reinstate his court's verdict. On July 17 he drafted a death warrant: Sarah

Good, Elizabeth How, Susannah Martin, Rebecca Nurse, and Sarah Wilds having been found guilty of "the horrible crime of witchcraft," the Salem sheriff was to arrange for their execution. Stoughton this time gave him a week to prepare, ordering that the five women hang the following Tuesday morning.

There were some ironies, beginning with the fact that Stoughton—a dispassionate man who viewed New Englanders as the intemperate children of a beneficent father—was a lifelong bachelor. Few men in the colony had as little firsthand familiarity with teenage girls or, for that matter, with women.* While in the years since he had so forcefully preached that it was time to "declare for whom we are, and choose our side," he had proved an opportunistic shape-shifter, nearly invertebrate in his loyalties, Stoughton was in 1692 obdurate and uncompromising. In unseating Andros he had deplored the judicial practices of that administration. It acted high-handedly, plumped up charges, ignored respectful petitions, and leveled "inexorable persecutions." It detained suspects for long periods without cause. It decided verdicts in advance. It held hearings that—charged the chief justice who redirected the Nurse jury and sentenced her to death—were "unreasonably strict, and rigorous and very unduly ensnaring to plain unexperienced men."

EARLY ON THE stifling morning of July 19, the Salem sheriff and his deputies loaded five women in a wooden cart. They rode slowly west, along Essex Street, under armed guard. To the modern eye, the cart trundling through central Salem—past the meetinghouse, past Hathorne's home, past Stephen Sewall's and Corwin's homes, past gaping, hooting crowds of spectators—carried five shabbily dressed women, colorless and middle-aged if not older, their hands identically bound. They in fact made for a disparate group. At thirty-nine (she had celebrated a birthday in jail), the rancorous Sarah Good was the youngest. Her five-year-old

---

* The effervescent Noyes, a rarity among clergymen for never having married, necessarily spent time among his female parishioners.

daughter remained that morning shackled in Boston, where Good had lost the infant she nursed at the time of her arrest. At seventy-one, Rebecca Nurse and the vitriolic Amesbury widow Susannah Martin were the eldest. The five had spent the most wretched weeks of their lives in close confinement but had not all been acquainted previously. None was a member of Parris's congregation. One was impoverished, one well-off. Good and Martin were downwardly mobile, having sued over elusive inheritances. Martin was the sole widow. Sarah Good's husband had quickly agreed his wife was a witch; Francis Nurse devoted whole days to proving that his was not. Prosecuted for a very different set of miscellaneous crimes, they had little in common apart from their gender and their untidy appearance. Save for Rebecca Nurse, all had been in court before, which left them vulnerable. Galileo too had answered to charges of having missed Mass before his telescope troubles began.

"The widow Glover is drawn by to be hanged," Samuel Sewall had noted in his diary on November 16, 1688; five witches riding to their execution was not something one missed or was meant to miss. All awaited the clatter of hooves and cart wheels. All witnessed the same sight. Many made sense of it differently. When they looked at one another, the five women saw a band of innocents, some more conspicuously guiltless than others. Martin had questioned whether anyone other than the afflicted girls practiced witchcraft. For weeks the women had been stretched on that most pernicious of psychological racks: You are not what you think you are, they were hectored; you are what we think you are. What did those in the Salem street see as the cart creaked to the edge of town, to turn north over the town bridge? Some saw five benign, wretched, and disheveled older women. Many watched resolutions to nagging mysteries trundle by, disturbers of the peace, thorns in the side. A great majority saw five powerful witches. Plump with righteousness, they knew this to be what justice looked like. They found what they were looking for: an end to affliction, uncertainty, impurity. As Martha Corey herself had said of the first suspects, it was no wonder the devil recruited them. They were idle, slothful, malicious souls. Plenty of Rebecca Nurse's defenders believed her cart mates guilty. Some no doubt shrank with fear as the dusty procession passed. Others vowed to redouble their devotions. If Rebecca Nurse could wind up in the devil's snare, who was safe?

A good magistrate, Stoughton had preached in 1668, dared to follow his conscience. It was incumbent on him to remain alert to Satan's devices, to redirect divine wrath, to preserve unity and eradicate evil. He knew New England to be suffering under divine probation. It had been a season of terrible trials; they had stalled in their mission. He had proved correct about those evil forces in the middle distance. In conjunction with the ministry, the magistrates could prove that—as Stoughton put it twenty-four years earlier—New England had not "abated in our love and zeal, in our wise, tender and faithful management of that great duty of mutual watchfulness and reproof." On a natural stage, the ocean and woodlands and marshes and the orderly town of Salem spread out beneath them, they had reason to believe that they restored a community to grace, conducting evil to the ground. Speaking for the crowd that clambered up the steep hill, Mather agreed. The five, he would write later, were sorceresses, "impudently demanding of God a vindication of their innocence." Any trickle of doubt evaporated in the heat of the morning. A haze of free-floating spite alone remained. We have no hint of what the afflicted girls thought.

There was another possible way to make sense of the procession laboring up the scraggy hill, the eyes of all people upon them. It may not have been as conspicuous that stifling Tuesday as it is today. Fifty-three years earlier, a sloppy Massachusetts clerk had drawn Topsfield's boundary over that of Salem village. As a result, a portion of southwestern Topsfield was, by some reckonings, a portion of northern Salem. A pitched battle ensued, largely on account of the precious resource already in short supply, as Parris so well knew: timber. A New England family consumed thirty to forty cords of wood a year, which translated into over an acre of forest. A long-standing feud divided the Putnams of Salem and the Townes of Topsfield over the issue, inviting regular acts of trespass. On one occasion Topsfield men felled trees as a helpless Putnam farmer looked on; a tribe of ax-wielding Putnams shortly thereafter appeared on the disputed land. The Essex County courts heard again and again from the Putnams. They ruled four times in favor of the Townes. It was the same sturdy brand of family feud that had kept ministers rotating through Salem village, one faction undermining the other's candidate.

Rebecca Nurse had grown up in Topsfield. Her maiden name—like that of Sarah Cloyce and Mary Esty, both in prison that scorching Tuesday—was Towne. Many of the men who complained against Nurse had years earlier brandished axes on her brother's land. The Hows and the Estys were intimate; Elizabeth How and Rebecca Nurse were sisters-in-law. Sarah Wilds's husband had helped establish the contested boundary. In 1660 he allied himself with the Nurse, Towne, and Esty men in a suit over a missing mare, a bright bay with a black mane, later to turn up in the wrong barn. All occupied land claimed by Salem village. Was there a connection? Certainly the spine-tingling procession to the granite ledge cannot have been what the four men who braved a tempest to press the initial witchcraft charges anticipated; one was a Nurse son-in-law. Not a syllable concerning the long-standing dispute turned up in court testimony, although already New England was a place where certain things went unsaid, even in the midst of violent assaults. Half of the witchcraft complaints filed before July had been Thomas Putnam's, however. His daughter had accused each of the sallow women now blinking in the bright sunlight. Putnam filed his last complaint on July 1. Parris's niece Abigail also disappears from the scene at this time. Something had clearly been resolved, though that may have been a different matter from the one the judges had in mind. By July other wheels within wheels had taken over.

For a second time a grim procession paused at the edge of the outcropping. In the absence of a path, the condemned presumably walked the scruffy last yards to the summit of the hill, where from the distance they had glimpsed a primitive gallows. Given their infirmities it cannot have been a speedy affair. As their skirts were bound around their ankles, as hoods were lowered over their eyes, all five women insisted on their innocence. Noyes persisted in a tense contest. He remained hell-bent on confessions, crucial to both the civil and ecclesiastical narratives. Susannah Martin was unlikely to let Noyes's badgering pass unacknowledged. We know Sarah Good did not. Between the time she arrived on the hill and the moment she blindly climbed the ladder, Noyes reminded Good that she had engaged in great wickedness. She was a witch; it was high time she admitted as much. He underestimated his shabby opponent. Under the gallows from which she was to hang, Sarah Good shot back: "You are a liar. I am no more a witch than you are a wizard!" Having lost an inheritance, a home, and a child, she added a shrill curse. "And if you take away my life," she threatened, "God will give you blood to drink." It was a line familiar to a man who feasted on Revelation.* Never before had Good sounded so magnificently witchlike.

Someone edged the women's feet off the ladder, presumably in quick succession. The crowd recoiled from their terrible moans. The witches remained on display long enough to make an impression but not much longer. It was an oppressively hot summer; they were buried quickly, at least initially among the rocks on the hill.† Good's curse hung longer in the air; Sewall could not get it out of his mind. He was not alone. While the first hanging had resulted in a pause in afflictions and accusations, the second provoked more. In downtown Salem men encountered specters in the street, where they flew past, swift as birds. The next day at the village parsonage not only Parris's niece but, for the first time, Mrs. Parris too suffered fits. Fortunately Hathorne and Corwin had not relaxed their efforts. They had spent three days interrogating old Ann Foster, who had made the ill-fated flight from Andover. She divulged precise details of the

---

* And it was a line so good that Nathaniel Hawthorne lent it to a man. He gives it to Matthew Maule in *The House of the Seven Gables*. Good may have borrowed it from two Quakers who had perished on a Boston scaffold thirty years earlier.
† Legend has it that the families quietly recovered the bodies; Nurse's sons were said to have done so after nightfall that evening. No trace of the five women has been found.

conspiracy, affixing her mark—an uncertain, inverted *C*—to her epic account. To some it seemed as if God were working in miracles: no sooner had they executed five witches than the Lord sent in a new crew, who confessed to their depravity and revealed their lurid designs.

By week's end the new parsonage culprit revealed himself. He was eighteen years old, hardy and appealing. He lived in Andover. Hathorne got farther with him than Noyes had with Sarah Good. "Sometimes," confessed the abashed teenager, "the devil stirred me up to hurt the minister's wife." He had rolled up a handkerchief and imagined it to be Mrs. Parris. How had he come to work for the devil? That was his mother's doing. Not only had she flown to Salem on an unreliable pole with Ann Foster, she had made him a witch. Though in prison, she had visited him recently, as a cat. The devil had promised her she would be queen of hell, a position for which there is no biblical precedent but that, to a hierarchy-minded New England teenager, made perfect sense.

VIII

———— ❦ ————

IN THESE HELLISH MEETINGS

Doubt is not a pleasant condition, but certainty is absurd.
—VOLTAIRE

BY THE END of July it was clear that the devil was not up to his usual tricks, preying on the occasional malcontent. Having established himself in Massachusetts, having recruited widely, he had grandiose plans. He intended to topple the church and subvert the country. Certain patterns had begun to emerge as well, some familiar, others strikingly new. To cast aspersions on a bewitched girl, to visit one's imprisoned spouse too regularly, was to risk accusation. Questioning the validity of witchcraft, the legitimacy of the evidence, or the wisdom of the court bordered on the heretical; the more you resisted, the deeper you dug yourself in. Imputations proved impossible to outrun. The word of two ministers could not save an accused parishioner. Neither age, fortune, gender, nor church membership offered immunity. Prominent men stood accused alongside homeless five-year-old girls. Many braced for the knock at the door.

Accusations tended to begin at rural addresses—notably in pious, well-ordered homes—and radiate to the towns. They did not migrate in the opposite direction. Servants accused mistresses, but mistresses did not accuse servants. When adolescents named peers, they tended to name those of the opposite gender. Wives did not incriminate husbands, although they had earlier, examining them as they slept for telltale marks. Husbands filed no slander suits to vindicate wives. Few slaves stood accused; no Indian stood trial. For all their diabolical behavior, Quakers escaped prosecution. Families divided in their loyalties. Increasingly you slept under the same roof, if not in the same bed, as your accuser.* Old friendships dissolved instantaneously. Others fractured messily. A Salem villager both defended and accused John Procter; his father signed the petition for Rebecca Nurse while complaining of Elizabeth How. The trials seemed to reactivate and ratify doubts quietly stored in the cellar. They often involved trivial matters, although as Mather noted, the trivial matters added up. Contact with the frontier proved hazardous. By 1692 New England prosecuted women for spousal abuse as often as it did men; cruel husbands and disputatious wives wound up accused. Bewitched women choked with fits, where men— who stepped forward only once the trials had begun—tended to submit to paralyzing bedroom visits. (Ann Putnam Sr. alone managed both.) As a group, young men suffered most imaginatively, supplying the most outlandish testimony. No one ever experienced pains without being able to name a witch. And Stoughton did not issue reprieves. Never before, in North America or England, had a court managed a perfect conviction rate.

On May 11, puckish George Jacobs had exhorted his seventeen-year-old granddaughter not to admit to witchcraft. To do so, he warned, was to wind up complicit in her own death. He was wrong. With one exception, no confessor was so much as arraigned. Abigail Hobbs, Tituba, and Margaret Jacobs remained safely in jail along with nine other self-described witches, a break with all precedent. And while in the past the

---

* On her way to the gallows, the Goodwins' tormentor had implicated her daughter.

spellbound often found herself under clinical study, she had not before played an interpretive role. Justices and ministers alone unriddled witchcraft. In 1692 so did afflicted girls, with the farsighted, diagnostic powers that since Thomas Putnam's insinuating April letter were day after day visible to all.

Late in July a Salem man noted that God had lifted a scourge: there had been no case of smallpox in a year. The Lord had however sent down a new plague. Its agent of contagion appears to have been a well-meaning Andover farmer desperate to save the dying wife who in twenty years had borne him ten children. Joseph Ballard first confronted a forty-nine-year-old relative. Had he anything to do with the peculiar "pains and pressures" that had incapacitated Elizabeth since the spring? The in-law dabbled in fortune-telling and black magic but could not help. He knew nothing of the matter. Ballard applied to the authorities, who — reprising an early-sixteenth-century Spanish practice — encouraged him to send a horse and escort for the Salem visionaries. The group almost certainly included Parris's niece and Mary Walcott. At Elizabeth Ballard's bedside the girls fell into fits. Directly or indirectly, they named frail Ann Foster, the seventy-two-year-old Andover widow who had crashed in flight.

Shortly thereafter a constable carried Foster to Salem village, a more arduous trip on horseback than by air. A Ballard neighbor on the southern edge of town, Foster was the widow of a much older, kindly Andover farmer. On July 15 she submitted to the first of several interrogations. Beginning just after Stoughton had sentenced five witches to death, she finished two days after their execution. Initially she denied any involvement with sorcery. She soon enough began to unspool a Tituba-worthy tale. The devil had appeared to her as an exotic bird. He promised prosperity, along with the gift of the evil eye. She had not seen him in six months, but her neighbor Martha Carrier had been in touch on his behalf. If anyone remembered even to ask Foster about the ailing Elizabeth Ballard the record bears no trace.

At Carrier's direction, Foster had bewitched several children and a hog. She worked her sorcery with poppets. Carrier had announced the devil's Sabbath in May and arranged their trip. They were twenty-five in the meadow where Reverend Burroughs officiated. Three days later, from the Salem jail, Foster added the malfunctioning pole and the crash. She mentioned that two other men had attended the meeting, where she overheard a witch say they were three hundred and five in all. They would destroy the village. Stoughton had scheduled a hanging for the following morning; it was a hectic day for the justices, who ran out of time. John Hale asked if he might remain behind with the suspect. He was curious about a few particulars. By what conveyance, he asked, had Foster flown to Salem? How long had the trip taken? Where precisely was the meeting? It was Hale who heard first about the bread and cheese in Foster's pocket, details that do not appear in the court papers. He heard too of her anxiety: she shivered at the thought that George Burroughs and Martha Carrier would murder her for having spilled their secrets. Both sat chained nearby. They had appeared spectrally, with a sharp weapon; they intended to stab her to death. (Foster's son-in-law had slit her daughter's throat with a knife. And she hailed from a community that—unlike Salem—had suffered Indian attacks.) Confessing to witchcraft could save your life. It also proved taxing.

Both alone with Hale and before the justices, Foster appeared entirely cooperative. Soon enough they discovered that she had failed to come clean with them, however. It seemed that she and Carrier had flown and crashed on that Salem-bound pole with a third rider, who traveled silently behind Foster. So divulged forty-year-old Mary Lacey, a newly arrested Andover suspect, on July 20. Lacey lived on the north end of Andover; a search of her home turned up rag and quill bundles that looked suspiciously like poppets. Foster had also withheld the details of a chilling ceremony. Dipping their heads in water, six at a time, the devil baptized his recruits; henceforth they were his. He performed the sacrament in a nearby river to which he had carried Mary Lacey in his arms.

On July 21 Ann Foster appeared before the magistrates for a fourth time, to account for the omissions in her story. It made for a particularly sensational hearing: Mary Lacey, who supplied the missing details, was her daughter.

July 21 was a lecture day, the first after the mass hanging; the weather continued hot and uncommonly dry. The justices spoke as if from a great height, with a condescension veering into derision. "Goody Foster," one began—it was likely Hathorne—"you remember we have three times spoken with you, and do you now remember what you then confessed to us?" An officer read her statement aloud. She swore to its every word. The justice commended her; she could expect more mercy than the others for having admitted to her part in the "very great wickedness." But she had hardly been forthright. Why had she not mentioned that her daughter had flown with her? How long had her daughter been a witch? Here she was flustered. "Did you not know your daughter to be a witch?" persisted Hathorne. She did not, and was taken aback to hear as much. Would she recognize her confederates if she saw them? Had there been two companies of witches in the field? She knew only that Carrier had been at the meeting. Mary Warren helpfully chimed in; a specter affirmed that Foster had recruited her own daughter.

The authorities understood that she had done so about thirteen years earlier. Was that correct? "No, and I know no more of my daughter's being a witch than what day I shall die upon," replied the Andover widow, sounding as firm on the subject as she had been on the details of the misbegotten Salem flight. Again she was reminded of the value of unburdening herself: "You cannot expect peace of conscience without a free confession," coaxed a magistrate. If she knew anything more, Foster swore, she would reveal it. At this the magistrates called her youngest daughter. Forty-year-old Mary Lacey had barely entered the meetinghouse when she berated her mother: "We have forsaken Jesus Christ, and the devil hath got hold of us. How shall we get clear of this evil one?" Under her breath, Foster began to pray. "What God do witches pray to?" a justice needled. "I cannot tell, the Lord help me," replied the befuddled old woman as her daughter delivered up fresh details of their flight to the village green and of the satanic baptism, a staple of Andover witchcraft; the fear of Baptists seemed as ingrained there as that of Indian ambush. Her mother, Mary Lacey clarified, rode first on the stick. She elaborated on the satanic ceremony. Questions fertilizing answers, she supplied the "queen of hell" appellation.

Court officers removed the two older women, to escort their fresh-faced daughter and granddaughter into the room. Ballard had also accused lovely, strong-minded eighteen-year-old Mary Lacey Jr. of having bewitched his wife. Mary Warren fell at once into fits; Mary Lacey Jr. was instructed to touch the arm of the convulsing girl, two years her senior. The Procter maid recovered. At first the Andover teenager was unhelpful. "Where is my mother who made me a witch, and I knew it not?" she cried, a yet more disturbing question than the one posed in June, when a suspect wondered whether she might be a witch and not know it. Asked to smile at Warren without hurting her, Mary Lacey failed; Warren collapsed to the floor. "Do you acknowledge now that you are a witch?" Lacey was asked. She could only agree, although she seemed to be working from a different definition. A recalcitrant child, she had caused her parents plenty of trouble. She had run away from home for two days; she gave her mother regular cause to wish that the devil would carry her off. But she had, she insisted, signed no pact. The justices reminded her of her options: if she desired to be saved by Christ, if she expected mercy, she would confess. "She then proceeded," noted the court reporter. She was more profligate with the details than her mother or grandmother; it was a hallmark of Salem that the younger generation—Cotton Mather included—could be relied upon for the most luxuriant reports. Mary Lacey Jr. had some practice already with flights of fancy. It appeared easier to describe satanic escapades when an adolescent had already been told, or believed, that she cavorted with the devil. The record allows a fleeting glimpse of her sense of herself. "I have been a disobed—" she began, after which the page is torn. She gave naughty Abigail Hobbs a run for her money.

The eighteen-year-old also picked up precisely where Abigail had left off; it is impossible to believe the two had not met. Twice in the night a strange noise had disturbed Mary in her bed. That had been the previous week, a year earlier, sixteen months before—the details morphed as they emerged. The devil visited the first time in the shape of a horse, the second as "a round, grey thing." Had he appeared to her when she ran away from home, asked the magistrates, conflating supernatural crimes with adolescent misdemeanors? "No," Mary replied, "but he put such thoughts in my mind as not to obey my parents." He did direct her to afflict several people, including Elizabeth Ballard, mentioned now for the first time. Mary worked her sorcery with poppets. She implicated her mother and grandmother, Martha Carrier, and Carrier's teenage son Richard. What form did her satanic worship take? "He bid me pray to him and serve him and said he was a God and lord to me," she admitted. The bargain too got more lavish; she would want for nothing. She implicated another Carrier son before divulging something else. "Does the devil require anything of you besides hurting persons?" asked a magistrate. Indeed he did. The witches were to recruit actively. They were to renounce their church baptisms, a prospect that struck at the very foundation of New England.

Mary Lacey Jr. unraveled the mysteries of how a man might manage to spend his day planting English corn while simultaneously communing with the devil and how his neighbors might fail to notice his flight. "Sometimes we leave our bodies at home, but at other times we go in our bodies," she explained, "and the devil puts a mist before their eyes and will not let them see us." She illuminated a more pressing matter, too. "Do you hear the devil hurts in the shape of any person without their consent?" asked the justices, who seemed to think a teenager might be able to solve their legal riddle. "When any person strikes with a sword or staff at a spirit or specter, will that hurt the body?" one asked. Lacey affirmed that it would. Both her mother and grandmother sported injuries. The revelation worked an immediate effect: with the validation of spectral evidence, Mary Warren stepped forward. She grasped Lacey's hand. This time the Procter servant suffered not a twinge of discomfort.

Only then was Mary Lacey Sr. returned to the room. As if affixing a caption to the stirring scene, one of the justices intoned: "Here is a poor miserable child, a wretched mother and grandmother." It took little more to provoke an emotional outburst. "Oh Mother, why did you give me to the devil twice or thrice over?" the eighteen-year-old pleaded, tears streaming down her face. Mary Lacey Sr. apologized. The teenager managed a spot of revenge: her mother had so often scolded that the devil should fetch her away. Her wish had come true! "Oh, my heart will break within me. Oh, that mother should have ever given me to the devil thus," she sobbed. She prayed that the Lord might expose all the witches. Officials returned her grandmother to the room. Three generations of enchantresses now stood before Higginson, Gedney, Hathorne, and Corwin in the village meetinghouse. Mary continued her rant: "Oh, grandmother, why did you give me to the devil? Why did you persuade me? And oh, grandmother, do not deny it. You have been a very bad woman in your time."

Either a new interrogator took over or Foster simply sank under her granddaughter's onslaught. The justices henceforth addressed her as "old woman." The teenager, a justice reminded Foster, showed signs of repentance. She could be pried from the devil's grasp; Foster herself courted devouring fire and everlasting flames. It was time she told the whole truth. With her granddaughter's help, Foster coughed up a few additional details. She had been a witch for about six years. (The eighteen-year-old immediately upped the number to seven. Foster acknowledged that "she did not know but it might be so.") The justices read Mary Lacey Jr.'s confession to the two older women. They confirmed having traveled together to the witches' meeting. They had signed the devil's book in red ink. They worked their sorcery with poppets. Carrier had boasted to Mary Lacey Sr. as well that the devil would make her queen of hell. Foster's daughter corroborated the flying accident. The three rode together to jail as a clutch of warrants made their way to Andover.

The next day eighteen-year-old Richard and sixteen-year-old Andrew Carrier appeared before the magistrates at Beadle's Tavern, where Burroughs had been held. They were to answer to charges of having afflicted Mary Warren. (Lost in the shuffle, Ballard's failing wife would live another five days.) Both Carriers were fine-looking young men, strapping and smart. Both denied any knowledge of witchcraft. The suspects were landing faster than the authorities could process them; hearings tended to overlap. Comely Mary Lacey Jr. lent a hand, prompting the justices and jogging defendants' memories. She answered for the boys. They had flown with the devil; at his instructions, Richard had plunged an iron spindle into a victim's knee. They had stabbed another man to death. Mary's mother protested that she had taken no part in that attack. Her daughter corrected her, as the eighteen-year-old had obviously so often been corrected herself: "Yes, Mother, do not deny it." Mary Lacey Sr. proceeded to confirm several names and to describe the torture instrument as well as a practice session in which the witches burned their victim with a pipe. Her daughter shared none of her mother's hesitation, picking up on each of Hathorne's suggestions and running with it. She was less successful with Richard Carrier, who contradicted everything, from the nocturnal flights to the pipe attack. In a tone that indicated a certain familiarity, Mary prodded him. They had murdered together! Did he not remember the conversations on their flights? What about his plans to recruit his brother and kill Ballard's wife? At this the afflicted began to tremble. Blood trickled from Mary Warren's mouth. The authorities hurried the boys into an adjoining room.

They proved less obstinate on their return. Richard appeared first, admitting to the charges in clipped sentences. For a full year he had served the black man. They had met for the first time in town, when the stranger surmised that Richard felt nervous about riding home in the dark and offered to accompany him. Richard had subsequently done his bidding. He had twice flown to Parris's pasture. The devil had baptized him with five others; Richard had lent him his likeness to torture Elizabeth Ballard. On Andrew's return to the room, his older brother greeted him with the news that he had confessed. The sixteen-year-old was a different witness this time around; where earlier Andrew had "stammered and stuttered exceedingly," he now expressed himself fluently. He had signed with the devil in June. They had met at night, in an Andover orchard. Both boys proved highly credible. With their clear-eyed assistance, the justices arrived finally at the explosive heart of the matter.

TWO MONTHS EARLIER, when most of Salem village had occupied itself with sheep-shearing, with churning sweet, spring milk into butter, with sowing Indian corn, a great swarm of witches had alighted in Parris's brilliantly green meadow. You might have heard the trumpet that summoned them; it resonated for miles around. The beating of a drum and a great commotion followed as, from as far away as Connecticut, over the course of hours, in a rustle of arrivals, witches descended on the village by every manner of aerial transport. Not all of them could say precisely how they swept into Salem. The Andover witches arrived in a matter of minutes. Mary Lacey Sr. of course sailed on the ill-designed stick with her mother and Martha Carrier. Richard Carrier did not recall the date of the assembly but—his memory refreshed—conceded that he had flown to the village with Mary Lacey Jr. They did so on an unwieldy contraption; assuming the shape of a horse, the devil carried the teenagers on a pole balanced across his shoulders. One farmer traveled alone on a branch. Most flew three or four to a pole. Ann Foster and Martha Carrier's picnic had preceded that flurry; others from the Andover contingent joined them. Foster counted only twenty-five witches. Richard Carrier reported they numbered about seventy in all. Mary Lacey Jr. estimated attendance at a hundred. The devil appeared in the shape of a black man with a high-crowned hat, another Swedish import. One celebrant noted a cloven foot.

The witches indulged in a satanic ceremony, all the more subversive as women officiated. Rebecca Nurse sat at the head of the communion table, at the devil's side; with an incantation, she and Elizabeth Procter handed around crimson-colored wine and bread. Nurse assured Abigail

Hobbs that the wine was blood "and better than our wine." Parris's niece confirmed that she saw the celebrants eat and drink. What was it they served? "They said it was our blood, and they had it twice that day," she testified, adding a vampiric twist. As for the bread, it was "as red as raw flesh." One participant watched Martha Carrier pour the wine. Mary Lacey Jr. recalled that there had not been enough bread to go around. Some had been reduced to stealing provisions, while others, like her grandmother, had brought their own. Not everyone partook. Even at a satanic congress, there were pockets of resistance, despite the phalanx of a hundred and five spectral swordsmen stationed nearby. Sixteen-year-old Andrew Carrier drank from an earthenware cup but did not eat. He was too far away to hear what the devil said when administering his sacrament. Abigail refused the sweet bread and wine; her mother passed up a tankard. Ann Foster kept her distance. A particularly disobliging recruit, Mercy Lewis spat at those who offered the red bread. "I will have none of it!" she howled. Some who accepted the drink found it bitter.

Reverend Burroughs officiated over the sacrament in the presence of two other men. Despite repeated interrogations no one could identify them, although at least one was a minister. The Coreys, the Procters, John Willard, and several other suspects attended, including four women who had now hanged. Several of the men sported very handsome apparel; Burroughs appeared in high spirits. The devil offered his great book, which all signed, some in blood, some with their fingers, others with sticks and pens, one on white bark, usually in red. Only one participant balked, to his immediate regret. He provoked "dreadful shapes, noises, and screeches, which almost scared him out of his wits." Most noted the names of their confederates on the page. They signed ordinarily for six to eight years; the pacts grew longer as the summer wore on. While there was some disagreement about the particulars—no one was better with the mind-boggling details than Mary Lacey Jr., who had the best memory in her family—there was none about the assignment. Beginning with the Parris household and continuing to Salem town, they were to destroy every church in Massachusetts Bay. In their place they would establish Satan's kingdom, where his recruits could expect happy days and better times.

The deviance was of a piece; desire comes in a wealth of luscious varieties. The devil seldom waved vaguely from a high mountain at garden-variety kingdoms below. He traded in specifics. He offered Richard Carrier new clothes and a horse; he enticed Carrier's brother with a house and land He would pay the debts of a struggling farmer with a large family. For an Andover carpenter, the devil proposed a captaincy in the militia. He promised Stephen Johnson, age fourteen, a pair of French fall shoes; he lured another teenage boy with a suit of clothes. He assured an Andover thirteen-year-old that he would pardon her sins. A child could have a black dog. He tempted an older Boxford woman with a classic: How did revenge on her enemies sound? The enticements could be gender-specific. A fifty-five-year-old would have the "abundance of satisfaction and quietness" she so desired. (He did not produce it; she grew only more miserable. Hanging their heads, many noted that the devil had failed to deliver on his promises, as if his reneging on his offer somehow invalidated the deal.) Theatrically inclined Mary Lacey Jr. could count on glory, a commodity unavailable at home. The devil spread around the grandiosity; several heard Martha Carrier boast that he offered her the queen-of-hell title. She would rule with a minister. Masquerading as Burroughs, the infernal one promised relief from all fear. To another recruit he held out something more spectacular yet. Not only did he intend to "abolish all the churches in the land," but he would make all men equal. Why not cancel Judgment Day and eliminate shame and sin? No one admitted to having signed his soul away without a reward.

Two days after the Carrier boys offered their rueful accounts, John Procter arranged for paper to be delivered to him. The first man to have been arrested, Procter had been in prison since April. Most of his family had joined him. In irons, he composed a petition on the Salem prison floor. He too had been deposing suspects; the blunt tavern owner who had bellowed early on that the unruly girls would benefit from a heating pieced events together differently, however. Indeed five people had confessed that week. He had spoken with each one; all had fabricated their accounts. How, asked the insanely literal-minded Salem farmer on July 23, could he have attended a diabolical sacrament when he had been shackled in prison? Among the five who had attended the Sabbath were the Carrier boys. Procter happened to know their fate. The court reporter had noted that the boys were carried out "and their feet and hands bound a little while." Procter revealed that to be something of a euphemism. Andrew Carrier had achieved sudden fluency for a reason: escorted from the room, the teenagers "would not confess anything 'til they tied them neck and heels till the blood was ready to come out of their noses." Only then had they divulged what they had never done. Procter was all the more outraged as his son too had been strung up, blood gushing from his nose. The torture would have continued overnight had a merciful official not intervened.*

Had Procter attended the hearings he might have commented on a different brand of torture: The authorities pummeled the Andover facts into shape. Mary Lacey Jr.'s testimony is shot through with prompts and leaps, suggestions and propositions; the court dangled deliverance before her as temptingly as the devil dangled glory. Accounts tended to conform in their general outlines, clearer by August, which made the confessions more precise too. As for the discrepancies, the justices wrote them down to satanic wiles. Too much consistency would, under the circumstances, have appeared suspect; the devil addled the brains of his recruits. It made perfect sense when Mary Lacey Sr. could not answer additional questions. The devil, she feared, had made off with her memory. As she climbed the stairs to her hearing, another suspect resolved to confess. Once inside the room she found she could not. The archfiend "doth carry things out of her mind," she explained.

---

* Massachusetts law prohibited torture with one exception: In a capital case, it could be employed to extract the names of confederates, with the provision that measures not prove "barbarous and inhumane." Though frowned upon, the procedure was not unfamiliar. A decade earlier, a man had strung up his servant "as butchers do beasts for the slaughter."

Procter knew that his trial had been set for August 2, along with that of George Burroughs; he wrote with some urgency. Addressing himself to five eminent Boston ministers, Increase Mather and Samuel Willard among them, Procter warned that a terrible miscarriage of justice was about to take place. He spoke not for himself but for his fellow prisoners. All were innocent. None could expect a fair hearing. They had conferred and could suggest no other explanation: the devil incensed the magistrates, ministers, juries, and people against them. Procter was characteristically forthright: The suspects were condemned before they set foot in Stoughton's courtroom. Already their estates had been decimated. He knew but did not include the details of his own: upon his arrest, George Corwin had descended on the Procters' fifteen-acre farm, selling and slaughtering the cattle. He confiscated the family's belongings, emptying a barrel of beer for the sake of a barrel, and a pot of broth for the pot. He left their young children without a scrap of food. Procter pleaded for either new judges or a less biased venue. The crowd in the Salem courtroom was as bloodthirsty as the magistrates. Might at least some of the ministers come to Salem to see for themselves?

He did not rail against the court, as had Cary, or against the charges, as had Alden. He cast no aspersions on the bewitched. While everyone else secured glory, happiness, and French fall shoes, he demanded only a fair trial. He sent his appeal to those men he surmised would be sympathetic; three hailed from Boston's First Church, a congregation that included no witchcraft judges. (Ironically, it had been Parris's Boston home.) He added a few lines designed to unsettle his correspondents. It was the highest of compliments that the devil insolently copied them, parodying baptisms and communions. But they themselves had begun to resemble their enemies. Stoughton's court, charged Procter, acted like a bunch of inquisitors, engaging in behavior "very like the Popish cruelties."* They too figured in a Puritan's worst nightmare; Cotton

---

* Procter was not the first defendant to invoke the Inquisition. In 1668 a fiery Salem ship carpenter landed in court after railing that Massachusetts magistrates acted like Spanish

Mather never hesitated to insert a word like "dragooning" into an account of a diabolical meeting. His father had credited Catholicism with heedless witchcraft prosecutions. Indeed the court seemed to have fallen under the spell of all it reviled.

IF IT WAS supremely difficult to outwit the devil, it was more arduous yet, plain-speaking John Procter would discover, to pry open a padlocked mind. If he received a response to his letter, it would not be in the form of a change of venue. He took the stand as scheduled in Salem twelve days later. But Procter chose the correct address for his petition. Insofar as there was resistance — or at least rumbling — in the ranks, it occurred among the most prominent clergymen, the Bostonians to whom the magistrates would appeal for guidance, the experts on the invisible world, with which most had firsthand experience. Increase Mather had published the influential 1684 volume to which his son's *Memorable Providences* stood as a sort of salute. The elder Mather had explicitly questioned various witchcraft claims. "It is also true," he had observed, "that the world is full of fabulous stories concerning some kind of familiarities with the devil, and things done by his help, which are beyond the power of creatures to accomplish." Witches could no more transform themselves into horses, wolves, or cats than they could work miracles. Willard had famously treated his strangled, pinched, and roaring sixteen-year-old servant in 1671. When he wrote up the episode, he termed it "a strange and unusual providence of God," resisting both the words "witchcraft" and "possession." Each of the five ministers to whom Procter wrote had prayed with John Goodwin in 1688. Three had endorsed *Memorable Providences*. Most had signed off on the publication of Lawson's Salem village sermon.*

---

inquisitors. Once arrested, he held, a man "had as good be hanged." Three witnesses testified to the truth of his diatribe while stipulating that they had no idea what the Inquisition was.

* Reverend John Bailey had taken in an afflicted Goodwin boy. Witchcraft touched the other two First Church ministers personally as well; in June, Reverend Moody's wife was accused, a charge that fell on deaf ears. Reverend James Allen still held the title to the three-hundred-acre Nurse estate. He received annual payments from the widower of an executed witch.

While the Salem ministers, magistrates, juries, and people marched in lockstep, as Procter complained, the Boston clergy lurched all over the place. The day after Rebecca Nurse was hanged, a group of ministers could be found at the home of Captain John Alden, in his seventh week in prison. Like Sewall, Alden was a longtime member of Willard's Third Church, the sole Boston congregation that supplied both witchcraft suspects and judges. Along with several ministers, a group of prominent Bostonians took turns leading prayers and singing psalms for the feisty sea captain. Samuel Sewall himself read a sermon. The presence in the room of a witchcraft judge indicates either some calculation or some confusion on the ministers' parts; when they entreated the Lord to intervene on Alden's account, did they pray for justice or innocence? Either way they were at least willing to address the Almighty on his behalf. In prison John Procter begged Reverend Noyes for some consolation, to be flatly rejected "because he would not own himself to be a witch." Together Alden's friends prayed through the afternoon of July 20, concluding with the 103rd Psalm: "The Lord works righteousness and justice for all the oppressed." Some prayers at least were answered; a drenching, much-needed rain fell that evening.

Among themselves the clergy wrangled still with the question that so perplexed the Salem magistrates that they were reduced to soliciting advice from an eighteen-year-old girl. Might the devil impersonate someone without his knowledge or cooperation? They had settled on that question for discussion at the end of June; it acquired a greater urgency by the time they climbed to Harvard's airy, second-floor library on the morning of August 1. Their participation in the Alden fast would seem to suggest that some indeed believed an innocent could be abused. Eight ministers attended the August meeting, including three to whom Procter had appealed. Increase Mather moderated in a room strongly redolent of tobacco. All agreed: the August answer to the question of whether you might be a witch and not know it was yes. (In June the Salem justices had said no.) At the same time, the ministers wriggled a little. While such a thing was possible, it was "rare and extraordinary."

The heist of an innocent was unusual, "especially when such matters come before civil judicature." In other words, the blameless infrequently wound up in court. That statement validated the justices and their proceedings. It also provided a loophole through which the ministers could, if necessary, drag someone they might need to exonerate.

At least a few of those men exerted themselves to see that some cases never landed in court. If only tacitly, they agreed with John Procter: while there were witches in Massachusetts, there were no reprieves in Stoughton's courtroom. (More cynically, there were witches in Massachusetts, but not among their friends.) Two days after the Salem justices ordered a new set of Andover arrests, Captain Cary's wife somehow managed to slip her eight-pound Cambridge chains. It is noteworthy that we have the report from Sewall, who expresses neither outrage at her escape nor fear that a murderous witch, whom his court was meant to prosecute, might be on the loose in the Boston area. Already a few Salem men had vanished into thin air. (John Alden would disappear in mid-September, to be hidden in Duxbury.) Before the court reconvened for its next session, Joshua Moody, among the ministers to whom Procter appealed, assisted in another escape.

Although repeated warrants had gone out for his arrest, forty-one-year-old Philip English could not be found through the month of May. A hulking, heavyset man, Salem's most prominent shipowner spent at least some of that time crouching behind bags of dirty laundry at a Boston home, where officials failed to locate him.* Born Philippe l'Anglois on the Channel island of Jersey, English had flourished in Salem, where by 1692 he had acquired fourteen buildings, a warehouse, a wharf, and a fleet. A devout, especially well-educated thirty-nine-year-old, his wife, Mary, descended from one of the town's first families. She was arrested on April 21, the day Thomas Putnam dispatched his portentous letter.

---

* Life as a fugitive was not cheap. English estimated that his weeks in hiding cost him about fifty pounds, a sum greater than the entire Bishop estate.

Until that time the couple occupied an ornate, many-gabled home, among the finest in Salem town. They employed a large staff, unsurprising as the entrepreneurial Philip English imported Jerseyan servants to Massachusetts. He traded extensively with French, Spanish, and West Indian ports; his twenty-one ships plied the coast from Nova Scotia to Virginia. English was a leader of the community, if one who interpreted his constabulary duties as he saw fit, a matter the hard-driving businessman had found himself explaining to the court years earlier. Until July he had occupied the town pew next to Stephen Sewall's. He did business with Justice Sewall. He was as well the landlord of court reporter Ezekiel Cheever.

A glint in the eye, English was not above offering up a corner of one neighbor's land to another, only to explode when afterward accused of fraud. He proved among the more inexhaustible of New England litigants, suing aggressively and rapaciously. By one count he had appeared in court as a plaintiff at least seventeen times over the previous two decades; by any count he displayed a fierce faith in Massachusetts justice. A conspicuously successful immigrant with an unapologetically independent spirit, English spoke with an accent, hailed from an Anglican island that belonged to a Catholic country, and contributed to the support of a Huguenot refugee community on whom the Dominion government smiled where the local populace did not. He preferred the Andros regime to Phips's, in part because he admired competence. He had made the familiar ascent from juryman to constable to selectman, a post to which the town had elected him in March. English might have been accused of many things, but—aside from his seemingly magical money-minting ability—he could hardly have imagined witchcraft to figure among them.

Thomas Putnam filed the original complaint against Philip English on behalf of four Salem village girls, but Susannah Shelden, the eighteen-year-old orphan, nearly single-handedly carried on the campaign against the couple. English lunged over the pews to pinch her in meeting. He bit her; he threatened to slit her throat. He consorted with a figure in a high-crowned hat. He had drowned a man at sea. It was English who intended to kill their governor. Shelden saw Mary English with a yellow bird at her breast. She had been a witch for twenty years. By June, six weeks after the initial warrant, English joined his wife in custody. His name came up regularly in court over those weeks. While in the nonspectral world he did business with several justices, in the spectral world he routinely consorted with Burroughs and Procter.

English too may have been—or was expected to be—on the docket for August 2. In any event as the details of the diabolical Sabbath emerged, the Salem merchant and his wife consulted with Reverend Moody. A senior clergyman, Moody was an especially warm, witty man. He had experience with the frontier—where he had served as both a minister and a Phips army chaplain—and the supernatural. He had supplied tales for Increase Mather's volume. He too had been hunted by the authorities for an ungodly infraction. Under the Dominion government eight years earlier, he had refused to offer communion in New Hampshire according to Church of England rites. Friends attempted to persuade him "providentially to be out of the province." He had ignored them, to wind up with a six-month prison sentence for contempt of His Majesty's laws. (He remained in custody for thirteen weeks, longer than English had now been.) Late in July Moody preached from Matthew 10:23, a text that includes the line, "If they persecute you in one city, flee to another." His message was transparent, though subjected to some debate by the prisoners, who reviewed it with Moody and Samuel Willard. Had they absorbed his message? asked Moody, probably on July 31. English wondered if he might elaborate. The minister insisted he escape. English hesitated. He had known life on the lam. He had his principles. His business affairs were already in a state of disarray. "God will not permit them to touch me," he is purported to have said. His wife demurred. Did he believe, she asked, that the six who had hanged were witches? Her husband did not. What was to prevent their deaths too?

"Take Mr. Moody's advice," she pleaded. More commonly a stickler for discipline, Moody evidently insisted that if English did not carry his wife to safety, he would do so himself. Already he had arranged for several Bostonians to convey the couple out of Massachusetts. The suspects fled.

Days after they had done so, the grand jury heard testimony that English had murdered a neighbor's son with witchcraft. (The neighbor could also report that, while riding home after having informed a friend of English's designs on his land, he had suffered a nosebleed so severe that it soaked his handkerchief and sullied his horse's mane.) A sixteen-year-old Salem servant swore that the couple had threatened to tear him to pieces. By the time he testified, the fugitives were miles from Salem, en route to New York, where Governor Benjamin Fletcher was said to have offered them asylum. That was entirely possible, although Fletcher did not arrive until August 30. New York would play a crucial role in the crisis but not yet. The two colonies were in close touch if on an uncordial footing, their agendas very much at odds. Fletcher would observe that the North American colonies were "as much divided in interest and affection as Christian and Turk." They had little inclination to extend any favors to the new Massachusetts administration.*

PHILIP AND MARY ENGLISH submitted the same questions to the Boston clergy that John Procter had so eloquently posed a week earlier. They got different answers. They escaped because they had the ear of moderate, influential ministers, men who could privately circumvent a system they publicly supported. But Alden, Cary, and the Englishes escaped as well for the same reason that so many stumbled and stammered and went blank before the Salem magistrates. Even in 1692, the rich were different. From the beginning New England's founders had harped on hierarchy. Still aboard ship, John Winthrop had in 1630 declared that the Lord had

---

* It did not help that many of the New York authorities were Dominion officials who had done jail time in the wake of the Massachusetts coup. New York's attorney general had shared a cramped, swampy cell with Andros.

seen to it in his wisdom that "in all times some must be rich, some poor, some high and eminent in power and dignity, others mean and in submission." While all served under the Lord, Stoughton had reminded his 1668 audience, "some are stewards in higher, some in inferior ranks and capacities." As some enjoyed greater abilities, so some stood to prosper more fully. We were not born equal, and we would not die so. Why, then, pretend to be in the course of our lives?*

There was an elite even among servants. (Tituba figured amid the lowest of the low.) Providence occupied various tiers, with cherubim and seraphim, archangels and angels. All devils were not created equal; there were trifling and dominant ones, mighty fiends and base goblins, some better qualified and more accomplished than others. "There is a monarchy among them," noted Cotton Mather, apishly copying the visible world. As Philip English, or Massachusetts's self-made governor, or even John Richards, the witchcraft judge who had arrived in Massachusetts as an immigrant servant, demonstrated, financial ranks could be fluid. Largely static and self-perpetuating, caste was less so. And as uncertain as you might be of your place in the universe, you rarely lost sight of your standing in society. The social register of meetinghouse seating—inviting feuds and grudges, invasions of laps and elbows in the ribs—was but one manifestation of that hierarchy. So serious was that business that Woburn required a committee to seat its seating committee. A Newbury woman would proceed, in a manner "altogether unbecoming her sex, to climb, ride, or stride over" a five-foot pew, disturbing the congregation, to make her point, in a seat by the wall. Those who assumed places not their own paid heavy fines.† There was every reason why a

---

* One group that did benefit from New World social fluidity was the clergy. They enjoyed little social status in England but leapfrogged to the head of the line in North America, where—in the absence of gentry—they occupied a rank just below the magistrates. If anyone in town had a fine cushion or a looking glass, it was usually a minister. Their position proved enviable enough that in 1699, several impostor ministers arrived in Boston.
† A number of creative equivalents were coined in the name of social harmony. The Deerfield authorities, for example, deemed that "the second seat in the front gallery and the hind seat in the front gallery shall be equal in dignity with the fifth seat in the body of the meetinghouse."

middle-aged Andover farmer with a large family should hunger for an equal society as there was every reason to associate one with the devil. "Whoever is for a parity in any society, will in the issue reduce things into an heap of confusion," warned an early Ipswich minister. Parris was acutely sensitive to class for a reason: in Barbados he hailed from a distinct elite. The island concentrated power and property in a very few hands. In the same way, his daughter—and her afflictions—attracted an attention no other village girl could have commanded.

Status was on abundant display at all times: at home, in the seating arrangement around the table, on the street. The village girls knew well who enjoyed social distinction and who did not, as they knew who was worth what. Pride in apparel was a privilege reserved for the rich; the devil promised silks and fine clothes as much for what they advertised as for how they looked. Only a gentleman could sport a gold-laced coat. Exceeding one's rank in apparel was an offense for which men answered in court as often as women.* Infractions occurred with regularity. Any number of women defended themselves against the charge of illegally donning silk hoods, a privilege afforded to those whose husbands' estates were worth above two hundred pounds, a category that did not include the wives of John Procter, Samuel Parris, or Thomas Putnam. (It did include the mother of Nicholas Noyes, who successfully challenged an accusation that she dressed above her station. The number who fended off such charges spoke less to sumptuous Puritan dress than to lavish New England envy.) Social rank determined the order of Harvard graduates. Cotton Mather took second place to a cousin, the then governor's grandson. Stoughton led his class. Higginson's eldest son was first among the 1670 graduates, Burroughs last. The alphabet did not suggest itself as an alternative means of ranking students until 1769.

Justice was even-handed but punishments contingent on social rank. Unless his crime was particularly egregious, a gentleman was not whipped;

---

* Dress was aspirational, even dangerously so, for both sexes. A piece of silk stolen by the Hales' maid wound its way around a hat worn by Dorcas Hoar's son.

a master and his servant accomplice received different sentences. When convicted in 1684, Reverend Moody requested he be spared the common jail, "it being so cold and nasty a place, that it would be cruelty to send me thither, considering my education and manner of living." He served his sentence in a private home. Sumptuary laws existed to keep people in their place. A witchcraft trial did too, while jostling the social order. Indian servants did not normally tussle on the ground with ship captains' wives any more than adolescent girls normally tutored learned men on jurisprudence. At the same time, no one who escaped in 1692 was without a fortune or a close relationship with a minister willing to collude on his behalf, essentially the same thing. Witchcraft too proved hierarchical and patriarchal. Witches drew their powers from a figure who was above a wizard. He was, as Ann Putnam Jr. early on revealed, a conjurer. He also happened to be a man who never, in all his many mutations, changed gender.

Ann Foster could fly across Essex County at high speed, but—the widow of an Andover farmer, even a prosperous one—she could not escape. One Rowley man broke his sister-in-law out of the Ipswich prison. She did not get very far; he paid a fine. When a warrant went out for sixteen-year-old Elizabeth Colson, accused by the village girls in May, she was nowhere to be found. Word had it that, poised to flee Massachusetts, she hid in Boston or Cambridge. Early in September the constable and his men tracked her to the home of her Reading grandmother. (Her mother, grandmother, and aunt had been rounded up in the meantime.) When they came for Elizabeth on a Sabbath morning, the men found the house locked tight. The deputy constable called to a colleague for assistance; suddenly they heard the back door fly open. Out sprinted the teenager. Sticks in hand, the constables gave chase, bounding across a neighbor's field. Nearly upon Elizabeth, one breathlessly called out: Why did she bother to run when he would surely catch her? He got no reply. The sixteen-year-old continued as fast as her legs would carry her and her skirts would allow, stumbling in the field, picking herself up again, shaking her hand behind her as if striking at her pursuers. Outrun, the two men sent their dog ahead. He leaped around the teenager but did not attack. The chase continued to a stone wall at the edge of some brush. By the time the constable reached the thicket Elizabeth had vanished. He beat the scrub; a great cat raced toward him, to stare him in the face. It scrambled off when the official attempted to strike it with his stick. It took little to understand that Colson had transformed herself. Hers was a daring escape, a fox hunt in which the fox prevailed. It left two grown men scratching their heads. Colson nonetheless wound up in the Cambridge jail ten days later. Meanwhile the whereabouts of Mary and Philip English appears to have been an open secret. No one tracked the couple — dogs at their heels and sticks in hand — as had been the case with fugitives in earlier capital cases.

Nor were arresting officers a suspect's worst enemies. When the authorities came for sixteen-year-old Martha Tyler, an Andover blacksmith's daughter, she attempted no headlong lunge for the back door. A pious girl, she had no crime to which to confess. That was before the ride to Salem, which she made with her brother or stepbrother. He spent the three-hour trip goading her. She begged him to stop; she knew nothing of witchcraft. On their Salem arrival she was led into a room, her brother on one side of her and John Emerson, the Gloucester minister, on the other. Emerson could see the devil before her. He swatted him away with his hand. The two men pressed her, Emerson mercilessly: "Well, I see you will not confess! Well, I will now leave you; and then you are undone, body and soul, forever." A schoolmaster, he knew something about extracting truths from adolescents. Her brother commanded Martha to stop lying. She was a witch. "Good brother," she pleaded, "do not say so; for I shall lie if I confess, and then who shall answer unto God for my lie?" He stood firm, insisting that her complicity was established, "that God would not suffer so many good men to be in such an error about it, and that she would be hanged if she did not confess." Martha capitulated. She preferred any dungeon to more psychological bludgeoning, as others would discover that they preferred to confess than to suffer long periods on their feet, without sleep, under ruthless interrogation. Many no longer knew what to believe. Others came to believe what they were told.

As the August court session approached, time seemed to accelerate; apprehensions built all around. Even as the grand jury assembled in Salem town, to which there was a general migration, Hathorne and Corwin continued their village hearings. On the Saturday that Elizabeth Cary escaped from prison, they interrogated Mary Toothaker in the village. A midwife, she had been widowed six weeks earlier, when her husband of thirty-seven years — an accused Billerica folk healer — had died in jail. Her eldest daughter had already confessed. Given the fact that Toothaker's younger sister was Martha Carrier, the justices must have examined Toothaker intently. She resisted their allegations, having promised herself twenty times over that she would prefer to die on the gallows "than say anything but that she was innocent." But perhaps, she now realized, wavering, that had been the devil speaking? With no clobbering minister or relative at her side, she pummeled herself. Was she having trouble confessing because she was innocent, she brooded, or because the devil silenced her? He sometimes interfered with her prayers. Might she unwittingly have covenanted with him? Warily she felt her way, trying to satisfy the authorities without mutilating the truth. To stand firm on her innocence was, she understood, to prove guilty of sinful intractability. Bewitched girls meanwhile tumbled about her. She finally confessed. By gripping a dishcloth tight in her hands, she had afflicted a long-suffering Andover man. She was convinced — or she convinced herself — that she was a witch. She had been one for just under two years. The devil promised her happy days with her son.

In the course of her July 30 confession Toothaker implicated eleven others, including her sister, her nephew, her daughter, and Burroughs, whose meetings she had twice attended in the Parris pasture. More than anyone she illuminated how those accounts came about. She proceeded by fits and starts, as if she were choking or hyperventilating. Throughout she has her doubts. She *thought* she was at the meetings. She *thought* she set her hand to a book there. She *thought* the idea was to topple the church; she *thought* she heard the sound of a trumpet. She could not be certain as to which eminence deposed her. "The devil is so subtle that when she would confess he stops her," noted the court reporter. Satan deluded her with Scripture. Which verse? asked a magistrate. The psalm that included the line "Let my enemies be confounded," Toothaker replied. It led her uncharitably to wish her accusers dead.

Her approach to her faith was equally instructive; against the riptide of piety ran an undertow of doubt. Toothaker felt herself worse off for her baptism. She had not improved substantially since. The fear of Indians paralyzed her that spring; she woke regularly from nightmares in which she fended off assaults. In the throes of her anxieties, a tawny man appeared. He would protect her, after which she was to pray to him. She readily consented. Perhaps, she now realized, she had been doing business with Satan all along! There was much confusion as to who the enemy was and if he might well be you. In the end Mary Toothaker made her deal with the devil, because he promised "to deliver her from the Indians," a rescue she mentioned three times. It turned out to be a brilliant bargain. Forty-eight hours after she confessed to witchcraft, Indians attacked Billerica.

WHEN YOU DESIGNATE yourselves "a flock in the wilderness," you are very nearly advertising for predators. A host of them had preyed—or been expected to prey—on New England since its founding. In the words of Mary Rowlandson (who may have had ministerial help with them), the Indians were "ravenous wolves," "roaring lions and savage bears." In Mather's pages Native Americans regularly turned up as tigers, the devil as a tiger or a roaring lion. The Quakers comported themselves as "grievous wolves." They joined the French and Indians to complete New England's diabolical menagerie, its lions, tigers, and bears. Bewitched at her May hearing, Ann Putnam Sr. went stiff as a plank. Only outside the meetinghouse did she find relief from the "paws of those roaring lions and jaws of those tearing bears"—words she borrowed from Lawson's

March 25 sermon. As physical and moral boundaries blurred, so did the rampaging, ravaging predators. (Parris was far from alone in his thinking when, in a May sermon, he lumped together Louis XIV, his Catholic confederates, and a witch-and-wizard-instigating devil, at least two of whom were nowhere in the neighborhood.)* In most statements you could substitute the word "Indian" for "Catholic" without altering the meaning of the phrase. Inevitably it entailed subversion.†

The Indians were of course also "horrid sorcerers and hellish conjurers." That made sense; the wilderness qualified as a sort of "devil's den." Since the time of Moses, the Prince of Darkness had thrived there. He was hardly pleased to be displaced by a convoy of Puritans, in "a corner of the world where he had reigned without any control for many ages." In fact he was livid about it, asserted Mather, who regularly muddied the zoological waters. Indians, wolves, and devils constituted the "dragons of the wilderness." To join the Church of England was, in Mather's estimation, to be bewitched. Quakers were a leprous people in the devil's snare. He deemed their religion every bit as wholesome as "juice of toads." Given the symbiotic relationship of an oppressed people and an inhospitable climate, it was from there but a short step to a colluding axis of evil.

The muddled fears produced a snarl of blame. When fire broke out in Boston, it was said to be the work of Baptists. Who slit the throats of the sheep grazing late on Cambridge Common? It had been wolves, but it made sense, late in 1691, to ban Frenchmen anyway. In 1689, agitating against Andros, Mather referred to the (fictitious) decade-old Popish Plot, still vivid in the New England mind. The new Indian war seemed "a branch of the plot to bring us low." Mather ascribed Phips's disastrous Quebec campaign to the Anglican presence in Boston; it made the Lord

---

* Baptists too were few and far between. Cotton Mather referred to the French monarch as "Louis le loup."
† When in 1676 Nathaniel Saltonstall, the onetime witchcraft judge, wrote of the Indian ambush that carried off Mary Rowlandson, he reported on a "flying rabble of barbarous heathens." He might just as well have been describing the heretics who swarmed into Salem village on poles.

angry. It helped that conspiracies came as naturally as did covenants to a New Englander, with his sense of sanctified mission and his insistence on purity. As an Indian informant put it, the colonists were as "apt to believe as children."* They felt themselves stalked on all sides. The Puritans had a natural Anglo-Saxon love of plot; as religion stood at the center of their lives, those became diabolical plots. Reverend Moody commented, in 1688, on the "unaccountable intrigues" that were afoot. Samuel Willard and Salem's John Higginson, moderate, prudent men, fiercely contended that Papist cabals either targeted or would soon target Massachusetts. Well before spectral Frenchmen infiltrated Gloucester, rumors flew that a crew of Irishmen headed to Massachusetts to establish Roman Catholicism in New England. Of course the shape-shifting, satanic saboteurs served an additional purpose: New England's enemies were its church's friends. They filled the pews. Particularly after a season of political storms, the common fears provided solid reason to band together. "O do not quarrel any more," pleaded Mather in 1690, "but unite immediately against your more united enemies."†

In deposing Andros, the colonial elite had charged that their governor schemed to deliver them to "a foreign power." (That conspiracy too featured menacing redcoats and a crown, if not a high-crowned hat.) Cotton Mather spoke to the same fears in 1690, when he preached on New England in a state of "distress and danger as it never saw before." His was a law-enforcing, discipline-endorsing address; in their sins and discontents they had brought down "whole armies of Indians and Gallic blood hounds." The authorities had failed in protecting the flock. Without a charter, New England stood at the mercy of wild beasts. A Mather sermon on witchcraft could sound indistinguishable from a tirade against a royal governor, as was clear early in August when Mather addressed the

---

* The Native Americans fully exploited that gullibility. Every year since they had arrived, the settlers heard of Indian conspiracies, often from opposing factions of Indians.
† Or as Macaulay has it in his *History of England:* "The most rigid discipline that can be enforced within a religious society is a very feeble instrument of purification, when compared with a little sharp persecution from without."

Salem crisis head-on. He borrowed Mary Rowlandson's Indian imagery wholesale; en route to their "hellish rendezvous," the diabolical monsters dragged "the poor people out of their chambers, and carry them over trees and hills, for diverse miles together." What exactly did an "army of devils" look like? Imagine "vast regiments of cruel and bloody French dragoons," Mather urged his parishioners, and they would get the idea. There was a crucial difference, however. When it came to marauding Indians, to "bloody and barbarous heathens," as Stoughton would term the French, you were gut-wrenchingly helpless. Witches you could do something about. When Indians raided Billerica on August 1, they butchered two women, their infants, and their teenage daughters, ages thirteen and sixteen. The judges traveled the same day to Salem, where all roads seemed that sweltering week to lead.

The Court of Oyer and Terminer reconvened in August with a new attorney general. For political reasons, Thomas Newton was replaced by Anthony Checkley, twenty-five years his senior and a friend of Justice Corwin's. Newton was a level-headed, affable, and conscientious civil servant, though not a barrister by training. Checkley had greater experience of the courts. He had prosecuted an earlier witchcraft case; he had served as attorney general in the Dominion government. He transferred at least eight suspects to Salem. They included no widows, folk healers, or acid-tongued beggar woman. Checkley instead prepared to prosecute four men, one of whom had attempted to elude arrest (John Willard) and one of whom had petitioned the authorities for a change of venue (Procter). George Jacobs, who guffawed that he was as much a buzzard as a wizard, joined them, as did Reverend Burroughs, the conjurer. Yet again it was clear where to begin. At ten in the morning on August 2, Stoughton opened the court with the case against Martha Carrier, the caustic queen of hell, Ann Foster's Andover flying companion, a woman so guilty she had been a witch two years before she was born, who had alleged the girls were dissembling and out of their wits, whose own sons had accused her, and who had last been seen on May 31 as she was escorted off, hands and feet bound, from the tumultuous hearing that had left the outgoing attorney general slack-jawed in disbelief.

Carrier's grand jury was only just under way when word reached Massachusetts that a massive earthquake had weeks earlier devoured Jamaica. A third of the island's population perished; the town of Port Royal disappeared into the sea. Houses had been swept away and mountains overturned. The calamity had a biblical dimension to it, the more so in Cotton Mather's retelling: Forty ships capsized, though none from New England. Jamaica's Puritan minister escaped with his life. Mather had already decided to preach that Thursday from the book of Revelation. Hastily he incorporated the newest scourge into his August 4 sermon. Earthquakes too had diabolical origins; the devil raged among them, knowing his time to be short.

All of Boston turned out that Thursday for a citywide fast. Sermons on such occasions adhered to a formula; matching sins to afflictions, they warned of greater terrors were reform not in the offing. Mather worked effectively with the news. The people of Jamaica had been "pulled into the jaws of the gaping and groaning earth, and many hundreds of the inhabitants buried alive." More, he prophesied, was to come: "You shall oftener hear about apparitions of the devil, and about poor people strangely bewitched, possessed, and obsessed by infernal fiends." Addressing the events in Salem, he supplied details that had never turned up in court testimony, including more primitive practices than those to which a wily villain would need to reduce himself, like stolen money that floated into the palms of his recruits. More than twenty witches had now confessed, some as young as seven. They berated the parents who had sold them to the devil. "It would break a heart of stone to have seen what I have lately seen," Mather allowed, the first hint that he had visited Salem, though he did not attend a court session, for which he seemed strategically to be setting the scene. Multitudes of devils, swarms of devils, droves of devils descended upon "the distressed county of Essex." With invisible instruments of torture, they nearly ruined the site of the first gathered church in the colony. The plague, he warned, was spreading from town to town, near and wide.

Mather addressed a related peril. There was much "agitated controversy among us," he allowed, nodding to the skeptics, not as quiet in 1692 as they seem to have been today. He urged moderation. Passion and rumor had run away with the story. He denounced the slandering and backbiting that encouraged the devil in the first place. Tipping his hand, he called once for compassion for the accused, twice for pity for the judges. They were up against the greatest sophist in existence. He appeared to have entwined New England in a finer thread than had ever been used before. The worthy judges labored to restore the innocent while excising the diabolical; it made for an arduous, hazardous operation. Mather was satisfied with the brand of evidence with which the magistrates had thus far prosecuted the "witch gang." But what of those for whom only spectral evidence existed? So snarled was the question that the honored magistrates had reason to cry, like Jehoshaphat, "We know not what to do!" The devil obscured matters by the minute so that they were all "sinfully, yea hotly, and madly, mauling one another in the dark."

Where the clergy assisted in escapes one minute and endorsed prosecutions the next (even Mather's August 4 sermon reads as both admonishment and encouragement); where a villager accused a neighbor, later to sign a petition defending her; where a justice of the peace could submit his examination of a witch to the authorities with the proviso that he was entirely out of his depth; where an accused witch could not determine if the voice in her head was God's or the devil's—in short, where everyone else remained lost in the mist, one man continued entirely clear-eyed. It was incumbent on him to perform the hazardous procedure Mather described, excising the diabolical without lopping off innocents in the process. And as of August 1, when preparations for a new Maine expedition consumed Phips, that man happened to be both the head of the witchcraft court and the acting governor of Massachusetts. Phips authorized him to proceed in his absence, although he remained in Boston that week. Having made an art of exceeding orders, he shrugged off the Salem mauling, which he left in the hands of his lieutenant governor and former political enemy, the ever-capable William Stoughton.

ON AUGUST 3 Martha Carrier appeared before a large crowd, one that included a flock of black-suited ministers, Lawson, Hale, Parris, and surely Noyes among them. We know nothing of her appearance, though — given her two months in an airless prison — Mather may well have been within his rights immortalizing the thirty-eight-year-old as a "rampant hag." Called to the bar, she acknowledged her identity with a raised hand. The court charged her with having "wickedly and feloniously" practiced witchcraft. She pleaded not guilty. If she again expressed the magnificent disdain she had in May, it went unrecorded. Court officers led in a group of village girls, whose depositions paled beside the eye-rolling fits that accompanied them. Carrier apparently had manifested little sympathy. She seemed to feel as she had in May, when she had chided the justices: "It is a shameful thing that you should mind these folks that are out of their wits." Ann Foster's fifty-five-year-old son revealed that Carrier had said that it made no difference to her if the girls' heads twisted right off. There seem to have been some poisonous looks on all sides.

The evidence against Carrier had piled up steadily since her May hearing. Her older sister, two of her children, and a niece had confessed to having attended satanic meetings in her company. Susannah Shelden turned up to testify with her wrists again soldered together. They could not be separated. Thomas Putnam described the tortures his daughter and four other Salem girls had endured at Carrier's hands since May; their limbs nearly dislocated. Ann Foster's daughter dolefully confessed that she and Carrier had together taken the diabolical sacrament. Carrier had undone her entire family "by enticing them into the snare of the devil." Short-tempered and sharp-tongued, she tended to claw at the social fabric, she clapped her hands in young men's faces and wished graphic misfortunes on neighbors. Those curses worked wonders; a land dispute produced a swollen foot or a boil on the groin. Carrier's twenty-two-year-old nephew had returned to Andover from the war with a gaping, four-inch-deep wound. Before his aunt's arrest, he could sink a four-inch knitting needle into it. She assured him it would never heal; since her arrest, it miraculously had. (The neighbor's groin sores had as well.) He made no mention of church-toppling plots. He could however be said to have shed some light on a phenomenon Beverly's John Hale observed: "The more there were apprehended, the more still were afflicted by Satan." That may not only have been the result of a creeping diabolical plot. Carrier's nephew had lost his accused father; he had died in prison six weeks earlier. His mother and sister had been detained. A cousin had confessed to witchcraft. As suspicions puddled around whole families, an accusation was an effective means of escaping the toxic spill. The fears went both ways. Even those who insisted their families were innocent pointed crooked fingers elsewhere. A Nurse relative testified against Carrier.

Both Procters stood trial as well that week. Very little testimony against them survives. What does survive implicates Elizabeth—now nine months pregnant—rather than John. In the wake of their appearance, a powerful petition went to Boston. A separate appeal went to the court. Ipswich minister John Wise drafted the Boston document and presumably solicited the signatures. Yet again, he reminded the authorities of the devil's habit of impersonating innocents. God's ways remained unsearchable. The most punctilious court could discern only so much; a little charity was in order. None of the petition's thirty-two signers had detected the slightest glimmer of wickedness in the couple, who enjoyed "the clearest reputation as to any such evils." They were good neighbors and dedicated churchgoers. Their case might have raised the greatest doubts about their accusers, had anyone been listening. Skepticism had led directly to accusation. It was after accusing Elizabeth Procter that one of the girls had explained that they spun their tales for sport. Two men testified they had overheard the Putnams feeding Mercy Lewis her lines. It made little difference. The court found both Procters guilty of witchcraft.

A contemporary of Parris, whom he had known at Harvard, John Wise ministered in Ipswich to a flock of about the same size and on similar terms. He had blazed a very different trail, applying his contentious spirit to the commonweal rather than to his forty cords of wood and eight loads of marsh hay. Wise had some original ideas about the role of government and about taxation without representation. An appealing man with a sprightly sense of humor, he easily succeeded in enlisting others to his cause; five years earlier, he had led Ipswich in a protest against Andros-imposed taxes. They infringed on New England liberties, contended Wise. He incited neighboring towns to resist, getting as far as Topsfield before his arrest. As he later made clear, Wise believed that very little separated aristocracy and monarchy. From there it was but one small step to tyranny. For his principles he spent twenty-one days in prison. Stoughton headed the court that heard his case; it was he who delivered the guilty verdict, one that Wise believed the justices imposed on the jury. It may well have been Stoughton who informed Wise and his friends that they were mistaken if they thought the laws of England followed them to the ends of the earth. They had, the court informed them, "no more privileges left you than not to be sold as slaves."*

Sensitive to liberties infringed and juries coerced, Wise had particular reason to speak out. He mistrusted authority. He believed cowardice a difficult word to pronounce but a more egregious thing of which to be guilty. He had reason to challenge Stoughton, for whom he may have felt some residual animosity. Certainly the tenor of the Ipswich minister's later remarks was very different from the chief justice's; Wise believed government owed its existence to the community that submitted to it, not the other way around. In his discourse he preferred "the very

---

* With Andros's demise, Wise's insubordination mutated into heroism. His court case is gloriously reprised in the pamphlets justifying the coup against royal authority without any hint that the sentencing magistrate had been Stoughton.

native dress of matter of fact" to any brand of oratorical finery. Wise was immensely popular, considered by his congregants a match for Cotton Mather. He sounds as if he had swallowed a healthy dose of John Locke.

Chains dangling from his wrists, John Procter that week rewrote his will. George Burroughs did not. Even while "a vast concourse of people" journeyed to Salem for his August 5 trial, even while each of the confessed witches designated him their leader, he had reason for confidence. On the eve of the trial, seven men examined him for witch marks. They found nothing. Burroughs held firm to his faith, encouraging his children — to whom he wrote with "solemn and savory instructions" — to do the same. He had supporters, some of whom persuaded a potential witness for the prosecution to make himself scarce that Friday. (The tenor of the times was such that he showed up anyway.) Friends visited Burroughs in prison to confer about his case. He did not intend to rely on the shoulder-shrugging of his May hearing. He knew enough about village affairs to impeach the credibility of his accusers; he had faith in the system. That confidence was all the greater as he knew not only some of his judges but also the attorney general; Burroughs had worked thirteen years earlier for the father of Checkley's first wife, the mother of the attorney general's five children. Burroughs was to appear before his equals. He expressed himself easily. And he sounded like his judges, speaking in the educated, variegated, Anglo-American accent of the day. He thought in — and could readily interpret — Scripture. All else aside, he was a Harvard-educated minister. In his pocket he carried a scrap of paper that would moreover clinch his defense.

Having been named over and over as the ringleader, Burroughs would have known that his trial was the one all awaited; he walked that Friday afternoon into a packed Salem courtroom. He assumed an active role, challenging prospective jurors as they stepped forward to be sworn in, a right other defendants do not appear to have exercised. He may have called witnesses as well. Narrow-faced, high-cheekboned, ethereal-looking Increase Mather was in the room, an event in itself. Burroughs could reassure himself that the elder Mather had, in *Illustrious Provi-*

Salem
1692

The County of Essex is Dr to William
Dounton Goale Keeper in Salem
Decembthe. 1693.

To: Sarah Osburne is m dyeth in
prison. Except 3 Roem part — 0: 07. 0

To: Sarah Good 6 weekes and for
her child Dorit. Good 1 mo dyet — 1: 01: 03

To: Giles Cory & his wife dyet 3 weeke
remaines there of — 3. 11. 03

To William Hobs 3 w. dyet — 1. 07. 06
To. Delvi Hobs 12 monsth dyet — 4. 10. 00
To: Abigail Hobs 12 m dyet — 4. 10. 00
To: Eliz Scargen 6 m Dyet and
for her child 4 mo Dyet — 4: 00: 00
To: Alce parker 9 weekes dyet — 1. 00 00
To. Mary Post haker 37 w dyet — 3: 07. 00
To: Hen Salter 16 w: dyet — 2: 00. 00
To: Rachel Hafell. 10 w dyet — 1. 05. 00
To: y two Jacksons 4 weeke dyet Each — 1: 00: 00
To. In Collen 4 w. dyet — 0. 10. 00
To: Edwr Wooland — 3. 00: 0

To: 9 years Salery at 5 p Anum — 27: 09: 00
agreed on & sealed. out of wch
only Rec 23s. Rest due 43: 17: 00

                    Allowed Wm Dounton for
william   Salery since y Resolution
Dounton   or S Edm Andros Gou wch   12: 11: 00
                    it might be due before
                    his s Gouernmt in full

Alowed   40: 00: 00

william Stoughton.

Sam Sewall

William Stoughton, the starchy chief justice and Harvard benefactor, among the most eminent of New England legal authorities. The survivor of four previous Massachusetts administrations, Stoughton also served as deputy governor in 1692. *(Harvard Art Museums / Fogg Museum, H37)*

Samuel Sewall as he appeared in 1729, thirty-two years after he publicly repented for his role on the Salem court. Eager for political stability and intent on consensus, Sewell tripped occasionally over his conscience. *(Peabody Essex Museum)*

S. Willard

Samuel Willard, the Boston minister who tactfully deviated from his colleagues: Satan could work his evil without entering into a formal pact with an accomplice; he could assume "the image of any man in the world." A generation earlier, Willard had conversed with the devil through a possessed sixteen-year-old servant girl.

(Harvard Art Museums / Fogg Museum, H18)

Buccaneering Massachusetts governor Sir William Phips, who absented himself from the trials, to wail afterward that "some who should have done their Majesties and this Province better service" had acted precipitously, a criticism aimed squarely at his deputy governor. The witchcraft stymied all official business; Phips's enemies exploited it, he complained, to undermine his fledgling administration.

(Courtesy of Cory Gardiner)

Margaret Sewall, the wife of court recorder Stephen Sewall, "that pearl of yours" in Cotton Mather's estimation. As a much younger woman, Mrs. Sewall took in Betty Parris, whom the devil followed, promising the enchanted nine-year-old anything her heart desired.

(Peabody Essex Museum)

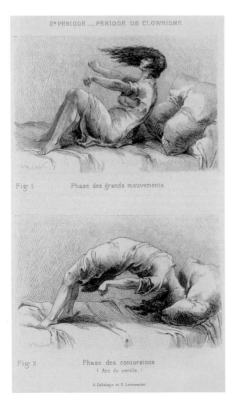

witnesses against Sarah Good

William Allen
John Hughes
Samuell Brabrooke
mary walkut
mercy Lewis.
Sarah Bibber
Abigail Williams
Elizabeth Hubberd
Ann Putman
Tittube indian
Richard Patch

An early list of witnesses against Sarah Good, the first deposed witch. Tituba and Abigail Williams appear; though included in the original complaint, Betty Parris does not. The last name is that of a forty-four-year-old Salem town man. The trial list would include William Good, the defendant's husband. *(From the records of the Court of Oyer and Terminer, 1692, property of the Supreme Judicial Court, Division of Archives and Records Preservation. On deposit at the Peabody Essex Museum)*

Convulsions and contortions as illustrated for an 1881 study of hysteria, prefaced by the artist's mentor, Jean-Martin Charcot. The pioneering French neurologist suggested a connection between trauma and hysterical symptoms, on which Freud would build *(From* Etudes Cliniques sur la Grande Hystérie ou Hystéro-Epilepsie, *Division of Rare and Manuscript Collections, Cornell University Library)*

An indictment against Reverend George Burroughs for having "tortured, afflicted, pined, consumed, wasted and tormented" Ann Putnam and "also for sundry other acts of witchcraft." The Procters' servant, the doctor's maid, and Ann's cousin Mary testified to the afflictions, observed at Burroughs's May hearing. (MSS 401, Phillips Library, Peabody Essex Museum)

Detail from a seventeenth-century German engraving of a witches' Sabbath, a more symphonic production. The Puritan preoccupations are missing but certain notes chime: male and female participants fly to a clearing; winged lions and monkey-goblins join them; frogs drop from the air. A woman tumbles from her uncooperative mount, as did the little Swedish girl and the elderly Ann Foster.

(Walpurgisnacht, by Michael Herr: akg-images)

Fifteenth-century French fliers. Among the earliest depictions of witches on brooms, the two are heretics rather than sorceresses — ironically, proto-Protestants from a sect that held that laypeople, of either sex, could preach. While enchanted brooms turned up in Salem, they conveyed no one through the air.

(akg-images)

From a 1670 illustration of Sweden's witchcraft epidemic, to play a defining role at Salem. Families travel here as they did in Essex County; women did not elsewhere load broomsticks with their children. "Several have confessed against their own mothers," observed a minister in the Salem courtroom, marveling that girls of eight or nine accused mothers of coercing them to sign diabolical pacts.

(National Library of Sweden)

11 September. Lords day

Sister Martha Kory taken into the Church. 27. April. 1690. was after examination upon suspicion of Witchcraft. 27. March. 1691/2 committed to Prison for that Fact, & was condemned to the Gallows for the same yesterday. And was this day in Publick by a general consent voted to be excommunicated out of the Church; & Lt. Nathanael Put-man, & the 2. Deacons chosen to signify to her with the Pastor the mind of the Church herein. Accordingly this. 14. Sept. 1692. The 3. aforesd. Brethren went with the Pastor to her in Salem Prison, whom we found very obdurate, justifying her self, & condemning all that had done any thing to her just discovery, or condemnation. Whereupon after a little discourse (for her imperiousness would not suffer much) & prayer (which she was willing to decline) the dreadful sentence of excommunication was pronounced against her.

Martha Kory Excommuni-cated.

Reverend Parris's account of his prison visit with Martha Corey. He found the self-described "gospel woman" obdurate and imperious, reluctant to pray with him. He pronounced her an excommunicate; she hanged eight days later. *(Courtesy Danvers Archival Center)*

From Martha Corey's deposition six months earlier. "Tell us who hurts these children," ordered Hathorne as the girls convulsed around her. "I do not know," she replied. She had no acquaintance with witchcraft. "You speak falsely," a court reporter chided, leading Corey ultimately to ask, "Can an innocent person be guilty?" Parris recorded her testimony for the court. *(MSS 401, Phillips Library, Peabody Essex Museum) dences,* expressed his doubts about witchcraft. Devils got altogether too much credit.

Sixteen people had given evidence at Burroughs's May hearing; nearly twice as many testified on August 5. Eight confessed witches revealed that Burroughs had been promised a kingship in Satan's reign. Nine other witnesses credited the short, muscular minister—that "very puny man"—with feats that would have taxed a giant. Elizabeth Hubbard, the doctor's niece, reported that Burroughs bragged of his rank. He was a conjurer, "above the ordinary rank of witches." Mercy Lewis, his former servant, emerged from a trance to share her Matthew-inflected account of Burroughs having carried her to the high mountain, to promise her the "mighty and glorious" kingdoms below. It is not easy to shake the sense that a sturdy, canny man, one who fascinated the village girls, was on trial for having survived wives and resisted Indians.

The bewitched delivered up their accounts with difficulty, falling into testimony-stopping trances, yelping that the forty-two-year-old minister bit them. They had the teeth marks to prove it! They displayed their wounds for court officials, who inspected Burroughs's mouth. The imprints matched perfectly. Choking and thrashing stalled the proceedings; the court could do nothing but wait for the girls to recover. During one such delay Stoughton appealed to the defendant. What, the chief justice asked his prisoner, did he think throttled them? Burroughs replied plainly; he assumed it was the devil. "How comes the Devil then to be so loath to have any testimony born against you?" challenged Stoughton, a brainteaser of a question and one that left Burroughs without an answer. He was equally bewildered when ghosts began to flit about the overcrowded room. They unsettled more than did the specters; some who were not bewitched saw them too. Directly before Burroughs, a girl recoiled from a horrible sight; she stared, she explained, at his dead wives. Their faces bloodred, the ghosts demanded justice. Stoughton called in several other bewitched children. Each described the apparitions. What, Stoughton inquired, did Burroughs make of this? The minister was appalled but could himself see nothing.

If those in the court did not already know that, as Mather would put it later, Burroughs "had been infamous for the barbarous use of his two late wives, all the country over," they did soon enough. It was asserted that he kept them "in a strange kind of slavery." He had brought them "to the point of death." Adding Lawson's wife and daughter to the list of casualties, one of the girls provided a motive for their murders: Burroughs resented his Salem successor for tending to a congregation that had mistreated him. The farrago of charges ultimately came together: someone testified that Burroughs had coerced his wives into swearing never to reveal his secrets. His former brother-in-law, a town tavern owner, testified—the entire family in the room—about the strawberry-picking expedition when Burroughs was said to have read his wife's mind. What did he have to say to that? asked Stoughton. The two had left a man with him, Burroughs explained. His brother-in-law objected. Stoughton demanded the man's name. A cloud crossed Burroughs's face. He had no answer. Burroughs may not have been conjurer material after all; either he was half starved and debilitated after three months in a damp, dark hole or someone exaggerated his might. He stammered and wavered. Was it possible, suggested the chief justice, that that man—a black man, at least in Mather's retelling—had stepped aside with Burroughs to fit him, along the path, with some sort of invisibility cloak?

Burroughs's answer is lost not because he failed to make one but because Mather deemed it not "worth considering"; the evidence dwarfed the objections. Burroughs does seem to have bungled his defense. Asked to account for his preternatural strength, he explained that an Indian had assisted him in firing the musket as if it were but a pistol. It was foolish to suggest an accomplice who could so easily be turned into a "black man"; Mather tended to insert demons casually into the literature and did here. Moreover, no one else had seen Burroughs's assistant. Called upon to explain his prowess with the barrels, Burroughs discovered himself without his best defense. He had managed that feat four years earlier at the home of his patron, the attorney general's father-in-law. Checkley was nowhere to be found; he appears to have kept his distance. Nor did Burroughs make more than a feeble attempt at discrediting his accusers. He was less eager to engage in gossip than the parishioners of whom he had abruptly taken his departure, who had sued him, and who transformed a minister into a wizard. His contrary streak remained on display; he reached instinctively to Scripture in the wake of a devastating Indian attack but was not going to gratify a hectoring official with an account of his children's baptisms.

He repeatedly stumbled, offering contradictory answers, a luxury afforded only the accusers. As for "his tergiversations, contradictions, and falsehoods," chided Mather, "now there never was a prisoner more eminent for them." Lawson found his Salem predecessor unconvincing on every score. Despite the senseless fits and the multitude of witnesses, the trial moved quickly; Burroughs stood before the bench for several hours at most. Out of excuses, he reached finally for the deal-clincher in his pocket. Extracting the scrap of paper, he handed it to the jury. The forty-two-year-old minister did not contest the validity of spectral evidence. With a few lines he proposed something more inflammatory still: Burroughs asserted that "there neither are, nor ever were witches, that having made a compact with the devil can send a devil to torment other people at a distance." It was a shot across the bow and the most objectionable thing he could have suggested. If diabolical compacts did not exist, if the devil could not subcontract out his work, the Court of Oyer and Terminer had sent six innocents to their deaths.

A tussle ensued over not only the substance of the lines but their source. Stoughton—who had graduated from Harvard the year Burroughs was born—recognized them at once: Burroughs had lifted the lines from the work of Thomas Ady. A leading English skeptic, Ady argued that witchcraft and the Bible were different things. He seemed to believe the latter an allegory. He inveighed against "groundless, fantastical doctrines," fairy tales and old wives' tales, the results of middle-of-the-night imaginings, excessive drinking, and blows to the head. Witches existed but they were rare; Ady believed them a convenient excuse for the ignorant physician. He suggested that one should not, when misfortune struck, try to remember who had last come to the door.* Burroughs denied having borrowed the passage, then emended his answer; he tended to be forthright at the most inconvenient moments. A visitor had passed him the text in manuscript. He had transcribed it. Burroughs had already several times agreed that witches plagued New England; it was too late in the day for such a dangerous gambit, about which we have but a portion of the story in the form of Mather's redacted version. The jury arrived promptly at a verdict. It was one that gratified the chief justice.

As he left the courtroom that afternoon, John Hale felt a tug of doubt about his former colleague, whose ordination he had witnessed and with whom he had worked closely for several years. Hale pulled aside a confessed witch. She swore she had attended a meeting at which Burroughs exhorted his confederates to topple the church and establish a kingdom of the devil. "You are one that bring this man to death," the equable minister reminded her. The situation was grave. "If you have charged anything upon him that is not true, recall it before it be too late, while he is alive." The woman had no misgivings. Hale clearly did but did not commit them to paper. Cotton Mather would himself glide past church-subverting schemes, which Hale understood to be the reason for his colleague's conviction. They seemed inconclusive proof of witchcraft. The same went for the ghosts and the expert marksmanship. Mather stipulated that neither played a role in the case, laboring so hard to keep spectral evidence in its place and out of the picture that he essentially concluded that Burroughs was found to be a wizard for having had the character of one. For his part, Increase Mather found Burroughs's superhuman strength damning; the minister had performed too many acts no man could manage without diabolical help. He believed the case airtight.

---

* Ady's denunciation of "witch-mongers"—and of "the wrongful killing of innocents under the name of witches"—was well known to Increase Mather. He had bought the volume a year earlier in London; he annotated it closely as he read.

"Had I been one of his judges," the elder Mather would allow, "I could not have acquitted him."

The convicted wizard did not disagree. At some point after the verdict had been announced Burroughs spoke with Hale. The minister might not respect wives but he did respect authority; he could quibble with neither the judges nor the jury that had convicted him. The evidence against him indeed appeared overwhelming. The only problem, Burroughs contended, was that it was all false. We do not know how he reconciled himself to his plight. In an equally dire situation he had bowed to divine displeasure. "The course of God's most sweet and rich promises and gracious providences may justly be interrupted by the sins of his people," he had noted seven months earlier, after the York atrocities. Along with both Procters, John Willard, George Jacobs, and Martha Carrier, Stoughton sentenced the minister to hang.

IX

◇

OUR CASE IS EXTRAORDINARY

WITCH, n. (1) Any ugly and repulsive old woman, in a wicked league with the devil. (2) A beautiful and attractive young woman, in wickedness a league beyond the devil.
—AMBROSE BIERCE

THE CONVICTION OF the mastermind behind the demonic conspiracy— "the chief of all the persons accused of witchcraft or the ringleader of them all," as the terrified Salem village tanner saw him—might have been thought to spell an end to witch-hunting. It did nothing of the sort. A blaze of confessions consumed August; the flames shot higher still over the first weeks of September. On the morning of Burroughs's trial, Increase Mather visited the Salem prisoners, interviewing several witches. Massachusetts's most distinguished minister pronounced himself satisfied with their reports of "hellish obligations and abominations." Days later, Martha Carrier's ten-year-old son admitted he had been a witch for a week. His mother had arranged for his demonic baptism, dipping him, naked, in the river that ran between the Carrier and Foster properties. He had flown to a meeting with three men and six women. They traveled on two poles. He did not mention his little sister but by August 10 did not need to; the Andover justice of the peace who deposed him spoke with her the same day. The conversation left him uneasy, though it would be some time before the distaste fully registered. He submitted his notes to Hathorne and Corwin with a rattled disclaimer, apologizing for "being unadvisedly entered upon service I am wholly unfit for." He hoped his account would prove helpful all the same.

Indeed it did. Sarah Carrier rode to Salem the following day. She chatted amiably along the way with the constables or before her hearing with Hathorne, who knew her story before he questioned her. She had been a witch since she was six. "And how old are you now?" Hathorne asked, for the record. "Near eight years old, brother Richard says," she replied brightly. "I shall be eight years old in November next." Sarah afflicted her victims with the spear her mother had given her and in the company of the same individuals her brother had named. Though bodily in prison, Martha Carrier appeared to her in the guise of a black cat. "How did you know that it was your mother?" inquired Hathorne. "The cat told me so," chirped the seven-year-old, more certain that she was a sorceress than that she was seven.

Plenty of black cats and red books had emerged in Salem too, but Andover witchcraft was to be substantially different. For starters, there was more of it. Witchcraft engulfed much of eastern Massachusetts and, briefly, a corner of Connecticut in 1692. It spread from Salem to twenty-four other communities. None succumbed so completely to it as Andover, where the epidemic moved faster and more furiously and produced more accused witches than both Salems combined. Between the time Martha Carrier stood trial and the time the Andover official's distaste finally caught up with him a month later, fifty witches turned up in a town of six hundred people. A family affair, Andover witchcraft moved in a less haphazard fashion. Children incriminated grandparents and mothers their sons. Siblings turned on one another. Nearly all of the witches belonged to five clans; in concert with the Salem girls, a dozen people named all the names. Accusations outflew even rumors, as cries of "You are a witch!" and "You are guilty!" ricocheted about town. Some gloated about who would be carried off next. Others glowered, further compromising themselves.

Along with a fresh cast, Andover provided a revised narrative. Ghosts tended not to disturb that community. Andover preferred satanic baptisms—in rivers, ponds, wells, or pails of water—something that had played no previous role in New England, although they had in Sweden. Nor in more prosperous Andover did neighbors normally enchant one another's hay or pigs; they focused on the diabolical, preferring spears, satanic sacraments, and witches' meetings, things of which Tituba had never dreamed. Forgotten and in her sixth month in prison—she had neither testified nor been indicted—she set the Salem stage. Andover's story tumbled fully formed out of Mary Lacey Jr.'s devil-toppling conspiracy. At its heart was Burroughs's diabolical sacrament, of which nearly every Andover confessor supplied some account and of which a consistent picture emerged, even if in Andover the devil could still appear as, depending on the witness, a colt, a mouse, a fly, a bird, a cat, a woman, a pig, a black man, a bear. Tituba aside, only Andover witches knew how to fly.

What had happened? Burroughs's conviction had unsettled, inviting a gritty dust of suspicion to permeate Andover. Closer to the frontier, the town was more vulnerable to Indian raids, to the unorthodox, and to smallpox. But it was also true that by August the authorities knew better what they were looking for. Both the questions and the answers were familiar after the Court of Oyer and Terminer's third session. From the beginning, Hathorne had engaged in skillful prompting. By August, he knew what he wanted to hear; it aligned neatly with what some wanted to say. The satanic bread grows visibly red and redder as, under questioning, his witness warms up. "Had you any hot irons or knitting needles?" Hathorne asked Foster's daughter. She obliged with an iron spindle. "Did you used at any time to ride upon a stick or pole?" he quizzed Foster's granddaughter. She had. "But doth not the devil threaten to tear you in pieces if you do not do what he says?" he challenged a Boxford woman.

"Yes, he threatens to tear me in pieces," she agreed. Only rarely did a witness disappoint. Were there not two ministers at the witches' meeting? Hathorne asked Mary Lacey Jr., who could not say and who never helped him find his man.

Partly as a result, something happened in Salem that had not happened before. Prior to 1692, only four New Englanders had admitted to witchcraft, one of whom probably had only a dim idea as to what she was saying. In the first three months of the trials, only eight confessed, including a four-year-old, Tituba, two suspects who would later recant, and cheeky Abigail Hobbs. By August, confessions bloomed faster than afflictions, accompanied by credit-bolstering displays of self-flagellating and hand-wringing. Nearly every one of the accused Andover witches confessed to the crime. Judicial coercion—"buzzings and chuckings of the hand," as one observer termed them; chains removed in exchange for confessions, dungeons threatened if they were withheld—was not the sole means to extract them. The fifty-two-year-old Boxford woman conceded she had been in the devil's employ for seven years. She later revealed that Abigail Hobbs and Mary Lacey Jr. had taunted her for days, "mocking me and spitting in my face, saying they knew me to be an old witch and if I would not confess it, I should very speedily be hanged." They frightened her out of her wits. She had no idea what she said at her trial and little of what was said to her; she caught only the formidable words "Queen Mary." There was little need for the brand of arm-twisting that, though it left no trace on paper, had in April led Mary Warren to yowl: "I will tell, I will tell!"

At the outset of her fourth interrogation, Hathorne had reminded Ann Foster that she could expect no peace without a full confession. Trading mercy for material, the bench encouraged her granddaughter, proffering something the family had not: God would forgive her if she confessed, a justice assured the wayward teenager. "I hope he will," she replied sincerely. Seventeen-year-old Margaret Jacobs was offered either the dungeon or her life. In his May letter, Cotton Mather early on recommended lesser punishments for those who renounced the devil; after mid-July, no one needed to be reminded of the price of noncompliance. In a strange Salem twist, Stoughton spared confessed witches, convicting only those who refused to acknowledge guilt.* If you could save your life by admitting that you flew through the air on a pole, wouldn't you?

Confession came naturally to a people who believed it the route to salvation, who submitted spiritual autobiographies when they entered into church membership, who did not entirely differentiate sin from crime. It stood at the heart of the New England enterprise; there was an art and a form to it, as witch-cake baker Mary Sibley demonstrated. By the craggy logic of the day, if you were named, you must have been named for a reason. Little soul-searching was required to locate a kernel of guilt. A sagging conscience bordered in any event on satanic complicity; to wrestle with one's faith was to wrestle with the devil. It was not difficult to get an eleven-year-old girl to confess to consorting with diabolical accomplices when already "she knew she was made up of all manners of sin," something she might perfectly well conclude on her own, without the advantage Mary Lacey Jr. had of regular maternal reminders. Learning of the extraordinary charge hurtling her way, Rebecca Nurse had racked her brain: For what sin had she possibly failed to atone? As had been true in Sweden, women, children, and young men tended to confess most readily. It was easier to extract confessions from women, less certain of their worth and more convinced of that of the magistrates, one reason why four middle-aged men—one of whom had suggested he was as likely to be a buzzard as a wizard—were scheduled to hang on August 19.

Something else haunted those who came before the Salem authorities. Mary Toothaker felt unworthy of her baptism. It imposed an expectation of progress; inevitably, one came up short. Many desperately wished themselves more receptive to Scripture, a yearning the devil

---

* It is unclear what Stoughton meant to do with the confessors, all of whom returned to prison. It made sense to keep them on hand to corroborate evidence and identify confederates as the trials proceeded. At least some of them expected to hang.

never offered to satisfy. They dreaded spiritual numbness, a condition akin to what a suspect described when her specter went off to afflict, leaving her "in a cold dumpish melancholy condition." "Methinks," moaned Cotton Mather, "I am but a very parrot in religion!" In the snow, her body raw, her dying six-year-old in her lap, Mary Rowlandson meditated before the campfire on how she had not used her Sabbaths to best effect. Mary Toothaker had no name other than the devil for the doubting, carping, tempting voice in her head. If you tried to pray and could not, who else could be stopping you? She, anyway, had no better answer. Any number of confessors lamented that they had wrung less than they wished from their devotions. An Andover carpenter may have had the same spiritual torpor in mind when he reported that the devil interrupted as he led his family in prayer.

While women tended to lament their vile natures, earlier misdeeds tumbled out too: an attempted suicide, a theft, a bout of drinking, an abortion, an adulterous liaison. Margaret Jacobs's mother wailed in prison about a daughter, drowned in a well seven years earlier. She believed she had killed the child. The hand-wringing, soul-baring confessing not only cleared one's name but promised to assist jailed relatives. The Laceys may have believed they were doing one another a favor as each fell in turn upon her narrative sword. And if you were going to confess, doing so in religious terms — if inverted religious terms — made sense. It put you on the road to grace. Renouncing the devil spelled relief, even if your confession had little to do with the charges at hand.

As the mystery reader knows, denials tend toward the convoluted. Confessions are refreshingly simple. Nothing is more expedient for a prosecutor, spared a time-consuming trial. From a 1692 witchcraft judge's point of view, confessions took pressure off tenuous spectral evidence. They were eagerly received and deeply reassuring, the more so as almost by definition, folded into each one — a sort of certificate of authenticity — came a gleaming bit of shrapnel in the form of an accusation. Not everyone was as careful as Tituba had been to name as coconspirators only those already under arrest. When Richard Carrier returned from his harrowing, upside-down ordeal, he delivered eleven names. On one count he remained stalwart: he did not incriminate his mother.

Martha Carrier and Ann Foster, across-the-river neighbors as well as flying companions, went their separate ways under interrogation. Foster buckled. Carrier gave no quarter. Both made their homes on the southern edge of Andover, very nearly in Middlesex rather than Essex County, at the town's newer, less desirable end. They lived as far as one could live from the meetinghouse and still remain in Andover. With the confessions of August 11, witchcraft crept into the heart of the community. Both of Carrier's younger children implicated twenty-two-year-old Elizabeth Johnson Jr., who supplied a familiar version of the witch meeting: they were about eighty in all, bent on dismantling Christ's kingdom. Johnson was a granddaughter of Andover's longtime minister, Francis Dane. That day Dane's pregnant forty-year-old daughter appeared before Hathorne and Corwin. Although a touch of her hand delivered the Procters' maid from her fits, Abigail Faulkner Sr. would not confess. Her niece urged her on "for the credit of her town." Faulkner stood her ground, according to the court report, insisting that "God would not require her to confess that she was not guilty of." She held out even after invisible forces yanked lovely Mary Warren under the examiners' table. Again Faulkner's hand delivered the Procter servant from her distress. But, objected Faulkner, she had looked at those girls when they had visited Andover earlier without affecting them in the least! That, the justices informed her, had been before she had begun to practice witchcraft.

Fifteen days later she would admit to having been furious at her niece's arrest. She "did look with an evil eye" on the bewitched. She hoped they would suffer; they were destroying her family. Again witchcraft inscribed a vicious circle. (In a similar sort of spell-casting, a Reading woman confessed that she had wished ill of her accusers.) It did not help that—though she expressed compassion for the girls—Abigail Faulkner Sr. shed no tear on their account. Nor could it have helped that she was a cousin of both Martha Carrier and Mary Toothaker and related by marriage to Elizabeth How, who had hanged on July 19. Within weeks, Faulkner's seven- and twelve-year-old daughters were detained as well. Both confessed. By mid-September, two of Reverend Dane's daughters, a daughter-in-law, four grandchildren, and various nieces and nephews would be in custody. Dane was to discover that he was related to no fewer than twenty witches.

Having married into one of Andover's foremost families, Francis Dane had served as Andover's minister since before Samuel Parris was born. He had taken it upon himself to serve simultaneously as village schoolmaster; most of the adult men in Andover who learned to write had done so under his tutelage. Andover knew few fractious land disputes; ministerial wars had not trampled local egos. Still, the town had reason to resent its autocratic, arthritic senior minister who refused to retire. Half lame, he could manage only some of his duties. The town hired a younger, more orthodox man, a Parris schoolmate, to replace their sixty-five-year-old preacher. Dane sued. Andover wound up paying both men, immediate neighbors, two generations apart, who shared a pulpit if not a worldview. Dane ruled with a strong hand, Thomas Barnard with a sharper edge. Barnard had complained that the schoolhouse in which he taught prior to his Andover ordination could have doubled as a pigsty. And ultimately the younger man would cost the town more than the seasoned one. No one accused Barnard or his young family, while over the next weeks Dane's family would be systematically targeted. He could not have shrugged off the sense that an accusation headed his way; Massachusetts now sentenced ministers to death. At least one congregant attempted to ride to his rescue. Before a September grand jury, an Andover matron recounted the flight to her diabolical baptism. She and a church deacon shared a pole with two other witches. Did she know if the devil could afflict in the shape of an accomplice without that accomplice's consent? asked the magistrates. She assured them he could not. Only the Monday before, she and Mrs. Dane had borrowed the reverend's specter in an attempt to implicate him. Their ploy had not worked. What hindered it? asked the authorities. "The Lord would not suffer it so to be, that the devil should afflict in an innocent person's shape," she explained.

Salem's whirlwind of a third act began now as—doubts and cavils nipping at the proceedings—the pace of arrests, confessions, and convictions accelerated wildly. There were to be no steely John Procters or dismissive Martha Carriers after August 19. When Carrier's children were called in, they confessed. The avowals touched on a fundamental New England problem. When could you deem yourself sufficiently reformed? Once you began confessing, there was no end in sight. The Salem magistrates sat nearly daily from the end of August through September, to hear a litany of variations on a familiar, harrowing tale. If a common jail did not guarantee that the particulars would agree, the method of interrogation and the price of resistance did. It is unclear if Ann Foster volunteered that she had flown through the air or if she was first asked if she had. She embellished as she went. She did not mention that flight in her initial hearing. She predated her pact and described the crash in her second, adding the Sabbath in the third. An Andover woman denied any part of witchcraft until she did not. A farmer belatedly inserted a satanic baptism into his confession; the devil had dipped his head in water and announced that he "was his for ever and ever." Somehow he had forgotten that detail earlier. It helped that no one knew precisely how a witch worked; Hale's curiosity was understandable. A part-biblical, part-folkloric, vaguely Swedish and less vaguely Indian construct, a witch was someone who in July pinched and strangled but in August toppled kingdoms.

By September, only minor matters failed to align. Had the argument been over a barn or a scythe? Did witches need an ointment to fly? (In New England they did not.) Was John Willard an old man or a young man? Hathorne inquired of Richard Carrier, testing his witness. Eighteen-year-old Carrier did not want to disappoint: "He is not an old man," he answered carefully. Asked how she had traveled to the Salem witches' meeting, Reverend Dane's daughter confessed she had done so on horseback. "But afterwards," notes the court reporter, she emended her answer, revealing that "she was carried thither on a pole." The "afterwards" is left to our imaginations. Tituba's hairy imp and flying monkey vanished, as did subversive plots against governors. Blue boars, bewitched oxen, dead cows, and even another ornery laundress turned up, but by September, satanic conspiracy took center stage. In court daily, with parents and guardians, the Salem girls assisted with the continuity. The star attraction, Mary Warren, fell into violent fits, on September 2 approaching the justices with "a pin run through her hand, and blood running out of her mouth." Before the court, a red stain spread across her bonnet; the mere mention of a suspect's name could level her. It was impossible to deny witchcraft in the girls' presence, tantamount to a corpse in the courtroom. You might well refute your neighbor's claim that he had seen your head on the body of a dog. But you could not discredit the bloodcurdling screams, the acrobatic postures, or counter the effect of Mary Warren crashing lifeless to the floor. Those displays sent even a self-assured twenty-nine-year-old man toward a confession. And the confessions agreed, with near-scientific accuracy, deeply reassuring to the hardworking Salem justices. It would be some time before their self-replicating nature would appear suspect rather than as proof that a deadly conspiracy had taken hold. Meanwhile, most of Essex County seemed to be flying through the air, on very crowded sticks.

WHILE THE AUTHORITIES flushed out the demonic conspiracy in Andover, they exposed something else in the process: a swarm of superstitions nested under the plain Puritan floorboards. Dane's daughter ultimately confessed to witchcraft but first squelched the rumor that she had practiced folk magic. She had decidedly not conjured with a sieve, a sort of seventeenth-century Ouija board. Weeks later a Dane in-law acknowledged that a bit of sieve-turning had indeed taken place in her household; she knew the incantation from Reverend Barnard's maid. On August 11 Faulkner's sister-in-law produced for the court a full collection of poppets, two of rag, a third of birch bark, one with three pins still stuck in it. Andover turned out to be rife with not only sorcery but also folk magic, religion's popular, wayward stepsister. It settled comfortably into parsonages. The Barnard and Dane households, like those of Higginson and Hale, were infested. Ironically, only the Parris household seemed immune.

If women were traditionally the wonder-workers—and excitable adolescent girls the fortune-teller's bread and butter—Andover turned those conventions too on their heads. The town's most gifted soothsayer proved to be a forty-nine-year-old Exeter-born carpenter, the feckless, free-spirited father of seven, something of a local celebrity. Samuel Wardwell peered into palms, casting his eyes meaningfully to the ground as he delivered his forecasts. He had predicted that the constable's wife would bear five girls before she delivered a boy. He had announced that Elizabeth Ballard would succumb to witchcraft before she did. A fair amount of expiation rippled through the testimony against Wardwell. None of those whose futures he so eerily foretold had minded at the time, not the young man whom Wardwell warned would fall from his horse, nor the one whose underage love he had divined, nor the one who learned that his sweetheart would betray him. All had gathered closely around the silver-tongued carpenter. Even in the presence of their adolescent daughters, Andover farmers begged him to reveal their fates. The sixty-five-year-old blacksmith who testified that Wardwell was "much addicted" to soothsaying had himself eagerly pulled up a chair.

Wardwell reluctantly confessed to witchcraft on September 1. Perhaps he had too often invoked the devil. It was difficult not to when cursing the stray animals that wreaked havoc in his fields.* He admitted he had met the prince of the air. Wardwell—whose affairs suffered while he pursued more frivolous interests—was the Andover man whom the

---

* There appeared to be some confusion about swearing. If you metaphorically wished the devil to carry off someone or something—a cow, a daughter—did that actually constitute an invitation? You had to be careful with those imprecations, Cotton Mather would warn. When you call the devil, he comes.

devil had assured of a militia captaincy. Soon enough the constable returned to the isolated Wardwell farm to arrest his wife of twenty years, their two eldest daughters, and an infant. The family disclosed that one brand of sorcery invited the other; Wardwell's stepdaughter allowed that she had experimented with a sieve and scissors in the spring. The devil had appeared to her, with propositions. She had subsequently met him three times, including once at the village meeting, where she had seen a dozen people riding on poles. The dabbling in the occult further fueled the confessions; many admitted easily to folk magic, about which they already felt guilty and at which they had been caught red-handed.*

Protestantism reared from magic, but—especially when it came to witch-hunting—the two had a tendency to blur. Lawson had inveighed in March against most of the practices to which Andover residents would confess, warning against the temptation to "charm away witchcraft." Mary Sibley's experiment had earned her a very public rebuke. Martha Carrier's niece had earlier attempted to kill a witch by bottling and baking an afflicted person's urine. Mary Toothaker consulted a book of astrology. On September 6 Reverend Hale testified to Dorcas Hoar's regular fortune-telling. Years earlier he had insisted she get rid of her book of palmistry, which his children had seen. Hoar had also taught herself to make predictions based on marks around the eye. At her trial the court measured her (four-foot-seven-inch-long) elf-lock. They ordered the matted tail cut off. Hoar quailed; if they did so, she protested, she would fall ill if not die. The court prevailed.

Mather acknowledged that in the presence of evil, many turned to illicit "burnings, and bottles and horseshoes and I know not what magical ceremonies" for relief. At the same time, the seventeenth-century minister distinguished more ably than do we between "Catholic nonsense" (horseshoes, urine cakes, touch tests) and proper Puritan theology. The line proved not so much unclear as perforated. Too late for George

---

* Reverend Dane would disclaim all knowledge of such charms and experiments. And after forty four years in the village, living in close contact with his parishioners, he would, he insisted with some embarrassment, have known of such things!

Jacobs, Increase Mather denounced sticking witch suspects with pins. What if the pin was itself enchanted? He wrote off the swim test used to identify witches as idle superstition. (His son endorsed the practice.) Was it faith healing to call in the girls to ask what ailed someone, as Parris did in mid-June when he sent for Mercy Lewis, who, in a trance, diagnosed a bewitched Putnam? Did boiling a lock of an afflicted child's hair in a skillet over the fire constitute medicine or superstition?* What was the difference between Samuel Wardwell warning that Ballard's wife would fall ill and Increase Mather growling—after Sewall's altercation with his son—that harm would befall the Sewalls? In 1676, Increase Mather set aside a day of prayer on which to beg the Lord to smite the stalwart Indian leader, King Philip. It worked, like a charm and within the week. How to distinguish between a prayer and a spell—or between a spell and an alchemical balm that cured wounds from a distance? The Lord's Prayer was understood to be a sort of "holy charm" before which ghosts and goblins fled.†

If the occult, religion, folklore, and medicine tended to overspill their bounds, they did so as profligately in wealthy households as anywhere. A December 1692 statute would deem locating hidden treasure a kind of witchcraft; the Massachusetts governor owed his career to that very pursuit. Phips had consulted a London fortune-teller who predicted a glorious future, a prediction not altogether different from the assurances Cotton Mather received from a glimmering, winged angel in his study. Several Salem judges owned volumes of astrology. Many dabbled in alchemy. All read almanacs. Wait Still Winthrop's library was particularly rich in mystical literature, in tables of astrological houses and treatises on magic. He shared the ministerial addiction to portents and prodigies.

---

* It caused the child agonies. And it brought to the door a neighbor who purported to be selling chickens. Assumed to have been conjured by the experiment, she would be accused, tried, and hanged on September 22.
† Mather would later be called on to defend himself for having conjured the devil in order to cure the Goodwins. In a detractor's view, his prayers resembled less divine revelation than the "charms and spells of superstitious persons."

The message could moreover be mixed. Increase Mather railed against various countercharms while acknowledging that they worked. Samuel Sewall consulted a minister as to whether the timing was propitious for an addition to his home. The supernatural hovered always nearby, in and out of religious dress. On his sickbed, at age twelve, the future Marblehead minister had spoken with an ethereal figure who supplied three magical pills. They cured him; he thereafter assumed his visitor to have been an angel. When another young woman who had communed with an angel began to terrorize those around her with divine edicts, Mather declared the spirit a devil for the sake of neighborhood peace. The Massachusetts ministers conjured with the question still in 1694, when they settled on it for their September meeting: How to differentiate a diabolical from an angelic visitation? Witchcraft and divine providence could easily be confused, as could a scowl and the evil eye, a prophecy and an educated guess, sin and diabolical collusion.

When it came to writing up the trials, when it came to hawking his beloved Swedish blueprint for Salem, Cotton Mather gave the folkloric a free pass. He knew the hidden world was there somewhere; he would relinquish no tool to exhibit it. He performed scientific calculations with the Bible to determine the date of the end of the world. In 1705 he applied Mosaic history to a mastodon tooth unearthed in New York. The angelic visitations in the study and demonic ones in the parlor spoke to the same anxieties and served similar ends. Sarah Good seemed to put curses on her neighbors. Cotton Mather so wished an odious son-in-law ill that he prayed for his death for three days on end. The entreaties worked; Mather took full credit for having dispatched the wicked young man, previously in the pink of health. His demise was "a wondrous thing."

AS SALEM PREPARED to execute five additional witches, four of them men, one a minister, misgivings made their way to the authorities from likely and unlikely addresses. Seventy-six-year-old Robert Pike had missed Phips's May swearing-in because he was busy taking testimony against Amesbury widow Susannah Martin. He lost part of his summer to the case against the Salisbury minister's mother-in-law, Mary Brad-bury, who — transforming herself into a blue boar — scrabbled under a horse's hooves, upsetting the rider. A popular Massachusetts council member, Pike was a longtime militia captain and Salisbury's most eminent citizen. The previous spring he had traveled to Maine with Stoughton and Gedney to negotiate an Indian truce. He was acquainted with Burroughs, having quarreled with him years earlier. Pike's son had been a Harvard classmate of Parris's; he was married to Joshua Moody's daughter. And his daughter had married a Putnam, which put him in a delicate position as far as the blue boar was concerned. Mary Bradbury's accusers were family, as, briefly, she had been as well; a fellow selectman, her husband was among Pike's closest friends. Pike was a devout man of wide reading and firm, fearless convictions. Decades earlier he had challenged a ruling on religious freedom. Found guilty of defaming the court, he was banned from public office.*

As mid-August crowds began to converge on Salem, Pike may have been the first public official to register qualms about the proceedings. In a long letter to Justice Corwin, he reviewed the logic of the case. He believed in witches, though observed that they were rare in the Old Testament. (As others had pointed out, most were also men.) Not for a minute did he doubt the devil's powers. The Old Deluder had made off with the Lord himself, torturing him with "temptations of horrid blasphemy." Surely any good man could suffer the same fate? For that matter, faulty character should not prove grounds for conviction. There were, Pike pointed out, plenty of "innocent persons that are not saints." He had particular trouble with ghosts; people simply did not return from their graves. And how could a man be simultaneously at Salem and Cambridge? Pike hinted that some fraud might be afoot. Personally he did not believe so. He agreed that their case was exceptional.

Which brought him to the oracular girls. Pike had not seen them in

---

* Salisbury could not live without him. It disregarded the order.

action but had heard plenty, as had everyone in Massachusetts. Here he stuttered a little. Whatever they were doing was either divine or diabolical. But for the record, communing with those who had been publicly and plainly buried happened to be unlawful. Leviticus warned specifically against consulting mediums or spirits. Why was it less likely that God racked and tormented the girls than that Satan did, "especially when some things that they tell are false and mistaken"? Pike wondered who might be abetting whom. The devil could work his art without human help; the opposite was not true. The visionary girls could know what they did only from the father of lies. How could they bear valid witness? The same went for the confessors, whom he was the first to skewer. Then there was that other logical pothole: it made no sense whatever that the accused should practice witchcraft in court while pleading innocent. "Self-interest," noted Pike, "teaches every one better." Whatever his perversities, the devil had no incentive to purge the world of witches. Pike worried that superstition played too great a role in the matter. He did not subscribe to witch marks. Hardly the first to do so, he wished Scripture were more clear. To his mind, it was better to allow a guilty man to live than execute an innocent, for two reasons: The heavens managed these matters better than did men. And a guilty person could be prosecuted later, on better evidence, while an innocent "cannot be brought again to life when once dead."*

If Pike received a response, it has not survived. Cotton Mather wrangled with a similar query on August 17, over a quiet week, as anticipation of a hanging registered as a pause in the proceedings.† One of Boston's

---

* Pike was not the only person to note that there are few witches in the Old Testament, fewer still in the New Testament. He also observed that Old Testament sorcerers were not so very clever. They could not even interpret Pharaoh's dream!

† In Salem village, Parris was of a very different mood. Following the psalm on Sunday, August 14, he dismissed his congregation with a prayer and a blessing. He asked that the men remain behind. Had they noticed that several parishioners had recently forgone communion, rarely bothering even to attend meeting? He called for volunteers to look into the matter, one that hardly required an investigation: The empty pews belonged to the families of Rebecca Nurse's son and sons-in-law. The volunteers had trouble locating Peter

wealthiest merchants, council member John Foster, appealed to Mather. Did he still believe a horrid witchcraft was afoot? Mather feared he did. Ten weeks had elapsed since he had set out his freewheeling thoughts for Justice Richards. Six witches had been executed in the interim. Five more were scheduled to hang in forty-eight hours. Again Mather warned against spectral evidence. Nevertheless, he saw that some use could be made of it. Its effects, he conceded, could well serve to "strengthen other presumptions." All Protestant writers agreed that the devil abused innocents. As if heading off a jinx, Mather twice mentioned that he should not be surprised were his specter to begin to molest his neighbors. Again he stressed that neither the touch test nor the evil eye should offer grounds for conviction. Again he opted for lesser punishments. Why not set bail, at least for those imprisoned solely on spectral charges? (That category did not include a malefactor against whom God had "strangely sent in other, and more human, and most convincing testimonies." The allusion was clear: the court had not sentenced Burroughs on invisible evidence alone.) He would be happier if reprieves were offered, if those under suspicion were simply deported. Again he could not write a letter on the subject without recourse to the word "nevertheless." With reason, he apologized for the "incoherency of my thoughts." They had grown no more lucid since May.

Mather steered clear of the illogic that so troubled Pike. He added a new refrain, however, harping on the virtues of the magistrates, "so eminent for their justice, wisdom, and goodness," discerning men for whom no one had "a greater veneration" than he. Whatever their personal beliefs, they would not, he assured Foster, proceed on a contested principle. A master of inconsistency, the devil might act the same way nineteen times, only to reverse course the twentieth. "It is our singular happiness," Mather assured Foster, "that we are blessed with judges who are

---

Cloyce, rarely at home, the church record drily notes, "being often with his wife in prison, at Ipswich, for witchcraft."

aware of this danger." He hoped Foster would strengthen their hands. He broadly hinted that the court might include a minister or two. In an English case a generation earlier, a clergyman had seen to it that an outbreak of witchcraft was extinguished. (No fewer than eighteen, including a vicar, had been executed in that outbreak.) "Our case is extraordinary," he too concluded.

The following day another Harvard-trained minister heard of a different set of misgivings. Seventeen-year-old Margaret Jacobs had been shackled in the foul Salem prison since early May, when Parris's niece had accused her. Margaret may have been on hand when her grandfather had guffawed that Hathorne and Corwin could burn him or hang him, he was as likely a buzzard as a wizard. Arrested the same day, she had quickly confessed at Beadle's Tavern. She was a witch. She had signed the devil's book. (Held next door, Jacobs was appalled to learn as much. He had urged her not to make herself an accessory to her own death, an outburst that further incriminated him.) The following day Margaret accused a Salem woman. She became a regular at that week's hearings; she watched an iridescent Burroughs bite the Procters' maid. She had been in manacles ever since. Her father and uncle had fled. Her half-crazed mother was in chains, awaiting trial.

On August 18 she could bear it no longer. Her grandfather was scheduled to hang the next morning, along with Burroughs and John Willard, whom she had helped to convict. There was a problem with her confession, the teenager announced on the eve of their execution; it was "altogether false and untrue." At her hearing, the afflicted girls had crumpled at the sight of her, startling Margaret. The justices had offered her a choice. "They told me, if I would not confess, I should be put down into the dungeon and would be hanged, but if I would confess I should have my life," she explained. She had opted for her life. She had since suffered "in such horror of conscience that I could not sleep for fear the devil should carry me away for telling such horrid lies."

Miserable, she requested permission to speak with Burroughs, whom she would have known as a child. She begged her former minister's forgiveness. Burroughs prayed "with and for her," in chains, as ever resolute in his faith. Margaret was a conscientious, emotional girl with a lively mind. She shared her grandfather's facility with language. She was also one of the "false witnesses" whom Burroughs blamed for his conviction. It is unclear when the news that she had recanted escaped the prison; she was one of only two suspects to do so. (The fortune-telling Wardwell would be the other.) It did Margaret little good; the magistrates would not believe her. For her reversal, they consigned her to the stifling dungeon. Fortunately she discovered that she preferred "death with a quiet conscience" to a load of crippling guilt. From the dungeon she wrote her father. She had seen her mother, who remained insane but sent her love. She knew her family was effectively ruined. She was wretched, not knowing how soon she would hang. She assured her father that she anticipated "a joyful and happy meeting in heaven." She remained his dutiful daughter.

Others remembered the evening of August 18 differently. While in the dungeon Burroughs comforted the sobbing teenager who had helped convict him, he managed to preside over a witches' meeting in central Andover, where he administered the sacrament. Removing his hat, he took solemn leave of his recruits. He urged them to continue steadfast; they should admit nothing. He does not appear to have explained why he elected not to torture the confessors who had betrayed him. An old farmer warmly expressed his hope that he would see Burroughs again. The spectral minister demurred. He did not think that likely.

Early the next morning officials led George Burroughs, John Willard, John Procter, and George Jacobs through the Salem prison yard and into a cart. Martha Carrier—Ann Foster's flying guide, the queen of hell, and the intemperate mother of five children, all but one of whom were now incarcerated—joined them, convicted for having served alongside Burroughs, whom she had no reason ever to have met before their trials. Though sentenced to die on the same day as her husband, Elizabeth Procter did not. Stoughton had granted a stay of execution in light of her pregnancy. The largest throng to date turned out to inspect the first men Massachusetts was to execute for witchcraft. Two Boxford constables carrying a suspect to her village examination crossed paths with the procession as it wound its way up the rocky slope; they dropped the accused witch at a house at the foot of the hill so as not to miss the affecting spectacle. As Parris had noted in a 1689 sermon: "To see a man taking his last steps, and going to the place of execution (though worthily) moves everyone whose heart is not harder than adamant." Unlike the pirates and murderers whose hangings had attracted crowds and whose execution sermons thousands had flocked to hear, all five insisted as the cart creaked up the hill that they were falsely accused. They hoped the real witches would soon be revealed; they "declared their wish that their blood might be the last innocent blood shed upon that account." Willard and Procter struck one onlooker as especially dignified. So "sincere, upright, and sensible of their circumstances" did they remain that they provoked tears all around. They forgave their accusers, the justices, the jury. They did not snarl that suffering children would continue to suffer after their death, as had Glover in 1688. They prayed they would be pardoned for their actual sins.

They did so before an especially distinguished crowd. As Increase Mather had made a courtroom appearance to observe the Burroughs conviction, so Cotton Mather journeyed to Salem for his execution. The presence of Mather—tall, clear-eyed, handsome, an imposing figure at any time—spoke to the significance of the occasion. At least some of the condemned appealed to him, in heartrending terms. Would he prepare them spiritually for the journey ahead? It is unclear if Mather did so or if he held to the same hard line as Noyes, who did not pray with witches. Some hearts remained adamantine.

By a corollary to the logic that determined that he should be tried last, forty-two-year-old Burroughs was executed first. He mounted the ladder with composure, pausing midway to offer what many expected to be a long-delayed confession. Again the dark little man—a wisp of his former self after fourteen weeks in the dungeon—proved a contrarian. Perched above a crowd that included his former in-laws and parishioners, a noose around his neck, he burst into an impassioned speech. He had a full command of Scripture; he had had time to prepare. He outdid himself. Burroughs knew how to deliver a sermon, gravely and fervently, his voice rising for emphasis and sinking for effect, producing an awe "like that would be produced on the fall of thunderbolts." Those he cast down that Friday earned, noted an eyewitness, "the admiration of all present." He spoke genuinely, heart-meltingly, the hangman a few steps below him on the ladder. With his last breaths, Burroughs entrusted himself to the Almighty. Tears rolled down cheeks all around before he concluded with some heart-stoppingly familiar lines. "Our Father, who art in Heaven," he began, continuing, from the ladder, with a blunder-free recitation of the Lord's Prayer, an impossible feat for a wizard, one any number of other suspects had not managed. Burroughs left his audience flustered. For a few moments it seemed—tears welling in the eyes even of prominent men—as if the crowd would obstruct the execution.

That feat on the part of a bona fide wizard called for an explanation, one his accusers speedily furnished. The devil stood beside Burroughs, dictating to him. Who else could preach so eloquently? Minutes later the minister dangled from a semi-finished beam. The life had not gone from his body when Mather stepped in to smother the sparks of discontent. He spoke firmly, always with much deliberation. From his horse, the lanky, light-haired twenty-nine-year-old reminded the spectators that Burroughs had never been ordained. (That was also true of Bayley and Lawson, at least one of whom was on the hill that day, but made the dying minister seem unorthodox.) What better disguise might the devil choose on such an occasion than to masquerade as "an angel of light"? It was a time-honored tactic. In the encyclopedia of backhanded compliments, that one qualified among the greatest; to the last, George Burroughs was to be condemned for his gifts. His sentence had been a just one, Mather assured the crowd. The protests quieted, as did the minister who dangled in midair. He may have heard a portion of Mather's remarks. Willard and Procter climbed the ladder next, followed by Martha Carrier and glib George Jacobs, Margaret's grandfather.

When cut down, the bodies were apparently dragged by their nooses to a common grave, about two feet deep, between the rocks. According to the sole surviving account, Burroughs's shirt and pants were removed and his corpse fitted with a shabbier set; one did not waste a fine pair of pants. The man who eleven years earlier, in the presence of Ann Putnam's father, had agreed to settle among the villagers and "live and die in the works of the ministry among them" was then buried carelessly, with Willard and Carrier, "one of his hands and his chin, and a foot of one [of] them being left uncovered."

THE EXECUTION OF a beguiling, articulate, Scripture-spouting minister who protested his innocence to the end created nearly as much disquiet as the idea that a beguiling, articulate, Scripture-spouting minister had actively recruited for the devil. The material facts—as even Procter and Willard acknowledged en route to their deaths—were not in dispute. Only the question of liability was. Did John Higginson, who had seen nearly everything there was to see in his fifty-three years in the Salem ministry, who had resisted offering Andros the answer the royal governor sought, and who had reprimanded the Salem villagers in 1687 for their "uncharitable expressions and uncomely reflections," their "settled prejudice and resolved animosity," truly believe his jailed daughter to be a witch? Evidently so. While she acknowledged that she had helped to convict innocents, even Margaret Jacobs thought witches flew about Salem. The August executions sent Cotton Mather to his desk, scrambling to make sense of the story. Samuel Sewall had been elsewhere that Friday, but in his diary entry for August 19, he almost unconsciously allowed his former schoolmate the last word. "Mr. Mather," Sewall wrote of the executed five, "says they all died by a righteous sentence." He continued, in a less comfortable vein: "Mr. Burroughs, by his speech, prayer, protestation of his innocence, did much move unthinking persons." Sewall permitted himself no note of sympathy for a colleague he and his family had entertained at their table over the years, who was never to see the refurbished Sewall kitchen. Nor did he allow a hint of doubt to creep into his lines.

Six days after the Burroughs execution, Hathorne and Corwin examined an eighteen-year-old Andover girl, a niece of Elizabeth How's. She denied any knowledge of witchcraft until, learning that her older sister had accused her, she admitted she had met the devil the previous winter. She submitted to a satanic baptism, flew on a pole, and attended a meeting of two hundred witches. (The older sister confirmed that figure but warned that five hundred witches infested Massachusetts.) The eighteen-year-old incriminated two additional sisters in the process. She also fielded several questions not posed before Burroughs had been hanged: Did she know of any innocents in jail? (She did, but only one.) And was it possible, the magistrates asked, suddenly rounding an unfamiliar corner, that the bewitched girls were themselves witches? "No," the teenager assured them. "They were honest persons that helped to bring out the witches." Either flustered by Pike's queries or for their own reasons, the Salem justices cast about for reassurance.

It arrived in floods of confessions. As the summer wore on they grew quicker, the poles more crowded. More witches were named in August than in July. Yet more identified themselves in September, in uniform accounts that continued prominently to feature Reverend Burroughs. Forty-six-year-old William Barker and forty-nine-year-old Samuel Wardwell, the Andover fortune-teller, confessed within days of each other. Both were financially strapped Andover farmers. Wardwell made no mention of the diabolical Sabbath, only of the afflictions he had caused. He had signed a decades-long pact with the devil. It would expire when he was sixty. Barker was a newer recruit. He supplied one of the largest estimates of the diabolical crew — in his version, it was more than half as large as Salem village — and the most compelling story line. He too fielded the court's unsettling new questions, to which he provided new answers. Did he know of any jailed innocents? He did not. What did he make of the girls? They performed an invaluable service. He warned the court against misinterpretation. Furious at having been discovered, the witches connived to make the bewitched appear guilty.

As Stoughton prepared to empanel jurors for the next court session, Barker delivered up additional riches. Little notoriety rivals courtroom notoriety; a rapturous moment in the spotlight was another diabolical lure. And Barker considered himself on a mission. Begging forgiveness of the honorable magistrates and all God's people, he pledged "to set to my heart and hand to do what in me lyeth to destroy such wicked worship." He offered a rationale for the choice of the Salem meadow for the infernal assembly, an explanation that gratified the authorities, Parris in particular: the devil aimed to destroy the villagers because they bickered among themselves and with their ministers. (In fairness, were those the criteria, Satan would have had his choice of New England congregations.) He confirmed what the court had warned the villagers seventeen years earlier: in their incessant squabbling, they had given Satan a leg up.* Barker revealed the devil's plan, one that demanded urgent attention all around: the archfiend intended to see to it that "there should be no day of resurrection or judgment and neither punishment nor shame for sin." He promised that "all persons should be equal," an equally heretical notion in 1692.

Andover meanwhile could not seem to get enough of the Salem soothsayers. They sent for the village girls on multiple occasions, stationing them in sickrooms, at the head and the feet of the ailing. Probably early in September, the junior Andover minister, Thomas Barnard, convened them for another purpose. Without explanation, he assembled seven local women in the meetinghouse. They included a thirteen-year-old girl and her mother, as well as Dane's forty-one-year-old daughter. Barnard led the group in prayer, then blindfolded them. As the Salem girls twitched and tumbled, Barnard instructed the Andover women to

---

* Cotton Mather spun a similarly ego-bolstering theory: it was because the justices were so great that the devil had touched down in Essex County, where he could be assured of a fair match.

lay their hands upon the visitors. Each calmed immediately. The seven were arrested and carried off, trembling. "We were all exceedingly astonished, and consternated and affrighted even out of our reason," they reported. Their examiners hectored them, "telling us that we were witches, and they knew it, and we knew it."

As the confessions piled up, the accusations did too, which meant new arrests and more intricate accounts. The first time she confessed, fifty-one-year-old Rebecca Eames had not been baptized by the devil; had been in his employ for seven years; was reluctant to agree her son was a wizard; did not name names. After twelve days in prison, she had practiced witchcraft for twenty-six years and been baptized. She revealed her son had been a wizard half as long. She named names. Five Andover sisters confessed. It had been a long time since anyone dared ask if the justices were all out of their wits or chuckled that he was as likely to be a buzzard as a wizard; Martin and Jacobs had both hanged. Just as everyone had known a victim of King Philip's War, everyone now knew an accused witch. In the free-for-all men accused women, girls their elders, children their mothers. Eleven members of one family stood accused, nine by relatives. The newly accused ranged in age from seven to eighty; nearly half were teenagers. Husbands continued to prove ready to believe the worst of their wives. Elizer Keyser, whose fireplace Burroughs had enchanted, accused another man, a Manchester cordwainer.

From the outset there were holes in the record. As Stephen Sewall explained, it was simply impossible to get everything down on paper. Several scribes were minimalists to begin; any number of accusations went unrecorded. After a point in the summer, denials barely materialized on the page. The toll of the trials registered across the judicial system, which—its magistrates tied up in daily witchcraft hearings—deferred all less pressing business. Exhaustion made itself felt from the highest levels on down; it was "difficult and troublesome work," the attorney general himself pointed out, the more so because he enjoyed no settled salary. The wealth of detail was too much for anyone. Even Hale, writing later, grew "weary with relating particulars."

For the jail keeps and for tavern keepers like the Ingersolls, the trials were good business. For everyone else, they introduced a season of hardships. Local constables worked overtime as they rode great distances to deliver warrants, escort suspects to and from hearings, track down escapees, and arrange jail transfers. The strain—at once brain-teasingly epistemological and entirely mundane—manifested in different ways. The Andover justice of the peace who had worried that he was unfit for the service he had entered upon signed his last arrest warrant toward mid-September. He had issued nearly forty summonses. Whether doubt or fatigue cramped his hand is unclear; he simply refused to sign another. The result was predictable, similar to what had happened after (the late) John Procter scoffed that the girls should be returned to their spinning and (the late) John Willard hesitated to round up suspects: the official and his wife were accused of witchcraft. His brother was named as well, along with his nonspectral dog accomplice, on which he was seen riding about. Both families—the men descended from Governor Bradstreet and poet Anne Bradstreet and could claim any number of minister relatives—fled north. The dog was put to death, one of Andover's two canine victims. The other sent the girls into frenzies each time it looked at them. It was shot.

All around hay went unhayed, corn unharvested, fences unrepaired, crops untended. Orchards were neglected and woodpiles depleted. Meanwhile a breeze began to lift off the water; the nights grew brisk. The most labor-intensive weeks of the year lay ahead. Fall was cider-making season, the time to dry and salt and pickle winter stores, to pick turnips and apples, husk corn and gut carcasses. It was difficult to do so among divided families, between prison visits—Mary Esty's husband rode to see her twice every week for five months—short-handed, after long days in court, or while tending to bewitched, or bewitching, relatives. (It was yet more difficult to do so in custody. As Stoughton's closest political associate complained in the wake of the Andros coup, how was he to run his farm, on which his family depended, from prison?) Many found themselves near ruin, having sold off livestock at bargain prices to support jailed relatives. It is almost impossible not to feel sorry for the deputy sheriff who at the end of the year pleaded not only exhaustion but penury. Since March he had done nothing but serve warrants, apprehend suspects, attend arraignments and trials, and convey witches from prison to prison. Those activities had "taken up my whole time and made me incapable to get anything for the maintenance of my poor family." He was now impoverished. (It did not help that Massachusetts believed paying public servants to be optional.) The sheriff begged Phips and Stoughton for assistance "this hard winter that I and my poor children may not be destitute of sustenance and so inevitably perish." He was depleted from serving his king and country, the more so as—having been bred a gentleman—he was "not much used to work." The Middlesex county sheriff and the Cambridge jail keep had paid for horses and men on the road and wood for the prison, for guards to accompany carts and for the constables who raised a hue and cry to pursue suspects, all from their own funds. They had devoted countless hours to those in their custody, for whom they bought provisions. They received no reimbursement. John Higginson Jr., the minister's son serving as clerk, found himself in debt solely given the expense of his public appearances.

It is more difficult to sympathize with Justice Corwin's twenty-five-year-old nephew, the Essex County sheriff. George Corwin wore himself out dismantling the households of the accused. He would have been within his rights emptying them after convictions; he did not always wait so long. Even as she begged Reverend Burroughs's forgiveness, Margaret Jacobs knew that Corwin had ransacked her grandfather's riverside estate. He and his men stripped the household bare, confiscating cattle, hay, barrels of apples and bushels of corn, a horse, five pigs, the beds and blankets, two brass kettles, a quantity of pewter, the chickens, and the chairs. They removed even the gold wedding ring from the finger of Margaret's mother. She managed to reclaim it but was left with no choice but to buy provisions from Corwin. While the Englishes safely escaped, their gabled mansion did not. Corwin unblushingly looted the property, afterward leaving it open to plunder. Furniture, household goods, and family portraits disappeared, a haul worth some fifteen hundred pounds. Only a single servant's bed remained. (Here Corwin was surely overeager. The Englishes had not been convicted, having fled before they could be tried.) After a sixty-one-year-old woman hanged in September, a deputy rode to her central Andover home. He seized the family's cattle, corn, and hay, and advised her sons to speak with Sheriff Herrick to avoid the sale of what remained of their possessions. In that conversation, Herrick—the born gentleman—kindly offered "an opportunity to redeem" the property, suggesting the sum of ten pounds. He settled for six, so long as the bribe materialized within the month.

The seizures introduced another complication. What to do with the orphaned children? Many were left to shift for themselves, the Procters' without a scrap of food or a pot in which to cook. Soon after Burroughs's arrest, his third wife "laid hands on all she could secure," including her husband's library. She then sold the family's goods and loaned out money, at interest. With her daughter she headed south, deserting her seven stepchildren, of whom the eldest was sixteen. "We were left, a parcel of small children of us, helpless," they petitioned later. They retained not even a token by which to remember their father. Late in September, the Andover selectmen turned for guidance to the Ipswich court. Both the fortune-telling Wardwell and his wife were in prison.* What to do with the couple's seven children? They were in "a suffering condition," one the town could not alleviate. The court ordered that most or all of them be placed with "good and honest families." The youngest had just turned five. The eldest wound up with his uncle, John Ballard, whose brother had accused Wardwell and conducted him to jail.

Hathorne, Corwin, and Gedney devoted the greatest number of hours to witchcraft. They conducted hearings every week and sat on the

---

* In fact Wardwell had gone to his death four days earlier. He did not live to be sixty, when his pact with the devil was set to expire.

court through September. Parris made the five-mile trip to town count-less times a week, devoting what has been estimated to be fifty days between late March and early September to witchcraft. He neglected duties at home to do so; family prayer must have fallen regularly to over-taxed, overwrought Elizabeth Parris. At night he returned to a disor-dered household, resounding still with Abigail's shrieks. He would not write in his sermon notebook for months. (Nor did he bleat about his salary, which went unpaid.) He accompanied his niece to court, testify-ing against ten suspects. He felt it his duty to assist in the mission at hand, a mission in which no one proved as tireless as Chief Justice Stoughton. Laboring to clear the land of witches once and for all, Stoughton con-vened the Court of Oyer and Terminer for a third session, to begin at noon on Tuesday, September 6.

The court that week indicted nineteen witches, the greatest number to date. It did so on more meager evidence and at an accelerated pace; Stoughton had a crisis to contain. He also met with several complica-tions. While her own niece testified against her, Mary Esty confounded the court, which had already once found it difficult to reconcile the gen-tle fifty-eight-year-old with witchcraft charges. In September even the Ipswich prison keepers defended the mother of seven, a model prisoner, unfailingly civil and sober. In nearly the same words—there were cam-paigns on all sides—the Boston jailers weighed in as well. Esty submit-ted a petition to the bench. She had been removed from her vast Topsfield farm in April, arrested and rearrested. Her eldest sister had been hanged in July. She and her sister Sarah Cloyce had but three requests. The court allowed them neither counsel nor the privilege of pleading their case under oath. Would the judges advocate for them? Second, might they call witnesses on their behalf? Topsfield's minister stood ready to swear to their innocence. Echoing Robert Pike, they asked if they might be tried by some other evidence than—the wording is notable—"the testimony of witches, or such as are afflicted, as is supposed, by witches." The women requested "a fair and equal hearing of what may be said for us, as well as against us." With each demand they subtly censured the court; English law guaranteed those rights. Stoughton sentenced both sisters to hang.

He met with another headache as the grand jury heard the attorney general's case against Giles Corey. At least seven Salem girls attested to the village farmer's supernatural gifts. ("I verily believe in my heart that Giles Corey is a dreadful wizard," swore Mercy Lewis. "I verily believe that Giles Corey is a dreadful wizard," swore Ann Putnam Jr. "I verily think he is a wizard," swore Elizabeth Hubbard.) He had turned up spectrally in their beds, in the meetinghouse (where he claimed a prime seat; witches attended a surprising number of sermons), at Bishop's hanging. When called before the grand jury on September 9, Corey stepped forward, raising his hand. The charges read, he pleaded not guilty. The court then inquired: "Culprit, how will you be tried?" Only with the words "By God and my country" could the trial proceed. Corey had uttered those five words in front of sentencing magistrates before; that September Friday he withheld them, stalling his case. Corey proved no more amenable to the attorney general's demands than he had to those of his wife when in March she had attempted to unsaddle his horse. (The court had convicted Martha the previous day.)

Fortunately for Stoughton, a few men remained ready to rally the troops and circle the wagons. On September 2 Cotton Mather wrote to the chief justice. The world knew well of his "zeal to assist" in Stoughton's weighty, worthy task. Already Mather had done more behind the scenes than Stoughton could possibly know. (The claim rather upended the muddled, equivocal letters to Foster and Richards.) He had been fasting almost weekly through the summer for an end to the sulfurous assault. He felt the ministers ought to support the court on its extraordinary mission; none had yet done so. He volunteered to step into the breach. He had begun to write up a little something, partially "to set our calamity in as true a light as I can." He promised to dispel any doubts about endangered innocents, a passage he underlined. He hoped to "flatten the fury, which we now so much turn upon one another." Mather promised to submit every syllable of his narrative to Stoughton so that "there may not be one word out of point." (He knew full well that he could publish nothing without permission, but had in mind an official history.) He would recount the Swedish epidemic, stressing those aspects that most resembled Salem's, an exercise analogous to reconstituting a person from his shadow. Might Stoughton and his colleagues sign off on his little labor, which would remind the people of their duties in such a crisis? As he knew how many momentous matters weighed on the chief justice, he troubled him with only a partial manuscript. He could skip its first thirty-four pages. In a singular valediction, Mather wished Stoughton "success in your noble encounter with hell." Unlike Mary Esty, Mather got the answer he wanted. Stoughton began his fulsome reply on the verso. The best account we have of 1692 comes down to us then—shaped by the swelling public outcry in August—as a propaganda piece.

Parris knew firsthand of the furies of which Mather spoke. As Stoughton pressed ahead, the village minister sounded very much like a man who understood that the destruction of the church was to begin at his home. He chose Revelation 17:14 as his September 11 text. Surveying the battle at hand, he cribbed shrilly and liberally from Cotton Mather. The war in which they engaged had long been prophesied. It pitted "the devil and his confederates" against Christ and his followers. They were the chosen; they would prevail. Besieged by doubters as much as by devils, Parris tamped down dissent; those who opposed the court were no better than those "mutinous and murmuring Israelites" who rebelled against Moses, wondering if it might be better to return to Egypt than die in the wilderness. To resist the magistrates was to side with the devil. A call to unity as much as piety, Parris's was a fiery address and doubtless a rousing one. In its wake Parris asked for a vote to excommunicate Martha Corey, who in March had derided Parris's niece and her coevals as "poor, distracted children." The vote carried but was not unanimous.

That Wednesday Parris visited Martha Corey in prison, accompanied by Nathaniel Putnam and the church deacons, two of them uncles of afflicted girls. Corey greeted her callers coolly, without the eagerness with which she had received them six months earlier, when she had looked forward to enlightening magistrates and ministers. She was no less forthright; Parris—who had transcribed the record of her husband's hearing—found her "very obdurate, justifying herself and condemning all that had done anything to her just discovery and condemnation." He suggested they pray. The self-described gospel woman had no interest; her callers did so largely for themselves. Afterward Parris pronounced "the dreadful sentence of excommunication" against his embittered parishioner, cutting her off from all church privileges and expectations and delivering her soul to Satan, perhaps a redundant exercise. The visit was brief.

ON SEPTEMBER 1, three days after William Barker exposed Satan's depraved scheme to make all men equal, witchcraft judge John Richards married in Boston. A little rough around the edges, Richards was a relative newcomer to Massachusetts, if a vastly successful one. He took as his bride Ann Winthrop, Wait Still Winthrop's sister. Stoughton performed the ceremony, which Samuel Sewall attended. Two other justices likely joined them; the shipbuilder Bartholomew Gedney was a Winthrop relative by marriage. The bride's sister was Mrs. Jonathan Corwin.* That no fewer than four witchcraft judges found themselves related by marriage and together on a Thursday afternoon was not unusual. Narrow to begin, the Massachusetts power base was yet more attenuated at the top. Just as the same men served as deacons and selectmen, the colony's largest taxpayers, its most storied names, dominated civic, legal, and religious affairs. Drawn from a tiny cohort, they made for a self-perpetuating elite precisely because of unions like the Richards-Winthrop one. The

---

* The festivities took place at the home of Bridget Usher, whose husband was then or was about to be in hiding, having been accused of witchcraft.

marriage was Richards's second. His first wife had also been a Winthrop, an aunt of his new bride.*

Ministerial circles overlapped and intersected in the same ways. The wife of Salem court clerk Stephen Sewall, the woman who cared for Betty Parris, was the daughter of an influential, conservative Cambridge minister, a longtime friend of the Mathers. Reverends Noyes and Hale were related by marriage, as were Hale and Gloucester's John Emerson, as were Samuel Parris and the Milton minister. As a group, the clergy—like the court—was somewhere between close-knit and inbred, a fraternity as much as a family.† They shared beds when they gathered for meetings. They laid relatives to rest in one another's tombs. Nicholas Noyes felt so close to the family of senior Salem minister John Higginson that he plunged directly into their personal affairs with but the barest-boned of apologies.

As Chief Justice Stoughton had taken nearly every political side over the previous tumultuous decade, it could not be said that the members of the court always saw eye to eye politically. Politics and business—and the politics of defending their commercial interests—joined the justices, however. Nearly every one had sizable interests in the frontier. They had suffered the greatest financial losses in 1689 and 1690, when Indians destroyed their mills. Stoughton and Sewall had traveled to New York together to enlist support for a joint attack on Montreal; Hathorne and Corwin had traveled to Maine and New Hampshire to review frontier defenses. In 1681 Stoughton was chosen to sail again to London to attempt to negotiate a new charter, an errand that fell to Richards—Stoughton had heard enough about New England insolence—when he refused.

Samuel Sewall socialized regularly with most of the other justices. Stoughton and Winthrop figured among his closest friends; he was more

---

* The relations stretched back a generation as well. Sewall's parents had been married by Saltonstall's father. Stoughton had served for years alongside Hathorne's father. Winthrop settled Corwin's father's estate. Sewall's and Cotton Mather's fathers were friendly; Winthrop's and Stoughton's had come to blows.
† Some carried this to extremes. Increase Mather lost his wife, who was also his stepsister, in 1714. He afterward married his nephew's widow.

intimate yet with Noyes. The frantically busy Sheriff Corwin—on October 7 attempting another confiscation—was the nephew of Justice Winthrop and the son-in-law of Justice Gedney. The same pattern prevailed all over New England, where a tight weave bound a small number of families. The witchcraft judges—and the ministers to whom they appealed, whose salaries they largely paid—observed fasts and debated the meaning of Revelation together, prayed, dined, swam, and sailed together. They baptized, taught, and mourned one another's children (Willard would baptize and bury seven of Samuel Sewall's); courted one another's widows; settled one another's estates. They would bear one another's coffins.

Together they had conspired against and toppled a government. Cotton Mather had written the declaration justifying the revolt against Andros, read to a vast crowd from the council chamber gallery. Surrounded by several future witchcraft judges, Stoughton had censured the deposed governor inside the town house. In London Increase Mather had lobbied hard for the new charter; he would defend himself for having betrayed his compatriots in agreeing to it for some time. Lieutenant Governor Stoughton—who also happened to be the chief justice and the senior Massachusetts statesman—had every reason to prove that they had returned the colony to a stable footing. Having agitated for the coup, having advertised cabals well in advance of a coven, those men needed to demonstrate that New England could regulate its own affairs. It could repel invaders. For a bunch of nonconformists, they took well to lockstep; it was some time before a hint of disaffection escaped the court. They had every inclination to fall in line and every political incentive to do so. Increase Mather's 1691 boast that "there is not a government in the world that has been laid under greater obligations by a particular man than the government here has been by me" had as much to do with what happened in Salem as any flying monkeys or chimney jellyfish. Writing in October, a critic of the court prefaced his remarks with a disclaimer: he would prefer to chew off his own fingers than "willingly cast dirt on authority, or anyway offer reproach to it." A member of Willard's congregation, he was a Sewall intimate. He would soon be related to Winthrop by marriage.

Through the parched summer, the story belonged purely to those who accused and confessed. Their accounts hung together. As of mid-September, the court repeatedly hit snags. Around midmonth, Reverend Hale's wife was named; the mother of three young children, she was seven months pregnant. Hale had raised some unpleasant questions, as he did at the Burroughs trial. (The charge introduced another awkwardness as well; Mrs. Hale was Reverend Noyes's first cousin.) It was about now that Andover justice of the peace Dudley Bradstreet, finding no reason to detain another witch, rested his pen. Nor had Stoughton heard the last from Mary Esty, who submitted a second petition. This time she addressed herself to the bench and beyond it, to Governor Phips. Scheduled to hang in a week, she was reconciled to her fate. "I petition to your Honors not for my own life," she wrote, "for I know I must die." The court was doing its best to eradicate witchcraft. But it proceeded wrongly. She ventured a few thoughts. Might the justices carefully depose the afflicted girls—and separate them for an interval? She recommended they try a confessed witch. Several had perjured themselves.

It remained to be seen what to do with old Giles Corey, with whom the court made no progress. Late in July, in the Ipswich prison, "very weak in body but in perfect memory," he had written his will, leaving his hundred-acre farm to two of his sons-in-law. John Procter, the neighbor with whom Corey alternately tussled in court and drank conciliatory toasts, had been hanged. Excommunicated Martha was to hang in a matter of days. Her husband had no intention of confessing, less of gratifying the justices, before whom he appeared several times, refusing on each occasion to deliver up the essential phrase. Obstinate to begin, he was all the more so having made the tour of New England prisons. He knew that anyone who set foot in Stoughton's courtroom was doomed. The girls would prattle on about his turtle familiars and his see-through knives all over again.

Entirely the man who boasted that he had never had recourse to the term "frightened" in his life, Corey declined to utter the obligatory five words. Failure to do so, Stoughton warned him, would result in the dreadful, medieval sentence of *peine forte et dure,* or "painful and severe punishment." Stones and lead would be piled atop him; the procedure was to be repeated until the suspect relented or died. It was a punishment invoked but never before used in New England. When last it had been threatened the 1638 defendant—a woman accused of having murdered her three-year-old—opted for the gallows.

Probably on September 17 guards led Corey either to the enclosed Salem prison yard or across the street to a field. He removed his shoes and stripped to near nakedness before stretching out spread-eagled on the cool ground. Officials covered him with a plank, on which they piled rocks; Dounton, the overemployed jail keep, presumably assisted. The authorities worked directly from established legal code. It called for the defendant to be pressed under "as great a weight as he could bear, and more." Corey was to "have no sustenance, save only, on the first day, three morsels of the worst bread, and, on the second day, three draughts of standing water, that should be nearest to the prison door." In its earliest hours the torture could yield results. After a certain point it was too late. Spectators clustered around, among them a friend of Corey's, a prosperous, truculent Nantucket sea captain. Salem-born, he had served as a selectman. He understood the situation as well as the odds; a brother-in-law counted among the fugitives. He attempted to reason with Corey.

While Giles Corey no doubt had a great deal to say between labored breaths, the sacrosanct phrase did not figure among his pronouncements. He repented but would not reconsider his obstinacy. For a second time that week the church excommunicated a Corey; the sentence appears to have been delivered in the midst of the torture. As he could not be declared guilty of witchcraft, he was excommunicated as a suicide. In the last moments of his multiple-day ordeal, his tongue protruded from his mouth; evidently Sheriff Corwin "with his cane, forced it in again." The old man expired soon after, at about noon on September 19. Corwin ventured out immediately to claim his estate, a curious irony as forty-three years earlier Giles Corey had made his first court appearance for having stolen wheat, tobacco, bacon, and a host of other goods from the sheriff's family. A son-in-law managed to hold off Corwin by agreeing to a ruinous fine.

As George Burroughs won the distinction of being the sole Harvard graduate to hang for witchcraft, Giles Corey would prove the only individual pressed to death in America. We have no record of how Martha—who could not have guessed where a quarrel over a saddle was to lead—received the news or if, in prison, the condemned woman heard her husband's groans. Others shrank from the abominable ordeal as they had shuddered at the execution of a minister. The extent of the revulsion can be read in a letter dispatched the following day to Justice Sewall. As Corey gasped under boulders, witches again assaulted Ann Putnam Jr. They threatened to press her to death that Sabbath evening, even before Corey expired. She finally had some respite when—reported her father—a ghost materialized. It delivered a convoluted tale that Putnam felt compelled to share with Justice Sewall. The ghost was that of the man Corey had allegedly murdered years earlier. He reported that while the devil had promised Corey that he would not hang, God decreed he would suffer a painful and appropriate death. Ann's ghostly conversation, Putnam marveled, was unusual for two reasons. He himself had known Corey's victim. The report was true! Yet it had all happened before his daughter was born. The twelve-year-old seemed to be in charge of the past as well as the future.

Why had no one mentioned this earlier? wondered Putnam. "Now, Sir, this is not a little strange to us; that nobody should remember these things, all the while that Giles Corey was in prison, and so often before the court." The earlier jury had found him guilty of murder, "but as if some enchantment had hindered the prosecution of the matter, the Court proceeded not against Giles Corey." (Putnam explained that magic: the verdict had cost Corey a hefty sum.) Sewall read the letter just after Corey's death and in precisely the spirit in which it was intended. The righteous had prevailed. The Sabbath-evening apparition reassured;

again, the pieces fit together with a satisfying click, though Sewall only half grasped them. From the letter, he took the ghost to be Corey's. And Sewall understandably inferred that Corey had "stamped and pressed a man to death." (Putnam had written that he had murdered his victim "by pressing him to death with his feet.") What the jury had heard in 1676 was that Corey had delivered nearly a hundred blows with a stick. It had also found him not guilty.

Martha Corey was to be a widow for only two days. Under colorless skies on the morning of September 22 she made the plodding trip across Salem to what would be known much later as Gallows Hill. It was a lecture day, probably chosen as such. Mary Esty rode with her, as did Samuel Wardwell and five others. Although scheduled to join them, Dorcas Hoar did not. Shorn of her elf-lock, Hoar was still very much alive. She preferred to remain so; days earlier, she had confessed to "the heinous crime of witchcraft." Noyes and Hale intervened on her behalf, appealing to Phips or Stoughton—they were unclear as to whether the governor or his deputy was in charge—for a stay of execution. Hale could not explain why Hoar had signed the devil's book but was sensitive to her confession. Given her distress, might she have a month, pleaded the ministers, "to perfect her repentance" and "prepare for death and eternity"? She posed no further danger. They dangled some bait, adding that Hoar was divulging names of her confederates. The stay was granted. Sewall noted that this was the first time a condemned witch confessed. It would also be the only time.

Others displayed more concern for their souls than their lives in the days leading up to the September execution. Fortune-telling Samuel Wardwell too experienced a change of heart. He had no interest in hearing further reports that he had attended a June sermon, muscling his way into the middle of the men's pews, when he had been roasting in prison that day. He was not a witch. How could the court convict him solely on spectral evidence? He recanted, only to discover that it was not as easy to renounce a diabolical baptism as a proper one. By the logic of the day, Dorcas Hoar—declaring herself guilty—remained in prison, while

Wardwell—maintaining his innocence—rode to the gallows.* He discouraged those who might have considered following in his footsteps; Wardwell would be the sole confessor to hang. He may have guessed as much but preferred, like Margaret Jacobs, not to live with a mutilated conscience. Corwin's men swooped in to seize Wardwell's livestock, carpenter's tools, eight loads of hay, and six acres of corn, which they presumably picked themselves. A little prematurely, Corwin showed up at the Hoar address as well. He rode off with the curtains and bed.

As the ox-drawn cart trundled up the path that parched, dull Thursday, a wheel stuck. It was some time in being liberated. The girls narrated: the devil hindered its progress. (The truth may have been more prosaic. Wheeled vehicles tended to be useless outside town on rough, rutted paths. This one was overloaded.) Asserting her innocence to the end, Martha Corey, the Salem gospel woman, ended her life with an ardent prayer, delivered from the ladder. As Wardwell addressed the crowd, a cloud of smoke from the executioner's pipe drifted into his face. He began to choke; the devil interrupted him, sneered his accusers, who could not have liked what the freewheeling Wardwell had to say. He was innocent. No court could prove otherwise. The extended Nurse family sobbed as Mary Esty climbed the ladder, bidding husband, children, and friends farewell. She spoke in the selfless, sober tones of her petition. Nearly all present found themselves in tears as the executioner fixed a hood over Esty's head and nudged her from the rung.

Nicholas Noyes remained dry-eyed. Turning to the bodies dangling from the primitive structure, he scoffed: "What a sad thing it is to see eight firebrands of hell hanging there!" None left a trace in Mather's history, on which he was already well advanced; they died a little out of time. They denied any part of witchcraft, as had, over four sessions, every one of the twenty-seven suspects who had come before the court, each of whom it sentenced to death. All were convicted for having tor-

* One wonders if the result would have been different were the genders reversed. Men tended to fare less well once in the clutches of the witchcraft court.

tured the Salem village girls, of whom some had never heard, and upon whom most had never before set eyes. Many in the Bay Colony kept careful count. With less exactitude but much relish, Puritan enemies marveled at the Massachusetts frenzy. They were eagerly "hanging one another" for precisely the crime, noted two Quaker merchants who visited Salem that fall, of which they liked to accuse their supposedly devilworshipping sect. Indeed they were "hotly and madly, mauling one another in the dark," as Cotton Mather wailed. Witch-hunting seemed to encourage you to act like the very creatures—Catholics, Frenchmen, wizards—you abhorred.

X

---⋈---

PUBLISHED TO PREVENT FALSE
REPORTS

For prophecy is history antedated; and history is postdated prophecy:
the same thing is told in both.
—NICHOLAS NOYES, 1698

ONE HUNDRED AND TWENTY soiled, underfed witch suspects were that fall in custody. Some were pregnant. Several had fallen dangerously ill; others had nursed now-dead suspects. Living atop one another in squalid hives of rumor, they made for unruly company. Nearly half had confessed. Reverend Dane's daughter-in-law and William Barker's sister-in-law described frantic, exhausting accusations, impossible for "timorous women to withstand." They had agreed to all that was imputed to them, "our understandings, our reason, our faculties almost gone." Bewildered and ashamed, they had little idea what to expect. Should confessed and accused witches anticipate the same fate? Some had insisted as fiercely on their innocence as others had testified to diabolical pacts. The satanic recruits hissed and spat at the holdouts. They knew perfectly well they were witches too! The confessors meanwhile reinforced one another's accounts. But where through the summer their uniformity had corroborated a diabolical plot, by late September it began to strain credibility.

The scope of the crisis disconcerted as well. Was it truly possible, John Hale would wonder, his disquiet growing, "that in a place of so much knowledge, so many in so small compass of land should abominably leap into the devil's lap at once?" The court met with mounting resistance. They needed an authoritative version of the invasion, one that would validate their hard work, underscore the present danger, and ease all doubts. Fortunately, they already had their volunteer.

Early in September Cotton Mather had requested the court transcripts from Stephen Sewall. The Salem clerk agreed to provide them but did not deliver. It is difficult to read anything into his hesitation. The court sat almost continuously through mid-September; Sewall's wife was pregnant with their fourth child. He fielded all kinds of requests and queries, including those from Parris, regularly in town, and the Nurses, repeatedly on his doorstep. He had enough paperwork to manage without transcribing additional copies of trial documents. Impatiently, cloyingly, Mather attempted again to wink the pages out of him days before the September 22 hanging. So that he might prove "the more capable to assist in lifting up a standard against the infernal enemy," he begged Sewall to make good on his promise. He needed accounts of only six or—were Sewall feeling indulgent—a dozen of the principal cases. The additional effort would pale in light of its benefits.* Mather reminded him that he was going out on a limb for the sake of their friends. He did not need to point out that one of those friends was Sewall's elder brother.

Recasting a favor as a command, Mather dictated his terms. The court recorder should submit the pages to him in narrative form. At the very least, he should elaborate on what he had so often related; would Sewall repeat what he had said about the confessors' credibility, about the dumbfounded jurors and their interpretation of spectral evidence? Mather did not sound like a man who had repeatedly inveighed against

---

* That argument came easily to Cotton Mather, who wrote as naturally as he breathed. His biographer has cause for gratitude, his bibliographer for paralysis. While he claimed his life was "almost a continual conversation with heaven," Mather managed to produce 437 books, 26 of them between 1692 and 1696.

it. He wanted the most convincing morsels; he would take Sewall's account and run with it. Witchcraft was after all more difficult to disbelieve now that eleven witches had hanged. (He had an additional reason to jump promptly into the fray: Both Hale and Noyes contemplated books of their own. Whatever they were witnessing, the Salem participants recognized it to be historic.) In a postscript Mather pulled out the heavy artillery: He worked at the command of their governor. He hinted at dire political repercussions.

Sewall had little opportunity to delay further; he and his family traveled the following day to Boston. He may have delivered a clutch of documents then, although he was never to furnish the eyewitness account. That Thursday found Stephen Sewall at his brother's richly appointed mansion—the decor was all oak and mahogany—with Stoughton, Hathorne, John Higginson Jr., and Cotton Mather. On September 22, as Salem hanged eight witches, the men wrangled with criticisms of the court. All continued fully satisfied with their work, including even Higginson, whose sister was jailed and who had signed a warrant for the arrest of a new Gloucester suspect days earlier. It was imperative that the justices, rather than Mary Esty or Giles Corey, remain the heroes; they were in the business of exterminating witches, not creating martyrs. It was a lecture day; they joined in prayer. If they were looking for a nod of divine approval, it arrived that evening in the form of a torrential, much-needed downpour.

Although on his May arrival Governor Phips had found his constituents miserably plagued by "a most horrible witchcraft or possession of devils," he had left the infestation entirely to Stoughton, preferring visible enemies, or at least those he could properly bludgeon. He could afford to ignore it no longer. On September 29 he returned to "agitated controversy." It impeded all other business. Those inclined to malign the new charter and administration exploited the trials to discredit Phips, coaxing the "strange ferment of dissatisfaction" into an open contest. Even if he had expected politically to sidestep the issue, he could not personally escape it; by fall he found himself related to an afflicted child and an accused witch. In his absence, his wife too had been named.* Phips grappled with the future of the court, scheduled to reconvene in October.

The justices labored, Mather had noted, "under heart-breaking solicitudes, how they might therein best serve God and man," another way of saying that they were downright confused. A squeak of dissent soon escaped the court; several justices shared their concerns with the governor. They feared they had been overly severe. Were they to sit again, they allowed, "they would proceed differently." (We do not know the names of the dissenters. They were most likely the newlywed Richards, or both Richards and Boston merchant Peter Sergeant. Richards—whose mother had fended off a witchcraft accusation years earlier—had already applied for direction. Sergeant was protected by a large fortune and free from the web of business associations that bound the rest of the court. Sewall deferred to Stoughton; Winthrop did not take stands. The three Salem justices remained steadfast.) Eminent churchmen posed good and pointed questions. Other esteemed citizens stood accused, even while a prominent Bostonian carried his ailing child the twenty miles to Salem, suddenly the Lourdes of New England, to be evaluated by the village girls. He incurred the wrath of Increase Mather. Was there "not a God in Boston," exploded Harvard's president, the most illustrious of New England ministers, "that he should go to the Devil in Salem for advice?" Things were wholly out of hand when a Boston divine was up against an adolescent oracle.

Again a golden age of witchcraft coincided with a golden age of witchcraft literature; both Mathers toiled away at books. Increase Mather finished first. On Monday, October 3, the association of ministers assembled in the bright Harvard library, just above the hall where most of them had years earlier attended chapel and lectures. They had expected to tackle a

---

* As her trial date approached, a prisoner had appealed to Lady Phips for help. She took it upon herself to sign a release warrant, which the jail keep honored. The retaliation was swift; the governor's wife was immediately accused.

question of propriety: Might a clergyman administer communion to a neighboring congregation that found itself without a minister? More urgent matters had intervened. As moderator, Cotton Mather read aloud late that morning from his father's newly completed *Cases of Conscience*, pages that had grown out of the association's August discussion. The essay constituted a nod to a 1646 English work that Increase Mather recommended to witchcraft jurors. He enlarged upon and urgently reiterated his May argument, dismantling spectral evidence. For a third time he insisted that although the devil could impersonate innocents, his ruse rarely succeeded.* Courts seldom convicted wrongfully, "so that perhaps there never was an instance of any innocent person condemned in any court of justice on earth" through sheer satanic delusion, a sentence contorted in its syntax—it included another court-clearing, twelve-ton "nevertheless"—if not its logic. Nor did the devil ordinarily arrange for persons to fly for miles through the air. Indeed he had done so in Sweden. But the visible and invisible worlds tended not to intermingle so freely.

Increase Mather set out to countenance a court; he dealt largely with forensics. While spectral sight existed, it was by no means certain that the Salem girls enjoyed it. Nor was it even clear that they were bewitched. He suspected possession.† (Except in his son's pages, the two words would be conjoined from this point on.) Possession easily accounted for the convulsions, the elastic limbs, the prophetic statements, the lunges into fireplaces, and the girls' blooming health. In his estimation, the evil eye was "an old fable." If witches emitted a physical venom from their eyes, all within their range of vision would be affected. (Alden had made the same point in vain.) As for the touch test: "Sometimes the power of imagination is such as that the touch of a person innocent and not

---

* The argument went like this: If the devil assumed the guise of innocents to work witchcraft, then he might just as well borrow their forms to commit theft and murder. And if he did, reasoned Mather, "there would be no living in the world."

† Martha Corey had come the closest to making that point in March, when—to Hathorne's and Noyes's fury—she had suggested that the girls were "distracted."

accused shall have the same effect." He rejected those "magical experiments" as he did the witch cake, a "great folly." (Mary Sibley could have had no idea how an idle afternoon's experiment would be immortalized.) Familiar with every detail of the proceedings, Mather knew even of the diabolical dog, shot for having afflicted a bewitched girl. "This dog was no devil," he explained, "for then they could not have killed him." He mentioned no other Massachusetts fatality in the body of his text. Nor did he mention that the court had disregarded every shred of the minister's June advice.

What constituted sufficient proof of witchcraft? A "free and voluntary confession" remained the gold standard. That said, some innocent blood had been shed in Sweden several years after their great epidemic, when a youngster accused her mother of having flown her to nocturnal meetings. The woman burned. The daughter afterward came before the court "crying and howling." She had accused her mother falsely, to settle a score. Evidence of spell-casting or secret-divining was dispositive, as were feats of unusual strength. (Both Mathers went out of their way to squelch doubts about Burroughs, who raised a special flurry of them.) When credible men and women in full possession of their faculties attested to these things, the evidence was sound; fifty-three-year-old Mather had no patience for mewling teenage girls. If one did not accept testimony from "a distracted person or of a possessed person in a case of murder, theft, felony of any sort, then neither may we do it in the case of witchcraft."* He cast a vote for clemency: "I would rather," he wrote that fall, "judge a witch to be an honest woman than judge an honest woman as a witch."

Eight ministers endorsed Mather's October 3 statement. By the time the pages went to press, six more had joined them, including some whose parishioners had been executed and others whose parishioners awaited trial. On the morning that Cotton Mather read his father's cogent essay

---

* Montaigne's terse, sixteenth-century corollary: "It is, after all, putting a rather high price on conjecture to roast a man alive for it."

aloud, the Salem justices heard testimony against a thirty-four-year-old Lynn witch. Oversize cats galloped ferociously across a roof. A grown man had for three nights been too terrified to sleep in his own home. "A black thing of a considerable bigness" brushed past a woman as she dressed. The justices summoned a writhing Mary Warren. A touch of the suspect's hand calmed her. With two glances the woman struck Mary to the floor. Warren went home, the Lynn witch to jail. The wind had shifted but gusted still in two countervailing directions at once. Around this time, Phips or someone in his confidence dispatched a series of questions to a group of New York clergymen, applying for a crash course in witchcraft. At least some believed the Massachusetts ministers out of their depth.

For the first time, seven suspects went home on bail the following day. All were under the age of eighteen. The youngest were Carrier's seven-year-old daughter and Reverend Dane's eight-year-old granddaughter. Among the eldest was Mary Lacey Jr., Ann Foster's headstrong, voluble eighteen-year-old granddaughter. Not everyone felt reassured by those releases; three suspects escaped from the Boston prison that week. William Barker, the Andover farmer who revealed the diabolical plan to make all men equal, seized the moment, as did a couple who had spent over nine months in custody. Sheriff Corwin promptly turned up to confiscate what was left of their Salem village estate. He had already once paid a call, rounding up cattle with which to settle their prison bill. Twelve children remained on the farm; on October 7 an elder son managed to hold off Corwin with a ten-pound bribe. It was the last attempted forfeiture. Wrote a Boston merchant that week to a friend in New York: "We here hope that the greatest heat and fury has stopped."

THROUGH OCTOBER, ONLY the silence had proved as eerie as the caterwauling girls. Even men who had boldly deposed English governors and landed in prison for civil disobedience went mute. Skeptics kept to themselves. Former deputy governor Thomas Danforth had conducted the

April hearing at which Parris's niece first mentioned the assembly of witches in her backyard, at which the girls thrust hands into mouths rather than identify Elizabeth Procter, at which Mrs. Pope had levitated and Abigail's hand was singed. Since that time Charlestown's largest landowner had had his doubts. He seems to have remained quiet, allowing only in mid-October that he did not believe the court could continue without the support of the people and the clergy. Its practices were dangerously divisive. Michael Wigglesworth, the renowned sixty-one-year-old clergyman, author of the much-read *The Day of Doom,* endorsed *Cases of Conscience* on October 3 but voiced no opinion on the trials until much later. The cost was high, the confidence in intelligent, able-bodied Stoughton higher still. All too often dissenters wound up named or fined. Fifty-two-year-old Samuel Willard, Increase Mather's only equal among ministers, had sounded notes of caution all along. He assisted the Englishes in their escape; he participated in the private fast for John Alden. In exchange, he met with "unkindness, abuse, and reproach"—and with a witchcraft accusation.

When finally the tide turned, it did so abruptly. Those who had flinched silently exhaled loudly. Fingers were pointed; tempers flared. Husbands berated themselves for having bullied wives into confessions. As soon as it was safe to do so, all began to speak at once, rarely with Increase Mather's circle-squaring, institution-sparing delicacy. When accused, a distinguished Bostonian filed a thousand-pound defamation suit. Cotton Mather observed that as the witchcraft intensified it was as if they fell under a spell, "enchanted into a raging, railing, scandalous and unreasonable disposition." As that spell lifted, they were more than ever "like mad men running against one another."

The shift came about less for any single reason than for twenty of them. Terror had worn out its welcome; the system and men's spirits were exhausted. The court had moved too aggressively and too expansively. It was a tricky business; the government was after all an Increase Mather creation. When the justices applied for advice, they reached out to him. No one had a greater investment in the Phips administration. Nor had the colony any more accomplished civil servant than the masterful, Mather-appointed Stoughton. He seemed now to stand with the more orthodox rural ministers, Reverends Parris, Noyes, Barnard, and Hale, who rejected all doubts about spectral evidence. The lack of modulation surprised some; how could "any man, much less a man of such abilities, learning and experience as Mr. Stoughton," subscribe to such a belief? a London correspondent, following events at a distance, would inquire in January. It was destitute of all reason and counter to the facts of history. Anyone who asked the kind of probing question Justice Richards had in May was unlikely to look on equably as a minister hanged; Burroughs's speech on the gallows rattled more even than had Corey's stubborn silence. The monolith shuddered a little.

Few could have felt so wholly torn as Samuel Sewall, who heartily endorsed the motto that "agreement makes kingdoms flourish," who skittered away from the controversial or confrontational. Early in October, his brother Stephen fell ill with a serious and prolonged fever. It is impossible not to wonder about causation; there may have been some soul-searching all around. The illness did not abate. Late in the month the Salem court clerk pledged to serve the Lord better if his life were spared. In and around Boston, his older brother spent October talking and reading about witchcraft, a subject on which everyone had an opinion. Some of the commentary was solicited. Much was not. Quakers predicted that witches would continue to prey on Massachusetts until the colony repented for having hanged their co-religionists.

On a damp Friday morning at the end of the first week of October, Sewall and Samuel Willard rode north to call on a trusted colleague. Sewall regularly appealed to Wenham minister Samuel Torrey for career advice, about legal matters, even about a trip to England. Widowed a month earlier, Torrey was lonely; in his kitchen, the three men discussed the crisis decimating the colony. The Wenham minister believed there had been irregularities. Those could be corrected, he felt, after which the court should resume its vital work. Heartened, Sewall left under a wintry drizzle. Strong winds moved in by morning. A hard frost fell the following night. Snow followed behind as Sewall settled in for some difficult reading. He may have had a preview of the pages Willard had composed to preface Mather's *Cases;* he already knew the opinion of his minister. It was not what a judge who had sent eleven to their deaths cared to hear.

As early as April, Willard had lectured on a celebrated instance of Satan abusing an innocent; the serpent in the Garden of Eden had been a mere instrument in his hands. The creature could not be blamed for actions "besides its nature, and beyond its apprehension." (As Willard exonerated the snake in Boston, Hathorne in Salem ensnared Bridget Bishop with his timeless logic—how could she claim she was not a witch when she did not know what a witch was?) Willard did not doubt the diabolical mischief. When detected, witches were to be exterminated. But the God who had declared as much (Exodus 22:18) also mandated two witnesses to a capital crime (Deuteronomy 17:6). Given the severity of the punishment, more rather than less proof was in order; Willard made an impassioned case for innocent until proven guilty. Nor was prosecution always desirable. Nowhere did God decree that every capital case be pursued. To do so was to "subvert this government" and "reduce a world into chaos"—a Puritan nightmare. In his preface to Mather's pages can be heard the roiling October objections to the crisis: "overhasty suspecting" "too resolute conclusions," "too precipitant judging," "bold usurpations," the dangers of "being misinformed."

Sewall had only admiration for his minister. He preached with uncommon genius; he delivered even a substandard sermon with aplomb. A man of discretion and equanimity, he did not pause in the pulpit when a parishioner fainted dead away. He came running when you had a teenager in despair; Sewall would appeal to him for assistance with his fifteen-year-old's heart-stabbing crisis of faith. Among Massachusetts ministers, only Cotton Mather would exceed Willard's literary output. When it came to experience with "evil angels" and "hellish designs," no one in New England could rival that of Boston's Third Church minister. As a young clergyman in remote Groton — fifty miles west of Salem village and yet more isolated, also in a snowy season — Willard had found himself contending with some earlier oddities. In 1671, his sixteen-year-old servant had begun to roar and shriek, erupt in "immoderate and extravagant laughter," engage in "foolish and apish gestures," and leap about the house. She fell wailing to the ground. She found herself alternately strangled and senseless. She endured forty-eight-hour-long fits of such intensity that six men could not restrain her. Elizabeth Knapp too saw enchanted creatures in the fireplace.

It was all a reprise of Salem, except that it had occurred twenty-one years earlier, seventeen years before the Goodwin children. Where those youngsters had barked like dogs and purred like cats, Elizabeth Knapp barked like a dog and bleated like a calf. She drowned out prayer. She struck at and spit in the faces of the adults who tended her. She met with Satan. Anticipating Cotton Mather, she could report that there were more devils than men in this world, a claim that sounded especially plausible in an outpost like Groton. Willard called in a doctor to treat Elizabeth. He diagnosed a stomach disorder, "occasioning fumes in her brain and strange fancies." After a second examination, he refused to administer to her further. Whatever ailed the teenager was diabolical in origin.

Elizabeth was much visited that winter — Willard noted that her afflictions peaked under observation and grew more violent as the crowd increased — but no one spent as much time at her side or came in for as much abuse as her master himself. He devoted full days to the sixteen-year-old, praying with her, reasoning with her, consoling her. She too accused a respectable neighbor of having bewitched her. She too acknowledged having signed a satanic pact. The devil had promised "money, silks, fine cloths, ease from labor, to show her the whole world." He gathered firewood for her even after she refused his help. In the reprieves between fits she wept uncontrollably. She confessed to a cascade of sins: she had snarled at her parents, neglected prayer, contemplated suicide. Willard remained calm throughout, even when Elizabeth revealed that the devil had instructed her to murder the minister and his children; she was to toss the youngest in the fire. Elizabeth was by turns incoherent, violent, accusatory, apologetic, "sottish and stupid," entranced, and utterly lucid. She too suffered from a magnetic pull into the fireplace. She nearly dove into a well. She contradicted herself hourly. It was the devil; it was the neighbor; it was the devil disguised as the neighbor; it was all fancies; she met the devil on the parsonage stairs; she had signed a seven-year compact in blood; she had signed no such thing.

It had just been affirmed that she was not possessed when — on a dark Sabbath afternoon in December — a low, male growl began to emanate from her body. Elizabeth's family rushed to her side from meeting. Willard followed, directly from the pulpit. "Oh! You are a great rogue," she greeted him, in a husky, adult voice, her lips motionless. Willard's blood ran cold. "Daunted and amazed," he called for a light. Some gimmick was surely at work. He challenged the devil to show himself, conversing with the gruff spirit through the teenager for some time. "You tell the people a company of lies," it taunted him. Willard answered, "Satan, thou art a liar and a deceiver, and God will vindicate his own truth one day." Ultimately he asked the company to kneel in prayer at Elizabeth's bedside. Louder this time, the devil growled, "Hold your tongue, hold your tongue, get you gone, you black rogue." Willard took careful, copious notes but resisted conclusions. One could counterfeit a great deal but this, he was certain, one could not. (Deodat Lawson had sworn the same of the Salem girls. No one could screw her body into such positions by natural means.) As to whether or not Elizabeth had truly covenanted with the devil, "I think," Willard concluded, "this is a case unanswerable." More comfortable with irresolution than Parris or either Mather, Willard stopped there, noting, among other curiosities, Elizabeth's ability to pronounce *P*s and *M*s without the slightest motion of her mouth. He kept her under close observation at an inconvenient time of year. And he did something more taxing yet: he suspended belief.

Elizabeth eventually recovered. No one hanged. Willard's fine-grained, clinical study of what seemed in the end a clear case of demonic possession circulated widely. Increase Mather would refer to it in *Cases;* he had included it earlier in *Illustrious Providences.* (He added a few Matherian twists to that infernal assault. In his 1684 version, the devil "belched forth most horrid and nefandous blasphemies.") Elizabeth Knapp would turn up again thirty years later in Cotton Mather's epic *Magnalia,* by which time her case was iconic, one of fourteen preternatural wonders of the invisible world. Under different circumstances, the Parris children too might have wound up in a condition that merited only compassion and that created no ripples beyond Salem village.* Willard assigned no blame, though he did wring evangelical mileage from the episode. Satan had targeted Groton for a reason. The inhabitants needed to examine how they had invited that cloven foot into their village; together they needed to drive it out. In 1692 Samuel Willard was one of the few men in Massachusetts who understood, firsthand, the trials of Samuel Parris, who had equal cause to ask himself what he had done to bring down a plague on his own home.

Four years after the Knapp case, Indians descended upon Groton, burning part of the town.† Willard and his family fled to Boston. Already published, a tireless preacher with a mellifluous voice, he had little difficulty finding employment. Willard was newly associated with the Third Church when in 1677 several Quaker women rushed, half dressed, their hair flying, faces black with ash, into the meetinghouse, causing "the greatest and most amazing uproar" Samuel Sewall had yet witnessed. A decade later Andros appropriated Willard's congregation, Boston's wealthiest, for Anglican services. In short order then, light-haired, even-featured Willard, a cool, logical thinker with a deeply philosophical bent, had known demonic, Indian, Quaker, and Anglican invasions. He had reason

* In September 1674 Elizabeth Knapp married a young man who worked for a next-door neighbor. We do not know what she thought of the events of 1692, by which time she was the mother of eight.
† "What will you do for a house to pray in now we have burnt your meetinghouse?" they taunted Willard at the parsonage.

to be as orthodox as anyone. A *Book of Common Prayer* had sullied his pulpit. His meetinghouse had been reduced to ash. He had conversed if not
with the devil then with some spirit in his employ.

Willard served on Harvard's governing board alongside Increase
Mather. He was happy to endorse a text that questioned the court's methods without undermining its verdicts. But he found he had more to say
than he could insert into the introduction to his colleague's essay. At
some point before October, Willard penned a few additional pages. He
expressed himself in the only way a distinguished Massachusetts minister could that fall: by tiptoeing into print with a piece of samizdat literature, passed hand to hand and attributed to P.E. and J.A., the initials of
two accused wizards Willard had helped to escape. Willard wrote to illu-
minate rather than indict, crafting an imaginary dialogue between two
level-headed adversaries working from the same texts. Published anony-
mously in Boston, the pages bore a false Philadelphia imprint.

In *Some Miscellany Observations on Our Present Debates Respecting Witchcrafts,* S. and B.—presumably Salem and Boston, as the Bostonians had
begun to separate themselves from their rural colleagues—agree on
two matters: witchcraft plagues New England. And dissatisfaction
regarding the court fosters treacherous animosities. Willard reinforced
the points he had made in his Mather preface but went much further,
reiterating warnings against state subversion. Judicial restraint alone
could avert it. S. objects: But good men might well be sacrificed to the
devil in the meantime! B. reminds his interlocutor that wherever the
blame ultimately falls, graver matters are at stake. As he could not
do elsewhere, Willard questioned the trial evidence. Preternatural
knowledge, argues B., has no place in an earthly courtroom. Whether
bewitched, possessed, or both, the girls were in league with the devil.
How else could they offer their eerie predictions, report on things that
had happened before they were born, or accuse people they had
never met?

Does B. really mean to "altogether invalidate the testimony of our afflicted?" objects S. Indeed, B. does. How could a distracted, discontented person qualify as a competent witness or testify about people she did not know? And how could the court trust a witness who did not even face the prisoner at the bar, as was required by law? ("That was because the witches smite them down with their poisoned looks," S. explains.) The two-witness rule happens to be crucial, B. reminds S., who disagrees. "If one man say that he saw lions in Africa last year, and another comes and says that he saw lions there this year; though it was not at the same time, nor likely the same individual lions: why then may it not do in this case?"

Although neither man has attended a trial, S. assures B. that no suspect has wound up incarcerated solely on spectral evidence. B. begs to differ. S. consoles himself that the touch test and the evil eye never fail; B. quibbles with both practices.* But what of the baptisms, the meetings, the sacraments? persists S. Again B. asks how a confessed witch might offer credible testimony. "Do you really believe that all the persons accused are witches?" he challenges. Because the scale of the attack seems implausible. S. agrees, leading B. to attempt to persuade him that the accusers either lie or suffer delusions. The two ultimately, fearfully agree to disagree. S. cannot resist a parting shot. "You are an admirable advocate for witches," he informs B., who sighs. He has heard the charge before. It was the label that attached itself to anyone who dared question the court before October.

HOW OFTEN WILLARD had been so labeled—and how often he had been pilloried for his views—became clear in another paper that began to circulate privately, probably among very few hands, on October 8.

---

* Willard appears to have used the touch test with Elizabeth Knapp. He in any event claimed that the sixteen-year-old could distinguish the accused neighbor's hand from that of all others. New England knew Knapp's story from *Illustrious Providences,* in which Increase Mather also used the word "touch." By the time Cotton Mather included Elizabeth's story in his *Magnalia,* she merely sensed—her eyes shut tight—the afflicting woman's approach; the two do not come in physical contact.

From it we know more of what Willard could not express but was by that fall everywhere discussed. The paper's author was thirty-four-year-old Thomas Brattle, an Anglican-leaning, Harvard-educated merchant, son of one of the richest men in Massachusetts. Brattle wrote to an unnamed minister who, midstorm, solicited his views. Thoughtfully Brattle provided them. He was uniquely well positioned to do so, as one of the best-read men in Massachusetts who neither preached nor held government office. On close terms with the court, he had no familial ties to the Phips administration. Like many of Boston's ministers, he was a man of science. Unlike many of them, he had regularly observed Salem arraignments and trials. He had been on hand for Stoughton's initial jury instructions, for Mary Bradbury's September 9 turn as a blue boar, and for the August 19 hanging.

Nearly a generation younger than Sewall, the youngest of the witchcraft judges, Brattle sounded like the kind of man who had had to teach himself Euclidean geometry at Harvard, as indeed he was; the subject was beyond the ken of his tutors. He had taken precise measurements of a comet sighted in New England over a decade earlier. As critically, to Brattle a comet was just a comet. He had missed the commotion over the Goodwin children, having spent much of the 1680s in England, in part working with chemist Robert Boyle. Even before that trip, Brattle had chafed at New England provincialism. He tended to believe simple solutions the best ones, a novel idea in Boston; in many ways he seemed to have parachuted into 1692 from another century altogether. As much as he today makes his compatriots sound like an extinct species engaging in a medieval rite, he was no rabble-rouser. It was Brattle who prefaced his remarks with the caveat that he preferred to bite off his fingertips than cast aspersions on authority. He did not however believe men to be infallible. When they erred, it was essential to speak up. He dissociated himself from the fractious types stirring up Boston. He had no political agenda; he did not oppose the new charter. But sometimes silence was unconscionable. Covering himself as he waded ahead—he hoped he was not walking into a snare by speaking his mind; Reverend Milborne had been arrested for far less—he undermined every assumption of Stoughton's court. He also avoided signing his letter.

As Brattle saw it, the trials were remarkable for irregularities of all kinds. How could a worldly, longtime associate of John Alden's—a captain of industry, Bartholomew Gedney had made and lost fortunes—turn on Alden because his touch appeared to relieve a poor child of her suffering? How could Reverend Noyes, "a learned, a charitable, and a good man," trust in the evil eye? It was all claptrap, the kind of village nonsense practiced by "the ruder and more ignorant sort." Who did not have an unusual mark somewhere on his body? Since when did a failure to cry indicate guilt? (Hathorne, Corwin, and Gedney were particularly fierce on that point.) The bulk of the charges moreover had nothing to do with witchcraft. Brattle balked at judicial procedures: The court was partial, its methods benighted, its hearings a travesty. Did the magistrates really claim they had never convicted on spectral evidence alone? That was patently untrue. And only a man out of his wits would accept it as legal evidence. Why was Justice Corwin's mother-in-law—accused several times—still at large? The court allowed confessed witches, who had renounced God and Christ, to swear under oath; Brattle quibbled over the very term "confessors." Testimony had been extracted by force, and from some of the most pious women in New England.

He went far beyond Willard, who could not bring himself to criticize the court. Brattle stressed the human cost: whole families had been torn apart. Those miserable Andover husbands who had believed the words of the village children over those of their own wives! They could now only "grieve and mourn bitterly." Indeed, fifty-five had confessed to diabolical plots. But some had maintained their innocence for over eighteen hours, "after most violent, distracting, and dragooning methods had been used with them." They thought themselves near death. He made clear how it was that "most would have chosen to have fallen into the hands of the barbarous enemy than"—as a later critic phrased it—"the hands of their brethren in church fellowship."

Brattle did not inquire how this remarkable mishap had come about, more dismayed by where events were leading. He had a few ideas as to culprits, however. While he choked on court procedures, he reserved special scorn for the bewitched. Who had deemed them visionaries? For the record, if they named people they had never met, that information could only come from the devil. (The same went for the confessors, their accounts riddled with contradictions.) If truly they suffered, how—here he specifically contradicted Stoughton's instructions to the jury that the intent to work witchcraft alone mattered—did they appear "hale and hearty, robust and lusty" day after day? As for spectral sight, the scientist in Brattle railed. It did not require an education in optics to grasp that it was "an utter impossibility" to see with one's eyes shut. That was not vision. It was imagination. There was as much reason to imprison Elizabeth Knapp as to countenance Salem's "blind, nonsensical girls." They were just as likely to turn out to have been delusional. At worst they were possessed. He was not the only one who thought of Knapp, whose history hung heavily over the proceedings. Willard alone left her out of both his public pronouncements and his underground one, even while the possession thesis continued to clunk around. Others had raised the Knapp case with Stoughton. The chief justice spoke of her uncharitably, "as though," reported Brattle, "he believed her to be a witch to this day."

Like everyone else, he had the greatest of respect for Stoughton and for the chief justice's wisdom and integrity. But as everyone who had observed him agreed, he was on this issue a brutal zealot, impatient with anything that challenged his opinions. Along with Stoughton, the Salem justices (or "the Salem gentlemen," as Brattle had them) constituted the prime movers. Hathorne, Corwin, and Gedney—and, at their sides, Reverends Noyes, Parris, and Higginson—frowned on queries, even those posed by their closest friends. Criticism of any kind rankled, eliciting irate answers.

Brattle found risible the idea of an unprecedented, infernal assault on New England's churches. He feared a different diabolical design. Turning the tables, he suggested—one wonders who his correspondent was, as Brattle was well beyond sedition by his sixth paragraph—that the court participated in "an hellish design to ruin and destroy this poor land." He had no time for Willard's chary, painstakingly open-ended conclusions. If people were imprisoned purely on complaints of the afflicted, and the afflicted acted on information provided by the devil, then the justices themselves collaborated with the devil. The infernal agents sat, in their dark gowns, on the bench; the Salem gentlemen were actually the ones possessed, "with ignorance and folly." Brattle reserved his compassion not for the convulsing girls, as did the authorities, or the hardworking justices, as did the Mathers, but for the husbands who had mistrusted and misled wives, for John Willard and John Procter, who had displayed such nobility in their last minutes, and for New England itself.* He alone voiced several wider concerns. How might anyone involved in the trials not later "look back upon these things without the greatest of sorrow and grief imaginable?" He trembled at the thought, the first to anticipate an indelible stain on New England, one that ages would not remove.

Brattle knew the future of the court was among the first matters to be discussed at the meeting of the legislative assembly on October 12, four days after he wrote. He hoped the assembly would disband it. If not, "I think we may conclude that N.E. is undone and undone." Just before that session, Phips received the second opinion he had sought in New York. Its Protestant clergymen fielded eight concise questions, moving from the global—did witches exist?—to the particular. What proof served to convict, what role did a fine reputation or a prior transgression play, and was spectral evidence sufficient for conviction? It is clear from the queries what the sticking points had become; Brattle was not alone in won-

* Although he demolished the idea that witches revealed their secrets to adolescent girls, he did not suggest that the devil might masquerade as a minister. Those who defended the court tended to steer clear of Burroughs; those who criticized it did not. Burroughs was somehow tainted goods. The attack on York created a martyr of Sewall's cousin, the butchered Maine minister. It worked the opposite effect on Burroughs.

dering about the village girls. Could the French Huguenot and three Dutch Calvinist ministers explain how those daily fending off diabolical assaults remained in such strapping good health?

The New York ministers and the Massachusetts ministers communicated in their sole common language, which was Latin. Fellow Calvinists, they saw eye to eye. The New Yorkers shared the Massachusetts missive as well with an especially learned, idealistic young Trinity graduate, newly arrived in New York as chaplain to the English forces and, at that point, the sole working Episcopal clergyman in the province.* All agreed; the devil indeed made cunning use of "lies, miracles, promises, fictitious or real sensual indulgences, honors, riches, and other innumerable allurements." He lured some into commerce with him; witchcraft consisted of that very pact. As to prior malice and unblemished reputations, the ministers had better news for the late Sarah Good than for the late Rebecca Nurse. The first was immaterial. Even a good man could find cause to dislike his neighbor. A fine reputation was worth little. Yet again a panel of experts deemed spectral evidence insufficient for conviction. To rely on that evidence alone "would be the greatest imprudence." As for the girls, their robust health should give no pause. The devil, explained the New York ministers, could see to it that his victims grew stronger under their affliction, craving and swallowing "greater quantities of nourishment than before." He operated as a kind of steroid. He could reverse all effects of torture.

That response arrived as Justice Sewall read Cotton Mather's *Wonders of the Invisible World*. Mather had been hurtling toward the deadline of the October legislative session; he finished in the nick of time. On October 11, both Sewall and Stoughton attested to the accuracy of his account, in every possible respect different from Brattle's. They also presented Mather's pages as having been written at the direction of the governor. Phips had them—or Mather himself—on hand when he wrote to

---

* John Miller was happy to offer an opinion. He was less than pleased with New England ways. His advice, he later noted, was requested and "generously given" though no one was so civil as to thank him for it.

London the following day, for the first time, of New England's preter-natural plague. At Stoughton's advice, the governor had established a special court. He had subsequently been out of the province almost without interruption. He returned to mayhem. Many condemned the justices. Moreover, the devil had begun to impersonate innocents. For that reason, he now postponed further prosecutions. Wherever possible, he prohibited additional arrests. He made a point of specifying that he did so entirely on his own and before anyone prevailed upon him to do so. The situation was explosive; the king's business suffered; the clamor endangered the fledgling administration. Some public servants had overreached; he was sorry to report that a few who owed the Crown better service had acted rashly. Phips's enemies schemed to use the witchcraft against him, a matter of enough concern that he mentioned it twice. Those who preferred the old charter and envied his appointment sought to blacken his name. He awaited Their Majesties' command.

That was the first the English authorities had officially heard of Massachusetts witchcraft. Phips's October letter was also a tissue of lies. He had by no means been largely absent from the colony. He sounded as if he were writing from Sweden rather than Boston; he borrowed details from Mather's description of that plague. He insisted the court ruled only with empirical evidence; a false claim, as Brattle, Dane, Willard, Wardwell, and later even Lawson confirmed. (Phips would speak always of "witchcraft or possession" but could not lean too heavily on the latter, given all that had happened. A Dutch minister would afterward refer to the Massachusetts epidemic as a "pretended witchcraft, or an unknown sickness.") Phips had hardly acted without having been prevailed upon, and urgently; he had heard regularly from the Nurses. He concerned himself less with protecting Their Majesties' innocent subjects than with safeguarding his precarious political position. He too sensed a plot afoot: they conspired to blame him! For the sake of public order, he had banned all publications concerning the witchcraft in any way, "because I saw a likelihood of kindling an inextinguishable flame." (That was not without precedent in Massachusetts, where an energetic printer had eked out a newssheet in 1690, published to prevent false reports. He was shut down within four days.*) Phips awaited orders, a statement that was impractical if not disingenuous. Letters between the two worlds were, it was noted, "like the production of elephants, once almost in two years." And if indeed he had decided to disband the court and halt prosecutions, he had not yet informed either his lieutenant governor or his legislature.

The ban on publications moreover applied only to volumes that did not bear the name Mather on the cover. Both *Cases of Conscience* and *Wonders of the Invisible World* slipped swiftly into print, artfully postdated 1693. The latter qualified as America's first instant book. Garlanded in credentials, it advertised itself as having been "published by the special command of His Excellency the Governor." Its publisher was Benjamin Harris, who had fared as well with *Memorable Providences* as he had poorly with the 1690 newssheet. Harris was no doubt delighted; he knew a bestseller when he saw one. Stoughton wrote a preface for the volume, with which he professed himself mildly surprised but immensely gratified. What a timely account, so carefully and moderately composed! The chief justice was particularly grateful for Mather's painstaking efforts, "considering the place that I hold in the Court of Oyer and Terminer, still laboring and proceeding in the trial of the persons accused and convicted for witchcraft." He especially appreciated the millenarian note; Mather drew from the stupendous events a rosy hint of the Second Coming. He had of course seen every shred of paper from which Mather worked.

It was a charade all around. Mather claimed he had been enlisted to write a book by which Stoughton professed himself abashedly gratified

---

* He had in mind a threefold mission: to enlighten the public and remind them of instances of divine providence; to help them better understand public affairs; and to cure "the spirit of lying, which prevails amongst us." Included in the offending materials was a report that Andros had armed the Indians. Massachusetts would wait another fourteen years for its first newspaper.

at a time when the governor pretended to have banned all books on witchcraft. Conceived as a propaganda piece, billed as a felicitous accident, advertised in the author's own words, *Wonders of the Invisible World* was published when books on witchcraft could not be. Indeed there were wheels within wheels, if not the kind which Thomas Putnam had envisioned.

PHIPS MIGHT WELL have wished himself in Sweden over the next weeks. Every sort of appeal came his way. Even as he reported to London, nine Andover men petitioned on behalf of their starving wives and children. Might they be sent home? "Penitent confessors," they could surely be trusted to remain under house arrest until their cases were called. As it was they suffered horribly, given the hardships of prison life, the hunger, the cold of the season, "their inward grief and trouble." The expense weighed heavily on their families. In exchange for a bond very few in Andover could have afforded, one twelve-year-old girl walked out of Salem prison three days later. A different kind of appeal went to Phips on October 18, from many of the same men and their relations. Their minister joined them. Twenty-six Andover men fervently wished that the land might be cleared of witches. But "distempered persons" had misrepresented their blameless friends and neighbors who had confessed only under duress, pounded by friends and interrogators. (Changing tack, Reverend Barnard signed the petition, which either he or Reverend Dane presumably wrote.) Their town's troubles stood only to increase if the court did not reconsider its methods. Already more witches were named. "And we know not who can think himself safe," pleaded the men, "if the accusations of children and others who are under a diabolical influence shall be received against persons of good fame." They too gently hinted that the court might have it backward. Might the girls themselves be the diabolical agents? From Ipswich, from Reading, others weighed in on behalf of miserable relatives. Might they have their wives back? "It is deplorable," wrote a Lynn man of his spouse, "that in old age the poor decrepit woman should lie under confinement so long in a stinking jail when her circumstances rather require a nurse to attend her." She had been in custody for nearly five months.

Brattle in tow, Increase Mather set out to investigate. In Salem's jail, struggling not to gag, they learned a great deal both about court methods and the human imagination. From eight aggrieved, ashamed, unkempt, and very hungry women, they heard the same story. The prisoners had afflicted no one, signed no pacts, attended no meetings, submitted to no diabolical baptisms. They had however been frightened out of their wits. Their confessions, they sobbed, had been "wholly false." William Barker's thirty-six-year-old sister-in-law was especially inconsolable. Repeatedly her examiners had promised her "she *did* know of their being witches, and *must* confess it, that she did know of their being baptized, etc., and must confess it." She had at last surrendered. She found the shame unbearable, as did sixteen-year-old Martha Tyler, bludgeoned by her brother on one side and her minister on the other. To save her eternal soul (and to save her life, as her brother reminded her), Martha had agreed to every allegation. The prisoners wept bitterly for having implicated others.

But how—the women faced a new barrage of queries in October, from friendlier interrogators—had they invented those vivid details? Brattle too was interested in specifics, although he asked different questions than had Reverend Hale, so curious about the mechanics of Ann Foster's flight. A fifty-five-year-old Andover woman who had flown on a pole to her satanic baptism elucidated; it was like watching the Wicked Witch of the West molt back into Miss Gulch. Forced to choose a date for her diabolical baptism, she had settled on one twelve years earlier. She had just had her last child. She had been ill and melancholy, "and so thought that that time might be as proper a time to mention as any." But why confess that Satan appeared as a cat? Having convinced her she was a witch, the magistrates pressed her to say what shape the devil assumed. Shortly before her arrest she had seen a cat outside her front door. It was the first thing that popped into her mind.* Most of the women had been blindfolded in Barnard's touch test, an experiment the junior minister now regretted. It left one forty-nine-year-old still in doubt. She assured the visitors that she had never spoken with the devil or afflicted anyone. As to whether she might be a witch, she remained of two minds. The howls of the girls rang still in her ears; she could not discount them. And three of the younger women in prison told an entirely different tale. They persisted in their accounts of flying, of choking victims, of stabbing poppets with thorns. Before their visitors, George Jacobs's servant convulsed, tortured, a cellmate explained, by Margaret Jacobs. For good reason Samuel Sewall wrote that day to an English cousin: "We desire your prayers for us relating to the witchcraft."

It was into that volatile, muddled, intemperate climate that Cotton Mather introduced *Wonders of the Invisible World*. Well aware of the "mire and mud" into which he trudged, Mather prefaced the volume with a tribute to his own courage. It was however crucial that proper use be made of the "stupendous and prodigious things that are happening among us." He did so only, he professed, because no one else volunteered. (Weeks earlier he had promised that his work would in no way interfere with that of Noyes or Hale, whom he effectively cut off at the pass.) He outlined his intentions: He set out "to countermine the whole plot of the devil against New England." He aimed his account abroad. And he published to head off "false reports." He said nothing about vindicating the court but did not need to; the objective is clear on every page, as in Stoughton's fulsome preface.

---

* How did cats come in for such abuse? Their association with the devil goes back to antiquity, though possibly not as far back as their association with overdeveloped female sexuality, which dates to Aristotle. Black cats in particular bound themselves up with the diabolical; "the archenemy of mankind himself," they made for the perfect witches' familiars. Black dogs too recur in the Salem literature, although historically British witches tended to prefer feline to canine form. Cats arguably make the more fitting (and feminine) sorcerers' apprentices; fickle, undeferential, unpredictable, coy, they go limp with pleasure one minute and brandish their claws the next. By turns purring and predatory, they spring into action at night, slinking through locked doors and pouncing on chests. They detach themselves from the darkness where least expected.

The two Mather volumes went their own ways. Where his father dealt in the abstract, defending innocents, Cotton Mather reveled in the occult, condemning witches. He took as much pride in the assault on New England as he had in observing a Goodwin girl reeling from a Mather volume. He wrote to prove that catastrophe remained possible — he was at his best when anticipating the worst — and, as crucially, that the storm had been foretold. More than forty years earlier, a condemned witch had predicted a "horrible plot against the country by witchcraft, and a foundation of witchcraft then laid, which if it were not seasonably discovered, would probably blow up, and pull down all the churches in the country."* That fate was now upon them, exactly as forecast! The acid test of a prediction is whether it comes true, as fortune-telling Dorcas Hoar knew. She had warned that various children would die; the families who suffered losses alone remembered her words. In 1676 Increase Mather had quickly turned out a history of King Philip's War as proof that his prophecies had been correct, an agile, efficient use of terror. It is a dangerous thing to have the same men in both the prophecy and the history business.

Mather confessed he would not be surprised if the witchcraft reached even farther than was suspected; he hardly sounded like a man intent on putting out a fire. Into his volume he folded a gloss on the experts, his August 4 sermon, and an account of a celebrated thirty-year-old English case, similar to Salem's, except perhaps for a combusting toad. He chose that trial with reason: it was one in which the prosecution rested on spectral evidence. Only in the second half of his pages does Mather launch into the account he has been, as he asserts, commanded to provide, a claim as disingenuous as Stoughton's introductory purr of surprise. Mather either received fewer cases than he had hoped for or found fewer

---

* No executed witch precisely fits his description, nor does the prophecy survive. It is not impossible Margaret Jones made one; a healer rumored to have a malignant touch and a gift for forecasting, she was the likely candidate, at the right time. Like Ann Putnam Jr., Cotton Mather was, in any case, reporting on events that had occurred before he was born.

that fit his narrative needs. Occasionally he seems to have embroidered on court reports, with details that appear nowhere in the surviving papers: the smell of brimstone, money raining down, a corner of sheet ripped from an invisible specter, pins the justices themselves removed from the girls' flesh. Otherwise he adhered closely to the evidence at hand while working some magic with his pages. No Nurse acquittal, no Esty petition, no witness in Elizabeth How's defense figures in *Wonders*. Mather included all the crowd-pleasing spectral stories while issuing regular reminders that flights and pacts played only supporting roles in the convictions.

He expressed his fervent hope that some of the accused might prove innocent. They deserve "our most compassionate pity, till there be fuller evidences that they are less worthy of it." That was a falsehood. Sixteen pages later he wrote of George Burroughs: "Glad should I have been if I had never known the name of this man." His very initials revolted Mather. (Burroughs alone remained so powerful a wizard that he could not be named.) He was essential to the story, its linchpin and mastermind, as Mather acknowledged in his next line: the government had specifically requested that he include that case in his volume—a claim that may even have been accurate. The about-face with Burroughs was nothing compared to the rest of the book. Mather had previously denounced the touch test and the evil eye. He had written off spectral evidence. He had called for exquisite caution. In *Wonders* he suggested that the touch of a hand, the ocular effects, the flights through the air, the vanishing acts, were part of the devil's blasphemous imitations of Christ. How the brute delighted in mocking church sacraments!

Having discharged his obligations, Mather tossed in a few more "matchless curiosities." In went a précis of Sweden, New England's blueprint. The devil's red beard and long gartered stockings did not travel. Nor did the satanic feasting and dancing. Mather sifted out the more memorable passages, enlisting some typographical help. In bold he emphasized the details that accorded precisely with Salem. The words "suffering children," "cut finger," "enchanted tools," "freely confessing," and "attempted to murder the judges but could not" leap from the page.

He included the late Swedish story of the little girl who recanted, a Mather family favorite. In as well went Thomas Putnam's incriminating letter about Giles Corey and the murder charge.* Mather claimed to have labored over the pages as he had labored over nothing before. If so, the artful design he had promised Stoughton is little in evidence; the work is jumbled, lumpy, at times deliriously incoherent. Mistakes had surely been made. But how to manage more adroitly when Satan toyed with them, injecting falsehood and cheats into the proceedings? The devil burned with jealousy at New England's wise magistrates. He raged at their fine new government. Spectral evidence might not be sufficient for conviction, but nor was it negligible.

As quickly as Cotton Mather had worked, *Wonders of the Invisible World* arrived as a case of too much too late. Conceived as a justification, published to prevent false reports, the pages read as a full-throated apologia. Between mid-September and mid-October—as Phips weighed disbanding the court, or weighed breaking the news that he had disbanded the court—the churning tide had turned. There was another problem as well. Where the father had no taste for the trials, the son appeared to urge them on. Cotton Mather worried less about condemning an innocent than about allowing a witch to walk free. He found himself under immediate fire, not only for his fawning embrace of the court but for an adolescent infraction to which New England was particularly sensitive: filial disrespect. He had not endorsed his father's volume; he undermined his position. Among all the freewheeling accusations in 1692, not once had a father accused a son or a son implicated a father. "With what sinful and raging asperity I have been since treated, I had rather forget than

---

* *Wonders of the Invisible World* was in print before the end of the year in London. Even in 1692 some words sold books more effectively than others; on the title page, the English publisher cannily enlarged "trials," "New England," and "several witches." He subsequently advertised the work as "The Trials of Several Witches Lately Executed in New England," discarding Mather's original title along with most of his theology. By the time a second edition appeared in February, "Mather's witch book"—shorn of its sermons and much of its supporting matter—had shrunk to its sensationalistic details. Its publisher hawked it as a sort of oddity from those curious, credulous colonists.

relate," Mather wailed, days after the publication of *Wonders*. A cataract of "unkindness, abuse, and reproach" roared his way. People said lovely things to his face and hideous things behind his back. He had meant only to tamp down dissent at a critical time! How could he be said to oppose his father and the rest of the New England ministry when his critics were themselves madly impaling one another? He could see little to do but die. (He was twenty-nine.)

As he explained it, the two had made a concerted effort to cover all bases. Cotton Mather had worried that *Cases* on its own would undermine the court and "everlastingly stifle any further proceedings of justice." He dreaded an open attack on the magistrates, whose work might expose them to "the rashest mobs." (He added the "rashest" afterward, for emphasis.) Father and son shared the Second Church pulpit. They saw each other daily and collaborated closely. Earlier, from opposite sides of the Atlantic, they had worked in concert to justify a coup, one man urging moderation on the restless colony, the other playing for sympathy in the mother country; they were unlikely to have forgotten their careful choreography now. More plausibly Cotton Mather felt the two books to be logical extensions of the same equivocal statement. "The Return of Several Ministers" was nothing if not elastic, a document that simultaneously extended goodwill to the court and mercy to the accused. Increase's *Cases* became the plea for "exquisite caution"; Cotton's *Wonders* the overgrown "nevertheless."* As Mather saw it, he made a case for prosecuting the guilty, his father for protecting the innocent. Were they not saying the same thing?

Wonders was published under what Mather felt was Stoughton's protection. It proved insufficient. His father rode to the rescue; the Phips administration could ill afford a rift at this juncture. As his pages went to press and probably hours before they did so, Increase Mather appended a backtracking postscript to *Cases*, to bring the two books into closer align-

* If indeed the Mathers' work was a clumsy case of good cop/bad cop, they might have reversed the assignment. It fell to Cotton, the less gifted politician, to address public order. He overstepped too in his starry-eyed defense of the chief justice, a man his father wholly supported but was less inclined to gush over.

ment. He may have heard from Stoughton personally. The elder Mather remained fully convinced that witches roamed the land; the confessions he had heard while visiting the imprisoned confirmed as much. He meant not to deny witchcraft, only to make its prosecution more exact. Nor did he intend to cast aspersions on the ever-worthy justices. They deserved "pity and prayers rather than censure." He was most grateful to his son for having established that no one had been convicted on spectral evidence alone. Increase Mather too made a point of mentioning Burroughs, the only witch he cited by name. The minister had deserved to hang. Burroughs had, Mather assured his readers, accomplished things that no one who "has not a devil to be his familiar could perform."

From a lofty altitude, Increase Mather indicated that he had heard that some believed the two books at odds. What strange things men imagined! He had vetted *Wonders* before its publication. He had not endorsed it only out of an aversion to nepotism. If he was containing his distaste for his son's runaway book, he did so convincingly. On one issue father and son were in perfect accord: whatever the fate of the witchcraft court, civil order must not suffer. The justices—and the government, which the trials jeopardized, inviting the new charter's critics to pounce—must not be compromised. Increase Mather offered not a word on court procedures. Only later, in his diary, would Cotton Mather assert that while he spoke honorably of the judges, he could not abide their methods. It was a difficult balancing act all around. At the head of the court sat after all the most trusted legal authority in Massachusetts, a chief justice altogether intent on his mission, confident he was on the side of the angels, and delighted that young Mather was, with his forthcoming account, not only to allay doubts but, in his zeal and wisdom, "to lift up a standard against the infernal enemy, that hath been coming in like a flood upon us." Stoughton borrowed most of the line from the volume's author.

HOW RADICALLY THE wind had shifted was clear from Samuel Parris's October 23 sermon. That Sunday he delivered a sweet, sensual discourse on reconciliation. He worked hard on the address, pouring a good deal of himself into it. We know nothing of the circumstances under which he wrote, if in the parsonage Abigail continued to convulse, if Betty Parris had yet returned from the Sewalls, how the two healthy Parris children weathered a crisis in which they played an imperceptible part, how Ann Putnam Jr. fared. Changing his tune more nimbly than had Mather, Parris ventured beyond words, to embraces. He took the Song of Solomon as his text, offering a rapturous catalog of kisses: There were lustful kisses, holy kisses, treacherous kisses, kisses of valediction, of subjection, of approbation, of reconciliation. A kiss betokened love and goodwill. Kisses were sweet among friends "after some jars and differences." The imagery was not uncommon; divine love translated naturally enough into a full-body immersion in grace.* But nothing could have constituted more of an about-face from Parris's divisive September 11 sermon than that singular, radiant discourse. It came as close to a tonic as one could expect from a man whose home and parish had been turned upside down, whose pews had been depleted, who contended still with a group of rogue parishioners and who had lost others permanently. Only in his conclusion did Parris revert to form. The Lord had sent Christ into the world to offer his love. Who would deny him? "His kisses are most sweet," lectured Parris. "If you will not be kissed by him, you shall, you must, be cursed by him." At those curses even devils roared.

Three days later, the legislative assembly considered a bill that contained a loaded disclaimer of its own. Satan roamed about Massachusetts "with a great rage and serpentine subtlety." A sterling commission had done its best to contain him. "Notwithstanding the indefatigable endeavors of those worthy gentlemen," the plague continued unabated. The colony remained under "dismal clouds of darkness." Was a fast day not in order, to apply for divine direction? It seemed prudent for a group of

---

* He was not the first to catalog kisses. The great English preacher Richard Sibbes had done so decades earlier, in a sermon Parris may have known. Sibbes ends on a note of sweet communion. Parris ends with a choice between Christ's kisses or curses.

ministers to meet with Phips's council to determine a course of action. They stood sorely in need of wisdom, the devil's rage threatening "the utter ruin and destruction of this poor country." A vote for the bill constituted a direct attack on the Court of Oyer and Terminer. The session proved highly contentious; the question neatly divided the assembly. After a bruising debate, the bill passed, by a vote of thirty-three to twenty-nine. Some of those who had complimented Cotton Mather on his pages did so sincerely.

Sewall—who had voted against the bill—supposed that the court should immediately consider itself dismissed. Not everyone agreed. The assembly had addressed the matter only obliquely; the court was scheduled still to reconvene in six days. Stoughton pressed Phips for a decision. He found it elusive. Cotton Mather might well have been speaking for Stoughton when he discoursed that Thursday on perseverance. Both men agreed that the court's fall would be destabilizing, an admission of error and an invitation to further witchcraft. Both believed its work unfinished. Stoughton made regular trips to Boston in an attempt to pry an answer out of Phips; lieutenant governor and chief justice though he was, he could not extract one. The two men had not been close but on this issue the bluff governor seemed downright cowed by his deputy, a man of great political dexterity who could run intellectual circles around him. On one such effort amid storms on October 28, Stoughton wound up drenched after his ride from Dorchester over a flooded causeway. Not for the first time he sought refuge in the Sewall household. He sent home for a change of clothes. If he did not recognize the torrent as an omen he should have: in his absence the following day Phips officially disbanded the Court of Oyer and Terminer.

The petitions continued to pile up. Ten accused Ipswich witches pleaded for their release. They were unlikely to be tried that winter; already they were freezing. They would soon "perish with cold." Some were nearly eighty. One was pregnant, another nursing a nine-week-old. In the year that his daughter had languished in prison, a Chelmsford father had had sole charge of her two- and five-year-old children. He was without resources. A young Ipswich man suddenly recanted his May testimony against Elizabeth Procter. On January 27 she gave birth on the floor of the Salem prison. She named the infant John, after her dead husband. Sentenced in August to hang, she had been reprieved only on account of her pregnancy. She awaited an execution date. Also convicted, Reverend Dane's daughter applied directly to Phips for a pardon. She had spent four months in close confinement. Her accusers admitted they had lied; she was pregnant. (She believed she would already have been hanged were she not.) She was entirely innocent, with an incapacitated husband and six children. On December 14 Abigail Hobbs's father walked free when two Topsfield neighbors posted a two-hundred-pound bond for him.

Not everyone had yet finished with the visionary girls. Gloucester sent for them early in November. On November 7 three more witches were arrested, including a Higginson in-law. Fresh indictments turned up amid the old. On the last day of 1692 Elizabeth Colson — who had led the constables on the wild-goose chase through the fields, confounding even their dog — was finally imprisoned in Cambridge. Elizabeth Hubbard continued to convulse and accuse into November. Pinched, pricked, and hauled under tables, Mary Warren was still testifying against suspects in January of 1693.

On a particularly dark and biting December day, the Massachusetts councillors seated a new court to try the remaining witchcraft suspects. By unanimous vote, they named Stoughton its chief justice. Three of his former Oyer and Terminer colleagues joined him, as did Thomas Danforth, who in April had elicited the first mention of the witches' meeting. On December 22 Phips swore in the newly established superior court. Each man took the oath to, as Sewall summed it up, "impartially administer justice according to our best skill." In accordance with the new charter, the December jurymen consisted of men whose estates rather than church membership qualified them for service. As such they were less likely to bow to the whims of the justices. While not intimately acquainted with Salem village affairs, they had all the same been touched by the crisis; some had entered accusations, while others were related to witches. Once seated, they applied to the bench for guidance. What use should they make of spectral evidence? None, came the answer. The court tried fifty-two cases early in January and acquitted all but three of the accused. Reverend Dane's twenty-two-year-old granddaughter was convicted. His daughter was not. The jury found the widow of fortune-telling Samuel Wardwell guilty but his daughter innocent. (Both had accused the dead father and husband.) The court cleared Margaret Jacobs, whose plea survives. She alone refers to her accusers as "possessed persons."

Stoughton continued to hold tenaciously to the validity of spectral evidence. He considered himself on a crusade, one he fully intended to finish. Hurriedly he signed three execution warrants, adding five for those suspects convicted in 1692, Elizabeth Procter, Dorcas Hoar, and Mary Lacey Jr. among them. He scheduled a hanging for February 1 and ordered graves to be dug. He seemed intent on proving that the laws of England indeed reached North America and indeed followed the guilty to the ends of the earth. Phips meanwhile conferred with attorney general Checkley, who feared he could no longer distinguish innocents from the guilty. Phips countermanded the execution, reprieving the eight convicted witches. It is unclear how Stoughton learned as much; he did not hear the news directly from Phips. Flying into a rage, he fumed: "We were in a way to have cleared the land of these!" He did not know who had obstructed justice but warned that the accused delivered the colony into diabolical hands. As he stormed off the bench, he spat, "The Lord have mercy on this country," his last recorded words on witchcraft. He did not appear on February 2, when Danforth took his place. Among the suspects who appeared over the next days was an eighty-year-old widow, the grandmother of the fleet-footed Reading girl. She uttered barely a word in her defense. Thirty witnesses testified against her. Paranormal things tended to happen to those who crossed her, exactly as she predicted they would. "If any in the world were a witch," noted Lawson, on hand for the trial, "she was one." She walked free.

By February 21, 1693, Phips was ready to declare the epidemic over. And he made plain to whom he had alluded in his earlier letter to London when he suggested that some public servants had overreached. It was on one man's account alone that the 1692 trials had been "too violent and not grounded upon a right foundation." That was the justice who had stomped off the court weeks earlier, "enraged and filled with passionate anger." Stoughton had been reckless, overly precipitous, possibly even corrupt. He had authorized unlawful seizures of estates and disposed of them without Phips's knowledge or consent. Phips had questioned his methods; Stoughton proceeded despite multiple warnings and a vigorous outcry. Where earlier Phips had followed the sage counsel of his deputy governor, he now seemed as much beleaguered by Stoughton as by witchcraft. He sounds as if he is squealing to their parents about the misdeeds of a gifted, favored older sibling. Phips shut down the trials until someone better versed in law might weigh in, he reported, crediting Increase Mather and the New York ministers with his decision. (Over the intervening weeks Stoughton boycotted council meetings. He reported that he had taken a fall.) Phips had stepped in decisively, every bit the savior the Mathers would later advertise. "The black cloud that threatened the province with destruction" was, he assured Their Majesties' secretary of state, behind them. Given the danger to lives, estates, reputations, and official business, the matter, Phips huffed, "has been a great vexation to me!" All was now well. Their Majesties' business could continue unimpeded. "People's minds before divided, and distracted, by different opinions concerning this matter, are now well composed," he exulted.

Phips and the council had already designated Thursday, February 23, as a colony-wide day of thanksgiving, for, among other happy events, the "restraint of enemies with the check given to the formidable assault of witchcrafts." The administration returned to focusing on the original "source of all our mischiefs"—the French. They began to reimburse Essex County for the extraordinary costs of the trials; they would raise taxes to cover bills from innkeepers, constables, jail keeps, blacksmiths. A year of false witness, false confessions, false friends, false dichotomies, and false books published to prevent false reports had come to an end. The jails emptied. Accusations ceased. Most afflictions abated. As early as April 3, 1693, Phips referred to the events of 1692, to which he had put a stop, as "a supposed witchcraft." That month a letter applauding his leniency began winging its way from London to New England, that far-off terrarium. It arrived in July. Phips was by then more than ever convinced that a little backslapping seemed in order. He had, in halting the proceedings, single-handedly saved New England from ruin.

Still, the confessions tugged at some. There was a reason the October vote on the future of the court had been so close. Cotton Mather continued to fret that not enough had been done to exterminate witches. When he visited Salem in September 1693, he was unsurprised to hear a church woman predict a new storm of witchcraft, a punishment for the court having been dissolved before its work was complete. Well-informed, mild-mannered men subscribed to the same fear. Had the times proved more stable, a second inquest would, asserted John Hale, have been in order. "Yet considering the combustion and confusion this matter had brought us into, it was thought safer to underdo rather than overdo," he concluded. They preferred to rest their case. They could correct any mistakes later. "Thus the matter ended somewhat abruptly," noted Hale, who knew that it had begun in the same fashion. Grappling alongside Parris for a diagnosis, he had observed Abigail and Betty in their initial fits. He had heard Tituba's rock-solid prison confession. He had testified against Dorcas Hoar and Bridget Bishop; he had coaxed the particulars of her flight and crash-landing from Ann Foster. "I inquired what she did for victuals," Hale would remember. Foster had then explained about the bread and cheese and described the refreshing stream.

It was to Hale as well that Foster confided her fears of George Burroughs and Martha Carrier, not yet established as the king and queen of hell. She believed they would murder her, as their specters threatened. She outlived them both, barely. Among the last casualties, Foster died in prison on December 9, 1692. Her son paid six pounds and ten shillings — the price of a fine cow — to recover her body. The first to sign a diabolical pact, Tituba was the last to be released. Having lent the previous year its shape, having introduced flights and familiars into the proceedings, having illuminated New England with her pyrotechnic confession but neither questioned nor so much as named since, she appeared before the grand jury for having covenanted with the devil on May 9, 1693. It declined to indict her.

XI

———◁▷———

THAT DARK AND MYSTERIOUS
SEASON

The truly terrible thing is that everyone has his reasons.
—JEAN RENOIR

STOUGHTON'S WORK CAME to a sudden halt; the return to normality took a little longer. Economically and emotionally, disenchantment came at a price. Orchards and cellars, fences and woodpiles had been sacrificed to justice, which had consumed a prodigious number of hours. Twenty-five years earlier the Salem farmers had warned that households suffered when husbands rode off to battle invaders; they languished when wives rode off to probe for witch marks as well. The lucky families were those who, at crippling expense, welcomed home relatives, in some cases relatives who they themselves had denounced. Festering neighborhood grudges evaporated, supplanted by graver matters, the common cold wiped out by plague. Sorcery had engulfed them; at issue was the punishment rather than the crime. Spectral evidence was extinct. The belief in witchcraft was not.

There were some awkwardnesses. What of the woman whom you had accused from several feet away and who was back on her farm across the stream? Reprieved witches sat suddenly in the next pew. How to embrace the six-year-old who had sworn her now-dead mother had made her a witch? Mary Lacey Sr. went back to cooking and spinning alongside the eighteen-year-old who had publicly scolded, "Oh Mother, why did you give me to the devil?" At least some Essex County residents must have wrangled with the commandment against false witness. Any number of trusts had been betrayed, by parents, children, neighbors, spouses, in-laws, by the paragons of piety. Was it possible to listen to Reverend Noyes, who had interrupted defendants, or Reverend Barnard, who had organized the surprise Andover touch test, or Reverend Hale, who had testified against parishioners, in quite the same way again? How did Francis Dane minister to the congregation that had denounced nearly his entire family? Nearly 10 percent of Andover had been accused. The averted gaze must have been as well practiced as the strained neck. What kind of marriage prospects could a girl anticipate when her mother had been hanged for witchcraft, implicating her in the process?

There were losses of faith as well as fortune. Newly returned to Boston, John Alden failed to turn up for communion on December 18. While his friends may have prayed for him in his absence, he had every reason to believe that they had sold him down the river. Reverend Willard's wife spoke sharply about the matter to Sewall, whom she held responsible. Months later he called on the Aldens. He regretted their troubles. He delighted in the captain's rehabilitation. His was a rare gesture; at least initially, recriminations preceded explanations and far outnumbered apologies. The Nurse and Tarbell families continued to boycott Salem village services; while the door-slamming, sermon-interrupting Sarah Cloyce had survived, her two elder sisters had hanged. She resettled in Boston with her husband. Philip English returned after nearly nine months of allegations against him to a ransacked house, looted down to the thimbles. He soon began rowing from Salem to Marblehead for Anglican services. Religious affiliations aside, it was difficult to believe he would ever again care to pray alongside Stephen Sewall. English began petitioning for restitution in April 1693. He was still doing so twenty-five years later.

The Sunday after Alden absented himself from the Third Church pews, Deodat Lawson preached in Charlestown. He spoke of family discipline, reminding the heads of households of their obligations to children, servants, slaves. Lawson warned against distraction and the rote discharge of duties. Parents should be neither overly formal nor overtedious. Ministers could be as remiss as anyone on those fronts; they too could prove "saints abroad and devils at home." For whatever reason, he aimed his lament specifically at children "twelve, fourteen, or sixteen years of age," a neglected and indulged cohort. Were those youngsters not the cause of New England's afflictions? No wonder Satan managed to frighten them "into subjection to him, and covenant with him." Their parents had forsaken them; confusion, rebellion, disobedience, and diabolical pacts followed. Lawson published the text—armored with an Increase Mather endorsement and a Sewall dedication—in 1693. The pages could only have discomfited Samuel Parris. Lawson had strayed some distance from his earlier claim that the pious home was the vulnerable home.

There was as much cause for soul-searching at the Salem village parsonage as anywhere; five accusers and four of the afflicted lived at that address, more than at any other. Parris was not insensitive to the burdens his family had placed on the community. (One wonders what the villagers thought as they passed his much-contested, much-discussed meadow.) Weeks after Lawson's sermon, Parris offered to forgo six pounds of his 1692 salary, "to gratify neighbors and to attempt the gain of amity." He would do the same again the coming year. (He could not resist adding that he made the sacrifice although events had cost him dearly, too.) He made no move to retrieve Tituba, an embarrassment and an expense. As the court was disbanded, as prisons emptied and families reunited, she remained behind bars. Someone paid her jail costs at the end of 1693, effectively buying her. She left Massachusetts.

For some, the return to normality proved impossible. The taint of witchcraft endured; one forever carried about one an "indefinable peculiarity."* Before his death, John Procter had warned that suspects were condemned before their trials. They remained so after their acquittals. His widow's case was worse than most: he had made no provision for Elizabeth in his will, which left her contending in vain with her relatives, "for they say," she informed the court, "I am dead in the law." They had ample reason to want to wash their hands of a temperamental and tainted stepmother. (She moved to Lynn, where she remarried.) Reverend Dane's daughter—also reprieved on account of pregnancy—returned to her ailing husband and her six older children. She lived "only as a malefactor." Having been accused of "the most heinous crime that mankind can be supposed to be guilty of," her life was in tatters, her family, she feared, vulnerable to new charges. Nor was what she termed the "perpetual brand of infamy" the sole burden. Martha Carrier's strapping sons had survived torture. Having confessed to flying through the air to a witch meeting, they had helped convict their mother. Orphaned, they discovered themselves to be related to a woman immortalized as the queen of hell.

While the hangings relieved afflictions, the trials crippled many more. Sarah Cloyce emerged from prison decrepit, having spent five months with irons on her hands and legs. Mary English returned from exile an invalid, to die in 1694, at forty-two. At least four witch suspects perished in prison. At the time of her release, little Dorothy Good had spent eight and a half months in miniature manacles. Her infant sister died before her eyes. She had watched her mother, against whom she had testified, head defiantly off to the gallows. Dorothy went insane; she would require care for the rest of her life. Mary Esty and Susannah Martin each left seven children. There were a great number of orphans.

Witchcraft demanded long memories and accountability; no one had

---

* In its permanence, a witchcraft accusation resembled an Internet rumor. The majority of the women who were hanged had faced earlier accusations or were daughters of women who had. Indelible stains did not attach themselves to accusers in 1692.

a taste for either in 1693, when villagers who once forgot nothing suddenly found themselves amnesiac. Insofar as any of them searched for reasons, they asked what had brought down the "damned crew of devils or witches" in the first place. Their descent called for piety rather than apologies; Andover and Salem must not become as notorious as Sweden. New England did not care to be remembered as "New Witch-land!" It would be some time before anyone asserted that you could not possibly fly through the air to a remote destination and return in an hour or so (for one thing, you would not be able to breathe, John Hale would point out in 1697), far longer before anyone suggested that twenty innocents had been put to death. (Hale went to his grave believing otherwise.)

As for Brattle's assertion that when men err, we are duty-bound to point out as much, it too evaporated. Shame obliterated blame; few agreed that there is nothing so honorable as admitting a mistake. The passive tense has rarely had such a workout; in the end the only one who dared point a finger was unruly Governor Phips. He reproached his crusading, calculating chief justice. Stoughton felt no need to defend his decisions, nor did anyone care for him to. Confessors disavowed their stories, some claiming that they had invented them in order to save their lives. Several accusers and witnesses were, it was revealed, "persons of profligate and vicious conversation." A few admitted they had lied; others insisted that they remembered nothing of what they had testified. It was as if all simply, suddenly awoke, shaking off their strange tales, from a collective preternatural dream.

The Mathers would go on prophesying the Second Coming and calculating its date, which in mid-1693 Cotton Mather promised was but a few years in the future. In the same sermon he railed against Salem's "matchless enchantments and possessions." The two words henceforth traveled in tandem. Witches reverted to "evil angels." Only occasionally did anyone allude to cheats or "distempered creatures," to "wicked and malicious people who feigned themselves bewitched, possessed or lunatic." Unneighborly behavior was again just unneighborly behavior; wives could again drag husbands from taverns without being accused of witchcraft. You could be lewd, just plain wicked, or raving mad. Women disturbed men in their sleep and transformed themselves into cats—as they had done for decades and would continue to well into the nineteenth century—but they no longer wound up in court for these offenses. It has been noted that in the years immediately following the trials women did not have an easy time getting convicted for anything. Villagers scratched their heads over enchanted fireplaces, ambulatory trees, and misplaced saucers but were more circumspect about those oddities, participating in another New England specialty: that of leaving things unsaid. After the acoustical runaway of the witchcraft crisis—the voices rising to a fever pitch—1692 left in its wake a thundering reticence. Naturally most of what Essex County labored to forget is precisely what we want to know.

Some wrongs were immediately righted. In June 1693, John Ruck, the grand jury foreman, became the guardian of George Burroughs's orphaned, abandoned sons. He arranged for their baptisms. Also that month, the widow of George Jacobs, the salty, stooped wizard, married the widower of Sarah Wilds, the hay-enchanting Topsfield misfit. Their spouses had traveled together to prison in the same mid-May convoy. John Willard's widow, who had cowered under the stairs after his beatings, married a Towne in 1694.* Much remained the same. Released from prison, Mary Toothaker had no home to which to return, Indians having destroyed Billerica. Two years later they returned to slaughter her, carrying her twelve-year-old daughter into captivity. The fall of 1693 meant renewed carnage in Maine as well. Massachusetts girls continued to disrupt sermons and convulse; by the fall of 1693 Cotton Mather was at work on a new case of possession, the first of two with which he conjured post-Salem.

The only brooms that played a role in the witch hunt were wielded

---

* Normality took some unusual forms. Eleven months after her husband was hanged, Reverend Burroughs's widow remarried. Having sworn months earlier that he wished he had never so much as heard Burroughs's name, Cotton Mather performed the ceremony.

afterward by men, to sweep the year under the carpet. The authorities who had fallen all over themselves to vindicate the ouster of a royal governor four years earlier felt no need to justify themselves in 1693. On May 31, every member of the witchcraft court was reelected to the Massachusetts council—Stoughton by the widest margin, and Sewall with more votes than Saltonstall, who had stepped off the court. (Hathorne, Sewall, and Corwin still sat together on the bench twenty years later.) In his blundering fashion, Phips would continue to alienate every Massachusetts constituency. By 1693 many had come to agree with the New York governor's description of him, as "a machine moved by every fanatical finger, the contempt of wise men and sport of the fools," a state of affairs that would soon land the lieutenant governor, his popularity undimmed, in Phips's office. Having prosecuted witches and then advised Phips against the proceedings, Checkley remained attorney general for at least a decade.

Maniacal record keepers, New Englanders did not like for things to fall "in the grave of oblivion." They made an exception for 1692, as they had for the Burroughs years, when Thomas Putnam retranscribed the village book of transactions, omitting those entries that "have been grievous to any of us in time past or that may be unprofitable to us for time to come." That account jumps from January 27, 1692, to December 7, leapfrogging over all arrests and trials.* The eagerness to forget was as great as, for nine months, had been the strong-arming to remember. Parris kept a scrupulous record of village deaths. They included two he attributed to witchcraft and one that others did, but no mention of Giles Corey or any villager who had hanged. One family lopped an accuser off the family tree. Others camouflaged themselves with alternate spellings of their names, not altogether difficult given the extant variations. No one noted precisely where the hangings took place. (It appears to have

---

* The villagers were not alone in believing that destroying paper reverses history. Raiding Indians made off with Andover's land deeds in 1676 in the hope they might send the Englishmen home.

been the triangle of land bounded today by Proctor, Pope, and Boston Streets.) For a hundred and fifty years, Giles Corey's ghost would haunt the field in which he was thought to have been pressed to death. A monument to the events of 1692 would wait another hundred and fifty.

Sewall practically bypasses the events in his diary, an omission he would address five years later. The 1692 pages of the Milton minister— who recorded every thunderclap and haircut—are lost. Even critics of the trials, even men who in the clearest of hands preserved every detail of colonial life—Thomas Danforth was both—left no record. Willard's sermons for the summer disappeared from his published body of work and from an attentive churchgoer's notebook. Wait Still Winthrop's 1692 and 1693 letters are missing from his family correspondence. In what has been described as retrospective glosses, Mather collapsed his account of the trials into a few pages. His writing about 1692 is all rewriting. (He so much aimed his remarks at posterity that he referred to himself in the third person, a different brand of transparent, out-of-body experience.) Anyone looking for a true ghost story might ask what happened to the court's official record book, of which Stephen Sewall took special care and which he surely kept close at hand. That silence would be the real conspiracy of 1692.*

Even those who had reason to believe themselves unpardonably wronged remained tongue-tied. Petitioning for redress, the Corey children noted that their father had been pressed under stones. They could bring themselves to say about their mother only that she was "put to death also, though in another way." The word "witches" figures nowhere in the heaps of pasteurized reparations claims. Families referred instead

---

* The court papers are thought to have disappeared on August 26, 1765, when a mob ransacked the home of Massachusetts's last royal governor, splitting open Thomas Hutchinson's doors and tossing his books into the street. If indeed the papers met that muddy end, it was by the greatest of ironies: the Stamp Act had occasioned the riot. The cost of colonial defense prompted the tax on official documentation, England's attempt to recoup expenses of the French and Indian War. The colonists resisted the continued English military presence; no foreign enemies plagued them. They had no use for overinvolved paternal authorities. In any event, the trial records were not seen again.

to the "sufferers of the year 1692," to loved ones who had endured the "late troubles at Salem," to events precipitated by "the powers of darkness" in the course of "that dark and mysterious season."

LIKE THE MINISTER's fence, pastoral relations in Salem village appeared beyond repair. Phips had not yet written London of his expert management of the witchcraft crisis when Parris invited five churchmen to meet with representatives from the disaffected Nurse clan at the parsonage on the afternoon of February 7. He needed to coax them back into the fold; their refusal to participate in the sacrament spiritually compromised the entire congregation. After a prayer, he inquired into the men's grievances. They were unforthcoming. Parris suggested they return in two weeks' time. He knew their position perfectly well; the three had called unexpectedly earlier that morning, when he heard them out in his study. (On that occasion he took pains to separate the parties.) In appealing to the girls to name witches, Parris indulged in the same brand of shameless superstition practiced by witch-cake bakers. How could he have sworn in court that anyone had been raised by a touch or felled by a glance? Had it not been for him, raged a Nurse son and son-in-law, each for over an hour, Rebecca Nurse would still be alive. To their minds Parris was "the great prosecutor." The men refused to accept communion from their minister until he apologized.

The bulk of witchcraft literature on his side, Parris saw no cause to reconsider his views. And he remained a stickler. The "displeased brethren," as he dubbed them, returned the following day. Sarah Cloyce's husband climbed to the parsonage study first. A full church member accompanied him. Parris insisted on a second disinterested party. Both sides believed they were resolving their disputes according to the dictates of Matthew 18, a text that mandated two witnesses to a grievance procedure; the disagreement devolved into the proper interpretation of three verses of Scripture. Late in March 1693, the men produced an unsigned, undated petition calling for a church council to determine "blameable cause," two words that most in Essex County kept painstakingly apart that year. Displeased to discover that the men had consulted with neighboring clergymen, Parris asked who, precisely, subscribed to their document. The Nurse contingent allowed only that they spoke for many in the province. Parris stuck the petition in his pocket. "I told them I would consider of it," he noted. It was a year to the date since the incendiary, one-of-you-is-a-devil sermon that had sent Sarah Cloyce storming from the meetinghouse. The same day, in Boston, Cotton Mather and his wife lost a newborn son, a death Mather attributed to witchcraft.*

When an April delegation called—a group that included widowed Francis Nurse—Parris informed them that he could not talk. He was off to a private prayer meeting. Flanked by various Putnams and his deacons, he met the following week with his detractors. Plucking their paper from his pocket, Parris read it aloud. What did they call such a document? Because he termed it a libel. The Nurses produced a second copy, bearing forty-two signatures. Parris cried fraud. All the signatures appeared in the same hand! Had anyone even signed the document— the charge was staggering in light of events—of his own free will? And was he answering to disaffected villagers or to disaffected church members? Because this happened to be purely an ecclesiastical matter. The two sides went back and forth until nightfall. They were evenly matched. In cogent petitions and dramatic exits, no family had expressed themselves as energetically as the Nurses. And no one was so intent on justice or exactitude as Samuel Parris, who—having devoted nine months of his life to meticulous testimony—now found himself accused of having produced garbled notes. (He was a far more conscientious reporter than many, including Thomas Putnam.)

A large meeting took place at the parsonage a month later. If the Parris children still convulsed, they did so with cause: belligerent, grim-

---

* Maria Mather suffered a fright when she met a horrible apparition on her porch in her last weeks of pregnancy; the specters that tormented the newly afflicted Boston girl claimed responsibility. Immediately after the birth, Increase Mather also received a venomous letter in which a woman—probably one accused in 1692—warned that Cotton "little knew what might quickly befall some of his posterity." It was Sarah Good all over again.

faced men tramped in and out of their home for a series of interminable, bruising debates. Already well familiar with a regime that rarely accepted apologies and issued none, that dealt in chapter-and-verse accusations and fussy, hoop-jumping technicalities, the children grew accustomed to the heavy footfalls in the entryway porch. After prayers that Thursday, Parris turned to the dissenters. What had they to say? They asked to air their grievances publicly. Parris managed to hold them off. Some fierce, un-Christian name-calling ensued, the kisses on which Parris had so tenderly expounded in October nowhere in evidence. The dissenters appealed to Phips and the provincial authorities. They got nowhere. In the fall of 1694 they turned to the Boston clergy. Willard directed Noyes, Hale, and Higginson to persuade Parris to settle the festering matter before a council of ministers. The word "witchcraft" figured nowhere in those communications.

Cotton Mather was in Salem town that fall and surely reiterated the message: Parris was causing a scandal. (It was on that visit that specters made off with Mather's papers. He returned home to find his young neighbor Margaret Rule tormented by eight demons—and asking, unprompted, about his missing notes. The seventeen-year-old had heard specters brag that they had stolen them.) Parris explained the village feud to his well-meaning colleagues. He had not been obstructionist. He did however insist on order. The dissenters subjected him to repeated abuse. He had tried to coax them back with his sermons; the church doors, insisted Parris, remained open. ("And as you are my sheep, I expect you hear my voice" did not strike the Nurses as an invitation, much less an olive branch.) He felt he had attempted any number of "kind and heart-affecting wooings." Still the defectors would not return for the Lord's Supper. His troubles, Parris insisted, were without parallel. The stalemate persisted. The Nurse men would not share the particulars of their grievances until Parris named a council. Parris would not name a council until he had reviewed the grievances.

On the afternoon of November 13, 1693, still unable to agree on how to proceed, Parris read his own complaints aloud to his critics. He had seventeen. The Nurse clan breached the covenant. They set an evil example. They were disorderly, accusatory, uncharitable. They reproached the community at home and defamed it abroad. They libeled their minister and harassed him in his own home, spreading word—to the governor, the court, and the Boston ministers—that Parris was "unpeacable." They claimed that he had made prayer impossible for over a year when they had been in their pews long after "the breaking forth of the late horrid witchcraft." The meeting consumed an afternoon. Two weeks later Parris informed the Nurses that the church had rejected their demand for a council. They might care to consider what Scripture had to say about making peace. He suggested a few texts. A full year went by.

Weeks after Phips had finally received a reply from the Crown to his February 1693 letter regarding the trials—Queen Mary signed off on a vague response, commending the care with which the governor had managed the crisis and advising him to proceed against any future witchcraft or possession with "the greatest moderation and all due circumspection"—seven ministers again exhorted Parris to resolve the dispute. He spent July 5, 1694, praying, fasting, and mulling over the issue with his stalwarts. He also rejected the ministers' advice. Weeks later they wondered if they had been unclear. They outlined a simple arbitration strategy. Parris was to resolve the matter before winter. Anglican and Baptist steeples had begun to rise in Boston. Mary Esty climbed to the gallows two years earlier.

In the record book over these months Parris's hand grows steadily more crabbed and cramped. The strain on him was great; the pressure to settle immense. On the afternoon of November 18, 1694, he returned to the meetinghouse to read aloud a statement several colleagues had vetted, the first public avowal that mistakes had been made in 1692, a paper he termed his "Meditations for Peace." (It included nine points, in contrast to his seventeen grievances.) Parris considered it a "very sore rebuke and humbling providence" that the witchcraft had broken out in his household. His family included both accusers and accused; he confessed that "God has been righteously spitting in my face." He denounced the superstitious practices to which others had resorted in his absence. Acknowledging that he had erred in his "management of those mysteries," he conceded that he had been wrong about spectral evidence; the devil could well afflict "in the shape of not only innocent but pious persons." The girls who saw Rebecca Nurse torturing them spoke accurately. So did Rebecca Nurse when she disclaimed responsibility. Here a rustle must have gone through the room; Nurse was both dead and excommunicated. He should not have relied on the girls as diagnosticians. He regretted any inadvisable remarks he had made from the pulpit as well as any mistakes he had committed in recording testimony, a job for which he had not volunteered. He extended his sympathy to all who had suffered. Humbly he beseeched the Lord's pardon for "all of my mistakes and trespasses in so weighty a matter." He did the same of his congregants. Might they put "all bitterness and wrath and anger and clamor and evil-speaking" behind them, to move forward in love?

Parris expressed his desire that the congregation "heartily, sincerely, and thoroughly" forgive one another, which is different from extending an apology. He added too the deal-breaking disclaimer that undercuts all such demands: he begged forgiveness for offenses his parishioners believed he had committed rather than for those he believed he had. As a peace offering however the statement was substantial. Visibly moved, Nurse's son-in-law allowed that if their minister had acknowledged half as much earlier, a great deal of unpleasantness might have been averted. A public meeting was called for November 26. The dissenters took seats together, joined by a few outsiders. Pressed to share their reasons for withdrawing from the church, the men produced their paper, again refusing to allow it into the minister's hands. They had no intention of retailing the charges against him until they stood before the proper authorities. Parris prevailed.

On November 26, 1694, more than two years after the witchcraft court had fallen, Parris read a scathing condemnation of his ministry from the pulpit, Francis Nurse following along with the original on his lap to make sure that his reverend omitted nothing. Parris had fostered a climate of accusation. The girls made prayer impossible; the aggrieved families preferred to attend meeting where they might actually hear the sermon. Given the reckless allegations, they had feared for their lives. They refused to accept communion from the hand of a man so at odds with accepted doctrine, one who expressed no charity and who pursued unfounded methods with the "bewitched or possessed persons." (They made Parris seem like a bit of a madman, out of step with the rest of the clergy. They nowhere accused him of having manufactured a crisis, however.) He had testified against the accused. His court accounts were faulty, his doctrine unsound, his self-justifications offensive. When he had finished, Parris asked—needlessly—if the issues were solely with him. They were. Did the parishioners withdraw from communion on account of anyone else? inquired a deacon. They did not. Amid frantic whispering and scurrying, Parris launched for a second time into his "Meditations for Peace." Were they satisfied with his remarks? After an agitated conference, Tarbell replied that they would need to reflect a little. Four nights later they called at the parsonage, to insist on a church council. They found Parris's apology mincing.

Parris was not alone in being called upon to justify himself that fall. In November 1694 William Phips sailed for London to answer to charges of misconduct. They ranged from embezzlement to assault; in thirty months as governor, he had failed to satisfy a single Boston faction. Stoughton threw him a farewell dinner, one the guest of honor boycotted. Parris's travails continued well after. In April 1695 an arbitration council that included Willard, both Mathers, and the ministers from Parris's former Boston congregation assembled in the village. They found fault on all sides. Parris had taken any number of "unwarrantable and uncomfortable steps" in the "late and dark time of the confusions." He needed to extend some compassion to the Nurse families. Unless the congregation wished to continue to devour one another—it was the 1687 advice of the Salem elders turned witchcraft judges all over again—they needed to accept his apology. Should reconciliation prove impossible, Parris must go.

A month later a different group of ministers made themselves more explicit. It was time Parris move on. (He was at least making out better than Phips, who died shortly after arriving in London. Stoughton—who did a wizardly job compiling the charges against him—stepped in as acting governor, in which office he served almost without interruption until his death.) Having performed Mary Walcott's April wedding ceremony, Parris preached his last Salem sermon on June 28, 1696. Weeks later, forty-eight-year-old Elizabeth Parris died. The third minister to lose a wife in the parsonage, her husband buried her in the village, where her stone remains.* Most of the community remained behind Parris, who refused to leave Salem without his salary. They had lost three pastors already; losing a fourth would only exacerbate matters. They petitioned for him to remain. Suit and countersuit followed. In July 1697 the matter went to three arbitrators, including two former witchcraft judges. To them the Nurse family complained that Parris led his congregants into "dangerous errors, and preached such scandalous immoralities" that he ought be dismissed from his profession. He had stifled some accusations while encouraging others. He had sworn to falsehoods. Both sides reached to hyperbole; as his critics saw it, Parris had "been the beginner and procurer of the sorest afflictions, not to this village only, but to this whole country, that did ever befall them." The arbitrators ruled against him. Parris returned to Stow, the remote hamlet where he had preached earlier. Immediately embroiled in a salary dispute, he lasted a year.

ON AUGUST 12, 1696, Samuel Sewall, burly, flushed-faced, his gray hair thinning, was stung by a sharply worded comment. Out of the blue, an Amsterdam-born friend remarked that he would not think twice about it

---

* The funeral was far more elaborate than the one Burroughs had held for his wife and for which he was to pay such a high price. Parris too was slow in paying off the debt.

were a man to claim he had hoisted Boston's Beacon Hill on his back, carted it off, then returned it to its rightful place. The gullibility of witch-craft judges and the claims of "foolish people" who believed in diabolical pacts had long astonished him. He was a Boston constable; his implication was clear and pointed. The inexplicably athletic George Burroughs had hanged almost exactly four years earlier. The comment set in motion a process that Parris's slow fade may have delayed. However grudgingly it had been extracted and at whatever cost to his congregation, Parris's apology still qualified as the sole public admission of wrongdoing. A dark cloud of shame hung about.

Sewall was not alone in shuddering at the unfinished business. On Sunday, September 16, 1696, Stoughton, the council, and the Massachu-setts assembly met for a day of prayer in the Boston town house. Five ministers officiated. When his turn came, Reverend Willard castigated the authorities. Innocents had perished. Why had no official order been promulgated to entreat God's pardon? The cumulative, collective sin weighed all the more heavily in a dispirited season, when God frowned on New England in crop failures, in swarms of flies, in epidemic illness, in Indian ambushes, in failed expeditions against the French. Mather's prediction that the millennium would begin in 1697 began to feel mis-placed. That winter proved the most brutal in New England memory. Thick ice paralyzed Boston Harbor. With trade at a standstill, grain prices rose to unprecedented heights. Food was scarce. The momentum to address 1692 grew, urged along by the occasional scold.

In mid-November Samuel Sewall rode north for a disconcerting trial. Even before Thomas Maule had built Salem town's small Quaker meet-inghouse, he had taken it upon himself to inform Reverend Higginson that he preached lies. The shrewd merchant seemed to have been sent to New England expressly to irritate its authorities; in a society that afforded little room to flex a nonconformist muscle, he exercised every one. It had been Maule who preferred to beat his servant rather than sell her, Maule who had chastised Hale when the minister prayed for Bridget Bishop at the gallows. She had killed one of Maule's children!* In 1695 Maule published a book, printed in New York, lambasting Massachusetts for its Quaker persecutions. With delight, he noted that the volume created "a great hurly-burly of confusion." Stoughton ordered his home searched for the offending publication; Sheriff Corwin saw to the task, removing thirty copies and arresting its author, transported to the Salem jail, a less crowded address than it had been earlier. The books burned.†

By the time the case came to trial in November, Maule was on the stand for both his blasphemous publication and his obstreperous, insulting behavior at his preliminary hearing. Sewall joined two other justices for a headache of an afternoon. It did not help that Maule—the kind of man who showed up for a hearing with a Bible under his arm and who breezily referred to the "High Court of Injustice"—hastened to equate Quaker persecutions with witch-hunting. The authorities were as odious as they had made Burroughs out to be. They had fought witchcraft with witchcraft. He mocked the village girls, with their absurd visionary powers. How could anyone imagine them to be "the true martyrs of Jesus Christ"? In November Maule went further, ridiculing the magistrates. Five times imprisoned and twice whipped, he was fearless. Did the court truly dare to sit in judgment of him, decrying his wickedness, when it had executed innocents? Those sanctimonious souls preferred their children to wind up "rogues and whores" rather than Quakers. And presto! Here was Reverend Higginson's daughter transformed into a witch.

The king's case presented, Maule addressed the jury. The court, he reminded them, had brought the wrath of God down upon the province.

---

* Maule himself backtracked. His wife had testified against Bishop, whom the couple believed a witch. At Bishop's June hanging, he announced that most of those in prison were as well.

† Naturally Maule went on to write about his imprisonment and trial in the 1697 *New England Persecutors Mauled with Their Own Weapons*. For their oppressive tactics, he compared the Massachusetts authorities to Jesuits, monks, and friars. They did the devil's work, while living regally on plundered estates. And he proposed an alternative interpretation: it was for crimes like those of 1692 that the Lord afterward delivered New England into the hands of barbarous Indians.

How could they prosecute him for his "notorious wicked lies" when they had murdered innocents and never repented? They had squandered all credibility; he did not need to point out that they had done so in that very room. It was no easier to speak or publish freely in 1696 than it had been earlier. But it was more difficult to be convicted. Maule had a rather novel defense as well, one that could work only that dismal winter. Indeed his name appeared on the offending volume. But the jurors would need to confer with the New York printer. How else to prove that the words "Thomas Maule" on the title page corresponded to the man who stood before them any more than a man did to his specter?

Maule cautioned the jury: They should deliberate with care. They did not want to incur the same load of guilt under which other Essex County jurors now squirmed. Any ruling was theirs alone, the judges but their clerks, a biting allusion to the reversed Nurse verdict. To the shock of the bench, the twelve men found Maule not guilty. How was that possible, exploded a Sewall colleague; Maule's odious book sat before them! Patiently the jurors explained that they found the evidence insufficient. The printer had set Maule's name to the page. Mere mortals could not corroborate what those words represented. The justice sputtered that Maule might have escaped the judgment of man but would not escape that of God, to which the defendant, aglow with triumph, had a retort: the jury delivered him from unrighteous men who worked unrighteous deeds.

In December, momentum built—under conditions similar to those that had produced a witchcraft scare; New England appeared to be "upon the brink of ruin"—for a public acknowledgment. The task of drafting the bill fell to Cotton Mather. He continued to hold that while he could not support their principles, he could speak only honorably of the judges. (There was a "nevertheless" in that statement too.) They had been prudent, pious, patient. They had comported themselves far better than the common people, who had entirely succumbed to delirious brains and discontented hearts. He drew up a laundry list of impieties for the fast day, inserting "wicked sorceries" about midway through the thicket of drinking, cursing, and insubordinate children, the embarrassing item you buried among sundries at the pharmacy counter. They had brought down storms from the invisible world that had led "unto those errors whereby great hardships were brought upon innocent persons, and (we fear) guilt incurred, which we have all cause to bewail." To Mather's draft others appended language acknowledging "neglects in the administration of justice." The council—on which sat every Salem justice—erupted in fury; Sewall had never seen it so incensed. The "wicked sorceries" could remain. The miscarriage of justice must go. It fell to him to rewrite the bill. In the end the much abbreviated proclamation included neither references to injustice nor the word "witchcraft" or "sorcery." Massachusetts would repent for whatever errors had been committed on all sides in "the late tragedy."

The wrangling, and Maule's imputations, weighed on Sewall. So did the chapter of Revelation he turned over in his mind those weeks, as heavy snow blanketed Boston. Through it he trudged two days after the debate, in distress, to fetch his minister. Both Sewall's wife and his two-year-old daughter, Sarah, were ill. The former witchcraft judge was that winter more susceptible to guilt, just as the Maule jury had been less susceptible to evidence; the same week a Boston woman upbraided him regarding another verdict, one into which he knew he had been "wheedled and hectored." The following morning at dawn little Sarah Sewall unexpectedly died in her nurse's arms. In the family's grief, the tiny corpse still in the house, Sewall's sixteen-year-old son read from Matthew 12, in Latin. His father shuddered at the seventh verse, with its reference to innocents condemned.* It "did awfully bring to mind the Salem tragedy," he brooded, his first private use of that word in connection with the witchcraft. After the funeral he spent a few melancholy

---

* "If ye had known what this meaneth, I will have mercy and not sacrifice, ye would not have condemned the guiltless."

minutes alone, underground, in the bitter cold, communing with the dead in the family crypt. Sarah was the second child he buried in 1696. In five years he had suffered repeated losses. He was miserable.

On January 14, 1697, the colony observed the province-wide fast of repentance. All work ceased as communities beseeched the Lord to "pardon all the errors of his servants and people," with special reference to Salem. As the minister passed Sewall on his way to the pulpit that afternoon, the witchcraft judge handed him a note. It may have been extracted; Sewall had sensed Willard's disfavor through the gloomy season. He was stung by slights; he felt himself ostracized. Midway through the service, the open-faced minister signaled to Sewall, who stood in his pew, head bowed. Before the full congregation, in the presence of Sewall's grieving wife and children, his minister read his words aloud. Given the "reiterated strikes of God upon himself and his family," Sewall was acutely aware of the guilt he had contracted on the witchcraft court. He beseeched God to forgive his sin and punish neither anyone else nor New England for his misstep.* When Willard had finished reading what was in effect a single, jam-packed sentence — one that included "blame," "shame," "sin," and "guilt," four words Parris had studiously avoided — Sewall bowed from the waist. He then took his seat.

It must have been an agonizing moment for a man who shrank from criticism and who preferred not to stand alone; his was an act of public penance of which he knew Stoughton, at the very least, disapproved. The chief justice snubbed him afterward. Evidently he felt an apology unnecessary; the bill ordering the fast sufficed. In condemning the Andros administration, Stoughton had pointed to unreasonable, ensnaring judicial procedures. Out of favor afterward, he had declared himself "willing to make any amendment for the miscarriages of the late government." He saw no need to address off-kilter contests or legal missteps in

---

* Among the "reiterated strikes" that year was fifteen-year-old Betty Sewall's spiritual meltdown. Weeks earlier the self-proclaimed reprobate was still weeping so profusely she could barely read. Newly returned from Salem, she sat across the aisle from her father on January 14.

1697. That evening Sewall transcribed the text of the note carefully in his diary. A few blocks away, Mather fretted at his desk over "divine displeasure." Might it "overtake my family, for my not appearing with vigor enough to stop the proceedings of the judges, when the inextricable storm from the invisible world assaulted the country?" The guilt lifts from the page. He prayed to the same end the following morning, receiving heavenly assurances that there would be no retribution.

Others also took advantage of the fast day to unburden themselves. Twelve Salem jurors—including at least some of the men who had found Rebecca Nurse not guilty before Stoughton suggested they reconsider—that afternoon begged pardon of God and of all those they had offended. They would never do "such things again on such grounds for the whole world." Inching toward a justification, they acknowledged that they had been "under the power of a strong and general delusion." They had made poor decisions. Their statement carries light notes of reproach. No one had managed to enlighten them on the woolly matter; others had joined in shedding innocent blood. Cotton Mather preached that afternoon on the subject to the North Church congregation, including a salute to the magistrates and ministers who had suffered for their righteous service. Afterward Robert Calef, a Boston merchant and constable, accosted him. The two had already been in correspondence for some time. In his remarks Mather defined witchcraft as a pact with the devil. What, demanded Calef, was his source? Mather doubtless knew that Calef had posted Thomas Maule's bail. He could not have imagined the troubles the exasperating forty-eight-year-old Boston wool dealer was to cause him.

In 1693 Calef had begun work on *More Wonders of the Invisible World*, its very title a provocation. Completed in 1697, the book was later printed in London. Already Calef had circulated a salacious paper accusing Mather of attempting to ignite another Salem with his treatment of seventeen-year-old Margaret Rule, who had delivered the news of Mather's missing notes. Calef suggested that both Mathers had handled the teenager indecently. They had done no such thing, Mather assured him. He had not asked how many witches sat on Margaret; he had expressly asked she *not* reveal names. His father had by no means touched her belly. Why would he, when the imp that afflicted her was said to be on her pillow? (He worked over those lines with uncharacteristic care, crossing out more than was his habit.) A Mather friend supplied Calef with the minister's account of Margaret's bedroom ravings and levitations, which Calef shared, a wholesale embarrassment five years after Salem. Mather denounced him from the pulpit and nearly had him arrested for libel. Calef agreed that witches existed but argued that Scripture provided no reliable means of identifying them. Hanging them in no way inconvenienced the devil. Men, Calef believed, should desist from dabbling in divine affairs. They tended to make a botch of them.

The immediate wrangling was with reputations rather than consciences; for the most part it was easier to settle than offer accounts. When George Corwin died on a snowy spring day in 1696, Philip English evidently threatened to seize the body. He would return it, he bellowed, only in exchange for some portion of the fifteen-hundred-pound estate the late sheriff had confiscated.* The sight of his bobtailed cow in Corwin's yard infuriated him. English turned up repeatedly in court thereafter for withholding his church taxes (an offense that landed him in jail) and for undermining the authority of the Salem selectmen (an office to which he had been elected weeks before his accusation). He called ministers and justices robbers. He refused to worship in a meetinghouse "infested" by Puritans. Salem's was "the devil's church." He was still blasting the clergy in 1722, when the court indicted him for calling Nicholas Noyes—dead for twenty-one years—a murderer. Family lore has him excoriating Hathorne on his deathbed.

Naturally no one took more shots at an analysis than Cotton Mather. Typically he inched closer and closer to the scene, placing himself more

---

* Of the male victims', only Burroughs's estate escaped Corwin's pillage. Part of it rode off with Mrs. Burroughs instead.

often at Salem than he had suggested in 1692; a reader of his later pages would assume he had attended the trials. Given how insistently he positioned himself at the center of events, it is understandable that he would come to be blamed for them, when he had urged every kind of moderation, denounced spectral evidence, attended no hearing, and played no prosecutorial role.* For once causality was not a burning issue; the origin of the plague of evil angels interested Mather less than its utility. So that proper use might be made of those "stupendous and prodigious things," he had written *Wonders of the Invisible World*. He regretted no page of that volume, despite the abuse the "reviled book" had earned him. Nor did he for a moment question the judges' "unspotted fidelity." He put his finger on something that remained invisible to him: political considerations had grossly disfigured moral ones. Mather did have one theory, either late in 1692 or very soon thereafter. Was this infestation of evil angels, he mused in his diary, not "intended by *hell,* as a particular defiance, unto *my* poor endeavors, to bring the souls of men into *heaven?*" He credited others with that idea.†

Mather folded something more of an explanation into his 1697 life of William Phips, a fairy tale written to exonerate a disastrous administration and the men behind it. In those pages he attributed the Salem epidemic to youthful spell-casting and fortune-telling. Books of superstition had poisoned adolescent minds, inviting down devils in "as astonishing a manner as was ever heard of." He insisted still on diabolical compacts but

---

* He was not unaware of those labors. "And why," he wondered later, "after all my unwearied cares and pains, to rescue the miserable from the lions and bears of hell which had seized them, and after all my studies to disappoint the devils in their designs to confound my neighborhood, must I be driven to the necessity of an apology?" He made none, comparing the thankless service he had rendered to "ten thousand steps over a rocky mountain filled with rattlesnakes." He registered only one regret: he should not have invited so many viewers into the "haunted chambers" of the Boston afflicted.

† The more he considered the matter, the more he resolved to battle the devil. Naturally that required the composition of another volume, in which he explicitly set out a covenant for his readers to sign. He planned to distribute copies of the text weekly where it might prove most beneficial. He was not unaware that—in pressing a book upon the unsuspecting and demanding their signatures—he was himself imitating Satan.

jettisoned the witches' meetings. Fortunately Phips had arrived in the nick of time to assemble a distinguished court. The judges had acted effectively, perhaps too effectively. Government subversion was at stake, however; Satan attempted to wrest their hard-won new charter from their hands. Mather reprinted the June "Return of Several Ministers," or did in part; he omitted the introductory call to arms as well as the concluding recommendation for "a speedy and vigorous prosecution." Writing to political ends, Mather was thrilled to report, upon publication, that his enemies were "in much anguish at the book."

He did not forget Sweden, although he no longer advertised the smile of God he had promised the witchcraft justices in exchange for their labors. Rather he allowed that that affair too had ended in confusion. How could Massachusetts Bay have fared better when the kingdom of Sweden could not penetrate their witchcraft? (They had. The children had lied.) Like the jurors, he fingered the devil and man's blinkered understanding. "Whole clouds of witnesses" could swear to what they had seen. As a last word on the subject he could only paraphrase a favorite early Christian writer: "Devils can cause men to see things that do not exist as if they did." Everyone was a victim.

Mather expressed no remorse; his doubts never escaped his diary. He could not however stay away from the subject, which he worried like a loose tooth. He would not let the curtain fall on the witchcraft, struggling for years afterward to keep it onstage, something he would have cause to regret. Stoughton took the silent route and escaped all odium. Mather wrote himself into the story. In his 1702 *Magnalia* — the epic New England history that would include the Phips hagiography — he devoted a full book to wonders. He elaborated on the Goodwin story. He slipped Indian chiefs into the Salem epidemic. He had long suspected that those "horrid sorcerers and hellish conjurers" had played the precipitating role in that "inexplicable war." An executed witch, he claimed, had seen them at the diabolical meetings, along with a crew of Frenchmen. In concert they plotted to ruin New England.

By the time the *Magnalia* was published, Beverly minister John Hale had produced a very different account of the trials. He had waited five years for someone else to make sense of the episode. No one had. Blind though he was to the pilfering in his household, Hale was uniquely qualified for the task. He had witnessed the girls' initial distress. He had spent countless hours in the courtroom, at hearings and hangings, alongside Parris and Noyes and in their confidence. He had testified against three women. He plainly labored to square the incontrovertible truth that innocents had died with the conviction that the judges had acted righteously. "But such was the darkness of that day," Hale lamented, "the tortures and the lamentations of the afflicted, and the power of former precedents, that we walked in the clouds, and could not see our way." Desperately he tried to dispense with the guilt—more must be done for the relief of those whose estates and reputations lay in ruins—and settle on a sufficient, safe method for the detection of witchcraft. He came closer to admitting error than anyone; still, he lurched confusedly. They might have been too vigorous in their prosecution but must not be too lenient in the future. Hale hints he had "special reasons" to address the matter before he died; he may or may not already have realized that he had testified against one woman thinking she was another. He settled on the same causes as did Mather, minus the Indians, the political agenda, and the personal affront. Hale admitted to what none of us does easily; the events of 1692 had brought him "to a more strict scanning of the principles I had imbibed, to question, and questioning at length, to reject many of them." He brushed uneasily past a half-articulated idea: the belief in witchcraft rather than witches themselves had unsettled Salem.

Crises invite two kinds of memoir: the don't-blame-me-I-wasn't-on-hand version, and the it-would-have-been-far-worse-had-I-not-been. Salem got only the first treatment. No heroes identified themselves. John Higginson, the senior town minister, introduced Hale's pages. He too fingered Satan. Twenty had met with a "tragical end." Some might have been innocent. Others who had escaped prosecution might have been guilty.

He acknowledged qualms about court procedures despite the impeccable judges and juries. He then dissociated himself entirely from the trials. "I stirred little," he wrote, deferring to his age (he had been seventy-six), "and was much disenabled (both in body and mind) from knowing and judging the occurrents and transactions of that time." Higginson had testified against no one but was intimately involved. He had offered courtroom prayers. He knew every detail of the proceedings. His son spent days recording testimony, his daughter some of 1692 in custody. Hale's was a brave essay on a perilous subject, one he chose not to publish in his lifetime. Surely by design, *A Modest Enquiry into the Nature of Witchcraft* appeared only in 1702, the year after Stoughton died.

Remarkably few traces of disapproval survive among or toward the authorities.* Parents still sent children to be educated by Reverend Noyes. Cotton Mather preached Moody's funeral sermon five years after Moody had helped the Englishes escape. Sewall dedicated a 1697 apocalyptic tract to Stoughton, who would devote his administration to fending off Indian incursions and frustrating French designs. Already chief justice, councillor, and lieutenant governor, Stoughton served for several years as commander in chief of the colony's troops; he assumed as well the responsibilities of judge of the admiralty. It would take several men to replace him. Sewall was at his bedside on July 4, 1701. "Pray for me!" were sixty-nine-year-old Stoughton's last words to his longtime colleague. He reached out a hand as his visitor left; Sewall kissed it. Three days later he was dead. Willard preached the funeral sermon, dwelling perhaps a note too long on the failure to repent. On occasion even the best of men provoked God, noted Willard, so that "though he loves their persons, yet he dislikes the things that are so done by them."

Two days after Sewall's visit, Stoughton had finalized his will. He opened it "most humbly begging and believing the pardon of all my great

* One of the few that does is from Wait Still Winthrop. In 1699 he classed Stoughton among men "who are fast to their own interest, but I know not to whose else." Any man who left the ministry for worldly affairs was, Winthrop huffed, by definition greedy, grasping, and untrustworthy.

and many sins both of heart and life," a formulaic phrasing. The document is a model of enlightened largesse; if a man can be judged by his last wishes, Stoughton was as compassionate as he was methodical. He forgot no one, from his housekeeper to the council doorkeeper to Harvard College, to which he left land, a four-story building, and scholarship monies. He provided for an indigent and deserving scholar. He stipulated that several Stoughton Hall rooms be reserved for Indian students, gratis. Separately, he set aside monies for Indian education. He settled a vast sum on Dorchester's school and forty acres on Milton's poor. For a century he had no rival among Harvard College benefactors.*

Mather and Maule continued their battle, Mather writing the Indian war down to Quakers, Maule the witchcraft down to *Wonders,* that "parcel of dark confused airy matter." Still the cloud would not dissipate; appeals for economic reparations and for the clearing of names piled up. As ever, they distinguished between the "errors and mistakes" in the trials and "the care and conscientious endeavor of the honorable judges," as a group of Topsfield petitioners had it, lobbying for relief. (Ministers submitted petitions for the convicted, although no Salem town or village minister signed one.) A curse lay on the land. Where once witches had explained God's frown, the bungled prosecution now did. As Brattle had warned, it was not easy to discharge the guilt. It festered, as the memory of an insult proves more potent than the insult itself, something 1692 had made abundantly clear.

Twelve years after Ann Foster, her daughter, and her granddaughter had incriminated one another, Michael Wigglesworth, the seventy-three-year-old Malden cleric, himself a punctilious and sensitive soul, weighed in, writing Increase Mather of his concerns.† An elder statesman, Wigglesworth had taught Sewall and both Mathers. As it so often

---

* The William Stoughton Fund continues to support several Harvard students a year, in accordance with his 1701 wishes.

† Wigglesworth appears to have gone quiet throughout the crisis, though the defecting Salem villagers shared their criticisms of their minister with him in 1693. Wigglesworth favored their appeal. He signed the letter insisting Parris depart a full year before the village minister did so.

does, the preoccupation with justice grew out of a perceived injustice. A drought that year threatened New England's farms; Wigglesworth feared "that God hath a controversy with us what was done in the time of witchcraft." The judges had been imposed upon by the devil or by "the devil's impostures." They had shed innocent blood, for which they had never personally assumed responsibility. He understood the subject was off-limits but no choice remained. He was especially appalled by the plundering of estates, something that had not accompanied earlier witchcraft prosecutions. (Nor had there been many wealthy witches before 1692.)* The failure properly to compensate families of those condemned in the "supposed witchcraft" compounded the shame; the curse would not lift until the court made proper amends. He urged Mather to pursue the matter. (Five years later, Philip English and twenty others still clamored for reparations, always with a respectful word for the judges. English submitted a claim for nearly twelve hundred pounds. He would receive three hundred in 1718.) No justice stepped forward, as Wigglesworth advised. The only one who had, regretted his courage soon enough; when in 1720 Samuel Sewall saw how the history books were being written, he was mortified. There was his humiliating confession for all posterity!

One bit of reckoning remained. On August 25, 1706, Ann Putnam Jr. stood amid the Salem village congregation to be admitted as a full church member. She was twenty-seven. Both her parents had died, leaving nine siblings in her care. Ann had not married. In more prosperous times, she had been afflicted by at least sixty-two people, among them her former minister, now dead; a neighbor, now dead; and teenage Dorothy Good, now insane. Of the nineteen who had been hanged, she had testified under oath against all but two. For over eight months whole communities had hung on her every syllable. She now stood silently as,

---

* It is unclear where the monies went. Stoughton took care to exempt Corwin and his heirs from liability in 1694, shielding them from restitution claims. Corwin evidently did not share any proceeds with Herrick, the impoverished undersheriff.

from the same pulpit on which she had wildly pointed to a yellow bird during Lawson's sermon, Salem's new minister read aloud her confession. The onetime prophet begged forgiveness of those whose relatives she had caused to be arrested or accused. She profoundly regretted the calamity she had caused. In particular she apologized to the Nurse, Esty, and Cloyce families, their ranks thin in the village pews by 1706. They were innocent. She twice reminded the congregation that she had acted in concert "with others." Whoever drafted her statement had the jurors' apology before him; as had they, Ann declared she had acted "ignorantly and unwittingly." She too had been neither able "to understand, nor able to withstand, the mysterious delusions of the powers of darkness and Prince of the air." Three times in her short statement she notes she had been an "instrument" in his designs.

There was no need to look any farther for a culprit. Their constant and implacable companion, so much in the air they breathed, an occupant of every Massachusetts town, had made them do it. In Salem village as elsewhere he crept back into the discourse. In a particularly ebullient 1693 address, Mather had devils everywhere in the air, "watching, wishing, snatching, to devour us." Meanwhile, the ground shifted gradually underfoot. The witches gradually became martyrs. It would be years before anyone asked whose delusion it had been anyway, before anyone dared to suggest that the judges were themselves the sorcerer's apprentices, that they rather than the village girls had been the "blind, nonsensical" parties, the ones possessed, if "with ignorance and folly." Which did not answer the question of what had happened either.

The petitions for redress grew increasingly emotional; in 1710 the Massachusetts legislature established a committee to process claims and clear Salem names. (Even in doing so they suggested they had simply prosecuted the wrong witch suspects.) In October 1711, the names of most victims were cleared and some families reimbursed for prison costs, still without any acknowledgment of responsibility. That ruling cleared jailers, constables, and sheriffs of any wrongdoing. It did not mention the justices. Many quarreled with the logic of the committee, which left open wounds and produced fresh indignities all around. Mather made a point of visiting Salem afterward "to endeavor an healing of all tendency to discord there." Abigail Hobbs was rewarded for her inflammatory confession. William Good, who had denounced his own wife, made out especially well. Pleas for further redress continued. Still no one scurried off in disgrace. We know of only one witness who recanted, on his deathbed, admitting that his charges against Bridget Bishop had been groundless. It seemed pointless to attribute blame, just as it seemed impossible to make sense of the events of 1692. Few were innocent aside from those who had been hanged.

BEFORE PARRIS CONCEDED they were bewitched, before they turned into visionaries or martyrs, before anyone dismissed them as "vile varlets," Abigail Williams and Betty Parris were thought to be diabolically possessed. They returned to that diagnosis as they grew to womanhood.* In every way the early Salem symptoms conformed to those of Elizabeth Knapp, the Goodwin children, and the two young women to whose bedsides Mather rushed post-Salem. We will never know what felled the girls, whether it had more to do with their souls or their chores, with parental attention or inattention. The prickling sensations, the twitching, stammering, and grimacing, the ulcerated skin and twisted limbs, the curled tongues and convex backs, the deliriums, the "furious invectives against imaginary individuals" do however conform precisely to what nineteenth-century neurologist Jean-Martin Charcot, with Freud following him, termed hysteria. Where the seventeenth-century authority saw the devil, we tend to recognize an overtaxed nervous system; what an earlier age called hysteria we term conversion disorder, the body literally translating emotions into symptoms. When sublimated, distress

---

* Even Cotton Mather executed an about-face, one he knew would sow confusion. To his father-in-law several years after Salem he admitted that "they who are usually look'd upon as *enchanted* persons, are generally, properly really *possessed* persons." As a consequence they made for unreliable witnesses.

will manifest physically, holding the body hostage. Charcot's drawings of convulsing hysterics agree in every detail with the scenes that left Deodat Lawson reeling.

Conditions favored such an outbreak. The talk around Betty and Abigail was fraught, angry, apocalyptic. The house was cold and growing colder. Disaffected churchmen thumped heavily in and out of the parsonage to air powerful resentments. Betty and Abigail had no escape from those furies in early 1692, the dark, bleak, and confined months when death felt closer, when witchcraft accusations tended to peak. It helped that the girls occupied the kind of small, sealed-off place that makes good theater (and good detective fiction); witchcraft charges less often emanated from urban addresses. In an isolated community, in a tightly wound household, the people who observed and conceivably caused the girls' distress were the only ones to whom they could appeal. Whether precipitated by a visit from Sarah Good, a message from the pulpit, or an interior anguish, something disabled them.

What they developed sounds to have been a form of emotional laryngitis; a sense of suffocation tends to accompany hysteria. The girls expressed in fits what they could not communicate in words, or what no one seemed to hear when they entrusted it to words.* Mather and Sewall were mistaken about lightning and its preference for parsonages.† But Parris was correct in noting that the devil targeted the most pious. Hysteria prefers decorous, sober households, where tensions puddle more deeply; it made sense that the Salem minister wound up with more witchcraft victims under his roof than anyone else. (The surprise was that he did not wind up with more. Two Parris children soldiered on, forgotten by history.) Instructed not to fidget, well-mannered, well-behaved Betty and Abigail writhed. They could not unburden themselves

---

* Freud relied on Virgil to introduce *The Interpretation of Dreams* with a line particularly suited to Salem: "If I cannot move the upper world," vows Juno, "I will move the underworld."

† Samuel Willard was in the half-destroyed Sewall kitchen that sultry 1695 afternoon as well. Eleven years later he baptized Benjamin Franklin, who would solve the lightning mystery.

as did those loudmouthed, plot-propelling bad girls Abigail Hobbs and Mary Lacey Jr., who may actually have believed they had signed pacts with the devil and sound as if they would have if they could. It would have been easier at the parsonage to have a vision than an opinion.

Conversion disorder also favors backwaters, women (especially young women), and the fatherless. It tends to break out in convents, schools, and hospitals, in tight-knit, emotionally charged environments. Freud noted that the especially visual, intellectually astute child will suffer first. Her symptoms are infectious, no doubt more so when she hails from the most conspicuous family in town. (By the same token, the devout tend to glimpse the devil more frequently. Possession rarely occurs in the absence of intense piety.) It was a full church member who introduced the witch cake, forcing Parris's hand, as it would be the more devout members of the community — and the more orthodox ministers — who leaped at the sacrament-subverting ceremony in the parsonage field. The girls may have been aware of the Goodwin case. The adults certainly were. And when your elders inform you that you are bewitched, you are unlikely to experience immediate relief of your symptoms. The pricks along your arms may grow just a little more intense, as the scalp tingles at the mention of lice.

Already at the center of the community, Betty and Abigail claimed its rapt attention, something others obviously craved. Mary Rowlandson was candid on that subject. "Before I knew what affliction meant," she admitted in her captivity narrative, "I was ready sometimes to wish for it." She could not have been the only New England woman who longed for a test by which to prove her holiness. Elizabeth Knapp sobbed not only that she led a spiritually unprofitable life, but that her "labor was burdensome to her." No one chastened an afflicted girl or sent her to gather firewood. Elizabeth Hubbard set off on no further terrifying errands, wolves nipping at her heels; any number of Cinderellas were relieved of their chores. (Ann Putnam Sr. — the first adult woman to be afflicted — wore herself out precisely because the girls on whose labor she relied contorted. She had cause for grief, for which there was little place in seventeenth-century Massachusetts. Elsewhere it manifested as crippling distress.) Parents looked on with tender concern, siblings no doubt with raging jealousy. In another outbreak, a young girl observed that her convulsing sisters "seemed to be more the object of their parents' care and love, as well as pity, than ever." It was not long before she assumed their symptoms.

Indictments described the bewitched as "consumed, pined, wasted, and tormented." No one who set eyes on the girls would have noticed the first three; never before had they been so cosseted. Doubtless that was a seduction in itself, an invitation to malingering. One witness for the defense noted that an afflicted girl fell into fits each time "her mother spoke to her with tartness." Not only did she remain healthy, but Elizabeth Knapp put on weight as her agonies increased. (Like the ministers, the girls appreciated a full house and a large theater. In 1693 an afflicted girl summoned the governor himself. Elizabeth warned she would not recover until a conclave of ministers met to pray over her in Boston, her own version of a trip to the Golden City.) She made clear that there was plenty of self-reproach and spiritual confusion and devilish temptation to discharge, the kind of anguish that left Sewall and the Goodwin children to sob they had squandered their lives. Already there was an Indian behind every bush, a spectral Frenchman in the yard.* Every child is on intimate terms with the raging monster inside. But adults too have awoken to discover an arm attached not to the comely hand of Henry Jekyll, but to the dusky, gnarled paw of Edward Hyde.

Did the afflicted truly feel pinched and pricked? The hysteric's skin is said to be uncommonly sensitive, especially late at night. It bruises easily.

---

* Vampiric practices could be conjured even without a teenage imagination. Reporting to the Lords of Trade on atrocities in 1689, a Dominion official claimed that the Indians made bloody sport of the colonists, "having killed 500 of them, roasting by slow fire more than 80 poor Christians, whose warm blood they drink, and sometimes eat their flesh, laying their sucking infants to the bleeding veins of their captives."

On two other counts, a seventeenth-century villager might feel metaphorically bitten or stabbed. You were meant to be pierced to the marrow by good preaching. And Cotton Mather termed winters "very pinching and piercing things."* There seemed, he noted, to be more hours in a winter day, allowing more time to reflect. The Puritans had stripped the calendar of every festival and holiday, to wind up with a work year of three hundred days. It contributed to their astonishing productivity. And it also left them with what has been deemed the "dullest calendar in Western civilization." The girls knew no respite during the most desolate, most interior months, the horizon low, the family oppressively close at hand.

Did they believe they saw Deliverance Hobbs on the beam, John Procter on the marshal's lap? They had spent a claustrophobic winter housebound, under ashen skies and drifted snow, between whitewashed walls, amid undecorated surroundings. Visual monotony has been known to produce hallucinations. (It is interesting that there were no olfactory hallucinations and only a rare disembodied voice.) It could not have been difficult to cough up visions under the feverish circumstances. On intimate terms with the supernatural, a girl well versed in Scripture supplied them all the more readily. Prayer works to clarify the mental imagery, to privilege the imaginary world over the actual one, at which the adolescent excels already. It was probably no accident that the best-educated village girls participated most ardently in the crisis. In Sweden, too, an intelligent, outspoken, orphaned eleven-year-old stood at the center of the outbreak. Past the window flew warped versions of the girls' fears, floating scenes from Scripture, linty household grudges, gurgling sins and guilts, the detritus of dreams and nightmares, scraps of gossip and political darts, a veritable Chagall of cats in the doorway and neighbors in the orchard. In a sense the afflicted engaged in a responsive read-

---

* An ingenious seventeenth-century English physician noted a correlation between the intruders that his mad patients believed leaped on or gnawed at their bodies and witches' familiars. The pests tended to be winged creatures, mice, rats, and dogs. Mather compared the imp that darted across Margaret Rule's 1693 pillow to a rat.

ing; having been fed a liturgical diet of tigers and dragons, they answered with black cats and wild beasts. In other words, as a modern historian has noted of our synchronized imaginations, "the Virgin Mary was more likely to appear to a French peasant in the seventeenth century than to a lowland Scot." The "bewitched" moreover made the imagery rhyme with their own stories. Susannah Shelden had survived Indian attack. She reported atrocities where Ann Putnam Sr. saw dead babies. Both delivered effigies of their apprehensions. It is true, as Brattle pointed out, that it is impossible to see with our eyes shut. But who can attest to what we see when we close them?

By the time the older girls began to contort, additional forces had come into play. The five who were to become the most vociferous accusers stepped in only after Tituba's high-voltage testimony. Every one was a servant. They had reached the age when one ecstatically ambushes the grown-ups, when dependence grades into revolt. They may have had an agenda, which they pursued more subtly than did Abigail Hobbs. They knew stresses the younger girls did not, having ventured farther into the forest of sin and temptation that Elizabeth Knapp so brilliantly charted. They were more attuned to adult collisions, demands, confidences, advances, to wolves in sheep's clothing. Was there a sexual element at play? One can make what one will of the piercing and pecking and pricking, of pitchforks thrown down, of backs arched suggestively upward and knees locked fiercely together. No concrete evidence survives. For the most part, men were the ones who complained of witches in their beds. But what about adolescence is not fraught with erotic fear and longing? The battle for a thrashing, moaning young woman's soul certainly titillated some at her bedside. And male, ministering hands were by no means undesirable. In 1693 Margaret Rule dismissed the women gathered around her, but not the men. She pleaded with one young caller in particular; grasping his hands, she maneuvered him back into his seat.

Hysteria is contagious and attention addictive; wanton self-abuse comes naturally to a teenager. It may have been difficult for a discontented, disenfranchised nineteen-year-old like Mercy Lewis to pass up the pleasure of planting herself in the spotlight.* Had anyone ever hung on her every pronouncement? George Burroughs certainly had not. For fatherless girls, the bewitched managed brilliantly, winning the company and compassion of every man they knew. (John Indian aside, no male accuser stepped in before Andover.) Many had cause for trauma; some surely played at their afflictions. Theater has long been the refuge of an unhappy childhood. It is possible that when Mary Walcott greeted Reverend Lawson on his return to the village she carried a message from a former parishioner. It is equally possible that she landed on Lawson's doorstep as a preview of the wonders at work; she was one of the two girls on whose spectral sight Parris particularly relied. The older girls colluded in some calculated way, with one another and with several adults. The telepathic courtroom displays could not have been orchestrated otherwise. Susannah Shelden had not bound her own wrists together. Ann Putnam Jr. and Elizabeth Hubbard did not arrive separately at the conclusion that the conjuring Burroughs ranked above a wizard, an unprecedented Massachusetts distinction. Despite her afflictions, Parris's niece managed to convey herself about a tavern and locate a young man who, with his rapier, might save her from a specter.

We will never know the extent of the counterfeiting. The bold prophecies doubled as stage directions, a touch of genius. They were not difficult to manage, at least for a persuasive child with a gift for words. In 1720, an identical case of witchcraft broke out thirty miles west of Salem village. At its center was a well-read eleven-year-old with a tenacious memory, a loyal younger sister, a pact of secrecy, and a ladder for the flying scenes. It turns out not to be so very difficult to pinch your own forehead or sink your teeth into your own arm. When you launch a muff across a meetinghouse — when you squarely hit your target with your shoe — you are more likely settling a score than suffering from either witchcraft or hysteria. And the loud hints endure: Accusers had attempted

---

* Calef noted that when families welcomed the Salem girls in their witch-hunting roles, "it was ordinary for other young people to be taken in fits, and to have the same spectral sight."

to recant. The girls admitted that they hungered for sport.* They were for once not cowering before their masters but running the show—or seemed to be; one justice broke his cane striking at a specter. In that respect too Salem upends convention. It is a cautionary tale turned on its head: a child misbehaves, and the world around her is punished.

Whether hallucinating or confabulating, the afflicted offered up what they absorbed from the adult world in warnings of invasion, in historical prophecies, in biblical imagery, in local gossip. They knew Sarah Good had a hole in her coat and Deliverance Hobbs a wound in her side, one she had incurred before the alleged tavern stabbing. They knew the names of eminent, unsavory, or adversarial members of other communities, including those of obstreperous Topsfield teenagers. The question is not why they retailed preposterous stories but why in 1692 they were believed; it is easier to understand their real or artificial visions than the vertiginous tales of everyone else. ("Indeed," notes a modern psychiatrist, "a sane adolescent would have something wrong with her.") Tituba's initial testimony had been largely religion-free. It was also rather vague. The adults transfigured the adolescent distress, attaching to it agendas (Putnam), convictions (Hathorne), obsessions (Mather, with his Swedish fixation), bestowing on the girls powers of which the teenagers may have been unaware.† Fairy tales too are collaborative exercises, old wives' tales polished and preserved by men. Hathorne asked leading questions and supplied partial answers, ghostwriting a familiar story, one reverse-engineered from all that was sacred, having originated in the Massachusetts pulpit. Was it coincidence that Hathorne happened to have taken down the 1689 affidavits regarding the alleged Andros conspiracy, that sinister plot to destroy Boston, win over all Massachusetts towns, and sacrifice the colonists to their heathen adversaries? Hathorne

---

* "These prayer meetings are about the only entertainment we have," complained a twentieth-century mill worker for whom religion—and religious enthusiasm—alone allowed for self-expression.

† "I have been wicked in my day, but I never thought a little girl like you would ever be able to melt me and end my wicked deeds," the Wicked Witch chides Dorothy, as she melts away.

discovered when he did so that Andros had bribed Indians to help him, distributing gold rings, money, and the text he insisted "was better than the Bible." That "horrid design" echoes throughout the Salem testimony, a political conspiracy recast as a religious one. Blind superstition delivered up the accusations. Deft politics—and close, patient, informed reading—accounted for the prosecutions.

Thomas Putnam's shoes stick out just a little too conspicuously from behind the curtain. Before he rode off that muddy late-February Monday to press witchcraft charges, he may have felt himself cursed, having lost two inheritances, land, children, a cow. He stood only to profit from wheels within wheels. He resented his encroaching Topsfield neighbors. H. L. Mencken's crack about the genius of Puritanism—"summoning the massive forces of the law to help in a private feud"—belongs to him. At the same time, Putnam had a much-loved, perceptive, desperately convulsing twelve-year-old at home. He was soon to have a deranged wife as well. It is difficult to believe he had a long-range strategy at the start. Certainly he intensified matters in person as he did on the page, layering on the adverbs, inserting exclamation marks with his letters to authorities. He complained against at least thirty-five and testified against seventeen, transcribing more than a hundred depositions. He appears to have written out all of his daughter's, Mercy Lewis's, and Mary Walcott's testimony. His minister shared his worldview, "believing the devil's accusations, and readily departing from all charity," as his detractors charged. It is difficult to say who served as whose proxy, the convulsing girls or the crusading parents.

The convulsions ratified the witchcraft, but the story belonged to the bench. Once in court, the women played secondary roles, as to some extent they may have done in the first place; sorcery allowed men to attack other men through wives or by way of daughters. (It is interesting that no one accused Francis Nurse.) All three town justices had suffered financial reverses; Putnam's February complaint may have found them in a score-settling mood. Hathorne did a great deal to see to it that the evidence fit his ideas, hanging political preoccupations on the clothesline of lore. Only after several weeks did a different brand of evidence emerge, when the girls began to produce tortured dead wives. Those revenants were another New England first. What men fear most came next: Wild beasts and devious, difficult women who took their breath away. The succubus—the suffocating, bed-invading female—is as ancient and pan-cultural as time itself. That heavy pressure—what Bishop evidently imposed on those men into whose beds she hopped—gives us the very word "nightmare."

The ministers added the apocalyptic overtones, buttressing context and extracting lessons. In their hands the witchcraft supplied a familiar tale of temptation and deliverance. They imposed design where there was none, but at a conspiracy-weaving, body-snatching moment they did not do so out of ignorance. The Massachusetts elite had read everything in sight, some of it too closely. As would be said of logic-loving Ipswich minister John Wise, those men were not so much the masters as the victims of their learning.* They had read and reread bushels of witchcraft texts. They parsed legal code. They knew their history. They worked in the sterling name of reason. They were less out of their depths than they were swimming in information, "poisoned," as Calef sniffed, "in their education."†

New England came to resemble Sweden primarily because Cotton Mather made sure that it did.‡ The Swedish epidemic began with a

---

* And as would be said of Mather's monumental New England history, the *Magnalia* would have been a better book if he had had a smaller library.
† When Calef and Mather began exchanging insults, each mocked the other for being the kind of men "who think that they have engrossed all the learning in the world." Calef suggested the Massachusetts ministers had gorged on the fables of Homer, Virgil, Horace, and Ovid. Brattle indicted the Harvard curriculum, heavy on Greek and Roman mythology.
‡ His father helped. In *Cases of Conscience,* Increase Mather granted that "it is not usual for devils to be permitted to come and violently carry away persons through the air, several miles from their habitations. Nevertheless, this was done in Swedeland, about 20 years ago, by means of a cursed knot of witches there."

nine-year-old and an eleven-year-old. It moved from mischief to heresy and—by way of satanic pacts and witches' meetings—to a kingdom-upending diabolical plot. Mather missed another similarity: the authorities shaped that story, inviting popular lore and local grudges into the courtroom, to be loaded with political and religious freight. The details Mather chose not to import—the devil's red beard, the brightly colored scarf around his high-crowned hat, the carnal Sabbath practices, the cat-transported milk pails, the golden witches' butter—never turned up in Massachusetts. Mather did touch on another affinity when describing the Swedish plague. "There is no public calamity," he cited from that report, "but some ill people will serve themselves of the sad providence, and make use of it for their own ends, as thieves when a house or town is on fire, will steal what they can."

He omitted the rest of that line, a nod to the truth in fables, the validity of rumors. People land in court because they are guilty, if not necessarily of the crime at hand. Had Salem village been asked to vote someone off the island, they would no doubt have settled on Sarah Good. They might soon enough have ejected Sarah Osborne as well. How Tituba wound up on the initial list is unclear. She may have exercised some unwelcome authority over the girls. She looked different from nearly everyone else in the community, where there were other slaves but few Indians. She had a magical narrative touch. The circle widened easily as the prosecution channeled fears, griefs, and antipathies, the gristle of communal life. Who doesn't have a bone to pick with a neighbor? There were as many reasons to accuse someone of witchcraft in 1692 as there were to denounce him under the Nazi occupation of France: envy, insecurity, political enmity, unrequited love, love that had run its course. Unruly households found themselves targeted, as did men who bludgeoned wives. Some wound up in court purely for their refusal to join in the proceedings. (Elizabeth Procter may have been sacrificed for her husband's misdeeds. There are few other ways to explain the fists jammed in mouths at her preliminary hearing. The girls had not expected to testify against her.) The unsavory, the meddlesome, the touchy and peevish fared poorly. So did the pillars of the community, the constables, jury members, fence surveyors and their wives, those men who had told people what they preferred not to hear. John Alden consorted too freely, and too profitably, with Maine Indians; he left Essex County feeling insecure. Witchcraft provided a means to eradicate all malignancies at once. One could not litigate thwarted wills or crumpled egos. But one could electrify a courtroom with tales of blighted animals and dancing hay.

While there is a consistency to the indignities, there is little discernible pattern to the charges. Much of what happened in Salem in 1692 had been written when tempers flared over the Topsfield border generations earlier, or in 1679 when the Putnams and Bradburys clashed, or in 1683 when Burroughs abandoned his congregants. To stare at it for too long is to clamber down the rabbit hole, to ask more of miasmic events than they will yield. If you spend enough time in seventeenth-century Salem, you begin to see patterns that are not necessarily there, like a hyperperspicacious assassination buff or an eminent minister in a renovated Boston kitchen or, for that matter, like a witchcraft judge.

More than half the women who were hanged in 1692 had previously been accused. Rebecca Nurse's, Mary Esty's, Elizabeth Procter's, and Mary English's mothers had been rumored to be witches. Samuel Wardwell had a Quaker uncle; the Nurses had raised a Quaker orphan; Alden had Quaker relations. Abigail Hobbs was happy to sell her parents down the river as only a fourteen-year-old will. She initiated the violent targeting in which the Willard and Wilds clans would engage, though intrafamilial treachery well predated 1692. Philip English and George Jacobs's brother-in-law had been voted Salem town selectmen weeks before they were accused; elections produce losers too. As the crisis widened, so did the reasons to name names. It became less dangerous to accuse than to object. Guilt played an active role in many denunciations, bursting in by any number of trapdoors. It explained why prayer—why the very word "prayer"—might grate on the ears, why so many seemed afraid of their own shadows. It may have powered the Sabbath-day afflictions, either because you were at home that afternoon (when Louder met

the flying monkey), or because you crossed paths at meeting with someone who unsettled you (and seemed to appear afterward in your bed in her
Sunday clothes), or because you heard terrifying things there.

DID ANN PUTNAM SR. name Rebecca Nurse because of the border dispute, because her husband opposed Parris and had opposed James Bayley, because—although relative latecomers—the Nurses had managed
to secure a large tract of village land, because Rebecca hailed from an
intolerably harmonious family, or because she took the sacrament in
Salem town, occupying a former Putnam pew in the village when she
did not? Would she have been named had she visited the parsonage girls,
which she did not do from fear of contagion?

Antipathies and temptations are written in invisible ink; we will
never know. Everyone was on edge. Witchcraft localized anxiety at a dislocated time, as atomic war powered McCarthy rumors in the 1950s.
Even those who knew themselves to be innocent believed a diabolical
plot afoot. Might Ann Putnam Sr. have named Rebecca Nurse simply
because the Nurses prospered where the Putnams did not? It is because
Miss Gulch owns half the property in town that Auntie Em cannot say
what she thinks of her to her face; witchcraft permitted a good Christian
woman to speak her mind. It was the men in Salem who complained of
being silenced, suffocated, and paralyzed in their beds—and who in
their testimony delivered the most outlandish tales.*

If you round up the old enemies, the skeptics, the deviants, the scolds,
the daughters of witches, the abusers and bullies, the arrivistes and the

---

* Several marked gender differences emerged in the course of the trials. Men crafted more
elaborate stories. They rarely saw ghosts, who were primarily female. Long lists of ancient
oddities did not attach themselves to men. Women tended to hallucinate more, or at least
to point more often to figures others could not see who violently ripped out their bowels.
Men appeared to have more difficulty accusing one another, although women arguably
acted more stoically. Mary Esty pleaded for the lives of others. John Procter did not.
Women neither incriminated husbands nor abandoned old friends. The men however
attracted more attention. Sewall mentions only suspected or convicted wizards in his
diary; Brattle singles out two men for their dignity en route to the gallows.

overly advantaged, only George Burroughs remains.* Of the five men who hanged—and every man who remained in prison was executed— most were related to witches. Burroughs traveled the farthest, to play the largest role. No other member of his family was accused. At the Mather household as on the Putnam farm, special animus was reserved for him. What was the minister's crime? He stood in the way of no one's inheritance. He had no designs on anyone's land. He was related to no female suspect. The Putnams carried a long-standing grudge, Burroughs having replaced their brother-in-law in the village pulpit. The minister was a difficult man and a secretive, disorderly houseguest, as much sinned against as sinning. More people testified against him than against anyone else. They were unlikely to have had the same reasons. Mather claimed that he had been requested specifically to include Burroughs in *Wonders*. He was happy to oblige; the loathing drips from his pen. Sewall may not have forgiven Burroughs for having had the temerity to survive when Maine's only ordained minister, a cousin, had not.

Hathorne had reason to dislike the Maine minister, his ex-brother-in-law, a dangerous man on another count. It was for the sake of frontiersmen like Burroughs that Massachusetts communities were left defenseless. His triple brush with heroism seems to have passed without comment before the justices, who may not have been able to forgive him their failures. They had removed militiamen from Maine in 1690; Casco had burned as a result. In indicting Burroughs, it has been suggested, the justices exonerated themselves. Burroughs had pleaded in 1691 for frontier troops and a commander. He no doubt had a great deal more to say off the page. The Dominion better protected Maine than did the post-Andros regime. Within weeks of the revolt, the frontier, deserted by troops, was overrun by Indians; its settlers had reason to feel as if they had been thrown to the wolves. Burroughs indeed appears to have been

---

* In the end only three Salem villagers were hanged. No original village covenant signer was accused.

lax in his religious practices, but his was just as likely a political infraction. He had cause to regret the Andros regime. If he said as much, he did so plainly. In either event there is as little evidence that he was the dreaded Baptist he posthumously became as there was that Tituba was black. He may well have voiced his displeasure before the abrupt departure from his parishioners, who had reason to expect a reprisal.

Across the board, strength of character fared poorly. Even when they did not thumb noses at authority, those who challenged the justices hanged. With one exception, those who confessed did not. (Here New England diverged not only from Sweden but from every other witchcraft trial on record.) More than fifty people falsely incriminated themselves, some purely to save their lives. But it was not difficult to believe in your monstrous powers when your glance knocked a child clear off her feet. Something lurked somewhere in the inner reaches, even if what you dredged up from the muck was not exactly sorcery. Sometimes what surfaced was simply a leaden feeling, the worry that one was impervious to faith. Someone or something stood in the way. "The design of the devil," Cotton Mather noted in 1695, "is to affright you into a hard and harsh opinion of yourselves." The boundary between a guilty conscience and diabolical collusion was not yet in place.

Accusers grasped at the names frequently bandied about: alleged witches, a minister's family, the woman whose daughter had been savagely murdered. (They had adult help. As Increase Mather observed in 1684: "It is evident that the peculiar antipathies of some persons are caused by the imaginations of their parents.") Andover caught the fever partly because the town suffered tensions of its own. It was on the verge of splitting in two; generations strained against one another in a community that had outgrown its land. But any town with a touch test–endorsing minister would have served just as well. By the time the witchcraft reached Andover, the justices had refined their methods of locating it. Confessions by no means require torture, although torture tends to produce the desired answers. Some were relieved to be spared from sharing a dungeon with Burroughs; others were happy to avoid humiliating public trials. Many cared only to please. From the tone of the reparations claims it is clear in what esteem the villagers held the authorities. John Hale was not the only one who felt, as he put it, "that the reverence I bore to aged, learned, and judicious persons caused me to drink in their principles."

A magistrate too can make you believe things of yourself that are not true. With a suggestible witness and an authority figure, it is not uncommon to wind up with a planted, potted memory. In the hands of the right adult, a child will swear that his day-care worker slaughtered rabbits, an elephant, a giraffe or "turned him into a mouse while he was in an airplane on the way to visit his grandmother." No one rested easily in a seventeenth-century prison; sleep deprivation also produces hallucinations. Where did Ann Foster find the details of her fantastic flight? For three well-spoken, well-dressed men she recycled familiar imagery. Satanic baptisms were all too credible, even if they were in short supply in Massachusetts, where no witch had flown before 1692. As for the aerial crash, what greater fear hounds the flier? Foster may not even have known that such things had happened, or been said to happen, in Sweden. She did not need to fabricate the aching leg. No seventy-two-year-old New England farm woman was without a pain somewhere.

What sets Salem apart is not the accusations but the convictions. At other times raving women had been said to be witches and men dreamed of the devil without anyone thinking twice about it. Why the unsparing prosecution in 1692? Mather implied that the Glover case played a role, the laundress having displayed her spells for all to see. Several on the Court of Oyer and Terminer were better at executing orders than at formulating them; they bent easily to the greater will. Hathorne, Corwin, and Gedney—the prime movers—acted in the interests of the ortho-doxy, which happened to align with their personal agendas. They knew who the troublemakers were, having been called upon to mediate in Salem village for years. As its "uncharitable expressions and uncomely reflections," its "settled prejudice, and resolved animosity" fermented into witchcraft, they promoted that transformation. Parris, Noyes, Barnard, and Hale eagerly backed them up. All signs point to their having been in the thrall of William Stoughton, their elder by a generation, nearly a father to young Mather.

With the question of why Stoughton—a political contortionist for over a decade—remained inflexible on witchcraft, one comes closest to the riddle of Salem. No documentation survives; it is more difficult to make sense of his intransigence than of Foster's flight to a satanic Sabbath. Both followed to some extent from their faith. Stoughton embraced spectral evidence, contrary to legal opinion; he departed from all precedent. After the hastily rearranged political allegiances, he took and held a stand. One may well account for the other. Firm hands were in order; Stoughton responded with clenched fists. He had known disfavor. He had no interest in returning to it.* Along with two other witchcraft justices, Stoughton had collaborated actively with the "alien incubus" that was Dominion rule.† Here was an opportunity for those men to rehabilitate themselves, to prove their mettle by dispelling a new intruder. They were now the righteous enforcers, the ones lifting that "standard against the infernal enemy." The only individual who could easily have slowed or reversed Salem's course, Stoughton elected not to do so. He believed as firmly in spectral evidence in 1693 as he had in 1692, or at least claimed to. He worked under an absent, weak governor who displayed little interest in the trials. Hathorne handed Stoughton a situation that was out of control well before Phips arrived and in which the new governor had no cause to involve himself. Afterward—as with the half-read May commission—he fumbled in attempting both to prove his piety to Massachusetts and his competence to London.

---

* He had a counterexample in his discredited political ally Joseph Dudley. "They look upon me," Dudley explained to an English correspondent in February 1692, "as a strange creature in their forests." Gedney too had been voted out of office "with great contempt and scorns" for his pro-English stance.
† William Barker dated his world-turned-upside-down pact with the devil to the year of the coup. Abigail Hobbs hinted at the same date, although she supplied several. There is as well a curious and perhaps wholly coincidental correlation between the length of a diabolical contract—generally between six and eight years—and that of an indenture agreement.

Stoughton labored to prove not only his constancy but a new government's legitimacy. He was as aware as anyone that to the Crown the colony appeared lax, impertinent, disorderly. They had paid a crushing price for having deviated from the laws of England. In prosecuting witches he simultaneously redeemed himself at home and broadcast New England's proficiency abroad; the colonists could govern themselves, in an orderly, Old World way. They were no riotous, irresponsible teenagers after all. They prosecuted subversives. They could show up those English officials who sniffed that Massachusetts was without law, courts, justice, or government. The crisis provided a great number of people—Barnard, Noyes, Cotton Mather, several adolescent girls, many Massachusetts authorities, the colony itself—a chance to show up their elders, all too happy to remind them, as the king assured New England, that they existed only by someone else's grace and favor.* What they had been given could also be taken away, nails on the blackboard of the adolescent mind.

The new charter reconstituted the judicial system, of which Andros had made a travesty and on which a new administration depended. The colony reeled still from those "barbarous usages." Stoughton may have set out to prove that New England was not, as the deposed governor had scoffed, "a place where none do and few care to understand (if they can help it) the laws or methods of England." They had much to lose, a reputation for civil disobedience to live down. Coursing public anger played a role; men who had overthrown a despot had no desire to face a mob. As an ousted Dominion official had warned in 1689, those who removed Andros were "like young conjurers, who had raised a devil they could not govern." Indeed the New England clergy had promoted the tale of that earlier implacable invader, the red-coated one with his sinister designs who had been heard to sneer that Puritans "were a people fit only

* The median age of the core accusers was seventeen. Even including thirty-year-old Ann Putnam Sr., the median age of sixteen of the nineteen who hanged was fifty-six. (We have no birth dates for three.)

to be rooted off the face of the earth." They lent it to a witch gang intent on establishing "perhaps a more gross *diabolism,* than ever the world saw before." They did not have to imagine that story, having themselves participated in it. The trials allowed them to dispel a stain of their own.

The clergy could resist in no meaningful way. They were known to have blown the bellows of sedition against the previous administration, to have preached up a rebellion, to have craftily incited a mob. They could not undermine a government that, at great cost, they had themselves installed. To vindicate the court was to vindicate the new charter; they too looked to prove themselves not in Boston but in London, where Mather aimed *Wonders.* Three years of anarchy and five of Dominion rule had been costly. The justices were moreover their patrons and sponsors, the men who paid their salaries. The ministers were as blindsided by the crisis as everyone else. But witchcraft allowed them to prove God's special stake in New England. It must be awfully important if Satan stood so intent on destroying it! The assault on Salem allowed a younger generation of clergymen to prove their worth in a cosmic battle. It fulfilled a prophecy too; here was the storm before the much advertised millennial calm, a last-ditch showdown with the devil.

For all of his 1692 fast days, for all of his warnings against spectral evidence, torture, and touch tests, for all of his hand-wringing, Cotton Mather did not find the assault of evil angels entirely unwelcome. In a 1693 document not meant for public consumption, he offered what may qualify as his most genuine assessment of the episode. It was certainly the most damning. Mather wrestled mightily with this statement; it is heavily blotted and redacted. What had Salem witchcraft yielded? No one of worth had been compromised. The "lively demonstrations of hell" had awakened many souls—young souls, especially, of both genders. Mather knew that calamity reliably filled the church; evangelically speaking, little rivaled an earthquake. "The devil got just nothing," reasoned Mather, as he meditated on the crisis, "but God got praises, Christ got subjects, the Holy Spirit got temples, the Church got addition, and the souls of men got everlasting benefits." Reversing his position on his own involvement, he preened a little: "I am not so vain as to say that any wisdom or virtue of mine did contribute unto this good order of things, but I am so just as to say I did not hinder this good." Any discomfort for having failed to shut down the trials had vanished. He decried only one monstrous injustice: the assault on his reputation.

Cases of Conscience, the advice of the New York ministers, Mary Esty's petition, and Giles Corey's gruesome death may have helped to extinguish the witchcraft. But as the casualties piled up, the terror rushed toward the authorities' front doors. When it did, the moment had passed. (The skeptic Robert Calef credited whoever had accused Mrs. Phips.) Blame could not be attributed, belonging as it did to too many addresses. Mystification yielded to mortification. It is unclear who actually heard Thomas Brattle's wise, unwelcome words; by October too many had been recalling (or inventing) twenty-five-year-old slights to be able to accuse anyone else of delusion. Firmly established, witchcraft exerted a magnetic pull on every glinting irritation, fear, grudge, peculiarity, offense; there was as much stray odium and animosity in Essex County as there were mangy dogs and marauding pigs. The community played the chorus, striking at empty air with canes, rapiers, and staffs, marveling as moths flew through the meetinghouse, chipping in oddities and old tales, rumored, recovered, invented. Everyone had his reasons.

The irony that they had come to the New World to escape an interfering civil authority was lost on the colonists, who unleashed on one another the kind of abuse they had deplored in royal officials. So was the fact that the embrace of faith, meant to buttress the church, would tear it irrevocably apart; the wonder tales harvested to prove New England's special status undermined it in the end. Political concerns outweighed all others, as political concerns had produced both *Illustrious Providences* and *Memorable Providences.* Mather's account of the witchcraft would be inseparable from his life of Phips; the authorities believed they protected a fledgling administration. They had contracted a kind of autoimmune disorder, deploying against themselves the very furies they so feared. There were in 1692 no perpetrators, and no consequences. Only a small, supernatural figure remained at the scene of the crime.* He did resolve one mystery while in Salem: indeed the devil needs conscious human collusion to work evil.

Witchcraft effectively aroused a lapsed, sluggish generation, though not as the clergy had anticipated. When the spell broke, the torrent of recriminations swept away a rich layer of faith. Massachusetts leaders would never again apply to the church for advice. Nor would an additional hint surface of a witches' meeting or an aerial mishap. As for the phantom Frenchmen and Indians, by 1698 the nattily dressed invaders were understood to be satanic agents, "demons in the shape of armed Indians and Frenchmen." The best minds in Essex County continued to believe them implicated somehow in the witchcraft. They never reappeared, fading imperceptibly away, like the indelible scene in the book you read as a child and never manage to find again.

---

* The sense that the devil had made them do it would find its echo years later in Hawthorne. As the traveler with the twisted staff informs Goodman Brown: "I have a very general acquaintance here in New England. The deacons of many a church have drunk the communion wine with me; the selectmen, of diverse towns, made me their chairman; and a majority of the Great and General Court are firm supporters of my interest. The governor and I, too—but these are state secrets."

XII

❖

A LONG TRAIN OF MISERABLE
CONSEQUENCES

People were chasing the wrong rabbit.
—DONALD RUMSFELD

ROUGHLY HALF OF the afflicted girls grew up, found husbands, and had children, if not necessarily in that order. Betty Parris married late and raised a family in Concord. No trace remains of her cousin Abigail, the exuberant witch hunter. She may have been the girl reported to have experienced "diabolical molestations to her death" and who died, still single, in 1697. Like Ann Putnam, Susannah Shelden failed to marry, highly uncommon in seventeenth-century New England. She wound up in Rhode Island charged as a "person of evil fame," which was more common. Betty Hubbard found a husband only at thirty-six. Sarah Churchill, the Jacobs servant, married at forty-two, having earlier paid a fine for fornication. Mercy Lewis, the Putnams' maid, bore an illegitimate child; she later married and moved to Boston. Mary Walcott, Abigail Hobbs, and Mary Lacey Jr. raised their families the old-fashioned way, several of them in the immediate area. For all of the deviations, at least some of the village girls appear to have turned out like the afflicted Goodwin girl, described in adulthood as "a very sober, virtuous woman"—and who never for a minute denied that she had witnessed witchcraft.

The village ministers fared less well. James Bayley, who had introduced the future Ann Putnam Sr. to the village, fell on hard times in Roxbury. Samuel Sewall visited with cakes, with money for firewood, and, less helpfully, with verses by Reverend Noyes. Suffering from pleurisy, Bayley died an excruciating death in 1707. Having provided the most indelible portrait of the Salem shrieks and teeth marks, Deodat Lawson returned to England. Hemming and hawing a little, he republished his witchcraft account in 1704, to lift the enduring censure on his friends and insist yet again on the "operations of the powers of darkness." The first to attempt to make sense of the epidemic, he remained the last retailing an account of it, the surviving 1963 Dallas Secret Service agent hawking his wares. Not long thereafter Lawson committed an indiscretion that left him issuing solemn apologies to the London ministry. He acknowledged having dishonored his profession with his "uneven and unwary conversation." He battled for several years to clear his name. The offense may have had nothing to do with sensationalistic witchcraft pronouncements; he may simply have drunk too much. He had however spoken carelessly, as he could be said to have done in 1692. By 1714 he lived in abject poverty, his family starving, his three young children infected with smallpox, his wife debilitated. He tried unsuccessfully to raise funds for a collection of sermons, throwing himself on the mercy of friends. If no relief were forthcoming, he warned, "we must unavoidably perish." He would be remembered as "the unhappy Mr. Deodat Lawson."

Samuel Parris remarried and fathered a second family. Trailed by the "difficulties and disturbances" of his ministry, he drifted about, landing in six communities over twelve years. He taught school, raised livestock, sold fabrics and sundries, preached in the smallest settlement in Massachusetts, and speculated in land. He overreached in one transaction; arrested for debt, he spent a few weeks of 1706 in jail in Cambridge. Having written and rewritten his will, Parris died in Sudbury at sixty-seven, a moderately wealthy man though one who continued to feel the world had shortchanged him. If he wrote another word on what he deemed that "very sore rebuke, and humbling providence," it has not survived. His estate did not include his Salem pasture, which he had sold earlier.

The village replaced Parris with a newly minted minister half his age. A Cambridge native, Joseph Green had been at Harvard in 1692; he well knew the singular history of the parsonage into which he moved, also with an Indian slave. A more temperate man, Green inherited a chastened flock. He welcomed back the dissenting brethren and reseated the meetinghouse, placing Nurses alongside Putnams, a daughter of Rebecca Nurse beside her accuser's mother, where the women would have heard Ann Putnam Jr.'s 1706 apology. Against much opposition, Green reversed Martha Corey's excommunication sentence.* It required less effort to convince his parishioners that they might breathe more easily in a new meetinghouse. They moved down the road, to the corner of Centre and Hobart Streets, where the First Church of Danvers stands today. The lumber of the old meetinghouse was left to decay, which it could not do quickly enough. Closure proved elusive; the Burroughs children petitioned still for redress in 1750. Green preached against fortune-telling a decade after Salem. Parishioners still slept in their pews. And Putnams complained of Salem village preaching.

A 1704 visitor found Massachusetts an uncomfortable place where no one knew "on his lying down to sleep, but that he might lose his life before the morning, by the hands of a merciless savage." Sewall woke from nightmares about the French in 1706. Mather nearly crossed paths with marauding Indians outside Andover that year; a niece disappeared into captivity at around the same time. While talk of evil angels quieted, the Apocalypse remained imminent. Mather forecast it for 1715. Sewall and Noyes still heatedly disputed passages of Revelation. Six-foot-long

---

* Salem town reversed those of Rebecca Nurse and Giles Corey in 1712.

mermen with forked tails appeared on the rocks of Branford, Connecticut, as Cotton Mather alerted London's Royal Society. In the early 1730s, the Boston clergy stepped in to heal "the mischievous unChristian divisions and contentions arising and prevailing" among the Salem town parishioners, their minister as "unpeacable" as Parris had been.

The trials did not upend the church, but—assisted by the new charter and in conjunction with forces already in motion—they did erode its foundation. Attempting to prove one thing, the Puritan orthodoxy had proved quite another. The very idea of confession had been contaminated. Mather had warned that the Lord sent down devils to "stop the mouths of the faithless"; not incorrectly, Robert Calef noted that those evil angels created a fair number of atheists. Hale was not alone in more strictly scanning his principles. When the new Massachusetts governor took the oath of office a decade after Salem, he did so in a traditional, Bible-kissing Anglican ceremony. Mather found himself ordaining Baptists. Sewall lived to see Christmas celebrated. There had been no flying before 1692 and there would be none afterward. People accused one another of witchcraft well into the eighteenth century, but Massachusetts would not execute another witch.*

We all apologize, or fail to, in our own ways. Increase Mather turned from the study of devils to the study of angels. In 1721, a smallpox epidemic raged through Boston. Cotton Mather faced down the entire medical establishment to advocate something that seemed every bit as dubious as spectral evidence: inoculation. He had studied medicine at Harvard; he had come to well understand infectious disease. Moving from imps and witches to germs and viruses, he finally located the devils we inhale with every breath. The battle turned so vitriolic that it dragged Salem out of hiding, allowing Mather to be bludgeoned for lunacy on two counts. (It also allowed him to drag the devil back onstage. Given the "cursed clamor," Satan seemed to have taken possession of Boston.)

---

* When in 1712 a Westfield girl accused her mother of witchcraft, the court found her guilty of having violated the Fifth, Sixth, and Ninth Commandments.

He remained as steadfast on the subject of inoculation as he had been equivocal on witchcraft. A homemade bomb came sailing in his window at three o'clock one morning. His reputation never recovered.*

The trials claimed more casualties than were clear at the time; the devil himself failed to recover. Present though the Old Deluder remained—if you committed adultery in Massachusetts in 1721, you did so "by insti-gation of the devil"—"the roaring lion, the old dragon, the enemy of all righteousness," as Parris had it in his apology, faded from the scene. He grew more abstract as evil retreated inside, less the master conspirator than the shadow of our poor judgment. By the end of Betty Parris's life-time, he had come, as a modern scholar has put it, to bear more resem-blance to "a leprechaun than to the old grandmaster of hell." Women also fared poorly after Salem, or at least went back to being invisible, where they remained, historically speaking, until a different scourge encouraged them to raise their voices, with suffrage and Prohibition.

In 1728, the year of Mather's death, a Medford minister could write off witchcraft as the stuff of fairy tales. Salem was very nearly ready to become one itself, to be recast and retold. At the same time Sewall resigned as chief justice. He lived two more years, attuned as ever to birdsong and rainbows, concerned with safeguarding the Massachusetts charter at all costs, to the end tripping over his conscience for the sake of consensus. In 1728 Topsfield and Salem resolved their border dispute. By the time of his death at 109, Martha Carrier's widower had the satisfac-tion of seeing that Salem witchcraft had become the "supposed witch-craft" and that the villain of the piece was no longer his wife, the queen of hell, or even her so-called confederates. Sorcery yielded to possession, by the middle of the eighteenth century to fraud. It would require only another few decades for Brattle's suggestion that the witches had more

---

* In the just-deserts department, he wound up with a high-strung third wife whose tan-trums he deemed "little short of a proper satanical possession." Lydia Mather made scenes, ran off to live at the neighbor's, cursed her husband, and at one point stole and defaced his diary.

likely been the accusers to register, for anyone to note that authorities get feverish, too.

The trials would take their place among those historical events that never happened until a generation or two after they did. Once they flickered back to life they refused to dim. Of all the portents and prophecies — those of the visionary girls, the boastful specters, the Mathers, the Salem woman who forecast a second storm of witchcraft — only Thomas Brattle's came true. Ages would not "wear off that reproach and those stains which these things will leave behind them upon our land."* John Adams cited the trials as a "foul stain upon this country," an irony for proceedings that had been intended to purify. The frenzy unleashed by a three-pence duty on tea seemed to one 1773 Massachusetts lawyer absurd, "and more disgraceful, to the annals of America than that of witchcraft." Salem came in especially handy over the second half of the nineteenth century; it provided an effective piece of shrapnel when North and South took aim at each other. Frederick Douglass asked how the belief in slavery was any bit less objectionable than that in sorcery. Abolition, argued others, was a hallucination on par with Salem witchcraft. The 1860 election of Lincoln struck terror in the slave-owning South, leading a popular magazine to screech: "The North, who having begun with burning witches, will end by burning us!" All could agree on one matter: when you wanted to reach the emotional high notes, you reached for Salem.

New England's enemies arguably did more than anyone to keep Salem alive, as for so long the church had sustained the devil. The South woke in the nineteenth century to the fact that "those bigoted, fanatical, mischief-making, would-be enlighteners" north of the Mason-Dixon Line wrote the schoolbooks, with lasting effects. Something needed to be done; the Salem misstep helped to remodel the New England past. In the midst of the Civil War, President Lincoln officially established

---

* Brattle married a daughter of Wait Still Winthrop and helped to found the more liberal Boston congregation that bears his name. Having blamed his alma mater for the "slips and imperfections" in his calculations, he endowed a Harvard fellowship in mathematics.

Thanksgiving, Pilgrim feasts being preferable to Puritan fasts. Decades earlier, Daniel Webster had delivered his Plymouth Rock oration, and people who had not persecuted witches or left a paper trail—or left much of any kind of trail at all—became the ur-Americans. Blameless, if colorless, the Pilgrims made better ancestors than did peevish, intolerant, urban, upper-class witch hunters. For a century or so they replaced their fanatical cousins.

It turns out to be eminently useful to have a disgrace in your past; Salem endures not only as a metaphor but as a vaccine and a taunt. It glares at us when fear paralyzes reason, when we overreact or overcorrect, when we hunt down or deliver up the alien or seditious. It endures in its lessons and our language. In the 1780s, enemies of the Federalists accused that party of launching a "detestable and nefarious conspiracy" to restore the monarchy. Anti-Illuminists warned of prowling Jesuits, of the Catholic serpent already coiled about, with sinister political designs. "We must awake," they warned in 1835, "or we are lost." The judge sentencing the Rosenbergs for espionage in 1951 termed theirs a "diabolical conspiracy to destroy a God-fearing nation." A network of subversives, night-and-day vigilance, the watchtowers of the nation, and reckless cruelty returned with the 1954 McCarthy hearings. It took very little in 1998 to turn Linda Tripp into the nosy Puritan neighbor and Ken Starr into a witch hunter.

English monarchs would continue to conspire—or appear to conspire—against the people. It is no surprise that the seventeenth-century Massachusetts authorities so often sounded like understudies for the Founding Fathers. Somewhere along the line those men had decided that obedience to God did not tally with allegiance to monarchs; it was less a love of democracy than a hatred of authority that is their chief contribution to the national DNA. As John Adams saw it, Massachusetts had compromised itself more by accepting Increase Mather's 1691 charter than by prosecuting witches. The same defiance, the same brooding sense of sanctified purpose that delivered the trials culminated in a revolution, the legacy of further hand-wringing about property lines, tax rates, and trespass.*

As dogma, the crusade against evil, and the ecstatic embrace of justice combined in Salem, they do too in what has been termed the paranoid style in American politics. When Richard Hofstadter described "the sense of heated exaggeration, suspiciousness, and conspiratorial fantasy," the national distempers that occasionally descend upon us, he could have been describing Essex County in 1692. That apocalyptic, absolutist strain still bleeds into our thinking. English officials in Massachusetts wrote off the ludicrous papist talk. "There are not two Roman Catholics betwixt this and New York," snorted an imprisoned Andros adviser in 1689; as for the rest of the designs against New England, they were delusional, "false and strangely ridiculous." But they very well might have been real. We are regularly being sacrificed to our heathen adversaries; in troubled times, we naturally look for traitors, terrorists, secret agents. Though in our imaginations, the business is indeed sometimes not imaginary. A little paranoia may even be salutary, though sometimes when you anticipate a hailstorm, one eerily comes crashing down on your head.

A great number of Americans have made the same startling discovery that Francis Dane did: They are related to witches. American presidents descend from George Jacobs, Susannah Martin, and John Procter. Nathan Hale was John Hale's grandson. Israel "Don't Fire Until You See the Whites of Their Eyes" Putnam was the son of John Putnam. Oliver Wendell Holmes and Louisa May Alcott descended from Samuel Sewall; Clara Barton from the Townes; Walt Disney from Burroughs. (In a nice twist, the colonial printer who founded the American Antiquarian Society, where Cotton Mather's papers reside today, was also a Burroughs descendant.) The Nurse family includes Lucille Ball, who testified before

---

* God would persist in testing the colonies, the colonies in interpreting those strikes as salutary. "I think we stood in need of a frown from heaven. I should have suspected that our cause had not been owned as a divine one if we had prospered without it," Benjamin Rush, the founder of American psychiatry, wrote in September 1776, recasting British victories as colonial godsends.

an investigator from the House Un-American Activities Committee. (Yes, she had registered with the Communist Party. No, she was not a Communist. In 1953, a husband leaped to a wife's defense: "The only thing red about Lucy is her hair," Desi Arnaz explained, "and even that's not legitimate.")

No one reprocessed the toxic spill of 1692 as creatively as did Nathaniel Hawthorne, at whom the guilt of his great-grandfather gnawed.* Hawthorne redeemed that most Puritan of legacies in kind: with a shelf of literature, chilly, twilit pages that fall somewhere between sermons and stories. Others had put Salem on the literary map before he wrote "Young Goodman Brown," *The Scarlet Letter,* or his 1851 bestseller, *The House of the Seven Gables,* but Hawthorne proved that territory still radioactive. Guilt and blame have grown up lushly on the scene, attracting writers from Walt Whitman to John Updike. Arthur Miller read the court papers under the spell of McCarthyism. He discovered, as New England itself had, that events must be absorbed before monuments can be raised. *The Crucible* was not a success in 1953. Only when it outgrew the headlines and matured into allegory did the play find its audience. The Puritans come to most of us today through *The Scarlet Letter* and *The Crucible*, which we read, appropriately enough, as adolescents.

AS GENERAL WASHINGTON was presiding over the Constitutional Convention on July 10, 1787, a mob attacked an old woman in the Philadelphia street outside. Accusing her of witchcraft, they pelted her with a slew of objects. She had cast a fatal spell on a child; weeks earlier, someone had cut her forehead "according to ancient and immemorial custom," as a newspaper had it—and precisely as a Salem visitor had attempted to slash Bridget Bishop. The 1787 woman died from her injuries. Witches might well rank among ghosts and fairies, as the Philadelphia papers

---

* He changed the spelling of his name, by some accounts adding the *w* to distance himself from the man who had branded Salem. That was unnecessary: Hawthorne also descended from Philip English, who went to his grave cursing Hathorne, never to know that his daughter would marry his persecutor's son.

noted, but they were not as easily dismissed. Alaska contended with a witchcraft epidemic in the late nineteenth century. In 1908 a Pennsylvania woman landed in jail for enchanting a cow. Sporadic assaults continue today, although the modern American witch is dangerous rather than malicious, more likely to exude steamy sexuality than to wield a scalding tongue. In a stunning inversion, empowered, nubile teenage witches — the new vampire-slayers — have taken over from the afflicted girls.

Salem village finally won its independence from Salem town in 1752. It renamed itself Danvers sixty years after the trials, which remained still the stuff of the recent unpleasantness. An 1895 reporter found town residents reluctant to talk about the past. When they did, it was to impress upon him that they had not *burned* a single witch. Years later Arthur Miller met with the same silence while researching *The Crucible.* "You couldn't get anyone to say anything about it," he complained of 1692. The two communities have since resolutely gone their separate ways. When current Danvers archivist Richard B. Trask began an excavation of the parsonage site in 1970, two elderly sisters waved fists at him from across the way, the kind of behavior that in another age elicited witchcraft accusations. "What are you bringing this up for?" they demanded. Meanwhile in Salem, Justice Corwin's gabled home has become "the Witch House," a misreading akin to making Dr. Frankenstein the monster. The town opted for brash commercialization, easier in the post-*Bewitched* era, when perky enchantresses twitched noses at vacuum cleaners. The mascot for Salem's sports teams is a witch on a broom. She sails across the local newspaper masthead and along doors of police cruisers; the best bakery in town has a Caffiend Club. In a turn of events that would have mystified Ann Foster, it is easy to buy a broomstick in Salem, home to a large Wiccan community. Hotels are booking now for next Halloween.*

When Massachusetts exonerated the Salem victims in 1710 it overlooked six women. They remained missing through the 1940s and 1950s,

---

* Ipswich and Topsfield tussle today over which town can properly claim the hay-enchanting Sarah Wilds, an undesirable in 1692.

as the commonwealth considered pardons but could not seem to make up its legislative mind. One lawyer appearing before a Senate committee objected to "fooling with history." Some legislators feared expensive suits for damages. Others hinted that a pardon might knock Salem's witches from their tourist-bewitching brooms. As the Commonwealth of Massachusetts had not existed in 1692, it surely had no jurisdiction over a verdict of Massachusetts Bay. On Halloween 2001 — weeks after we began to wonder anew about unseen evils — Massachusetts pardoned the last of the condemned. They included Susannah Martin and Bridget Bishop, who had transformed themselves into gleaming lights and disturbed men in their beds, afterward spending weeks together in a stifling prison. Parris had testified and Mather had written against both women. Bishop was not entirely sure she knew what a witch was. The convulsing girls wholly mystified her. "Do you think they are bewitched?" Hathorne asked Susannah Martin. "No," she had replied, three hundred and nine years before her pardon. "I do not think they are."

Acknowledgments

———— ❦ ————

In 2008 David D. Hall observed that his decades in the seventeenth century had convinced him that the past remains eternally open to fresh questions; he could hardly have suspected that someone might read that line as an invitation. Patiently, incisively, and all too frequently, he has fielded queries ranging from the elementary to the insane. It is a pleasure at last to acknowledge a gratitude equaled only by my admiration for his work. I owe an immeasurable debt as well to John Demos, who has made the seventeenth century a more congenial place than it could have been even on the sunniest, cider-soaked afternoon. There are not that many people who happen to know whether, if you were flying on a pole just above the treetops, heading southeast from Andover, in 1692, you would be able to glimpse the ocean in the distance. I am hugely grateful to Danvers town archivist Richard B. Trask, who does.

I have leaned, heavily at times, on the following experts: J. M. Beattie, Elizabeth Bouvier, Richard Godbeer, Evan Haefeli, Hendrik Hartog, Richard R. Johnson, David Thomas Konig, Eve LaPlante, Kenneth P. Minkema, John M. Murrin, Daniel C. Richman, Bernard Rosenthal, David Grant Smith, Roger Thompson, Douglas Winiarski, and Michael P. Winship. For help with and around archives, I am indebted to Kent Bicknell, Robin Briggs, Carolyn Broomhead, Nicholas Cronk, Rebecca Ehrhardt, David Ferriero, Amanda Foreman, Jonathan Galassi, Malcolm Gaskill, Birgitta Lagerlöf-Génetay, Paul LeClerc, Marie Lennersand,

Acknowledgments

Krishnakali Lewis, Maira Liriano, Megan Marshall, Scott McIsaac, Stephen Mitchell, Oliver Morley, Robert J. O'Hara, Eunice Panetta, Caroline Preston, Kathleen Roe, Rob Shapiro, and Abby Wolf. For archival assistance and for permission to quote from manuscript collections, I should particularly like to thank Irene Axelrod, Sidney E. Berger, Kathy M. Flynn, and Catherine Robertson at the Peabody Essex Museum; D. Brenton Simons, Bridget Donahue, Timothy Salls, and Suzanne M. Stewart at the New England Historic Genealogical Society; Barbara S. Meloni at the Harvard University Archives, Pusey Library; Amy Coffin at the Topsfield Historical Society; Inga Larson and Carol Majahad at the North Andover Historical Society; Kris Kobialksa at the First Church of Salem; Dana C. Street at the Martha's Vineyard Museum; Richard B. Trask at the Danvers Archival Center, Peabody Institute Library; Peter Drummey, Elaine Grublin, Elaine Heavey, and Brenda Lawson at the Massachusetts Historical Society; Elizabeth Watts Pope, Ashley Cataldo, and Kimberly Toney Pelkey at the American Antiquarian Society; Barbara Austen at the Connecticut Historical Society; Justine Sundaram and Andrew Isodoro at Boston College's John J. Burns Library; and Elizabeth Bouvier, head of archives at the Massachusetts Supreme Judicial Court.

Matthew J. Boylan, Ella Delaney, Kate Foster, the indefatigable Mary Mann, Rachel Reiderer, David Smith, Tim Wales, and Andy Young supplied research and fact-checking assistance. Tom Puchniak expertly tracked down images. Anne Eisenberg, Lis Bensley, Ellen Feldman, Patti Foster, Harry G. Frankfurt, Shelley Freedman, Laurie Griffith, Mitch Katz, Charlotte Kingham, Souad Kriska, Mameve and Howard Medwed, Carmen Marino, Ronald C. Rosbottom, Robin Rue, Andrea Versenyi, Will Swift, Strauss Zelnick, and William Zinsser provided various seventeenth-century interventions. Elinor Lipman read these pages in their earliest incarnation and improved every one. Eric Simonoff and Alicia Gordon are the most inspired—and patient—of agents.

It has been a privilege to work again with the impeccable Michael Pietsch. I am indebted to him for many things but especially for his consummate skill with an erasable blue pen. He could have used ball-point. Across the board, the Little, Brown team—in particular Reagan Arthur, Amanda Brower, Amanda Brown, Victoria Chow, Heather Fain, Liz Garriga, Jayne Yaffe Kemp, Marie Mundaca, the visionary, possibly wizardly Mario J. Pulice, Tracy Roe, and Tracy Williams—continues to astonish. Households suffer when women disappear into the archives too; if there is a way to thank Marc de La Bruyère and our children for thriving in my absence, I intend now to find it.

Notes

———— ❖ ————

Three centuries of documentation can add up to as many pages of source notes. Volumes that have shaped the text as a whole or that I have consulted regularly appear in the selected bibliography; they are cited below by author's last name and abbreviated title. Most accounts of 1692 have been printed and reprinted; I have tried to note them in their most readily accessible editions. The supporting seventeenth-century texts are available on Cornell University Library's Witchcraft Collection website; most sermons are online; the bulk of the original Salem documentation can be found at the University of Virginia's excellent Salem witch trials website. Principal sources — like the magisterial 2009 *Records of the Salem Witch-Hunt,* which for the first time offers up the extant record chronologically, lending the hunt its shape — are rendered as follows:

B&N Boyer and Nissenbaum, eds., *Salem-Village Witchcraft: A Documentary Record of Local Conflict in Colonial New England*
Burr *Narratives of the New England Witchcraft Cases*
CM Diary Mather, *Diary of Cotton Mather*
Magnalia Mather, *Magnalia Christi Americana*
MP Mather, *Memorable Providences*
WOW Mather, *Wonders of the Invisible World*
IP Mather, *Illustrious Providences*
JH *John Hale: A Man Beset by Witches*
SPN Cooper and Minkema, eds., *The Sermon Notebook of Samuel Parris*
RFQC *The Records and Files of the Quarterly Courts of Essex County*
R Rosenthal et al., eds., *Records of the Salem Witch-Hunt*
SS Diary Sewall, *The Diary of Samuel Sewall*
Sibley *Sibley's Harvard Graduates*
EIHC *Essex Institute Historical Collections*

Thomas Putnam — among the most prolific court reporters but by no means the most creative — alternately wrote "witch" and "wicth." An apparition was an "apperishtion," a "daughter" a "dafter," "melancholy" was "malloncely." For readability's sake I have modernized spellings and taken occasional liberties with punctuation. All proper names conform to the spellings in *Records of the Salem Witch-Hunt.* John Hale, Cotton Mather, Increase Mather, and Samuel Parris are abbreviated as JH, CM, IM, and SP; NE is New England. Names of principal archives appear as follows:

MHS	Massachusetts Historical Society
AAS	American Antiquarian Society
DAC	Danvers Archival Center, Peabody Institute Library
NEHGS	New England Historic Genealogical Society
PEM	Phillips Library, Peabody Essex Museum
PRO	Public Records Office, Kew

I: THE DISEASES OF ASTONISHMENT

3   "We will declare": Anton Chekhov, *Letters on the Short Story, the Drama, and Other Literary Topics* (New York: Benjamin Blom, 1964), 8.

3   voodoo arrived later: The nineteenth-century historian was Charles W. Upham. For Tituba and the voodoo, Bernard Rosenthal, "Tituba," *OAH Magazine of History* (July 2003), 48–50; Rosenthal, *Salem Story,* 10–31; Rosenthal, "Tituba's Story," *New England Quarterly* (June 1998): 190–203. On the educational eminence of Massachusetts: Lawrence A. Cremin, *American Education: The Colonial Experience* (New York: Harper and Row, 1970), 207. Gretchen Adams makes the fine point that the South supplied the witch-burning in the contentious 1850s: *The Specter of Salem* (Chicago: University of Chicago Press, 2010), 95–96.

4   exact number: It is elusive, given mistaken identities and impartial records. Boyer and Nissenbaum, in *Salem Possessed,* put it at 141; Rosenthal, *Salem Story,* at 156; Emerson W. Baker, in *A Storm of Witchcraft* (New York: Oxford, 2015), at 169 or 172; Koehler, *Search for Power,* at 204. A contemporaneous account indicates that more than two hundred were accused. If so, far more documentation has been lost than we realize.

4   a careful chronicler: *Magnalia,* 2: 411. It may have been a printer's error.

4   Might you be a witch: R, 392; the guilty innocent, R, 145.

4   Nearly as many theories: Scholars have weighed in from every discipline. In lieu of a complete bibliography and among the best overviews of the immense literature: John Demos, *The Enemy Within,* 189–215; David D. Hall, "Witchcraft and the Literature of Interpretation," *New England Quarterly* (June 1985): 253–81; John M. Murrin, "The Infernal Conspiracy of Indians and Grandmothers," *Reviews in American History* (December 2003): 485–94; Trask, *"The Devil Hath Been Raised,"* x. For generational hostility, Demos, *Entertaining Salem;* for regional difference and ethnic hostility, Elinor Abbot, *Our Company Increases Apace* (Dallas: SIL International, 2007), and Richard Slotkin, *Regeneration Through Violence* (New York: Harper, 1996);

for economic hostility, Boyer and Nissenbaum, *Salem Possessed*; for residual, imported regional hostility, Cedric B. Cowing, *The Saving Remnant* (Urbana: University of Illinois Press, 1995); for sexual hostility, Koehler, *Search for Power*; for an epidemic of encephalitis lethargica, Laurie Winn Carlson, *A Fever in Salem* (Chicago: Ivan R. Dee, 2000); for ergot, Linda R. Caporael, "Ergotism: The Satan Loosed in Salem?," *Science* 192 (April 1976): 21–26; for ecclesiastical strains, Richard Latner, "'Here Are No Newters': Witchcraft and Religious Discord in Salem Village and Andover," *New England Quarterly* (March 2006): 92–122. Benjamin C. Ray debunks the neat east-west split conceived by Boyer and Nissenbaum in *Salem Possessed* in his "The Geography of Witchcraft Accusations in 1692 Salem Village," *William and Mary Quarterly* 65 (July 2008): 449–78. On taxes: Noel D. Johnson and Mark Koyama, "Taxes, Lawyers, and the Decline of Witch Trials in France," MPRA, working paper no. 34266, October 2011; conspiracy, Enders A. Robinson, *The Devil Discovered: Salem Witchcraft 1692* (Prospect Heights, IL: Waveland, 1991). Emily Oster makes a case that frantic witch-hunting coincides with a little ice age in "Witchcraft, Weather, and Economic Growth in Renaissance Europe," *Journal of Economic Perspectives* 18 (Winter 2004): 215–28; the atmospheric conditions are from James Sullivan, *The History of the District of Maine* (Boston: Thomas and Andrews, 1795), 212. Ask today's female reenactors at Plimoth Plantation what they consider the most punishing month of the year; without hesitation, they will say February.

5   "There are departments": Chadwick Hansen, "Andover Witchcraft and the Causes of the Salem Witchcraft Trials," in *The Occult in America,* ed. Howard Kerr and Charles Crow (Urbana: University of Illinois, 1983), 53.

6   "with more purity": Nicholas Noyes, *New-England's Duty and Interest to Be an Habitation of Justice and Mountain of Holiness* (Boston, 1698).

6   "New English Israel": CM, *Small Offers Towards the Service of the Tabernacle in the Wilderness* (Boston, 1689).

6   what offended them: The "resistance to something" trope is from Henry Adams. See Stephen Innes, *Creating the Commonwealth: The Economic Culture of Puritan New England* (New York: W. W. Norton, 1995), 312.

6–7 "neither drive a bargain": Edward J. Ward, *Boston in 1682 and 1699: A Trip to New England* (Providence, RI: Club for Colonial Reprints, 1905), 54. Sewall and the courtship: SS *Diary,* 2: 966. New Hampshire's lieutenant governor: John Usher Papers, Ms. N-2071, 102, MHS. Danforth cites Saint John the Baptist in Roger Thompson, *Cambridge Cameos* (Boston: New England Historic Genealogical Society, 2005), 146. The prisoner is from Perley, *History of Salem,* 3: 186; the killer cat from R, 436; the ax in the hand (testimony in both cases against Susannah Martin) from R, 276.

7   church went flying: Ola Elizabeth Winslow, *Meetinghouse Hill* (New York: Macmillan, 1952), 54.

8   very different dark: No one is better on the subject than A. Roger Ekirch, *At Day's Close: A History of Nighttime* (London: Weidenfeld, 2005). I am grateful to John Demos for having called my attention to the book. Also for a sense of the wilderness among modern sources: Peter N. Carroll, *Puritanism and the Wilderness* (New York:

Columbia University Press, 1969); William Cronon, *Changes in the Land* (New York: Hill and Wang, 1983); John R. Stilgoe, *Common Landscape of America* (New Haven, CT: Yale University Press, 1982). The rabid hog: R, 359. Very often in the literature New Englanders refer to themselves as "ear-witnesses"; words—and sound— reigned supreme.

8 agents had stolen them: *CM Diary*, 1: 171–73. Outwitting the devil, he preached without them from memory. It was September 1693; CM had journeyed to Salem in part to see to it "that the complete history of the late witchcrafts and possessions might not be lost."

9 rest of the Bible intact: John Hull, *The Diaries of John Hull* (Boston: John Wilson, 1857), 231.

9 "diseases of astonishment": CM in Burr, 101.

11 "peevish and touchy": John Bowle, ed., *The Diary of John Evelyn* (Oxford: Oxford University Press, 1983), 2: 235. For a fine account of that "restrained hostility," Michael Garibaldi Hall, *Edward Randolph and the American Colonies, 1676–1703* (Chapel Hill: University of North Carolina Press, 1960).

11 venerable Salem minister: John Higginson to his son, August 31, 1692, Fam. Mss. 433, Higginson Family Papers, PEM; Norton, *In the Devil's Snare*, 13, maintains that SP burned his notes.

12 "a very wicked, spiteful manner": R, 127. On the multiply authored testimonies and records, their transcriptions and lacunae, see especially Marion Gibson, *Reading Witchcraft: Stories of Early English Witches* (London: Routledge, 1999); Peter Grund's superb "From Tongue to Text: The Transmission of the Salem Witchcraft Records," *American Speech* 82 (Summer 2007): 119–50; *Studia Neophilologica* 84 (2012), in particular essays by Matti Peikola, Matti Rissanen, Leena Kahlas-Tarkka; Grund et al., "Editing the Salem Witchcraft Records: An Exploration of a Linguistic Treasury," *American Speech* 79 (Summer 2004): 146–67; Grund, "The Anatomy of Correction," *Studia Neophilologica* 79 (2007): 3–14.

12 "I will tell": R, 196–97.

13 minister at odds: Samuel Willard, *A Compleat Body of Divinity* (Boston: B. Green, 1726), 627.

II. THAT OLD DELUDER

For the best portraits of the uncomfortable edge on which the Puritan lived: David D. Hall, "The Mental World of Samuel Sewall," *Proceedings of the MHS*, vol. 92 (1980), 21–44; Edward Eggleston, *The Transit of Civilization: From England to America in the Seventeenth Century* (Boston: Beacon, 1959); Eve LaPlante, *Salem Witch Judge: The Life and Repentance of Samuel Sewall* (New York: Harper, 2007); Silverman, *Life and Times of Cotton Mather;* Richard P. Gildrie, *The Profane, the Civil, and the Godly* (University Park: Pennsylvania State University Press, 1994). For the dark, the cold, and the external climate: Carroll, *Puritanism and the Wilderness;* Ekirch, *At Day's Close.* For the liturgical details, Charles E. Hambrick-Stowe, *The Practice of Piety: Puritan Devotional Disciplines in Seventeenth-*

Century New England (Chapel Hill: University of North Carolina Press, 1982). No one has ransacked the historical record for the texture of day-to-day life better (if with less notation) than Alice Morse Earle in her various works. See also George Francis Dow, "Domestic Life in New England in the Seventeenth Century," *Topsfield Historical Collections* 29 (1928); Jonathan L. Fairbanks, ed., *New England Begins: The Seventeenth Century* (Boston: Museum of Fine Arts, 1982); Roger Thompson, *Sex in Middlesex: Popular Mores in a Massachusetts County, 1649–1699* (Amherst: University of Massachusetts Press, 1986); Laurel Thatcher Ulrich, *Good Wives* (New York: Vintage, 1991); and Winslow, *Meetinghouse Hill*. For the lay of the land, Katherine Alysia Grandjean, "Reckoning: The Communications Frontier in Early New England" (PhD diss., Harvard, 2008). The sound: Richard Cullen Rath, *How Early America Sounded* (Ithaca: Cornell University Press, 2003). To Danvers town archivist Richard B. Trask, I owe countless other details.

15   "But who can tell": *CM Diary*, 1: 144.
15   Skimming groves: The flight is reconstructed from Foster and Carrier's testimony and that of their children and grandchildren: R, 467–75; Hale in Burr, 418; WOW, 158. The landscape derives from Cronon, *Changes in the Land*, 22–31; Joshua Scottow, *A Narrative of the Planting of the Massachusetts Colony, Anno 1628* (Boston, 1694); Hull, *Diaries*, 225; interviews with Richard Trask, November 28, 2012, and February 8, 2015. Glanvill reprinted the Swedish crash from Anthony Horneck, *An Account of What Happened in the Kingdom of Sweden* (London: St. Lownds, 1682), 10. Charles MacKay, *The Witch Mania* (extracted from *Memoirs of Extraordinary Popular Delusions and the Madness of Crowds* [London, 1841]), 550, adds the tremendous height. On Andover and the Scots, Abbot, *Our Company*. The impassable path: RFQC, 9: 69.
16   Sound echoed: For the eerie quiet, Ekirch, *At Day's Close*. The beaver's tail is from John Giles, *Memoirs of Odd Adventures, Strange Deliverances, Etc. in the Captivity of John Giles* (Cincinnati: Spiller and Gates, 1869), 40; "hideous noise with roaring": John Josselyn, *New-England's Rarities* (Boston: William Veazie, 1865), 48; screech of the crowd, SS *Diary*, 1: 509; flock of pigeons, CM in Silverman, *Selected Letters*, 34. Josselyn reported they were so thick they could obscure the sun. The freakish bellow: SS *Diary*, 1: 288; crack of timber, Gildrie, *The Profane*, xi; RFQC, 9: 580–84; tortoises propagating: Giles, *Memoirs*, 42.
16   phantom Frenchmen: *Magnalia*, 2: 537–40. See also Marshall W. S. Swan, "The Bedevilment of Cape Ann," *EIHC* 117 (July 1981): 153–77.
17   glow-in-the-dark jellyfish: R, 244; moved the landmarks: R, 258–59; a saucer: R, 412; the broom: R, 409.
17   lame Indian: SS *Diary*, 2: 750. The blinking went both ways. CM claimed that when Indians first saw a man on horseback, they took the "man and the horse to be one creature"; *MP*, 7.
17   The Sewall incident: SS *Diary*, 1: 331. Baxter had long before noted that lightning more often struck churches than castles, an observation to which CM would refer in *A Midnight Cry* (Boston, 1692). He insisted on its preference for ministers' homes in *Magnalia*, 2: 313.

18 "Horrid sorcerers": *Magnalia*, 2: 537. Four armed Indians: RFQC, 4: 230. House in ashes: Charles H. Lincoln, ed., *Narratives of the Indian Wars, 1675–1699* (1913; repr., New York: Barnes and Noble, 1959), 83.

18 "It is harder to find": *Magnalia*, 2: 515.

18 "Our men could see": Daniel Gookin, cited in Carroll, *Puritanism and the Wilderness*, 207. Essex County suffered proportionately more casualties than the rest of the colony. "I believe no town in this province has suffered more by the war than Salem," John Higginson Jr. wrote his brother in 1697; Higginson Family Papers, MHS Collections, 1838, 202. For King Philip's War, see Jill Lepore's superb *The Name of War: King Philip's War and the Origins of American Identity* (New York: Vintage, 1999).

18 devastating raids: See Emerson W. Baker and James Kences's fine "Maine, Indian Land Speculation, and the Essex County Witchcraft Outbreak of 1692," *Maine History* 40 (Fall 2001): 159–89. Casualties on the other side were yet more dreadful. By the best estimates, the Indian population of NE numbered around 100,000 in 1600. By the century's end—with some 90,000 Englishmen in America—it had fallen to about 10,000.

19 "The whole race": John Dunton, *John Dunton's Letters from New England* (Boston: Prince Society, 1867), 293.

19 "I Stand Here": RFQC, 5: 290.

19 murderer repented: Hugh Stone in *Magnalia*, 2: 356–62.

20 "spread the distemper": Cited in Karlsen, *The Devil*, 100; earlier suspicions of Carrier, R, 734.

20 late January: Tituba testified on March 2, 1692, that the enchantment had begun just over six weeks earlier; R, 135.

20 "invisible agents": JH in Burr, 413. JH reported the symptoms conformed exactly to those of the Goodwins; CM makes them more acute in *Magnalia*, 2: 409.

20 "foolish, ridiculous speeches": Robert Calef in Burr, 342.

20–21 "exemplary temper" to "intolerable anguish": *Magnalia*, 2: 396–403. Such epidemics had broken out at least three times previously; Koehler, *Search for Power*, 175. Since CM had set down the Goodwin history, another case of witchcraft had emerged. The Goodwin children had also relapsed. The "aerial steed": *MP*, 29. "Grievous fits" were not uncommon: see RFQC, 3: 54, and Demos, *Entertaining Salem*, 166–72; they were assumed to be sent by the devil. According to Joshua Moody, both Glover women were accused and jailed; letter to IM, MHS. The convicted Glover appears to have been Mary; Massachusetts Archive Series, vol. 35, 95–96, 254, Massachusetts State Archives.

21 "agitations, writhings": Richard Bernard, *A Guide to Grand-Jury Men* (London: Felix Kyngston, 1629), 45.

22 knitting, spooling: For Puritan chores, see Alice Morse Earle, *Child Life in Colonial Days* (Stockbridge, MA: Berkshire House, 1993); David Freeman Hawke, *Everyday Life in Early America* (New York: Harper and Row, 2003).

22 Others allotted: "Autobiography of the Rev. John Barnard," *Proceedings of the MHS*, vol. 5 (1836), 187. SP would not be remembered today for his sermons alone.

23 In a Connecticut case: See Richard Godbeer's concise and elegant *Escaping Salem: The Other Witch Hunt of 1692* (New York: Oxford University Press, 2005), 25. In a post-Salem case CM too made a point of rounding up "disinterested witnesses." For how seldom the sick were left alone, see for example Peter Thacher diary, P-186, MHS. On sickbeds, Hall, *Worlds of Wonder*, 197.

23 "odd postures": Calef in Burr, 242. CM noted that as many as fifty observers gathered around Mercy Short in 1693. The prayer and psalms, CM in Burr, 276.

23 "perniciously bad": Sanford J. Fox, *Science and Justice: The Massachusetts Witchcraft Trials* (Baltimore: Johns Hopkins University Press, 1968), 55. There were "wise, tender, and faithful" physicians, but they were physicians of the soul; doctors had often trained for the ministry.

23 basic medical kit: Harriet S. Tapley, "Early Physicians of Danvers," *Historical Collections of the Danvers Historical Society* 4 (1916): 73–88. The hedgehog fat is from Lawrence Hammond, *Diary Kept by Captain Lawrence Hammond, 1677–1694* (Cambridge: John Wilson and Son, 1892). For the raw state of medicine: George Francis Dow, *Every Day Life in the Massachusetts Bay Colony* (Boston: Society for the Preservation of New England Antiquities, 1935), 174–98; Patricia A. Watson, *The Angelical Conjunction: The Preacher-Physicians of Colonial New England* (Knoxville: University of Tennessee Press, 1991); and "Z. Endicott Book of Remedies," Frederick Lewis Gay Papers, Ms. N-2013, MHS.

24 William Griggs: See Anthony S. Patton, "The Witch Doctor," *Harvard Medical Alumni Bulletin* (Winter 1999): 34–39. See also Robinson, *The Devil Discovered*, 117–18.

24 "Am I bewitched": Thomas Ady, *A Candle in the Dark* (Boston, 1656), 120.

24 seizing, strangled Groton girl: Samuel Willard, "Samuel Willard's Account of the Strange Case of Elizabeth Knapp in Groton," Mather Papers, MHS.

24 "evil hand": JH in Burr, 413.

25 witchcraft versus possession: Mather on the affinity, Burr, 136; "It is an ordinary thing," David C. Brown, "The Salem Witchcraft Trials: Samuel Willard's *Some Miscellany Observations*," *EIHC* 122 (1986): 228. IM in *IP*, 198, asserted that you could suffer the two simultaneously. David Harley, "Explaining Salem: Calvinist Psychology and the Diagnosis of Possession," *American Historical Review* 101 (April 1996): 307–30, is best on the subject; as he notes, "New England at this time had no tradition of demonic possession" (313). Michael Dalton, *The Country Justice* (Boston, 1678), listed seven signs of bewitchment; IM offered six of possession. They overlap. Richard Raiswell and Peter Dendle, in "Demon Possession in Anglo-Saxon and Early Modern England," *Journal of British Studies* 47 (October 2008): 738–67, note that the symptoms are identical.

25–26 "angry and sending" to "spiritual enemies": *SPN*, 188–90.

26 "I am a man": *CM Diary*, 1: 471.

26 "If we want" and "den for devils": Goodwin in Burr, 131; "school of piety": *CM Diary*, 2: 265.

26 the concoction: John resorted to an old English recipe cited in previous cases on both sides of the Atlantic (and explicitly denounced by IM in *IP*). See Roger

Thompson, "Salem Revisited," *Journal of American Studies* 6 (December 1972): 332. A variation on the experiment would come up again in Salem testimony, R, 318 (in that version, the healer suggested you would find the witch dead the next morning). SP was explicit; the idea was Sibley's and the execution John's. He had no reason to minimize Tituba's role, especially as she was at the time he discussed the incident already in prison. She nonetheless comes down to us as a witch-cake baker, beginning with JH in Burr, 413, and Lawson in Burr, 162. JH either misremembered or elicited some information from Tituba on his own; see JH, 44. SP would later apologize for the behavior of his servants—plural.

27 "going to the devil": Parris in B&N, 278; "she has done": SP in the church record book for March 27.

28 town of Salem: See Richard Trask's invaluable "The Devil Amongst Us: A History of the Salem Village Parsonage," *Danvers Historical Society* (1971): 1–12; Richard P. Gildrie, *Salem, Massachusetts, 1626–1683: A Covenant Community* (Charlottesville: University Press of Virginia, 1975); and Gildrie, "Salem Society and Politics in the 1680s," *EIHC* 114 (October 1978): 185–206. There is much granular detail in the Higginson Family letters, MHS, 1838.

28–29 "in a wilderness" to "have been absent": B&N, 229–31. The petition dates from 1667.

30 "not seldom great": *SPN*, 184. For CM's twist, *CM Diary*, 2: 581.

31 Bayley meanwhile filed a slander suit: RFQC, 7: 248–49.

31 "that in case any difference": Salem Village Book of Transactions, November 25, 1680, DAC. See Hall, *Faithful Shepherd*, 187–94, on the rise of contractualism in ministers' contracts.

31–32 John Putnam had lent Burroughs funds: RFQC, 9: 30–32, 47–49. "When brother": B&N, 171; see also Perley, *History of Salem*, vol. 2, 172. Burroughs was not alone in borrowing money from the congregants who elected not to pay him.

32 "given to God": Lawson, October 6, 1713, Ms. Rawlinson, D839, Bodleian Library. There is no record of Lawson's having studied at or graduated from Cambridge, Oxford, or Trinity College, Dublin, although he claimed he had attended Cambridge, the center of Puritan learning. I am grateful to Suzanne M. Stewart of the NEHGS and Tim Wales in England for extensive Lawson research. For his turns of phrase, see May 22, 1680, Massachusetts Archives Collections, vol. 39, 658, Massachusetts State Archives. "God is not moved": Lawson, *The Duty and Property of a Religious Householder* (Boston, 1692). See also Charles Edward Banks, *The History of Martha's Vineyard* (Boston: George H. Dean, 1911), vol. 2, 149–50.

33 "uncharitable expressions" to "If you will unreasonably": B&N, 344–45.

33 pastor and flock: Silverman, *Life and Times of Cotton Mather*, 332.

34 warming pan: RFQC, 9: 448.

34 the Topsfield-Ipswich line: See George Francis Dow, *History of Topsfield, Massachusetts* (Topsfield, MA: Topsfield Historical Society, 1940), 320–30.

34 the demoralized clergy: Willard to IM, July 10, 1688, MHS; cheating and starving: CM, "New England's Choicest Blessing," 1679, 8; CM, "A Monitory Letter Concerning the Maintenance of an Able and Faithful Ministry, 1700; Konig, *Law and Society*, 98–108.

35 Harvard tuition: Samuel Eliot Morison, *Harvard College in the Seventeenth Century* (Cambridge, MA: Harvard University Press, 1936), 1: 103–6.

35 "Are you, sir, the parson": From Claude M. Fuess, *Andover: Symbol of New England* (Andover, MA: Andover Historical Society, 1959), 105. Hall, *Faithful Shepherd*, thinks the story apocryphal. The sentiment was very real.

35 "some nebulous and distant": Gildrie, *The Profane*, 148. Also on the ministers' maintenance, see Samuel Swett Green, *The Use of the Voluntary System in the Maintenance of Ministers* (Worcester, MA: Charles Hamilton, 1886).

35 "that might render": *CM Diary*, 1: 351.

35 "sit and sleep": IM, "Practical Truths Tending to Promote the Power of Godliness," 1682.

35 "useless whispering" and "unnecessary gazing": *SPN*, 290.

35–36 hours of sermons: Stout, *New England Soul*, 4. Stout estimates the average to have been 7000 sermons in a lifetime, for 15,000 listening hours.

36–37 On Parris: See Gragg, *Quest for Security*, and Gragg, "The Barbados Connection," *New England Historical and Genealogical Record* 140 (April 1986): 99–113; Gragg, "Samuel Parris: Portrait of a Puritan Clergyman," *EIHC* 119 (October 1983): 209–37. For the economic climate, Carl Bridenbaugh, *Cities in the Wilderness* (New York: Capricorn Books, 1964); Richard S. Dunn, "The Barbados Census of 1680: Profile of the Richest Colony in English America," *William and Mary Quarterly* 26 (1969): 3–30. In fairness, Parris's timing was lousy. The Barbados years were ones of devastating weather and, at the end of his stay, a smallpox epidemic. NE trade was next to impossible under Andros, who had strangled it with strict enforcement of the Navigation Acts. Interviews with David Hall, November 29, 2012, and September 21, 2013.

37 "The work was weighty": Cited in Samuel P. Fowler, *An Account of the Life, Character, Etc. of the Reverend Samuel Parris of Salem Village* (Salem: William Ives, 1857), 1. It was not unusual to emphasize the enormity of the task, though generally one did so differently, to point up one's inadequacies. See "Memoir of Rev. John Hale," *Proceedings of the MHS*, vol. 7 (1838), 257.

37 The Puritan mind: Perry Miller and Thomas H. Johnson, eds., *The Puritans: A Sourcebook of Their Writings* (New York: Harper, 1963), 1: 60. For the NE palette, see David Hackett Fischer, *Albion's Seed* (New York: Oxford University Press, 1989), 140. He credits it with Harvard's muddy crimson.

37 "this poor little": *SPN*, 84.

38 "rather discouraging": "A General Account of the Transaction between the Inhabitants of Salem Village and My Self, Samuel Parris," W. L. Clements Library, University of Michigan.

38 "Isn't that pretty soft": Alice Morse Earle, *The Sabbath in Puritan New England* (Charleston, SC: Bibliolife, 2008), 140. With two fireplaces, you needed 30 cords of wood—or an acre of standing timber—to survive the year; Hawke, *Everyday Life*, 55. The fine for cutting a tree of more than 24 inches in diameter was 100 pounds, or twice the annual ministerial salary. Journal of Lords of Trade, 2 September 1691, CO 391/7, 42–4, PRO. The new charter reserved all trees of that size for the Royal Navy.

38 "After much urging": SP, "A General Account," W. L. Clements Library, University of Michigan.

39 "You are to bear" to "love me best": *SPN*, 51. Interview with David Hall, September 21, 2013.

39 "consolations dropped": Dunton, *Dunton's Letters*, 255. He was citing Noyes. For Higginson, see *Proceedings of the MHS*, vol. 16 (1902), 478–520.

40 longtime ministerial service: Hall, *Faithful Shepherd*, 193. Beverly granted Hale a much smaller parsonage and two acres after three decades.

40–41 "I cannot preach" to "some other place": SP's October 28, 1690, list of proposals, Simon Gratz Collection, the Historical Society of Pennsylvania. On SP's church record book, Marilynne K. Roach's superb "Records of the Rev. Samuel Parris," *New England Historical and Genealogical Register* 157 (January 2003): 6–30. The record book is in the DAC.

41 "had scarce wood": Record book, 18 November 1691, DAC. The rattling coughs: Earle, *The Sabbath*, 53–63; Winslow, *Meetinghouse Hill*, 56.

41 too cold to go on: SP may well have dismissed the January congregants on account of the cold. Or he may have done so on account of the distractions in the pews, which could already have begun.

41 "So perplexing": Cited in David H. Flaherty, *Privacy in Colonial New England* (Charlottesville: University Press of Virginia, 1972), 135. Squirrel-killing: Joseph Green diary, DIA 72, PEM. See also Peter Thacher diary, P-186, MHS; "Autobiography of the Rev. John Barnard," 219, 233; CM, "A Monitory Letter," 1700.

43 the Cambridge meeting: *Proceedings of the MHS*, vol. 17 (1879), 263.

43 "one chief project": The Old Deluder Act of 1647, in the *Records of the Governor and Company of the Massachusetts Bay in NE* (1853), vol. 2, 203.

43 the delinquent father: RFQC, 5: 378.

43 three times through the Bible: "Autobiography of the Rev. John Barnard," 178. The dozen readings: William L. Joyce et al., eds., *Printing and Society in Early America* (Worcester, MA: AAS, 1983), 22.

43 "Wise parents": *SPN*, 236 on food, 318 on rod. For CM, see for example "Some Special Points, Relating to the Education of My Children," in Miller and Johnson, *The Puritans*, 2: 724–27. Exercises for his children recur throughout CM's diaries.

44 "seeing their young" to "farther off": *SPN*, 183, 193.

III: THE WORKING OF WONDERS

45 "I have seen too much": Arthur Conan Doyle, "The Man with the Twisted Lip," in *The New Annotated Sherlock Holmes* (New York: Norton, 2005), 183.

45 rainstorms: For the apocalyptic weather, Hammond diary, P-363, MHS. The farmers filed charges in all four names, although the Putnam household alone was affected.

45–46 Sin and crime: See Eli Faber, "Puritan Criminals: The Economic, Social, and Intellectual Background to Crime in Seventeenth-Century Massachusetts," *Perspectives in American History 11 (1978): 83–144; David Flaherty, "Law and the Enforcement of Morals in Early America," *Perspectives in American History* 5 (1971): 203–53.

46 local menace: Good fit even the skeptic's idea of a witch. See Reginald Scot's 1584 description of "these miserable wretches" in Katherine Howe, ed., *The Penguin Book of Witches* (New York: Penguin, 2014), 20; RFQC, 9: 579–80.

46–47 "turbulent a spirit" to "unusual manner": R, 423; similarly R, 411. The Herrick testimony: R, 424.

48 "shameful vanity": Sewall in 1714, cited in Richard Francis, *Judge Sewall's Apology* (New York: Harper and Row, 2005), 326. There does not appear to have been a copy of Shakespeare yet in America; no estate inventory included a painting. The organ: Thomas Wertenbaker, *The Puritan Oligarchy* (New York: Scribner's, 1947), 128.

48 seating was nearly toxic: See Abbot, *Our Company*, 181–82, for the baroque formulations; Robert J. Dinkin, "Seating the Meeting House in Early Massachusetts," *New England Quarterly* 43 (September 1970): 450–56.

48 Hathorne presided: See J. M. Beattie, *Crime and the Courts in England* (Princeton, NJ: Princeton University Press, 1986); John H. Langbein, *The Origins of Adversary Criminal Trial* (Oxford: Oxford University Press, 2003), 43; Langbein, "The Criminal Trial Before the Lawyers," *University of Chicago Law Review* 45 (Winter 1978): 263–316. Beattie points out that the emphasis in hearings was on preserving the witness's words rather than the defendant's, and that the task was less to prove the charges than the suspect's guilt; interview with J. M. Beattie, September 29, 2014. R, 127–30, for Good's hearing. Mercy Short would later describe her as having been in tatters. For the hearing choreography, R, 46.

48 evaluate Indian defenses: *Documentary History of the State of Maine* (Portland: Maine Historical Society, 1869), 5: 92–93.

49 "What day of the week": RFQC, 9: 398–99; reduced responsible men to gibberish: RFQC, 3: 398.

49–50 Sarah's muttering: See Matthew Hopkins, *The Discovery of Witches* (Essex, UK: Charles Clark's, 1837), 2; CM, *Optanda, Good Men Described and Good Things Propounded* (Boston: 1692), 88; Samuel Willard, *The Character of a Good Ruler* (Boston: 1694), 30; CM, *Fair Weather, or Considerations to Dispel the Clouds and Allay the Storms of Discontent* (Boston: 1692), 33, 37; CM, *The Present State of New England* (Boston: 1690), 42. "The devil's music" is from *Fair Weather,* 49.

50–51 "Her answers": R, 127. In her sleep: Ibid., 127–28.

52 "Order in the court": Interview with J. M. Beattie, September 9, 2014.

52 diligent search: JH, 73.

53 Tituba: See Chadwick Hansen, "The Metamorphosis of Tituba, or Why American Intellectuals Can't Tell an Indian Witch from a Negro," *New England Quarterly* 47 (March 1974): 3–12. Rosenthal, "Tituba's Story," is especially clear-minded about how Upham dismantled CM and installed Tituba, working in part from fictional sources. For a fine-grained study of Tituba and a case for her South American origins, see Elaine G. Breslaw, *Tituba, Reluctant Witch of Salem* (New York: New York University Press, 1996). On Tituba's testimony: See Matti Rissanen, "'Candy No

Witch, Barbados,'" in *Language in Time and Space*, ed. Heinrich Ramisch and Kenneth Wynne (Stuttgart: Franz Steiner, 1997), 183–93. Rissanen, 191, notes that we have 130 words of Good's versus 700 of Tituba's; Dawn Archer, "'Can Innocent People Be Guilty?,'" *Journal of Historical Pragmatics* (2002): 220, notes that in all, Hathorne asked Tituba 39 questions; Kathleen L. Doty, in "Telling Tales: The Role of Scribes in Constructing the Discourse of the Salem Witchcraft Trials," *Journal of Historical Pragmatics* (2007): 35, notes that the justices treat Tituba more gently than they had Sarah Good. See also Risto Hiltunen's excellent "'Tell Me, Be You a Witch?': Questions in the Salem Witchcraft Trials of 1692," *International Journal for the Semiotics of Law* 9 (1996): 17–37. Tituba had provided some clues to her testimony already: the court had enlisted a number of reporters, as if they expected something momentous; R, 128–36.

55 show more love: Alan Macfarlane, *The Family Life of Ralph Josselin* (Cambridge: Cambridge University Press, 1970), 145.

56 William Allen and John Hughes: R, 141; Sibley, R, 425. Rosenthal, *Salem Story*, 17–19, points out the inconsistencies in the accounts. Sibley strikes Tituba's back in one, her arm in the other.

57 "He tell me": R, 135.

58 actual pact with the devil: They turned up rarely in NE, but they had turned up; see David D. Hall, ed., *Witch-Hunting in Seventeenth-Century New England* (Boston: Northeastern University Press, 1991), 119. None had played a central role in a witch-craft case before. After Tituba, pacts were everywhere.

59 "a grave of the living": Dunton, *Dunton's Letters*, 119–20.

59 Prison breaks: RFQC, 4: 275; RFQC, 8: 31–32; RFQC, 9: 26.

59 "And it was thought": JH in Burr, 415.

60 mentioned God only once: The point is Kahlas-Tarkka's in "'I Am a Gosple Woman,'" *Studia Neophilologica* 84, 58.

60 "And thus": JH in Burr, 415.

60 "A witch is one": Joseph Glanvill, *Saducismus Triumphatus* (Gainesville, FL: Scholars' Facsimiles, 1966), 268. The volume dates from 1681. The etymology is of interest: "wizard" derives from the German root *wissen*, "to know," while "witch" derives from *wiccian*, "to bewitch."

61 toad into the family milk: RFQC, 4: 57.

61 the witch's mark: For the authority, see Dalton, *The Country Justice*, 73; Thomas, *Religion and the Decline of Magic*, 530; Koehler, *Search for Power*, 270. The witch's mark was a fairly new arrival.

61 what enchantment looked like: See Bernard, *A Guide to Grand-Jury Men*, for a description of the gnashing, frothing, and tumbling. Other signs align perfectly with the description in Dalton, *The Country Justice*, a copy of which Sewall carried about with him on the circuit; EIHC 129 (1993): 68–69.

61 the Cheshire cat: IM in *IP*, 165. For the taverns, see Richard P. Gildrie's excellent "Taverns and Popular Culture in Essex County, MA, 1678–1686," *EIHC* 124 (1988): 162.

62 "No wonder that": Cited in Louise A. Breen, *Transgressing the Bounds* (Oxford: Oxford University Press, 2001), 178; "the worst of drunkards," Gildrie, "Taverns and

Popular Culture," 163. The modern historian is Emil Oberholzer Jr., *Delinquent Saints: Disciplinary Action in Early Congregational Churches of Massachusetts* (New York: Columbia University Press, 1956), 152.

62–63 Witches had troubled New England: The literature is vast. I have relied especially on Robin Briggs, *Witches and Neighbors: The Social and Cultural Context of European Witchcraft* (London: Penguin, 1998); Fox, *Science and Justice*; Christina Larner, *Witchcraft and Religion: The Politics of Popular Belief* (London: Blackwell, 1984); Brian P. Levack, *The Witchcraft Sourcebook* (New York: Routledge, 2010); Alan Macfarlane, *Witchcraft in Tudor and Stuart England* (New York: Harper and Row, 1970); Brian A. Pavlac, *Witch Hunts in the Western World* (Westport, CT: Greenwood, 2009); Thomas, *Religion and the Decline of Magic*. There were exceptions on the orgies; a 1662 Connecticut case involved dancing and sex with the devil. The first known prosecution is from Fox, *Science and Justice*, who points out that there is no recorded history without witches. For the traditional witches' Sabbath: Carlo Ginzburg, *Ecstasies: Deciphering the Witches' Sabbath* (New York: Pantheon, 1991).

63 false memories: IM cited in Koehler, *Search for Power*, 271.

63 witch's ultimate target: Or as Samuel Willard put it in a June 1692 sermon, the devil "aims at the soul but if he cannot succeed there he will do his utmost against the body" (Sewall sermon notebook, Ms. N-905, MHS).

65 greatest hunts: Numerically speaking, Catholic Germany and northern France executed the greatest number of witches. The Channel island of Guernsey: Levack, *The Witchcraft Sourcebook*, 185. Though ecumenical, witches had their predilections. As John Gaule put it in his 1646 *Select Cases of Conscience*, a volume familiar to New England: "There has been, are, and are likely still to be more witches under the Popish than in the Protestant religion. For not only their popes, priests, friars, nuns (many of them) have been notorious witches: but their prestigious miracles and superstitious rites little better than kinds of witchcrafts."

65 The devil boasts: Edward K. Trefz, "Satan in Puritan Preaching," *Boston Public Library Quarterly* 8 (1956): 71–84; Trefz, "Satan as the Prince of Evil," *Boston Public Library Quarterly* (1955); 3–22; Andrew Delbanco, *The Death of Satan: How Americans Have Lost the Sense of Evil* (New York: Farrar, Straus and Giroux, 1995); Paul Carus, *The History of the Devil and the Idea of Evil* (La Salle, IL: Open Court, 1974).

66 Swedish girl who had plummeted from her stick: Demos, *The Enemy Within*, 90.

67 a pact with Satan: See Hall, *Witch-Hunting*, 24. For a NE history, see Demos, *Entertaining Salem*, 401–9.

67 disseminated an instructive account of her compact: MP, 1–44. The problem may have been CM's Gaelic; he concluded that the Irish used the same word to mean both "spirits" and "saints," 11. Martha Goodwin did name additional tormentors; CM kept the information to himself.

68 "never been in a place": *Journal of Jasper Danckaerts* (New York: Scribner's, 1913), 290.

68 "You have a neighbor": R, 370.

68 accused witch languishing: Rosenthal discovered her; R, 16.

68 Connecticut had been more troubled: Godbeer, *Escaping Salem*.

68 "We inclined to": JH in Burr, 412. On the leniency of the system, see David D. Hall, *A Reforming People* (New York: Knopf, 2013), 87. On the other hand, of the fifty-six people executed in Massachusetts between 1630 and 1692, the greatest number—by a factor of two—were for witchcraft.

69 spectral bear: Koehler, *Search for Power*, 291.

70 "Many things are done": Albert Kyper, cited in Stuart Clark, *Thinking with Demons: The Idea of Witchcraft in Early Modern Europe* (Oxford: Oxford University Press, 1999), 233.

70 to doubt the sun: William Perkins, *Discourse of the Damned Art of Witchcraft* (Cambridge: Cantrell Legge, 1618), 31. The colonists returned to Perkins again and again with their questions.

70 "We have the attestation" to "times and places": Glanvill, *Saducismus Triumphatus*, 67.

71 "Flashy people": *Magnalia*, 1: 187.

71 official 1692 version: CM in Burr, 261. The description, he noted, tallied with what they had heard from abroad. Interestingly, in Catholic countries, the devil interfered with the reading of "Popish books," where in NE, he made it impossible for a Puritan girl to read Mather volumes.

72 more devils than men: See, for example, IM, *Angelographia; or, A Discourse Concerning the Nature and Power of the Holy Angels* (Boston, 1696), 111.

72 "was nothing to him": RFQC, 8: 272. Epithets appear to have been different in other colonies, where you might be written off as a noodle, an ape, an old rogue; see John Demos, *Remarkable Providences* (Boston: Northeastern University Press, 1991), 288. John M. Murrin notes similarly that the NE court record is all sin and evil, sin and pollution, where other colonies counted in felonies and misdemeanors; see David Hall et al., eds., *Saints and Revolutionaries: Essays on Early American History* (New York: W. W. Norton, 1984), 188. See also Hall, *Witch-Hunting*, 87; Hall, *Worlds of Wonder*, 74. "had so much": RFQC, 7: 362. On the Indians and the devil, David S. Lovejoy, "Satanizing the American Indian," *New England Quarterly* 67 (December 1994): 603–21.

72 "the devil take you": David Hall, "The Uses of Literacy in New England, 1600–1850," in *Printing and Society in Early America*, 36.

72 foreigner in an unusual hat: From Bernard Bailyn, *The New England Merchants in the Seventeenth Century* (New York: Harper, 1955), 110. The overbearing English official was, in IM's estimation, "a child of the devil." Edward Randolph Papers, III: 329.

72 "it is the main drift": *SPN*, 184.

73 "Where will the Devil": *WOW*, 10.

73 "infernal fiends": CM in Levack, *The Witchcraft Sourcebook*, 112.

73 prosecutions stuttered: Carus, *The History*, 379–90.

73 the Apocalypse: In the 1640s, it was prophesied for the 1650s; Hall, *Faithful Shepherd*, 86; it had been imminent since 1655 according to David E. Stannard, *The Puritan Way of Death* (New York: Oxford University Press, 1977), 123.

74 Mather defied anyone: CM in Burr, 143.

74 "they would act": Lawson in ibid., 342. There may have been an additional reason to send off Betty. As Moody noted of the Goodwins in 1688: "If any step home they are immediately afflicted, and while they keep out are well."

74 That was the devil: Cited by Lawson in Burr, 160. Betty would not be mentioned again in a 1692 witchcraft complaint.

75–76 "I know what you are" to "nothing that was good": R, 149–50. On the previous marriage, see Eleanor V. Spiller, "Giles Corey," *Essex Genealogist* 5 (February 1985): 11–14.

77 "I will come" to "iron rod": R, 152–53. Martha Goodwin was propelled in much the same way through Mather's house, "dragged wholly by other hands."

77 "the people who make": CM, *Ornaments for the Daughters of Zion* (Boston, 1692). See Jane Kamensky's *Governing the Tongue: The Politics of Speech in Early New England* (New York: Oxford University Press, 1997). In her "Words, Witches, and Women Trouble: Witchcraft, Disorderly Speech, and Gender Boundaries in Puritan New England," *EIHC* 128 (October 1992), she provides a marvelous tour of the lexicon, with a chart of the forms of speech associated with the accused, 307.

77 Ann Putnam Sr.: Rosenthal believes she was not yet thirty; *Salem Story*, 229n and RFQC, 8: 348, 424.

78 "helping to tend" to "black pen": R, 160–61.

79 "I have perceived" to "heard nothing": R, 155.

IV. ONE OF YOU IS A DEVIL

80 "Two errors": Blaise Pascal, *Thoughts* (New York: Collier Press, 1910), 220.

80 "as rare an history": Lawson in Burr, 152. Lawson and SP could not have been out of touch; the copy of Perkins on SP's desk came from a deacon at Lawson's congregation. Lawson, CM, and SP regularly invoked the same imagery over these months.

80 could not have returned: Interview with David Hall, January 23, 2013.

81 "after I was removed": Lawson in Burr, 148.

82 "'Whish, whish, whish'": The cry resembled a 1637 German spell for takeoff: "Whoosh! Up the chimney, up the window hole!" Levack, *The Witchcraft Sourcebook*, 207.

82 "ought I know": Calef in Burr, 148–53.

83 "Now stand" to "enough of that": Lawson in Burr, 154.

83 Quaker women: Earle, *The Sabbath*, 96–97. Women spoke so often at Quaker meetings you might as well call them ministers, CM huffs in *Little Flocks Guarded Against Grievous Wolves* (Boston: 1691), 94.

83–84 "I know no doctrine" to "pathetic prayer": Lawson in Burr, 154–55.

83 "distracting and disturbing": B&N, 296.

84–87 "We did not send" to "prove she was a witch": R, 146; Lawson in Burr, 156.

87 delegation assembled: R, 162. Roach thinks the Nurse family requested the neighbors call: See Marilynne Roach, *Six Women of Salem* (New York: Da Capo, 2013), 130. On the family, see Lee Shai Weissbach, "The Townes of Massachusetts," *EIHC* 118 (1982): 200–220; RFQC, 5: 341.

89 Lawson called on Ann Putnam Sr.: Lawson in Burr, 157–58. Lawson had reason to hesitate; bibliomancy was strongly discouraged. The passage in question offered a

sort of litmus test as to where one stood on Judgment Day; it was a text designed to make the impious squirm; e-mail with David Hall, September 24, 2013. Ann was six weeks pregnant. In her trances Mercy Short tended to offer remarkably apt passages, CM in Burr, 275.

90 Rebecca Nurse stood before Hathorne and Corwin: R, 157–58, 160–61; Lawson remarks on her indifference in *Christ's Fidelity: The Only Shield Against Satan's Malignity* (London: J. Lawrence, 1704), 109.

91 shed only three tears: MacKay, *The Witch Mania,* 510.

92 He had prepared carefully: Lawson in Trask, *"The Devil Hath Been Raised,"* 65–106. He may have added to the sermon after its delivery and before publication, as he would again later.

93 Martha Corey's husband: The only men convicted of witchcraft in Massachusetts prior to 1692 had been married to witches. There was a reason for a husband to offer up incriminating remarks.

93 the arrest of Dorothy: R, 155–56, 163.

93–94 "terror, amazement": Lawson in Trask, *"The Devil Hath Been Raised,"* 95; "vile and wicked" to "is a devil": *SPN,* 194–98. On the sudden, sweeping swerve from hypocrisy to devils, interview with David Hall, November 29, 2012. By March, SP did not believe anyone colluded unwillingly with the devil. The door-slamming is from Lawson in Burr, 161, and interview with Richard Trask, November 28, 2012. Cloyce's exit: R, 415.

95 "thresh the devil": R, 538.

96 "sport, they must have": R, 537. The reporter had married into the Cloyce family.

96 rush to narrative: CM wrote his account of the Goodwins' enchantment in real time, which allowed Martha to read it over. She did so repeatedly, ridiculing the work and warning the author that he "should quickly come to disgrace by that history."

96 Scripture provided the bedrock: David D. Hall, "Toward a History of Popular Religion in Early New England," *William and Mary Quarterly* 41 (January 1984): 49–55. John Dane appealed to the Bible to decide to come to NE, where he would be safer from temptation; "John Dane's Narrative," *New-England Historical Genealogical Record* (April 1854): 154; the Sewalls retreated to bedrooms with the Bible after harsh words were exchanged. One woman used hers to deck a New Hampshire sheriff's assistant; Koehler, *Search for Power,* 372.

97 seer and watchman: See CM, *Midnight Cry;* Roger Thompson, " 'Holy Watchfulness' and Communal Conformism," *New England Quarterly* 56 (December 1983): 504–22; and Earle, *The Sabbath,* 75–77, for the watchful deacons. To mind other people's business was, asserted Edmund Morgan, to be a good Puritan.

97 the daughter's bonnet: *CM Diary,* 1: 369.

98 "If any people": Cited in Miller and Johnson, *The Puritans,* 1: 245.

98 "had willingly risked": Stout, *New England Soul,* 31. If one reviewed the record, God had been frowning on NE from the beginning. He would continue to do so; in 1701 you could still title a sermon "Prognosticks of Impending Calamities."

98 "ravening wolves" and "wild boars": Scottow, *A Narrative*, 28.

99 revoke their charter: David S. Lovejoy is especially fine on the period, *The Glorious Revolution in America* (New York: Harper and Row, 1972). For the end of prosperity, Timothy H. Breen and Stephen Foster, "The Puritans' Greatest Achievement: A Study of Social Cohesion in Seventeenth-Century Massachusetts," *Journal of American History* 60 (June 1973): 16.

99 "the petty differences": "Letter from New England," November 11, 1694, CO 5/858, PRO.

99 Andros asked John Higginson: Cited in *The Andros Tracts* (New York: Burt Franklin, 1868), 1: 26. Dunton described Higginson's speech as "a glimpse of heaven" in *The Life and Errors of John Dunton* (London: J. Nichols, 1818), 127.

99 "remote, rocky, barren": Edward Johnson, *Johnson's Wonder-Working Providence* (New York: Elibron Classics, 2005), 210.

100 in a military coup: Historians have happily noted that that revolt took place eighty-six years to the day before Paul Revere's ride. The Tower of Babel: Edward Randolph to the governor of Barbados, May 16, 1689, *Edward Randolph: Letters and Official Papers* (Boston: Prince Society, 1899), 4: 267.

100 "that strange agglomeration": Aldous Huxley, *The Devils of Loudun* (New York: Harper and Brothers, 1953), 39. The annunciation is from Ann M. Little, "Men on Top? The Farmer, the Minister, and Marriage in Early New England," *Pennsylvania History* 64 (Summer 1997): 134.

100 great Enlightenment thinkers: See Lawrence Stone, "The Disenchantment of the World," *New York Review of Books,* December 2, 1971, and David Stannard, "Death and the Puritan Child," *American Quarterly* (December 1974): 472.

101 Almanacs sold briskly: John Partridge, *Monthly Observations and Predictions for This Present Year, 1692* (Boston: Benjamin Harris, 1692), 4. The almanac's prediction for April was even more ominous: "If there is any roguery now against the government, be sure there is a woman up to the ears in it; but be it what it will, a woman is at the bottom, and the thing is villainous." On the overlap of science and magic, folklore and erudition, Hall's seminal 1990 *Worlds of Wonder;* Walter W. Woodward, *Prospero's America* (Chapel Hill: University of North Carolina Press, 2010); John Winthrop et al., "Scientific Notes from the Books and Letters of John Winthrop, Jr.," *Isis* 11 (December 1928): 325–42; Jon Butler, "Magic, Astrology, and the Early American Religious Heritage," *American Historical Review* 84 (April 1979): 317–46; and Ann Kibbey, "Mutations of the Supernatural: Witchcraft, Remarkable Providences, and the Power of Puritan Men," *American Quarterly* 34 (Summer 1982): 125–48 As a rule, the more intently you immersed yourself in science, the more interest you displayed in the supernatural.

101 best-educated community: Cremin, *American Education,* 189–207. There were more educated men in Massachusetts than in any other colony. There was also more witchcraft.

102 "prodigious witchcrafts": Harley, "Explaining Salem," 315.

102 best pig followed him: Michael P. Winship, "Encountering Providence in the Seventeenth Century," *EIHC* 126 (1990): 35. Luck had not yet entered the picture; it was

divine providence when the woodpile collapsed just after you had called the children away from it. Apocalypse practice: SS *Diary*, 1: 331.

102–103 inclement weather: Karen Kupperman, "Climate and Mastery of the Wilderness in Seventeenth-Century New England," in *Seventeenth-Century New England*, ed. David Hall and David Allen (Boston: Colonial Society of Massachusetts, 1984), 9. The overenjoyable sex: Edward Taylor, cited in Koehler, *Search for Power*, 80. The lame knee: "The Autobiography of Increase Mather," *Proceedings of the AAS* (Worcester, 1961), 350. See also Kibbey, "Mutations of the Supernatural."

103 "inquire, instruct, advise": "Records of the Cambridge Association of Ministers," October 13, 1690, *Proceedings of the MHS*, vol. 17 (1880), 264.

103 "I observe the law": Hull, *Diaries*, 136.

104 Cantlebery's wife: RFQC, 2: 101. Cantlebery had paid the call to complain that the neighbor's swine were in his peas. The neighbor's initial response had been to inform him he was a "rogue, whelp and toad."

104 land grants were defined: George Lee Haskins pointed out that the initial charter was based on two rivers parallel to each other only if you squinted; *Law and Authority in Early Massachusetts* (New York: Macmillan, 1960), 9.

104 rotten, decomposing fence: SP's October 28, 1690, list of proposals, Simon Gratz Collection, the Historical Society of Pennsylvania. CM described the devil as "the make-bait of the world" in "Things to Be Look'd For," 1691, 18.

105 "she would as soon": RFQC, 3: 54–55.

105 They sought revenge: Lawrence W. Towner, "'A Fondness for Freedom': Servant Protest in Puritan Society," *William and Mary Quarterly* 19 (April 1962): 212; Roger Thompson, "Adolescent Culture in Colonial Massachusetts," *Journal of Family History* (Summer 1984): 133; RFQC, 3: 66. "Because she was": RFQC, 8: 222–24. Maule was Quaker, the servant Irish Catholic; there was no contest. The case was dismissed.

105 the only explanation: CM in Burr, 95.

106 Ben Gould: R, 188.

107 A roll call: R, 172–73.

107 "stupendious revolution": CM, *Midnight Cry*, 21. The sermon—in which CM referred to devil's compacts and lawful convictions for them—was published immediately.

107 less rustic, better-lit town meetinghouse: Perley, *History of Salem*, vol. 3, 430–34.

107 blots on the page: See Meredith Marie Neuman, *Jeremiah's Scribes: Creating Sermon Literature in Puritan New England* (Philadelphia: University of Pennsylvania Press, 2013), 66.

108 Thomas Danforth: See Roger Thompson's expert sleuthing, especially "The Transit of Civilization: The Case of Thomas Danforth," in *The Transit of Civilization*, ed. Winfried Herget and Karl Ortseifen (Tubingen: Gunter Narr, 1986), 37–44, and Thompson, *Cambridge Cameos*.

108 Salem town meetinghouse: Town Records of Salem, MA, vol. 3 (Salem: Essex Institute, 1934), 201–2. Interview with Richard Trask, January 21, 2015.

108 On the imperfect records: Rosenthal, *Salem Story*, 125; Doty, "Telling Tales"; Gibson, *Reading Witchcraft*, 12–49. SP later acknowledged his mistakes.

108–109 "When did" through "dying fainting fit": R, 173–74.

110 "visionary girls": Letter appended to Deodat Lawson, *A Further Account of the Trials of the New England Witches* (Boston, 1693), 1.

110 "he would soon": R, 182.

110 He lurched forward and bit: Calef in Burr, 348.

111 "Oh you old witch": R, 181. Rosenthal thinks Procter may have been arrested; *Salem Story*, 110–11. No warrant survives.

112 Constable Herrick rounded up four more witches: R, 710–11.

112–113 Corey was an obvious target: RFQC, 1: 152, 172; RFQC, 7: 90–91, 134. The stinking water episode: RFQC, 1: 208–9. The "evil hand": RFQC, 7: 90. For some marvelous Corey detective work, David C. Brown, "The Case of Giles Corey," *EIHC* 121 (1985): 282–99; also Spiller, "Giles Corey."

113–114 "Which of you" to "temptation to witchcraft": R, 187–88.

114 Bridget Bishop: R, 184–85. In 1679 she had also appeared before someone who pointed to her and swore she had bewitched him "as now she stands before the court," RFQC, 7: 329; RFQC, 4: 90, 386. On the two Bishops, David L. Greene, *American Genealogist* 227 (July 1981): 131–38. It did not help that—as Marilynne Roach points out—there were no fewer than four Edward Bishops in the area. Even JH could not keep them straight.

116–117 "You were a little": R, 197; "torn in pieces": R, 203.

118 "I will speak": R, 189–94. Abigail does not mention Burroughs until her subsequent examination; see Rosenthal, *Salem Story*, 42–43. She had attended a great witches' assembly: R, 198.

120–121 "great care" to "high and dreadful": R, 204. Benjamin C. Ray, in *Satan and Salem* (Charlottesville: University of Virginia Press, 2015), calculated that Thomas Putnam wrote over 120 depositions and complaints, or one-third of the total; according to Ray, the signature Putnam phrase "most grievously" occurs 172 times in his documentation. Putnam filed the first complaint as well as the last, on September 17.

V: THE WIZARD

122 "In the terror": Charles Dickens, *Great Expectations* (New York: Oxford University Press, 1993), 65.

122 Any number of discrepancies: Breslaw, *Tituba*, 118, points out that one court reporter did not think Tituba's tall man from Boston even worthy of mention. Abigail and Deliverance Hobbs produced different versions of the witches' Sabbath, with different presiding deacons.

122 "not a tooth": Robert Calef, *More Wonders of the Invisible World* (London: Nath. Hillar, 1700), 165. Edward J. Ward was not impressed with Massachusetts dentistry; see Ward, *Boston in 1682 and 1699*, 53.

123 "managed in imagination": CM to John Richards, May 31, 1692, Cotton Mather Letters, John J. Burns Library, Boston College.

123 Reverend Nicholas Noyes: Dunton, *Dunton's Letters*, 255; Higginson Family Papers, MHS. On his verse, see Sibley, 245. The burning poppets: R, 464.

124 "cross and swift questions": CM to Richards, May 31, 1692, Cotton Mather Letters, John J. Burns Library, Boston College.

124 "with the doleful shrieks": *WOW*, 14. Joshua Scottow reported that the shrieks made it appear "as if hell and his furies had been let loose," *A Narrative*, 47.

124 "It is no rare thing": Bernard, *Guide to Grand-Jury Men*, cited in Trask, *"The Devil Hath Been Raised,"* 135. On the twofold importance of confession, Hall, *A Reforming People*, 86.

124–126 he designed an experiment: R, 211. The "tall black man": R, 213.

126 bloody battle waged: R, 207.

126–127 "I can deny it" to "are bewitched": R, 215. William Hobbs too hesitated to interpret the epidemic at hand.

127 "How did you know": R, 205. David C. Brown, in *A Guide to the Salem Witchcraft Hysteria of 1692* (self-published, 2000), suggests the girls did this on purpose to bolster their credibility.

127 agreed but steadily increased: R, 237; Lawson in Burr, 163; R, 555, 561–63.

127 "red bread": R, 220. Ten days later, Deliverance added roast and boiled meat; R, 237.

128 "What, are ministers witches": R, 505–6. In *The Country Justice*, Dalton recognized the distinction between conjurers and witches. The former claimed they could actually raise the devil.

128 little black man: R, 243. Elizabeth Hubbard was yet more helpful. He was "a little black-haired man" who wore "blackish apparel."

129 "as if the blood": Lawson's appendix to *Christ's Fidelity*, 99; cf. R, 246. If Burroughs failed to confess, the two women threatened they would reappear in court; see *Magnalia*, 1: 189, for the greater fear of ghosts. IM had said the difference between ghosts and specters was unclear; *IP*, 204. On Burroughs's wives, David L. Greene, "The Third Wife of the Rev. George Burroughs," *American Genealogist* 56 (1980): 43–45.

130 "a child of God": R, 243–44.

130 the devil promised: I am indebted to David Hall for a copy of his unpublished September 12, 2012, Huntington Library talk.

131 For the spelling: Upham, *Salem Witchcraft*, 143; Roach, *Six Women of Salem*, 29; "sublimely unaware": Henry Alexander, "The Language of the Salem Witchcraft Trials," *American Speech* 3 (June 1928): 392; Grund, "Editing the Salem Witchcraft Records," 158.

131 "did most grievously": R, 336–37.

131–132 tireless industry: CM, *Ornaments, Eureka: The Virtuous Woman Found;* the "prince and judge": Michael Walzer, *The Revolution of the Saints: A Study in the Origins of Radical Politics* (London: Weidenfeld, 1965), 190; "Well; and what if I am": CM in Burr, 270. Margaret Rule detains the young men, Burr, 327; "come to the gallows": Cited in Michael Hall, *The Last American Puritan: The Life of Increase Mather* (Middletown, CT: Wesleyan University Press, 1988), 143. "Charm the children": Cotton Mather, *Small Offers*, 48; "penal and wrathful": *SPN*, 117. Steven Mintz, *Huck's Raft: A History of American Childhood* (Cambridge, MA: Harvard University Press, 2004), 7–32. Also see Thompson, "The Case of Thomas Danforth," 34.

132 work diligently: The 1680 mother is cited in Earle, *Child Life*, 100.

132 "When the devil finds": CM, "A Discourse on the Power and Malice of the Devils," in *MP*, 15.

133 "put away childish": Ross W. Beales Jr., "In Search of the Historical Child," *American Quarterly* 27 (October, 1975): 384.

133 Betty's first yelp of terror: SS *Diary*, 1: 345–46, 348–49, 355, 359–60. Dunton on the furnishing, *Dunton's Letters*, 254. Stannard, "Death and the Puritan Child," 473. Betty would go on to marry, bear seven children, and die at thirty-four.

134–135 "I had rather": Thomas White, *A Little Book for Little Children* (Boston: 1702), 13, Faber, "Puritan Criminals," 91. Or as James Janeway had it, "They are not too little to die, they are not too little to go to hell." For the Sewall maid: *SS Diary*, 2: 731. For "that she was in the dark": *MP*, 46. Apocalyptic scenes could sound oddly like black Sabbaths, as women flew into the wilderness to wrangle with mythical beasts, Stout, *New England Soul*, 48. The blood-vomiting dragons: Cited in Joyce, *Printing and Society in Early America*, 42.

135 "To fail to be": Stannard, *Puritan Way of Death*, 70.

135 "lively and pungent": *CM Diary*, 2: 359. He fretted that the admonitions were not pungent enough. From the evidence, the children had more occasion to fear their birthdays than their father.

135 Indians did childhood differently: Peter Charles Hoffer, *Law and People in Colonial America* (Baltimore: Johns Hopkins University Press, 1998), 71; Mintz, *Huck's Raft*, 8; James Axtell, "The White Indians of Colonial America," in *Colonial America: Essays in Politics and Social Development*, ed. Stanley N. Katz and John M. Murrin (New York: Knopf, 1983), 43. "Let not English": Cotton Mather, *Small Offers*, 44; Stannard, "Death and the Puritan Child," 476; James. E. Kences, "Some Unexplored Relationships of Essex County Witchcraft to the Indian Wars of 1675 and 1689," *EIHC* 120 (July 1984): 186.

135 "entertain any frightful": Samuel Mather, "The Home Life of Cotton Mather," in *A Library of American Literature*, ed. Edmund Stedman and Ellen Hutchinson (New York: Charles Webster, 1891).

136 grisly tales: See Kathryn Zabelle Derounian, "The Publication, Promotion and Distribution of Mary Rowlandson's Indian Captivity Narrative in the Seventeenth Century," *Early American Literature* 23 (1988): 239–61. David Hall thinks these tales had seeped into the groundwater; interview with Hall, October 19, 2012.

136 Samuel Sewall dreamed: SS *Diary*, 1: 328.

137 Sewall children wept: Ibid., 145. Mary Rowlandson could not bear to be in the room with a corpse. On children and corpses, Michael MacDonald's highly original *Mystical Bedlam* (Cambridge: Cambridge University Press, 1981), 76.

137 reordered affections and complicated successions: RFQC, 8: 355, 424, 430; "Autobiography of the Rev. John Barnard," 179.

138 "art, craft, and mystery": Mintz, *Huck's Raft*, 33.

138 "Binding out": See Katz and Murrin, *Colonial America,* 136; Stannard, "Death and the Puritan Child," 466; Thompson, "Adolescent Culture," 129. Some aspects of the indenture agreements had a familiar ring: The apprentice was to serve his master faithfully, keep his secrets, obey his lawful commandments. In turn, the master agreed to provide the apprentice with "sufficient meat, drink, apparel, lodging, and washing." Those agreements were for seven years; diabolical ones were often said to last for six or eight.

138 "Puberty," it has been said: Adam Phillips, *Going Sane* (New York: Harper, 2007), 121. Demos notes, in *A Little Commonwealth: Family Life in Plymouth Colony* (New York: Oxford, 1999), 145, that a NE childhood was short-lived and that no seventeenth-century word existed for that period between puberty and adulthood.

138 a full inventory of harassments: Beales, "In Search of the Historical Child," 398; Faber, "Puritan Criminals," 101; RFQC, 8: 103; RFQC, 2: 238.

139 "A married man": William E. Nelson, "The Persistence of Puritan Law: Massachusetts, 1660–1760," *Willamette Law Review* (2013): 389.

139 "She is so fat": Cited in Alice Morse Earle, *Customs and Fashions in Old New England* (New York: Scribner's, 1896), 101. See also Faber, "Puritan Criminals"; RFQC, 7: 419; Peter Thacher diary, P-186, MHS; Towner, "'A Fondness for Freedom,'" 208.

139 "for they would know not": E. T. Fisher, *The Report of a French Protestant Refugee in Boston, 1687* (Boston, 1868), 21.

140 "this orphan plantation": Hull, *Diaries,* 130; Bowle, *Diary of John Evelyn,* 235. See Stout, *New England Soul,* 105–30, on the insubordination of the 1690s. Richard S. Dunn is incisive on the settlers' attempts to retain their dignity while following orders, *Puritans and Yankees: The Winthrop Dynasty of New England* (Princeton, NJ: Princeton University Press, 1962).

140 "disobedient, disobliging": Joshua Scottow, *Old Men's Tears for Their Own Declensions* (Boston: 1691), 12.

140 one of his servants had been stealing: RFQC, 7: 44–50.

141 Ministers devoted sermons: Towner, "'A Fondness for Freedom,'" 205–6; Cotton Mather, *A Good Master Well Served* (Boston, 1696), 5, 52.

141 "Pray sooth": From Sarah Knight's journal, in Miller and Johnson, *The Puritans,* 2: 434. For the best account of Puritan hooligans and practical jokers, Thompson, "Adolescent Culture," 134–35. The ideal adolescent—deferential, disciplined, sober, and chaste—remained a mythical creature.

141 "exceedingly addicted": RFQC, 7: 42–55.

142 "who were much given": *Publications of the Colonial Society of Massachusetts,* vol. 22 (Boston: Colonial Society, 1920), 274.

142 "could not tell ink" and "upon her head": RFQC, 1: 390; RFQC, 4: 108. Koehler, *Search for Power,* is best on the misbehavior; also see Ulrich, *Good Wives,* 184–202. A "flustered Cotton Mather": CM Diary, 1: 457. The "lousy slut": RFQC, 2: 10. They landed in court with regularity: N.E.H. Hull, *Female Felons: Women and Serious Crime in Colonial Massachusetts* (Urbana: University of Illinois Press, 1987). They managed to suffocate: R, 256–57, 372.

143 "has a better faculty": SS *Diary*, 1: 496. The biblical precedent: Cotton Mather, *Small Offers*, 30, 44. A group of Ipswich men petitioned: Winslow, *Meetinghouse Hill*, 128.

144 Cotton Mather said she did: With nine daughters on whom he doted, CM devoted a great deal of time to pondering women and their worth. They were no more evil or immoral than their male counterparts, though he could not help but note that they gossiped avidly and tended to be more lewd and vain. He knew however who filled his pews. Adapting Luther in *A Good Master Well Served*, 34, he preached that "the work of a poor milk maid, if it is done with an exercise of grace, is more glorious than the triumphs of Caesar."

144 the Holy Ghost: Hall, *Worlds of Wonder*, 41; "It amazes me": Oberholzer, *Delinquent Saints*, 228; "in a worse condition": Cited in Elizabeth Reis, *Damned Women: Sinners and Witches in Puritan New England* (Ithaca, NY: Cornell University Press, 1999), 43. CM practically reveled in his depravity. As he explained: "By loathing of himself continually, and being very sensible of what are his own loathsome circumstances, a Christian does what is very pleasing to Heaven." Women blamed their souls: See Reis, *Damned Women*, 121–64, and Reis, "Confess or Deny? What's a 'Witch' to Do?," *OAH Magazine of History* (July 2003): 11–13. She makes the fine point that in conversion narratives women tended to focus more on their vile nature while men cited drinking or gambling. For "ready to draw up," Peter Thacher diary, P-186, MHS. The non-eater, David Hall, ed., *Puritans in the New World: A Critical Anthology* (Princeton, NJ: Princeton University Press, 2004), 131.

144 The captivity narrative: E-mail with David Hall, December 27, 2013; Alden T. Vaughan and Edward W. Clark, eds., *Puritans Among the Indians: Accounts of Captivity and Redemption* (Cambridge, MA: Harvard University Press, 1981).

145 kept a horse saddled: Harriet S. Tapley, *Chronicles of Danvers* (Danvers, MA: Danvers Historical Society, 1923), 28.

146 Dorcas Hoar: R, 225–27, 593–94, for the hearing; R, 315, for stamping her feet. See also Barbara Ritter Dailey, " 'Where Thieves Break Through and Steal': John Hale Versus Dorcas Hoar," *EIHC* 128 (1992): 255–69. The elf-lock is from Lawson, appendix to *Christ's Fidelity*, 112.

147 Susannah Martin: See Karlsen, *The Devil*, 89–95; R, 228–29, 256, 392, 426; RFQC, 4: 129–35; Jesse Souweine, "Word of Mouth" (thesis, Cornell, 1996), 53–62.

147 "No, I do not think": A number of suspects stopped short of diagnosing witchcraft. Wilmott Reed would say only that the afflicted "were in a sad condition"; R, 209, 344.

149 Sarah Bibber: R, 242–43.

149 "or the other" to "If ever there were": SPN, 202–3. CM would also evoke the Baxter passage.

150 "Well, what will" to "take your prisoner": RFQC, 9: 48–49.

151–152 grandson of a Cambridge-educated: On Burroughs, Gilbert Upton, *The Devil and George Burroughs* (London: Wordwright, 1997); Mary Beth Norton, "George Burroughs and the Girls from Casco: The Maine Roots of Salem Witchcraft," *Maine History* 40 (Winter 2001/2002): 258–77; Edward E. Bourne, *The History of Wells and Kennebunk* (Portland: B. Thurston, 1875), 171–78. GB appears to have preached for IM in 1675. On

Burroughs and Church, see Francis Baylies, *An Historical Memoir of the Colony of New Plymouth* (Boston: Wiggin and Lunt, 1866), 75–78. For the raids, Lincoln, *Narratives of the Indian Wars,* 218–40; Benjamin Bullivant journal, *Proceedings of the MHS,* vol. 16 (1878), 103–8. For the Casco 1690 raid, John Usher and Colonel Lidget correspondence, CO 5/855, nos. 100, 101, PRO.

151 "could after tedious": Usher to the Earl of Nottingham, October 20, 1692, John Usher Papers.

153 "It is taken": Roland L. Warren, *Loyal Dissenter: The Life and Times of Robert Pike* (Lanham, MD: University Press of America, 1992), 167. As London heard it, Thomas Danforth informed the poor Maine settlers that if the Lord Jesus could not help them, he could not; Bullivant letter, April 11, 1690, CO 5/855, no. 103, PRO.

153 They were well armed: Josselyn, in Baker and Reid, *New England Knight,* 8.

153–154 "pillars of smoke" to "pluck you up": Burroughs letter of January 27, 1692, Massachusetts Archives Collection, vol. 37, 259, Massachusetts State Archives. See also Kences, "Some Unexplored Relationships," 190.

154 "barbarously murdered": Captain Lloyd letter of January 27, 1692, Massachusetts Archives Collection, vol. 38, 257, Massachusetts State Archives.

154 encouraged the enemy: *Andros Tracts,* 1: 176–78.

155 "no peace, order or safety": Bullivant letter, July 1690, CO 5/855, no. 103, PRO.

155 careful case against Burroughs: R, 241. The documentation for the preliminary examination is scant. Some of the charges against Burroughs may have surfaced only at the August trial, though the hearing notes indicate that all the themes were touched upon in May. Trask points out that some testimony was rewritten; R, 47. On the back of his account, SP scrawled a series of scriptural passages about purification.

156 "he was a very sharp": R, 246–47.

156 "My God makes known": R, 532. The Sarah Burroughs divorce, *Records of the Court of Assistants of the Colony of Massachusetts Bay* (Boston, 1901), 3: 146.

158 "an amazing" to "cannot name it": R, 241.

158 "a very puny": CM in Burr, 219.

158 "None of us could do": R, 249.

159–160 George Jacobs hobbled: R, 251–52. The location of the hearing is not clear. See Matti Rissanen, "Power and Changing Roles in Salem Witch Trials," *Studia Neophilologica* 84 (2012): 119–29; Rissanen, "'Candy No Witch, Barbados'"; Rissanen, "Salem Witchcraft Papers as Evidence of Early American English," *English Linguistics* (2003): 84–114. On the trespassing animals: RFQC, 5: 428.

160 another wizard nervously quipped: R, 288. It was John Willard.

160 "Hollowed be thy name": Calef in Burr, 347.

161 "I verily believe": R, 254 or 256 or 257; David L. Greene, "Salem Witches II: George Jacobs," *American Genealogist* 58 (April 1982): 65–76.

161 Mary Warren, the Procter maid, waffled: R, 356–57. Her tongue protruded from her mouth: R, 268–69.

162 "altogether false" to "believe her": R, 355.

162 Salem farmer Bray Wilkins: R, 527–28. Wilkins would live another decade, dying at ninety-two. The villagers complained that SP had recruited Mary Walcott and Abigail as visionaries; SP swore to an account Mercy Lewis had provided at a bedside as well, however. The idea that Willard balked at arrests originates with Upham.

163 "if he could": R, 281–82, 295, 296, 297.

163–164 "What do you say" to "really believe it": R, 286–88. On the proliferation of family in the Willard case, Rosenthal, *Salem Story*, 118–19.

164 "suburb of hell": Dunton, *Dunton's Letters*, 119. CM wrote down the impious household as the very suburb of hell in his *Batteries upon the Kingdom of the Devil* (1695), 62. A man had "better live in a prison, in a dungeon, than in such a family!"

VI. A SUBURB OF HELL

On the politics, Richard A. Johnson's very fine *Adjustment to Empire* (New Brunswick, NJ: Rutgers University Press, 1981); Owen Stanwood, *The Empire Reformed: English America in the Age of the Glorious Revolution* (Philadelphia: University of Pennsylvania Press, 2011); William Pencak, *War, Politics, and Revolution in Provincial Massachusetts* (Boston: Northeastern University Press, 1981); Viola Florence Barnes, *The Dominion of New England* (New York: Ungar, 1960); Edward Randolph, *Documents and Letters*. For excellent portraits of colonial administration, Gertrude Ann Jacobsen, *William Blathwayt: A Late Seventeenth-Century English Administrator* (New Haven, CT: Yale University Press, 1932), and Michael Hall, *Edward Randolph and the American Colonies*. Especially astute on the intercharter period—and the new, destabilizing role of the people in civic affairs—is Breen, *Puritans and Adventurers*, 81–105. The coup served the Puritan orthodoxy well. It also introduced them to an empowered populace, many of whom expected to make their voices heard.

165 "Hell seems a great deal": Flannery O'Connor, *A Prayer Journal* (New York: Farrar, Straus and Giroux, 2013), 6.

165 What could not yet happen. While there is general agreement that Governor Dudley Bradstreet held off, there is no hard evidence that he did so. The delay certainly allowed allegations to accumulate. See Benjamin C. Ray, "The Salem Witch Mania," *Journal of the American Academy of Religion* (2010): 5.

166 "between government and no government": Calef in Burr, 349.

166 "Salem is one of the few": Arthur Miller, introduction, *The Crucible* (New York: Penguin, 1995), ix.

166 Boston's majestic harbor: For Boston, see Samuel Maverick, "Account of New England," *Proceedings of the MHS*, vol. 1 (1884), 231–51; Josselyn, *New-England's Rarities*, 32; Fisher, *Report of a French Protestant Refugee*. For the lost cow: SS *Diary*, 1: 63; for hogs in the street: Bridenbaugh, *Cities in the Wilderness*, 56.

166 "shaken and shattered": *Magnalia*, 1: 183.

166 "thousand perplexities": CM, *The Present State*, 35.

166–167 The rugged forty-one-year-old: On the militiamen, Richard Trask interview, April 1, 2013. The best source on Phips is Baker and Reid's meticulously researched volume *New England Knight*. See also Viola F. Barnes, "The Rise of William Phips," *New England Quarterly* (July 1928): 271–94, and Barnes, "Phippius Maximus," *New England Quarterly* (October 1928): 532–53, from which come the Indian divers, and T. H. Breen, *The Character of a Good Ruler* (New York: W. W. Norton, 1974). For Keynes, see *A Treatise on Money* (London: Macmillan, 1930), vol. 2, 151. Philip F. Gura is excellent on CM's mythologizing of the governor; "Cotton Mather's Life of Phips," *New England Quarterly* 50 (September 1977): 440–57. For the Golden Fleece comparison: SS *Diary*, 1: 172. The arrival: Jacob Melyen letter book, May 25, 1692, AAS.

167 "did not care a turd": John Knepp journal, Egerton Ms. 2526, 5r, 9r, British Library.

168 "dropped from the machine": *Magnalia*, 1: 184.

168 "distressed, enfeebled": Cited in Silverman, *Life and Times of Cotton Mather*, 78. The charter was vacated on October 23, 1684; news that the colony no longer had one reached its governor on April 17, 1685. See Jacobsen, *William Blathwayt*, 128.

168 the delayed rite: *Magnalia*, 1: 165.

168 a clerk's art: Tamara Plakins Thornton, *Handwriting in America: A Cultural History* (New Haven, CT: Yale University Press, 1996), 39.

169 "a shameful and cowardly": Cited in Baker and Reid, *New England Knight*, 113.

169 "poor people": Benjamin Bullivant letter, May 19, 1690, CO 5/855, no. 94, PRO.

170 "a knot of people": *MP*, appendix 8.

170 "alien incubus": Cited in Johnson, *Adjustment to Empire*, 93.

171 "an unthankful murmuring": IM, *The Great Blessing of Primitive Counsellors* (Boston, 1693), 19–21.

171 "a people fit only": CM, *Midnight Cry*, 63.

171 "vultures and harpies" to ""breaches in God's hedge": CM, *Optanda*, 70–87. He recycled the "spit of reproach" from *The Present State*, 12.

172 One prominent New Englander: It was Elisha Cooke, far from alone in repudiating a document that reimposed royal authority.

172 "that the people": Nottingham to Blathwayt, Add. Ms. 37991, fol. 138r, British Library; IM to Nottingham, June 23, 1692, CO/5/571, no. 7, PRO.

173 "I found this province": Phips to William Blathwayt, October 12, 1692, R, 686.

173 Sweden's earlier scourge: That account, which reached NE via Glanvill, featured a more classically configured Miltonian devil who played harp for the children and arranged for dancing, feasting, and sex. See the English summary of Birgitta Lagerlöf-Génetay, *De Svenska Haxprocessernas Utbrottsskede 1668–1671* (Stockholm: Almquist and Wiksell, 1990); Thomas Wright, *Narratives of Sorcery and Magic* (London: Bentley, 1851), 2: 244–60. Wright notes that those elements derive from earlier French and German cases. Most of the visionaries were boys.

173 "with a remarkable smile": CM to Richards, May 31, 1692, Cotton Mather Letters, John J. Burns Library, Boston College.

173 "by reason of witchcrafts": IM, "The Autobiography of Increase Mather," May 14 entry, 344. The word "possession" does not turn up in the testimony until seventeen-year-old Margaret Jacobs used it in January 1693.

174 Carrier jostled a twelve-year-old: R, 510–11. The disembodied voice: CM in Burr, 243.

174 round up the extended family of George Jacobs: Calef in Burr, 371. On Jacobs, Greene, "Salem Witches II."

174 nineteen different afflictions: The tally is Norton's, *In the Devil's Snare*, 174.

175 Mercy Lewis hovered near death: R, 311–12, 624.

175 "enemy he had": R, 309.

175 "to sink that happy": *WOW*, 21.

175 Nathaniel Cary: R, 309–311. Bernard Rosenthal suspects that Elizabeth Cary may actually have been Hannah, as Upham suggested in "Salem Witchcraft and Cotton Mather," *The Historical Magazine*, September 1869. That would make sense of several dating discrepancies—as would Rosenthal's theory that two Cary women, Elizabeth and Hannah, were accused; Rosenthal e-mail, May 21, 2015. For an earlier Cary suit, see *Records of the Court of Assistants*, 1: 106. For the generous liquor allowances, Gildrie, "Taverns and Popular Culture," 178. For Tituba and John's presumed marriage, Rosenthal, "Tituba," 48.

176 the touch test: Brattle in Burr, 171; R, 34; Lawson, appendix to *Christ's Fidelity*, 102.

178 "to sit in the stocks": Cited in Adam Jay Hirsch, *The Rise of the Penitentiary: Prisons and Punishments in Early America* (New Haven, CT: Yale University Press, 1992), 34. See also Alice Morse Earle, *Curious Punishments of Bygone Days* (New York: Book League of America, 1929), 30.

179 facility announced itself: Randolph to Robert Chaplin, October 28, 1689, CO 5/855, no. 46, PRO; Beattie, *Crime and the Courts*, 299; R, 311; RFQC, 8: 335–57; Perley, *History of Salem*, vol. 3, 241. For the prison visit, Calef in Burr, 259–60. The released prisoners: RFQC, 7: 243.

179 "the fierceness": Dunton, *Dunton's Letters*, 120. The rain in the cell: Randolph to Robert Chaplin, October 28, 1689, CO 5/855, no. 103, PRO.

180 "a noisome place": RFQC, 2: 227; "almost poisoned": RFQC 8, 335. The ship captain who had jailed the sailor came regularly to rail at him at the top of his lungs. Fourteen weeks in a freezing, fetid prison was bad enough, the youngster complained. Did he really have to hear his father denounced in the street outside as "an Anabaptistical quaking rogue" in league with the devil?

180 William Dounton: Esther I. Wik, "The Jailkeeper at Salem in 1692," *EIHC* 111 (1975): 221–27; RFQC, 8: 31. Many suspects made the tour of prisons. Sarah Wilds, the constable's mother, spent April in Salem, to be removed for two months to Boston and afterward confined at Ipswich, before being moved again to Salem. The family was responsible for the costs of those guarded trips. Dounton was the official who met with a warming pan when collecting the minister's salary. He himself had attacked a fellow Salemite who resented his many appointments and opposed his nomination to yet another. It was probably no coincidence that he was relieved of the post shortly after the trials.

181 Phips established a special court: R, 322. A quorum of five would suffice, stipulated the order, so long as Stoughton, Richards, or Gedney was present.

181 One Scotswoman preferred to burn: MacKay, *The Witch Mania*, 505. See Thompson, *Cambridge Cameos*, 96, for the puddle-drinking.

182 Civic leaders produced civic leaders: Kenneth A. Lockridge and Alan Kreider, "The Evolution of Massachusetts Town Government," *William and Mary Quarterly* 23 (October 1966): 566; Gildrie, "Salem Society," 199. Samuel Sewall would be elected to the Massachusetts council thirty-three times.

182 "people of the best": Phips to the privy council, October 12, 1692, R, 686. On the Salem justices, Benjamin C. Ray, "Satan's War Against the Covenant in Salem Village, 1692," *New England Quarterly* 80 (March 2007): 72. As Baker points out in *A Storm of Witchcraft*, 180, Sergeant alone was not a substantial landowner. At least several of the same men presided over the Goodwin case; Norton, *In the Devil's Snare*, 382n; e-mail with Elizabeth Bouvier, May 5, 2015.

183 "all the councilors": *CM Diary*, 1: 148.

183–184 John Alden: Kences, "Some Unexplored Relationships," 191; Hull, *Diaries*, 159. Interview with Richard Johnson, August 20, 2014; Louise Breen, *Transgressing the Bounds*, 197–208.

184 "honest and lawful": R, 332. For their experience, Langbein, "The Criminal Trial," 276–77.

185 the Alden interrogation: R, 334. Norton, *In the Devil's Snare*, provides the estimate of the frontier trips, 186. For Alden and the munitions, Baker, *A Storm of Witchcraft*, 144–45. Alden in 1690 requisitioned Marblehead's cannon, leaving the town vulnerable. For the instructions with the "bears and wolves," Robinson, *The Devil Discovered*, 38. On Alden see also Louise Breen, *Transgressing the Bounds*, 199–206.

185–186 "They will dissemble" to "you will not believe": R, 335–36.

186 "she should be Queen": CM in Burr, 244.

186 "Staring in people's faces": R, 334.

187 "had always looked" to "these say of me": R, 334; similarly, Brattle in Burr, 170. For Alden and the Indian captives, *Magnalia*, 2: 360.

187 "I have beheld": R, 348.

188 It was not unusual: Oberholzer, *Delinquent Saints*, 215–16; Haskins, *Law and Authority*, 61. Nor was it surprising that Richards should do so. Along with Gedney and Stoughton, he had served on the court that presided over the Elizabeth Morse witchcraft case eleven years earlier. She was found guilty; reprieved; retried; reprieved a second time. There was cause for confusion.

188 Willard affirmed: Samuel Sewall, notes on sermons, May 29 entry, Ms. N-905, MHS; Mark Peterson, " 'Ordinary Preaching,' " *EIHC* 129 (1992): 95–98.

189 "murmuring frenzies" to "lisping witches": CM to Richards, May 31, 1692, Cotton Mather Letters, John J. Burns Library, Boston College. Already the colonists marked the date of the November 5, 1605, Gunpowder Plot. It would give way in the eighteenth century to effigies of the pope and the devil being paraded around Boston

and torched. Richards was not the first to confer with CM about Salem; there is evidence that Lawson already had and unmistakable hints that SP had, too.

190 Henry IV: Fox, *Science and Justice,* 80.

191 consulted precedent in witchcraft cases: Hale in Burr, 415–16.

192 "If there were a witch": Calef in Burr, 383.

192 A school occupied: For courtroom geography and process, see Trask on legal procedures, R, 44–63; Martha J. McNamara, "In the Face of the Court" *Winterthur Portfolio* 36 (Summer 2001): 125–39; William D. Northend, "Address Before the Essex Bar Association," *EIHC* 22 (1885): 276; interview with Richard Trask, January 21, 2015; interview with J. M. Beattie, September 9, 2014. Generally on the courtroom attitudes and procedures: Langbein, *Origins of Adversary Criminal Trial;* Langbein, "The Criminal Trial"; Beattie, *Crime and the Courts;* Edgar J. McManus, *Law and Liberty in Early New England: Criminal Justice and Due Process* (Amherst: University of Massachusetts Press, 1993); Murrin, "Magistrates, Sinners, and a Precarious Liberty: Trial by Jury in Seventeenth-Century New England," in Hall, *Saints and Revolutionaries,* 152–206. Interviews with John Murrin, December 11, 2014, and Richard Trask, November 29, 2012.

192 "that according to your best": R, 356.

193 "hurt, tortured, afflicted": R, 334.

193 witch's teats: Louis J. Kern, "Eros, the Devil, and the Cunning Woman," *EIHC* 129 (1993): 20, 31. Koehler, *Search for Power,* 84–85, notes that the language of female genitalia is altogether missing from Puritan literature. A panel of Connecticut women: Godbeer, *Escaping Salem,* 95. The woman at the gallows: Hall, *Witch-Hunting,* 79.

193 The heart that passes for a stomach: Watson, *Angelical Conjunction,* 141. On the literature of witch's marks, see Pavlac, *Witch Hunts.* Rosenthal, *Salem Story,* 77, thinks at least some of the women who examined the six suspects refused to sign anything, knowing what was at stake.

193 A Quaker woman: Thomas Maule, *Truth Held Forth and Maintained* (Boston, 1695), 214.

194 "a preternatural excrescence": R, 362.

194 William Stoughton called: Beattie, *Crime and the Courts,* 332; Langbein, *Origins of Adversary Criminal Trial,* 308; RFQC, 4: 153; interview with J. M. Beattie, September 9, 2014. CM on the trial, Burr, 223–29.

194 honest attorneys: Randolph to Povey, January 24, 1687, in Thomas Hutchinson, *A Collection of Original Papers Relative to the History of the Massachusetts Bay* (Boston: Thomas and John Fleet, 1769), 557.

196 caused an apple to fly: R, 367; the son of the miller: R, 331.

197 "smooth, flattering": R, 369.

197 "You devil" to "me and you": R, 368.

198 "answer was thought": Charles J. Hoadly, ed., *Records of the Colony and Plantation of New Haven* (Hartford, CT: Case, Tiffany, 1857), 260.

198 Bishop's trial proceeded smoothly and swiftly: Langbein, "The Criminal Trial," 282–85; Northend, "Address Before the Essex Bar Association," 258; interview with J. M. Beattie, September 29, 2014.

199 "There was little": CM in Burr, 223.

199 A seventeenth-century magistrate: Brattle in Burr, 187. See R, 35; even Bernard rejected spectral evidence as a basis for conviction. It would be used in England in 1690 and 1695 but—largely discredited—did not secure convictions.

199 "on diverse other days": R, 394.

200 Bishop appears to have been confused: Rosenthal, *Salem Story,* 72–81.

200 Nurse could account: R, 413–14.

200 "detestable arts": R, 366. The wording was standard.

200 Ann Dolliver: R, 390. For Dolliver's husband leaving Massachusetts, John J. Babson, *History of the Town of Gloucester* (Gloucester, MA: Procter Brothers, 1860), 81.

201 "crazed in her understanding": John Higginson Sr. to his son, August 31, 1692, Higginson Family Papers.

201 "Not with intent": R. 390.

201–202 "soft words but hard": Dunton, *Dunton's Letters,* 255. For Higginson on drinking, see his letter to the court, June 25, 1678, in *EIHC* 43 (1907): 180. It was probably he who warned the Salem villagers in 1687, when they were at odds over Lawson, "If you will unreasonably trouble yourselves, we pray you not any further to trouble us." The angry, obstinate Baptists: Hull, *Diaries,* 226.

202 "under the infirmities": Higginson in Burr, 401.

202 "and there cause her": R, 394. On the uncommonly severe phrasing, e-mail with Elizabeth Bouvier, April 30, 2015.

202–203 on the morning of June 10: Interview with Richard Trask, January 21, 2015. The five-syllable words: Earle, *Child Life,* 29. For details of earlier executions on which this one is based, see Hall, *Worlds of Wonder,* 178–84 (which includes the execution sermons, as well as the point about the suspenseful last-minute admissions); Dunton in Miller and Johnson, *The Puritans,* 2: 415–19; John Rogers, *Death the Certain Wages of Sin to the Impenitent* (Boston, 1701). At a later execution, all was "hurry and confusion, racket and noise, praying and oaths," according to Robert Ellis Cahill, *New England's Cruel and Unusual Punishments* (Salem, MA: Old Saltbox, 1994).

203 "in a frame extremely": *MP,* 63.

204 "and turned the knot": John Winthrop, *Winthrop's Journal* (New York: Scribner's, 1908), vol. 2, 319. The blow of an ax: Jacob Milborne execution, *Collections of the New-York Historical Society* (1868): 425–26. The agonized cries: SS *Diary,* 1: 509.

204 Corwin arranged for the corpse: R, 395. Roach thinks Corwin crossed out the line because someone claimed the body; *Six Women of Salem,* 252. Puritan interments were simple and in unconsecrated ground. For the site of the burial, Marilynne Roach, *Gallows and Graves* (Watertown, MA: Sassafras Grove, 1977); Sidney Perley, "Where the Salem Witches Were Hanged," *EIHC* 57 (January 1921): 1–19. According to Lawson, graves for a later hanging were dug in advance.

204 "painful, grotesque": Saul Bellow, *Herzog* (New York: Penguin, 1964), 23.

205 "a vexation to herself" to "recovered their senses": CM in Burr, 249.

205 "a formidable crew": *Magnalia,* 2: 534. That was the attack during which the Wells women fired at the enemy or, as CM proudly declared, "took up the Amazonian stroke."

205 "a very doleful time": *CM Diary,* 1: 150.

VII. NOW THEY SAY THERE IS ABOVE SEVEN HUNDRED IN ALL

206 "Nature has given": Samuel Johnson to the Reverend Dr. Taylor, August 18, 1763, in *The Letters of Samuel Johnson,* ed. Bruce Redford (Princeton, NJ: Princeton University Press, 1992), 1: 228.

206 "a relatively spontaneous bicker": Langbein, *Origins of Adversary Criminal Trial,* 253. See also Murrin, "Magistrates, Sinners, and a Precarious Liberty," *Saints and Revolutionaries,* 152–206; interview with Richard Trask, April 1, 2014; interview with J. M. Beattie, September 9, 2014.

206 "If you sued a lot": William Offutt Jr., cited in Hoffer, *Law and People,* 78. Offutt was speaking of Delaware Quakers.

207 "I am no thief": Langbein, *Origins of Adversary Criminal Trial,* 57.

207 "will pry": Bernard, *Guide to Grand-Jury Men,* 244.

207–208 "much harm and little good": SS *Diary,* 1: 277. For the Mather contretemps, ibid., 454–55; for the pardoned pirate, ibid., 250.

208 Willard's afternoon sermon: See Peterson, "'Ordinary Preaching,'" 95–98. Also on Willard, Stephen Robbins, "Samuel Willard and the Spectres of God's Wrathful Lion," *New England Quarterly* 60 (December 1987): 601; Brown, "The Salem Witchcraft Trials."

209 "now they say": Joshua Brodbent to Francis Nicholson, June 21, 1692, CO 5/1037, no. 112, fol. 227r, PRO.

209 "he has left the court": Brattle in Burr, 184. The facts are elusive, as no commission for the Court of Oyer and Terminer has come down to us.

210 "she was a witch": RFQC, 3: 420. The point about defamation is from Thompson, "'Holy Watchfulness,'" 504–22.

210 To fail to report: McManus, *Law and Liberty,* 68. Thompson, "'Holy Watchfulness,'" 521, makes the point that turning in a suspected witch shielded one from accusations of complicity. See Weisman, *Witchcraft, Magic, and Religion,* 204–8, for a chart of prior defamation suits involving witchcraft. David Hall thinks the lack of defamation actions indicates a shock to the system; interview with Hall, October 19, 2012.

211 "The Return of Several Ministers Consulted": June 15, 1692, B&N, 118–19. CM's original is in the Cotton Mather Letters, John J. Burns Library, Boston College. He would later claim to have offered to take in some of the afflicted, as he had Martha Goodwin; he may have done so now.

211 "that I should be": *CM Diary,* 1: 311. Mather wrote half of the published Massachusetts sermons to the end of 1692, before he had yet turned thirty.

212 "Several persons": R, 399; Milborne petition, Massachusetts council minutes, CO 5/785 PRO. On the Milborne brothers, David William Voorhees, "'Fanatiks' and 'Fifth Monarchists': The Milborne Family in the Seventeenth-Century Atlantic World," *New York Genealogical and Biographical Record* 129 (July 1998): 174–82.

212 "seditious and scandalous" to "public justice": R, 399.

213 Thomas Newton outlined his case: R, 409–13.

214 "The same evidence": The observation was Cary's, R, 311.

215 "all the delectable things": CM in Burr, 236.

215–216 "that some she-devil" to "creature in the world": CM in Burr, 232–34. Even those who knew Martin and had reason to be well inclined toward her did not rise to her defense. Thomas, *Religion and the Decline of Magic*, 649, cites a seventeenth-century observer on the vicious circle.

216–217 Topsfield's Elizabeth How: CM in Burr, 237–40; see also Philip Graystone, *Elizabeth Jackson of Rowley* (Hull, UK: Lampada Press, 1993). "If you are a witch": R, 438. Equal numbers of witnesses spoke for and against her.

217 "No, never" to "she is a witch": R, 373–74.

217 when Sarah Wilds came: Years earlier her stepsons had been accused of witchcraft as well; two stepdaughters soon would be. She had been whipped for fornication in 1649; RFQC, 1: 179.

218 "almost saw revenge": R, 462–63.

218 "as the child unborn": R, 349.

219 John Putnam Sr. seems to have been: R, 435, and R, 429. A. P. Putnam, *Rebecca Nurse and Her Friends* (Boston: Thomas Todd, 1894), 1–38.

220 "the most ancient, skillful": R, 412–13.

220 "the jury of women": R, 380.

220–221 the jury returned: Calef in Burr, 358. We know little of how a seventeenth-century jury worked. They did not proceed by ballot or formal vote; they did not always excuse themselves from the courtroom to deliberate; the majority seem to have deferred to the foreman; Beattie, *Crime and the Courts*, 396. On asking a jury to re-deliberate, e-mail with John Langbein, March 10, 2014. The opposite happened in Connecticut; see Godbeer, *Escaping Salem*, 119.

221 "I could not tell" to "evidence against her": R, 465.

221–222 "What? Do these persons": Calef in Burr, 359. On accomplices, interview with J. M. Beattie, September 9, 2014.

222 "hard of hearing": R, 465. The devil whispered at her ear: Lawson, appendix to *Christ's Fidelity*, 110; see also Thomas, *Religion and the Decline of Magic*, 546, on the roar in the courtroom.

222 nothing on paper: Cited by Trask, R, 53.

222–223 sentence of excommunication: David C. Brown, "The Keys of the Kingdom: Excommunication in Colonial Massachusetts," *New England Quarterly* 67 (December 1994): 531–66. For the language, David D. Hall, ed., *The Antinomian Controversy, 1636–1638* (Durham, NC: Duke University Press, 1990), 388; Demos, *Remarkable Providences*, 277; Hall, *Witch-Hunting*, 89, on Ann Hibbins; CM Diary 1: 180. Interview with David Hall, May 21, 2014.

223 late-summer meeting: *Proceedings of the MHS*, vol. 17 (1879), 268.

224 "struck dumb, deaf, blind": June 10, 1692, letter appended to Lawson, *A Further Account*.

224 "was mistaken": Calef in Burr, 360. She may have meant John Willard.

225 To the job Stoughton brought: On Stoughton, Convers Francis, *An Historical Sketch of Watertown* (Cambridge: Metcalf, 1830), 59; SS Diary, 1: 148; *Records of the First Church at Dorchester* (Boston: George H. Ellis, 1801), 50–65; Northend, "Address Before the

Essex Bar Association," 258n. A respected jurist, Stoughton had in 1680 reviewed and revised NE law. The assertion that there were but three qualified men in all of Massachusetts: Randolph to Blathwayt, in *Letters and Official Papers*, 6: 218.

226 "an impudent, saucy": Governor Fletcher, in John Usher to Nottingham, Colonial State Papers, January 31, 1693, CO 5/571, no. 18, PRO.

227 "Christ is against him": Stoughton, *New England's True Interest* (Boston, 1668), 18–23. On Stoughton and the seminal sermon: E-mails with David Hall, May 11, 2013, and October 3, 2014. Michael G. Hall, *The Last American Puritan*, 87, names Stoughton among the handful of men who created NE; Stoughton is cited in CM's *The Present State*, 36. On Stoughton and the pulpits, Hull, *Diaries*, 231.

227 public office and land speculation: John Frederick Martin, *Profits in the Wilderness* (Chapel Hill: University of North Carolina Press, 1991), 90–99. For the dense pine, Cronon, *Changes in the Land*, 75.

227 "amassed great quantities": Randolph to Blathwayt, May 21, 1687, *Letters and Official Papers*, 6: 221.

227 "I find all are mad": Randolph to Shrimpton in ibid., 3: 310. On WS in London, see especially Hall, *Edward Randolph*, 21–52.

228 enemy of the people: Everett Kimball, *The Public Life of Joseph Dudley* (London: Longmans, 1911), 17; Randolph letter, CO/1/54, no 51, fol. 121, PRO.

228 "he might thank himself": Mary Lou Lustig, *The Imperial Executive in America: Sir Edmund Andros* (Madison, NJ: Fairleigh Dickinson University Press, 2002), 196. She is best on the Andros coup. See also Charles M. Andrews, *Narratives of the Insurrections* (New York: Scribner's, 1915), 199–203.

228 skid off topic: See Wait Still Winthrop to Ashurst, 1699, *Collections of the Massachusetts Historical Society*, sixth series (1892): 46–50.

228 "rascally petty tyrant": From "The Revolution in New-England Justified," cited in Breen, *The Character of the Good Ruler*, 147–48.

229 "by having the windows": C.D., *New England's Faction Discovered* (London, 1690), 4.

229 knew only losses: Higginson Family Papers, 202.

229 "seek the subversion": Hull, *Diaries*, 217.

229 all was in disarray: Fisher, *Report of a French Protestant Refugee*, 17.

230 "worm" and "underminer of state": See Everett Emerson, *Letters from New England: The Massachusetts Bay Colony, 1629–1638* (Amherst: University of Massachusetts Press, 1976), 148. Given the convulsive state of Massachusetts politics, he was back in office shortly.

230 an English official had noted: Randolph to Blathwayt, July 2, 1686, *Letters and Official Papers*, 4: 99.

230 "Mr. Stoughton is a real friend": CM to IM, cited in Stoughton Sibley entry, 200. CM would extol Stoughton for his "unspotted fidelity"; *CM Diary* 1: 154. In fairness, he used the same term for Sewall later; see letter of September 17, 1712, NEHGS.

231 Nocturnal invasions: Kences, "Some Unexplored Relationships"; Swan, "Bedevilment of Cape Ann"; *Magnalia*, 2: 621–23. The Gloucester minister—who helped elicit Salem confessions—prayed that "those apparitions may not prove the sad omens of some future and more horrible molestations."

232 velvet saddles: Perley, *History of Salem*, vol. 3, 127.

232 Wait Still Winthrop: Dunn, *Puritans and Yankees*.

232 festivities surrounding Harvard's commencement: Morison, *Harvard College*, vol. 2, 465–70; Bridenbaugh, *Cities in the Wilderness*, 276; David Levin, *Cotton Mather: The Young Life of the Lord's Remembrancer* (Cambridge, MA: Harvard University Press, 1978), 54; Hall, *Worlds of Wonder*, 65; Thompson, *Cambridge Cameos*, 37, for the pineapples and anchovies; Hammond diary, P-363, reel 5.3, MHS. Alden's son was as well the worst offender in his class, twice fined for breaking windows.

232 "eat up the poor": Winthrop to Henry Ashurst, July 25, 1698, *Collections of the MHS*, sixth series, vol. 5, 1892, xix.

233 Phips might defraud: Barnes, "Phippius Maximus," 278.

233 prominent Dutch merchant: See Evan Haefeli's invaluable "Dutch New York and the Salem Witch Trials: Some New Evidence," *Proceedings of the AAS* 110 (October 2000): 277–308; Jacob Melyen letter book, AAS. Melyen was also friendly with Sewall, who registered no concerns about "foolish people." I am grateful to Joroen Janssen, David Sonnenberg, and Lili Lynton for translation assistance.

233 "dismal outcries": Calef in Burr, 359.

234 "the horrible crime": R, 466.

234 "declare for whom": Stoughton, *New England's True Interest*, 24.

234 "inexorable persecutions" to "unexperienced men": Cited in *Tracts and Other Papers Relating Principally to the Origin, Settlement and Progress of the Colonies of North America* (New York: Peter Smith, 1947), vol. 4, 52, 57.

235 "The widow Glover": SS *Diary*, 1: 183.

236 "abated in our love": Stoughton, *New England's True Interest*, 21.

236 "impudently demanding": CM to John Cotton, August 5, 1692, Silverman, *Selected Letters*, 40.

236 precious resource: The angry words Sewall exchanged with his father-in-law stemmed from his having been too profligate with February firewood; see Hull, *Diaries*, 253. On laws to forestall timber shortages, see David Grant Smith, "Crossing Boundaries: Space, Place, and Order in 17th Century Topsfield, MA," unpublished manuscript, Harvard Divinity School, 2009, 10–15. Already by 1653 the settlers had turned "close, clouded woods" into goodly cornfields; see also Johnson, *Johnson's Wonder-Working Providence*, 37.

237 All occupied land: Upham, *Salem Witchcraft*, 354; RFQC, 2: 204.

237 a primitive gallows: Interview with Richard Trask, April 1, 2013.

238 "You are a liar" to "blood to drink": Calef in Burr, 358. In her superb *Commerce and Culture: The Maritime Communities of Colonial Massachusetts* (New York: W. W. Norton, 1984), 115–16, Christine Leigh Heyrman notes that the threat was not new.

238 terrible moans: See CM, *Useful Remarks: An Essay upon Remarkables in the Way of Wicked Men* (Boston, 1723).

239 God were working in miracles: CM to John Cotton, August 5, 1692, Silverman, *Selected Letters*, 40.

239 "Sometimes," confessed the abashed: R, 481; CM in Burr, 243.

VIII. IN THESE HELLISH MEETINGS

On Andover: Philip Greven, *Four Generations: Population, Land, and Family in Colonial Andover Massachusetts* (Ithaca: Cornell University Press, 1970); Abbot, *Our Company Increases;* Enders Anthony Robinson, *Andover Witchcraft Genealogy* (Andover, MA: Goose Pond Press, 2013); Marjorie Wardwell Otten, *The Witch Hunt of 1692* (n.p., n.d.); Jeremy M. Sher, "Brand of Infamy: The Andover Witchcraft Outbreak of 1692" (senior thesis, Princeton, 2001); Sarah Loring Bailey, Historical Sketches of Andover (Boston: Houghton, 1880).

240 "Doubt is not a pleasant": Voltaire to Frederick William, November 28, 1770, in *Voltaire in His Letters* (New York: Putnam's, 1919), 232.

240 grandiose designs: Roger Wolcott to Henry Wolcott, July 25, 1692, Connecticut Historical Society.

241 Servants accused mistresses: See Nelson, "Persistence of Puritan Law," 337, for a man accused of witchcraft by a servant. Benjamin C. Ray discusses accusations leveled at the less wealthy in "Teaching the Salem Witch Trials" in *Past Time, Past Place: GIS for History* (Redlands, CA: ESRI Press, 2002), 26. Demos, *The Enemy Within,* 84, makes the point that no Native American was prosecuted. Nor were any Jerseyans accused with the exception of Philip English. Abbot, *Our Company,* explores ethnic tensions in Andover, which might have accounted for the targeting of Scotswomen like Carrier, and, by marriage, Foster. Sher, "Brand of Infamy," 98, observes that it was odd Thomas Carrier was not accused when he was the father of four witches and the husband of another. Sher points out that Carrier had in fact returned to town before the smallpox, which leveled her family (45). She had however also survived.

241 both defended and accused: James Holton, from Ray, "The Geography of Witchcraft Accusations," 463, and R, 945.

241 trivial matters added up: WOW, 152.

241 spousal abuse: Demos notes that that went in both directions; *A Little Commonwealth,* 95.

241 perfect conviction rate: Thomas, *Religion and the Decline of Magic,* 687.

242 a Salem man: Roger Wolcott to Henry Wolcott, July 25, 1692, Connecticut Historical Society. Joseph Ballard complained of the Laceys; his brother, constable John Ballard, had arrested Carrier in May.

242 "pains and pressures": R, 469; Brattle in Burr, 180. Rosenthal, *Salem Story,* 54, thinks the girls summoned would have been Ann Putnam Jr. and Mary Walcott. Norton, "George Burroughs," 233, prefers Mercy Lewis and Betty Hubbard. All had proved their ability to diagnose by the summer. We know Hubbard and Walcott signed indictments against Foster; R, 634. It is possible Foster was arrested before the Salem visionaries even arrived in Andover.

242–243 She soon enough began: R, 467. John Hale asked if he might remain: JH, 47.

244–245 Mary Lacey: R, 471–78; yet more disturbing question than the one posed in June: R, 392.

247–248 the witches' meeting: Reconstructed largely from testimony of Mary Toothaker, R, 491–92; Mary Barker, R, 559–61; William Barker Sr. (who caught the cloven foot), R, 561–66; the Laceys and Carriers, R, 479–82; Sarah Bridges, R, 553–54; Susannah Post, R, 555; Sarah Wardwell, R, 577–78; Elizabeth Johnson Jr., R, 543; Elizabeth Johnson Sr., R, 568; Ann Foster, R, 471–77; Mary Warren, R, 350; JH in Burr, 419; Lawson, appendix to *Christ's Fidelity*. Abigail Williams added the vampiric twist, R, 173. There are nearly fifty accounts in all. CM would retroactively insert Frenchmen and Indian chiefs into the meetings "to concert the methods of ruining New England"; he claimed to have heard as much from a confessed witch; Burr, 281–22. See Benjamin C. Ray's fine "They Did Eat Red Bread Like Man's Flesh," *Common-Place* 9 (July 2009). SP's field may have made sense for a diabolical gathering for reasons still audible today; with a swampy lowlands nearby, it hosted pond frogs, said by Josselyn, *New-England's Rarities*, 76, to "chirp in the spring like sparrows, and croak like toads in the autumn.

248 eighteen-year-old Richard and sixteen-year-old Andrew: R 479–83; Roger Wolcott to Henry Wolcott, July 25, 1692, Connecticut Historical Society. Twelve-year-old Phoebe Chandler would testify that when Richard Carrier looked her way in meeting, she experienced "a strange burning in the stomach" and missed all but two words of the subsequent prayers and psalms. The symptoms sound familiar even if they are not generally attributed to the evil eye; R, 511.

250 "dreadful shapes": CM in Burr, 236.

251 French fall shoes: R, 574. He lured fourteen-year-old William Barker Jr. and Joanna Tyler with clothes as well; R, 571, 661. Pardon her sins: R, 560; revenge on her enemies, R, 547; "abundance of satisfaction": R, 608; Mary Lacey Jr. could count on glory: R, 474, 569. In an earlier case, the devil tempted a woman into witchcraft by acting as her much-loved dead child; Demos, *Entertaining Salem*, 170. "abolish all the churches": Barker, R, 563. Interestingly, no one seems to have applied for eternal youth.

251 he composed a petition: R, 486. He would have known he had been on an earlier docket as well. The couple had been sent to Salem in time for the initial trial.

252 "and their feet": R, 480.

252 "doth carry things": R, 573.

252 "barbarous and inhumane": William H. Whitmore, ed., *The Colonial Laws of Massachusetts* (Boston, 1889), 187.

253 Already their estates: Calef in Burr, 361.

253 devil insolently copied them: CM made the same point; Burr, 245.

254 credited Catholicism: *IP*, 179.

254 "It is also true": *IP*, 175. IM included a summary of the Knapp case in *IP*, as would CM in *Magnalia*.

254 "had as good be hanged": RFQC, 4: 78–82.

255 Alden's friends: SS *Diary*, 1: 293; interview with David Hall, May 18, 2014.

255 airy, second-floor library: Morison, *Harvard College*, vol. 2, 428–30; the August answer: R, 392. "rare and extraordinary": *Proceedings of the MHS*, vol. 17 (1879), 268.

256 Joshua Moody: Calef in Burr, 371; R, 918. Moody had been Willard's Harvard tutor; he had coauthored an appeal for the charter restoration with IM and supplied wonder tales in the past, reporting on the Goodwins. See Sibley, 374–77.

256–257 Philip English: Katharine Dana English, "Facts About the Life of Philip English of Salem," typescript, 1943, PEM; William Bentley, *The Diary of William Bentley* (Gloucester, MA: Peter Smith, 1962), vol. 2, 22–25; George F. Cheever, "Philip English," *EIHC* (1860), vol. 1, 67–181; vol. 2, 21–204, 237–72; vol. 3, 17–120; Henry W. Belknap, "Philip English, Commerce Builder," *Proceedings of the AAS* 41 (1931): 17–24; Phyllis Whitman Hunter, *Purchasing Identity in the Atlantic World* (Ithaca: Cornell University Press, 2001), 40–52; Bryan F. Le Beau, "Philip English and the Witchcraft Hysteria," *Historical Journal of Massachusetts* (January 1987): 1 20. Le Beau, 4, beautifully unpacks the Beale testimony vs. R, 500 and supplies the figure of seventeen court appearances. See also RFQC, 6: 346–48, for an English suit, and RFQC, 7: 108, on his conviction that debtors should pay their debts. On the French in Salem, Gildrie, "Salem Society," 192. Susannah Shelden appears to have handled the campaign against the Englishes, although that may be an illusion of the surviving documentation, which is meager.

259 a nosebleed so severe: R, 500; the Salem servant, R, 523. Haefeli, "Dutch New York," 306, has the Aldens and Englishes in New York by early October.

259 "as much divided": Fletcher to Blathwayt, November 10, 1693, CO 5/1083, PRO. Fletcher knew something of persecution himself, having, as a Protestant, been dismissed from the Irish army seven years earlier.

260 "in all times": John Winthrop, *A Model of Christian Charity* (Boston, 1630).

260 "some are stewards": Stoughton, *New England's True Interest*, 14. As Winthrop had it, "For once in the history of the world, the sovereign places were filled by the sovereign men." On the tiers of servitude, Towner, "'A Fondness for Freedom,'" 202. "There is a monarchy": CM, *Batteries Upon the Kingdom of the Devil*, 6, also *WOW*, 45. Gildrie, "Salem Society," 186, observes that wealth and status were not coterminous.

260 on the clergy and social status: The point is David Hall's in *Faithful Shepherd*, 68, 152. Ministers ranked among the top 15 percent of colonists (183). It helped, notes Hall, that they constituted fine matches for merchant daughters.

260 "altogether unbecoming": RFQC, 4: 136.

260 "the second seat": Cited in Warren, *Loyal Dissenter*, 33.

261 "Whoever is for a parity": William Hubbard, *The Happiness of a People in the Wisdom of Their Rulers* (Boston, 1676), 8.

261 a distinct elite: See Dunn, "The Barbados Census," 10. Generally on the Barbados planters, Carl and Roberta Bridenbaugh, *No Peace Beyond the Line: The English in the Caribbean* (Oxford: Oxford University Press, 1972).

261 Exceeding one's rank: Boston dog-owning too was regulated, by a 1697 edict.

261 piece of silk: Barbara Ritter Daily, "'Where Thieves Break Through and Steal,' John Hale vs. Dorcas Hoar, 1672–1692," *EIHC* 128 (October 1992): 258.

262 "it being so cold": Moody in Sibley, 373.

262 One Rowley man: R, 675.

262 Elizabeth Colson: R, 626.

263 Martha Tyler and "Well, I see" to "did not confess": R, 694. To confuse matters, Martha Sprague was also known as Martha Tyler; R, 773.

264–265 "than say anything" to "from the Indians": R, 491–94. She was not alone in her anxiety; IM worried that his faith itself might be a delusion.

265 "a flock in the wilderness": Scottow, *A Narrative,* 14.

266 "a branch of the plot": *Andros Tracts,* 1: 18.

266 "flying rabble": Lincoln, *Narratives of the Indian Wars,* 80; in "a corner of the world," CM, *The Present State,* 38; "dragons of the wilderness," CM, *Fair Weather,* 91; "juice of toads," CM, *Little Flocks,* 15.

267 "apt to believe": Cited in Grandjean, "Reckoning," 152. On inventing enemies for harmony's sake, Hall, *Faithful Shepherd,* 245–47; similarly, James Axtell, *The School Upon a Hill: Education and Society in Colonial New England* (New York: W. W. Norton, 1976), 35.

267 "O do not quarrel": CM, *The Present State,* 40.

267 "distress and danger": Ibid., 28. Richard Godbeer underlines the similarity between a Mather sermon and an anti-Andros tract in *The Devil's Dominion* (Cambridge: Cambridge University Press, 1994), 189.

267 "The most rigid discipline": Thomas Macaulay, *History of England* (London: Heron Books, 1967), 1: 129–30.

268 "the poor people": WOW, 81.

268 "bloody and barbarous": Stoughton to the Council of Trade and Plantations, September 30, 1697, CO 5/859, no. 124, PRO.

268 Anthony Checkley: He later claimed to be generally in the dark regarding his powers and duties and pleaded for better instructions; R, 829. The salary too was all vagueness. Checkley added a line that every NE minister could have borrowed: "I am willing to serve you if you do not starve me." See Anne Powell, "Salem Prosecuted: The Role of Thomas Newton and Anthony Checkley in the Salem Witchcraft Crisis" (undergraduate paper for Mary Beth Norton, Cornell, 1993).

269 a massive earthquake: CM very much had Revelation on his mind these months; e-mail with David Hall, July 6, 2014; CM to John Cotton, August 5, 1692, in Silverman, *Selected Letters,* 40–41. "pulled into the jaws": WOW, 61.

269 "You shall oftener hear": WOW, 82–83.

269 "It would break": WOW, 102. The expression was formulaic; he used it as well of the Goodwin children in their fits, as did his father, of the imprisoned Andover matrons.

270 Tipping his hand: WOW, 100, 104. Like so many images, the fine infernal thread turns up in Lawson as well. CM and Lawson shared the "brand plucked from the burning," an uncommon phrase; they were in close touch over these months. In *Magnalia,* 1: 187, CM included court details that had appeared nowhere else, among them burned rags in mouths and poison stains on pillows.

270 "We know not" to "in the dark": WOW, 84.

270 out of his depth: R, 540.

271 "rampant hag" and the Carrier trial: CM in Burr, 241–44. Her indifference: R, 512.

271 wrists seemingly soldered: From Wigglesworth comes a thrilling description of hell: "With iron bands they bind their hands and cursed feet together"; see Bruce C. Daniels, *Puritans at Play* (New York: St. Martin's, 1995), 39.

272 "The more there were": Hale in Burr, 421.

272 a powerful petition: R, 533–36. They included the names of some who had signed depositions against them; R, 534, 539.

272 Ipswich minister John Wise: R, 334. "the clearest reputation": R, 535. On Wise, see George Allan Cook, *John Wise: Early American Democrat* (New York: Columbia University Press, 1952), especially 50–57. Also Hall, *Ways of Writing*, 182; *Proceedings of the MHS*, vol. 15 (1902): 281–302; Wise in Miller and Johnson, *The Puritans*, 1: 256–69. Evidently his works would inspire some eighteenth-century crusaders who thrilled to his rousing anthem: "The end of all good government is to cultivate humanity, and promote the happiness of all, and the good of every man in all his rights, his life, liberty, estate, honor, etc. without injury or abuse done to any."

273 "no more privileges": Cited in Emory Washburn, *Sketches of the Judicial History of Massachusetts* (Boston: Little, Brown, 1840), 106. The court fined and suspended Wise, although he was rehabilitated in time to serve as chaplain on Phips's 1690 expedition. See "Revolution in New-England Justified," 10, for Wise's heroism. The insults bore repeating; IM repeated them when petitioning the Crown; 1688, CO 1/65, no. 52, PRO; CM reproduced them in *Magnalia*, 1: 161.

274 "a vast concourse": CM to John Cotton, August 5, 1692, in Silverman, *Selected Letters*, 40.

274 "solemn and savory": B&N, 88.

274–276 his trial was the one: CM in Burr, 215–22. Anne Powell, "Salem Prosecuted," for the relationship with the Checkleys and for Checkley distancing himself from the trial; see Lawson, appendix to *Christ's Fidelity*, 114–15. Several members of the extended Nurse family had been in the Wells garrison during the 1691 siege; none appears to have stepped forward to defend Burroughs. We have the Burroughs account only from Lawson, who was present for it, and from CM, who accurately summarized those depositions to which his version can be compared. He also inserted flourishes, freely editorialized, and elided. For Burroughs's reply to the question about reading his wife's mind, Mather leaves us with "The prisoner now at the bar had nothing to answer unto what was thus witnessed against him that was worth considering." Lawson reported that nothing that Burroughs said sounded convincing; appendix to *Christ's Fidelity*, 99, 115. Testimony regarding GB's miraculous feats with the musket and the molasses barrel was enhanced by court reporters nearly a month after he hanged, R, 646–47; evidently some uneasiness lingered. The Salem man who entered those charges had seen his mother hang for witchcraft.

277 "tergiversations, contradictions": CM in Burr, 222. CM evidently had Gaul's 1646 *Select Cases of Conscience* at his elbow; he used passages of it verbatim to malign Burroughs.

277 "there never was": CM in Burr, 222. See Ady, *A Candle in the Dark*, 142–64; I am grateful to Kent Bicknell for his notes on IM's edition of Ady. CM trips over Burroughs the plagiarist as he does over Burroughs the skeptic. He was himself a master

compiler and copyist, never above retailing—and improving upon—the work of his closest friends.

278 "You are one" to "he is alive": Hale in Burr, 421.

278 Hale did but did not: CM makes clear JH's dissatisfaction in *Magnalia*, 2: 537.

278 character of one: As Langbein, *Origins of Adversary Criminal Trial*, 192, makes clear, that was perfectly acceptable. You might well enter court as "a notorious cheat and shoplift," to leave convicted of fraud.

279 "Had I been one": IM, *Cases of Conscience*, in *Proceedings of the AAS* 10 (1896), postscript.

279 "The course of God's": George Burroughs to the governor and council at Boston, January 27, 1692, vol. 37, 259, Massachusetts State Archives.

IX. OUR CASE IS EXTRAORDINARY

280 "WITCH, n.": Ambrose Bierce, *The Devil's Dictionary* (Cleveland, OH: World Publishing, 1944), 367.

280 "the chief of all": R, 244. Richard Latner is especially good on Andover and on the syncopated, geographic rhythm of the accusations, which spike suddenly and just as suddenly subside; Latner, "The Long and Short of Salem Witchcraft: Chronology and Collective Violence in 1692," *Journal of Social History* 42 (Fall 2008): 137–56. Richard Gildrie, "Visions of Evil: Popular Culture, Puritanism, and the Massachusetts Witchcraft Crisis of 1692," *Journal of American Culture* 8 (1985): 27, provides the one-in-fifteen-accused figure for Andover. By some calculations the figure is closer to one in ten.

280 "hellish obligations": IM, *Cases of Conscience*, postscript.

281 "being unadvisedly entered": R, 540.

281 "And how old" to "cat told me so": R, 539.

282 "You are a witch": R, 686–87. Others glowered: R, 543.

282 a revised narrative: Rosenthal, *Salem Story*, 132–36, tracks the change in narrative direction. Abigail Hobbs mentioned no meeting and no subversion. She did not fly; she had signed a covenant with the devil in now-forgotten Maine.

282 "Had you any hot": R, 479. "Did you used": R, 473. "But doth not the": R, 548. No more than six or seven accused Andover witches denied the allegations.

283 "buzzings and chuckings": Brattle in Burr, 189.

283 "mocking me": R, 705–6.

283 "hope he will": R, 474–75.

284 Confession came naturally: On the centrality of confession to NE life, see Hall, *Worlds of Wonder*, 174–96, and Reis, *Damned Women*, 131. Reis is especially good on sin and women and on how men and women confessed differently; 121–64. "she knew she was": Mintz, *Huck's Raft*, 25. On confession generally, see Kathleen Doty and Risto Hiltunen, "'I Will Tell, I Will Tell': Confessional Patterns in the Salem Witchcraft Trials, 1692," *Journal of Historical Pragmatics* (2002): 299–335. Margo Burns's superb "'Other Ways of Undue Force and Fright': The Coercion of False

Confessions by the Salem Magistrates," *Studia Neophilologica* 84 (2012): 24–39. In his *Discourse on the Damned Art of Witchcraft,* Perkins suggested that a confession is all the more substantial when it contains an accusation. Rosenthal cannily observes that some of the remembered slights may have been invented ones; "Witchcraft, Magic, and Religion in Seventeenth-Century Massachusetts," *New England Quarterly* 57 (December 1984): 601.

285 "in a cold dumpish": R, 568. On the spiritual torpor and confessions, see Hall, *Worlds of Wonder,* 144–47. Similarly, see R, 367–68, 576, 608–9, 630, 680.

285 "Methinks," moaned Cotton: *CM Diary,* 1: 22.

286 "for the credit" to "look with an evil": R, 542–43; a Reading woman confessed: R, 585.

287 no fewer than twenty witches: Again, the number is fluid. Depending on how one defines members of the Dane clan, it varies from nineteen to forty-five. Baker, in *A Storm of Witchcraft,* 10, notes that nearly a third of the accused belonged, directly or indirectly, to ministerial families.

287 simultaneously as village schoolmaster: RFQC, 7: 100. Barnard and the pigsty: Sibley, 175.

288 "The Lord would not": R, 608.

288 "was his for ever": R, 571.

288 "He is not an old": R, 788.

289 "But afterwards": R, 530.

289 "a pin run through": R, 578.

289 a swarm of superstitions: On the interpenetration of superstition and religion, all roads lead to Hall, *Worlds of Wonder.* It would have come as quite a shock to IM to learn that he was written off by his English political enemies in the 1680s as "that star-gazer, that half distracted man" (Randolph to Bradstreet, September 4, 1684, *Letters and Official Papers,* 3: 322).

290 "much addicted": R, 644. For Wardwell's background, Marjorie Wardwell Otten, *Essex Genealogist* 21 (May 2001): 85–88.

290 careful with those imprecations: "Discourse on Witchcraft," MP, 28; R, 576–77.

291 sieve and scissors: R, 573. The same week, Mary Warren swore that an Andover man had both practiced witchcraft and experimented with the sieve; R, 598.

291 "charm away witchcraft": Lawson, *Christ's Fidelity,* 73.

291 "burnings, and bottles": "Discourse on Witchcraft," MP, 29.

292 "charms and spells": George Keith, *A Refutation of Three Opposers of Truth* (Philadelphia: William Bradford, 1690), 72.

292–293 Wait Still Winthrop's library: Winthrop, "Scientific Notes"; three magical pills: "Autobiography of the Rev. John Barnard," 181.

293 "a wondrous thing": *CM Diary,* 2: 349.

293 Robert Pike: Warren, *Loyal Dissenter;* Kences, "Some Unexplored Relationships"; "Journal of Reverend John Pike," *Proceedings of the MHS,* vol. 14 (1875), 121–50. Pike took depositions when the Carr estate was contested from those who insisted that Ann Putnam Sr.'s father had been in perfect possession of his faculties on his deathbed and those who swore he had not; RFQC, 8: 353.

294–295 "temptations of horrid" to "when once dead": Pike, in Upham, *Salem Witchcraft*, 697–705.

296–297 "strengthen other" to "case is extraordinary": CM to John Foster, August 17, 1692, in Silverman, *Selected Letters*, 41–42.

297 "altogether false" to "such horrid lies": R, 743.

298 "a joyful and happy": R, 549. A sixteen-year-old boy would accuse her weeks later of threatening to run a skewer through him if he refused to sign her book. Teenage confessors in prison accused her as well. As her grandfather had, John Willard had tried to dissuade her from confessing; she had survived tremendous strain.

298 spectral minister demurred: R, 558.

299 "To see a man": *SPN*, 76.

299 "declared their wish" to "upon that account": Brattle in Burr, 177.

300 "like that would be": Sibley on IM.

300 "admiration of all present" to "angel of light": Calef in Burr, 360–61. Murrin, "The Infernal Conspiracy," 342, reads the account as indicating that the crowd nearly surges forth to rescue Burroughs. I have followed Sewall's order for the hangings. Lawson too reported that some saw the devil on the gallows prompting the condemned "when they were just ready to be turned off; even while they were making their last speech."

301 "live and die": RFQC, 9: 31.

301 "one of his hands": Calef in Burr, 361.

302 several questions: R, 553.

303 "to set to my heart" to "shame for sin": R, 562–64. Barker was distantly related to Ann Foster. Of the Andover fliers, he was the best raconteur.

304 "We were all": R, 738. On the manhandling: Brattle in Burr, 180, 189.

304 Sewall explained: R, 374–75.

304 "difficult and troublesome": R, 828–29.

304 "weary with relating": Hale in Burr, 421.

305 dog was put to death: Calef in Burr, 372; IM, *Cases of Conscience*, 60.

306 "taken up my whole" to "used to work": R, 711. Dounton too waited for his salary; R, 839.

306 dismantling the households: See David C. Brown's excellent "The Forfeitures at Salem, 1692," *William and Mary Quarterly* 50 (January 1993): 85–111. He finds that Corwin acted in most cases in accordance with English (if not colonial) law; the escapees were the only exceptions. Corwin did not confiscate land.

307 "laid hands on all" to "helpless": R, 914.

307 "a suffering condition": R, 674.

308 Parris made the five-mile trip: Gragg, *Quest for Security*, 132; on ministers' overtaxed wives: Earle, *The Sabbath*, 133.

308 had but three requests: R, 620. They had help with their petition. As Rosenthal points out, R, 36n, their language comes very close to Bernard's and other experts'.

309 "I verily believe": R, 617–19; Brown, "The Case of Giles Corey"; interview with J. M. Beattie, September 9, 2014. Corey knew what he was doing. Langbein, *Origins of Adversary Criminal Trial*, 279, notes that in over a century and thousands of cases, no one exercised the right to remain silent. As he puts it, "The right to remain silent

was literally the right to commit suicide." A Massachusetts man had attempted to do so, refusing to plead in a 1689 piracy case. The bench begged him to reconsider, and "he at last came to and pleaded to his indictment"; Samuel Melyen Commonplace Book, Ms. SBd-7, MHS.

309 "flatten the fury": CM to WS, September 2, 1692, Cotton Mather Letters, John J. Burns Library, Boston College. Reproduced in part in Silverman, *Selected Letters*, 43–44. CM prayed for the release of NE from the "evil angels" who had ensnared them. He prayed as well that the Lord would direct him in publishing "such testimonies as might be serviceable to the occasion."

309–310 "zeal to assist" to "encounter with hell": CM to Stoughton, September 2, 1692, Cotton Mather Letters, John J. Burns Library, Boston College.

310 "mutinous and murmuring": *SPN*, 203–5.

311 "very obdurate" to "of excommunication": B&N, 280.

311 witchcraft judges found themselves related: For the web of relations among the justices, see Baker, *A Storm of Witchcraft*, 168, and his fine chart, 163. CM had dedicated *MP* to Winthrop; Sergeant and Sewall were partners in a Braintree ironworks and a sawmill. An alliance that may have proved crucial in 1692 was that between Willard and Joseph Dudley, twice related by marriage. It was evidently Dudley, Stoughton's disgraced political ally, who applied to the New York ministers for some answers to Massachusetts's witchcraft questions. Also not incidentally, Mrs. Parris was related to court recorder Stephen Sewall.

313 Together they had conspired: Eight years earlier Dominion officials had ordered Winthrop to arrest CM for sedition; he neglected to do so. On Stoughton greeting Andros, Lustig, *Imperial Executive*, 196. As the English saw it, the coup had been encouraged by "crafty ministers"; the Mathers were its prime movers. Indeed NE preferred to answer to God than to a king.

313 "there is not a government": IM, "The Autobiography of Increase Mather," 351. He felt the charter with which he returned was one for which his countrymen would, a few years earlier, have happily traded half their estates.

313 "willingly cast dirt": Brattle in Burr, 169.

314 "I petition": R, 658.

315 guards led Corey: By some accounts the torture began on September 16; it lasted several days. For the details, C. L'Estrange Ewen, ed., *Witch Hunting and Witch Trials* (New York: Dial, 1929), 28; "have no sustenance": Brown, "The Case of Giles Corey," 288. On repenting for his obstinacy, Richard D. Pierce, ed., *The Records of the First Church in Salem* (Salem, MA: Essex Institute, 1974), 218. The Salem-born Nantucket friend was a brother-in-law of an accused man then in hiding.

315 "with his cane": Calef in Burr, 367.

316 "Now, Sir" to "against Giles Corey": R, 671. For the earlier Corey case, RFQC, 6: 190.

317 "stamped and pressed": SS *Diary*, 1: 296. A quiet note of resistance sounded about now. Instructed at her hearing to recite the Lord's Prayer, a Gloucester suspect provided a variation. To the line "Forgive us our trespasses as we forgive them that trespass against us," she added a plucky "So do I"; R, 672.

317 "the heinous crime" to "death and eternity": R, 673.

318–319 "hanging there": Calef in Burr, 367–69. The careful account-keepers included Lawrence Hammond, *Diary,* Ms. SBd-98, MHS. "hanging one another": Thomas Wilson and James Dickinson, November 11, 1692, in the Library of the Society of Friends, vol. 1, portfolio 31/93, partly summarized in *The Epistle to the monthly and Quarterly Meetings of Friends of England, Wales and Elsewhere, from Our Yearly Meeting* (London, 1693).

319 "hotly and madly": WOW, 84. The English seemed forever to undo themselves quarreling, far more than did other peoples, clucked CM, a statement that revealed him to be a man who, for all his erudition, traveled little.

X. PUBLISHED TO PREVENT FALSE REPORTS

320 "For prophecy is history": Noyes, *New-England's Duty.*

320 "timorous women": R, 739; also R, 687–88, 697. For the inventory, Francis Foxcroft to Colonel Lidget, October 6, 1692, Frederick L. Gay Family Papers, Ms. N-131, box 1, MHS. He reported 120 in jail and twice as many accused.

321 "that in a place of so much": Hale in Burr, 423.

321 "the more capable": CM to Stephen Sewall, September 20, 1692, NEHGS.

321 "almost a continual conversation": *CM Diary,* 2: 267.

322 On September 22: The Sewall interior is from LaPlante, Salem Witch Judge, 22; SS *Diary,* 1: 297; e-mail with David Hall, July 6, 2014.

322 "a most horrible": Phips letter of October 12, 1692; R, 686–78.

322 "agitated controversy": WOW, 84; "strange ferment": R, 686. CM too referred to the "dreadful ferment."

323 "they would proceed differently": Phips to Nottingham, February 21, 1693; R, 810. Brattle indicated as much in early October; these men were ready to "throw up their commissions."

323 "not a God in Boston": Brattle in Burr, 179–80.

324–325 "so that perhaps" to "honest woman as a witch": IM, *Cases of Conscience.* On the meeting, *Proceedings of the MHS,* vol. 17 (1879), 267–68.

325 "It is, after all": Michel de Montaigne, *Essais* (Paris: Flammarion, 1979), 244.

326 "A black thing": R, 681.

326 "We here hope": Haefeli, "Dutch New York," 306.

327 "unkindness, abuse": Brattle in Burr, 187.

327 "enchanted into a raging": *CM Diary,* 1: 151.

327 "like mad men": CM to John Cotton, October 20, 1692, John J. Burns Library, Boston College.

328 "any man, much less": To IM, January 9, 1693, cited in Thomas Hutchinson, *History of the Colony and Province of Massachusetts Bay* (Cambridge, MA: Harvard University Press, 1936), vol. 2, 18.

329 "besides its nature": Samuel Willard, Sermon 53, April 19, 1692, in *Compleat Body of Divinity,* 184.

329 "subvert this government" to "misinformed": Willard preface to IM, *Cases of Conscience*.

330–332 Elizabeth Knapp: See Willard, "Samuel Willard's Account." In a 1679 case that, like Knapp's, IM included in *IP*, 151, a Newbury boy "barked like a dog, and clucked like a hen." IM discussed Knapp in *IP*; see Burr, 21–23; CM included her in *Magnalia*, 2: 390–91, reducing the story to four paragraphs. Both also bled the pathos from it. She comes off more as a curiosity than a girl in pain, either bored or frightened out of her wits. As he did with Salem, CM emphasized her cries of "Money! Money!" He took liberties with the neighbor, who causes Knapp "grievous agonies," something she did not have in the original. And he inserted a demon into the story. On Willard and his matchless preaching, Seymour Van Dyken, *Samuel Willard, 1640–1707: Preacher of Orthodoxy in an Era of Change* (Grand Rapids, MI. Eerdmans, 1972), 44. For not pausing in his preaching, SS *Diary*, 1: 287. "belched forth": IM in Burr, 22. I am grateful to Robert J. O'Hara for information on Elizabeth Knapp's fate and to Reverend Nancy S. Taylor for details about Willard's arrival at the Third (Old South) Church. Willard wrung evangelical mileage: See Samuel Willard, *Useful Instructions for a Professing People in Times of Great Security and Degeneracy* (Cambridge, MA: Samuel Green, 1673), 29–43.

332 "What will you do": *Magnalia*, 2: 493.

332 "the greatest and most amazing": SS *Diary*, 1: 44.

333 S. objects: Brown, "The Salem Witchcraft Trials." Mary Rhinelander McCarl is excellent on the 1692 publishing climate; see "Spreading the News of Satan's Malignity in Salem: Benjamin Harris, Printer and Publisher of the Witchcraft Narratives," *EIHC* 129 (January 1993): 39–61. Haefeli, "Dutch New York," 279, suspects Willard wrote the piece in reaction to IM's about-face of a postscript to *Cases*.

335 Thomas Brattle: Reproduced in Burr, 168–90; see also Rick Kennedy's splendid "Thomas Brattle and the Scientific Provincialism of New England," *New England Quarterly* (December 1990): 584–600. Brattle went on to master trigonometry; he qualifies as one of those rare men who could legitimately blame his college education for his future miscalculations. He and Sewall had contemplated another riddle together several years earlier, in Stonehenge. The identity of his 1692 correspondent remains a mystery. The men he identified as the prime movers were also those who had endorsed Lawson's March sermon. His letter is notably lacking in scriptural references.

339 the New York ministers: Joseph Dudley, who directed the Glover trial, appears to have submitted the questions; Burr, 195n; *Proceedings of the MHS*, vol. 50 (1884), 348–53; Calef claimed he did as well. If so, neither the Mathers nor Stoughton enlisted him to do it. Thomas Newton or Willard (twice his brother-in-law, and in close touch with the New York clergymen) might have done so. Interview with David Hall, January 12, 2013, the letter constituted a clear brush-off toward the Massachusetts clergy. In John Miller, *New Yorke Considered and Improved A.D. 1695*, ed. Victor Hugo Paltsits (New York, 1901), 123. John Miller said an uneasy Phips requested the advice. See also Selyns letter of December 30, 1692, in *Ecclesiastical Records: State of New York*, vol. 7 (Albany: University of the State of New York, 1916), 1046.

339 "generously given": Miller, *New Yorke Considered*, 15.

339 "lies, miracles" to "nourishment than before": *Proceedings of the MHS,* vol. 1 (1884), 353–58.

340 Phips's October letter: Phips in Burr, 196–98. He hews closely to IM's *Cases.* In a separate letter that day he touched on subjects he preferred to sorcery, reporting on his success in battling the French and Indians, proposing a new attempt on Canada. He assured London the country was behind him. With six hundred men he had defeated NE's enemies; with sufficient ships, he could rout them in the spring. He sounds eminently capable if not downright invincible; see Phips to Nottingham, October 12, 1692, UK file, CO 5/751, no. 15, PRO. Norton, in *In the Devil's Snare,* 237–39, first noted that Phips's absence from Boston was fictitious.

341 "the spirit of lying": David D. Hall, *Ways of Writing: The Practice and Politics of Text-Making in Seventeenth-Century New England* (Philadelphia: University of Pennsylvania Press, 2008), 185. See McCarl, "Spreading the News," 49–50; Bridenbaugh, *Cities in the Wilderness,* 130–31. As for wheels within wheels, Benjamin Harris's business partner was the nephew of Reverend James Allen, a Mather intimate, a signatory to *Cases,* a minister to whom Procter appealed, and a participant at the Sewall fast for Alden.

341 "like the production of elephants": Cited in Jacobsen, *William Blathwayt,* 476. On communication between the two worlds, David Cressy, *Coming Over: Migration and Communication Between England and New England in the Seventeenth Century* (New York: Cambridge University Press, 1989).

342 "considering the place": Stoughton preface to *WOW,* 6.

342 "Penitent confessors" to "and trouble": R, 687–88.

342 "distempered persons" to "good fame": R, 690. That a change was in the air is clear from the penmanship; justice of the peace Dudley Bradstreet had resurfaced. The petition is strangely lacking in Fosters and Laceys.

342 "It is deplorable": R, 692.

343 "and so thought": R, 693. IM has been credited with that visit. As Rosenthal and others make clear, R 694n, there is no hard evidence that he did. Brattle was surely on the scene, if not the sole witness to the recantations. Either he had already paid a visit or this is the visit to which he refers in the October 8 letter. The women do not sound as if they are talking to a minister. And the scientific nature of the questions seems more like Brattle than anyone else. The touch test, R, 737–38.

344 How did cats: Briggs, *Witches and Neighbors,* 28–30, 108–10.; Dennis C. Turner and Patrick Bateson, eds. *The Domestic Cat: The Biology of Its Behavior* (Cambridge: Cambridge University Press, 2000), 189–90. Witches had long been known to prefer feline to canine form; British witches had confessed as much. The "archenemy": MacKay, *The Witch Mania,* 491.

344 "We desire your prayers": Sewall letter book, 1685/86–1737, Ms. N-905, MHS. The letter is dated October 19, 1692.

344 "mire and mud": *WOW,* 22; "false reports": *WOW,* 5. Again CM and Lawson's language chimed: The devil launched his attack from the heart of NE piety, "the first-born of our English settlements." Both men mention courtroom pins, brimstone, a

suspect nearly hanged before their very eyes ("one thing which I had like to forget," as Lawson put it), none of which appears in the extant documentation.

345 "horrible plot against": WOW, 14. Calef took CM to task for this in *More Wonders*: Was it not enough for things to happen; must they also turn out to have been prophesied? For IM proving how correct his forecasts had been with King Philip's War, Hall, *Faithful Shepherd*, 241.

346 "our most compassionate": WOW, 100. The reluctance to name GB may have indicated Burroughs had allies; interview with David Hall, January 4, 2015. In vain, CM had also denounced torture.

346 "matchless curiosities": WOW, 159. The typographical help: WOW, 167.

347 the English publisher: See Albert B. Cook, "Damaging the Mathers: London Receives the News of Salem," *New England Quarterly* 65 (June 1992): 302–8; *Athenian Mercury*, December 24 and 31, 1692, January 14, 1693.

347 "With what sinful" to "rashest mobs": CM to John Cotton, October 20, 1692, Cotton Mather Letters, John J. Burns Library, Boston College.

348 Father and son shared: David Levin, "Did the Mathers Disagree About the Salem Witchcraft Trials?," *Proceedings of the AAS* (1985): 19–37. They did not see eye to eye even on the specifics; IM had warned against the Lord's Prayer experiment, which CM endorsed. They differed too on the swim test.

349 "pity and prayers" to "could perform": IM postscript to *Cases*.

349 "to lift up a standard": Stoughton preface to WOW, 7. He was quoting from CM to Stephen Sewall, September 20, 1692, NEHGS.

350 "after some jars" to "cursed by him": SPN, 211–15; interview with David Hall, October 29, 2012; e-mail with David Hall, August 6, 2014. See Richard Sibbes, "The Spouse, Her Earnest Desire After Christ," in *The Complete Works of Richard Sibbes* (Edinburgh: James Nichol, 1862), 200–208. Increase Mather owned a copy of the Sibbes; one of the Mathers may well have suggested the sermon to SP.

350 "with a great rage" to "clouds of darkness": R, 696. On the acrimony, SS *Diary*, 1: 299; Murrin, "The Infernal Conspiracy," 343. Among those in the room were Dudley Bradstreet and a Bradbury son-in-law, whose presence surely made an impression. The charter empowered Phips to dissolve the court unilaterally.

351 "perish with cold": R, 697.

352 Dane's daughter: R, 705. The cause of her husband's incapacity was fits, of which he now suffered his second bout in five years.

352 "impartially administer": SS *Diary*, 1: 302. No such qualifying rule had existed before November, although it should have.

353 What use should they make: Calef in Burr, 382.

353 "We were in a way" to "this country": Calef, *More Wonders*, 152, and Lawson, letter appended to *A Further Account*.

354 "If any in the world": Lawson, letter appended to *A Further Account*; R, 833. She died in jail before her release.

354 "too violent" to "well composed": Phips letter of February 21, 1693, in R, 810–11.

354 taken a fall: Colonial State Papers, Massachusetts council minutes, February 22, 1693, CO 5/940, no. 201, PRO.

354 "restraint of enemies": Massachusetts council minutes, February 2, 1693, February 23, 1693, CO 5/785, fols. 108v–109v, PRO.

355 "a supposed witchcraft": Phips to Lords of Trade and Plantations, April 3, 1693, CO 5/857, no. 46, PRO.

355 a little backslapping: Phips to the Earl of Nottingham, September 11, 1693, CO/751, no. 37, PRO.

355 new storm: *CM Diary,* 1: 172.

355 "Yet considering" to "abruptly": Hale in Burr, 422. "I inquired": Hale in Burr, 418.

356 declined to indict: R, 820. See Rosenthal, *Salem Story,* 31, 226n, for her fate. She appears to have spent twenty-two months in prison.

XI. THAT DARK AND MYSTERIOUS SEASON

357 "The truly terrible": *The Rules of the Game,* Jean Renoir (1939).

358 "Oh Mother": Hale in Burr, 419.

358 10 percent of Andover: Sher, "Brand of Infamy," 2.

358 John Alden failed to turn up: SS *Diary,* 1: 302, 310; e-mail from David Hall, August 6, 2014. Alden was acquitted in April of 1693; R, 733. Sewall would be in the room when Alden died in March 1702. The Aldens had taken in an English daughter when the couple fled; R, 917.

358 Philip English returned: See Le Beau, "Philip English"; R, 687.

359 "saints abroad" to "covenant with him": Lawson, *The Duty and Property.* Delivered on December 25, 1692, the sermon was published in 1693 with a dedication to Samuel Sewall. David Hall thinks Lawson may also have intended the rebuke for parents of unbaptized children.

359 "to gratify neighbors": January 17, 1693, Corwin Family Papers, Mss. 45, PEM.

360 "indefinable peculiarity": Nathaniel Hawthorne, *The House of the Seven Gables* (Mineola, NY: Dover, 1999), 15.

360 "for they say": R, 844.

360 "only as a malefactor" to "brand of infamy": R, 848.

361 "damned crew" to "New Witch-land": Scottow, *A Narrative,* 43–44.

361 "persons of profligate": R, 889; Hale in Burr, 422; *Magnalia,* 1: 191–92.

361 "matchless enchantments": CM, The Day, and the Work of the Day (Boston, 1693), 65.

361 "wicked and malicious": Melyen letter of January 12, 1693, cited in Haefeli, "Dutch New York," 308. For his background, Reis, *Damned Women,* 129n.

362 the widow of George Jacobs: Many marriages took place among families of the survivors. It is unclear if it did so because they had known a similar trauma or because no one else would go near them. Roach, *Six Women of Salem,* 379, notes that Bridget Bishop's widowed son-in-law married the daughter of another executed witch.

362 Burroughs's widow: Greene, "The Third Wife"; Ian Nelson Glade, "Mary (Burroughs) (Homier) (Hall) Tiffany," *American Genealogist* 48 (1972): 141–43. The marriage was short; a year later, her new husband would be in court for abusing her.

363 "a machine moved": Benjamin Fletcher to Earl of Nottingham, March 8, 1693, CO 5/1081, no. 31, fols. 139r–140r, PRO.

363 "have been grievous": Salem Book of Records, February 18, 1687, DAC.

363 Raiding Indians: I am grateful to Carol Majahad at the North Andover Historical Society for the observation.

363 lopped an accuser: It was Susannah Shelden. On commemoration, Kenneth E. Foote's astute "To Remember and Forget: Archives, Memory, and Culture," *American Archivist* (Summer 1990): 378–92. The entire year disappeared from other journals, like that of John Marshall, MHS; Willard did not include his mid-June warning against spectral evidence in his *Compleat Body of Divinity*. On Danforth, see Roger Thompson's fine "The Case of Thomas Danforth." For Norton on Winthrop, see *In the Devil's Snare*, 2003, 13; Peterson on Bromfield's Willard notes, *EIHC* 129, 101. As for the court record book, Higginson never let those pages out of his sight during the Hutchinson trial.

364 retrospective glosses: David Levin, "When Did Cotton Mather See the Angel?," *Early American Literature* 15 (Winter 1980): 271–75; David Levin, "Cotton Mather's Misnamed Diary," *American Literary History* 2 (Summer 1990): 183–202.

365 the disaffected Nurse clan: B&N, 280–312; "the great prosecutor": B&N, 283. Not only had Parris testified against Rebecca Nurse, but so had no fewer than six members of Deacon Putnam's family.

366 "little knew": *CM Diary*, 1: 163–64.

367 Cotton Mather was in Salem: *CM Diary*, 1: 171. The Mrs. Carver who felt the witch business abandoned prematurely was probably Dorothy Carver, whose husband had recently been held hostage by pirates.

368 "the greatest moderation": R, 800.

370 William Phips sailed: Gura, "Cotton Mather's Life of Phips," 442. Phips had managed to cane not only an English sea captain but one whose right arm was in a sling at the time, then to imprison the royal officer "in the common jail, amongst witches and other felons." On boycotting the farewell dinner, Baker and Reid, *New England Knight*, 246.

371 they petitioned for him: The witch-cake baker, the farmers whom the spectral Sarah Good had terrified, Ingersoll, Dr. Griggs, and the men whom Martha Corey had warmly greeted on her doorstep in March 1692 all signed.

371 "been the beginner": B&N, 266. The search for a new minister began that July. Among the eight candidates interviewed was the village's first minister, James Bayley, which suggests that the Putnams may earlier have angled for his return.

372 "foolish people" and Beacon Hill: SS *Diary*, 1: 354. It was Melyen. As early as November 22, Sewall prayed both that the Lord would save NE from witches and that he would vindicate the judges. However he understood that pardon, he believed that the court had something for which to answer.

372–374 a disconcerting trial: SS *Diary*, 1: 359. Thomas Maule, *New England Persecutors Mauled with Their Own Weapons* (Boston, 1697). On Maule, see Matt Bushnell Jones, "Thomas Maule, the Salem Quaker, and Free Speech in Massachusetts Bay," *EIHC* (January 1936): 1–42. From "rogues and whores" to "wicked lies": Maule, *New England Persecutors*, 36–37. The sputtering justice was Danforth, who had deposed the girls in April then sat out the next months, uneasy about the witchcraft court and (seemingly) silent.

374 "upon the brink": *CM Diary*, 1: 211. The other "nevertheless": Ibid., 151.

375 "unto those errors": George H. Moore, "Notes on the History of Witchcraft in Massachusetts," *AAS Proceedings* (1882): 174; *CM Diary*, 1: 214–16, 361–63. Also see William DeLoss Love Jr., *The Fast and Thanksgiving Days of New England* (Boston: Houghton, 1895), 265–69; Calef in Burr, 385–86.

375 "wheedled and hectored" to "Salem tragedy": SS *Diary*, 1: 363–64. The entire household was on edge, eighteen-year-old Sam weeping about leaving home, Betty at her prospects for salvation.

376 "pardon all the errors": Calef, *More Wonders*, 154.

376 "reiterated strikes": For Sewall's apology, SS *Diary*, 1: 366–67; LaPlante, *Salem Witch Judge*, 199–205. Two of Sewall's court colleagues may well have been present that day. On Stoughton's disapproval, SS *Diary*, 1: 403. Easily slighted, he did not like to take a stand alone; SS *Diary*, 11: 1027; David S. Lovejoy, "Between Hell and Plum Island: Samuel Sewall and the Legacy of the Witches," *New England Quarterly* 70 (1997): 355–67.

376 ensnaring judicial procedures: "A Narrative of the Proceedings of Sir Edmund Andros and His Complices," by several gentlemen who were of his Council, 1691, 10. Stoughton was named chief justice again in 1695, three years after Salem.

376 "willing to make": Sibley, 200.

377 "divine displeasure" to "assaulted the country": *CM Diary*, 1: 216. It was his last explicit note of regret.

377 "such things" to "general delusion": Calef in Burr, 387–88. They are the only twelve jurors whose apology survives — or who made one.

378 worked over those lines: "Another Brand Pluck'd," in CM Papers, Ms. N-527, MHS.

378 English evidently threatened: Suffolk Files Collection, vol. 144, 135–38, General Sessions of the Peace Record Book, 4: 76–78, Massachusetts State Archives. He imitated Noyes at prayer "in a scoffing ridiculous manner"; he charged the Salem ministers and justices in particular with having murdered Rebecca Nurse and John Procter. Indicted, he apologized, August 2, 1722. On English and the evolving legend of Corwin's corpse, Marilynne K. Roach, "The Corpse in the Cellar," *New England Ancestors* (Fall 2007): 42–43. See also Belknap, "Philip English"; Cheever, "Philip English," 198; Le Beau, "Philip English," 8–10; Calef, *More Wonders*, 119.

379 "And why": CM on Margaret Rule, reproduced in Burr, 320; "haunted chambers," ibid., 322. Calef wrote as much to indict Mather as to attack the trials, as Mather had written as much to exonerate friends as to elucidate events.

379 "intended by *hell*": *CM Diary*, 1: 156.

379 "as astonishing a manner": *Magnalia*, 1: 136. See also Gura, "Cotton Mather's Life of Phips," and David H. Watters, "The Spectral Identity of Sir William Phips," *Early*

American Literature 18 (Winter 1983): 219–32. Calef accused CM of erecting the monument to Phips as an elaborate decoy from the witchcraft. He was not wrong. As Watters emphasizes in CM's retelling, the arrival of Phips and the new charter brings down the devil, intent on establishing a rival kingdom.

380 "in much anguish": *CM Diary* 1: 245. Trading shepherding for nautical metaphors, CM has Massachusetts befogged in what another minister called "the mortiferous sea of witchcraft," with Phips steering it from shipwreck. CM stole the image and most of the line.

380 "Whole clouds of witnesses": *Magnalia*, 1: 193.

380 "horrid sorcerers": *Magnalia*, 2: 537. The retrofitted Indians and Frenchmen, Burr, 281–82. CM could not help himself.

381 "But such was the darkness": JH, 131. It was probably no accident that Hale wrote immediately following the 1697 retractions. Still, the project discomfited Sewall, who feared Hale would upset the apple cart all over again. "Special reasons" and "to a more strict scanning": Hale in Burr, 404–5. CM takes light, interesting liberties with JH's account in *Magnalia*, 2: 409–16.

381–382 "tragical end" to "of that time": Higginson in Burr, 400–401.

382 "who are fast": Wait Still Winthrop to Ashurst, August or September 1699, *Collections of the MHS*, sixth series, vol. 5, 1892, 50.

382 "Pray for me": SS *Diary*, 1: 450.

382 "though he loves": Willard, Prognosticks of Impending Calamities," 12. Stephen Foster, in *The Long Argument: English Puritanism and the Shaping of New England Culture, 1570–1700* (Chapel Hill: University of North Carolina Press, 1991), 266–67, notes the Mather potshots.

382 "most humbly begging": Stoughton's will, Suffolk County Probate, 2675, judicial archives, Massachusetts State Archives. I am grateful to Tamara Elliott Rogers for the information on Stoughton's enduring Harvard College bequest.

383 "parcel of dark": Thomas Maule, *An Abstract of a Letter to Cotton Mather* (New York, 1701), 17.

383 "errors and mistakes" to "honorable judges": R, 851.

384 "that God hath" to "impostures": Wigglesworth to IM, Mather Papers, MHS. Increasingly, the witchcraft became the "supposed witchcraft."

384 he was mortified: SS *Diary*, 2: 948.

384 Stoughton took care: R, 713, 889. See Rosenthal, *Salem Story*, 195–200.

385 "ignorantly" to "Prince of the air": Her apology is in the Salem minister's record book, DAC; Interview with Richard Trask, April 1, 2015. Again, the numbers vary; Ann was bewitched by between sixty-two and sixty-eight people.

385 "watching, wishing": CM, *Winter Meditations: Directions How to Employ the Leisure of the Winter for the Glory of God* (Boston, 1693), 59.

385 "blind, nonsensical" and "ignorance and folly": Brattle in Burr, 172, 188.

386 "to endeavor an healing": *CM Diary*, 2: 112. William Good demanded compensation for the infant Sarah lost in prison, R, 871.

386 one witness who recanted: Calef in Burr, 356.

386 "vile varlets": Calef, *More Wonders,* 7.

386 "furious invectives": Charcot, as cited in Hansen, *Witchcraft at Salem,* 17. Pierre Janet in 1907 described hysteria's symptoms as beginning with pains in the lower body that spread upward to the throat, where they produced choking sensations and facial rictus.

386 "they who are usually": "Mather-Calef Paper on Witchcraft," *Proceedings of the MHS,* vol. 47 (1914), 244.

387 death felt closer: Hambrick-Stowe, *The Practice of Piety,* 171–72; Kenneth Lockridge, cited in Weissbach, "Townes of Massachusetts," 207; Oster, "Witchcraft, Weather." Elizabeth Knapp convulsed in November; the Goodwins toward midsummer. It is doubtful that anyone would have had time for a witchcraft crisis in November, the busiest month of the year. As Larner, *Witchcraft and Religion,* has pointed out, such panics did not break out under actual alien occupation. Elaine Showalter, *Hystories: Hysterical Epidemics and Modern Media* (New York: Columbia University Press, 1997), 19, notes that epidemics of hysteria tend to erupt at jittery ends of centuries.

387 Hysteria prefers: See George Rosen, *Madness in Society* (New York: Harper, 1968); Josef Breuer and Sigmund Freud, *Studies on Hysteria* (New York: Basic Books, 2000); and Sander L. Gilman et al., eds., *Hysteria Beyond Freud* (Berkeley: University of California Press, 1993).

387 "If I cannot move": Cited in Carol Gilligan, *Joining the Resistance* (New York: Polity, 2011), 87. The line is alternately translated: "If I cannot deflect the will of heaven, I shall move hell."

388 "Before I knew what affliction": Mary Rowlandson, *A Narrative of the Captivity and Restoration of Mrs. Mary Rowlandson* (Cambridge: Cambridge University Press, 1902), 72.

388 "labor was burdensome": Willard, "Samuel Willard's Account," 565.

389 "seemed to be more": Ebenezer Turell, "Detection of Witchcraft," MHS, 15. Margaret Rule too fretted about salvation just before her symptoms began, Burr, 310.

389 "consumed, pined": R, 82.

389 "her mother spoke": R, 373–74.

389 The hysteric's skin: Huxley, *The Devils,* 253. Ekirch, in *At Day's Close,* 294, points out that skin tends to be most sensitive at 11:00 p.m. For "very pinching": CM, *Winter Meditations,* introduction, 70. See William Ames, *The Marrow of Theology* (Durham, NC: Labyrinth Press, 1968), 57–59, on the pricking, piercing words from the pulpit.

389 "having killed 500": Randolph to the Lords of Trade, October 24, 1689, CO 5/855, no. 41, fols 117r-188v, PRO.

390 ingenious seventeenth-century physician: MacDonald, *Mystical Bedlam,* 202–9.

390 "dullest calendar": Hawke, *Everyday Life,* 91; Innes, *Creating the Commonwealth,* 17–18.

390 clarify the mental imagery: Prayer works that effect for women more often than men. See T. M. Luhrmann's brilliant *When God Talks Back* (New York: Vintage, 2012), especially 216–26. Or as Ambrose Bierce defined the word *ghost:* "the outward and visible sign of an inward fear."

390 an intelligent, outspoken, orphaned eleven-year-old: See the English summary of Lagerlöf-Génetay, *De Svenska Haxprocessernas;* E. William Monter, "Scandinavian

Witchcraft in Anglo-American Perspective," in *Early Modern European Witchcraft,* ed. Bengt Ankarloo and Gustav Henningsen (Oxford: Clarendon Press, 1993), 425–34. The majority of the afflicted Swedish children could read, according to Horneck, *An Account,* 3; Sweden alone had a higher literacy rate than NE.

391 "In other words": Richard P. Gildrie, "The Salem Witchcraft Trials as a Crisis of Popular Imagination," *EIHC* 128 (June 1992): 276. As Luhrmann points out in *When God Talks Back,* Buddhists tend to have visions of Buddha. On what we see with our eyes closed, Oliver Sacks, *Hallucinations* (New York: Vintage, 2012).

391 erotic fear and longing: No one is better on the subject than Demos, *Entertaining Salem,* 2004. See especially Mary Warren and her struggle with John Procter in her spectral lap, R, 263; the routine trip to grandmother's house can drip with sexual menace too. On the sexual thrill for the spectators, Delbanco, *The Death of Satan,* 60; for the flirtations, afflicted Margaret Rule, in Calef, Burr, 327.

392 an identical case: Turell, "Detection of Witchcraft," 6–22. In his account, the minister blamed "unguarded tenderness and affection" for encouraging the children in their folly. Rosenthal, *Salem Story,* sees more conspiring than he does hallucinating; interview with Bernard Rosenthal, January 15, 2015. As Bernard warned in his 1627 *Guide to Grand-Jury Men,* 54, those who counterfeited witchcraft symptoms did so for gain, for revenge, to please others, "some of a pleasure they take to gull spectators, and to be had in admiration."

392 "it was ordinary": Calef, *More Wonders,* 120. There was adult collaboration too. Reverend Noyes plucked pins from throats of the bewitched; R, 514. The broken cane: Calef in Burr, 355.

393 hungered for sport: R, 537. "These prayer meetings": Cited in Rosen, *Madness in Society,* 220.

393 "a sane adolescent": Phillips, *Going Sane,* 97.

394 "was better than the Bible": "Revolution in New-England Justified," 31. Murrin, "The Infernal Conspiracy," 345, describes a massive act of transference on the part of those who had collaborated with the Dominion government. To expiate their sins in plotting to undermine a holy commonwealth, they prosecuted others. Norton is convincing on the subject, *In the Devil's Snare.* T. H. Breen, *Puritans and Adventurers: Change and Persistence in Early America* (New York: Oxford University Press, 1980), 105, puts it differently: "If the Massachusetts government had been able to defend the colonists from the French and Indians, the witch hunting episode might never have occurred, much less gotten out of hand."

394 "summoning the massive": Mencken, cited in Adams, *Specter of Salem,* 150. Nor could the girls have guessed the extent of their powers. L. Frank Baum did: "Didn't you know water would be the end of me?" asked the witch in a wailing, despairing voice. "Of course not," answered Dorothy, "how should I?"

394 "believing the devil's accusations": B&N, 266. From the smoldering Reichstag in 1933 to weapons of mass destruction, there is nothing like a specter to legitimize power or rally the troops. See Randolph letter of May 16, 1689, on the colonists' bending the French and Indian threat to their own ends. Certainly there was a

great deal of redirected guilt, a hot-potato emotion as Arthur Miller noted in *Timebends*, xiii.

395 the very word "nightmare": Only the rare incubus turned up in Essex County. When women complained of bedroom attacks, they tended to name other women. On sleep paralysis: Owen Davies, "The Nightmare Experience, Sleep Paralysis, and Witchcraft Accusations," *Folklore* (August 2003): 181–203; David J. Hufford, *The Terror That Comes in the Night* (Philadelphia: University of Pennsylvania Press, 1982); Selma R. Williams, *Riding the Nightmare: Women and Witchcraft* (New York: Athenaeum, 1978); R, 27.

395 read everything in sight: Cremin, *American Education*, 212, observes that Massachusetts may have represented the most educated commonweal in the history of the world to that point. The John Wise remark is in Sibley, 435. Mather's library, Dunton, cited in Larzer Ziff, *Puritanism in America: New Culture in a New World* (New York: Viking, 1973), 11.

395 "poisoned," as Calef sniffed: In Richard M. Gummere, *Seven Wise Men of Colonial America* (Cambridge, MA: Harvard University Press, 1967), 23. C. S. Lewis wrote about the fever that turned into Narnia in *On Stories and Other Essays on Literature* (New York: Mariner, 2002): 46. He began with two images, "a queen on a sledge, a magnificent lion. At first there wasn't even anything Christian about them; that element pushed itself in of its own accord. It was part of the bubbling."

395 Swedish epidemic: That epidemic too was built on a preexisting myth and allowed children to target their own families. See Lagerlöf-Génetay, *De Svenska Haxprocessernas;* Monter, "Scandinavian Witchcraft." Calef, *More Wonders,* 19, notes that a white spirit turned up in Salem as it did in Sweden; Mather tended to bury it. Bengt Ankarloo points out that the clergy and justices shaped that narrative; see Ankarloo's "Blakulla, ou le sabbat des sorciers scandinaves," in *Le sabbat des sorciers en Europe* (Grenoble, France: Millon, 1993), 251–58. The Bury St. Edmunds trials too — to which both JH and CM turned in their accounts of Salem, as did the justices — began with entranced, Scripture-resistant, pin-spitting preadolescent girls.

395 "who think that they have": Calef, cited in "Mather-Calef Papers on Witchcraft," 250.

395 "it is not usual": IM, in *Cases,* 20.

396 "There is no public": *WOW,* 171. CM cleaned up Horneck's language a little.

396 fists jammed in mouths: Fists went into mouths at the Esty hearing as well; R, 208. It may not have been a coincidence that Foster and Carrier were of Scots clans. Or it may have been a perfect coincidence.

398 "had she visited": Some intuited that it could also be dangerous to leave the room. When Margaret Rule asked those at her bedside to withdraw, "One woman said, I am sure I am no witch, I will not go." Rule's other callers followed suit; it was impossible to know what might be asserted in your absence. Calef in Burr, 326.

398 gender differences: For women hallucinating more, see Gildrie, "The Salem Witchcraft Trials," 276. It is Roger Thompson who observes that women come off better. The tongue-holding good Christian woman appears only in the movie of *Oz.* The male victims claim Sewall's attention; CM gave Burroughs top billing.

399 original village covenant: Over 70 percent of the accused were however non-church members. Ray, *Satan and Salem*, 190.

399 it has been suggested: The point is Norton's, *In the Devil's Snare*. CM located "the most unanimous resolution perhaps that ever was known to have inspired any people" behind the Andros coup. That was essential to the deed; Burroughs would have been unlikely to have subscribed to it. Maule too acknowledged the clergy's hatred of Burroughs in *Truth Held Forth*, 189. He does not say he was a Baptist. For the inability to protect the frontier post-Andros, see Bullivant to Col. Lidget, CO 5/855, no. 103, PRO. As one Crown official put it seven years later, the Massachusetts leaders "have not a public spirit and, so long as they can sleep securely in this town of Boston, they [think] nor look no further"; Earl of Bellemont to the Council of Trade, August 28, 1699, CO 5/860, no. 65, PRO.

400 "The design of the devil": CM, *Batteries Upon the Kingdom of the Devil*, 24.

400 "It is evident that": IM, *IP*, 102.

401 "that the reverence I bore": Hale in Burr, 404.

401 day-care worker: Debbie Nathan and Michael Snedeker, *Satan's Silence: Ritual Abuse and the Making of a Modern Witch Hunt* (New York: Basic Books, 1995), 157. "turned him into a mouse": Dorothy Rabinowitz, *No Crueler Tyrannies: Accusation, False Witness, and Other Terrors of Our Times* (New York: Free Press, 2003), 13. With child-abuse scandals, Rabinowitz points out, 29, it was understood that if a child said he had been molested, he told the truth. If he denied the abuse, he was simply not ready to talk yet. For a modern case of hysteria and hallucination, Lawrence Wright's extraordinary two-part "Remembering Satan," *New Yorker*, May 17 and May 24, 1993.

401 "uncharitable expressions": B&N, 344. At other times raving women were said to be witches and men dreamed of the devil without anyone thinking twice about it, Hull *Diaries*, 181.

402 "They look upon me": Dudley to Blathwayt, February 25, 1692, cited in Philip Ranlet, *Enemies of the Bay Colony* (Lanham, MD: University Press of America, 2006), 184.

403 English officials who sniffed: Edward Randolph Papers IV: 283.

403 "a place where none do": Andros to Lord Sunderland, March 30, 1687, in John Russell Bartlett, ed., *Records of the Colony of Rhode Island and Providence Plantations* (Providence: Knowles, 1858), 3: 224.

403 "like young conjurers": Randolph cited in Ranlet, *Enemies of the Bay Colony*, 107. In deriding the coup that unseated him, an English official wondered if rebellion was not akin to the sin of witchcraft; Palmer in *Andros Tracts*, 1: 36. Some liked to harp on the chaos there. "New England is worse than bedlam," Randolph scoffed in a March 14, 1693, dispatch. Boston was in the grip of "fantastical delusions," its people "more stupid than their governer." Randolph Papers, 7: 433–44.

403 "were a people fit only": Cited in Lustig, *Imperial Executive*, 213, and echoed by CM, *Midnight Cry*, 63.

404 "perhaps a more gross *diabolism*": WOW, 16.

404 "preached up a rebellion": Randolph to Samuel Shrimpton, July 26, 1684, *Letters and Official Papers*, 3: 318.

404 ministers were as blindsided: The point is David Hall's; interview with Hall, January 12, 2013.

404–405 "lively demonstrations" to "hinder this good": CM in Burr, 322–23.

405 Calef credited: Calef, *More Wonders*, 164–65.

405 all wonder tales harvested: For the political utility of those tales, Perry Miller, *The England Mind from Colony to Province* (Cambridge, MA: Harvard University Press, 1981), 142–45.

405–406 small, supernatural figure: When Mary Marston confessed in August, she literally said the devil had made her do it; R, 565.

406 "demons in the shape": *Magnalia*, 2: 541. John Emerson, who wrote up the chimerical invaders, had been minister at Salmon Falls when the town was burned in 1690. He had also earlier warned the authorities of Gloucester's distress. So many of their men were off at the frontier that the town felt utterly exposed, "every day and night in expectation" of assault, all the more so given their harbor, the best in NE. So depleted were their forces that they could barely man a watch; they preferred to abandon the town than to "live in continual hazard and fear of their lives." They sound precisely like the Salem villagers begging off town-watch duty in 1667.

XII. A LONG TRAIN OF MISERABLE CONSEQUENCES

Whole volumes have been devoted to Salem's legacy. See, in particular, Gretchen Adams's sterling 2010 work *The Specter of Salem* as well as her "The Specter of Salem in American Culture," *OAH Magazine of History* (July 2003): 24–27; Owen Davies, *America Bewitched: The Story of Witchcraft After Salem* (New York: Oxford University Press, 2013); Dane Anthony Morrison and Nancy Lusignan Schultz, eds., *Salem: Place, Myth, and Memory* (Boston: Northeastern University Press, 2004). On digesting history more generally, see Foote, "To Remember and Forget."

407 "long train of miserable": "Return of Several Ministers Consulted," B&N, 117–18.

407 "People were chasing": Cited in Mark Danner, "Donald Rumsfeld Revealed," *New York Review of Books*, January 9, 2014, 65.

407 Betty Parris married: See Marilynne Roach's excellent "'That Child, Betty Parris': Elizabeth (Parris) Barron and the People in Her Life," *EIHC* 124 (January 1988): 1–27.

407 "diabolical molestations": Norton, "George Burroughs," 311, suggests this was Shelden; Baker, *A Storm of Witchcraft*, 109, thinks Warren or Shelden; Roach, "'That Child,'" thinks Abigail.

408 "a very sober": Cited in Justin Winsor, *The Memorial History of Boston* (Boston: James R. Osgood, 1881), vol. 2, 146.

408 "operations of the powers": Lawson in Burr, 149. Burr theorized that Lawson left NE because of his role in the Salem proceedings. There is no evidence to support that assertion.

408 "uneven and unwary": Lawson letters of October 6, 1713, and July 12, 1715, Ms. Rawlinson, D839, fol. 169r, Bodleian Library.

408 "we must unavoidably perish": Lawson to Jeremy Dummer and Henry Newman, December 24 1714, Ms. Rawlinson, C128, fol. 12r, Bodleian Library.

408 "the unhappy Mr. Deodat": Edmund Calamy, *A Continuation of the Account of the Ministers, Lecturers, Masters and Fellows of Colleges and Schoolmasters, Who Were Ejected and Silenced After the Restoration* (London: R. Ford, 1727), 11: 629.

408 "difficulties and disturbances": Journal of the Rev. Israel Loring, January 25, 1720, Sudbury, Massachusetts, archives. The best source on the later years is again Gragg, *Quest for Security*, 153–75; see B&N, 195–96, for the will.

409 Joseph Green: Joseph Green diary, DIA 72, PEM; Sibley.

409 lumber of the old meetinghouse: Richard B. Trask, *The Meetinghouse at Salem Village* (Danvers, MA: Danvers Alarm List, 1992), 20.

409 "on his lying down": John Kendall, *The Life of Thomas Story* (Philadelphia: Crukshank, 1805), 172. When John Alden sailed to England twelve years later with an official request for matériel, he was captured by the French. Dudley Bradstreet was taken prisoner by Indians in his snowbound house.

409–410 Six-foot-long mermen: CM, July 5, 1716, in Silverman, *Selected Letters*, 211.

410 "the mischievous unChristian": *A Faithful Narrative of the Proceedings of the Ecclesiastical Council Convened at Salem in 1734* (Boston: Henchman, 1735), 3.

410 Calef noted: Calef, *More Wonders*, 7.

410 smallpox epidemic: See Ernest Caulfield, "Pediatric Aspects of the Salem Witchcraft Tragedy," *American Journal of Diseases of Children* (1943): 788–802; *CM Diary*, 2: 632, 657, for "cursed clamor" and the bomb. It is interesting that CM, who—while studying medicine at Harvard, claimed to contract "almost every distemper that I read of in my studies"—seemed not to ponder a psychosomatic angle in 1692. Naturally both IM and CM claimed to have foretold the 1721 epidemic.

410 a Westfield girl: Oberholzer, *Delinquent Saints*, 124.

411 "by instigation of": Francis, *Judge Sewall's Apology*, 321.

411 "a leprechaun": Delbanco, *The Death of Satan*, 64–69; similarly, Reis, *Damned Women*, 164–93.

411 "little short of a proper satanical": *CM Diary*, 2: 749. For a fresh analysis of the marriage, see Virginia Bernhard, "Cotton Mather's 'Most Unhappy Wife': Reflections on the Uses of Historical Evidence," *New England Quarterly* (September 1987): 351. As she notes, it is not difficult to make the case that CM had a touch of paranoia. As Arthur Miller observed, paranoia however secretes its pearl around a grain of fact.

412 "wear off that reproach": Brattle in Burr, 190.

412 "foul stain": Cited in Adams, *Specter of Salem*, 36.

412 "The North": Ibid., 118.

413 Pilgrim feasts: See Peter Gomes's wonderful "Pilgrims and Puritans: 'Heroes' and 'Villains' in the Creation of the American Past," *Proceedings of the MHS*, vol. 95 (1983): 1–16.

413 "detestable and nefarious": Cited in Jesse Walker, *The United States of Paranoia: A Conspiracy Theory* (New York: HarperCollins, 2013), 113.

413 "We must awake": Cited in Richard Hofstadter, *The Paranoid Style in American Politics and Other Essays* (New York: Vintage, 2008), 20.

413 "diabolical conspiracy": Cited in Michael Heale, *The United States in the Long Twenti-eth Century* (London: Bloomsbury, 2015), 133.

413 obedience to God: Best on the point is Innes, *Creating the Commonwealth,* 200.

413 John Adams: Adams, *Specter of Salem,* 35. He was voicing precisely the sentiment Phips and IM battled.

414 "the sense of heated": Hofstadter, *The Paranoid Style,* 3. The line appeared in a November 1964 *Harper's;* it is reworked slightly.

414 "There are not two": Andros Tracts, 1: 37. The official reply and these assertions fell to Samuel Sewall.

414 American presidents: See Gary Boyd Roberts, "Notable Kin: The Progeny of Witches and Wizards," *Nexus* (June 1992).

414 "I think we stood": Cited in Joseph J. Ellis, *Revolutionary Summer* (New York: Knopf, 2013), 50.

415 *The Crucible* was not a success: Miller, *Timebends,* 347–49; Miller, "Why I Wrote 'The Crucible,'" *New Yorker,* October 21, 1996, 164.

415 "according to ancient": *Independent Journal,* July 18, 1787; *Massachusetts Centinel,* August 1, 1787; *Pennsylvania Evening Herald,* October 27, 1787. For Edmund S. Morgan on the incident, "The Witch and We, the People," *American Heritage* 34 (August 1983), 6–11. The last colonial trial for witchcraft took place in Virginia in 1706.

416 "You couldn't get": Cited in Morrison and Schultz, *Salem: Place, Myth, and Memory,* 55. See also Miller, *Timebends,* 335–49; Miller felt the town began exploring and exploiting its past only after *The Crucible.*

416 "What are you": Interview with Richard Trask, April 2, 2015.

416 tussle today over Sarah Wilds: I am grateful to Topsfield archivist Amy Coffin for the detail.

417 "fooling with history": Daniel Lang, "Poor Ann," *New Yorker,* September 11, 1954, 100. Lang follows the history of the remaining six unexonerated women. An earlier refusal to exonerate them seemed ridiculous; the 1959 Massachusetts senate did not care to make itself "a laughing stock in the eyes of enlightened society all around the world." The 2001 Act (Session Laws, Acts of 2001, chapter 122) makes no refer-ence to executions.

417 "Do you think" to "think they are": R, 230. In his draft, SP records Hathorne's ques-tion differently: "Do not you think they are bewitched?" he has the chief justice ask, R, 228. Her answer remains the same.

Selected Bibliography

Baker, Emerson W., and John G. Reid. *The New England Knight: Sir William Phips, 1651–1695.* Toronto: University of Toronto Press, 1998.

Boyer, Paul, and Stephen Nissenbaum. *Salem Possessed: The Social Origins of Witchcraft.* Cambridge, MA: Harvard University Press, 1974.

———. *Salem-Village Witchcraft: A Documentary Record of Local Conflict in Colonial New England.* Boston: Northeastern University Press, 1993.

Burr, George Lincoln. *Narratives of the New England Witchcraft Cases.* Mineola, NY: Dover, 2002.

Cooper, James. F., Jr., and Kenneth P. Minkema. *The Sermon Notebook of Samuel Parris, 1689–1694.* Boston: Colonial Society of Massachusetts, 1993.

Demos, John. *The Enemy Within: 2,000 Years of Witch-Hunting in the Western World.* New York: Viking, 2008.

———. *Entertaining Salem: Witchcraft and the Culture of Early New England.* New York: Oxford University Press, 2004.

Dow, George Francis, ed. *The Records and Files of the Quarterly Courts of Essex County.* 9 vols. Essex Institute, 1911–1975.

Felt, James Barlow. *Annals of Salem.* 2 vols. Boston: James Munroe, 1845.

Gragg, Larry. *A Quest for Security: The Life of Samuel Parris.* New York: Greenwood, 1990.

Hall, David D. *The Faithful Shepherd: A History of the New England Ministry in the Seventeenth Century.* Cambridge, MA: Harvard University Press, 2006.

———. *Ways of Writing: The Practice and Politics of Text-Making in Seventeenth-Century New England.* Philadelphia: University of Pennsylvania Press, 2008.

———. *Worlds of Wonder, Days of Judgment: Popular Religious Belief in Early New England.* Cambridge, MA: Harvard University Press, 1990.

Hansen, Chadwick. *Witchcraft at Salem.* New York: George Braziller, 1969.

Harris, Marguerite L., et al. *John Hale: A Man Beset by Witches.* Beverly, MA: Hale Family Association, 1992.

Karlsen, Carol F. *The Devil in the Shape of a Woman: Witchcraft in Colonial New England.* New York: Norton, 1998.

Koehler, Lyle. *A Search for Power: The "Weaker Sex" in Seventeenth-Century New England.* Urbana: University of Illinois Press, 1980.

Konig, David Thomas. *Law and Society in Puritan Massachusetts.* Chapel Hill: University of North Carolina Press, 1981.

Mather, Cotton. *Diary of Cotton Mather.* 2 vols. New York: Frederick Ungar, 1911.

———. *Magnalia Christi Americana, or the Ecclesiastical History of New England.* Hartford, CT: Silas Andrus, 1820.

———. *Memorable Providences Relating to Witchcrafts and Possessions.* EEBO Editions, n.d.

———. *The Wonders of the Invisible World.* Forgotten Books, 2012.

Mather, Increase. *An Essay for the Recording of Illustrious Providences.* EEBO Editions, n.d.

Norton, Mary Beth. *In the Devil's Snare: The Salem Witchcraft Crisis of 1692.* New York: Vintage, 2003.

Perley, Sidney. *The History of Salem, Massachusetts, 1626–1716.* 3 vols. Salem, MA, 1924.

"Perspectives on Witchcraft: Rethinking the Seventeenth-Century New England Experience," *Essex Institute Historical Collections,* vols. 128 and 129, October 1992 and January 1993.

Phillips, James Duncan. *Salem in the Seventeenth Century.* Boston: Houghton Mifflin, 1933.

Roach, Marilynne K. *The Salem Witch Trials: A Day-by-Day Chronicle of a Community Under Siege.* Lanham, MD: Taylor Trade, 2004.

Rosenthal, Bernard. *Salem Story: Reading the Witch Trials of 1692.* New York: Cambridge University Press, 1999.

Rosenthal, Bernard, et al., eds. *Records of the Salem Witch-Hunt.* New York: Cambridge University Press, 2009.

Sewall, Samuel. *The Diary of Samuel Sewall.* 2 vols. New York: Farrar, Straus and Giroux, 1973.

Sibley, John Langdon. *Biographical Sketches of Graduates of Harvard University in Cambridge, MA.* Vols. 2 and 3. Cambridge, MA: C. W. Sever, 1873–1885.

Silverman, Kenneth. *The Life and Times of Cotton Mather.* New York: Welcome Rain, 2002.

Silverman, Kenneth, ed. *Selected Letters of Cotton Mather.* Baton Rouge: Louisiana State University Press, 1971.

Stout, Harry S. *The New England Soul: Preaching and Religious Culture in Colonial New England.* New York: Oxford, 1986.

Thomas, Keith. *Religion and the Decline of Magic.* London: Penguin, 1991.

Thompson, Roger. *The Witches of Salem.* London: Folio Society, 1982.

Trask, Richard B. *"The Devil Hath Been Raised": A Documentary History of the Salem Village Witchcraft Outbreak of March 1692.* Danvers, MA: Yeoman, 1997.

Upham, Charles W. *Salem Witchcraft.* 1867. Reprint, Mineola, NY: Dover, 2000.

Weisman, Richard. *Witchcraft, Magic, and Religion in Seventeenth-Century Massachusetts.* Amherst: University of Massachusetts Press, 1984.

Index

Ady, Thomas, 277–78, 278n

Alden, John: arrest warrant for, 183–84; capture by French, 479n; charges against, 253, 358; death of, 470n; disappearance of, 256, 259, 333, 359; on evil eye, 324; imprisonment of, 187, 232, 255; and Indians, 397; private fast for, 255, 327, 468n; witchcraft hearing of, 184–87, 336, 450n

Andros, Edmund: colonists' revolt against, 100, 107, 140, 166, 168, 170, 175, 212, 228–29, 229n, 232, 234, 266, 267, 273n, 305, 313, 363, 399, 400, 403, 439n, 477n; enforcement of Navigation Acts, 431n; and Philip English, 257; and John Hathorne, 393–94; and John Higginson, 99–100, 201, 301, 439n; and Indians, 341n, 394; and land titles, 229, 229n; and Maine, 154; on prison conditions, 179, 180; and Nathaniel Saltonstall, 209; and William Stoughton, 228, 234, 305, 376; supporters of, 172; taxes levied by, 171, 273; and Samuel Willard, 332

Anglican Church, 6, 99, 100, 151, 209, 229, 258, 266, 332, 359

Ballard, Elizabeth, 242, 245, 246, 248, 290, 292

Ballard, John, 307, 457n

Ballard, Joseph, 242, 245, 248, 307, 457n

Baptist Church, 151, 202, 212, 266

Barker, Mary, 320, 343

Barker, William, 302–3, 311, 320, 326, 343, 402n, 464n

Barnard, Thomas, 287, 289, 290, 303–4, 328, 342, 344, 358

Baxter, Richard, 191, 210, 427n, 445n

Bayley, James: death of, 408; education of, 151; and Ann Putnam, Sr., 129, 137, 398; as Salem village minister, 30–31, 33, 42, 77, 228, 300, 471n; slander suit filed by, 31, 430n

Bernard, Richard, 191, 211, 452n, 475n

Bibber, Sarah, 149, 210, 214, 219, 220, 224

Bishop, Bridget: conviction of, 199–200, 200n, 209; examination for witch marks, 193, 194, 198, 200; execution of, 202–5, 209, 309, 373, 373n; and Jonathan Hale, 372–73; imprisonment of, 181–82, 194, 195–96, 200, 202; indictment of, 192, 193; pardon for, 417; plea of, 194, 195; poppets of, 198, 199; preliminary hearing of, 114–16, 120, 123, 192, 195, 196, 197, 329, 441n; trial of, 195–97, 207, 215, 216, 223; witchcraft trial of 1680, 114–15, 188, 192, 193, 196; witnesses against, 195–98, 197n, 198n, 199, 213, 355, 373n, 386, 395

Bishop, Edward, 110, 114–15, 204, 213, 441n

Boyle, Robert, 73, 101n, 335

Bradbury, Mary, 17, 294, 335

Bradbury family, 397, 469n

Bradstreet, Dudley, 165, 314, 447n, 468n, 469n, 479n

Brattle, Thomas: on Court of Oyer and Terminer, 335–38, 338n, 340, 466n; education of, 335, 412n, 467n; investigation of jails, 343, 468n; opinions of Salem witch trials, 361, 383, 391, 398n, 405, 411–12

Burroughs, George: arrest of, 128–29, 145–46, 161, 212, 248, 442n; and Sarah Bibber, 210; borrowing money from congregants, 31, 430n; Thomas Brattle on, 338n; and Anthony Checkley, 268, 274, 276–77;

410–11; on Elizabeth Knapp, 467n; and Deodat Lawson, 80, 437n; letter on assignment of Court of Oyer and Terminer, 188–91, 199, 224; on lightning striking churches, 387, 427n; *Magnalia*, 332, 334n, 380, 381, 395n; on Maine, 154; on Susannah Martin, 216; on medical treatments, 23–24; on meetings of witches, 253–54, 458n; *Memorable Providences*, 21, 25n, 38, 72–73, 102, 191, 254, 341, 405; and William Milborne, 212–13; as minister, 182; and Joshua Moody, 382; and New York ministers, 467n; on observers of Mercy Short, 429n; on pact with devil, 67, 435n, 440n; on parenting, 135, 135n, 443n; parenting of, 42, 44n, 135, 135n, 137–38; and Samuel Parris, 367, 370; and William Perkins, 66, 69–70; and William Phips, 166n, 168, 171, 266, 322, 339, 348, 354, 379–80, 405, 473n; and possession cases, 362; publishing and writing of, 211n, 245, 321n, 323, 329, 347n, 364, 414, 453n, 465n; on punishments, 283, 296; reaction to afflictions, 331; relations with other clergy, 312, 312n; "The Return of Several Ministers Consulted," 211–12, 348, 380; on Revelation, 269, 460n; and John Richards, 183, 188–91, 190n, 211, 232, 296, 309, 450n, 451n; on Salem witch trials, 11, 172, 173, 197n, 198n, 199, 211, 215–17, 218, 268, 269, 270, 293, 295–96, 301, 309–10, 318, 319, 321–22, 342, 344, 345–47, 345n, 347n, 348n, 364, 374–75, 377, 378–80, 379n, 381, 386, 401, 417, 460n, 466n, 469n; and Second Coming, 100, 341, 361; sermons of, 141, 171, 201, 205, 211n, 267–68, 270, 345, 361, 453n; on servants, 260; on Samuel Sewall, 208, 321, 455n; and social hierarchy, 261; on spectral evidence, 190, 211, 270, 278, 296, 324, 345, 346, 347, 349, 379, 404; and William Stoughton, 229, 230, 309–10, 339, 341–42, 345, 347, 348n, 349, 402, 455n; on support for ministers, 34, 35, 42, 72; on swim test for witches, 292, 469n; on torture, 469n; on watchfulness, 97, 104; John Wise compared to, 274; on witchcraft debate, 70, 71, 73–74, 324, 327, 355, 377; on witchcraft executions, 236, 322; on witchcraft in imagination, 123; on witchcraft in Sweden, 173, 189, 340, 346–47, 380, 393, 395–96; on witchcraft judges, 296–97, 303n, 323, 338, 348, 349, 374, 380; on witchcraft versus possession, 25n; and witnesses for witchcraft cases, 429n; on women, 77, 142n, 143, 144, 445n, 452n;

Wonders of the Invisible World, 339–40, 341, 342, 344, 345–48, 347n, 351, 379, 383, 399, 404, 468–69n; on youths, 132

Mather, Increase: and Thomas Ady, 278n; on angels, 410; on Apocalypse, 121, 361; Boston parish of, 33; and George Burroughs, 274–75, 276, 277, 278–79, 299, 325, 349, 445n; *Cases of Conscience*, 324–26, 327, 329, 332, 333, 341, 345–46, 347, 348–49, 395n, 405; on Catholicism, 254; and charter, 100, 166, 169, 170, 170n, 171, 172n, 209, 231, 313, 327, 413, 459n, 465n; on devil, 63, 72, 255, 275, 324, 324n, 436n; and doubts concerning Court of Oyer and Terminer, 233; English enemies' opinions of, 463n; explanations for calamities, 103; on faith, 460n; on folk magic, 291–93, 292n; on ghosts contrasted with specters, 442n; and Joseph Glanvill, 66; on Harvard's governing board, 333; and Harvard University, 232; *Illustrious Providences*, 71, 101–2, 254, 274–75, 332, 334n, 405; on imprisoned Andover women, 460n; investigation of jails, 343, 349, 468n; on King Philip's War, 102, 345; and Deodat Lawson, 359; and Joshua Moody, 258; negotiations of colony's grievances, 100; and New York ministers, 467n; and Samuel Parris, 370; and William Phips, 169, 170, 328, 348, 354; on prevalence of witchcraft, 62n; and John Procter, 253; reaction to afflictions, 331; relations with other clergy, 312, 312n; on Salem witch trials, 172, 347, 348, 348n, 469n; on sleeping parishioners, 35; on William Stoughton, 228, 229, 230, 349; on touch test, 324–25; venomous letter received by, 366n; visits with prisoners, 280; and Michael Wigglesworth, 383–84; Samuel Willard compared to, 188; on witchcraft accusers, 323, 325; on witchcraft debate, 327, 349; and witchcraft judges, 327–28, 349; on witchcraft versus possession, 25n, 173n, 324, 429n; on youths, 132

Mather, Maria, 366, 366n

Maule, Thomas, 105, 372–74, 373n, 375, 377, 383, 440n, 477n

Milborne, William, 212–13, 212n, 336

Miller, Arthur, 3, 11, 166, 415, 416, 476n, 479n

Moody, Joshua: assisting in escapes, 256; and charter, 459n; and Philip English, 258, 259, 382; on Glover women, 428n; on Goodwin children, 436n, 459n; on plots, 267; sermons of, 258; and social hierarchy, 262; wife accused of witchcraft, 254n

Index

witchcraft executions: in France, 435n; in
Germany, 435n; of Massachusetts Bay
Colony, 3, 62, 67–68, 69, 202–5, 202n, 234,
235–36, 244, 258, 293, 299, 322, 326, 335, 353,
436n; spectators of, 202–4, 202n, 234,
235–36, 299

witchcraft judges: and criticism of Court of
Oyer and Terminer, 323, 466n; education
of, 207, 207n, 208; and establishment of
Court of Oyer and Terminer, 181–83; and
establishment of new court, 352–53;
interrogation of suspects and accusers, 198;
Cotton Mather on virtues of, 296–97, 303n,
323, 338, 348, 349, 374, 380; Cotton Mather's
advice to, 189–91; Cotton Mather's
friendships with, 183; in Cotton Mather's
sermons, 205; Increase Mather's advice to,
327–28, 338; William Phips on, 206; and
precedents in witchcraft cases, 191;
questioning of verdicts, 220–21, 225, 302;
relationships of, 311, 312n, 313, 465n;
resignation of, 209; and witchcraft
confessions, 285; workload of, 304. *See also
specific judges*

witches: ages of, 4; beliefs about, 13, 25, 69, 156;
blaming for misfortune, 105–6; cats
associated with, 344n, 468n; conceptions
of, 60–66, 70–71, 433n; conjurers
distinguished from, 262, 442n; etymology
of, 434n; European witches, 62–66, 73; and
evil eye, 190, 211, 223, 242, 286, 296, 324, 334,
336, 346; familiars of, 60–61, 63, 65; flight of,
15–16, 18, 28, 55, 62–63, 64, 346, 427n, 437n;

Joseph Glanvill's definition of, 60; inability
to cry, 91; as marginals, 53; meetings of,
108–9, 118–19, 120, 123, 127, 192, 195, 243, 247,
248, 249–50, 258, 264, 282, 286, 302, 327, 352,
359, 441n, 442n, 458n; men as, 3, 67, 106, 111,
127n, 294, 398n, 438n; pacts with devil, 57,
58, 61, 63, 65, 67, 118, 136, 203, 208, 233, 245,
277, 288, 320, 339, 346, 377, 388, 434n, 435n,
440n; poppets of, 61, 67, 123, 190, 198, 199,
201, 243, 246, 290; prosecution of, 64–65;
Sabbaths of, 63, 65, 108–9, 112, 128, 213, 243,
441n, 443n; swim test, 190, 190n, 292, 469n;
touch test, 176, 178, 184, 186, 187, 195, 211,
223, 245, 286, 296, 324–25, 326, 334, 344, 346,
358

witch marks: Thomas Brattle on, 336;
distinguishing, 190, 190n; William
Dounton searching prisoners for, 180;
examination of witch suspects for, 193–94,
200, 451n; and Sarah Good, 51, 52; and
George Jacobs, 161, 174; Cotton Mather on,
190; and pact with devil, 61, 65; Robert Pike
on, 295; purpose of, 194n; and Tituba, 59;
wives examining husbands for, 241

women: assaults on, 104–5, 138–39; compared to
devil, 72; confessions of, 285;
excommunication of, 142–43; geographical
mobility of, 217; ideal of, 133, 137, 142;
Cotton Mather on, 77, 142n, 143, 144, 445n,
452n; piety of, 144–45, 144n, 445n; and
power, 64; prosecution for spousal abuse,
241; Quaker women, 83; wartime efforts of,
143, 144, 452n

About the Author

STACY SCHIFF is the author of *Véra (Mrs. Vladimir Nabokov)*, winner of the Pulitzer Prize; *Cleopatra: A Life*, a #1 bestseller and winner of the PEN/Jacqueline Bograd Weld Award for biography; *Saint-Exupéry*, a Pulitzer Prize finalist; and *A Great Improvisation: Franklin, France, and the Birth of America*, winner of the George Washington Book Prize and the Ambassador Book Award. Schiff has received fellowships from the Guggenheim Foundation, the National Endowment for the Humanities, and the Center for Scholars and Writers at the New York Public Library. The recipient of an Academy Award in Literature from the American Academy of Arts and Letters, Schiff has contributed to *The New Yorker*, the *New York Times*, and the *Washington Post*, as well as many other publications. She lives in New York City.